P. B. Shelley

The Works of
P. B. Shelley

with an Introduction and Bibliography

Wordsworth Poetry Library

This edition published 1994 by Wordsworth Editions Ltd,
Cumberland House, Crib Street, Ware, Hertfordshire SG12 9ET.

ISBN 1-85326-408-3

Printed and bound in Denmark by Nørhaven.

The paper in this book is produced from pure wood
pulp, without the use of chlorine or any other substance
harmful to the environment. The energy used in its
production consists almost entirely of hydroelectricity
and heat generated from waste materials, thereby
conserving fossil fuels and contributing little to the
greenhouse effect.

INTRODUCTION

O N 5 August 1822 the London *Courier* announced: 'Shelley, the writer of some infidel poetry, has been drowned; *now* he knows whether there is a God or no'. This brutally facetious and dismissive note gives some clue as to the problems surrounding Shelley's reputation and life. He was barely twenty-nine when he died, and his parents forbade any biography. Later his widow and, more oppressively, his Victorian daughter-in-law did much to bowdlerize the impassioned radical politics, the unconventional but idealistic sexual morality and the flaunting atheism of the poet. For the rest of the 19th century and much of this, readers have known Shelley largely through his more lyrical (and less controversial) writing; have been given images of Shelley as 'Ariel' or a stricken deer, the doomed romantic youth, rather than as the revolutionary social and political thinker who emerges so clearly from Richard Holmes's incomparable biography, *Shelley: The Pursuit*.

Percy Bysshe Shelley was born in August 1792, son of the prosperous and conventional Timothy Shelley, soon to become an M.P. His eary life, at Field Place in Sussex, was happy, with an adoring company of younger sisters (a domestic situation he seems to have attempted to replicate throughout his life). But his school days were wretched: at Eton he was known as 'mad Shelley' and 'atheist Shelley'. He was already writing sensational 'Gothick' tales and his career at Oxford was cut short when he, with his friend Thomas Jefferson Hogg, published a pamphlet, *The Necessity of Atheism*. This marked the beginning of a widening rift with his family. It is difficult now to realise with what horror atheism was viewed then, but this was a time – not long after the French Revolution – humming with new political ideas which woke a strong repressive reaction in the British Isles. Shelley's political thought was fiercely radical, and he saw all authority, inlcuding that of established religion, as inherently wicked. In August 1811, aged just nineteen, he eloped with Harriet Westbrook, herself only seventeen, and, though he deeply disapproved of marriage (partly because of the rights it denied women), married her in Edinburgh. They were accompanied by her much older sister, Eliza, who lived with them for much of their married life. Hogg joined them in York, where there seems to have been some botched notion of free love between Harriet and Shelley's friend. Shelley and the dauntless Harriet embarked on an uncomfortably nomadic life, travelling all over the British Isles and as far as Dublin. Their daughter, Ianthe, was born in 1813. Financial difficulties and some curious alarums and excursions constantly worked against the Shelleys' dream of founding a utopian community of 'like spirits', but he continued to write political tracts. His ideas are clearly stated in *Queen Mab*, the long visionary poem of 1813. Here he mounts explicit attacks on monarchy, war, commerce and religion, and champions republicanism, vegetarianism, free love and atheism. The poem was to become a text for the Chartists.

Shelley had long been influenced by the radical philosopher, William Godwin, and in 1814 he met Godwin's daughter by Mary Wollstone-craft, the fifteen-year-old Mary. Although Harriet was pregnant, Shelley now eloped with Mary to Italy, taking with them her step-sister Jane (later calling herself 'Claire') Clairmont, four months Mary's junior. The excursion, though comfortless (France was ravaged by the recent war), produced their joint *History of a Six Weeks Tour*. The death of Shelley's baronet grandfather and some painful and protracted negotiations with his father made the financial situation easier, though they were rarely to stay in one place for long. Their son, William (Shelley's beloved 'Willmouse') was born and Shelley wrote the long poem *Alastor* (published in 1816 to Shelley's first favourable reviews) which deploys much of the imagery and preoccupations which recur throughout Shelley's work: an alienated hero, 'Gentle and brave and generous', who ignores the submissive ministrations of an 'Arab maid' and surrenders to an onanistic vision of a 'veiled maid'' before embarking on a visionary river journey and dying. The vividly evoked landscapes have here, as in his later work, explicit congruence with inner emotional states.

In 1816 Shelley and the two very young women spent the summer on Lake Geneva, close to the newly-exiled Byron, by whom Claire was pregnant, and Mary embarked on her novel, *Frankenstein*. Shelley started his philosophical and somewhat Wordsworthian poems, 'Mont Blanc' and the 'Hymn to Intellectual Beauty'. But that autumn Harriet drowned herself in the Serpentine, and Shelley was to lose both Ianthe and the son born after his departure. This experience produced some desolate poetry:

> The moon made thy lips pale, beloved –
> The wind made thy bosom chill –
> The night did shed on thy dear head
> Its frozen dew

Nevertheless the trio began to make new friends, and settled at Marlow, on the Thames, where Shelley continued his political pamphleteering. Thomas Love Peacock, who was to become a lifelong friend, observed the lively, intellectual menage and was to draw an affectionately satirical portrait of Shelley as Scythrop Glowry in *Nightmare Abbey*. And now Shelley started work on what can be seen as the first of his mature poems. Originally entitled *Laon and Cythna*, this long, diffuse poem celebrates the French Revolution in an exotic oriental disguise and, in order to reinforce the revolutionary message, makes the heroes an incestuous brother and sister. Although the tyrants seem to win there is an ecstatic apotheosis in which (another boat journey) the heroes sail to a visionary political paradise. Modified to escape prosecution it was published as *The Revolt of Islam* in 1818.

By then an exhibition of Egyptian antiquities had inspired the great sonnet 'Ozymandias' which shows the fleetingness of earthly power. The monumental statue commissioned by a tyrant – 'Look on my works, ye Mighty, and despair!' – is now only a 'colossal wreck':

> Two vast and trunkless legs of stone
> Stand in the desert . . . Near them on the sand,
> Half sunk, a shattered visage lies . . .
> . . . Round the decay . . .
> The lone and level sands stretch far away.

In his poem, 'Rosalind and Helen', Shelley depicted someone who became 'A spirit of unresting flame/Which goaded him in his distress/Over the world's vast wilderness', and in 1818 this sense of being a goaded exile took him with Mary and Claire and their children to Italy. They resumed their nomadic ways, living in eight places in less than two years, during which Mary found Claire's presence increasingly trying. Certainly a *ménage a trois* invited malicious gossip, and we shall never know the details of Shelley's undoubtedly close and loving relationship with the spirited Claire. But she remained obsessed with Byron (who refused to see her), and not only because of the arguments over their daughter, Allegra, which Shelley mediated with tact and kindness. It was the friendship with Byron which inspired Shelley's delightful poem of argument 'Julian and Maddalo'. This was a difficult time: a mysterious child was born in Naples, almost certainly Shelley's, and fostered out in spite of his warm paternal feelings. These were further harrowed by the deaths of his daughter Clara, partly because of Shelley's thoughtlessness, and of Willmouse. Mary retreated into terrible depression which was only partially lifted by the birth of Percy in 1819.

Nevertheless, it was a time of amazing fecundity for Shelley. *Prometheus Unbound* shows Aeschylus's Titan tortured eternally for bringing fire to mankind, as the people's hero against tyranny (represented by the father-figure Jupiter).

> He gave man speech, and speech created thought,
> Which is the measure of the universe; . . .
> Man looks on his creation like a God,
> And sees that it is glorious,

But the evil of tyranny makes mankind 'the wreck of his own will, the scorn of earth,/The outcast, the abandoned, the alone'. Prometheus is rescued by both the power of ideal love, personified in his beloved, Asia, and by the brute revolutionary force of Demogrogon who overthrows Jupiter. *The Mask of Anarchy*, written in furious response to the Peterloo massacre, uses the ballad form with stinging effect to pillory Britain's repressive government:

> I met Murder on the way
> He had a mask like Castlereagh –
> Very smooth he looked, yet grim;
> Seven bloodhounds followed him . . .

> Last came Anarchy: he rode
> On a white horse, splashed with blood;
> He was pale even to the lips,
> Like Death in the Apocalypse.

'Ode to the West Wind', written in the wind-lashed woods above Florence, effortlessly handles the difficult *terza rima* form (inspired by Dante) in beautiful and closely-observed nature writing which also figures metaphorically for Shelley's own state of mind. The wind is a 'Wild Spirit . . . Destroyer and Preserver' (an image later echoed by Claire in her journal: 'a great Poet . . . is a Creator and a Destroyer'), and Shelley is 'too like thee: tameless and swift and proud'. More realistic now about the liklihood of revolution, he retains hopes of being at least an inspiration:

> Drive my dead thoughts over the universe
> Like withered leaves to quicken a new birth! . . .
>
> Scatter, as from an unextinguished hearth,
> Ashes and sparks, my words among mankind!

Peter Bell the Third is a savage lampoon on Wordsworth, that 'solemn and unsexual man', who, Shelley believed, had betrayed his youthful ideals. *The Cenci*, Shelley's only complete theatrical work, returns to the incestuous theme in a melodramatic Venetian tale of revenge and murder. The move to a more settled existence at Pisa produced his famous and ringing *Defence of Poetry*. The death of Keats early in 1819 inspired *Adonais*, which owed much to Shelley's knowledge of Greek (he was a skilled and sensitive translator from Latin, Greek, Italian and Spanish) and to Milton's *Lycidas*. As Mary observed, 'There is much in the *Adonais* which seems to be more applicable to Shelley himself than to the young and gifted poet whom he mourned'. He gives the self-portrait of 'a pard-like spirit, beautiful and swift', along with sketches of Byron, 'the pilgrim of eternity' and the radical *litterateur*, Leigh Hunt, 'the gentlest of the wise'. The young Emilia Viviani, imprisoned in a convent, evoked Shelley's extraordinary statement of his life, loves and philosphy in *Epipsychidion*. Sorting uneasily with what purports to be a platonic love poem – and platonic the relationship had to remain – are the autobiographical passages in which Mary figures as the moon, Emilia as the Sun and Claire as a 'Comet, beautiful and fierce . . ./Alternating attraction and repulsion'. Here too is the central statement of Shelley's ideas about love:

> I never was attached to that greater sect,
> Whose doctrine is, that each one should select
> Out of the crowd a mistress or a friend,
> And all the rest, though fair and wise, commend
> To cold oblivion . . .
> With one chained friend, perhaps a jealous foe,
> The dreariest and the longest journey go.

With echoes of the quests in *Alastor* and the 'Hymn to Intellectual

Beauty' he declares, 'In many mortal forms I rashly sought/The shadow of that idol of my thought', and sees himself as 'a hunted deer that could not flee' until redeemed by Emilia's love.

The arrival of Byron in Pisa, and an invitation to Leigh Hunt to edit a liberal-radical journal there, bear witness to Shelley's renewed hopes of founding a community of like minds. But Byron's presence was inhibiting, and Shelley wrote little more than the verse drama, *Hellas*, which more optimistically than *The Revolt of Islam*, looked forward to liberation from tyranny and a revivified world, and the incomplete play, *Charles I*, which includes the beautiful little lyric, 'A widow bird sate mourning for her love'.

In spring 1822, after Shelley with Mary and Claire had moved to the seaside at Lerici, they heard of the death of Byron's little daughter Allegra. This grief touched Shelley, and was compounded by Mary's bad miscarriage. He was however able to write some of his most charming lyrics for Jane Williams, a friend living nearby. It is appropriate that one of these takes the names 'Miranda' and 'Ariel' from Shakespeare's sea-suffused play, *The Tempest*. Images of water pervade much of Shelley's poetry, along with journeys by boat and dark intuitions of drowing. In August Shelley, along with Edward Williams and an English cabin boy, was drowned in a storm which overtook their yacht as they returned from visting Byron. Now, like his Keats/*Adonais*, Shelley

> . . . has outsoared the shadow of our night;
> Envy and calumny and hate and pain,
> And that unrest which men miscall delight,
> Can touch him not and torture not again;
> From the contagion of the world's slow stain
> He is secure, and now can never mourn
> A heart grown old, a head grown grey in vain;
> Nor, when the spirit's self has ceased to burn,
> With sparkless ashes load an unlamented urn.

FURTHER READING

F.L. Jones (ed.), *The Letters of Percy Bysshe Shelley* (Oxford, 1964).

F.L. Jones (ed.), *Mary Shelley's Journal* (Oklahoma, 1947).

F.L. Jones (ed.), *The Letters of Mary Shelley* (Oklahoma, 1944).

Marion Kingston Stocking (ed.), *The Journals of Claire Clairmont* (Harvard, 1968).

Mary Shelley, *Frankenstein: or, The Modern Prometheus* (London, 1818).

Thomas Love Peacock, *Nightmare Abbey* (London, 1818).

Richard Holmes, *Shelley: The Pursuit* (London, 1974).

James Rieger, *The Mutiny Within: the Heresies of Percy Bysshe Shelley* (New York, 1967).

Judith Chernaik, *The Lyrics of Shelley* (Australia, 1972).

CONTENTS

                                                                PAGE
ŒDIPUS TYRANNUS; OR, SWELLFOOT THE TYRANT: A TRAGEDY
    IN TWO ACTS   271
    Advertisement.   271
    Act I   271
    Act II   279

EARLY POEMS   285
    A SUMMER-EVENING CHURCHYARD   285
    MUTABILITY   286
    ON DEATH   286
    TO COLERIDGE   287
    TO WORDSWORTH   287
    LINES: "THE COLD EARTH SLEPT BELOW"   .   .   .   287
    STANZAS: APRIL, 1814   288
    FEELINGS OF A REPUBLICAN ON THE FALL OF BONAPARTE   .   .   288

POEMS WRITTEN IN 1816.   289
    THE SUNSET   289
    HYMN TO INTELLECTUAL BEAUTY   290
    MONT BLANC   291

POEMS WRITTEN IN 1817   294
    PRINCE ATHANASE   294
    FRAGMENTS OF PRINCE ATHANASE   296
        Fragment I   296
        Fragment II   297
        Fragment III   298
        Fragment IV   299
    MARIANNE'S DREAM.   299
    DEATH   301
    TO CONSTANTIA, SINGING   302
    TO CONSTANTIA   302
    SONNET: OZYMANDIAS   302
    TO THE LORD CHANCELLOR   303
    LINES TO A CRITIC   304
    LINES: "THAT TIME IS DEAD FOR EVER, CHILD"   .   .   304
    ON FANNY GODWIN.   304

POEMS WRITTEN IN 1818   305
    ADVERTISEMENT TO ROSALIND AND HELEN   .   .   .   305
    ROSALIND AND HELEN   305
    LINES WRITTEN AMONG THE EUGANEAN HILLS   .   .   .   322
    JULIAN AND MADDALO   325
    THE WOODMAN AND THE NIGHTINGALE   336
    MISERY: A FRAGMENT   337
    TO MARY——.   338
    PASSAGE OF THE APENNINES   338
    ON A FADED VIOLET   338
    STANZAS, WRITTEN IN DEJECTION, NEAR NAPLES   .   .   .   339
    SONG FOR TASSO   339
    THE PAST   340
    MAZENGHI   340
    SONNET: "LIFT NOT THE PAINTED VEIL WHICH THOSE WHO LIVE".   341

CONTENTS

THE POETICAL WORKS OF
PERCY BYSSHE SHELLEY

TO HARRIET *****

WHOSE is the love that, gleaming through
the world,
Wards off the poisonous arrow of its
scorn ?
Whose is the warm and partial praise,
Virtue's most sweet reward ?

Beneath whose looks did my reviving
soul
Riper in truth and virtuous daring grow?
Whose eyes have I gazed fondly on,
And loved mankind the more ?

Harriet ! on thine :—thou wert my purer
mind ;
Thou wert the inspiration of my song ;
Thine are these early wilding flowers,
Though garlanded by me.

Then press into thy breast this pledge of
love,
And know, though time may change and
years may roll,
Each flow'ret gathered in my heart
It consecrates to thine.

QUEEN MAB

I

How wonderful is Death,
Death and his brother Sleep !
One, pale as yonder waning moon,
With lips of lurid blue ;
The other, rosy as the morn
When throned on ocean's wave,
It blushes o'er the world :
Yet both so passing wonderful !

Hath then the gloomy Power
Whose reign is in the tainted sepul-
chres
Seized on her sinless soul
Must then that peerless form
Which love and admiration cannot
view
Without a beating heart, those
azure veins   [of snow,
Which steal like streams along a field
That lovely outline, which is fair
As breathing marble, perish ?
Must putrefaction's breath
Leave nothing of this heavenly
sight
But loathsomeness and ruin ?
Spare nothing but a gloomy theme,

On which the lightest heart might
moralise ?
Or is it only a sweet slumber
Stealing o'er sensation,
Which the breath of roseate morn-
ing
Chaseth into darkness ?
Will Ianthe wake again,
And give that faithful bosom joy
Whose sleepless spirit waits to
catch
Light, life, and rapture, from her
smile ?

Yes ! she will wake again,
Although her glowing limbs are mo-
tionless,
And silent those sweet lips,
Once breathing eloquence
That might have soothed a tiger's
rage,
Or thawed the cold heart of a con-
queror.
Her dewy eyes are closed,
And on their lids, whose texture
fine
Scarce hides the dark blue orbs be-
neath,

The baby Sleep is pillowed :
Her golden tresses shade
The bosom's stainless pride,
Curling like tendrils of the para-
 site
Around a marble column.

Hark ! whence that rushing
 sound?
'Tis like the wondrous strain
That round a lonely ruin swells,
Which, wandering on the echo-
 ing shore,
The enthusiast hears at even-
 ing :
'Tis softer than the west wind's
 sigh ;
'Tis wilder than the unmeasured
 notes
Of that strange lyre whose strings
The genii of the breezes sweep :
Those lines of rainbow light
Are like the moonbeams when
 they fall
Through some cathedral window, but
 the teints
Are such as may not find
Comparison on earth.

Behold the chariot of the Fairy
 Queen !
Celestial coursers paw the un-
 yielding air ;
Their filmy pennons at her word
 they furl,
And stop obedient to the reins of
 light :
These the Queen of Spells drew
 in,
She spread a charm around the
 spot,
And leaning graceful from the
 ethereal car,
Long did she gaze, and silently,
 Upon the slumbering maid.

Oh ! not the visioned poet in his
 dreams,
When silvery clouds float through the
 wildered brain,
When every sight of lovely, wild,
 and grand,
  Astonishes, enraptures ele-
  vates—
  When fancy at a glance com-
  bines

The wondrous and the beau-
 tiful,—
So bright, so fair, so wild a
 shape
Hath ever yet beheld,
As that which reined the coursers
 of the air,
And poured the magic of her gaze
Upon the sleeping maid.

 The broad and yellow moon
 Shone dimly through her
  form—
That form of faultless sym-
 metry ;
The pearly and pellucid car
 Moved not the moonlight's
  line ;
 'Twas not an earthly page-
  ant ;
Those who had looked upon
 the sight,
 Passing all human glory,
 Saw not the yellow moon,
 Saw not the mortal scene,
 Heard not the night-wind's
  rush,
 Heard not an earthly sound,
 Saw but the fairy pageant,
 Heard but the heavenly
  strains
That filled the lonely dwell-
 ing.

The Fairy's frame was slight ; yon
 fibrous cloud,
That catches but the palest tinge
 of even,
And which the straining eye can
 hardly seize
When melting into eastern twi-
 light's shadow,
Were scarce so thin, so slight ; but
 the fair star,
That gems the glittering coronet
 of morn,
 Sheds not a light so mild, so
  powerful,
As that which, bursting from the
 Fairy's form,
 Spread a purpureal halo round
  the scene,
  Yet with an undulating
  motion,
  Swayed to her outline grace-
  fully.

From her celestial car
The Fairy Queen descended,
And thrice she waved her wand
Circled with wreaths of amaranth :
Her thin and misty form
Moved with the moving air,
And the clear silver tones,
As thus she spoke, were such
As are unheard by all but gifted ear.

Fairy. Stars ! your balmiest influence shed !
Elements ! your wrath suspend !
Sleep, Ocean, in the rocky bounds
That circle thy domain !
Let not a breath be seen to stir
Around yon grass-grown ruin's height,
Let even the restless gossamer
Sleep on the moveless air !
Soul of Ianthe ! thou,
Judged alone worthy of the envied boon
That waits the good and the sincere ;
that waits
Those who have struggled, and with resolute will
Vanquished earth's pride and meanness, burst the chains,
The icy chains of custom, and have shone
The day-stars of their age ;—Soul of Ianthe !
Awake ! arise !

Sudden arose
Ianthe's Soul ; it stood
All beautiful in naked purity,
The perfect semblance of its bodily frame.
Instinct with inexpressible beauty and grace,
Each stain of earthliness
Had passed away, it reassumed
Its native dignity, and stood
Immortal amid ruin.

Upon the couch the body lay,
Wrapt in the depth of slumber :
Its features were fixed and meaningless,
Yet animal life was there,
And every organ yet performed
Its natural functions ; 'twas a sight
Of wonder to behold the body and soul.
The self-same lineaments, the same
Marks of identity were there ;
Yet, oh how different ! One aspires to heaven,
Pants for its sempiternal heritage,
And ever-changing, ever-rising still,
Wantons in endless being.
The other, for a time the unwilling sport
Of circumstance and passion, struggles on ;
Fleets through its sad duration rapidly ;
Then like a useless and worn-out machine,
Rots, perishes and passes.

Fairy. Spirit ! who hast dived so deep ;
Spirit ! who hast soared so high ;
Thou the fearless, thou the mild,
Accept the boon thy worth hath earned,
Ascend the car with me.

Spirit. Do I dream ? Is this new feeling
But a visioned ghost of slumber ?
If indeed I am a soul,
A free, a disembodied soul,
Speak again to me.

Fairy. I am the Fairy MAB : to me
'tis given
The wonders of the human world to keep.
The secrets of the immeasurable past,
In the unfailing consciences of men,
Those stern, unflattering chroniclers, I find :
The future, from the causes which arise
In each event, I gather : not the sting

QUEEN MAB

Which retributive memory implants
In the hard bosom of the selfish man;
Nor that ecstatic and exulting throb
Which virtue's votary feels when he
  sums up
The thoughts and actions of a well-
  spent day,
Are unforeseen, unregistered by me:
And it is yet permitted me, to rend
The veil of mortal frailty, that the
  spirit,
Clothed in its changeless purity, may
  know
How soonest to accomplish the great
  end
For which it hath its being, and may
  taste
That peace, which, in the end, all life
  will share.
This is the meed of virtue; happy
  Soul,
  Ascend the car with me!

  The chains of earth's immurement
    Fell from Ianthe's spirit;
They shrank and brake like bandages
    of straw
  Beneath a wakened giant's strength.
    She knew her glorious change,
    And felt in apprehension uncon-
      trolled
      New raptures opening round:
    Each day-dream of her mortal
      life,
    Each frenzied vision of the slum-
      bers
      That closed each well-spent day
    Seemed now to meet reality.

  The Fairy and the Soul pro-
      ceeded;
    The silver clouds disparted;
And as the car of magic they as-
    cended,
    Again the speechless music
      swelled,
    Again the coursers of the air
Unfurled their azure pennons, and the
    Queen,
      Shaking the beamy reins,
      Bade them pursue their way.

    The magic car moved on.
  The night was fair, and countless
    stars
  Studded heaven's dark blue
    vault,—

    Just o'er the eastern wave
  Peeped the first faint smile of
    morn:—
    The magic car moved on—
    From the celestial hoofs
  The atmosphere in flaming sparkles
    flew,
    And where the burning wheels
  Eddied above the mountain's lofti-
    est peak,
    Was traced a line of lightning.
  Now it flew far above a rock,
    The utmost verge of earth,
  The rival of the Andes, whose dark
    brow
      Lowered o'er the silver sea.

  Far, far below the chariot's
      path,
    Calm as a slumbering babe,
    Tremendous Ocean lay.
  The mirror of its stillness
    showed
    The pale and waning stars,
    The chariot's fiery track,
    And the grey light of morn
    Tinging those fleecy clouds
    That canopied the dawn.
  Seemed it, that the chariot's
    way
Lay through the midst of an immense
    concave,
Radiant with million constellations,
    tinged
      With shades of infinite col-
        our,
      And semicircled with a belt
      Flashing incessant meteors.

    The magic car moved on.
    As they approached their
      goal,
  The coursers seemed to gather
      speed;
  The sea no longer was distinguished;
    earth   [sphere;
    Appeared a vast and shadowy
    The sun's unclouded orb
    Rolled through the black con-
      cave;
      Its rays of rapid light
Parted around the chariot's swifter
      course,   [spray
    And fell, like ocean's feathery
      Dashed from the boiling
        surge
      Before a vessel's prow.

The magic car moved on.
Earth's distant orb appeared
The smallest light that twinkles in the
heaven ;
Whilst round the chariot's way
Innumerable systems rolled,
And countless spheres diffused
An ever varying glory.
It was a sight of wonder : some
Were hornèd like the crescent
moon ;
Some shed a mild and silver beam
Like Hesperus o'er the western
sea ;
Some dashed athwart with trains
of flame,
Like worlds to death and ruin
driven ;
Some shone like suns, and as the char-
iot passed,
Eclipsed all other light.

Spirit of Nature ! here !
In this interminable wilderness
Of worlds, at whose immensity
Even soaring fancy staggers,
Here is thy fitting temple.
Yet not the lightest leaf
That quivers to the passing
breeze
Is less instinct with thee :
Yet not the meanest worm
That lurks in graves and fattens on
the dead
Less shares thy eternal breath.
Spirit of Nature ! thou !
Imperishable as this scene,
Here is thy fitting temple !

II

If solitude hath ever led thy steps
To the wild ocean's echoing shore,
And thou hast lingered there,
Until the sun's broad orb
Seemed resting on the burnished
wave,
Thou must have marked the lines
Of purple gold, that motionless
Hung o'er the sinking sphere :
Thou must have marked the bil-
lowy clouds
Edged with intolerable radiancy,
Towering like rocks of jet
Crowned with a diamond wreath.
And yet there is a moment,
When the sun's highest point

Peeps like a star o'er ocean's western
edge,
When those far clouds of feathery
gold,
Shaded with deepest purple, gleam
Like islands on a dark blue sea ;
Then has thy fancy soared above the
earth,
And furled its wearied wing
Within the Fairy's fane.

Yet not the golden islands
Gleaming in yon flood of light,
Nor the feathery curtains
Stretching o'er the sun's bright
couch,
Nor the burnished ocean-waves,
Paving that gorgeous dome,
So fair, so wonderful a sight
As Mab's ethereal palace could afford.
Yet likest evening's vault, that fairy
Hall !
As Heaven, low resting on the wave, it
spread
Its floors of flashing light,
Its vast and azure dome,
Its fertile golden islands
Floating on a silver sea ;
Whilst suns their mingling beamings
darted
Through clouds of circumambient
darkness,
And pearly battlements around
Looked o'er the immense of Heaven.

The magic car no longer moved.
The Fairy and the Spirit
Entered the Hall of Spells :
Those golden clouds
That rolled in glittering billows
Beneath the azure canopy,
With the ethereal footsteps trembled
not :
The light and crimson mists,
Floating to strains of thrilling melody
Through that unearthly dwelling,
Yielded to every movement of the will.
Upon their passive swell the Spirit
leaned,
And, for the varied bliss that pressed
around,
Used not the glorious privilege
Of virtue and of wisdom.

Spirit ! the Fairy said,
And pointed to the gorgeous
dome,

This is a wondrous sight
And mocks all human gran-
     deur ;
But, were it virtue's only meed, to
     dwell
In a celestial palace, all resigned
To pleasurable impulses, immured
Within the prison of itself, the will
Of changeless nature would be unful-
     filled.
Learn to make others happy. Spirit,
     come !
This is thine high reward :—the past
     shall rise ;
Thou shalt behold the present ; I will
     teach
     The secrets of the future.

     The Fairy and the Spirit
Approached the overhanging battle-
     ment.—
     Below lay stretched the universe !
     There, far as the remotest line
     That bounds imagination's flight,
     Countless and unending orbs
In mazy motion intermingled,
Yet still fulfilled immutably
     Eternal Nature's law.
     Above, below, around
     The circling systems formed
A wilderness of harmony ;
Each with undeviating aim,
In eloquent silence, through the
     depths of space
     Pursued its wondrous way.

     There was a little light
That twinkled in the misty distance :
     None but a spirit's eye
     Might ken that rolling orb ;
     None but a spirit's eye,
     And in no other place
But that celestial dwelling, might be-
     hold
Each action of this earth's inhabit-
     ants.
     But matter, space and time,
In those aerial mansions cease to act ;
And all-prevailing wisdom, when it
     reaps
The harvest of its excellence, o'er-
     bounds
Those obstacles, of which an earthly
     soul
     Fears to attempt the conquest.

The Fairy pointed to the earth.
The Spirit's intellectual eye
Its kindred beings recognised.
The thronging thousands, to a passing
     view,
Seemed like an ant-hill's citizens.
     How wonderful ! that even
The passions, prejudices, interests,
That sway the meanest being, the
     weak touch
     That moves the finest nerve,
     And in one human brain
Causes the faintest thought, becomes
     a link
     In the great chain of nature.

     Behold, the Fairy cried,
Palmyra's ruin'd palaces !—
     Behold !   where   grandeur
     frowned
     Behold ! where pleasure smiled;
What now remains ?—the memory
     Of senselessness and shame—
     What is immortal there ?
     Nothing—it stands to tell
     A melancholy tale, to give
     An awful warning : soon
Oblivion will steal silently
     The remnant of its fame.
     Monarchs and conquerors there
Proud o'er prostrate millions trod—
The earthquakes of the human
     race,—
Like them, forgotten when the ruin
     That marks their shock is past.

     Beside the eternal Nile
     The Pyramids have risen.
Nile shall pursue his changeless
     way ;
     Those Pyramids shall fall ;
Yea ! not a stone shall stand to tell
     The spot whereon they stood ;
Their very site shall be forgotten,
     As is their builder's name !

     Behold yon sterile spot ;
Where now the wandering Arab's
     tent
     Flaps in the desert-blast.
There once old Salem's haughty
     fane
Reared high to heaven its thousand
     golden domes,
     And in the blushing face of day
     Exposed its shameful glory.

QUEEN MAB

7

Oh ! many a widow, many an orphan
    cursed
The building of that fane ; and
    many a father,
Worn out with toil and slavery, im-
    plored
The poor man's God to sweep it from
    the earth,
And spare his children the detested
    task
Of piling stone on stone, and poison-
    ing
    The choicest days of life,
    To soothe a dotard's vanity.
There an inhuman and uncultured
    race
Howled hideous praises to their De-
    mon-God ;
They rushed to war, tore from the
    mother's womb
The unborn child,—old age and in-
    fancy
Promiscuous perished ; their victori-
    ous arms
Left not a soul to breathe. Oh ! they
    were fiends :
But what was he who taught them
    that the God
Of nature and benevolence had given
A special sanction to the trade of
    blood ?
His name and theirs are fading, and
    the tales
Of this barbarian nation, which im-
    posture
Recites till terror credits, are pursu-
    ing
    Itself into forgetfulness.

Where Athens, Rome, and Sparta
    stood,
    There is a moral desert now :
    The mean and miserable huts,
    The yet more wretched palaces,
Contrasted with those ancient fanes,
Now crumbling to oblivion ;
The long and lonely colonnades,
Through which the ghost of Free-
    dom stalks,
    Seem like a well-known tune,
Which in some dear scene we have
    loved to hear,
    Remembered now in sadness.
    But, oh ! how much more
      changed,
    How gloomier is the contrast

Of human nature there !
Where Socrates expired, a tyrant's
    slave,
A coward and a fool, spreads death
    around—
    Then, shuddering, meets his
      own.
Where Cicero and Antoninus lived,
    A cowled and hypocritical monk
    Prays, curses, and deceives.

    Spirit ! ten thousand years
    Have scarcely passed away,
Since, in the waste where now the
    savage drinks
His enemy's blood, and, aping Eu-
    rope's sons,
    Wakes the unholy song of war,
    Arose a stately city,
Metropolis of the western continent :
    There, now, the mossy column-
      stone,
Indented by Time's unrelaxing grasp,
    Which once appeared to brave
    All, save its country's ruin ;
    There the wide forest scene,
Rude in the uncultivated loveliness
    Of gardens long run wild,
Seems, to the unwilling sojourner,
    whose steps
    Chance in that desert has delayed,
Thus to have stood since earth was
    what it is.
Yet once it was the busiest haunt,
Whither, as to a common centre,
    flocked,
    Strangers, and ships, and merchan-
      dise :
    Once peace and freedom blest
    The cultivated plain :
    But wealth, that curse of man,
Blighted the bud of its prosperity :
Virtue and wisdom, truth and liberty,
Fled, to return not, until man shall
    know
That they alone can give the bliss
    Worthy a soul that claims
    Its kindred with eternity.

    There's not one atom of yon
      earth
    But once was living man ;
    Nor the minutest drop of rain,
    That hangeth in its thinnest
      cloud,
    But flowed in human veins :
    And from the burning plains

Where Lybian monsters yell,
From the most gloomy glens
Of Greenland's sunless clime,
To where the golden fields
Of fertile England spread
Their harvest to the day,
Thou canst not find one spot
Whereon no city stood.

How strange is human pride !
I tell thee that those living things,
To whom the fragile blade of grass,
That springeth in the morn
And perisheth ere noon,
Is an unbounded world ;
I tell thee that those viewless be-
ings,
Whose mansion is the smallest par-
ticle
Of the impassive atmosphere,
Think, feel, and live like man ;
That their affections and anti-
pathies,
Like his, produce the laws
Ruling their moral state ;
And the minutest throb
That through their frame dif-
fuses
The slightest, faintest mo-
tion,
Is fixed and indispensable
As the majestic laws
That rule yon rolling orbs.

The Fairy paused. The Spirit,
In ecstacy of admiration, felt
All knowledge of the past revived ;
the events
Of old and wondrous times,
Which dim⁷tradition interruptedly
Teaches the credulous vulgar, were
unfolded
In just perspective to the view ;
Yet dim from their infinitude.
The Spirit seemed to stand
High on an isolated pinnacle ;
The flood of ages combating below,
The depth of the unbounded uni-
verse
Above, and all around
Nature's unchanging harmony.

III

FAIRY ! the Spirit said,
And on the Queen of Spells
Fixed her ethereal eyes,

I thank thee.   Thou hast given
A boon which I will not resign, and
taught
A lesson not to be unlearned.   I know
The past, and thence I will essay to
glean
A warning for the future, so that man
May profit by his errors, and derive
Experience from his folly :
For, when the power of imparting joy
Is equal to the will, the human soul
Requires no other heaven.

Mab.   Turn thee, surpassing Spirit !
Much yet remains unscanned.
Thou knowest how great is
man,
Thou knowest his imbecility :
Yet learn thou what he is ;
Yet learn the lofty destiny
Which restless Time prepares
For every living soul.

Behold a gorgeous palace, that, amid
Yon populous city, rears its thousand
towers
And seems itself a city. Gloomy
troops
Of sentinels, in stern and silent ranks,
Encompass it around : the dweller
there
Cannot be free and happy ; hearest
thou not
The curses of the fatherless, the groans
Of those who have no friend ? He
passes on :
The King, the wearer of a gilded chain
That binds his soul to abjectness, the
fool
Whom courtiers nickname monarch,
whilst a slave
Even to the basest appetites—that
man
Heeds not the shriek of penury ; he
smiles
At the deep curses which the destitute
Mutter in secret, and a sullen joy
Pervades his bloodless heart when
thousands groan
But for those morsels which his
wantonness
Wastes in unjoyous revelry, to save
All that they love from famine : when
he hears
The tale of horror, to some ready-made
face

Of hypocritical assent he turns,
Smothering the glow of shame, that,
    spite of him,
Flushes his bloated cheek.
            Now to the meal
Of silence, grandeur, and excess, he
    drags
His palled unwilling appetite. If gold,
Gleaming around, and numerous vi-
    ands culled
From every clime, could force the
    loathing sense
To overcome satiety,—if wealth
The spring it draws from poisons not,
    —or vice,
Unfeeling, stubborn vice, converteth
    not
Its food to deadliest venom ; then
    that king
Is happy ; and the peasant who ful-
    fils
His unforced task, when he returns at
    even,
And by the blazing faggot meets again
Her welcome for whom all his toil is
    sped,
Tastes not a sweeter meal.
            Behold him now
Stretched on the gorgeous couch ; his
    fevered brain
Reels dizzily awhile : but ah ! too
    soon
The slumber of intemperance sub-
    sides,
And conscience, that undying serpent,
    calls
Her venomous brood to their noctur-
    nal task.
Listen ! he speaks ! oh ! mark that
    frenzied eye—
Oh ! mark that deadly visage.
    King.   No cessation !
Oh ! must this last for ever ! Awful
    death,
I wish yet fear to clasp thee ! Not
    one moment
Of dreamless sleep ! O dear and
    blessed peace !
Why dost thou shroud thy vestal
    purity
In penury and dungeons ! wherefore
    lurkest
With danger, death, and solitude :
    yet shunn'st
The palace I have built thee ! Sacred
    peace !

Oh visit me but once, and pitying shed
One drop of balm upon my withered
    soul.

Vain man ! that palace is the virtu-
    ous heart,
And peace defileth not her snowy robe
In such a shed as thine. Hark ! yet
    he mutters ;
His slumbers are but varied agonies,
They prey like scorpions on the springs
    of life.
There needeth not the hell that bigots
    frame
To punish those who err : earth in it-
    self
Contains at once the evil and the cure ;
And all-sufficing nature can chastise
Those who transgress her law,—she
    only knows
How justly to proportion to the fault
The punishment it merits.
                Is it strange
That this poor wretch should pride
    him in his woe ?
Take pleasure in his abjectness, and
    hug
The scorpion that consumes him ? Is
    it strange
That, placed on a conspicuous throne
    of thorns,   mured-
Grasping an iron sceptre, and im-
Within a splendid prison, whose stern
    bounds
Shut him from all that's good or dear
    on earth,
His soul asserts not its humanity ?
That man's mild nature rises not in
    war
Against a king's employ ? No—'tis
    not strange,
He, like the vulgar, thinks, feels, acts,
    and lives
Just as his father did ; the uncon-
    quered powers
Of precedent and custom interpose
Between a *king* and virtue. Stranger
    yet,
To those who know not nature, nor
    deduce
The future from the present, it may
    seem,
That not one slave, who suffers from
    the crimes
Of this unnatural being ; not one
    wretch,

Whose children famish, and whose
nuptial bed
Is earth's unpitying bosom, rears an
arm
To dash him from his throne !
           Those gilded flies
That, basking in the sunshine of a
court,
Fatten on its corruption !—what are
they ?
—The drones of the community ;
they feed
On the mechanic's labour ; the starved
hind
For them compels the stubborn
glebe to yield
Its unshared harvests ; and yon squalid form,
Leaner than fleshless misery, that
wastes
A sunless life in the unwholesome
mine,
Drags out in labour a protracted
death,
To glut their grandeur ; many faint
with toil,
That few may know the cares and
woe of sloth.

Whence, thinkest thou, kings and
parasites arose ?
Whence that unnatural line of drones,
who heap
Toil and unvanquishable penury
On those who build their palaces, and
bring
Their daily bread ?—From vice,
black, loathsome vice ;
From rapine, madness, treachery, and
wrong ;
From all that genders misery, and
makes
Of earth this thorny wilderness ; from
lust,
Revenge, and murder.—And when
reason's voice,
Loud as the voice of nature, shall
have waked
The nations ; and mankind perceive
that vice
Is discord, war, and misery ; that vir-
tue
Is peace, and happiness, and harmony ;
When man's maturer nature shall disdain

The playthings of its childhood ;—
kingly glare
Will lose its power to dazzle ; its
authority
Will silently pass by ; the gorgeous
throne
Shall stand unnoticed in the regal hall,
Fast falling to decay ; whilst false-
hood's trade
Shall be as hateful and unprofitable
As that of truth is now.
           Where is the fame
Which the vain-glorious mighty of
the earth
Seek to eternise ? Oh ! the faintest
sound
From time's light footfall, the minut-
est wave
That swells the flood of ages, whelms
in nothing
The unsubstantial bubble. Ay ! to-
day,
Stern is the tyrant's mandate, red the
gaze
That flashes desolation, strong the arm
That scatters multitudes. To-mor-
row comes !
That mandate is a thunder-peal that
died   [flash
In ages past ; that gaze, a transient
On which the midnight closed, and on
that arm
The worm has made his meal.
           The virtuous man
Who, great in his humility, as kings
Are little in their grandeur ; he who
leads
Invincibly a life of resolute good,
And stands amid the silent dungeon-
depths
More free and fearless than the trem-
bling judge,
Who, clothed in venal power, vainly
strove
To bind the impassive spirit ;—when
he falls,
His mild eye beams benevolence no
more :
Withered the hand outstretched but
to relieve ;
Sunk reason's simple eloquence, that
rolled
But to appal the guilty. Yes ! the
grave
Hath quenched that eye, and death's
relentless frost

Withered that arm : but the unfading
  fame
Which virtue hangs upon its votary's
  tomb ;
The deathless memory of that man,
  whom kings
Call to their mind and tremble ; the
  remembrance
With which the happy spirit contem-
  plates
Its well-spent pilgrimage on earth,
Shall never pass away.

Nature rejects the monarch, not the
  man ;
The subject, not the citizen : for kings
And subjects, mutual foes, for ever
  play
A losing game into each other's hands,
Whose stakes are vice and misery.
  The man
Of virtuous soul commands not, nor
  obeys.
Power, like a desolating pestilence,
Pollutes whate'er it touches; and
  obedience,
Bane of all genius, virtue, freedom,
  truth,
Makes slaves of men, and of the hu-
  man frame
A mechanized automaton.
              When Nero,
High over flaming Rome, with sa-
  vage joy
Lowered like a fiend, drank with en-
  raptured ear
The shrieks of agonizing death, be-
  held   [felt
The frightful desolation spread, and
A new-created sense within his soul
Thrill to the sight, and vibrate to the
  sound ;
Thinkest thou his grandeur had not
  overcome
The force of human kindness ? and,
  when Rome,
With one stern blow, hurled not the
  tyrant down,
Crushed not the arm, red with her
  dearest blood,
Had not submissive abjectness des-
  troyed
Nature's suggestions ?
          Look on yonder earth :
The golden harvests spring ; the un-
  failing sun

Sheds light and life ; the fruits, the
  flowers, the trees,
Arise in due succession ; all things
  speak
Peace, harmony, and love.   The Uni-
  verse,
In nature's silent eloquence, declares
That all fulfil the works of love and
  joy,—
All but the outcast, Man.   He fabri-
  cates
The sword which stabs his peace ; he
  cherisheth
The snakes that gnaw his heart ; he
  raiseth up
The tyrant, whose delight is in his woe,
Whose sport is in his agony.   Yon
  sun,
Lights it the great alone ?   Yon sil-
  ver beams,
Sleep they less sweetly on the cottage
  thatch,
Than on the dome of kings ?   Is
  mother earth
A step-dame to her numerous sons,
  who earn
Her unshared gifts with unremitting
  toil ;
A mother only to those puling babes
Who, nursed in ease and luxury,
  make men
The playthings of their babyhood,
  and mar,
In self-important childishness, the
  peace
Which men alone appreciate ?

    Spirit of Nature ! no !
The pure diffusion of thy essence
    throbs
  Alike in every human heart.
    Thou, aye, erectest there
  Thy throne of power unappeal-
    able :
  Thou art the judge beneath
    whose nod
  Man's brief and frail authority
    Is powerless as the wind
    That passeth idly by.
Thine the tribunal which surpasseth
  The show of human justice,
    As God surpasses man.

    Spirit of Nature ! thou
Life of interminable multitudes ;
  Soul of those mighty spheres

Whose changeless paths through
    Heaven's deep silence lie ;
Soul of that smallest being,
    The dwelling of whose life
Is one faint April sun-gleam ;—
Man, like these passive things,
Thy will unconsciously fulfilleth :
Like theirs, his age of endless
    peace,
    Which time is fast maturing,
    Will swiftly, surely, come ;
And the unbounded frame, which
    thou pervadest,
    Will be without a flaw
Marring its perfect symmetry.

IV

How beautiful this night ! the
    balmiest sigh,
Which vernal zephyrs breathe in
    evening's ear,
Were discord to the speaking quiet-
    ude
That wraps this moveless scene.
    Heaven's ebon vault,
Studded with stars unutterably
    bright,
Through which the moon's unclouded
    grandeur rolls,
Seems like a canopy which love has
    spread
To curtain her sleeping world. Yon
    gentle hills,
Robed in a garment of untrodden
    snow ;
Yon darksome rocks, whence icicles
    depend,
So stainless that their white and
    glittering spires
Tinge not 'the moon's pure beam ;
    yon castled steep,
Whose banner hangeth o'er the time-
    worn tower
So idly, that rapt fancy deemeth it
A metaphor of peace ;—all form a
    scene
Where musing solitude might love to
    lift
Her soul above this sphere of earthli-
    ness ;
Where silence undisturbed might
    watch alone,
So cold, so bright, so still.
                    The orb of day,
In southern climes, o'er ocean's
    waveless field

Sinks sweetly smiling : not the
    faintest breath
Steals o'er the unruffled deep ; the
    clouds of eve
Reflect unmoved the lingering beam
    of day ;
And vesper's image on the western
    main
Is beautifully still. To-morrow
    comes :
Cloud upon cloud, in dark and deep-
    ening mass,
Roll o'er the blackened waters ; the
    deep roar
Of distant thunder mutters awfully ;
Tempest unfolds its pinion o'er the
    gloom
That shrouds the boiling surge ; the
    pitiless fiend,
With all his winds and lightnings,
    tracks his prey ;
The torn deep yawns,—the vessel
    finds a grave
Beneath its jagged gulf.
                    Ah ! whence yon glare
That fires the arch of heaven !—that
    dark red smoke
Blotting the silver moon ? The stars
    are quenched
In darkness, and the pure and
    spangling snow
Gleams faintly through the gloom
    that gathers round.
Hark to that roar, whose swift and
    deafening peals
In countless echoes through the
    mountains ring,
Startling pale midnight on her starry
    throne !
Now swells the intermingling din ;
    the jar   [bomb ;
Frequent and frightful of the bursting
The falling beam, the shriek, the
    groan, the shout,
The ceaseless clangor, and the rush
    of men
Inebriate with rage :—loud, and more
    loud
The discord grows ; till pale death
    shuts the scene,
And o'er the conqueror and the
    conquered draws
His cold and bloody shroud.—Of all
    the men
Whom day's departing beam saw
    blooming there

In proud and vigorous health ; of all
the hearts
That beat with anxious life at sun-set
there ;
How few survive, how few are beating
now !
All is deep silence, like the fearful
calm
That slumbers in the storm's por-
tentous pause ;
Save when the frantic wail of widowed
love
Comes shuddering on the blast, or the
faint moan
With which some soul bursts from the
frame of clay
Wrapt round its struggling powers.
          The grey morn
Dawns on the mournful scene ; the
sulphurous smoke
Before the icy wind slow rolls away,
And the bright beams of frosty morn-
ing dance
Along the spangling snow. There
tracks of blood
Even to the forest's depth, and scat-
tered arms,
And lifeless warriors, whose hard linea-
ments
Death's self could change not, mark
the dreadful path
Of the outsallying victors : far behind,
Black ashes note where their proud
city stood.
Within yon forest is a gloomy glen—
Each tree which guards its darkness
from the day,
Waves o'er a warrior's tomb.
          I see thee shrink,
Surpassing Spirit !—wert thou hu-
man else ?
I see a shade of doubt and horror fleet
Across thy stainless features : yet
fear not ;
This is no unconnected misery,
Nor stands uncaused, and irretriev-
able.
Man's evil nature, that apology
Which kings who rule, and cowards
who crouch, set up
For their unnumbered crimes, sheds
not the blood
Which desolates the discord-wasted
land :
From kings, and priests, and states-
men, war arose,

Whose safety is man's deep unbettered
woe,
Whose grandeur his debasement.
Let the axe
Strike at the root, the poison-tree will
fall ;
And where its venomed exhalations
spread
Ruin, and death, and woe, where mil-
lions lay
Quenching the serpent's famine, and
their bones
Bleaching unburied in the putrid blast,
A garden shall arise, in loveliness
Surpassing fabled Eden.
          Hath Nature's soul,
That formed this world so beautiful,
that spread
Earth's lap with plenty, and life's
smallest chord
Strung to unchanging unison, that
gave
The happy birds their dwelling in the
grove,
That yielded to the wanderers of the
deep
The lovely silence of the unfathomed
main,
And filled the meanest worm that
crawls in dust
With spirit, thought, and love ; on
Man alone
Partial in causeless malice, wantonly
Heaped ruin, vice, and slavery ; his
soul   [afar
Blasted with withering curses ; placed
The meteor happiness, that shuns his
grasp,
But serving on the frightful gulf to
glare,
Rent wide beneath his footsteps ?
          Nature !—no !
Kings, priests, and statesmen blast
the human flower,
Even in its tender bud ; their influ-
ence darts
Like subtle poison through the blood-
less veins
Of desolate society. The child,
Ere he can lisp his mother's sacred
name,
Swells with the unnatural pride of
crime, and lifts
His baby-sword even in a hero's mood.
This infant arm becomes the bloodiest
scourge

Of devastated earth ; whilst specious
  names
Learnt in soft childhood's unsuspecting hour,
Serve as the ʳsophisms with which
  manhood dims
Bright reason's ray, and sanctifies the
  sword
Upraised to shed a brother's innocent
  blood.
Let priest-led slaves cease to proclaim that man
Inherits vice and misery, when force
And falsehood hang even o'er the
  cradled babe,
Stifling with rudest grasp all natural
  good.

Ah ! to the stranger-soul, when first it
  peeps
From its new tenement, and looks
  abroad
For happiness and sympathy, how
  stern
And desolate a tract is this wide
  world !
How withered all the buds of natural
  good !
No shade, no shelter from the sweeping storms
Of pitiless power ! On its wretched
  frame,
Poisoned, perchance, by the disease
  and woe
Heaped on the wretched parent,
  whence it sprung,
By morals, law, and custom, the pure
  winds
Of heaven, that renovate the insect
  tribes,
May breathe not. The untainting
  light of day
May visit not its longings. It is
  bound
Ere it has life : yea, all the chains are
  forged
Long ere its being : all liberty and
  love
And peace is torn from its defence-
  lessness ;
Cursed from its birth, even from its
  cradle doomed
To abjectness and bondage !

Throughout this varied and eternal
  world
Soul is the only element, the block

That for uncounted ages has re-
  mained.
The moveless pillar of a mountain's
  weight
Is active living spirit. Every grain
Is sentient both in unity and part,
And the minutest atom comprehends
A world of loves and hatreds ; these
  beget
Evil and good : hence truth and
  falsehood spring ;
Hence will, and thought, and action,
  all the germs
Of pain or pleasure, sympathy or hate,
That variegate the eternal universe.
Soul is not more polluted than the
  beams
Of heaven's pure orb, ere round their
  rapid lines
The taint of earth-born atmospheres
  arise.

Man is of soul and body, formed for
  deeds
Of high resolve ; on fancy's boldest
  wing
To soar unwearied, fearlessly to turn
The keenest pangs to peacefulness,
  and taste
The joys which mingled sense and
  spirit yield.   [woe,
Or he is formed for abjectness and
To grovel on the dunghill of his fears,
To shrink at every sound, to quench
  the flame
Of natural love in sensualism, to know
That hour as blest when on his worth-
  less days
The frozen hand of death shall set its
  seal,
Yet fear the cure, though hating the
  disease.
The one is man that shall hereafter
  be ;
The other, man as vice has made him
  now.

War is the statesman's game, the
  priest's delight,
The lawyer's jest, the hired assassin's
  trade,
And, to those royal murderers, whose
  mean thrones
Are bought by crimes of treachery
  and gore,
The bread they eat, the staff on which
  they lean.

Guards, garbed in blood-red livery,
surround
Their palaces, participate the crimes
That force defends, and from a na-
tion's rage
Secure the crown, which all the curses
reach
That famine, frenzy, woe and penury
breathe.
These are the hired bravoes who de-
fend
The tyrant's throne—the bullies of
his fear:
These are the sinks and channels of
worst vice,
The refuse of society, the dregs
Of all that is most vile: their cold
hearts blend
Deceit with sternness, ignorance with
pride,
All that is mean and villainous, with
rage
Which hopelessness of good, and self-
contempt,
Alone might kindle; they are decked
in wealth,
Honour and power, then are sent
abroad
To do their work. The pestilence
that stalks
In gloomy triumph through some
Eastern land
Is less destroying. They cajole with
gold,
And promises of fame, the thought-
less youth
Already crushed with servitude: he
knows
His wretchedness too late, and
cherishes
Repentance for his ruin, when his
doom
Is sealed in gold and blood!
Those too the tyrant serve, who
skilled to snare
The feet of justice in the toils of law,
Stand, ready to oppress the weaker
still;
And, right or wrong, will vindicate for
gold,
Sneering at public virtue, which be-
neath
Their pitiless tread lies torn and
trampled, where
Honour sits smiling at the sale of
truth.

Then grave and hoary-headed hypo-
crites,
Without a hope, a passion, or a love,
Who, through a life of luxury and
lies,
Have crept by flattery to the seats of
power,
Support the system whence their
honours flow—
They have three words; well tyrants
know their use,
Well pay them for the loan, with
usury
Torn from a bleeding world!—God,
Hell, and Heaven.
A vengeful, pitiless, and almighty
fiend,
Whose mercy is a nick-name for the
rage
Of tameless tigers hungering for
blood.
Hell, a red gulf of everlasting fire,
Where poisonous and undying worms
prolong
Eternal misery to those hapless slaves
Whose life has been a penance for its
crimes.
And Heaven, a meed for those who
dare belie
Their human nature, quake, believe,
and cringe
Before the mockeries of earthly power.

These tools the tyrant tempers to his
work,
Wields in his wrath, and as he wills,
destroys,
Omnipotent in wickedness: the
while
Youth springs, age moulders, manhood tamely does
His bidding, bribed by short-lived
joys to lend
Force to the weakness of his trembling arm.
They rise, they fall; one generation
comes
Yielding its harvest to destruction's
scythe.
It fades, another blossoms: yet behold!
Red glows the tyrant's stamp-mark
on its bloom,
Withering and cankering deep its passive prime.

He has invented lying words and
    modes,
Empty and vain as his own coreless
    heart ;
Evasive meanings, nothings of much
    sound,
To lure the heedless victim to the
    toils
Spread round the valley of its para-
    dise.

Look to thyself, priest, conqueror, or
    prince !
Whether thy trade is falsehood, and
    thy lusts
Deep wallow in the earnings of the
    poor,
With whom thy master was :—or
    thou delight'st
In numbering o'er the myriads of thy
    slain,
All misery weighing nothing in the
    scale
Against thy short-lived fame ; or
    thou dost load
With cowardice and crime the groan-
    ing land,
A pomp-fed king. Look to thy
    wretched self !
Ay, art thou not the veriest slave
    that e'er
Crawled on the loathing earth ? Are
    not thy days
Days of unsatisfying listlessness ?
Dost thou not cry, ere night's long
    rack is o'er,
'When will the morning come' ? Is
    not thy youth
A vain and feverish dream of sensual-
    ism ?
Thy manhood blighted with unripe
    disease ?
Are not thy views of unregretted
    death
Drear, comfortless, and horrible ?
    Thy mind,
Is it not morbid as thy nerveless
    frame,
Incapable of judgment, hope, or love ?
And dost thou wish the errors to sur-
    vive
That bar thee from all sympathies of
    good,
After the miserable interest
Thou hold'st in their protraction ?
    When the grave

Has swallowed up thy memory and
    thyself,
Dost thou desire the bane that poisons
    earth
To twine its roots around thy coffined
    clay,
Spring from thy bones, and blossom
    on thy tomb,
That of its fruit thy babes may eat
    and die ?

v

Thus do the generations of the earth
Go to the grave, and issue from the
    womb,
Surviving still the imperishable
    change
That renovates the world ; even as
    the leaves
Which the keen frost-wind of the
    waning year
Has scattered on the forest soil, and
    heaped
For many seasons there, though long
    they choke,
Loading with loathsome rottenness
    the land,
All germs of promise. Yet when the
    tall trees
From which they fell, shorn of their
    lovely shapes,   [there,
Lie level with the earth to moulder
They fertilise the land they long de-
    formed,
Till from the breathing lawn a forest
    springs
Of youth, integrity, and loveliness,
Like that which gave it life, to spring
    and die.
Thus suicidal selfishness, that blights
The fairest feelings of the opening
    heart,
Is destined to decay, whilst from the
    soil
Shall spring all virtue, all delight, all
    love,
And judgment cease to wage unna-
    tural war
With passion's unsubduable array.
Twin-sister of religion, selfishness !
Rival in crime and falsehood, aping all
The wanton horrors of her bloody
    play ;
Yet frozen, unimpassioned, spiritless,
Shunning the light, and owning not
    its name ;

Compelled, by its deformity, to screen
With flimsy veil of justice and of
  right,
Its unattractive lineaments, that
  scare
All, save the brood of ignorance : at
  once
The cause and the effect of tyranny ;
Unblushing, hardened, sensual, and
  vile ;
Dead to all love but of its abjectness,
With heart impassive by more noble
  powers
Than unshared pleasure, sordid gain,
  or fame :
Despising its own miserable being,
Which still it longs, yet fears, to dis-
  enthrall.

Hence commerce springs, the venal
  interchange
Of all that human art or nature yield ;
Which wealth should purchase not,
  but want demand,
And natural kindness hasten to sup-
  ply
From the full fountain of its bound-
  less love,
For ever stifled, drained, and tainted
  now.
Commerce ! beneath whose poison-
  breathing shade
No solitary virtue dares to spring ;
But poverty and wealth with equal
  hand
Scatter their withering· curses, and
  unfold
The doors of premature and violent
  death,
To pining famine and full-fed disease,
To all that shares the lot of human
  life,
Which poisoned body and soul, scarce
  drags the chain
That lengthens as it goes and clanks
  behind.

Commerce has set the mark of selfish-
  ness,
The signet of its all-enslaving power,
Upon a shining ore, and called it gold :
Before whose image bow the vulgar
  great,
The vainly rich, the miserable proud,
The mob of peasants, nobles, priests,
  and kings,

And with blind feelings reverence the
  power
That grinds them to the dust of
  misery.
But in the temple of their hireling
  hearts
Gold is a living god, and rules in scorn
All earthly things but virtue.

Since tyrants, by the sale of human
  life,
Heap luxuries to their sensualism,
  and fame
To their wide-wasting and insatiate
  pride,
Success has sanctioned to a credulous
  world
The ruin, the disgrace, the woe of war.
His hosts of blind and unresisting
  dupes   [inet
The despot numbers ; from his cab-
These puppets of his schemes he
  moves at will,
Even as the slaves by force or famine
  driven
Beneath a vulgar master, to perform
A task of cold and brutal drudgery ;—
Hardened to hope, insensible to fear,
Scarce living pulleys of a dead ma-
  chine,
Mere wheels of work and articles of
  trade,
That grace the proud and noisy pomp
  of wealth !

The harmony and happiness of man
Yield to the wealth of nations ; that
  which lifts
His nature to the heaven of its pride,
Is bartered for the poison of his soul ;
The weight that drags to earth his
  towering hopes,
Blighting all prospect but of selfish
  gain,
Withering all passion but of slavish
  fear,
Extinguishing all free and generous
  love
Of enterprise and daring, even the
  pulse
That fancy kindles in the beating
  heart
To mingle with sensation, it de-
  stroys,—
Leaves nothing but the sordid lust of
  self,

The grovelling hope of interest and
 gold,
Unqualified, unmingled, unredeemed
Even by hypocrisy.
                 And statesmen boast
Of wealth! The wordy eloquence
 that lives
After the ruin of their hearts, can gild
The bitter poison of a nation's woe,
Can turn the worship of the servile
 mob
To their corrupt and glaring idol,
 Fame,
From Virtue, trampled by its iron
 tread,
Although its dazzling pedestal be
 raised
Amid the horrors of a limb-strewn
 field,
With desolated dwellings smoking
 round.
The man of ease, who, by his warm
 fireside,
To deeds of charitable intercourse
And bare fulfilment of the common
 laws
Of decency and prejudice, confines
The struggling nature of his human
 heart,
Is duped by their cold sophistry; he
 sheds   [wreck
A passing tear perchance upon the
Of earthly peace, when near his dwell-
 ing's door
The frightful waves are driven,—when
 his son
Is murdered by the tyrant, or religion
Drives his wife raving mad.   But
 the poor man,
Whose life is misery, and fear, and
 care;
Whom the morn wakens but to fruit-
 less toil;
Who ever hears his famished off-
 spring's scream,
Whom their pale mother's uncom-
 plaining gaze
For ever meets, and the proud rich
 man's eye
Flashing command, and the heart-
 breaking scene
Of thousands like himself; he little
 heeds
The rhetoric of tyranny, his hate
Is quenchless as his wrongs, he laughs
 to scorn

The vain and bitter mockery of words,
Feeling the horror of the tyrant's
 deeds,
And unrestrained but by the arm of
 power,
That knows and dreads his enmity.

The iron rod of penury still compels
Her wretched slave to bow the knee
 to wealth,
And poison, with unprofitable toil,
A life too void of solace to confirm
The very chains that bind him to his
 doom.
Nature, impartial in munificence,
Has gifted man with all-subduing
 will:
Matter, with all its transitory shapes,
Lies subjected and plastic at his feet,
That, weak from bondage, tremble as
 they tread
How many a rustic Milton has passed
 by,
Stifling the speechless longings of his
 heart,
In unremitting drudgery and care!
How many a vulgar Cato has com-
 pelled
His energies, no longer tameless then,
To mould a pin, or fabricate a nail!
How many a Newton, to whose pass-
 ive ken
Those mighty spheres that gem in-
 finity
Were only specks of tinsel, fixed in
 heaven
To light the midnights of his native
 town!

Yet every heart contains perfection's
 germ:
The wisest of the sages of the earth,
That ever from the stores of reason
 drew
Science and truth, and virtue's dread-
 less tone,
Were but a weak and inexperienced
 boy,
Proud, sensual, unimpassioned, unim-
 bued
With pure desire and universal love,
Compared to that high being, of
 cloudless brain,
Untainted passion, elevated will,
Which death (who even would linger
 long in awe

Within his noble presence, and be-
neath
His changeless eye-beam), might
alone subdue.
Him, every slave now dragging
through the filth
Of some corrupted city his sad life,
Pining with famine, swoln with lux-
ury,
Blunting the keenness of his spiritual
sense
With narrow schemings and unworthy
cares,
Or madly rushing through all violent
crime,
To move the deep stagnation of his
soul,—
Might imitate and equal.
                    But mean lust
Has bound its chains so tight about
the earth,
That all within it but the virtuous
    man   [reach
Is venal: gold or fame will surely
The price prefixed by selfishness, to all
But him of resolute and unchanging
will;
Whom, nor the plaudits of a servile
crowd,
Nor the vile joys of tainting luxury,
Can bribe to yield his elevated soul
To tyranny or falsehood, though they
wield
With blood-red hand the sceptre of
the world.

All things are sold: the very light of
heaven
Is venal; earth's unsparing gifts of
love,
The smallest and most despicable
things
That lurk in the abysses of the deep,
All objects of our life, even life itself,
And the poor pittance which the laws
allow
Of liberty, the fellowship of man,
Those duties which his heart of hu-
man love
Should urge him to perform instinct-
ively,
Are bought and sold as in a public
mart
Of undisguising selfishness, that sets
On each its price, the stamp-mark of
her reign.

Even love is sold; the solace of all
woe
Is turned to deadliest agony, old age
Shivers in selfish beauty's loathing
arms,
And youth's corrupted impulses prepare
A life of horror from the blighting
bane
Of commerce: whilst the pestilence
that springs
From unenjoying sensualism, has
filled
All human life with hydra-headed
woes.

Falsehood demands but gold to pay
the pangs
Of outraged conscience; for the slav-
ish priest
Sets no great value on his hireling
faith:
A little passing pomp, some servile
souls,
Whom cowardice itself might safely
chain,
Or the spare mite of avarice could
bribe
To deck the triumph of their languid
zeal,
Can make him minister to tyranny.
More daring crime requires a loftier
meed:
Without a shudder the slave-soldier
lends
His arm to murderous deeds, and
steels his heart,
When the dread eloquence of dying
men,
Low mingling on the lonely field of
fame,
Assails that nature whose applause he
sells
For the gross blessings of the patriot
mob,
For the vile gratitude of heartless
kings,
And for a cold world's good word,—
viler still!

There is a nobler glory which survives
Until our being fades, and, solacing
All human care, accompanies its
change;
Deserts not virtue in the dungeon's
gloom,

And, in the precincts of the palace,
  guides
Its footsteps through that labyrinth
  of crime ;
Imbues his lineaments with daunt-
  lessness,
Even when, from power's avenging
  hand, he takes
Its sweetest, last and noblest title—
  death ;
—The consciousness of good, which
  neither gold,
Nor sordid fame, nor hope of hea-
  venly bliss,
Can purchase ; but a life of resolute
  good,
Unalterable will, quenchless desire
Of universal happiness, the heart
That beats with it in unison, the brain,
Whose ever-wakeful wisdom toils to
  change
Reason's rich stores for its eternal
  weal.

This commerce of sincerest virtue
  needs
No mediative signs of selfishness,
No jealous intercourse of wretched
  gain,
No balancings of prudence, cold and
  long ;
In just and equal measure all is
  weighed,
One scale contains the sum of human
  weal,
And one, the good man's heart.
                        How vainly seek
The selfish for that happiness denied
To aught but virtue ! Blind and
  hardened, they
Who hope for peace amid the storms
  of care,
Who covet power they know not how
  to use,
And sigh for pleasure they refuse In
  give :—
Madly they frustrate still their own
  designs ;
And, where they hope that quiet to
  enjoy
Which virtue pictures, bitterness of
  soul,
Pining regrets, and vain repentances,
Disease, disgust, and lassitude, per
  vade
Their valueless and miserable lives.

But hoary-headed selfishness has felt
Its deathblow,   and is tottering to
  the grave :
A brighter morn awaits the human
  day,
When every transfer of earth's natural
  gifts
Shall be a commerce of good words
  and works ;
When poverty and wealth, the thirst
  of fame,
The fear of infamy, disease and woe,
War with its million horrors, and
  fierce hell,
Shall live but in the memory of
  time,
Who, like a penitent libertine, shall
  start,
Look back, and shudder at his younger
  years.

VI

ALL touch, all eye, all ear,
The Spirit felt the Fairy's burning
  speech.
O'er the thin texture of its frame,
The varying periods painted, chang-
  ing glows ;
  As on a summer even,
When soul-enfolding music floats
  around,
The stainless mirror of the lake
Re-images the eastern gloom,
Mingling convulsively its purple hues
  With sunset's burnished gold.

Then thus the Spirit spoke :
It is a wild and miserable world !
  Thorny, and full of care,
Which every fiend can make his prey
  at will.
O Fairy ! in the lapse of years,
  Is there no hope in store ?
  Will yon vast suns roll on
Interminably, still illuming
The night of so many wretched
  souls,
  And see no hope for them ?
Will not the universal spirit e'er
Revivify this withered limb of Hea-
  ven ?

The Fairy calmly smiled
to comfort, and a kindling gleam of
  hope
Suffused the Spirit's lineaments.

Oh! rest thee tranquil; chase those
     fearful doubts,
Which ne'er could rack an everlasting
     soul,
That sees the chains which bind it to
     its doom.
Yes! crime and misery are in yonder
     earth,
     Falsehood, mistake, and lust;
But the eternal world
Contains at once the evil and the cure.
Some eminent in virtue shall start up,
     Even in perversest time:
The truths of their pure lips, that
     never die,
Shall bind the scorpion falsehood with
     a wreath
     Of ever-living flame,
Until the monster sting itself to death.

     How sweet a scene will earth be-
          come!
Of purest spirits, a pure dwelling-
     place,
Symphonious with the planetary
     spheres;
When man, with changeless nature
     coalescing,
Will undertake regeneration's work,
When its ungenial poles no longer
     point
     To the red and baleful sun
     That faintly twinkles there.

     Spirit, on yonder earth,
Falsehood now triumphs; deadly
     power
Has fixed its seal upon the lip of
     truth!
     Madness and misery are there!
The happiest is most wretched! Yet
     confide
Until pure health-drops, from the cup
     of joy,
Fall like a dew of balm upon the
     world.
Now, to the scene I show, in silence
     turn,
And read the blood-stained charter of
     all woe,
Which nature soon, with re-creating
     hand,
Will blot in mercy from the book of
     earth.
How bold the flight of passion's wan-
     dering wing,

How swift the step of reason's firmer
     tread,
How calm and sweet the victories of
     life,
How terrorless the triumph of the
     grave!
How powerless were the mightiest
     monarch's arm,
Vain his loud threat, and impotent
     his frown!
How ludicrous the priest's dogmatic
     roar!
The weight of his exterminating curse
How light! and his affected charity,
To suit the pressure of the changing
     times,
What palpable deceit!—but for thy
     aid,
Religion! but for thee, prolific fiend,
Who peoplest earth with demons,
     hell with men,
And heaven with slaves!

Thou taintest all thou look'st upon!
     —the stars,
Which on thy cradle beamed so
     brightly sweet,
Were gods to the distempered play-
     fulness
Of thy untutored infancy: the trees,
The grass, the clouds, the mountains,
     and the sea,
All living things that walk, swim,
     creep, or fly,
Were gods: the sun had homage, and
     the moon
Her worshipper. Then thou be-
     camest a boy,
More daring in thy frenzies: every
     shape,   [wild,
Monstrous or vast, or beautifully
Which from sensation's relics, fancy
     culls;
The spirits of the air, the shuddering
     ghost,
The genii of the elements, the powers
That give a shape to nature's varied
     works,
Had life and place in the corrupt be-
     lief
Of thy blind heart: yet still thy
     youthful hands
Were pure of human blood. Then
     manhood gave
Its strength and ardour to thy
     frenzied brain;

Thine eager gaze scanned the stupendous scene,
Whose wonders mocked the knowledge of thy pride,
Their everlasting and unchanging
laws
Reproached thine ignorance. Awhile
thou stoodst
Baffled and gloomy ; then thou didst
sum up
The elements of all that thou didst
know ;
The changing seasons, winter's leaf-
less reign,
The budding of the heaven-breathing
trees,
The eternal orbs that beautify the
night,
The sunrise, and the setting of the
moon,
Earthquakes and wars, and poisons
and disease,
And all their causes, to an abstract
point
Converging, thou didst bend, and
call'd it God !
The self-sufficing, the omnipotent,
The merciful, and the avenging God !
Who, prototype of human misrule,
sits
High in heaven's realm, upon a gold-
en throne,
Even like an earthly king ; and whose
dread work,
Hell, gapes for ever for the unhappy
slaves
Of fate, whom he created in his sport,
To triumph in their torments when
they fell !
Earth heard the name ; earth trem-
bled, as the smoke
Of his revenge ascended up to heaven,
Blotting the constellations ; and the
cries
Of millions butchered in sweet confi-
dence
And unsuspecting peace, even when
the bonds
Of safety were confirmed by wordy
oaths
Sworn in his dreadful name, rung
through the land ;
Whilst innocent babes writhed on thy
stubborn spear,
And thou didst laugh to hear the
mother's shriek

Of maniac gladness as the sacred steel
Felt cold in her torn entrails !

Religion ! thou wert then in man-
hood's prime :
But age crept on : one God would not
suffice
For senile puerility ; thou framedst
A tale to suit thy dotage, and to glut
Thy misery-thirsting soul, that the
mad fiend
Thy wickedness had pictured, might
afford
A plea for sating the unnatural thirst
For murder, rapine, violence, and
crime,
That still consumed thy being, even
when
Thou heardst the step of fate ; —
that flames might light
Thy funeral scene, and the shrill
horrent shrieks
Of parents dying on the pile that
burned
To light their children to thy paths,
the roar,
Of the encircling flames, the exulting
cries
Of thine apostles, loud commingling
there,
    Might sate thy hungry ear
    Even on the bed of death !

But now contempt is mocking thy
grey hairs ;
Thou art descending to the darksome
grave,
Unhonoured and unpitied, but by
those
Whose pride is passing by like thine,
and sheds,
Like thine, a glare that fades before
the sun
Of truth, and shines but in the dreadful night
That long has lowered above the
ruined world.

Throughout these infinite orbs of
mingling light,
Of which yon earth is one, is wide diffused
A spirit of activity and life,
That knows no term, cessation, or
decay ;
That fades not when the lamp of
earthly life,

Extinguished in the dampness of the grave,
Awhile there slumbers, more than when the babe
In the dim newness of its being feels
The impulses of sublunary things,
And all is wonder to unpractised sense :
But, active, steadfast and eternal, still
Guides the fierce whirlwind, in the tempest roars,
Cheers in the day, breathes in the balmy groves,
Strengthens in health, and poisons in disease ;
And in the storm of change, that ceaselessly
Rolls round the eternal universe, and shakes
Its undecaying battlement, presides,
Apportioning with irresistible law
The place each spring of its machine shall fill ;
So that, when waves on waves tumultuous heap
Confusion to the clouds, and fiercely driven
Heaven's lightnings scorch the up-rooted ocean fords,
Whilst, to the eye of shipwrecked mariner,
Lone sitting on the bare and shuddering rock,
All seems unlinked contingency and chance :
No atom of this turbulence fulfils
A vague and unnecessitated task,
Or acts but as it must and ought to act.
Even the minutest molecule of light,
That in an April sunbeam's fleeting glow
Fulfils its destined, though invisible work,
The universal Spirit guides ; nor less
When merciless ambition, or mad zeal,
Has led two hosts of dupes to battle-field,
That, blind, they there may dig each other's graves
And call the sad work glory, does it rule
All passions : not a thought, a will, an act,
No working of the tyrant's moody mind,

Nor one misgiving of the slaves who boast
Their servitude, to hide the shame they feel,
Nor the events enchaining every will,
That from the depths of unrecorded time
Have drawn all-influencing virtue, pass
Unrecognised or unforeseen by thee,
Soul of the Universe ! eternal spring
Of life and death, of happiness and woe,
Of all that chequers the phantasmal scene
That floats before our eyes in wavering light,
Which gleams but on the darkness of our prison,
Whose chains and massy walls
We feel but cannot see.

Spirit of Nature ! all-sufficing Power.
Necessity ! thou mother of the world !
Unlike the God of human error, thou
Requirest no prayers or praises ; the caprice
Of man's weak will belongs no more to thee
Than do the changeful passions of his breast
To thy unvarying harmony : the slave,
Whose horrible lusts spread misery o'er the world
And the good man, who lifts, with virtuous pride,
His being, in the sight of happiness,
That springs from his own works ; the poison-tree,
Beneath whose shade all life is withered up,
And the fair oak, whose leafy dome affords [love
A temple where the vows of happy
Are register'd, are equal in thy sight :
No love, no hate thou cherishest ; revenge
And favouritism, and worst desire of fame,
Thou knowest not : all that the wide world contains
Are but thy passive instruments, and thou
Regardest them all with an impartial eye

Whose joy or pain thy nature cannot
feel,
  Because thou hast not human sense,
  Because thou art not human mind.

Yes! when the sweeping storm of
  time
Has sung its death-dirge o'er the
  ruined fanes
And broken altars of the almighty
  fiend
Whose name usurps thy honours, and
  the blood
Through centuries clotted there, has
  floated down
The tainted flood of ages, shalt thou
  live
Unchangeable! A shrine is raised to
  thee,
  Which, nor the tempest breath of
  time,
  Nor the interminable flood,
  Over earth's slight pageant rolling,
    Availeth to destroy,—
The sensitive extension of the world.
  That wondrous and eternal fane,
Where pain and pleasure, good and
  evil join,
To do the will of strong necessity,
  And life in multitudinous shapes,
Still pressing forward where no term
  can be,
  Like hungry and unresting flame
Curls round the eternal columns of its
  strength.

VII

Spirit. I was an infant when my
  mother went
To see an atheist burned. She took
  me there:
The dark-robed priests were met
  around the pile;
The multitude was gazing silently;
And as the culprit passed with dauntless mien,
Tempered disdain in his unaltering
  eye,
Mixed with a quiet smile, shone
  calmly forth:
The thirsty fire crept round his manly
  limbs;
His resolute eyes were scorched to
  blindness soon:
His death-pang rent my heart! the
  insensate mob

Uttered a cry of triumph, and I wept.
Weep not, child! cried my mother,
  for that man
Has said, There is no God.

Fairy.   There is no God!
Nature confirms the faith his death-
  groan seal'd:
Let heaven and earth, let man's re-
  volving race,
His ceaseless generations, tell their
  tale;
Let every part depending on the chain
That links it to the whole, point to the
  hand
That grasps its term! Let every seed
  that falls,
In silent eloquence unfold its store
Of argument: infinity within,
Infinity without, belie creation;
The exterminable spirit it contains
Is nature's only God; but human
  pride
Is skilful to invent most serious names
To hide its ignorance.
                    The name of God
Has fenced about all crime with holi-
  ness,   [pers,
Himself the creature of his worship-
Whose names and attributes and pas-
  sions change,
Seeva, Buddh, Foh, Jehovah, God, or
  Lord,
Even with the human dupes who
  build his shrines,
Still serving o'er the war-polluted
  world
For desolation's watchword; whether
  hosts
Stain his death-blushing chariot
  wheels, as on
Triumphantly they roll, whilst Brah-
  mins raise
A sacred hymn to mingle with the
  groans;
Or countless partners of his power
  divide
His tyranny to weakness; or the
  smoke
Of burning towns, the cries of female
  helplessness,
Unarmed old age, and youth, and in-
  fancy,
Horribly massacred, ascend to heaven
In honour of his name; or, last and
  worst,

Earth groans beneath religion's iron
   age, .
And priests dare babble of a God of
   peace,
Even whilst their hands are red with
   guiltless blood,
Murdering the while, uprooting every
   germ
Of truth, exterminating, spoiling all,
Making the earth a slaughter-house !

O Spirit ! through the sense
By which thy inner nature was ap-
   prised
   Of outward shows vague dreams
      have roll'd,
And varied reminiscences have
   waked
   Tablets that never fade ;
All things have been imprinted
   there,
The stars, the sea, the earth, the
   sky,
Even the unshapeliest lineaments
   Of wild and fleeting visions
      Have left a record there
         To testify of earth.

These are my empire, for to me is
   given
The wonders of the human world to
   keep,
And fancy's thin creations to endow
With manner, being, and reality ;
Therefore a wondrous phantom, from
   the dreams
Of human error's dense and purblind
   faith,
I will evoke, to meet thy questioning.
   Ahasuerus, rise !

   A strange and woe-worn wight
   Arose beside the battlement,
     And stood unmoving there.
His inessential figure cast no shade
   Upon the golden floor ;
His port and mien bore mark of many
   years,
And chronicles of untold ancientness
Were legible within his beamless eye. :
   Yet his cheek bore the mark of
      youth ;
Freshness and vigour knit his manly
   frame ;
The wisdom of old age was mingled
   there

   With youth's primeval daunt-
     lessness ;
   And inexpressible woe,
Chasten'd by fearless resignation,
   gave
An awful grace to his all-speaking
   brow.

Spirit. Is there a God ?

   Ahasuerus. Is there a God !—ay,
     an almighty God,
And vengeful as almighty ! Once
   his voice
Was heard on earth : earth shuddered
   at the sound ;
The fiery-visaged firmament ex-
   pressed
Abhorrence, and the grave of nature
   yawned
To swallow all the dauntless and the
   good
That dared to hurl defiance at his
   throne,
Girt as it was with power. None but
   slaves
Survived,—cold-blooded slaves, who
   did the work
Of tyrannous omnipotence ; whose
   souls
No honest indignation ever urged
To elevated daring, to one deed
Which gross and sensual self did not
   pollute.
These slaves built temples for the
   omnipotent fiend,
Gorgeous and vast : the costly altars
   smoked
With human blood, and hideous
   pæans rung
Through all the long-drawn aisles. A
   murderer heard
His voice in Egypt, one whose gifts
   and arts
Had raised him to his eminence in
   power,
Accomplice of omnipotence in crime,
And confidant of the all-knowing one.
   These were Jehovah's words.

From an eternity of idleness
I, God, awoke ; in seven days' toil
   made earth
From nothing ; rested, and created
   man :
I placed him in a paradise, and there
Planted the tree of evil, so that he

Might eat and perish, and my soul
 procure
Wherewith to sate its malice, and to
 turn,
Even like a heartless conqueror of
 the earth,
All misery to my fame. The race of
 men
Chosen to my honour, with impunity
May sate the lusts I planted in their
 heart.
Here I command thee hence to lead
 them on,
Until, with harden'd feet, their con-
 quering troops
Wade on the promised soil through
 woman's blood,
And make my name be dreaded
 through the land.
Yet ever-burning flame and ceaseless
 woe
Shall be the doom of their eternal
 souls,
With every soul on this ungrateful
 earth,
Virtuous or vicious, weak or strong,—
 even all
Shall perish, to fulfil the blind revenge,
(Which you, to men, call justice) of
 their God.

    · The murderer's brow
Quiver'd with horror.
      God omnipotent,
Is there no mercy ? must our punish-
 ment
Be endless ? will long ages roll away,
And see no term ? Oh ! wherefore
 hast thou made
In mockery and wrath this evil earth?
Mercy becomes the powerful—be but
 just :
O God ! repent and save.
      One way remains :
I will beget a son, and he shall bear
The sins of all the world ; he shall
 arise
In an unnoticed corner of the earth,
And there shall die upon a cross, and
 purge
The universal crime ; so that the few
On whom my grace descends, those
 who are mark'd
As vessels to the honour of their God,
May credit this strange sacrifice, and
 save

Their souls alive : millions shall live
 and die,
Who ne'er shall call upon their Savi-
 our's name,
But, unredeemed, go to the gaping
 grave.
Thousands shall deem it an old
 woman's tale,
Such as the nurses frighten babes
 withal :
These in a gulf of anguish and of flame
Shall. curse their reprobation end-
 lessly,
Yet tenfold pangs shall force them to
 avow,
Even on their beds of torment, where
 they howl,   [doom.
My honour, and the justice of their
What then avail their virtuous deeds,
 their thoughts
Of purity, with radiant genius bright,
Or lit with human reason's earthly
 ray ?
Many are called, but few will I elect.
Do thou my bidding, Moses.
     Even the murderer's cheek
Was blanched with horror, and his
 quivering lips
Scarce faintly uttered—O almighty
 one,
I tremble and obey !

O Spirit ! centuries have set their
 seal
On this heart of many wounds, and
 loaded brain,
Since the Incarnate came : humbly
 he came,
Veiling his horrible Godhead in the
 shape
Of man, scorned by the world, his
 name unheard,
Save by the rabble of his native town,
Even as a parish demagogue. He led
The crowd ; he taught them justice,
 truth, and peace,
In semblance ; but he lit within their
 souls
The quenchless flames of zeal, and
 blest the sword
He brought on earth to satiate with
 the blood
Of truth and freedom his malignant
 soul.
At length his mortal frame was led to
 death.

I stood beside him : on the torturing
cross
No pain assailed his unterrestrial
sense ;
And yet he groaned.   Indignantly I
summed
The massacres and miseries which his
name
Had sanctioned in my country, and I
cried,
Go ! go ! in mockery.
A smile of godlike malice reillumed
His fading lineaments.—I go, he cried,
But thou shalt wander o'er the un-
quiet earth
Eternally.——The dampness of the
grave
Bathed my imperishable front. I fell,
And long lay tranced upon the
charmèd soil.
When I awoke hell burned within my
brain,
Which staggered on its seat ; for all
around
The mouldering relics of my kindred
lay,
Even as the Almighty's ire arrested
them,
And in their various attitudes of death
My murdered children's mute and
eyeless skulls
Glared ghastly upon me.
                        But my soul,
From sight and sense of the polluting
woe
Of tyranny, had long learned to pre-
fer
Hell's freedom to the servitude of
heaven.
Therefore I rose, and dauntlessly be-
gan
My lonely and unending pilgrimage,
Resolved to wage unweariable war
With my almighty tyrant, and to hurl
Defiance at his impotence to harm
Beyond the curse I bore.   The very
hand
That barred my passage to the peace-
ful grave
Has crushed the earth to misery, and
given
Its empire to the chosen of his slaves.
These have I seen, even from the ear-
liest dawn
Of weak, unstable, and precarious
power ;

Then preaching peace, as now they
practise war,
So, when they turned but from the
massacre
Of unoffending infidels, to quench
Their thirst for ruin in the very blood
That flowed in their own veins, and
pitiless zeal
Froze every human feeling, as the
wife
Sheathed in her husband's heart the
sacred steel,
Even whilst its hopes were dreaming
of her love ;
And friends to friends, brothers to
brothers stood
Opposed in bloodiest battle-field, and
war,
Scarce satiable by fate's last death-
draught waged,
Drunk from the wine-press of the Al-
mighty's wrath ;
Whilst the red cross, in mockery of
peace,
Pointed to victory !   When the fray
was done,
No remnant of the exterminated faith
Survived to tell its ruin, but the flesh,
With putrid smoke poisoning the
atmosphere,
That rotted on the half-extinguished
pile.

Yes ! I have seen God's worshippers
unsheathe
The sword of his revenge, when grace
descended,
Confirming all unnatural impulses,
To sanctify their desolating deeds ;
And frantic priests waved the ill-
omened cross
O'er the unhappy earth : then shone
the sun
On showers of gore from the upflash-
ing steel
Of safe assassination, and all crime
Made stingless by the spirits of the
Lord,
And blood-red rainbows canopied the
land.

Spirit ! no year of my eventful being
Has passed unstained by crime and
misery,
Which flows from God's own faith.
I've marked his slaves,

With tongues whose lies are venom-
  ous, beguile
The insensate mob, and, whilst one
  hand was red
With murder, feign to stretch the
  other out
For brotherhood and peace ; and,
  that they now
Babble of love and mercy, whilst
  their deeds
Are marked with all the narrowness
  and crime
That freedom's young arm dares not
  yet chastise,
Reason may claim our gratitude, who
  now,
Establishing the imperishable throne
Of truth, and stubborn virtue, maketh
  vain
The unprevailing malice of my foe,
Whose bootless rage heaps torments
  for the brave,
Adds impotent eternities to pain,
Whilst keenest disappointment racks
  his breast
To see the smiles of peace around
  them play,
To frustrate or to sanctify their doom.

Thus have I stood,—through a wild
  waste of years
Struggling with whirlwinds of mad
  agony,
Yet peaceful, and serene, and self-
  enshrined,
Mocking my powerless tyrant's horr-
  ible curse
With stubborn and unalterable will,
Even as a giant oak, which heaven's
  fierce flame
Had scathed in the wilderness, to
  stand
A monument of fadeless ruin there ;
Yet peacefully and movelessly it
  braves
The midnight conflict of the wintry
  storm,
  As in the sunlight's calm it spreads
  Its worn and withered arms on high
To meet the quiet of a summer's noon.

  The Fairy waved her wand :
  Ahasuerus fled
Fast as the shapes of mingled shade
  and mist,
That lurk in the glens of a twilight
  grove,

Flee from the morning beam :
The matter of which dreams are
  made
Not more endowed with actual life
Than this phantasmal portraiture
Of wandering human thought.

VIII

The present and the past thou hast
  beheld :
It was a desolate sight.   Now Spirit,
  learn,
  The secrets of the future.—Time !
Unfold the brooding pinion of thy
  gloom,
Render thou up thy half-devoured
  babes,
And from the cradles of eternity,
Where millions lie lulled to their por-
  tioned sleep
By the deep murmuring stream of
  passing things,
Tear thou that gloomy shroud.—
  Spirit, behold
    Thy glorious destiny !

    Joy to the Spirit came.
Through the wide rent in Time's
  eternal veil,
Hope was seen beaming through the
  mists of fear.
    Earth was no longer hell ;
    Love, freedom, health, had
      given
Their ripeness to the manhood of its
  prime,
    And all its pulses beat
Symphonious   to   the   planetary
  spheres :
    Then dulcet music swelled
Concordant with the life-strings of the
  soul ;
It throbbed in sweet and languid
  beatings there,
Catching new life from transitory
  death.—
Like the vague sighings of a wind at
  even,
That wakes the wavelets of the slumbering sea,
And dies on the creation of its breath,
And sinks and rises, fails and swells
  by fits :
    Was the pure stream of feeling
    That sprang from these sweet
      notes,

And o'er the Spirit's human sym-
    pathies
With mild and gentle motion calmly
    flowed.

        Joy to the Spirit came,—
Such joy as when a lover sees
The chosen of his soul in happiness,
        And witnesses her peace
Whose woe to him were bitterer than
    death ;
        Sees her unfaded cheek
Glow mantling in first luxury
    of health,
        Thrills with her lovely eyes,
Which like two stars amid the heav-
    ing main
        Sparkle through liquid bliss.
Then in her triumph spoke the Fairy
    Queen :
I will not call the ghost of ages gone
To unfold the frightful secrets of its
    lore ;
        The present now is past,
And those events that desolate the
    earth
Have faded from the memory of Time,
Who dares not give reality to that
Whose being I annul. To me is
    given
The wonders of the human world to
    keep,
Space, matter, time, and mind.
    Futurity
Exposes now its treasure ; let the
    sight
Renew and strengthen all thy failing
    hope.
O human Spirit ! spur thee to the
    goal
Where virtue fixes universal peace,
And, 'midst the ebb and flow of human
    things,
Show somewhat stable, somewhat
    certain still,
A light-house o'er the wild of dreary
    waves.

The habitable earth is full of bliss ;
Those wastes of frozen billows that
    were hurled
By everlasting snow-storms round the
    poles,
Where matter dared not vegetate nor
    live,
But ceaseless frost round the vast soli-
    tude

Bound its broad zone of stillness, are
    unloosed ;
And fragrant zephyrs there from
    spicy isles
Ruffle the placid ocean-deep, that
    rolls
Its broad, bright surges to the sloping
    sand,
Whose roar is wakened into echoings
    sweet
To murmur through the heaven-
    breathing groves,
And melodise with man's blest nature
    there.

Those deserts of immeasurable sand,
Whose age-collected fervours scarce
    allowed
A bird to live, a blade of grass to
    spring,
Where the shrill chirp of the green
    lizard's love
Broke on the sultry silentness alone,
Now teem with countless rills and
    shady woods,
Corn-fields and pastures and white
    cottages ;
And where the startled wilderness be-
    held
A savage conqueror stained in kindred
    blood,
A tigress sating with the flesh of
    lambs
The unnatural famine of her tooth-
    less cubs,
While shouts and howlings through
    the desert rang
Sloping and smooth the daisy-spang-
    led lawn,
Offering sweet incense to the sunrise,
    smiles
To see a babe before his mother's
    door,
        Sharing his morning's meal
    With the green and golden
        basilisk
        That comes to lick his feet.

Those trackless deeps, where many a
    weary sail
Has seen above the illimitable plain,
Morning on night, and night on morn-
    ing rise,
Whilst still no land to greet the wan-
    derer spread
Its shadowy mountains on the sun-
    bright sea,

Where the loud roarings of the tem-
pest-waves
So long have mingled with the gusty
wind
In melancholy loneliness, and swept
The desert of those ocean solitudes,
But vocal to the sea-bird's harrowing
shriek,
The bellowing monster, and the rush-
ing storm ;
Now to the sweet and many mingling
sounds
Of kindliest human impulses respond.
Those lonely realms bright garden-
isles begem,
With lightsome clouds and shining
seas between,
And fertile valleys, resonant with bliss,
Whilst green woods overcanopy the
wave,
Which like a toil-worn labourer leaps
to shore,
To meet the kisses of the flowrets
there.

All things are recreated, and the flame
Of consentaneous love inspires all
life :
The fertile bosom of the earth gives
suck
To myriads, who still grow beneath
her care
Rewarding her with their pure per-
fectness :
The balmy breathings of the wind in-
hale
Her virtues, and diffuse them all
abroad : .
Health floats amid the gentle atmo-
sphere,
Glows in the fruits, and mantles on the
stream :
No storms deform the beaming brow
of heaven,
Nor scatter in the freshness of its pride
The foliage of the ever-verdant trees ;
But fruits are ever ripe, flowers ever
fair,
And autumn proudly bears her ma-
tron grace,
Kindling a flush on the fair cheek of
spring,
Whose virgin bloom beneath the
ruddy fruit
Reflects its tint, and blushes into love.

The lion now forgets to thirst for
blood :
There might you see him sporting in
the sun
Beside the dreadless kid ; his claws
are sheathed,
His teeth are harmless, custom's force
has made
His nature as the nature of a lamb.
Like passion's fruit, the nightshade's
tempting bane
Poisons no more the pleasure it be-
stows :
All bitterness is past ; the cup of joy
Unmingled mantles to the goblet's
brim,
And courts the thirsty lips it fled be-
fore.

But chief, ambiguous man, he that
can know
More misery, and dream more joy than
all ;
Whose keen sensations thrill within
his breast
To mingle with a loftier instinct there,
Lending their power to pleasure and
to pain,
Yet raising, sharpening, and refining
each ;
Who stands amid the ever-varying
world,
The burthen or the glory of the earth ;
He chief perceives the change ; his
being notes
The gradual renovation, and defines
Each movement of its progress on his
mind.

Man, where the gloom of the long
polar night
Lowers o'er the snow-clad rocks and
frozen soil,
Where scarce the hardiest herb that
braves the frost
Basks in the moonlight's ineffectual
glow,
Shrank with the plants, and darkened
with the night ;
His chilled and narrow energies, his
heart,
Insensible to courage, truth, or love,
His stunted stature and imbecile
frame,
Marked him for some abortion of the
earth,

Fit compeer of the bears that roamed
   around,
Whose habits and enjoyments were
   his own :
His life a feverish dream of stagnant
   woe,
Whose meagre wants, but scantily
   fulfilled,
Apprised him ever of the joyless length
Which his short being's wretchedness
   had reached ;
His death a pang which famine, cold,
   and toil,
Long on the mind, whilst yet the vital
   spark
Clung to the body stubbornly, had
   brought :
All was inflicted here that earth's
   revenge
Could wreak on the infringers of her
   law ;
One curse alone was spared—the
   name of God.

Nor, where the tropics bound the
   realms of day
With a broad belt of mingling cloud
   and flame,
Where blue mists through the un-
   moving atmosphere
Scattered the seeds of pestilence, and
   fed
Unnatural vegetation, where the land
Teemed with all earthquake, tempest,
   and disease,
Was man a nobler being ; slavery
Had crushed him to his country's
   blood-stained dust ;
Or he was bartered for the fame of
   power,   [ing,
Which, all internal impulses destroy-
Makes human will an article of trade ;
Or he was changed with Christians
   for their gold,
And dragged to distant isles, where to
   the sound
Of the flesh-mangling scourge, he does
   the work
Of all-polluting luxury and wealth,
Which doubly visits on the tyrants'
   heads
The long-protracted fulness of their
   woe ;
Or he was led to legal butchery,
To turn to worms beneath that burn-
   ing sun

Where kings first leagued against the
   rights of men,
And priests first traded with the
   name of God.

Even where the milder zone afforded
   man
A seeming shelter, yet contagion there,
Blighting his being with unnumbered
   ills,
Spread like a quenchless fire ; nor
   truth till late
Availed to arrest its progress, or cre-
   ate
That peace which first in bloodless
   victory waved
Her snowy standard o'er this favoured
   clime :
There man was long the train-bearer
   of slaves,
The mimic of surrounding misery,
The jackal of ambition's lion-rage,
The bloodhound of religion's hungry
   zeal.

Here now the human being stands
   adorning
This loveliest earth with taintless
   body and mind ;
Blest from his birth with all bland im-
   pulses,
Which gently in his noble bosom
   wake
All kindly passions and all pure de-
   sires.
Him (still from hope to hope the bliss
   pursuing,
Which from the exhaustless store of
   human weal
Draws on the virtuous mind) the
   thoughts that rise
In time-destroying infiniteness, gift
With self-enshrined eternity, that
   mocks
The unprevailing hoariness of age,
And man, once fleeting o'er the transi-
   ent scene
Swift as an unremembered vision,
   stands
Immortal upon earth ; no longer now
He slays the lamb that looks him in
   the face,
And horribly devours his mangled
   flesh,
Which, still avenging nature's broken
   law,

Kindled all putrid humours in his
    frame,
All evil passions, and all vain belief,
Hatred, despair, and loathing in his
    mind,
The germs of misery, death, disease,
  - and crime.
No longer now the winged inhabitants
That in the woods their sweet lives
    sing away,
Flee from the form of man; but gath-
    er round,
And prune their sunny feathers on
    the hands
Which little children stretch in friend-
    ly sport
Towards these dreadless partners of
    their play.
All things are void of terror: man has
    lost
His terrible prerogative, and stands
An equal amidst equals: happiness
And science dawn, though late, upon
    the earth;
Peace cheers the mind, health renov-
    ates the frame;
Disease and pleasure cease to mingle
    here,   [there;
Reason and passion cease to combat
Whilst each unfettered o'er the earth
    extends
Its all-subduing energies, and wields
The sceptre of a vast dominion there;
Whilst every shape and mode of
    matter lends
Its force to the omnipotence of mind,
Which from its dark mine drags the
    gem of truth
To decorate its paradise of peace.

IX

O HAPPY Earth! reality of Heaven!
To which those restless souls that
    ceaselessly
Throng through the human universe,
    aspire;
Thou consummation of all mortal
    hope!
Thou glorious prize of blindly-work-
    ing will!
Whose rays, diffused throughout all
    space and time,
Verge to one point and blend for ever
    there:
Of purest spirits thou pure dwelling-
    place!

Where care and sorrow, impotence
    and crime,
Languor, disease, and ignorance, dare
    not come:
O happy Earth, reality of Heaven!

Genius has seen thee in her passionate
    dreams;
And dim forebodings of thy loveliness,
Haunting the human heart, have there
    entwined
Those rooted hopes of some sweet
    place of bliss,
Where friends and lovers meet to part
    no more.
Thou art the end of all desire and will,
The product of all action; and the
    souls
That by the paths of an aspiring
    change
Have reached thy haven of perpetual
    peace,
There rest from the eternity of toil
That framed the fabric of thy perfect-
    ness.

Even Time, the conqueror, fled thee
    in his fear;
That hoary giant, who, in lonely pride,
So long had ruled the world, that na-
    tions fell
Beneath his silent footstep. Pyram-
    ids,
That for millenniums had withstood
    the tide
Of human things, his storm-breath
    drove in sand
Across that desert where their stones
    survived
The name of him whose pride had
    heaped them there.
Yon monarch, in his solitary pomp,
Was but the mushroom of a summer
    day,
That his light-winged footstep pressed
    to dust:
Time was the king of earth: all things
    gave way
Before him, but the fixed and virtuous
    will,
The sacred sympathies of soul and
    sense,
That mocked his fury and prepared
    his fall.

Yet slow and gradual dawned the
    morn of love;

Long lay the clouds of darkness o'er
  the scene,
Till from its native heaven they
  rolled away :
First, crime triumphant o'er all hope
  careered
Unblushing, undisguising, bold and
  strong ;
Whilst falsehood, tricked in virtue's
  attributes,
Long sanctified all deeds of vice and
  woe,
Till, done by her own venomous sting
  to death,
She left the moral world without a law,
No longer fettering passion's fearless
  wing.
Then steadily the happy ferment
  worked ;
Reason was free ; and wild though
  passion went
Through tangled glens and wood-
  embosomed meads,
Gathering a garland of the strangest
  flowers,
Yet, like the bee returning to her
  queen,   [brow,
She bound the sweetest on her sister's
Who, meek and sober, kissed the sport-
  ive child,
No longer trembling at the broken rod.

Mild was the slow necessity of death :
The tranquil Spirit failed beneath its
  grasp.
Without a groan, almost without a
  fear,
Calm as a voyager to some distant
  land,
And full of wonder, full of hope as he.
The deadly germs of languor and dis-
  ease
Died in the human frame, and purity
Blessed with all gifts her earthly wor-
  shippers.
How vigorous then the athletic form
  of age !
How clear its open and unwrinkled
  brow !
Where neither avarice, cunning, pride,
  nor care,
Had stamped the seal of grey deform-
  ity
On all the mingling lineaments of time.
How lovely the intrepid front of
  youth !

Which meek-eyed courage decked
  with freshest grace ;
Courage of soul, that dreaded not a
  name,
And elevated will, that journeyed on
Through life's phantasmal scene in
  fearlessness,
With virtue, love, and pleasure, hand
  in hand.
Then, that sweet bondage which is
  freedom's self,
And rivets with sensation's softest tie
The kindred sympathies of human
  souls,
Needed no fetters of tyrannic law.
Those delicate and timid impulses
In nature's primal modesty arose,
And with undoubting confidence dis-
  closed
The growing longings of its dawning
  love,
Unchecked by dull and selfish chast-
  ity,
That virtue of the cheaply virtuous,
Who pride themselves in senselessness
  and frost.
No longer prostitution's venomed
  bane
Poisoned the springs of happiness and
  life ;
Woman and man, in confidence and
  love,
Equal and free and pure, together trod
The mountain-paths of virtue, which
  no more
Were stained with blood from many
  a pilgrim's feet.

Then, where, through distant ages,
  long in pride
The palace of the monarch-slave had
  mocked
Famine's faint groan, and penury's
  silent tear,
A heap of crumbling ruins stood, and
  threw
Year after year their stones upon the
  field,
Wakening a lonely echo ; and the
  leaves
Of the old thorn, that on the topmost
  tower
Usurped the royal ensign's grandeur,
  shook
In the stern storm that swayed the
  topmost tower,

And whispered strange tales in the
whirlwind's ear.
Low through the lone cathedral's roof-
less aisles
The melancholy winds a death-dirge
sung :
It were a sight of awfulness to see
The works of faith and slavery, so vast,
So sumptuous, yet so perishing with-
al !
Even as the corpse that rests beneath
its wall.
A thousand mourners decked the
pomp of death
To-day, the breathing marble glows
above
To decorate its memory, and tongues
Are busy of its life : to-morrow, worms
In silence and in darkness seize their
prey.

Within the massy prison's moulder-
ing courts,
Fearless and free the ruddy children
played,
Weaving gay chaplets for their inno-
cent brows
With the green ivy and the red wall-
flower,
That mock the dungeon's unavailing
gloom ;
The ponderous chains, and gratings
of strong iron,   [stone,
There rusted amid heaps of broken
That mingled slowly with their native
earth :
There the broad beam of day, which
feebly once
Lighted the cheek of lean captivity
With a pale 'and sickly glare, then
freely shone
On the pure smiles of infant playful-
ness :
No more the shuddering voice of
hoarse despair
Pealed through the echoing vaults, but
soothing notes
Of ivy-fingered winds and gladsome
birds
And merriment were resonant around.
These ruins soon left not a wreck be-
hind :
Their elements, wide scattered o'er the
globe,
To happier shapes were moulded, and
became

Ministrant to all blissful impulses :
Thus human things were perfected,
and earth,
Even as a child beneath its mother's
love,
Was strengthened in all excellence,
and grew
Fairer and nobler with each passing
year.   [scene
Now Time his dusky pennons o'er the
Closes in steadfast darkness, and the
past
Fades from our charmed sight. My
task is done :
Thy lore is learned. Earth's wonders
are thine own,
With all the fear and all the hope
they bring.
My spells are past : the present now
recurs.
Ah me ! a pathless wilderness re-
mains
Yet unsubdued by man's reclaiming
hand.

Yet, human Spirit ! bravely hold thy
course,
Let virtue teach thee firmly to pursue
The gradual paths of an aspiring
change :
For birth and life and death, and that
strange state
Before the naked soul has found its
home,
All tend to perfect happiness, and urge
The restless wheels of being on their
way,
Whose flashing spokes, instinct with
infinite life,
Bicker and burn to gain their des-
tined goal.   [sense
For birth but wakes the spirit to the
Of outward shows, whose unexperi-
enced shape
New modes of passion to its frame
may lend ;
Life is its state of action, and the store
Of all events is aggregated there
That variegate the eternal universe ;
Death is a gate of dreariness and
gloom,
That leads to azure isles and beaming
skies,
And happy regions of eternal hope,
Therefore, O Spirit ! fearlessly bear
on :

Though storms may break the prim-
  rose on its stalk,
Though frosts may blight the freshness of its bloom,
Yet spring's awakening breath will
  woo the earth,
To feed with kindliest dews its favourite flower,
That blooms in mossy banks and
  darksome glens,
Lighting the greenwood with its sunny
  smile.

Fear not then, Spirit, death's disrob-
  ing hand ;
So welcome when the tyrant is awake,
So welcome when the bigot's hell-
  torch burns ;
'Tis but the voyage of a darksome
  hour,
The transient gulf-dream of a startling
  sleep.
Death is no foe to virtue : earth has
  seen
Love's brightest roses on the scaffold
  bloom,
Mingling with freedom's fadeless lau-
  rels there,
And presaging the truth of visioned
  bliss.
Are there not hopes within thee,
  which this scene
Of linked and gradual being has con-
  firmed,
Whose stingings bade thy heart look
  further still,
When to the moonlight walk, by
  Henry led,
Sweetly and sadly thou didst talk of
  death ?
And wilt thou rudely tear them from
  thy breast,
Listening supinely to a bigot's creed,
Or tamely crouching to the tyrant's
  rod,
Whose iron thongs are red with hu-
  man gore ?
Never : but bravely bearing on, thy
  will
Is destined an eternal war to wage
With tyranny and falsehood, and up-
  root
The germs of misery from the human
  heart.
Thine is the hand whose piety would
  soothe

The thorny pillow of unhappy crime,
Whose impotence an easy pardon
  gains,
Watching its wanderings as a friend's
  disease :
Thine is the brow whose mildness
  would defy
Its fiercest rage, and brave its stern-
  est will,
When fenced by power and master of
  the world.
Thou art sincere and good ; of reso-
  lute mind,
Free from heart-withering custom's
  cold control,
Of passion lofty, pure and unsubdued.
Earth's pride and meanness could not
  vanquish thee,
And therefore art thou worthy of the
  boon
Which thou hast now received : virtue
  shall keep
Thy footsteps in the path that thou
  hast trod,
And many days of beaming hope shall
 . bless
Thy spotless life of sweet and sacred
  love.
Go, happy one ! and give that bosom
  joy,
Whose sleepless spirit waits to catch
Light, life and rapture from thy
  smile.

The Fairy waves her wand of
  charm.
Speechless with bliss the Spirit mounts
  the car,
That rolled beside the battlement,
Bending her beamy eyes in thankful-
  ness.
Again the enchanted steeds were
  yoked,
Again the burning wheels inflame
The steep descent of heaven's untrod-
  den way.
Fast and far the chariot flew :
The vast and fiery globes that rolled
  Around the Fairy's palace-gate
Lessened by slow degrees, and soon
  appeared
Such tiny twinklers as the planet orbs
That there attendant on the solar
  power
With borrowed light pursued their
  narrower way.

Earth floated then below :
The chariot paused a moment there ;
The Spirit then descended :
The restless coursers pawed the un-
genial soil,
Snuffed the gross air, and then, their
errand done,   [heaven,
Unfurled their pinions to the winds of
The Body and the Soul united then ;
A gentle start convulsed Ianthe's
frame ;

Her veiny eyelids quietly unclosed ;
Moveless awhile the dark blue orbs
remained :
She looked around in wonder, and be-
held
Henry, who kneeled in silence by her
couch,
Watching her sleep with looks of
speechless love,
And the bright beaming stars
That through the casement shone.

ALASTOR : OR, THE SPIRIT OF SOLITUDE

Nondum amabam, et amare amabam, quærebam quid amarem amans amare.
Confess. St. August.

PREFACE

THE poem entitled "Alastor," may be considered as allegorical of one of the most interesting situations of the human mind. It represents a youth of uncorrupted feelings and adventurous genius, led forth by an imagination inflamed and purified through familiarity with all that is excellent and majestic, to the contemplation of the universe. He drinks deep of the fountains of knowledge, and is still insatiate. The magnificence and beauty of the external world sinks profoundly into the frame of his conceptions, and affords to their modifications a variety not to be exhausted. So long as it is possible for his desire to point towards objects thus infinite and unmeasured, he is joyous, and tranquil, and self-possessed. But the period arrives when these objects cease to suffice. His mind is at length suddenly awakened, and thirsts for intercourse with an intelligence similar to itself. He images to himself the Being whom he loves. Conversant with speculations of the sublimest and most perfect natures, the vision in which he embodies his own imaginations, unites all of wonderful, or wise, or beautiful, which the poet, the philosopher, or the lover could depicture. The intellectual faculties, the imagination, the func-

tions of sense, have their respective requisitions on the sympathy of corresponding powers in other human beings. The Poet is represented as uniting these requisitions, and attaching them to a single image. He seeks in vain for a prototype of his conception. Blasted by his disappointment, he descends to an untimely grave.

The picture is not barren of instruction to actual men. The Poet's self-centred seclusion was avenged by the furies of an irresistible passion pursuing him to speedy ruin. But that Power which strikes the luminaries of the world with sudden darkness and extinction, by awakening them to too exquisite a perception of its influences, dooms to a slow and poisonous decay those meaner spirits that dare to abjure its dominion. Their destiny is more abject and inglorious, as their delinquency is more contemptible and pernicious. They who, deluded by no generous error, instigated by no sacred thirst of doubtful knowledge, duped by no illustrious superstition, loving nothing on this earth, and cherishing no hopes beyond, yet keep aloof from sympathies with their kind, rejoicing neither in human joy nor mourning with human grief ; these, and such as they, have their apportioned curse. They languish, because none feel

with them their common nature.
They are morally dead. They are
neither friends, nor lovers, nor fathers,
nor citizens of the world, nor bene-
factors of their country. Among
those who attempt to exist without
human sympathy, the pure and tender-hearted perish through the inten-
sity and passion of their search after
its communities, when the vacancy
of their spirit suddenly makes itself
felt. All else, selfish, blind, and torpid, are those unforeseeing multitudes
who constitute, together with their
own, the lasting misery and loneliness of the world. Those who love
not their fellow-beings, live unfruit-
ful lives, and prepare for their old age
a miserable grave.

> The good die first,
> And those whose hearts are dry as sum-
> mer's dust
> Burn to the socket !
> *December* 14, 1815.

EARTH, ocean, air, beloved brother-
hood !
If our great mother have imbued my
soul
With aught of natural piety to feel
Your love, and recompense the boon
with mine ;
If dewy morn, and odorous noon, and
even,
With sunset and its gorgeous ministers,
And solemn midnight's tingling silentness ;
If autumn's hollow sighs in the sere
wood,
And winter robing with pure snow
and crowns
Of starry ice the grey grass and bare
boughs ;
If spring's voluptuous pantings when
she breathes
Her first sweet kisses, have been dear
to me ;
If no bright bird, insect, or gentle
beast
I consciously have injured, but still
loved
And cherished these my kindred ;—
then forgive
This boast, beloved brethren, and
withdraw

No portion of your wonted favour
now !

Mother of this unfathomable world !
Favour my solemn song, for I have
loved
Thee ever, and thee only ; I have
watched
Thy shadow, and the darkness of thy
steps,
And my heart ever gazes on the
depth
Of thy deep mysteries. I have made
my bed
In charnels and on coffins, where black
death
Keeps record of the trophies won from
thee.
Hoping to still these obstinate ques-
tionings
Of thee and thine, by forcing some lone
ghost,
Thy messenger, to render up the tale
Of what we are. In lone and silent
hours,
When night makes a weird sound of
its own stillness,
Like an inspired and desperate
alchymist
Staking his very life on some dark
hope,
Have I mixed awful talk and asking
looks
With my most innocent love, until
strange tears,
Uniting with those breathless kisses,
made
Such magic as compels the charmed
night
To render up thy charge : and, though
ne'er yet
Thou hast unveiled thy inmost sanc-
tuary ;
Enough from incommunicable dream,
And twilight phantasms, and deep
noonday thought,
Has shone within me, that serenely
now
And moveless, as a long-forgotten lyre
Suspended in the solitary dome
Of some mysterious and deserted fane,
I wait thy breath, Great Parent, that
my strain
May modulate with murmurs of the
air,
And motions of the forests and the sea,

And voice of living beings, and woven
    hymns
Of night and day, and the deep heart
    of man.

  There was a Poet whose untimely
    tomb
No human hands with pious reverence
    reared,
But the charmed eddies of autumnal
    winds
Built o'er his mouldering bones a
    pyramid
Of mouldering leaves in the waste
    wilderness ;
A lovely youth,—no mourning maiden
    decked
With weeping flowers, or votive cy-
    press wreath,
The lone couch of his everlasting sleep :
Gentle, and brave, and generous, no
    lorn bard
Breathed o'er his dark fate one melo-
    dious sigh :
He lived, he died, he sang in solitude.
Strangers have wept to hear his pas-
    sionate notes,
And virgins, as unknown he passed,
    have pined
And wasted for fond love of his wild
    eyes.
The fire of those soft orbs has ceased
    to burn,
And Silence too, enamoured of that
    voice,
Locks its mute music in her rugged
    cell.

  By solemn vision and bright silver
    dream,
His infancy was nurtured. Every
    sight
And sound from the vast earth and
    ambient air
Sent to his heart its choicest impulses.
The fountains of divine philosophy
Fled not his thirsting lips : and all
    of great,
Or good, or lovely, which the sacred
    past
In truth or fable consecrates, he felt
And knew. When early youth had
    past, he left
His cold fireside and alienated home,
To seek strange truths in undiscovered
    lands.

Many a wide waste and tangled wil-
    derness
Has lured his fearless steps ; and he
    has bought
With his sweet voice and eyes, from
    savage men,
His rest and food. Nature's most
    secret steps
He, like her shadow, has pursued,
    where'er
The red volcano overcanopies
Its fields of snow and pinnacles of ice
With burning smoke : or where bitu-
    men lakes,
On black bare pointed islets ever beat
With sluggish surge, or where the se-
    cret caves,
Rugged and dark, winding among the
    springs,
Of fire and poison, inaccessible
To avarice or pride, their starry domes
Of diamond and of gold expand above
Numberless and immeasurable halls,
Frequent with crystal column, and
    clear shrines
Of pearl, and thrones radiant with
    chrysolite.
Nor had that scene of ampler majesty
Than gems of gold, the varying roof
    of heaven
And the green earth, lost in his heart
    its claims
To love and wonder ; he would linger
    long
In lonesome vales making the wild his
    home,
Until the doves and squirrels would
    partake
From his innocuous hand his blood-
    less food,
Lured by the gentle meaning of his
    looks,
And the wild antelope, that starts
    whene'er
The dry leaf rustles in the brake, sus-
    pend
Her timid steps, to gaze upon a form
More graceful than her own.
                His wandering step,
Obedient to high thoughts has visited
The awful ruins of the days of old :
Athens, and Tyre, and Balbec, and the
    waste
Where stood Jerusalem, the fallen
    towers
Of Babylon, the eternal pyramids,

Memphis and Thebes, and whatsoe'er
  of strange
Sculptured on alabaster obelisk,
Or jasper tomb, or mutilated sphynx,
Dark Ethiopia on her desert hills
Conceals.   Among the ruined temples
  there,
Stupendous columns, and wild images
Of more than man, where marble de-
  mons watch
The Zodiac's brazen mystery, and
  dead men
Hang their mute thoughts on the
  mute walls around,
He lingered, poring on memorials
Of the world's youth, through the
  long burning day
Gazed on those speechless shapes, nor,
  when the moon
Filled the mysterious halls with float-
  ing shades
Suspended he that task, but ever
  gazed
And gazed, till meaning on his vacant
  mind
Flashed like strong inspiration, and
  he saw
The thrilling secrets of the birth of
  time.

  Meanwhile an Arab maiden brought
  his food,
Her daily portion, from her father's
  tent,
And spread her matting for his couch,
  and stole
From duties and repose to tend his
  steps :
Enamoured, yet not daring for deep
  awe
To speak her love :—and watched
  his nightly sleep,
Sleepless herself, to gaze upon his lips
Parted in slumber, whence the regular
  breath
Of innocent dreams arose :   then,
  when red morn
Made paler the pale moon, to her cold
  home,
Wildered, and wan, and panting, she
  returned.

  The Poet wandering on, through
  Arabie
And Persia, and the wild Carmanian
  waste,

And o'er the aërial mountains which
  pour down
Indus and Oxus from their icy caves,
In joy and exultation held his way ;
Till in the vale of Cachmire, far with-
  in
Its loneliest dell, where odorous plants
  entwine
Beneath the hollow rocks a natural
  bower,
Beside a sparkling rivulet he stretched
His languid limbs.   A vision on his
  sleep
There came, a dream of hopes that
  never yet
Had flushed his cheek.   He dreamed
  a veiled maid
Sate near him, talking in low solemn
  tones.
Her voice was like the voice of his own
  soul
Heard in the calm of thought ;   its
  music long,
Like woven sounds of streams and
  breezes, held
His inmost sense suspended in its web
Of many-coloured woof and shifting
  hues.
Knowledge and truth and virtue
  were her theme,
And lofty hopes of divine liberty,
Thoughts the most dear to him, and
  poesy,
Himself a poet.   Soon the solemn
  mood
Of her pure mind kindled through all
  her frame
A permeating fire ;   wild numbers then
She raised, with voice stifled in tre-
  mulous sobs
Subdued by its own pathos :   her fair
  hands
Were bare alone, sweeping from some
  strange harp
Strange symphony, and in their
  branching veins
The eloquent blood told an ineffable
  tale.
The beating of her heart was heard to
  fill
The pauses of her music, and her
  breath
Tumultuously accorded with those
  fits
Of intermitted song.   Sudden she rose,
As if her heart impatiently endured

Its bursting burthen : at the sound
  he turned,
And saw by the warm light of their
  own life
Her glowing limbs beneath the sinuous veil
Of woven wind ; her outspread arms
  now bare,
Her dark locks floating in the breath
  of night,
Her beamy bending eyes, her parted
  lips
Outstretched, and pale, and quivering
  eagerly.
His strong heart sank and sickened
  with excess
Of love. He reared his shuddering
  limbs, and quelled
His gasping breath, and spread his
  arms to meet
Her panting bosom :—she drew back
  awhile,
Then, yielding to the irresistible joy,
With frantic gesture and short breath-
  less cry   [arms.
Folded his frame in her dissolving
Now blackness veiled his dizzy eyes,
  and night
Involved and swallowed up the
  vision ; sleep,
Like a dark flood suspended in its
  course,
Rolled back its impulse on his vacant
  brain.

  Roused by the shock, he started
    from his trance—
The cold white light of morning, the
  blue moon
Low in the west, the clear and garish
  hills,
The distinct valley and the vacant
  woods,
Spread round him where he stood.
  Whither have fled
The hues of heaven that canopied his
  bower
Of yesternight ? The sounds that
  soothed his sleep,
The mystery and the majesty of
  Earth,
The joy, the exultation ? His wan
  eyes
Gaze on the empty scene as vacantly
As ocean's moon looks on the moon in
  heaven.

The spirit of sweet human love has
  sent
A vision to the sleep of him who
  spurned
Her choicest gifts. He eagerly pur-
  sues
Beyond the realms of dream that fleet-
  ing shade ;
He overleaps the bounds. Alas !
  alas !
Were limbs and breath and being
  intertwined
Thus treacherously ? Lost, lost, for
  ever lost
In the wide pathless desert of dim
  sleep,
That beautiful shape ! Does the dark
  gate of death
Conduct to thy mysterious paradise,
O Sleep ? Does the bright arch of
  rainbow clouds,
And pendent mountains seen in the
  calm lake,
Lead only to a black and watery
  depth,
While death's blue vault with loath-
  liest vapours hung,
Where every shade which the foul
  grave exhales
Hides its dead eye from the detested
  day,   [realms ?
Conduct, O Sleep, to thy delightful
This doubt with sudden tide flowed on
  his heart,
The insatiate hope which it awakened,
  stung
His brain even like despair.
                    While daylight held
The sky, the Poet kept mute confer-
  ence
With his still soul. At night the pas-
  sion came,
Like the fierce fiend of a distempered
  dream,
And shook him from his rest, and led
  him forth
Into the darkness.—As an eagle
  grasped
In folds of the green serpent, feels her
  breast
Burn with the poison, and precipi-
  tates
Through night and day, tempest, and
  calm and cloud,
Frantic with dizzying anguish, her
  blind flight

O'er the wide aëry wilderness : thus
　driven
By the bright shadow of that lovely
　dream,
Beneath the cold glare of the deso-
　late night,
Through tangled swamps and deep
　precipitous dells,
Startling with careless step the moon-
　light snake,
He fled. Red morning dawned upon
　his flight,
Shedding the mockery of its vital hues
Upon his cheek of death. He wan-
　dered on,
Till vast Aornos, seen from Petra's
　steep, ·
Hung o'er the low horizon like a
　cloud ;
Through Balk, and where the deso-
　lated tombs
Of Parthian kings scatter to every
　wind
Their wasting dust, wildly he wan-
　dered on,
Day after day, a weary waste of hours,
Bearing within his life the brooding
　care
That ever fed on its decaying flame.
And now his limbs were lean ; his
　scattered hair
Sered by the autumn of strange suffer-
　ing,
Sung dirges in the wind ; his listless
　hand
Hung like dead bone within its with-
　ered skin ;
Life, and the lustre that consumed it,
　shone
As in a furnace burning secretly
From his dark eyes alone. The cot-
　tagers,
Who ministered with human charity
His human wants, beheld with won-
　dering awe
Their fleeting visitant. The moun-
　taineer,
Encountering on some dizzy precipice
That spectral form, deemed that the
　Spirit of wind
With lightning eyes, and eager breath,
　and feet
Disturbing not the drifted snow, had
　paused
In his career ; the infant would con-
　ceal

His troubled visage in his mother's
　robe
In terror at the glare of those wild
　eyes,
To remember their strange light in
　many a dream
Of after times ; but youthful maidens,
　taught
By nature, would interpret half the
　woe
That wasted him, would call him with
　false names
Brother, and friend, would press his
　pallid hand
At parting, and watch, dim through
　tears, the path
Of his departure from their father's
　door.

　　At length upon the lone Choras-
　mian shore
He paused, a wide and melancholy
　waste
Of putrid marshes. A strong im-
　pulse urged
His steps to the sea-shore. A swan
　was there,
Beside a sluggish stream among the
　reeds.
It rose as he approached, and with
　strong wings
Scaling the upward sky, bent its
　bright course
High over the immeasurable main.
His eyes pursued its flight :—" Thou
　hast a home,
Beautiful bird ! thou voyagest to
　thine home,
Where thy sweet mate will twine her
　downy neck
With thine, and welcome thy return
　with eyes
Bright in the lustre of their own fond
　joy.
And what am I that I should linger
　here,
With voice far sweeter than thy
　dying notes,
Spirit more vast than thine, frame
　more attuned
To beauty, wasting these surpassing
　powers
In the deaf air, to the blind earth,
　and heaven
That echoes not my thoughts ? " A
　gloomy smile

Of desperate hope wrinkled his
    quivering lips.
For sleep, he knew, kept most relent-
    lessly
Its precious charge, and silent death
    exposed,
Faithless perhaps as sleep, a shadowy
    lure,
With doubtful smile mocking its own
    strange charms.

    Startled by his own thoughts, he
        looked around :
There was no fair fiend near him, not
    a sight
Or sound of awe but in his own deep
    mind.
A little shallop floating near the shore
Caught the impatient wandering of
    his gaze.
It had been long abandoned, for its
    sides
Gaped wide with many a rift, and its
    frail joints
Swayed with the undulations of the
    tide.
A restless impulse urged him to em-
    bark
And meet lone Death on the drear
    ocean's waste ;
For well he knew that mighty Shadow
    loves
The slimy caverns of the populous
    deep.

    The day was fair and sunny : sea
        and sky
Drank its inspiring radiance, and the
    wind
Swept strongly from the shore, black-
    ening the waves.
Following his eager soul, the wanderer
Leapt in the boat, he spread his cloak
    aloft
On the bare mast, and took his lonely
    seat,
And felt the boat speed o'er the tran-
    quil sea
Like a torn cloud before the hurricane.

    As one that in a silver vision
        floats
Obedient to the sweep of odorous
    winds
Upon resplendent clouds, so rapidly
Along the dark and ruffled waters fled

The straining boat. A whirlwind
    swept it on,
With fierce gusts and precipitating
    force,
Through the white ridges of the chafed
    sea.
The waves arose.   Higher and higher
    still
Their fierce necks writhed beneath the
    tempest's scourge
Like serpents struggling in a vulture's
    grasp.
Calm and rejoicing in the fearful war
Of wave running on wave, and blast on
    blast
Descending, and black flood on whirl-
    pool driven
With dark obliterating course, he sate :
As if their genii were the ministers
Appointed to conduct him to the
    light
Of those beloved eyes, the Poet sate
Holding the steady helm.   Evening
    came on,
The beams of sunset hung their rain-
    bow hues
High mid the shifting domes of
    sheeted spray
That canopied his path o'er the waste
    deep ;
Twilight, ascending slowly from the
    east,
Entwined in duskier wreaths her
    braided locks
O'er the fair front and radiant eyes of
    day ;
Night followed, clad with stars.   On
    every side
More horribly the multitudinous
    streams
Of ocean's mountainous waste to
    mutual war
Rush'd in dark tumult thundering, as
    to mock
The calm and spangled sky.   The
    little boat
Still fled before the storm ; still fled,
    like foam
Down the steep cataract of a wintry
    river ;
Now pausing on the edge of the riven
    wave ;
Now leaving far behind the bursting
    mass
That fell, convulsing ocean.   Safely
    fled—

As if that frail and wasted human
   form
Had been an elemental god.
                At midnight
The moon arose : and lo ! the ether-
   eal cliffs
Of Caucasus, whose icy summits shone
Among the stars like sunlight, and
   around
Whose caverned base the whirlpools
   and the waves,
Bursting and eddying irresistibly,
Rage and resound for ever.—Who
   shall save ?—
The boat fled on,—the boiling torrent
   drove,—
The crags closed round with black
   and jagged arms,
The shattered mountain overhung
   the sea,
And faster still, beyond all human
   speed,
Suspended on the sweep of the smooth
   wave,
The little boat was driven.   A cavern
   there
Yawned, and amid its slant and wind-
   ing depths
Ingulphed the rushing sea.   The
   boat fled on
With unrelaxing speed.   " Vision and
   Love ! "
The Poet cried aloud, " I have beheld
The path of thy departure.   Sleep and
   death
Shall not divide us long."
              The boat pursued
The windings of the cavern.   Day-
   light shone
At length upon that gloomy river's
   flow :
Now, where the fiercest war among
   the waves
Is calm, on the unfathomable stream
The boat moved slowly.   Where the
   mountain, riven,
Exposed those black depths to the
   azure sky,
Ere yet the flood's enormous volume
   fell
Even to the base of Caucasus, with
   sound
That shook the everlasting rocks, the
   mass
Filled with one whirlpool all that
   ample chasm ;

Stair above stair the eddying waters
   rose,
Circling immeasurably fast, and laved
With alternating dash the gnarled
   roots
Of mighty trees, that stretched their
   giant arms
In darkness over it.   I' the midst was
   left,
Reflecting, yet distorting every cloud,
A pool of treacherous and tremend-
   ous calm,
Seized by the sway of the ascending
   stream,
With dizzy swiftness, round, and
   round, and round,
Ridge after ridge the straining boat
   arose,
Till on the verge of the extremest
   curve,
Where, through an opening of the
   rocky bank,
The waters overflow, and a smooth
   spot
Of glassy quiet 'mid those battling
   tides
Is left, the boat paused shuddering.
   Shall it sink
Down the abyss ?   Shall the revert-
   ing stress
Of that resistless gulf embosom it ?
Now shall it fall ?   A wandering
   stream of wind,
Breathed from the west, has caught
   the expanded sail,
And, lo ! with gentle motion between
   banks
Of mossy slope, and on a placid
   stream,   [hark !
Beneath a woven grove, it sails, and,
The ghastly torrent mingles its far
   roar,
With the breeze murmuring in the
   musical woods.
Where the embowering trees recede,
   and leave
A little space of green expanse, the
   cove
Is closed by meeting banks, whose
   yellow flowers
For ever gaze on their own drooping
   eyes,
Reflected in the crystal calm.   The
   wave
Of the boat's motion marred their
   pensive task,

Which nought but vagrant bird, or
    wanton wind,
Or falling spear-grass, or their own
    decay
Had e'er disturbed before.   The Poet
    longed
To deck with their bright hues his
    withered hair,
But on his heart its solitude returned,
And he forbore.   Not the strong im-
    pulse hid
In those flushed cheeks, bent eyes,
    and shadowy frame
Had yet performed its ministry : it
    hung
Upon his life, as lightning in a cloud
Gleams, hovering ere it vanish, ere the
    floods
Of night close over it.
            The noonday sun
Now shone upon the forest, one vast
    mass
Of mingling shade, whose brown mag-
    nificence
A narrow vale embosoms. There,
    huge caves,
Scooped in the dark base of those
    aëry rocks
Mocking its moans, respond and roar
    for ever.
The meeting boughs and implicated
    leaves   led
Wove twilight o'er the Poet's path, as
By love, or dream, or god, or mightier
    Death,
He sought in Nature's dearest haunt,
    some bank,
Her cradle, and his sepulchre.   More
    dark
And dark the shades accumulate—
    the oak,
Expanding its immense and knotty
    arms,
Embraces the light beech.   The
    pyramids
Of the tall cedar overarching, frame
Most solemn domes within, and far
    below,
Like clouds suspended in an emerald
    sky,
The ash and the acacia floating hang
Tremulous and pale.   Like restless
    serpents, clothed
In rainbow and in fire, the parasites,
Starr'd with ten thousand blossoms,
    flow around

The grey trunks, and, as gamesome
    infants' eyes,
With gentle meanings, and most inno-
    cent wiles,
Fold their beams round the hearts of
    those that love,
These twine their tendrils with the
    wedded boughs
Uniting their close union ; the woven
    leaves
Make network of the dark blue light
    of day,
And the night's noontide clearness,
    mutable
As shapes in the weird clouds.   Soft
    mossy lawns
Beneath these canopies extend their
    swells,
Fragrant with perfumed herbs, and
    eyed with blooms
Minute, yet beautiful.   One darkest
    glen
Sends from its woods of musk-rose,
    twined with jasmine,
A soul-dissolving odour, to invite
To some more lovely mystery.
    Through the dell,
Silence and Twilight here, twin sis-
    ters, keep
Their noonday watch, and sail among
    the shades,
Like vaporous shapes half-seen ; be-
    yond, a well,
Dark, gleaming, and of most trans-
    lucent wave,
Images all the woven boughs above,
And each depending leaf, and every
    speck
Of azure sky, darting between their
    chasms ;
Nor aught else in the liquid mirror
    laves   [star
Its portraiture, but some inconstant
Between one foliaged lattice twinkl-
    ing fair,
Or painted bird, sleeping beneath the
    moon,
Or gorgeous insect, floating motion-
    less,
Unconscious of the day, ere yet his
    wings
Have spread their glories to the gaze
    of noon.

Hither the Poet came.   His eyes
    beheld

Their own wan light through the reflected lines
Of his thin hair, distinct in the dark depth
Of that still fountain ; as the human heart,
Gazing in dreams over the gloomy grave,
Sees its own treacherous likeness there. He heard
The motion of the leaves, the grass that sprung
Startled and glanced and trembled even to feel
An unaccustomed presence, and the sound
Of the sweet brook that from the secret springs
Of that dark fountain rose.   A Spirit seemed
To stand beside him—clothed in no bright robes
Of shadowy silver or enshrining light,
Borrow'd from aught the visible world affords
Of grace, or majesty, or mystery ;—
But undulating woods, and silent well,
And rippling rivulet, and evening gloom
Now deepening the dark shades, for speech assuming
Held commune with him, as if he and it
Were all that was,—only—when his regard
Was raised by intense pensiveness,—two eyes,
Two starry eyes, hung in the gloom of thought,
And seemed with their serene and azure smiles
To beckon him.
                   Obedient to the light
That shone within his soul, he went, pursuing
The windings of the dell.—The rivulet
Wanton and wild, through many a green ravine
Beneath the forest flowed.   Sometimes it fell
Among the moss, with hollow harmony
Dark and profound.   Now on the polished stones

It danced ; like childhood laughing as it went :
Then, through the plain in tranquil wanderings crept,
Reflecting every herb and drooping bud
That overhung its quietness.—" O stream !
Whose source is inaccessibly profound,
Whither do thy mysterious waters tend ?
Thou imagest my life.   Thy darksome stillness,
Thy dazzling waves, thy loud and hollow gulfs,   [course
Thy searchless fountain, and invisible
Have each their type in me : And the wide sky,
And measureless ocean may declare as soon
What oozy cavern or what wandering cloud
Contains thy waters, as the universe
Tell where these living thoughts reside, when stretched
Upon thy flowers my bloodless limbs shall waste
I' the passing wind ! "
                   Beside the grassy shore
Of the small stream he went ; he did impress
On the green moss his tremulous step, that caught
Strong shuddering from his burning limbs.   As one
Roused by some joyous madness from the couch
Of fever, he did move ; yet, not like him,
Forgetful of the grave, where, when the flame
Of his frail exultation shall be spent,
He must descend.   With rapid steps he went
Beneath the shade of trees, beside the flow
Of the wild babbling rivulet ; and now
The forest's solemn canopies were changed
For the uniform and lightsome evening sky.
Grey rocks did peep from the spare moss, and stemmed
The struggling brook : tall spires of windlestrae

Threw their thin shadows down the
  rugged slope,
And nought but gnarled roots of
  ancient pines
Branchless and blasted, clenched
  with grasping roots
The unwilling soil.   A gradual change
  was here,
Yet ghastly.   For, as fast years flow
  away,
The smooth brow gathers, and the
  hair grows thin
And white ; and where irradiate
  dewy eyes
Had shone, gleam stony orbs : so
  from his steps
Bright flowers departed, and the beau-
  tiful shade
Of the green groves, with all their
  odorous winds
And musical motions.   Calm, he still
  pursued
The stream, that with a larger volume
  now
Rolled through the labyrinthine dell ;
  and there
Fretted a path through its descend-
  ing curves
With its wintry speed.   On every side
  now rose
Rocks, which, in unimaginable forms,
Lifted their black and barren pin-
  nacles
In the light of evening, and its preci-
  pice
Obscuring the ravine, disclosed above,
'Mid toppling stones, black gulfs,
  and yawning caves,
Whose windings gave ten thousand
  various tongues
To the loud stream.   Lo ! where the
  pass expands
Its stony jaws, the abrupt mountain
  breaks,
And seems, with its accumulated
  crags,
To overhang the world : for wide ex-
  pand
Beneath the wan stars and descend-
  ing moon
Islanded seas, blue mountains, mighty
  streams,
Dim tracks and vast, robed in the lustrous gloom
Of leaden-coloured even, and fiery
  hills

Mingling their flames with twilight, on
  the verge
Of the remote horizon.   The near
  scene,
In naked and severe simplicity,
Made contrast with the universe.   A
  pine,
Rock-rooted, stretched athwart the
  vacancy
Its swinging boughs, to each incon-
  stant blast
Yielding one only response, at each
  pause,
In most familiar cadence, with the
  howl
The thunder and the hiss of homeless
  streams
Mingling its solemn song, whilst the
  broad river,
Foaming and hurrying o'er its rugged
  path,
Fell into that immeasurable void,
Scattering its waters to the passing
  winds.

Yet the grey precipice, and solemn
  pine
And torrent, were not all ;—one silent
  nook
Was there.   Even on the edge of that
  vast mountain,
Upheld by knotty roots and fallen
  rocks,
It overlooked in its serenity
The dark earth, and the bending
  vault of stars.
It was a tranquil spot, that seemed to
  smile
Even in the lap of horror.   Ivy
  clasped
The fissured stones with its entwining
  arms,
And did embower with leaves forever
  green,
And berries dark, the smooth and
  even space
Of its inviolated floor, and here
The children of the autumnal whirl-
  wind bore,
In wanton sport, those bright leaves,
  whose decay,
Red, yellow, or ethereally pale,
Rival the pride of summer.   'Tis the
  haunt
Of every gentle wind, whose breath
  can teach

The wilds to love tranquillity. One step,
One human step alone, has ever broken
The stillness of its solitude :—one voice
Alone inspired its echoes ;—even that voice
Which hither came, floating among the winds,
And led the loveliest among human forms
To make their wild haunts the depository
Of all the grace and beauty that endued
Its motions, render up its majesty,
Scatter its music on the unfeeling storm,
And to the damp leaves and blue cavern mould,
Nurses of rainbow flowers and branching moss,
Commit the colours of that varying cheek,
That snowy breast, those dark and drooping eyes.

The dim and horned moon hung low, and poured
A sea of lustre on the horizon's verge
That overflowed its mountains. Yellow mist
Filled the unbounded atmosphere, and drank
Wan moonlight even to fulness : not a star
Shone, not a sound was heard ; the very winds,
Danger's grim playmates, on that precipice
Slept, clasped in his embrace.—O, storm of death !
Whose sightless speed divides this sullen night :
And thou, colossal Skeleton, that, still
Guiding its irresistible career
In thy devastating omnipotence,
Art king of this frail world, from the red field
Of slaughter, from the reeking hospital,
The patriot's sacred couch, the snowy bed
Of innocence, the scaffold and the throne,

A mighty voice invokes thee. Ruin calls
His brother Death. A rare and regal prey
He hath prepared, prowling around the world ;
Glutted with which thou mayst repose, and men
Go to their graves like flowers or creeping worms,
Nor ever more offer at thy dark shrine
The unheeded tribute of a broken heart.

When on the threshold of the green recess
The wanderer's footsteps fell, he knew that death
Was on him, Yet a little, ere it fled,
Did he resign his high and holy soul
To images of the majestic past,
That paused within his passive being now,
Like winds that bear sweet music, when they breathe
Through some dim latticed chamber. He did place
His pale lean hand upon the rugged trunk
Of the old pine. Upon an ivied stone
Reclined his languid head, his limbs did rest,
Diffused and motionless, on the smooth brink
Of that obscurest chasm ;—and thus he lay,
Surrendering to their final impulses
The hovering powers of life. Hope and despair,
The torturers, slept : no mortal pain or fear
Marred his repose, the influxes of sense,
And his own being unalloyed by pain,
Yet feebler and more feeble, calmly fed
The stream of thought, till he lay breathing there
At peace, and faintly smiling :—his last sight
Was the great moon, which o'er the western line
Of the wide world her mighty horn suspended
With whose dun beams inwoven darkness seemed

To mingle. Now upon the jagged
hills
It rests, and still as the divided frame
Of the vast meteor sunk, the Poet's
blood,
That ever beat in mystic sympathy
With nature's ebb and flow, grew
feebler still :
And when two lessening points of
light alone
Gleamed through the darkness, the
alternate gasp
Of his faint respiration scarce did stir
The stagnate night :—till the minut-
est ray
Was quenched, the pulse yet lingered
in his heart.
It paused—it fluttered. But when
heaven remained
Utterly black, the murky shades in-
volved
An image, silent, cold, and motion-
less,
As their own voiceless earth and va-
cant air.
Even as a vapour fed with golden
beams
That ministered on sunlight, ere the
west
Eclipses it, was now that wondrous
frame—
No sense, no motion, no divinity—
A fragile lute, on whose harmonious
strings
The breath of heaven did wander—a
bright stream
Once fed with many-voiced waves—
a dream
Of youth, which night and time have
quenched for ever,
Still, dark, and dry, and unremembered now.

O, for Medea's wondrous alchymy,
Which wheresoe'er it fell made the
earth gleam
With bright flowers, and the wintry
boughs exhale
From vernal blooms fresh fragrance !
O, that God,
Profuse of poisons, would concede the
chalice
Which but one living man has drained,
who now,
Vessel of deathless wrath, a slave that
feels

No proud exemption in the blighting
curse
He bears, over the world wanders for
ever,
Lone as incarnate death ! O, that
the dream
Of dark magician in his visioned cave,
Raking the cinders of a crucible
For life and power, even when his
feeble hand
Shakes in its last decay, were the true
law
Of this so lovely world ! But thou
art fled
Like some frail exhalation, which the
dawn
Robes in its golden beams,—ah !
thou hast fled !
The brave, the gentle, and the beau-
tiful,
The child of grace and genius. Heart-
less things
Are done and said i' the world, and
many worms
And beasts and men live on, and
mighty Earth
From sea and mountain, city and
wilderness,
In vesper low or joyous orison,
Lifts still its solemn voice :—but thou
art fled—
Thou canst no longer know or love
the shapes
Of this phantasmal scene, who have to
thee
Been purest ministers, who are, alas !
Now thou art not. Upon those pal-
lid lips
So sweet even in their silence, on
those eyes
That image sleep in death, upon that
form
Yet safe from the worm's outrage, let
no tear
Be shed—not even in thought. Nor,
when those hues
Are gone, and those divinest linea-
ments,
Worn by the senseless wind, shall live
alone
In the frail pauses of this simple
strain,
Let not high verse, mourning the
memory
Of that which is no more, or painting's
woe

Or sculpture, speak in feeble imagery
Their own cold powers. Art and
　　eloquence,
And all the shows o' the world, are
　　frail and vain
To weep a loss that turns their light
　　to shade.
It is a woe " too deep for tears," when
　　all
Is reft at once, when some surpassing
　　Spirit

Whose light adorned the world around
　　it, leaves
Those who remain behind nor sobs
　　nor groans,　　　　　　　[hope ;
The passionate tumult of a clinging
But pale despair and cold tranquil-
　　lity,
Nature's vast frame, the web of
　　human things,
Birth and the grave, that are not as
　　they were.

THE REVOLT OF ISLAM

A POEM IN TWELVE CANTOS

Ὅσαις δὲ βροτὸν ἔθνος ἀγλαίαις ἀπτόμεσθα
Περαίνει πρὸς ἔσχατον
Πλόον· ναυσὶ δ' οὔτε πεζὸς ἰὼν ἂν εὕροις
Ἐς ὑπερβορέων ἀγῶνα θαυματὰν ὁδόν.

Πινδ. Πνθ. x.

PREFACE

The Poem which I now present to the
world, is an attempt from which I
scarcely dare to expect success, and
in which a writer of established fame
might fail without disgrace. It is an
experiment on the temper of the public mind, as to how far a thirst for a
happier condition of moral and political society survives, among the enlightened and refined, the tempests
which have shaken the age in which
we live. I have sought to enlist the
harmony of metrical language, the
ethereal combinations of the fancy,
the rapid and subtle transitions of
human passion, all those elements
which essentially compose a Poem, in
the cause of a liberal and comprehensive morality ; and in the view of
kindling within the bosoms of my
readers, a virtuous enthusiasm for
those doctrines of liberty and justice,
that faith and hope in something
good, which neither violence, nor misrepresentation, nor prejudice can ever
totally extinguish among mankind.

For this purpose, I have chosen a
story of human passion in its most
universal character, diversified with
moving and romantic adventures,
and appealing, in contempt of all
artificial opinions or institutions, to
the common sympathies of every
human breast. I have made no attempt to recommend the motives
which I would substitute for those at
present governing mankind, by me-
thodical and systematic argument.
I would only awaken the feelings so
that the reader should see the beauty
of true virtue, and be incited to those
inquiries which have led to my moral
and political creed, and that of some
of the sublimest intellects in the
world. The Poem, therefore (with
the exception of the first Canto, which
is purely introductory), is narrative,
not didactic. It is a succession of
pictures illustrating the growth and
progress of individual mind aspiring
after excellence, and devoted to the
love of mankind ; its influence in
refining and making pure the most
daring and uncommon impulses of the
imagination, the understanding, and
the senses ; its impatience at " all
the oppressions which are done under
the sun " ; its tendency to awaken
public hope and to enlighten and improve mankind ; the rapid effects of
the application of that tendency ; the
awakening of an immense nation
from their slavery and degradation
to a true sense of moral dignity and

freedom ; the bloodless dethronement of their oppressors, and the unveiling of the religious frauds by which they had been deluded into submission : the tranquillity of successful patriotism, and the universal toleration and benevolence of true philanthropy ; the treachery and barbarity of hired soldiers ; vice not the object of punishment and hatred, but kindness and pity ; the faithlessness of tyrants ; the confederacy of the Rulers of the World, and the restoration of the expelled Dynasty by foreign arms : the massacre and extermination of the Patriots, and the victory of established power ; the consequences of legitimate despotism, civil war, famine, plague, superstition, and an utter extinction of the domestic affections ; the judicial murder of the advocates of Liberty ; the temporary triumph of oppression, that secure earnest of its final and inevitable fall ; the transient nature of ignorance and error, and the eternity of genius and virtue. Such is the series of delineations of which the Poem consists. And if the lofty passions with which it has been my scope to distinguish this story, shall not excite in the reader a generous impulse, an ardent thirst for excellence, an interest profound and strong, such as belongs to no meaner desires—let not the failure be imputed to a natural unfitness for human sympathy in these sublime and animating themes. It is the business of the Poet to communicate to others the pleasure and the enthusiasm arising out of those images and feelings, in the vivid presence of which within his own mind, consists at once his inspiration and his reward.

The panic which, like an epidemic transport, seized upon all classes of men during the excesses consequent upon the French Revolution, is gradually giving place to sanity. It has ceased to be believed, that whole generations of mankind ought to consign themselves to a hopeless inheritance of ignorance and misery, because a nation of men who had been dupes and slaves for centuries, were incapable of conducting themselves with the wisdom and tranquillity of freemen so soon as some of their fetters were partially loosened. That their conduct could not have been marked by any other characters than ferocity and thoughtlessness, is the historical fact from which liberty derives all its recommendations, and falsehood the worst features of its deformity. There is a reflux in the tide of human things which bears the shipwrecked hopes of men into a secure haven, after the storms are past. Methinks, those who now live have survived an age of despair.

The French Revolution may be considered as one of those manifestations of a general state of feeling among civilised mankind, produced by a defect of correspondence between the knowledge existing in society and the improvement or gradual abolition of political institutions. The year 1788 may be assumed as the epoch of one of the most important crises produced by this feeling. The sympathies connected with that event extended to every bosom. The most generous and amiable natures were those which participated the most extensively in these sympathies. But such a degree of unmingled good was expected, as it was impossible to realise. If the Revolution had been in every respect prosperous, then misrule and superstition would lose half their claims to our abhorrence, as fetters which the captive can unlock with the slightest motion of his fingers, and which do not eat with poisonous rust into the soul. The revulsion occasioned by the atrocities of the demagogues and the re-establishment of successive tyrannies in France was terrible, and felt in the remotest corner of the civilised world. Could they listen to the plea of reason who had groaned under the calamities of a social state, according to the provisions of which, one man riots in luxury whilst another famishes for want of bread ? Can he who the day before was a trampled slave, suddenly become liberal-minded, forbearing, and independent ? This is the consequence of the habits of a state of society to be produced by resolute perseverance and indefatigable hope, and long-suffering and long-believing courage, and the systematic efforts of generations of men of intellect and virtue. Such is the lesson which experience teaches now. But on the first reverses of hope in the progress of French liberty, the sanguine eagerness for good overleapt the solution of these questions, and for a time extinguished itself in the unexpectedness of their result. Thus many of the most ardent and tender-hearted of the worshippers of public good have been morally ruined, by what a partial glimpse of the events they deplored, appeared to show as the melancholy desolation of all their cherished hopes. Hence gloom and misanthropy have become the characteristics of the age in which we live, the solace of a disappointment that unconsciously finds relief only in the wilful exaggeration of its own despair. This influence has tainted the literature of the age with the hopelessness of the minds from which it flows. Metaphysics,[1] and inquiries into moral and political science, have become little else than vain attempts to revive exploded superstitions, or sophisms like those[2] of Mr. Malthus, calculated to lull the oppressors of mankind into a security of everlasting triumph. Our works of fiction and poetry have been overshadowed by the same infectious gloom. But mankind appear to me to be emerging from their trance. I am aware, methinks, of a slow, gradual, silent change. In that belief I have composed the following Poem.

I do not presume to enter into competition with our greatest contemporary Poets. Yet I am unwilling to tread in the footsteps of any who have preceded me. I have sought to avoid the imitation of any style of language or versification peculiar to the original minds of which it is the character, designing that even if what I have produced be worthless, it should still be properly my own. Nor have I permitted any system relating to mere words, to divert the attention of the reader from whatever interest I may have succeded in creating, to my own ingenuity in contriving to disgust them according to the rules of criticism. I have simply clothed my thoughts in what appeared to me the most obvious and appropriate language. A person familiar with nature, and with the most celebrated productions of the human mind, can scarcely err in following the instinct, with respect to selection of language, produced by that familiarity.

There is an education peculiarly fitted for a Poet, without which genius and sensibility can hardly fill the circle of their capacities. No education, indeed, can entitle to this appellation a dull and unobservant mind, or one, though neither dull nor unobservant, in which the channels of communication between thought and expression have been obstructed or closed. How far it is my fortune to belong to either of the latter classes, I cannot know. I aspire to be something better. The circumstances of my accidental education have been favourable to this ambition. I have been familiar from boyhood with mountains and lakes, and the sea, and the solitude of forests : Danger, which sports upon the brink of precipices, has been my playmate. I have trodden the glaciers of the Alps, and lived under the eye of Mont Blanc. I have been a wanderer among distant fields. I have sailed down mighty rivers, and seen the sun rise and set, and the stars come forth, whilst I have sailed night and day down a rapid stream among mountains. I have seen populous

[1] I ought to except Sir W. Drummond's *Academical Questions;* a volume of very acute and powerful metaphysical criticism.

[2] It is remarkable, as a symptom of the revival of public hope, that Mr. Malthus has assigned, in the later editions of his work, an indefinite dominion to moral restraint over the principle of population. This concession answers all the inferences from his doctrine unfavourable to human improvement, and reduces the *Essay on Population,* to a commentary illustrative of the unanswerableness of *Political Justice.*

cities, and have watched the passions which rise and spread, and sink and change, amongst assembled multitudes of men. I have seen the theatre of the more visible ravages of tyranny and war, cities and villages reduced to scattered groups of black and roofless houses, and the naked inhabitants sitting famished upon their desolated thresholds. I have conversed with living men of genius. The poetry of ancient Greece and Rome, and modern Italy, and our own country, has been to me like external nature, a passion and an enjoyment. Such are the sources from which the materials for the imagery of my Poem have been drawn. I have considered Poetry in its most comprehensive sense, and have read the Poets, and the Historians, and the Metaphysicians [1] whose writings have been accessible to me, and have looked upon the beautiful and majestic scenery of the earth as common sources of those elements which it is the province of the Poet to embody and combine. Yet the experience and the feelings to which I refer, do not in themselves constitute men Poets, but only prepare them to be the auditors of those who are. How far I shall be found to possess that more essential attribute of Poetry, the power of awakening in others sensations like those which animate my own bosom, is that which, to speak sincerely, I know not; and which, with an acquiescent and contented spirit, I expect to be taught by the effect which I shall produce upon those whom I now address.

I have avoided, as I have said before, the imitation of any contemporary style. But there must be a resemblance, which does not depend upon their own will, between all the writers of any particular age. They cannot escape from subjection to a common influence which arises out of an infinite combination of circumstances belonging to the times in which they live, though each is in a degree the author of the very influence by which his being is thus pervaded. Thus, the tragic Poets of the age of Pericles; the Italian revivers of ancient learning; those mighty intellects of our own country that succeeded the Reformation, the translators of the Bible, Shakspeare, Spenser, the Dramatists of the reign of Elizabeth, and Lord Bacon [2]; the colder spirits of the interval that succeeded;—all resemble each other, and differ from every other in their several classes. In this view of things, Ford can no more be called the imitator of Shakspeare, than Shakspeare the imitator of Ford. There were perhaps few other points of resemblance between these two men, than that which the universal and inevitable influence of their age produced. And this is an influence which neither the meanest scribbler, nor the sublimest genius of any era, can escape; and which I have not attempted to escape.

I have adopted the stanza of Spenser (a measure inexpressibly beautiful), not because I consider it a finer model of poetical harmony than the blank verse of Shakspeare and Milton, but because in the latter there is no shelter for mediocrity: you must either succeed or fail. This perhaps an aspiring spirit should desire. But I was enticed, also, by the brilliancy and magnificence of sound which a mind that has been nourished upon musical thoughts, can produce by a just and harmonious arrangement of the pauses of this measure. Yet there will be found some instances where I have completely failed in this attempt, and one, which I here request the reader to consider as an erratum, where there is left most inadvertently an alexandrine in the middle of a stanza.

But in this, as in every other respect, I have written fearlessly. It is the misfortune of this age, that its Writers, too thoughtless of immor-

---

[1] In this sense there may be such a thing as perfectibility in works of fiction, notwithstanding the concession often made by the advocates of human improvement that perfectibility is a term applicable only to science.

[2] Milton stands alone in the age which he illumined.

tality, are exquisitely sensible to temporary praise or blame. They write with the fear of Reviews before their eyes. This system of criticism sprang up in that torpid interval when Poetry was not. Poetry, and the art which professes to regulate and limit its powers, cannot subsist together. Longinus could not have been the contemporary of Homer, nor Boileau of Horace. Yet this species of criticism never presumed to assert an understanding of its own : it has always, unlike true science, followed, not preceded, the opinion of mankind, and would even now bribe with worthless adulation some of our greatest Poets to impose gratuitous fetters on their own imaginations, and become unconscious accomplices in the daily murder of all genius either not so aspiring or not so fortunate as their own. I have sought therefore to write, as I believe that Homer, Shakspeare, and Milton wrote, in utter disregard of anonymous censure. I am certain that calumny and misrepresentation, though it may move me to compassion, cannot disturb my peace. I shall understand the expressive silence of those sagacious enemies who dare not trust themselves to speak. I shall endeavour to extract from the midst of insult, and contempt, and maledictions, those admonitions which may tend to correct whatever imperfections such censurers may discover in this my first serious appeal to the Public. If certain Critics were as clear-sighted as they are malignant, how great would be the benefit to be derived from their virulent writings ! As it is, I fear I shall be malicious enough to be amused with their paltry tricks and lame invectives. Should the public judge that my composition is worthless, I shall indeed bow before the tribunal from which Milton received his crown of immortality, and shall seek to gather, if I live, strength from that defeat which may nerve me to some new enterprise of thought which may *not* be worthless. I cannot conceive that Lucretius, when he meditated that poem whose

doctrines are yet the basis of our metaphysical knowledge, and whose eloquence has been the wonder of mankind, wrote in awe of such censure as the hired sophists of the impure and superstitious noblemen of Rome might affix to what he should produce. It was at the period when Greece was led captive, and Asia made tributary to the Republic, fast verging itself to slavery and ruin, that a multitude of Syrian captives, bigoted to the worship of their obscene Ashtaroth, and the unworthy successors of Socrates and Zeno, found there a precarious subsistence by administering, under the name of freedmen, to the vices and vanities of the great. These wretched men were skilled to plead, with a superficial but plausible set of sophisms, in favour of that contempt for virtue which is the portion of slaves, and that faith in portents, the most fatal substitute for benevolence in the imaginations of men, which, arising from the enslaved communities of the East, then first began to overwhelm the western nations in its stream. Were these the kind of men whose disapprobation the wise and lofty-minded Lucretius should have regarded with a salutary awe ? The latest and perhaps the meanest of those who follow in his footsteps, would disdain to hold life on such conditions.

The Poem now presented to the Public occupied little more than six months in the composition. That period has been devoted to the task with unremitting ardour and enthusiasm. I have exercised a watchful and earnest criticism on my work as it grew under my hands. I would willingly have sent it forth to the world with that perfection which long labour and revision is said to bestow. But I found that if I should gain something in exactness by this method, I might lose much of the newness and energy of imagery and language as it flowed fresh from my mind. And although the mere composition occupied no more than six months, the thoughts thus arranged were slowly gathered in as many years.

I trust that the reader will carefully distinguish between those opinions which have a dramatic propriety in reference to the characters which they are designed to elucidate, and such as are properly my own. The erroneous and degrading idea which men have conceived of a Supreme Being, for instance, is spoken against, but not the Supreme Being itself. The belief which some superstitious persons whom I have brought upon the stage entertain of the Deity, as injurious to the character of his benevolence, is widely different from my own. In recommending also a great and important change in the spirit which animates the social institutions of mankind, I have avoided all flattery to those violent and malignant passions of our nature, which are ever on the watch to mingle with and to alloy the most beneficial innovations. There is no quarter given to Revenge, or Envy, or Prejudice. Love is celebrated everywhere as the sole law which should govern the moral world. 1817.

DEDICATION

There is no danger to a Man, that knows
What life and death is: there's not any law
Exceeds his knowledge: neither is it lawful
That he should stoop to any other law.

CHAPMAN.

TO MARY ———

I

So now my summer-task is ended, Mary,
And I return to thee, mine own heart's home;
As to his Queen some victor Knight of Faëry,
Earning bright spoils for her enchanted dome;
Nor thou disdain, that ere my fame become
A star among the stars of mortal night,
If it indeed may cleave its natal gloom,
Its doubtful promise thus I would unite
With thy beloved name, thou Child of love and light.

II

The toil which stole from thee so many an hour
Is ended—and the fruit is at thy feet!
No longer where the woods to frame a bower
With interlaced branches mix and meet,
Or where with sound like many voices sweet,
Water-falls leap among wild islands green,
Which framed for my lone boat a lone retreat
Of moss-grown trees and weeds, shall I be seen:
But beside thee, where still my heart has ever been.

III

Thoughts of great deeds were mine, dear Friend, when first
The clouds which wrap this world from youth did pass.
I do remember well the hour which burst
My spirit's sleep: a fresh May-dawn it was,
When I walked forth upon the glittering grass,
And wept, I knew not why: until there rose
From the near school-room, voices, that, alas!
Were but one echo from a world of woes—
The harsh and grating strife of tyrants and of foes.

IV

And then I clasped my hands and looked around,
But none was near to mock my streaming eyes,
Which poured their warm drops on the sunny ground—
So without shame, I spake :—" I will be wise,
And just, and free, and mild, if in me lies
Such power, for I grow weary to behold
The selfish and the strong still tyrannize
Without reproach or check." I then controlled
My tears, my heart grew calm, and I was meek and bold.

V

And from that hour did I with earnest thought
Heap knowledge from forbidden mines of lore,
Yet nothing that my tyrants knew or taught
I cared to learn, but from that secret store
Wrought linked armour for my soul, before
It might walk forth to war among mankind ;
Thus power and hope were strengthened more and more
Within me, till there came upon my mind
A sense of loneliness, a thirst with which I pined.

VI

Alas, that love should be a blight and snare
To those who seek all sympathies in one !—
Such once I sought in vain ; then black despair,
The shadow of a starless night, was thrown
Over the world in which I moved alone :—
Yet never found I one not false to me,
Hard hearts, and cold, like weights of icy stone
Which crushed and withered mine, that could not be
Aught but a lifeless clog, until revived by thee.

VII

Thou Friend, whose presence on my wintry heart
Fell, like bright Spring upon some herbless plain,
How beautiful and calm and free thou wert
In thy young wisdom, when the mortal chain
Of Custom thou didst burst and rend in twain,
And walked as free as light the clouds among,
Which many an envious slave then breathed in vain
From his dim dungeon, and my spirit sprung
To meet thee from the woes which had begirt it long.

VIII

No more alone through the world's wilderness,
Although I trod the paths of high intent,
I journeyed now : no more companionless,
Where solitude is like despair, I went.—
There is the wisdom of a stern content
When Poverty can blight the just and good,
When Infamy dares mock the innocent,
And cherished friends turn with the multitude
To trample : this was ours, and we unshaken stood !

IX

Now has descended a serener hour,
And with inconstant fortune, friends return ;

Though suffering leaves the knowledge and the power
Which says :—Let scorn be not repaid with scorn.
And from thy side two gentle babes are born
To fill our home with smiles, and thus are we
Most fortunate beneath life's beaming morn :
And these delights, and thou, have been to me
The parents of the Song I consecrate to thee.

x

Is it, that now my inexperienced fingers
But strike the prelude of a loftier strain ?
Or, must the lyre on which my spirit lingers
Soon pause in silence, ne'er to sound again,
Though it might shake the Anarch Custom's reign,
And charm the minds of men to Truth's own sway,
Holier than was Amphion's ? I would fain
Reply in hope—but I am worn away,
And Death and Love are yet contending for their prey.

xi

And what art thou ? I know, but dare not speak :
Time may interpret to his silent years.
Yet in the paleness of thy thoughtful cheek,
And in the light thine ample forehead wears,
And in thy sweetest smiles, and in thy tears,
And in thy gentle speech, a prophecy
Is whispered, to subdue my fondest fears :
And through thine eyes, even in thy soul I see
A lamp of vestal fire burning internally.

xii

They say that thou wert lovely from thy birth,
Of glorious parents thou aspiring Child !
I wonder not—for One then left this earth
Whose life was like a setting planet mild,
Which clothed thee in the radiance undefiled
Of its departing glory ; still her fame
Shines on thee, through the tempests dark and wild
Which shake these latter days ; and thou canst claim
The shelter, from thy Sire, of an immortal name.

xiii

One voice came forth from many a mighty spirit,
Which was the echo of three thousand years ;
And the tumultuous world stood mute to hear it,
As some lone man who in a desert hears
The music of his home :—unwonted fears
Fell on the pale oppressors of our race,
And Faith, and Custom, and low-thoughted cares,
Like thunder-stricken dragons, for a space
Left the torn human heart, their food and dwelling-place.

xiv

Truth's deathless voice pauses among mankind !
If there must be no response to my cry—
If men must rise and stamp with fury blind
On his pure name who loves them,—thou and I,

Sweet Friend ! can look from our tranquillity
Like lamps into the world's tempestuous night,—
Two tranquil stars, while clouds are passing by
Which wrap them from the foundering seaman's sight,
That burn from year to year with unextinguished light.

CANTO I

I

WHEN the last hope of trampled France had failed
Like a brief dream of unremaining glory,
From visions of despair I rose, and scaled
The peak of an aërial promontory,
Whose caverned base with the vexed surge was hoary
And saw the golden dawn break forth, and waken
Each cloud, and every wave :—but transitory
The calm : for sudden, the firm earth was shaken,
As if by the last wreck its frame were overtaken.

II

So as I stood, one blast of muttering thunder
Burst in far peals along the waveless deep,
When, gathering fast, around, above, and under,
Long trains of tremulous mist began to creep,
Until their complicating lines did steep
The orient sun in shadow :—not a sound
Was heard ; one horrible repose did keep
The forests and the floods, and all around
Darkness more dread than night was poured upon the ground.

III

Hark ! 'tis the rushing of a wind that sweeps
Earth and the ocean. See ! the lightnings yawn
Deluging Heaven with fire, and the lashed deeps
Glitter and boil beneath : it rages on,
One mighty stream, whirlwind and waves upthrown,
Lightning, and hail, and darkness eddying by,
There is a pause—the sea-birds, that were gone
Into their caves to shriek, come forth to spy
What calm has fall'n on earth, what light is in the sky.

IV

For, where the irresistible storm had cloven
That fearful darkness, the blue sky was seen
Fretted with many a fair cloud interwoven
Most delicately, and the ocean green,
Beneath that opening spot of blue serene,
Quivered like burning emerald : calm was spread
On all below ; but far on high, between
Earth and the upper air, the vast clouds fled,
Countless and swift as leaves on autumn's tempest shed.

V

For ever as the war became more fierce
Between the whirlwinds and the rack on high,
That spot grew more serene ; blue light did pierce
The woof of those white clouds, which seemed to lie

Far, deep, and motionless ; while through the sky
The pallid semicircle of the moon
Past on, in slow and moving majesty ;
Its upper horn arrayed in mists, which soon
But slowly fled, like dew beneath the beams of noon.

VI

I could not choose but gaze ; a fascination
Dwelt in that moon, and sky, and clouds, which drew
My fancy thither, and in expectation
Of what I knew not, I remained :—the hue
Of the white moon, amid that heaven so blue
Suddenly stained with shadow did appear ;
A speck, a cloud, a shape, approaching grew,
Like a great ship in the sun's sinking sphere
Beheld afar at sea, and swift it came anear—

VII

Even like a bark, which from a chasm of mountains,
Dark, vast, and overhanging, on a river
Which there collects the strength of all its fountains,
Comes forth, whilst with the speed its frame doth quiver,
Sails, oars, and stream, tending to one endeavour ;
So, from that chasm of light a winged Form
On all the winds of heaven approaching ever
Floated, dilating as it came : the storm
Pursued it with fierce blasts, and lightnings swift and warm.

VIII

A course precipitous, of dizzy speed,
Suspending thought and breath ; a monstrous sight !
For in the air do I behold indeed
An Eagle and a Serpent wreathed in fight :—
And now, relaxing its impetuous flight
Before the aërial rock on which I stood,
The Eagle, hovering, wheeled to left and right,
And hung with lingering wings over the flood,
And startled with its yells the wide air's solitude.

IX

A shaft of light upon its wings descended,
And every golden feather gleamed therein—
Feather and scale inextricably blended.
The Serpent's mailed and many-coloured skin
Shone through the plumes ; its coils were twined within
By many a swollen and knotted fold, and high
And far, the neck receding lithe and thin,
Sustained a crested head, which warily
Shifted and glanced before the Eagle's steadfast eye.

X

Around, around, in ceaseless circles wheeling
With clang of wings and scream, the Eagle sailed
Incessantly—sometimes on high concealing
Its lessening orbs, sometimes as if it failed,
Drooped through the air ; and still it shrieked and wailed,

And casting back its eager head, with beak
And talon unremittingly assailed
The wreathed Serpent, who did ever seek
Upon his enemy's heart a mortal wound to wreak.

XI

What life, what power, was kindled and arose
Within the sphere of that appalling fray !
For, from the encounter of those wondrous foes,
A vapour like the sea's suspended spray
Hung gathered : in the void air, far away,
Floated the shattered plumes ; bright scales did leap,
Where'er the Eagle's talons made their way,
Like sparks into the darkness ;—as they sweep,
Blood stains the snowy foam of the tumultuous deep.

XII

Swift chances in that combat—many a check,
And many a change, a dark and wild turmoil ;
Sometimes the Snake around his enemy's neck
Locked in stiff rings his adamantine coil,
Until the Eagle, faint with pain and toil,
Remitted his strong flight, and near the sea
Languidly fluttered, hopeless so to foil
His adversary, who then reared on high
His red and burning crest, radiant with victory.

XIII

Then on the white edge of the bursting surge,
Where they had sunk together, would the Snake
Relax his suffocating grasp, and scourge
The wind with his wild writhings ; for to break
That chain of torment, the vast bird would shake
That strength of his unconquerable wings
As in despair, and with his sinewy neck
Dissolved in sudden shock those linked rings,
Then soar—as swift as smoke from a volcano springs.

XIV

Wile baffled wile, and strength encountered strength,
Thus long, but unprevailing :—the event
Of that portentous fight appeared at length :
Until the lamp of day was almost spent
It had endured, when lifeless, stark, and rent,
Hung high that mighty Serpent, and at last
Fell to the sea, while o'er the continent,
With clang of wings and scream the Eagle past,
Heavily borne away on the exhausted blast.

XV

And with it fled the tempest, so that ocean
And earth and sky shone through the atmosphere—
Only, it was strange to see the red commotion
Of waves like mountains o'er the sinking sphere
Of sunset sweep, and their fierce roar to hear
Amid the calm : down the steep path I wound
To the sea-shore—the evening was most clear

And beautiful, and there the sea I found
Calm as a cradled child in dreamless slumber bound.

XVI

There was a woman, beautiful as morning,
Sitting beneath the rocks upon the sand
Of the waste sea—fair as one flower adorning
An icy wilderness—each delicate hand
Lay crossed upon her bosom, and the band
Of her dark hair had fallen, and so she sate
Looking upon the waves ; on the bare strand
Upon the sea-mark a small boat did wait,
Fair as herself, like Love by Hope left desolate.

XVII

It seemed that this fair Shape had looked upon
That unimaginable fight, and now
That her sweet eyes were weary of the sun,
As brightly it illustrated her woe ;
For in the tears which silently to flow
Paused not, its lustre hung ; she watching aye
The foam-wreaths which the faint tide wove below
Upon the spangled sands, groaned heavily,
And after every groan looked up over the sea.

XVIII

And when she saw the wounded Serpent make
His path between the waves, her lips grew pale,
Parted and quivered ; the tears ceased to break
From her immovable eyes ; no voice of wail
Escaped her ; but she rose, and on the gale
Loosening her star-bright robe and shadowy hair,
Poured forth her voice ; the caverns of the vale
That opened to the ocean, caught it there,
And filled with silver sounds the overflowing air.

XIX

She spake in language whose strange melody
Might not belong to earth. I heard, alone,
What made its music more melodious be,
The pity and the love of every tone ;
But to the snake those accents sweet were known,
His native tongue and hers : nor did he beat
The hoar spray idly then, but winding on
Through the green shadows of the waves that meet
Near to the shore, did pause beside her snowy feet.

XX

Then on the sands the Woman sate again,
And wept and clasped her hands, and all between,
Renewed the unintelligible strain
Of her melodious voice and eloquent mien ;
And she unveiled her bosom, and the green
And glancing shadows of the sea did play
O'er its marmoreal depth :—one moment seen,
For ere the next, the Serpent did obey
Her voice, and, coiled in rest, in her embrace it lay.

XXI

Then she arose, and smiled on me with eyes
Serene yet sorrowing, like that planet fair,
While yet the daylight lingereth in the skies
Which cleaves with arrowy beams the dark-red air,
And said : To grieve is wise, but the despair
Was weak and vain which led thee here from sleep :
This shalt thou know, and more, if thou dost dare
With me and with this Serpent, o'er the deep,
A voyage divine and strange, companionship to keep.

XXII

Her voice was like the wildest, saddest tone,
Yet sweet, of some loved voice heard long ago.
I wept.   Shall this fair woman all alone
Over the sea with that fierce Serpent go ?
His head is on her heart, and who can know
How soon he may devour his feeble prey ?
Such were my thoughts, when the tide 'gan to flow ;
And that strange boat, like the moon's shade did sway
Amid reflected stars that in the waters lay.

XXIII

A boat of rare device, which had no sail
But its own curved prow of thin moonstone,
Wrought like a web of texture fine and frail,
To catch those gentlest winds which are not known
To breathe, but by the steady speed alone
With which it cleaves the sparkling sea ; and now
We are embarked, the mountains hang and frown
Over the starry deep that gleams below
A vast and dim expanse, as o'er the waves we go.

XXIV

And as we sailed, a strange and awful tale
That Woman told, like such mysterious dream
As makes the slumberer's cheek with wonder pale !
'Twas midnight, and around, a shoreless stream,
Wide ocean rolled, when that majestic theme
Shrined in her heart found utterance, and she bent
Her looks on mine ; those eyes a kindling beam
Of love divine into my spirit sent,
And, ere her lips could move, made the air eloquent.

XXV

Speak not to me, but hear ! much shalt thou learn,
Much must remain unthought, and more untold,
In the dark Future's ever-flowing urn :
Know then, that from the depth of ages old
Two Powers o'er mortal things dominion hold,
Ruling the world with a divided lot,
Immortal, all-pervading, manifold,
Twin Genii, equal Gods—when life and thought
Sprang forth, they burst the womb of inessential Nought.

XXVI

The earliest dweller of the world alone

Stood on the verge of chaos : Lo ! afar
O'er the wide wild abyss two meteors shone,
Sprung from the depth of its tempestuous jar :
A blood-red Comet and the Morning Star
Mingling their beams in combat—as he stood
All thoughts within his mind waged mutual war
In dreadful sympathy—when to the flood
That fair star fell, he turned and shed his brother's blood.

XXVII

Thus evil triumphed, and the Spirit of Evil,
One Power of many shapes which none may know,
One Shape of many names ; the Fiend did revel
In victory, reigning o'er a world of woe,
For the new race of man went to and fro,
Famished and homeless, loathed and loathing, wild,
And hating good—for his immortal foe
He changed from starry shape, beauteous and mild.
To a dire Snake, with man and beast unreconciled.

XXVIII

The darkness lingering o'er the dawn of things,
Was Evil's breath and life : this made him strong
To soar aloft with overshadowing wings ;
And the great Spirit of Good did creep among
The nations of mankind, and every tongue
Cursed, and blasphemed him as he past ; for none
Knew good from evil though their names were hung
In mockery o'er the fane where many a groan,
As King, and Lord, and God, the conquering Fiend did own.

XXIX

The Fiend, whose name was Legion ; Death, Decay,
Earthquake, and Blight, and Want, and Madness pale,
Winged and wan diseases, an array
Numerous as leaves that strew the autumnal gale ;
Poison, a snake in flowers, beneath the veil
Of food and mirth, hiding his mortal head ;
And, without whom all these might nought avail,
Fear, Hatred, Faith, and Tyranny, who spread
Those subtle nets which snare the living and the dead.

XXX

His spirit is their power, and they his slaves
In air, in light, and thought, and language dwell ;
And keep their state from palaces to graves,
In all resorts of men—invisible ;
But when, in ebon mirror, Nightmare fell,
To tyrant or impostor bids them rise.
Black winged demon forms—whom, from the hell,
His reign and dwelling beneath nether skies,
He loosens to their dark and blasting ministries.

XXXI

In the world's youth his empire was as firm
As its foundations—soon the Spirit of Good,
Though in the likeness of a loathsome worm,

Sprang from the billows of the formless flood,
Which shrank and fled ; and with that fiend of blood
Renewed the doubtful war—thrones then first shook,
And earth's immense and trampled multitude,
In hope on their own powers began to look,
And Fear, the demon pale, his sanguine shrine forsook.

XXXII

Then Greece arose, and to its bards and sages,
In dream the golden-pinioned Genii came,
Even where they slept amid the night of ages
Steeping their hearts in the divinest flame
Which thy breath kindled, Power of holiest name !
And oft in cycles since, when darkness gave
New weapons to thy foe, their sunlike fame
Upon the combat shone—a light to save,
Like Paradise spread forth beyond the shadowy grave.

XXXIII

Such is this conflict—when mankind doth strive
With its oppressors in a strife of blood,
Or when free thoughts, like lightnings, are alive ;
And in each bosom of the multitude
Justice and truth, with custom's hydra brood,
Wage silent war ;—when priests and kings dissemble
In smiles or frowns their fierce disquietude,
When round pure hearts, a host of hopes assemble,
The Snake and Eagle meet—the world's foundations tremble .

XXXIV

Thou hast beheld that fight—when to thy home
Thou dost return, steep not its hearth in tears ;
Though thou mayst hear that earth is now become
The tyrant's garbage, which to his compeers,
The vile reward of their dishonoured years,
He will dividing give.—The victor Fiend
Omnipotent of yore, now quails, and fears
His triumph dearly won, which soon will lend
An impulse swift and sure to his approaching end.

XXXV

List, stranger, list ! mine is a human form,
Like that thou wearest—touch me—shrink not now !
My hand thou feel'st is not a ghost's, but warm
With human blood.—'Twas many years ago,
Since first my thirsting soul aspired to know
The secrets of this wondrous world, when deep
My heart was pierced with sympathy, for woe
Which could not be mine own—and thought did keep
In dream, unnatural watch beside an infant's sleep.

XXXVI

Woe could not be mine own, since far from men
I dwelt, a free and happy orphan child,
By the sea-shore, in a deep mountain glen ;
And near the waves, and through the forests wild,
I roamed, to storm and darkness reconciled,

For I was calm while tempest shook the sky :
But, when the breathless heavens in beauty smiled,
I wept sweet tears, yet too tumultuously
For peace, and clasped my hands aloft in ecstasy.

XXXVII

These were forebodings of my fate.—Before
A woman's heart beat in my virgin breast,
It had been nurtured in divinest lore :
A dying poet gave me books, and blest
With wild but holy talk the sweet unrest
In which I watched him as he died away—
A youth with hoary hair—a fleeting guest
Of our lone mountains—and this lore did sway
My spirit like a storm, contending there alway.

XXXVIII

Thus the dark tale which history doth unfold,
I knew, but not, methinks, as others know,
For they weep not ; and Wisdom had unrolled
The clouds which hide the gulf of mortal woe :
To few can she that warning vision show,
For I loved all things with intense devotion ;
So that when Hope's deep source in fullest flow,
Like earthquake did uplift the stagnant ocean
Of human thoughts—mine shook beneath the wide emotion.

XXXIX

When first the living blood through all these veins
Kindled a thought in sense, great France sprang forth
And seized, as if to break, the ponderous chains
Which bind in woe the nations of the earth.
I saw, and started from my cottage hearth ;
And to the clouds and waves in tameless gladness
Shrieked, till they caught immeasurable mirth—
And laughed in light and music : soon sweet madness
Was poured upon my heart, a soft and thrilling sadness.

XL

Deep slumber fell on me ;—my dreams were fire,
Soft and delightful thoughts did rest and hover
Like shadows o'er my brain ; and strange desire
The tempest of a passion, raging over
My tranquil soul, its depths with light did cover,
Which past ; and calm, and darkness, sweeter far
Came—then I loved ; but not a human lover !
For when I rose from sleep, the Morning Star
Shone through the woodbine wreaths which round my casement were.

XLI

'Twas like an eye which seemed to smile on me.
I watched till, by the sun made pale, it sank
Under the billows of the heaving sea ;
But from its beams deep love my spirit drank,
And to my brain the boundless world now shrank
Into one thought—one image—yea for ever !
Even like the day's-spring, poured on vapours dank,
The beams of that one star did shoot and quiver
Through my benighted mind—and were extinguished never.

XLII

The day past thus : at night, methought in dream
A shape of speechless beauty did appear ;
It stood like light on a careering stream
Of golden clouds which shook the atmosphere ;
A winged youth, his radiant brow did wear
The Morning Star : a wild dissolving bliss
Over my frame he breathed, approaching near,
And bent his eyes of kindling tenderness
Near mine, and on my lips impressed a lingering kiss,

XLIII

And said : A Spirit loves thee, mortal maiden,
How wilt thou prove thy worth ? Then joy and sleep
Together fled ; my soul was deeply laden,
And to the shore I went to muse and weep ;
But as I moved, over my heart did creep
A joy less soft, but more profound and strong
Than my sweet dream ; and it forbade to keep
The path of the sea-shore : that Spirit's tongue
Seemed whispering in my heart, and bore my steps along.

XLIV

How, to that vast and peopled city led,
Which was a field of holy warfare then,
I walked among the dying and the dead,
And shared in fearless deeds with evil men,
Calm as an angel in the dragon's den—
How I braved death for liberty and truth,
And spurned at peace, and power, and fame, and when
Those hopes had lost the glory of their youth,
How sadly I returned—might move the hearer's ruth.

XLV

Warm tears throng fast ! the tale may not be said—
Know then, that when this grief had been subdued,
I was not left, like others, cold and dead ;
The Spirit whom I loved in solitude
Sustained his child : the tempest-shaken wood,
The waves, the fountains, and the hush of night—
These were his voice, and well I understood
His smile divine when the calm sea was bright
With silent stars, and Heaven was breathless with delight.

XLVI

In lonely glens, amid the roar of rivers,
When the dim nights were moonless, have I known
Joys which no tongue can tell ; my pale lip quivers
When thought revisits them :—know thou alone,
That after many wondrous years were flown,
I was awakened by a shriek of woe ;
And over me a mystic robe was thrown,
By viewless hands, and a bright star did glow
Before my steps—the Snake then met his mortal foe.

XLVII

Thou fear'st not then the Serpent on thy heart ?
Fear it ! she said with brief and passionate cry,

And spake no more : that silence made me start—
I looked and we were sailing pleasantly,
Swift as a cloud between the sea and sky,
Beneath the rising moon seen far away ;
Mountains of ice, like sapphire, piled on high
Hemming the horizon round, in silence lay
On the still waters,—these we did approach alway.

XLVIII

And swift and swifter grew the vessel's motion,
So that a dizzy trance fell on my brain—
Wild music woke me : we had past the ocean
Which girds the Pole, Nature's remotest reign—
And we glode fast o'er a pellucid plain
Of waters, azure with the noon-tide day.
Ethereal mountains shone around—a Fane
Stood in the midst, girt by green isles which lay
On the blue sunny deep, resplendent far away.

XLIX

It was a Temple, such as mortal hand
Has never built, nor ecstasy, or dream,
Reared in the cities of enchanted land :
'Twas likest Heaven, ere yet day's purple streak
Ebbs o'er the western forest, while the gleam
Of the unrisen moon among the clouds
Is gathering—when with many a golden beam
The thronging constellations rush in crowds,
Paving with fire the sky and the marmoreal floods.

L

Like what may be conceived of this vast dome,
When from the depths which thought can seldom pierce
Genius beholds it rise, his native home,
Girt by the deserts of the Universe,
Yet, nor in painting's light, or mightier verse,
Or sculpture's marble language, can invest
That shape to mortal sense—such glooms immerse
That incommunicable sight, and rest
Upon the labouring brain and over-burthened breast.

LI

Winding among the lawny islands fair,
Whose bloomy forests starred the shadowy deep,
The wingless boat paused where an ivory stair.
Its fretwork in the crystal sea did steep,
Encircling that vast Fane's aërial heap :
We disembarked, and through a portal wide
We passed—whose roof of moonstone carved, did keep
A glimmering o'er the forms on every side,
Sculptures like life and thought ; immovable, deep-eyed.

LII

We came to a vast hall, whose glorious roof
Was diamond, which had drunk the lightning's sheen
In darkness, and now poured it through the woof
Of spell-inwoven clouds hung there to screen

Its blinding splendour—through such veil was seen
That work of subtlest power, divine and rare ;
Orb above orb, with starry shapes between,
And horned moons, and meteors strange and fair,
On night-black columns poised—one hollow hemisphere !

LIII

Ten thousand columns in that quivering light
Distinct—between whose shafts wound far away
The long and labyrinthine aisles—more bright
With their own radiance than the Heaven of Day ;
And on the jasper walls around, there lay
Paintings, the poesy of mightiest thought,
Which did the Spirit's history display ;
A tale of passionate change, divinely taught,
Which, in their winged dance, unconscious Genii wrought.

LIV

Beneath, there sate on many a sapphire throne,
The great, who had departed from mankind,
A mighty Senate ; some whose white hairs shone
Like mountain snow, mild, beautiful, and blind.
Some female forms, whose gestures beamed with mind ;
And ardent youths, and children bright and fair ;
And some had lyres whose strings were intertwined
With pale and clinging flames, which ever there
Waked faint yet thrilling sounds that pierced the crystal air.

LV

One seat was vacant in the midst, a throne,
Reared on a pyramid like sculptured flame,
Distinct with circling steps which rested on
Their own deep fire—soon as the woman came
Into that hall, she shrieked the Spirit's name
And fell ; and vanished slowly from the sight.
Darkness arose from her dissolving frame,
Which gathering, filled that dome of woven light,
Blotting its sphered stars with supernatural night.

LVI

Then first two glittering lights were seen to glide
In circles on the amethystine floor,
Small serpent eyes trailing from side to side,
Like meteors on a river's grassy shore,
They round each other rolled, dilating more
And more—then rose, commingling into one,
One clear and mighty planet hanging o'er
A cloud of deepest shadow which was thrown
Athwart the glowing steps and the crystalline throne.

LVII

The cloud which rested on that cone of flame
Was cloven : beneath the planet sate a Form,
Fairer than tongue can speak or thought may frame,
The radiance of whose limbs rose-like and warm
Flowed forth, and did with softest light inform

The shadowy dome, the sculptures, and the state
Of those assembled shapes—with clinging charm
Sinking upon their hearts and mine—He sate
Majestic yet most mild—calm, yet compassionate.

LVIII

Wonder and joy a passing faintness threw
Over my brow—a hand supported me,
Whose touch was magic strength : an eye of blue
Looked into mine, like moonlight, soothingly ;
And a voice said—Thou must a listener be
This day—two mighty spirits now return,
Like birds of calm, from the world's raging sea,
They pour fresh light from Hope's immortal urn ;
A tale of human power—despair not—list and learn !

LIX

I looked, and lo ! one stood forth eloquently,
His eyes were dark and deep, and the clear brow
Which shadowed them was like the morning sky,
The cloudless Heaven of Spring, when in their flow
Through the bright air, the soft winds as they blow
Wake the green world—his gestures did obey
The oracular mind that made his features glow,
And where his curved lips half open lay,
Passion's divinest stream had made impetuous way.

LX

Beneath the darkness of his outspread hair.
He stood thus beautiful : but there was One
Who sate beside him like his shadow there,
And held his hand—far lovelier—she was known
To be thus fair by the few lines alone
Which through her floating locks and gathered cloak,
Glances of soul-dissolving glory, shone :—
None else beheld her eyes, in him they woke
Memories which found a tongue, as thus he silence broke.

CANTO II

I

The starlight smile of children, the sweet looks
Of women, the fair breast from which I fed,
The murmur of the unreposing brooks,
And the green light which, shifting overhead,
Some tangled bower of vines around me shed,
The shells on the sea-sand, and the wild flowers,
The lamplight through the rafters cheerly spread,
And on the twining flax—in life's young hours
These sights and sounds did nurse my spirit's folded powers.

II

In Argolis beside the echoing sea,
Such impulses within my mortal frame
Arose, and they were dear to memory,
Like tokens of the dead :—but others came
Soon, in another shape : the wondrous fame

Of the past world, the vital words and deeds
Of minds whom neither time nor change can tame,
Traditions dark and old, whence evil creeds
Start forth, and whose dim shade a stream of poison feeds.

III

I heard, as all have heard, the various story
Of human life, and wept unwilling tears,
Feeble historians of its shame and glory,
False disputants on all its hopes and fears,
Victims who worshipped ruin,—chroniclers
Of daily scorn, and slaves who loathed their state ;
Yet flattering power had given its ministers
A throne of judgment in the grave—'twas fate,
That among such as these my youth should seek its mate.

IV

The land in which I lived, by a fell bane
Was withered up. Tyrants dwelt side by side,
And stabled in our homes,—until the chain
Stifled the captive's cry, and to abide
That blasting curse men had no shame—all vied
In evil, slave and despot ; fear with lust
Strange fellowship through mutual hate had tied,
Like two dark serpents tangled in the dust,
Which on the paths of men their mingling poison thrust.

V

Earth, our bright home, its mountains and its waters,
And the ethereal shapes which are suspended
Over its green expanse, and those fair daughters,
The clouds, of Sun and Ocean, who have blended
The colours of the air since first extended
It cradled the young world, none wandered forth
To see or feel : a darkness had descended
On every heart : the light which shows its worth,
Must among gentle thoughts and fearless take its birth.

VI

This vital world, this home of happy spirits,
Was as a dungeon to my blasted kind,
All that despair from murdered hope inherits
They sought, and in their helpless misery blind,
A deeper prison and heavier chains did find,
And stronger tyrants :—a dark gulf before,
The realm of a stern Ruler, yawned ; behind,
Terror and Time conflicting drove, and bore
On their tempestuous flood the shrieking wretch from shore.

VII

Out of that Ocean's wrecks had Guilt and Woe
Framed a dark dwelling for their homeless thought,
And, starting at the ghosts which to and fro
Glide o'er its dim and gloomy strand, had brought
The worship thence which they each other taught.
Well might men loathe their life, well might they turn
Even to the ills again from which they sought

Such refuge after death !—well might they learn
To gaze on this fair world with hopeless unconcern !

VIII

For they all pined in bondage ; body and soul,
Tyrant and slave, victim and torturer, bent
Before one Power, to which supreme control
Over their will by their own weakness lent,
Made all its many names omnipotent ;
All symbols of things evil, all divine ;
And hymns of blood or mockery, which rent
The air from all its fanes, did intertwine
Imposture's impious toils round each discordant shrine.

IX

I heard, as all have heard, life's various story,
And in no careless heart transcribed the tale ;
But, from the sneers of men who had grown hoary
In shame and scorn, from groans of crowds made pale
By famine, from a mother's desolate wail
O'er her polluted child, from innocent blood
Poured on the earth, and brows anxious and pale
With the heart's warfare ; did I gather food
To feed my many thoughts :—a tameless multitude.

X

I wandered through the wrecks of days departed
Far by the desolated shore, when even
O'er the still sea and jagged islets darted
The light of moonrise ; in the northern Heaven,
Among the clouds near the horizon driven,
The mountains lay beneath one planet pale ;
Around me broken tombs and columns riven
Looked vast in twilight, and the sorrowing gale
Waked in those ruins grey its everlasting wail !

XI

I knew not who had framed these wonders then,
Nor had I heard the story of their deeds;
But dwellings of a race of mightier men,
And monuments of less ungentle creeds
Tell their own tale to him who wisely heeds
The language which they speak ; and now, to me
The moonlight making pale the blooming weeds,
The bright stars shining in the breathless sea,
Interpreted those scrolls of mortal mystery.

XII

Such man has been, and such may yet become !
Ay, wiser, greater, gentler, even than they
Who on the fragments of yon shattered dome
Have stamped the sign of power—I felt the sway
Of the vast stream of ages bear away
My floating thoughts—my heart beat loud and fast—
Even as a storm let loose beneath the ray
Of the still moon, my spirit onward past
Beneath truth's steady beams upon its tumult cast.

XIII

It shall be thus no more ! too long, too long,
Sons of the glorious dead ! have ye lain bound
In darkness and in ruin—Hope is strong,
Justice and Truth their winged child have found—
Awake ! arise ! until the mighty sound
Of your career shall scatter in its gust
The thrones of the oppressor, and the ground
Hide the last altar's unregarded dust,
Whose Idol has so long betrayed your impious trust.

XIV

It must be so—I will arise and waken
The multitude, and like a sulphurous hill,
Which on a sudden from its snows had shaken
The swoon of ages, it shall burst, and fill
The world with cleansing fire ; it must, it will—
It may not be restrained !—and who shall stand—
Amid the rocking earthquake steadfast still,
But Laon ? on high Freedom's desert land
A tower whose marble walls the leagued storms withstand !

XV

One summer night, in commune with the hope
Thus deeply fed, amid those ruins grey
I watched beneath the dark sky's starry cope ;
And ever from that hour upon me lay
The burthen of this hope, and night or day,
In vision or in dream, clove to my breast :
Among mankind, or when gone far away
To the lone shores and mountains, 'twas a guest,
Which followed where I fled, and watched when I did rest.

XVI

These hopes found words through which my spirit sought
To weave a bondage of such sympathy
As might create some response to the thought
Which ruled me now—and as the vapours lie
Bright in the outspread morning's radiancy,
So were these thoughts invested with the light
Of language ; and all bosoms made reply
On which its lustre streamed, whene'er it might
Thro' darkness wide and deep those tranced spirits smite.

XVII

Yes, many an eye with dizzy tears was dim,
And oft I thought to clasp my own heart's brother,
When I could feel the listener's senses, swim,
And hear his breath its own swift gaspings smother
Even as my words evoked them—and another,
And yet another, I did fondly deem,
Felt that we all were sons of one great mother ;
And the cold truth such sad reverse did seem,
As to awake in grief from some delightful dream.

XVIII

Yes, oft beside the ruined labyrinth
Which skirts the hoary caves of the green deep,

Did Laon and his friend on one grey plinth,
Round whose worn base the wild waves hiss and leap,
Resting at eve, a lofty converse keep :
And that his friend was false, may now be said
Calmly—that he like other men could weep
Tears which are lies, and could betray and spread
Snares for that guileless heart which for his own had bled.

XIX

Then, had no great aim recompensed my sorrow,
I must have sought dark respite from its stress—
In dreamless rest, in sleep that sees no morrow—
For to tread life's dismaying wilderness
Without one smile to cheer, one voice to bless,
Amid the snares and scoffs of human kind,
Is hard—but I betrayed it not, nor less
With love that scorned return, sought to unbind
The interwoven clouds which make its wisdom blind.

XX

With deathless minds, which leave where they have past
A path of light, my soul communion knew ;
Till from that glorious intercourse, at last,
As from a mine of magic store, I drew
Words which were weapons ;—round my heart there grew
The adamantine armour of their power,
And from my fancy wings of golden hue
Sprang forth—yet not alone from wisdom's tower,
A minister of truth,—these plumes young Laon bore.

XXI

An orphan with my parents lived, whose eyes
Were lodestars of delight, which drew me home
When I might wander forth ; nor did I prize
Aught human thing beneath Heaven's mighty dome
Beyond this child : so when sad hours were come,
And baffled hope like ice still clung to me,
Since kin were cold, and friends had now become
Heartless and false, I turned from all to be,
Cythna, the only source of tears and smiles to thee.

XXII

What wert thou then ? A child most infantine,
Yet wandering far beyond that innocent age
In all but its sweet looks and mien divine ;
Even then, methought, with the world's tyrant rage
A patient warfare thy young heart did wage,
When those soft eyes of scarcely conscious thought,
Some tale, or thine own fancies, would engage
To overflow with tears, or converse fraught
With passion, o'er their depths its fleeting light had wrought.

XXIII

She moved upon this earth a shape of brightness,
A power, that from its objects scarcely drew
One impulse of her being—in her lightness
Most like some radiant cloud of morning dew

Which wanders through the waste air's pathless blue,
To nourish some far desert ; she did seem
Beside me, gathering beauty as she grew,
Like the bright shade of some immortal dream
Which walks, when tempest sleeps, the wave of life's dark stream.

XXIV

As mine own shadow was this child to me,
A second self, far dearer and more fair ;
Which clothed in undissolving radiancy
All those steep paths which languor and despair
Of human things had made so dark and bare,
But which I trod alone—nor, till bereft
Of friends, and overcome by lonely care,
Knew I what solace for that loss was left,
Though by a bitter wound my trusting heart was cleft.

XXV

Once she was dear, now she was all I had
To love in human life—this playmate sweet,
This child of twelve years old—so she was made
My sole associate, and her willing feet
Wandered with mine where earth and ocean meet,
Beyond the aërial mountains whose vast cells
The unreposing billows ever beat,
Through forests wide and old, and lawny dells,
Where boughs of incense droop over the emerald wells.

XXVI

And warm and light I felt her clasping hand
When twined in mine : she followed where I went,
Through the lone paths of our immortal land.
It had no waste, but some memorial lent
Which strung me to my toil—some monument
Vital with mind : then Cythna by my side,
Until the bright and beaming day were spent,
Would rest, with looks entreating to abide,
Too earnest and too sweet ever to be denied.

XXVII

And soon I could not have refused her—thus
For ever, day and night, we two were ne'er
Parted, but when brief sleep divided us :
And, when the pauses of the lulling air
Of noon beside the sea had made a lair
For her soothed senses, in my arms she slept,
And I kept watch over her slumbers there,
While, as the shifting visions over her swept,
Amid her innocent rest by turns she smiled and wept.

XXVIII

And, in the murmur of her dreams, was heard
Sometimes the name of Laon :—suddenly
She would arise, and, like the secret bird
Whom sunset wakens, fill the shore and sky
With her sweet accents—a wild melody !
Hymns which my soul had woven to Freedom, strong
The source of passion, whence they rose to be

Triumphant strains, which, like a spirit's tongue,
To the enchanted waves that child of glory sung.

XXIX

Her white arms lifted through the shadowy stream
Of her loose hair—oh, excellently great
Seemed to me then my purpose, the vast theme
Of those impassioned songs, when Cythna sate
Amid the calm which rapture doth create
After its tumult, her heart vibrating,
Her spirit o'er the ocean's floating state
From her deep eyes far wandering, on the wing
Of visions that were mine, beyond its utmost spring.

XXX

For, before Cythna loved it, had my song
Peopled with thoughts the boundless universe,
A mighty congregation, which were strong
Where'er they trod the darkness to disperse
The cloud of that unutterable curse
Which clings upon mankind :—all things became
Slaves to my holy and heroic verse,
Earth, sea, and sky, the planets, life, and fame,
And fate, or whate'er else binds the world's wondrous frame.

XXXI

And this beloved child thus felt the sway
Of my conceptions, gathering like a cloud
The very wind on which it rolls away :
Hers too were all my thoughts, ere yet, endowed
With music and with light, their fountains flowed
In poesy ; and her still and earnest face,
Pallid with feelings which intensely glowed
Within, was turned on mine with speechless grace,
Watching the hopes which there her heart had learned to trace.

XXXII

In me, communion with this purest being
Kindled intenser zeal, and made me wise
In knowledge, which in hers mine own mind seeing,
Left in the human world few mysteries :
How without fear of evil or disguise
Was Cythna !—what a spirit strong and mild,
Which death, or pain, or peril, could despise,
Yet melt in tenderness ! what genius wild,
Yet mighty, was enclosed within one simple child !

XXXIII

New lore was this—old age with its grey hair,
And wrinkled legends of unworthy things,
And icy sneers, is nought ; it cannot dare
To burst the chains which life for ever flings
On the entangled soul's aspiring wings,
So is it cold and cruel, and is made
The careless slave of that dark power which brings
Evil, like blight on man, who, still betrayed,
Laughs o'er the grave in which his living hopes are laid.

XXXIV

Nor are the strong and the severe to keep
The empire of the world : thus Cythna taught
Even in the visions of her eloquent sleep,
Unconscious of the power through which she wrought
The woof of such intelligible thought,
As from the tranquil strength which cradled lay
In her smile-peopled rest, my spirit sought
Why the deceiver and the slave has sway
O'er heralds so divine of truth's arising day.

XXXV

Within that fairest form, the female mind
Untainted by the poison clouds which rest
On the dark world, a sacred home did find :
But else, from the wide earth's maternal breast,
Victorious Evil, which had dispossest
All native power, had those fair children torn,
And made them slaves to soothe his vile unrest,
And minister to lust its joys forlorn,
Till they had learned to breathe the atmosphere of scorn.

XXXVI

This misery was but coldly felt, till she
Became my only friend, who had indued
My purpose with a wider sympathy ;
Thus, Cythna mourned with me the servitude
In which the half of humankind were mewed,
Victims of lust and hate, the slaves of slaves :
She mourned that grace and power were thrown as food
To the hyæna lust, who, among graves,
Over his loathed meal, laughing in agony, raves.

XXXVII

nd I, still gazing on that glorious child,
Even as these thoughts flushed o'er her :—" Cythna sweet,
Well with the world art thou unreconciled ;
Never will peace and human nature meet,
Till free and equal man and woman greet
Domestic peace ; and ere this power can make
In human hearts its calm and holy seat,
This slavery must be broken "—as I spake
From Cythna's eyes a light of exultation brake.

XXXVIII

She replied earnestly :—" It shall be mine,
This task, mine, Laon !—thou hast much to gain;
Nor wilt thou at poor Cythna's pride repine,
If she should lead a happy female train
To meet thee over the rejoicing plain,
When myriads at thy call shall throng around
The Golden City."—Then the child did strain
My arm upon her tremulous heart, and wound
Her own about my neck, till some reply she found.

XXXIX

I smiled, and spake not.—" Wherefore dost thou smile
At what I say ? Laon, I am not weak,

And, though my cheek might become pale the while,
With thee, if thou desirest, will I seek
Through their array of branded slaves to wreak
Ruin upon the tyrants. I had thought
It was more hard to turn my unpractised cheek
To scorn and shame, and this beloved spot
And thee, O dearest friend, to leave and murmur not.

XL

" Whence came I what I am ? Thou, Laon, knowest
How a young child should thus undaunted be ;
Methinks, it is a power which thou bestowest,
Through which I seek, by most resembling thee,
So to become most good, and great, and free ;
Yet far beyond this Ocean's utmost roar
In towers and huts are many like to me,
Who, could they see thine eyes, or feel such lore
As I have learnt from them, like me would fear no more.

XLI

" Thinkest thou that I shall speak unskilfully,
And none will heed me ? I remember now,
How once, a slave in tortures doomed to die,
Was saved, because in accents sweet and low
He sang a song his Judge loved long ago,
As he was led to death.—All shall relent
Who hear me—tears as mine have flowed, shall flow,
Hearts beat as mine now beats, with such intent
As renovates the world ; a will omnipotent !

XLII

" Yes, I will tread Pride's golden palaces,
Through Penury's roofless huts and squalid cells
Will I descend, where'er in abjectness
Woman with some vile slave her tyrant dwells,
There with the music of thine own sweet spells
Will disenchant the captives, and will pour
For the despairing, from the crystal wells
Of thy deep spirit, reason's mighty lore,
And power shall then abound, and hope arise once more.

XLIII

" Can man be free if woman be a slave ?
Chain one who lives, and breathes this boundless air
To the corruption of a closed grave !
Can they whose mates are beasts, condemned to bear
Scorn, heavier far than toil or anguish, dare
To trample their oppressors ? In their home
Among their babes, thou knowest a curse would wear
The shape of woman—hoary crime would come
Behind, and fraud rebuild religion's tottering dome.

XLIV

" I am a child :—I would not yet depart.
When I go forth alone, bearing the lamp
Aloft which thou hast kindled in my heart,
Millions of slaves from many a dungeon damp

Shall leap in joy, as the benumbing cramp
Of ages leaves their limbs—no ill may harm
Thy Cythna ever—truth its radiant stamp
Has fixed, as an invulnerable charm,
Upon her children's brow, dark falsehood to disarm.

XLV

" Wait yet awhile for the appointed day—
Thou wilt depart, and I with tears shall stand
Watching thy dim sail skirt the ocean grey ;
Amid the dwellers of this lonely land
I shall remain alone—and thy command
Shall then dissolve the world's unquiet trance,
And, multitudinous as the desert sand
Borne on the storm, its millions shall advance,
Thronging round thee, the light of their deliverance.

XLVI

" Then, like the forests of some pathless mountain,
Which from remotest glens two warring winds
Involve in fire, which not the loosened fountain
Of broadest floods might quench, shall all the kinds
Of evil catch from our uniting minds
The spark which must consume them ;—Cythna then
Will have cast off the impotence that binds
Her childhood now, and through the paths of men
Will pass, as the charmed bird that haunts the serpent's den.

XLVII

" We part !—O Laon, I must dare, nor tremble,
To meet those looks no more !—Oh, heavy stroke !
Sweet brother of my soul ; can I dissemble
The agony of this thought ? "—As thus she spoke
The gathered sobs her quivering accents broke,
And in my arms she hid her beating breast.
I remained still for tears—sudden she woke
As one awakes from sleep, and wildly prest
My bosom, her whole frame impetuously possest.

XLVIII

" We part to meet again—but yon blue waste,
Yon desert wide and deep, holds no recess
Within whose happy silence, thus embraced
We might survive all ills in one caress :
Nor doth the grave—I fear 'tis passionless—
Nor yon cold vacant Heaven :—we meet again
Within the minds of men, whose lips shall bless
Our memory, and whose hopes its light retain
When these dissevered bones are trodden in the plain."

XLIX

I could not speak, though she had ceased, for now
The fountains of her feeling, swift and deep,
Seemed to suspend the tumult of their flow ;
So we arose, and by the starlight steep
Went homeward—neither did we speak nor weep,

But pale, were calm.—With passion thus subdued,
Like evening shades that o'er the mountains creep,
We moved towards our home; where, in this mood,
Each from the other sought refuge in solitude.

CANTO III

I

WHAT thoughts had sway o'er Cythna's lonely slumber
That night, I know not; but my own did seem
As if they might ten thousand years outnumber
Of waking life, the visions of a dream,
Which hid in one dim gulf the troubled stream
Of mind; a boundless chaos wild and vast,
Whose limits yet were never memory's theme:
And I lay struggling as its whirlwinds past,
Sometimes for rapture sick, sometimes for pain aghast.

II

Two hours, whose mighty circle did embrace
More time than might make grey the infant world,
Rolled thus, a weary and tumultuous space:
When the third came, like mist on breezes curled,
From my dim sleep a shadow was unfurled:
Methought, upon the threshold of a cave
I sate with Cythna; drooping briony, pearled
With dew from the wild streamlet's shattered wave,
Hung, where we sate, to taste the joys which Nature gave.

III

We lived a day as we were wont to live,
But nature had a robe of glory on,
And the bright air o'er every shape did weave
Intenser hues, so that the herbless stone,
The leafless bough among the leaves alone,
Had being clearer than its own could be,
And Cythna's pure and radiant self was shown
In this strange vision, so divine to me,
That if I loved before, now love was agony.

IV

Morn fled, noon came, evening, then night descended,
And we prolonged calm talk beneath the sphere
Of the calm moon—when, suddenly was blended
With our repose a nameless sense of fear;
And from the cave behind I seemed to hear
Sounds gathering upwards!—accents incomplete,
And stifled shrieks,—and now, more near and near,
A tumult and a rush of thronging feet
The cavern's secret depths beneath the earth did beat.

V

The scene was changed, and away, away, away!
Through the air and over the sea we sped,
And Cythna in my sheltering bosom lay,
And the winds bore me;—through the darkness spread
Around, the gaping earth then vomited

Legions of foul and ghastly shapes, which hung
Upon my flight ; and ever as we fled,
They plucked at Cythna—soon to me then clung
A sense of actual things those monstrous dreams among.

VI

And I lay struggling in the impotence
Of sleep, while outward life had burst its bound,
Though, still deluded, strove the tortured sense
To its dire wanderings to adapt the sound
Which in the light of morn was poured around
Our dwelling—breathless, pale, and unaware
I rose, and all the cottage crowded found
With armed men, whose glittering swords were bare,
And whose degraded limbs the tyrant's garb did wear.

VII

And ere with rapid lips and gathered brow
I could demand the cause—a feeble shriek
It was a feeble shriek, faint, far, and low,
Arrested me—my mien grew calm and meek,
And, grasping a small knife, I went to seek
That voice among the crowd—'twas Cythna's cry !
Beneath most calm resolve did agony wreak
Its whirlwind rage :—so I past quietly
Till I beheld, where bound, that dearest child did lie.

VIII

I started to behold her, for delight
And exultation, and a joyance free,
Solemn, serene, and lofty, filled the light
Of the calm smile with which she looked on me :
So that I feared some brainless ecstasy,
Wrought from that bitter woe, had wildered her—
" Farewell ! farewell ! " she said, as I drew nigh.
" At first my peace was marred by this strange stir,
Now I am calm as truth—its chosen minister.

IX

" Look not so, Laon—say farewell in hope :
These bloody men are but the slaves who bear
Their mistress to her task—it was my scope
The slavery where they drag me now, to share,
And among captives willing chains to wear
Awhile—the rest thou knowest—return, dear friend !
Let our first triumph trample the despair
Which would ensnare us now, for in the end,
In victory or in death our hopes and fears must blend."

X

These words had fallen on my unheeding ear,
Whilst I had watched the motions of the crew
With seeming careless glance ; not many were
Around her, for their comrades just withdrew
To guard some other victim—so I drew
My knife, and with one impulse, suddenly
All unaware three of their number slew,

And grasped a fourth by the throat, and with loud cry
My countrymen invoked to death or liberty !

XI

What followed then, I know not—for a stroke
On my raised arm and naked head came down,
Filling my eyes with blood—when I awoke,
I felt that they had bound me in my swoon,
And up a rock which overhangs the town,
By the steep path were bearing me : below
The plain was filled with slaughter,—overthrown
The vineyards and the harvests, and the glow
Of blazing roofs shone far o'er the white Ocean's flow.

XII

Upon that rock a mighty column stood,
Whose capital seemed sculptured in the sky,
Which to the wanderers o'er the solitude
Of distant seas, from ages long gone by,
Had many a landmark ; o'er its height to fly
Scarcely the cloud, the vulture, or the blast,
Has power—and when the shades of evening lie
On Earth and Ocean, its carved summits cast
The sunken daylight far through the aërial waste.

XIII

They bore me to a cavern in the hill
Beneath that column, and unbound me there :
And one did strip me stark ; and one did fill
A vessel from the putrid pool ; one bare
A lighted torch, and four with friendless care
Guided my steps the cavern paths along,
Then up a steep and dark and narrow stair
We wound, until the torches' fiery tongue
Amid the gushing day beamless and pallid hung.

XIV

They raised me to the platform of the pile,
That column's dizzy height :—the grate of brass
Through which they thrust me, open stood the while,
As to its ponderous and suspended mass,
With chains which eat into the flesh, alas !
With brazen links, my naked limbs they bound :
The grate, as they departed to repass,
With horrid clangour fell, and the far sound
Of their retiring steps in the dense gloom was drowned.

XV

The noon was calm and bright :—around that column
The overhanging sky and circling sea
Spread forth in silentness profound and solemn
The darkness of brief frenzy cast on me,
So that I knew not my own misery :
The islands and the mountains in the day
Like clouds reposed afar ; and I could see
The town among the woods below that lay,
And the dark rocks which bound the bright and glassy bay.

XVI

It was so calm, that scarce the feathery weed
Sown by some eagle on the topmost stone
Swayed in the air :—so bright, that noon did breed
No shadow in the sky beside mine own—
Mine, and the shadow of my chain alone.
Below the smoke of roofs involved in flame
Rested like night, all else was clearly shown
In the broad glare, yet sound to me none came,
But of the living blood that ran within my frame.

XVII

The peace of madness fled, and ah, too soon !
A ship was lying on the sunny main ;
Its sails were flagging in the breathless noon—
Its shadow lay beyond—that sight again
Waked, with its presence, in my tranced brain
The stings of a known sorrow, keen and cold :
I knew that ship bore Cythna o'er the plain
Of waters, to her blighting slavery sold,
And watched it with such thoughts as must remain untold.

XVIII

I watched, until the shades of evening wrapt
Earth like an exhalation—then the bark
Moved, for that calm was by the sunset snapt.
It moved a speck upon the Ocean dark :
Soon the wan stars came forth, and I could mark
Its path no more ! I sought to close mine eyes,
But, like the balls, their lids were stiff and stark ;
I would have risen, but, ere that I could rise,
My parched skin was split with piercing agonies.

XIX

I gnawed my brazen chain, and sought to sever
Its adamantine links, that I might die :
O Liberty ! forgive the base endeavour,
Forgive me, if, reserved for victory,
The champion of thy faith e'er sought to fly.—
That starry night, with its clear silence, sent
Tameless resolve which laughed at misery
Into my soul—linked remembrance lent
To that such power, to me such a severe content.

XX

To breathe, to be, to hope, or to despair
And die, I questioned not ; nor, though the sun
Its shafts of agony kindling through the air
Moved over me, nor though in evening dun,
Or when the stars their visible courses run,
Or morning, the wide universe was spread
In dreary calmness round me, did I shun
Its presence, nor seek refuge with the dead
From one faint hope whose flower a dropping poison shed.

XXI

Two days thus past—I neither raved nor died—
Thirst raged within me, like a scorpion's nest

Built in mine entrails ; I had spurned aside
The water-vessel, while despair possest
My thoughts, and now no drop remained ! The uprest
Of the third sun brought hunger—but the crust
Which had been left, was to my craving breast
Fuel, not food.   I chewed the bitter dust,
And bit my bloodless arm, and licked the brazen rust.

XXII

My brain began to fail when the fourth morn
Burst o'er the golden isles—a fearful sleep,
Which through the caverns dreary and forlorn
Of the riven soul, sent its foul dreams to sweep
With whirlwind swiftness—a fall far and deep,—
A gulf, a void, a sense of senselessness—
These things dwelt in me, even as shadows keep
Their watch in some dim charnel's loneliness,
A shoreless sea, a sky sunless and planetless !

XXIII

The forms which peopled this terrific trance
I well remember—like a quire of devils,
Around me they involved a giddy dance ;
Legions seemed gathering from the misty levels
Of ocean, to supply those ceaseless revels,
Foul, ceaseless shadows :—thought could not divide
The actual world from these entangling evils,
Which so bemocked themselves, that I descried
All shapes like mine own self, hideously multiplied.

XXIV

The sense of day and night, of false and true,
Was dead within me.   Yet two visions burst
That darkness—one, as since that hour I knew,
Was not a phantom of the realms accurst,
Where then my spirit dwelt—but of the first
I know not yet, was it a dream or no.
But both, though not distincter, were immersed
In hues which, when through memory's waste they flow,
Make their divided streams more bright and rapid now.

XXV

Methought that grate was lifted, and the seven
Who brought me thither, four stiff corpses bare,
And from the frieze to the four winds of Heaven
Hung them on high by the entangled hair ;
Swarthy were three—the fourth was very fair :
As they retired, the golden moon upsprung,
And eagerly, out in the giddy air,
Leaning that I might eat, I stretched and clung
Over the shapeless depth in which those corpses hung.

XXVI

A woman's shape, now lank and cold and blue,
The dwelling of the many-coloured worm,
Hung there, the white and hollow cheek I drew
To my dry lips—what radiance did inform

Those horny eyes ? whose was that withered form ?
Alas, alas ! it seemed that Cythna's ghost
Laughed in those looks, and that the flesh was warm
Within my teeth !—a whirlwind keen as frost
Then in its sinking gulfs my sickening spirit tost.

XXVII

Then seemed it that a tameless hurricane
Arose, and bore me in its dark career
Beyond the sun, beyond the stars that wane
On the verge of formless space—it languished there,
And, dying, left a silence lone and drear,
More horrible than famine :—in the deep
The shape of an old man did then appear,
Stately and beautiful ; that dreadful sleep
His heavenly smiles dispersed, and I could wake and weep.

XXVIII

And, when the blinding tears had fallen, I saw
That column, and those corpses, and the moon,
And felt the poisonous tooth of hunger gnaw
My vitals, I rejoiced, as if the boon
Of senseless death would be accorded soon ;—
When from that stony gloom a voice arose,
Solemn and sweet as when low winds attune
The midnight pines ; the grate did then unclose,
And on that reverend form the moonlight did repose.

XXIX

He struck my chains, and gently spake and smiled :
As they were loosened by that Hermit old,
Mine eyes were of their madness half beguiled
To answer those kind looks.—He did enfold
His giant arms around me to uphold
My wretched frame, my scorched limbs he wound
In linen moist and balmy, and as cold
As dew to drooping leaves :—the chain, with sound
Like earthquake, through the chasm of that steep stair did bound,

XXX

As, lifting me, it fell !—What next I heard,
Were billows leaping on the harbour bar,
And the shrill sea-wind, whose breath idly stirred
My hair ;—I looked abroad, and saw a star
Shining beside a sail and distant far
That mountain and its column, the known mark
Of those who in the wide deep wandering are,
So that I feared some Spirit, fell and dark,
In trance had lain me thus within a fiendish bark.

XXXI

For now, indeed, over the salt sea billow
I sailed : yet dared not look upon the shape
Of him who ruled the helm, although the pillow
For my light head was hollowed in his lap,
And my bare limbs his mantle did enwrap,

Fearing it was a fiend : at last, he bent
O'er me his aged face ; as if to snap
Those dreadful thoughts the gentle grandsire bent,
And to my inmost soul his soothing looks he sent.

XXXII

A soft and healing potion to my lips
At intervals he raised—now looked on high,
To mark if yet the starry giant dips
His zone in the dim sea—now cheeringly,
Though he said little, did he speak to me.
" It is a friend beside thee—take good cheer,
Poor victim, thou art now at liberty ! "
I joyed as those a human tone to hear,
Who in cells deep and lone have languished many a year.

XXXIII

A dim and feeble joy, whose glimpses oft
Were quenched in a relapse of wildering dreams,
Yet still methought we sailed, until aloft
The stars of night grew pallid, and the beams
Of morn descended on the ocean streams,
And still that aged man, so grand and mild,
Tended me, yet even as some sick mother seems
To hang in hope over a dying child,
Till in the azure East darkness again was piled.

XXXIV

And then the night wind, steaming from the shore,
Sent odours dying sweet across the sea,
And the swift boat the little waves which bore,
Were cut by its keen keel, though slantingly ;
Soon I could hear the leaves sigh, and could see
The myrtle blossoms starring the dim grove,
As past the pebbly beach the boat did flee
On sidelong wing into a silent cove,
Where ebon pines a shade under the starlight wove.

CANTO IV

I

THE old man took the oars, and soon the bark
Smote on the beach beside a tower of stone ;
It was a crumbling heap whose portal dark
With blooming ivy trails was overgrown ;
Upon whose floor the spangling sands were strown,
And rarest sea-shells, which the eternal flood,
Slave to the mother of the months, had thrown
Within the walls of that great tower, which stood
A changeling of man's art, nursed amid Nature's brood.

II

When the old man his boat had anchored,
He wound me in his arms with tender care,
And very few but kindly words he said,
And bore me through the tower adown a stair,
Whose smooth descent some ceaseless step to wear

For many a year had fallen.—We came at last
To a small chamber, which with mosses rare
Was tapestried, where me his soft hands placed
Upon a couch of grass and oak-leaves interlaced.

III

The moon was darting through the lattices
Its yellow light, warm as the beams of day—
So warm, that to admit the dewy breeze,
The old man opened them ; the moonlight lay
Upon a lake whose waters wove their play
Even to the threshold of that lonely home :
Within was seen in the dim wavering ray,
The antique sculptured roof, and many a tome
Whose lore had made that sage all that he had become.

IV

The rock-built barrier of the sea was past,—
And I was on the margin of a lake,
A lonely lake, amid the forests vast
And snowy mountains :—did my spirit wake
From sleep, as many-coloured as the snake
That girds eternity ? in life and truth,
Might not my heart its cravings ever slake ?
Was Cythna then a dream, and all my youth,
And all its hopes and fears, and all its joy and ruth ?

V

Thus madness came again,—a milder madness,
Which darkened nought but time's unquiet flow
With supernatural shades of clinging sadness ;
That gentle Hermit, in my helpless woe,
By my sick couch was busy to and fro,
Like a strong spirit ministrant of good :
When I was healed, he led me forth to show
The wonders of his sylvan solitude,
And we together sate by that isle-fretted flood.

VI

He knew his soothing words to weave with skill
From all my madness told : like mine own heart,
Of Cythna would he question me, until
That thrilling name had ceased to make me start,
From his familiar lips—it was not art,
Of wisdom and of justice when he spoke—
When 'mid soft looks of pity, there would dart
A glance as keen as is the lightning stroke
When it doth rive the knots of some ancestral oak.

VII

Thus slowly from my brain the darkness rolled,
My thoughts their due array did re-assume
Through the enchantments of that Hermit old ;
Then I bethought me of the glorious doom
Of those who sternly struggle to relume
The lamp of Hope o'er man's bewildered lot,
And, sitting by the waters in the gloom

Of eve, to that friend's heart I told my thought—
That heart which had grown old, but had corrupted not.

VIII

That hoary man had spent his livelong age
In converse with the dead, who leave the stamp
Of ever-burning thoughts on many a page,
When they are gone into the senseless damp
Of graves !—his spirit thus became a lamp
Of splendour, like to those on which it fed,
Through peopled haunts, the City and the Camp,
Deep thirst for knowledge had his footsteps led,
And all the ways of men among mankind he read.

IX

But custom maketh blind and obdurate
The loftiest hearts :—he had beheld the woe
In which mankind was bound, but deemed that fate
Which made them abject would preserve them so ;
And in such faith, some steadfast joy to know,
He sought this cell ; but, when fame went abroad
That one in Argolis did undergo
Torture for liberty, and that the crowd
High truths from gifted lips had heard and understood,

X

And that the multitude was gathering wide,
His spirit leaped within his aged frame ;
In lonely peace he could no more abide,
But to the land on which the victor's flame
Had fed, my native land, the Hermit came ;
Each heart was there a shield, and every tongue
Was as a sword of truth—young Laon's name
Rallied their secret hopes, though tyrants sung
Hymns of triumphant joy our scattered tribes among.

XI

He came to the lone column on the rock,
And with his sweet and mighty eloquence
The hearts of those who watched it did unlock,
And made them melt in tears of penitence.
They gave him entrance free to bear me thence.
" Since this," the old man said, " seven years are spent
While slowly truth on thy benighted sense
Has crept ; the hope which wildered it has lent,
Meanwhile, to me the power of a sublime intent.

XII

" Yes, from the records of my youthful state,
And from the lore of bards and sages old,
From whatsoe'er my wakened thoughts create
Out of the hopes of thine aspirings bold,
Have I collected language to unfold
Truth to my countrymen ; from shore to shore
Doctrines of human power my words have told ;
They have been heard, and men aspire to more
Than they have ever gained or ever lost of yore.

XIII

" In secret chambers parents read, and weep,
My writings to their babes, no longer blind ;
And young men gather when their tyrants sleep,
And vows of faith each to the other bind ;
And marriageable maidens, who have pined
With love, till life seemed melting through their look,
A warmer zeal, a nobler hope now find ;
And every bosom thus is wrapt and shook,
Like autumn's myriad leaves in one swoln mountain brook.

XIV

" The tyrants of the Golden City tremble
At voices which are heard about the streets ;
The ministers of fraud can scarce dissemble
The lies of their own heart ; but when one meets
Another at the shrine, he inly weets,
Though he says nothing, that the truth is known ;
Murderers are pale upon the judgment-seats,
And gold grows vile even to the wealthy crone,
And laughter fills the Fane, and curses shake the Throne.

XV

" Kind thoughts, and mighty hopes, and gentle deeds
Abound, for fearless love, and the pure law
Of mild equality and peace succeeds
To faiths which long have held the world in awe,
Bloody, and false, and cold :—as whirlpools draw
All wrecks of Ocean to their chasm, the sway
Of thy strong genius, Laon, which foresaw
This hope, compels all spirits to obey,
Which round thy secret strength now throng in wide array.

XVI

" For I have been thy passive instrument—
(As thus the old man spake, his countenance
Gleamed on me like a spirit's)—thou hast lent
To me, to all, the power to advance
Towards this unforeseen deliverance
From our ancestral chains—ay, thou didst rear
That lamp of hope on high, which time, nor chance,
Nor change may not extinguish, and my share
Of good was o'er the world its gathered beams to bear.

XVII

" But I, alas ! am both unknown and old,
And though the woof of wisdom I know well
To dye in hues of language, I am cold
In seeming, and the hopes which inly dwell
My manners note that I did long repel ;
But Laon's name to the tumultuous throng
Were like the star whose beams the waves compel
And tempests, and his soul-subduing tongue
Were as a lance to quell the mailed crest of wrong.

XVIII

" Perchance blood need not flow, if thou at length
Wouldst rise ; perchance the very slaves would spare

)

Their brethren and themselves ; great is the strength
Of words—for lately did a maiden fair,
Who from her childhood has been taught to bear
The tyrant's heaviest yoke, arise, and make
Her sex the law of truth and freedom hear ;
And with these quiet words—' for thine own sake
I prithee spare me,'—did with ruth so take

XIX

" All hearts, that even the torturer, who had bound
Her meek calm frame, ere it was yet impaled,
Loosened her weeping then ; nor could be found
One human hand to harm her—unassailed
Therefore she walks through the great City, veiled
In virtue's adamantine eloquence,
'Gainst scorn, and death, and pain, thus trebly mailed,
And blending in the smiles of that defence,
The Serpent and the Dove, Wisdom and Innocence.

XX

" The wild-eyed women throng around her path :
From their luxurious dungeons, from the dust
Of meaner thralls, from the oppressor's wrath,
Or the caresses of his sated lust,
They congregate :—in her they put their trust ;
The tyrants send their armed slaves to quell
Her power ; they, even like a thunder gust
Caught by some forest, bend beneath the spell
Of that young maiden's speech, and to their chiefs rebel.

XXI

" Thus she doth equal laws and justice teach
To woman, outraged and polluted long ;
Gathering the sweetest fruit in human reach
For those fair hands now free, while armed wrong
Trembles before her look, though it be strong ;
Thousands thus dwell beside her, virgins bright,
And matrons with their babes, a stately throng !
Lovers renew the vows which they did plight
In early faith, and hearts long parted now unite.

XXII

" And homeless orphans find a home near her,
And those poor victims of the proud, no less,
Fair wrecks, on whom the smiling world with stir,
Thrusts the redemption of its wickedness :—
In squalid huts, and in its palaces
Sits Lust alone, while o'er the land is borne
Her voice, whose awful sweetness doth repress
All evil, and her foes relenting turn,
And cast the vote of love in hope's abandoned urn.

XXIII

" So in the populous City, a young maiden
Has baffled Havoc of the prey which he
Marks as his own, whene'er with chains o'erladen
Men make them arms to hurl down tyranny,

False arbiter between the bound and free;
And o'er the land, in hamlets and in towns
The multitudes collect tumultuously,
And throng in arms; but tyranny disowns
Their claim, and gathers strength around its trembling thrones.

XXIV

" Blood soon, although unwillingly, to shed
The free cannot forbear—the Queen of Slaves,
The hood-winked Angel of the blind and dead,
Custom, with iron mace points to the graves
Where her own standard desolately waves
Over the dust of Prophets and of Kings.
Many yet stand in her array—' she paves
Her path with human hearts,' and o'er it flings
The wildering gloom of her immeasurable wings.

XXV

" There is a plain beneath the City's wall,
Bounded by misty mountains, wide and vast;
Millions there lift at Freedom's thrilling call
Ten thousand standards wide; they load the blast
Which bears one sound of many voices past,
And startles on his throne their sceptred foe:
He sits amid his idle pomp aghast,
And that his power hath past away, doth know—
Why pause the victor swords to seal his overthrow?

XXVI

" The tyrant's guards resistance yet maintain:
Fearless, and fierce, and hard as beasts of blood
They stand a speck amid the peopled plain;
Carnage and ruin have been made their food
From infancy—ill has become their good,
And for its hateful sake their will has wove
The chains which eat their hearts—the multitude
Surrounding them, with words of human love,
Seek from their own decay their stubborn minds to move.

XXVII

" Over the land is felt a sudden pause,
As night and day those ruthless bands around
The watch of love is kept:—a trance which awes
The thoughts of men with hope—as when the sound
Of whirlwind, whose fierce blasts the waves and clouds confound,
Dies suddenly, the mariner in fear
Feels silence sink upon his heart—thus bound,
The conqueror's pause, and oh! may freemen ne'er
Clasp the relentless knees of Dread, the murderer!

XXVIII

" If blood be shed, 'tis but a change and choice
Of bonds,—from slavery to cowardice,
A wretched fall!—uplift thy charmed voice,
Pour on those evil men the love that lies
Hovering within those spirit-soothing eyes—

Arise, my friend, farewell ! ''—As thus he spake,
From the green earth lightly I did arise,
As one out of dim dreams that doth awake,
And looked upon the depth of that reposing lake.

XXIX

I saw my countenance reflected there ;—
And then my youth fell on me like a wind
Descending on still waters—my thin hair
Was prematurely grey, my face was lined
With channels, such as suffering leaves behind,
Not age ; my brow was pale, but in my cheek
And lips a flush of gnawing fire did find
Their food and dwelling ; though mine eyes might speak
A subtle mind and strong within a frame thus weak.

XXX

And though their lustre now was spent and faded,
Yet in my hollow looks and withered mien
The likeness of a shape for which was braided
The brightest woof of genius, still was seen—
One who, methought, had gone from the world's scene,
And left it vacant—'twas her lover's face—
It might resemble her—it once had been
The mirror of her thoughts, and still the grace
Which her mind's shadow cast, left there a lingering trace.

XXXI

What then was I ?   She slumbered with the dead.
Glory and joy and peace, had come and gone.
Doth the cloud perish, when the beams are fled
Which steeped its skirts in gold ? or dark, and lone,
Doth it not through the paths of night unknown,
On outspread wings of its own wind upborne
Pour rain upon the earth ? the stars are shown,
When the cold moon sharpens her silver horn
Under the sea, and make the wide night not forlorn.

XXXII

Strengthened in heart, yet sad, that aged man
I left with interchange of looks and tears,
And lingering speech, and to the Camp began
My way.   O'er many a mountain chain which rears
Its hundred crests aloft, my spirit bears
My frame ; o'er many a dale and many a moor,
And gaily now me seems serene earth wears
The bloomy spring's star-bright investiture,
A vision which aught sad from sadness might allure.

XXXIII

My powers revived within me, and I went
As one whom winds waft o'er the bending grass,
Through many a vale of that broad continent.
At night when I reposed, fair dreams did pass
Before my pillow ; my own Cythna was
Not like a child of death, among them ever ;
When I arose from rest, a woeful mass

That gentlest sleep seemed from my life to sever,
As of the light of youth were not withdrawn for ever.

XXXIV

Aye, as I went, that maiden who had reared
The torch of Truth afar, of whose high deeds
The Hermit in his pilgrimage had heard,
Haunted my thoughts.—Ah, Hope its sickness feeds
With whatsoe'er it finds, or flowers or weeds !
Could she be Cythna ?—Was that corpse a shade
Such as self-torturing thought from madness breeds ?
Why was this hope not torture ? yet it made
A light around my steps which would not ever fade.

CANTO V

I

OVER the utmost hill at length I sped,
A snowy steep :—the moon was hanging low
Over the Asian mountains and outspread
The plain, the City, and the Camp, below,
Skirted the midnight Ocean's glimmering flow,
The City's moon-lit spires and myriad lamps,
Like stars in a sublunar sky did glow,
And fires blazed far amid the scattered camps,
Like springs of flame, which burst where'er swift Earthquake stamps

II

All slept but those in watchful arms who stood,
And those who sate tending the beacon's light,
And the few sounds from that vast multitude
Made silence more profound—Oh, what a might
Of human thought was cradled in that night !
How many hearts impenetrably veiled
Beat underneath its shade, what secret fight
Evil and good, in woven passions mailed,
Waged through that silent throng, a war that never failed !

III

And now the Power of Good held victory,
So, through the labyrinth of many a tent,
Among the silent millions who did lie
In innocent sleep, exultingly I went ;
The moon had left Heaven desert now, but lent
From eastern morn the first faint lustre showed
An armed youth—over his spear he bent
His downward face.—" A friend ! " I cried aloud,
And quickly common hopes made freemen understood.

IV

I sate beside him while the morning beam
Crept slowly over Heaven, and talked with him
Of those immortal hopes, a glorious theme !
Which led us forth, until the stars grew dim :
And all the while, methought, his voice did swim,
As if it drowned in remembrance were
Of thoughts which make the moist eyes overbrim :

At last, when daylight 'gan to fill the air,
He looked on me, and cried in wonder, " Thou art here ! "

V

Then, suddenly, I knew it was the youth
In whom its earliest hopes my spirit found ;
But envious tongues had stained his spotless truth,
And thoughtless pride his love in silence bound,
And shame and sorrow mine in toils had wound,
Whilst he was innocent, and I deluded.
The truth now came upon me, on the ground
Tears of repenting joy, which fast intruded,
Fell fast, and o'er its peace our mingling spirits brooded.

VI

Thus, while with rapid lips and earnest eyes
We talked, a sound of sweeping conflict spread,
As from the earth did suddenly arise ;
From every tent, roused by that clamour dread,
Our bands outsprung and seized their arms ; we sped
Towards the sound : our tribes were gathering far,
Those sanguine slaves amid ten thousand dead
Stabbed in their sleep, trampled in treacherous war,
The gentle hearts whose power their lives had sought to spare.

VII

Like rabid snakes, that sting some gentle child
Who brings them food, when winter false and fair
Allures them forth with its cold smiles, so wild
They rage among the camp ;—they overbear
The patriot host—confusion, then despair
Descends like night—when " Laon ! " one did cry ;
Like a bright ghost from heaven, that shout did scare
The slaves, and, widening through the vaulted sky,
Seemed sent from Earth to Heaven in sign of victory.

VIII

In sudden panic those false murderers fled,
Like insect tribes before the northern gale :
But, swifter still, our hosts encompassed
Their shattered ranks, and in a craggy vale,
Where even their fierce despair might nought avail,
Hemmed them around !—and then revenge and fear
Made the high virtue of the patriots fail :
One pointed on his foe the mortal spear—
I rushed before its point, and cried, " Forbear, forbear ! "

IX

The spear transfixed my arm that was uplifted
In swift expostulation, and the blood
Gushed round its point : I smiled, and—" Oh ! thou gifted
With eloquence which shall not be withstood,
Flow thus ! "—I cried in joy, " thou vital flood,
Until my heart be dry, ere thus the cause
For which thou wert aught worthy be subdued—
Ah, ye are pale,—ye weep,—your passions pause,—
'Tis well ! ye feel the truth of love's benignant laws.

X

" Soldiers, our brethren and our friends are slain.
Ye murdered them, I think, as they did sleep !
Alas, what have ye done ?   The slightest pain
Which ye might suffer, there were eyes to weep ;
But ye have quenched them—there were smiles to steep
Your hearts in balm, but they are lost in woe ;
And those whom love did set his watch to keep
Around your tents truth's freedom to bestow,
Ye stabbed as they did sleep—but they forgive ye now.

XI

" O wherefore should ill ever flow from ill,
And pain still keener pain for ever breed ?
We all are brethren—even the slaves who kill
For hire, are men ; and to avenge misdeed
'On the misdoer, doth but Misery feed
With her own broken heart !   O Earth, O Heaven !
And thou, dread Nature, which to every deed
And all that lives, or is to be, hath given,
Even as to thee have these done ill, and are forgiven.

XII

" Join then your hands and hearts, and let the past
Be as a grave which gives not up its dead
To evil thoughts."—A film then overcast
My sense with dimness, for the wound, which bled
Freshly, swift shadows o'er mine eyes had shed.
When I awoke, I lay 'mid friends and foes,
And earnest countenances on me shed
The light of questioning looks, whilst one did close
My wound with balmiest herbs, and soothed me to repose ;

XIII

And one, whose spear had pierced me, leaned beside
With quivering lips and humid eyes ;—and all
Seemed like some brothers on a journey wide
Gone forth, whom now strange meeting did befall
In a strange land, round one whom they might call
Their friend, their chief, their father, for assay
Of peril, which had saved them from the thrall
Of death, now suffering.   Thus the vast array
Of those fraternal bands were reconciled that day.

XIV

Lifting the thunder of their acclamation
Towards the City, then the multitude,
And I among them, went in joy—a nation
Made free by love ; —a mighty brotherhood
Linked by a jealous interchange of good ;
A glorious pageant, more magnificent
Than kingly slaves, arrayed in gold and blood ;
When they return from carnage, and are sent
In triumph bright beneath the populous battlement.

XV

Afar, the City walls were thronged on high,
And myriads on each giddy turret clung,

And to each spire far lessening in the sky,
Bright pennons on the idle winds were hung ;
As we approached, a shout of joyance sprung
At once from all the crowd, as if the vast
And peopled Earth its boundless skies among
The sudden clamour of delight had cast,
When from before its face some general wreck had past.

XVI

Our armies through the City's hundred gates
Were poured, like brooks which to the rocky lair
Of some deep lake, whose silence them awaits,
Throng from the mountains when the storms are there :
And, as we passed through the calm sunny air,
A thousand flower-inwoven crowns were shed,
The token flowers of truth and freedom fair,
And fairest hands bound them on many a head,
Those angels of love's heaven, that over all was spread.

XVII

I trod as one tranced in some rapturous vision :
Those bloody bands so lately reconciled,
Were, ever as they went, by the contrition
Of anger turned to love from ill beguiled,
And every one on them more gently smiled,
Because they had done evil :—the sweet awe
Of such mild looks made their own hearts grow mild,
And did with soft attraction ever draw
Their spirits to the love of freedom's equal law.

XVIII

And they, and all, in one loud symphony
My name with Liberty commingling, lifted,
" The friend and the preserver of the free !
The parent of this joy ! " and fair eyes, gifted
With feelings caught from one who had uplifted
The light of a great spirit, round me shone ;
And all the shapes of this grand scenery shifted
Like restless clouds before the steadfast sun,—
Where was that Maid ?   I asked, but it was known of none.

XIX

Laone was the name her love had chosen,
For she was nameless, and her birth none knew :
Where was Laone now ?—The words were frozen
Within my lips with fear ; but to subdue
Such dreadful hope, to my great task was due,
And when at length one brought reply, that she
To-morrow would appear, I then withdrew
To judge what need for that great throng might be,
For now the stars came thick over the twilight sea.

XX

Yet need was none for rest or food to care,
Even though that multitude was passing great,
Since each one for the other did prepare
All kindly succour.—Therefore to the gate

Of the Imperial House, now desolate,
I passed, and there was found aghast, alone,
The fallen Tyrant!—Silently he sate
Upon the footstool of his golden throne,
Which, starred with sunny gems, in its own lustre shone.

XXI

Alone, but for one child, who led before him
A graceful dance: the only living thing
Of all the crowd, which thither to adore him
Flocked yesterday, who solace sought to bring
In his abandonment!—She knew the King
Had praised her dance of yore, and now she wove
Its circles, aye weeping and murmuring
'Mid her sad task of unregarded love,
That to no smiles it might his speechless sadness move.

XXII

She fled to him, and wildly clasped his feet
When human steps were heard:—he moved nor spoke,
Nor changed his hue, nor raised his looks to meet
The gaze of strangers.—Our loud entrance woke
The echoes of the hall, which circling broke
The calm of its recesses,—like a tomb
Its sculptured walls vacantly to the stroke
Of footfalls answered, and the twilight's gloom
Lay like a charnel's mist within the radiant dome.

XXIII

The little child stood up when we came nigh;
Her lips and cheeks seemed very pale and wan,
But on her forehead and within her eye
Lay beauty, which makes hearts that feed thereon
Sick with excess of sweetness;—on the throne
She leaned.   The King, with gathered brow and lips
Wreathed by long scorn, did inly sneer and frown
With hue like that when some great painter dips
His pencil in the gloom of earthquake and eclipse.

XXIV

She stood beside him like a rainbow braided
Within some storm, when scarce its shadows vast
From the blue paths of the swift sun have faded.
A sweet and solemn smile, like Cythna's, cast
One moment's light, which made my heart beat fast,
O'er that child's parted lips—a gleam of bliss,
A shade of vanished days,—as the tears past
Which wrapt it, even as with a father's kiss
I pressed those softest eyes in trembling tenderness.

XXV

The sceptred wretch then from that solitude
I drew, and of his change compassionate,
With words of sadness soothed his rugged mood.
But he, while pride and fear held deep debate,
With sullen guile of ill dissembled hate

Glared on me as a toothless snake might glare :
Pity, not scorn, I felt, though desolate
The desolator now, and unaware
The curses which he mocked had caught him by the hair.

XXVI

I led him forth from that which now might seem
A gorgeous grave : through portals sculptured deep
With imagery beautiful as dream
We went, and left the shades which tend on sleep
Over its unregarded gold to keep
Their silent watch.—The child trod faintingly,
And, as she went, the tears which she did weep
Glanced in the starlight ; wildered seemed she,
And when I spake, for sobs she could not answer me.

XXVII

At last the tyrant cried, " She hungers, slave !
Stab her, or give her bread ! "—It was a tone
Such as sick fancies in a new-made grave
Might hear.   I trembled, for the truth was known,
He with this child had thus been left alone,
And neither had gone forth for food,—but he
In mingled pride and awe cowered near his throne,
And she, a nursling of captivity,
Knew nought beyond those walls, nor what such change might be.

XXVIII

And he was troubled at a charm withdrawn
Thus suddenly ; that sceptres ruled no more—
That even from gold the dreadful strength was gone
Which once made all things subject to its power—
Such wonder seized him, as if hour by hour
The past had come again ; and the swift fall
Of one so great and terrible of yore
To desolateness, in the hearts of all
Like wonder stirred, who saw such awful change befall.

XXIX

A mighty crowd, such as the wide land pours
Once in a thousand years, now gathered round
The fallen tyrant ;—like the rush of showers
Of hail in spring, pattering along the ground,
Their many footsteps fell, else came no sound
From the wide multitude : that lonely man
Then knew the burthen of his change, and found,
Concealing in the dust his visage wan,
Refuge from the keen looks which thro' his bosom ran.

XXX

And he was faint withal.   I sate beside him
Upon the earth, and took that child so fair
From his weak arms, that ill might none betide him
Or her ;—when food was brought to them, her share
To his averted lips the child did bear ;
But when she saw he had enough, she ate
And wept the while ;—the lonely man's despair

Hunger then overcame, and of his state
Forgetful, on the dust as in a trance he sate.

XXXI

Slowly the silence of the multitudes
Past, as when far is heard in some lone dell
The gathering of a wind among the woods—
And he is fallen ! they cry ; he who did dwell
Like famine or the plague, or aught more fell,
Among our homes, is fallen ! the murderer
Who slaked his thirsting soul as from a well
Of blood and tears with ruin ! He is here !
Sunk in a gulf of scorn from which none may him rear ;

XXXII

Then was heard—He who judged let him be brought
To judgment ! Blood for blood cries from the soil
On which his crimes have deep pollution wrought !
Shall Othman only unavenged despoil ?
Shall they, who by the stress of grinding toil
Wrest from the unwilling earth his luxuries,
Perish for crime, while his foul blood may boil,
Or creep within his veins at will ?—Arise !
And to high justice make her chosen sacrifice.

XXXIII

" What do ye seek ? what fear ye ? " then I cried,
Suddenly starting forth, " that ye should shed
The blood of Othman—if your hearts are tried
In the true love of freedom, cease to dread
This one poor lonely man—beneath Heaven shed
In purest light above us all, through earth,
Maternal earth, who doth her sweet smiles spread
For all, let him go free ; until the worth
Of human nature win from these a second birth.

XXXIV

" What call ye *justice* ? Is there one who ne'er
In secret thought has wished another's ill ?—
Are ye all pure ? Let those stand forth who hear,
And tremble not. Shall they insult and kill,
If such they be ? their mild eyes can they fill
With the false anger of the hypocrite ?
Alas, such were not pure—the chastened will
Of virtue sees that justice is the light
Of love, and not revenge, and terror and despite."

XXXV

The murmur of the people, slowly dying,
Paused as I spake ; then those who near me were,
Cast gentle looks where the lone man was lying
Shrouding his head, which now that infant fair
Clasped on her lap in silence ;—through the air
Sobs were then heard, and many kissed my feet
In pity's madness, and, to the despair
Of him whom late they cursed, a solace sweet
His very victims brought—soft looks and speeches meet.

XXXVI

Then to a home, for his repose assigned,
Accompanied by the still throng he went
In silence, where, to soothe his rankling mind,
Some likeness of his ancient state was lent;
And, if his heart could have been innocent
As those who pardoned him, he might have ended
His days in peace; but his straight lips were bent,
Men said, into a smile which guile portended,
A sight with which that child like hope with fear was blended.

XXXVII

'Twas midnight now, the eve of that great day,
Whereon the many nations at whose call
The chains of earth like mist melted away,
Decreed to hold a sacred Festival,
A rite to attest the equality of all
Who live.   So to their homes, to dream or wake
All went.   The sleepless silence did recall
Laone to my thoughts, with hopes that make
The flood recede from which their thirst they seek to slake.

XXXVIII

The dawn flowed forth, and from its purple fountains
I drank those hopes which make the spirit quail,
As to the plain between the misty mountains
And the great City, with a countenance pale
I went :—it was a sight which might avail
To make men weep exulting tears, for whom
Now first from human power the reverend veil
Was torn, to see Earth from her general womb
Pour forth her swarming sons to a fraternal doom ;

XXXIX

To see, far glancing in the misty morning,
The signs of that innumerable host,
To hear one sound of many made, the warning
Of Earth to Heaven from its free children tost,
While the eternal hills, and the sea lost
In wavering light, and, starring the blue sky
The city's myriad spires of gold, almost
With human joy made mute society
Its witnesses with men who must hereafter be.

XL

To see, like some vast island from the Ocean,
The Altar of the Federation rear
Its pile i' the midst ; a work, which the devotion
Of millions in one night created there,
Sudden, as when the moonrise makes appear
Strange clouds in the east ; a marble pyramid
Distinct with steps : that mighty shape did wear
The light of genius ; its still shadow hid
Far ships : to know its height the morning mists forbid :—

XLI

To hear the restless multitudes for ever
Around the base of that great Altar flow,

As on some mountain islet burst and shiver
Atlantic waves; and solemnly and slow
As the wind bore that tumult to and fro,
To feel the dreamlike music, which did swim
Like beams through floating clouds on waves below,
Falling in pauses from that Altar dim
As silver-sounding tongues breathed an aërial hymn.

XLII

To hear, to see, to live, was on that morn
Lethean joy! so that all those assembled
Cast off their memories of the past outworn:
Two only bosoms with their own life trembled,
And mine was one,—and we had both dissembled;
So with a beating heart I went, and one,
Who having much, covets yet more, resembled;
A lost and dear possession, which not won,
He walks in lonely gloom beneath the noonday sun.

XLIII

To the great Pyramid I came: its stair
With female choirs was thronged: the loveliest
Among the free, grouped with its sculptures rare.
As I approached, the morning's golden mist,
Which now the wonder-stricken breezes kist
With their cold lips, fled, and the summit shone
Like Athos seen from Samothracia, drest
In earliest light by vintagers, and one
Sate there, a female shape upon an ivory throne.

XLIV

A Form most like the imagined habitant
Of silver exhalations sprung from dawn,
By winds which feed on sunrise woven, to enchant
The faiths of men: all mortal eyes were drawn,
As famished mariners through strange seas gone,
Gaze on a burning watch-tower, by the light
Of those divinest lineaments—alone
With thoughts which none could share, from that fair sight
I turned in sickness, for a veil shrouded her countenance bright.

XLV

And, neither did I hear the acclamations
Which, from brief silence bursting, filled the air,
With her strange name and mine, from all the nations
Which we, they said, in strength had gathered there
From the sleep of bondage; nor the vision fair
Of that bright pageantry beheld,—but blind
And silent, as a breathing corpse did fare,
Leaning upon my friend, till, like a wind
To fevered cheeks, a voice flowed o'er my troubled mind.

XLVI

Like music of some minstrel heavenly-gifted,
To one whom fiends enthrall, this voice to me;
Scarce did I wish her veil to be uplifted,
I was so calm and joyous.—I could see

The platform where we stood, the statues three
Which kept their marble watch on that high shrine,
The multitudes, the mountains, and the sea ;
As when eclipse hath passed, things sudden shine
To men's astonished eyes most clear and crystalline.

XLVII

At first Laone spoke most tremulously :
But soon her voice that calmness which it shed
Gathered, and—" Thou art whom I sought to see,
And thou art our first votary here," she said :
" I had a dear friend once, but he is dead !—
And of all those on the wide earth who breathe,
Thou dost resemble him alone—I spread
This veil between us two, that thou beneath
Shouldst image one who may have been long lost in death.

XLVIII

" For this wilt thou not henceforth pardon me ?
Yes, but those joys which silence well requite
Forbid reply : why men have chosen me
To be the Priestess of this holiest rite
I scarcely know, but that the floods of light
Which flow over the world, have borne me hither
To meet thee, long most dear ; and now unite
Thine hand with mine, and may all comfort wither
From both the hearts whose pulse in joy now beats together.

XLIX

" If our own will as others' law we bind,
If the foul worship trampled here we fear ;
If as ourselves we cease to love our kind ! "—
She paused, and pointed upwards—sculptured there
Three shapes around her ivory throne appear ;
One was a Giant, like a child asleep
On a loose rock, whose grasp crushed, as it were
In dream, sceptres and crowns ; and one did keep
Its watchful eyes in doubt whether to smile or weep ;

L

A Woman sitting on the sculptured disk
Of the broad earth, and feeding from one breast
A human babe and a young basilisk ;
Her looks were sweet as Heaven's when loveliest
In Autumn eves.—The third Image was drest
In white wings swift as clouds in winter skies.
Beneath his feet, 'mongst ghastliest forms, represt
Lay Faith, an obscene worm, who sought to rise,
While calmly on the Sun he turned his diamond eyes.

LI

Beside that Image then I sate, while she
Stood, 'mid the throngs which ever ebbed and flowed
Like light amid the shadows of the sea
Cast from one cloudless star, and on the crowd
That touch, which none who feels forgets, bestowed ;

And whilst the sun returned the steadfast gaze
Of the great Image as o'er Heaven it glode,
That rite had place ; it ceased when sunset's blaze
Burned o'er the isles ; all stood in joy and deep amaze ;

LII

When in the silence of all spirits there
Laone's voice was felt, and through the air
Her thrilling gestures spoke, most eloquently fair.

1

" Calm art thou as yon sunset ! swift and strong
As new-fledged Eagles, beautiful and young,
That float among the blinding beams of morning ;
And underneath thy feet writhe Faith, and Folly,
Custom, and Hell, and mortal Melancholy—
Hark ! the Earth starts to hear the mighty warning
Of thy voice sublime and holy ;
Its free spirits here assembled,
See thee, feel thee, know thee now :
To thy voice their hearts have trembled,
Like ten thousand clouds which flow
With one wide wind as it flies !
Wisdom ! thy irresistible children rise
To hail thee, and the elements they chain
And their own will to swell the glory of thy train.

2

" O Spirit vast and deep as Night and Heaven !
Mother and soul of all to which is given
The light of life, the loveliness of being,
Lo ! thou dost re-ascend the human heart,
Thy throne of power, almighty as thou wert,
In dreams of Poets old grown pale by seeing
The shade of thee :—now, millions start
To feel thy lightnings through them burning :
Nature, or God, or Love, or Pleasure,
Or Sympathy, the sad tears turning
To mutual smiles, a drainless treasure,
Descends amidst us ;—Scorn and Hate,
Revenge and Selfishness, are desolate—
A hundred nations swear that there shall be
Pity and Peace and Love, among the good and free !

3

" Eldest of things, divine Equality !
Wisdom and Love are but the slaves of thee,
The Angels of thy sway, who pour around thee
Treasures from all the cells of human thought,
And from the Stars, and from the Ocean brought,
And the last living heart whose beatings bound thee.
The powerful and the wise had sought
Thy coming ; thou in light descending
O'er the wide land which is thine own,
Like the spring whose breath is blending
All blasts of fragrance into one,

Comest upon the paths of men !
Earth bares her general bosom to thy ken,
And all her children here in glory meet
To feed upon thy smiles, and clasp thy sacred feet.

4

" My brethren, we are free ! the plains and mountains,
The grey sea-shore, the forests, and the fountains,
Are haunts of happiest dwellers ; man and woman,
Their common bondage burst, may freely borrow
From lawless love a solace for their sorrow !
For oft we still must weep, since we are human.
     A stormy night's serenest morrow,
     Whose showers are pity's gentle tears,
     Whose clouds are smiles of those that die
     Like infants, without hopes or fears,
     And whose beams are joys that lie
     In blended hearts, now holds dominion ;
The dawn of mind, which, upwards on a pinion
Borne, swift as sunrise, far illumines space,
And clasps this barren world in its own bright embrace !

5

" My brethren, we are free ! the fruits are glowing
Beneath the stars, and the night winds are flowing
O'er the ripe corn, the birds and beasts are dreaming—
Never again may blood of bird or beast
Stain with its venomous stream a human feast,
To the pure skies in accusation steaming ;
Avenging poisons shall have ceased
     To feed disease and fear and madness,
     The dwellers of the earth and air
     Shall throng around our steps in gladness,
     Seeking their food or refuge there.
Our toil from thought all glorious forms shall cull,
To make this earth, our home, more beautiful,
And Science, and her sister Poesy,
Shall clothe in light the fields and cities of the free !

6

" Victory, Victory to the prostrate nations !
Bear witness, Night, and ye, mute Constellations,
Who gaze on us from your crystalline cars !
Thoughts have gone forth whose powers can sleep no more !
Victory ! Victory ! Earth's remotest shore,
Regions which groan beneath the Antarctic stars,
The green lands cradled in the roar
     Of western waves, and wildernesses
     Peopled and vast, which skirt the oceans
     Where morning dyes her golden tresses,
     Shall soon partake our high emotions :
Kings shall turn pale ! Almighty Fear,
The Fiend-God, when our charmed name he hear,
Shall fade like shadow from his thousand fanes,
While Truth with Joy enthroned o'er his lost empire reigns ! "

LIII

Ere she had ceased, the mists of night entwining
Their dim woof, floated o'er the infinite throng ;
She like a spirit through the darkness shining,
In tones whose sweetness silence did prolong,
As if to lingering winds they did belong,
Poured forth her inmost soul : a passionate speech
With wild and thrilling pauses woven among,
Which whoso heard was mute, for it could teach
To rapture like her own all listening hearts to reach.

LIV

Her voice was as a mountain stream which sweeps
The withered leaves of Autumn to the lake,
And in some deep and narrow bay then sleeps
In the shadow of the shores ; as dead leaves wake
Under the wave, in flowers and herbs which make
Those green depths beautiful when skies are blue,
The multitude so moveless did partake
Such living change, and kindling murmurs flew
As o'er that speechless calm delight and wonder grew.

LV

Over the plain the throngs were scattered then
In groups around the fires, which from the sea
Even to the gorge of the first mountain glen
Blazed wide and far : the banquet of the free
Was spread beneath many a dark cypress tree,
Beneath whose spires, which swayed in the red light
Reclining as they ate, of Liberty.
And Hope, and Justice, and Laone's name,
Earth's children did a woof of happy converse frame.

LVI

Their feast was such as Earth, the general mother,
Pours from her fairest bosom, when she smiles
In the embrace of Autumn ;—to each other
As when some parent fondly reconciles
Her warring children, she their wrath beguiles
With her own sustenance ; they relenting weep :
Such was this Festival, which from their isles,
And continents, and winds, and ocean's deep,
All shapes might throng to share, that fly, or walk, or creep.

LVII

Might share in peace and innocence, for gore
Or poison none this festal did pollute,
But piled on high, an overflowing store
Of pomegranates, and citrons, fairest fruit,
Melons and dates, and figs, and many a root
Sweet and sustaining, and bright grapes ere yet
Accursed fire their mild juice could transmute
Into a mortal bane, and brown corn set
In baskets ; with pure streams their thirsting lips they wet.

LVIII

Laone had descended from the shrine,
And every deepest look and holiest mind
Fed on her form, though now those tones divine
Were silent as she past ; she did unwind
Her veil, as with the crowds of her own kind
She mixed ; some impulse made my heart refrain
From seeking her that night, so I reclined
Amidst a group, where on the utmost plain
A festal watch-fire burned beside the dusky main.

LIX

And joyous was our feast ; pathetic talk,
And wit, and harmony of choral strains,
While far Orion o'er the waves did walk
That flow among the isles, held us in chains
Of sweet captivity, which none disdains
Who feels ; but, when his zone grew dim in mist
Which clothes the Ocean's bosom, o'er the plains
The multitudes went homeward, to their rest,
Which that delightful day with its own shadow blest.

CANTO VI

I

BESIDE the dimness of the glimmering sea,
Weaving swift language from impassioned themes,
With that dear friend I lingered, who to me
So late had been restored, beneath the gleams
Of the silver stars ; and ever in soft dreams
Of future love and peace sweet converse lapt
Our willing fancies, till the pallid beams
Of the last watch-fire fell, and darkness wrapt
The waves, and each bright chain of floating fire was snapt.

II

And till we came even to the City's wall
And the great gate, then, none knew whence or why,
Disquiet on the multitudes did fall :
And first, one pale and breathless past us by,
And stared and spoke not ; then with piercing cry
A troop of wild-eyed women, by the shrieks
Of their own terror driven,—tumultuously
Hither and thither hurrying with pale cheeks,
Each one from fear unknown a sudden refuge seeks—

III

Then, rallying cries of treason and of danger
Resounded : and—" They come ! to arms ! to arms !
The Tyrant is amongst us, and the stranger
Comes to enslave us in his name ! to arms ! "
In vain : for Panic, the pale fiend who charms
Strength to forswear her right, those millions swept
Like waves before the tempest—these alarms
Came to me, as to know their cause I leapt
On the gate's turret, and in rage and grief and scorn I wept !

IV

For to the North I saw the town on fire,
And its red light made morning pallid now,
Which burst over wide Asia.—Louder, higher,
The yells of victory and the screams of woe
I heard approach, and saw the throng below
Stream through the gates like foam-wrought waterfalls
Fed from a thousand storms—the fearful glow
Of bombs flares overhead—at intervals
The red artillery's bolt mangling among them falls.

V

And now the horsemen come—and all was done
Swifter than I have spoken—I beheld
Their red swords flash in the unrisen sun.
I rushed among the rout to have repelled
That miserable flight—one moment quelled
By voice, and looks, and eloquent despair,
As if reproach from their own hearts withheld
Their steps, they stood ; but soon came pouring there
New multitudes, and did those rallied bands o'erbear.

VI

I strove, as drifted on some cataract
By irresistible streams, some wretch might strive
Who hears its fatal roar : the files compact
Whelmed me, and from the gate availed to drive
With quickening impulse, as each bolt did rive
Their ranks with bloodier chasm : into the plain
Disgorged at length the dead and the alive,
In one dread mass, were parted, and the stain
Of blood from mortal steel fell o'er the fields like rain.

VII

For now the despot's bloodhounds with their prey
Unarmed and unaware, were gorging deep
Their gluttony of death ; the loose array
Of horsemen o'er the wide fields murdering sweep,
And with loud laughter for their tyrant reap
A harvest sown with other hopes ; the while,
Far overhead, ships from Propontis keep
A killing rain of fire :—when the waves smile
As sudden earthquakes light many a volcano isle.

VIII

Thus sudden, unexpected feast was spread
For the carrion fowls of Heaven.—I saw the sight—
I moved—I lived—as o'er the heaps of dead,
Whose stony eyes glared in the morning light,
I trod ; to me there came no thought of flight,
But with loud cries of scorn which whoso heard
That dreaded death, felt in his veins the might
Of virtuous shame return, the crowd I stirred,
And desperation's hope in many hearts recurred.

IX

A band of brothers gathering round me, made,
Although unarmed, a steadfast front, and still

Retreating, with stern looks beneath the shade
Of gathered eyebrows, did the victors fill
With doubt even in success; deliberate will
Inspired our growing troop; not overthrown
It gained the shelter of a grassy hill,
And ever still our comrades were hewn down,
And their defenceless limbs beneath our footsteps strown.

X

Immovably we stood—in joy I found,
Beside me then, firm as a giant pine
Among the mountain vapours driven around,
The old man whom I loved—his eyes divine
With a mild look of courage answered mine,
And my young friend was near, and ardently
His hand grasped mine a moment—now the line
Of war extended, to our rallying cry,
As myriads flocked in love and brotherhood to die.

XI

For ever while the sun was climbing Heaven
The horsemen hewed our unarmed myriads down
Safely, though when by thirst of carnage driven
Too near, those slaves were swiftly overthrown
By hundreds leaping on them : flesh and bone
Soon made our ghastly ramparts; then the shaft
Of the artillery from the sea was thrown
More fast and fiery, and the conquerors laughed
In pride to hear the wind our screams of torment waft.

XII

For on one side alone the hill gave shelter,
So vast that phalanx of unconquered men,
And there the living in their blood did welter
Of the dead and dying, which, in that green glen,
Like stifled torrents, made a plashy fen
Under the feet—thus was the butchery waged
While the sun clomb Heaven's eastern steep—but when
It 'gan to sink, a fiercer combat raged,
For in more doubtful strife the armies were engaged.

XIII

Within a cave upon the hill were found
A bundle of rude pikes, the instrument
Of those who war but on their native ground
For natural rights: a shout of joyance sent
Even from our hearts the wide air pierced and rent,
As those few arms the bravest and the best
Seized ; and each sixth, thus armed, did now present
A line which covered and sustained the rest,
A confident phalanx, which the foes on every side invest.

XIV

That onset turned the foes to flight almost ;
But soon they saw their present strength, and knew
That coming night would to our resolute host

Bring victory ; so dismounting close they drew
Their glittering files, and then the combat grew
Unequal but most horrible ;—and ever
Our myriads, whom the swift bolt overthrew,
Or the red sword, failed like a mountain river
Which rus es forth in foam to sink in sands for ever.

xv

Sorrow and shame, to see with their own kind
Our human brethren mix, like beasts of blood
To mutual ruin, armed by one behind,
Who sits and scoffs !—That friend so mild and good
Who like its shadow near my youth had stood,
Was stabbed !—my old preserver's hoary hair,
With the flesh clinging to its roots, was strewed
Under my feet ! I lost all sense or care,
And like the rest I grew desperate and unaware.

xvi

The battle became ghastlier, in the midst
I paused, and saw, how ugly and how fell,
O Hate ! thou art, even when thy life thou shedd'st
For love. The ground in many a little dell
Was broken, up and down whose steeps befell
Alternate victory and defeat, and there
The combatants with rage most horrible
Strove, and their eyes started with cracking stare,
And impotent their tongues they lolled into the air,

xvii

Flaccid and foamy, like a mad dog's hanging ;
Want, and Moon-madness, and the Pest's swift bane
When its shafts smite—while yet its bow is twanging—
Have each their mark and sign—some ghastly stain ;
And this was thine, O War ! of hate and pain
Thou loathed slave. I saw all shapes of death,
And minister'd to many, o'er the plain
While carnage in the sunbeam's warmth did seethe
Till twilight o'er the east wove her serenest wreath.

xviii

The few who yet survived, resolute and firm,
Around me fought. At the decline of day,
Winding above the mountain's snowy term,
New banners shone : they quivered in the ray
Of the sun's unseen orb—ere night the array
Of fresh troops hemmed us in—of those brave bands
I soon survived alone—and now I lay
Vanquished and faint, the grasp of bloody hands
I felt, and saw on high the glare of falling brands,

xix

When on my foes a sudden terror came,
And they fled, scattering.—Lo ! with reinless speed
A black Tartarian horse of giant frame
Comes trampling o'er the dead ; the living bleed
Beneath the hoofs of that tremendous steed

On which, like to an angel, robed in white,
Sate one waving a sword ; the hosts recede
And fly, as through their ranks, with awful might,
Sweeps in the shadow of eve that Phantom swift and bright ;

XX

And its path made a solitude.—I rose
And marked its coming ; it relaxed its course
As it approached me, and the wind that flows
Through night, bore accents to mine ear whose force
Might create smiles in death.—The Tartar horse
Paused, and I saw the shape its might which swayed,
And heard her musical pants, like the sweet source
Of waters in the desert, as she said,
" Mount with me, Laon, now "—I rapidly obeyed.

XXI

Then " Away ! away ! " she cried, and stretched her sword
As 'twere a scourge over the courser's head,
And lightly shook the reins.—We spake no word,
But like the vapour of the tempest fled
Over the plain ; her dark hair was dispread,
Like the pine's locks upon the lingering blast ;
Over mine eyes its shadowy strings it spread
Fitfully, and the hills and streams fled fast,
As o'er the glimmering forms the steed's broad shadow past,

XXII

And his hoofs ground the rocks to fire and dust,
His strong sides made the torrents rise in spray,
And turbulence, as if a whirlwind's gust
Surrounded us ;—and still away ! away !
Through the desert night we sped, while she alway
Gazed on a mountain which we neared, whose crest
Crowned with a marble ruin, in the ray
Of the obscure stars gleamed ;—its rugged breast
The steed strained up, and then his impulse did arrest.

XXIII

A rocky hill which overhung the Ocean :—
From that lone ruin, when the steed that panted
Paused, might be heard the murmur of the motion
Of waters, as in spots for ever haunted
By the choicest winds of Heaven, which are enchanted
To music by the wand of Solitude,
That wizard wild, and the far tents implanted
Upon the plain, be seen by those who stood
Thence marking the dark shore of Ocean's curved flood.

XXIV

One moment these were heard and seen—another
Past ; and the two who stood beneath that night,
Each only heard, or saw, or felt, the other ;
As from the lofty steed she did alight,
Cythna (for, from the eyes whose deepest light
Of love and sadness made my lips feel pale
With influence strange of mournfullest delight,

My own sweet Cythna looked,) with joy did quail,
And felt her strength in tears of human weakness fail.

XXV

And for a space in my embrace she rested,
Her head on my unquiet heart reposing,
While my faint arms her languid frame invested :
At length she looked on me, and half unclosing
Her tremulous lips, said : " Friend, thy bands were losing
The battle, as I stood before the King
In bonds.—I burst them then, and swiftly choosing
The time, did seize a Tartar's sword, and spring
Upon his horse, and swift as on the whirlwind's wing,

XXVI

" Have thou and I been borne beyond pursuer,
And we are here."—Then, turning to the steed,
She pressed the white moon on his front with pure
And rose-like lips, and many a fragrant weed
From the green ruin plucked, that he might feed ;—
But I to a stone seat that Maiden led,
And kissing her fair eyes, said, " Thou hast need
Of rest," and I heaped up the courser's bed
In a green mossy nook, with mountain flowers dispread.

XXVII

Within that ruin, where a shattered portal
Looks to the eastern stars, abandoned now
By man, to be the home of things immortal,
Memories, like awful ghosts which come and go,
And must inherit all he builds below,
When he is gone, a hall stood ; o'er whose roof
Fair clinging weeds with ivy pale did grow,
Clasping its grey rents with a verdurous woof,
A hanging dome of leaves, a canopy moon-proof.

XXVIII

The autumnal winds, as if spellbound, had made
A natural couch of leaves in that recess,
Which seasons none disturbed, but in the shade
Of flowering parasites, did spring love to dress
With their sweet blooms the wintry loneliness
Of those dead leaves, shedding their stars, whene'er
The wandering wind her nurslings might caress ;
Whose intertwining fingers ever there,
Made music wild and soft that filled the listening air.

XXIX

We know not where we go, or what sweet dream
May pilot us through caverns strange and fair
Of far and pathless passion, while the stream
Of life our bark doth on its whirlpools bear,
Spreading swift wings as sails to the dim air ·
Nor should we seek to know, so the devotion
Of love and gentle thoughts be heard still there
Louder and louder from the utmost Ocean
Of universal life, attuning its commotion.

XXX

To the pure all things are pure ! Oblivion wrapt
Our spirits, and the fearful overthrow
Of public hope was from our being snapt,
Though linked years had bound it there ; for now
A power, a thirst, a knowledge, which below
All thoughts, like light beyond the atmosphere,
Clothing its clouds with grace, doth ever flow,
Came on us, as we sate in silence there,
Beneath the golden stars of the clear azure air.

XXXI

In silence which doth follow talk that causes
The baffled heart to speak with sighs and tears,
When wildering passion swalloweth up the pauses
Of inexpressive speech :—the youthful years
Which we together past, their hopes and fears,
The blood itself which ran within our frames,
That likeness of the features which endears
The thoughts expressed by them, our very names,
And all the winged hours which speechless memory claims,

XXXII

Had found a voice :—and ere that voice did pass,
The night grew damp and dim, and through a rent
Of the ruin where we sate, from the morass,
A wandering Meteor, by some wild wind sent,
Hung high in the green dome, to which it lent
A faint and pallid lustre ; while the song
Of blasts, in which its blue hair quivering bent,
Strewed strangest sounds the moving leaves among ;
A wondrous light, the sound as of a spirit's tongue.

XXXIII

The Meteor showed the leaves on which we sate,
And Cythna's glowing arms, and the thick ties
Of her soft hair, which bent with gathered weight
My neck near hers, her dark and deepening eyes,
Which, as twin phantoms of one star that lies
O'er a dim well, move, though the star reposes,
Swam in our mute and liquid ecstasies,
Her marble brow, and eager lips, like roses,
With their own fragrance pale, which spring but half uncloses.

XXXIV

The Meteor to its far morass returned :
The beating of our veins one interval
Made still ; and then I felt the blood that burned
Within her frame, mingle with mine, and fall
Around my heart like fire ; and over all
A mist was spread, the sickness of a deep
And speechless swoon of joy, as might befall
Two disunited spirits when they leap
In union from this earth's obscure and fading sleep,

XXXV

Was it one moment that confounded thus
All thought, all sense, all feeling, into one

Unutterable power, which shielded us
Even from our own cold looks, when we had gone
Into a wide and wild oblivion
Of tumult and of tenderness ? or now
Had ages, such as make the moon and sun,
The seasons and mankind, their changes know,
Left fear and time unfelt by us alone below ?

XXXVI

I know not.   What are kisses whose fire clasps
The failing heart in languishment, or limb
Twined within limb ? or the quick dying gasps
Of the life meeting, when the faint eyes swim
Through tears of a wide mist, boundless and dim,
In one caress ?   What is the strong control
Which leads the heart that dizzy steep to climb,
Where far over the world those vapours roll,
Which blend two restless frames in one reposing soul ?

XXXVII

It is the shadow which doth float unseen,
But not unfelt, o'er blind mortality,
Whose divine darkness fled not from that green
And lone recess, where lapt in peace did lie
Our linked frames, till, from the changing sky,
That night and still another day had fled ;
And then I saw and felt.   The moon was high,
And clouds, as of a coming storm, were spread
Under its orb,—loud winds were gathering overhead.

XXXVIII

Cythna's sweet lips seemed lurid in the moon,
Her fairest limbs with the night wind were chill,
And her dark tresses were all loosely strewn
O'er her pale bosom :—all within was still,
And the sweet peace of joy did almost fill
The depth of her unfathomable look ;—
And we sate calmly, though that rocky hill,
The waves contending in its caverns strook,
For they foreknew the storm, and the grey ruin shook.

XXXIX

There we unheeding sate, in the communion
Of interchanged vows, which, with a rite
Of faith most sweet and sacred, stamped our union.—
Few were the living hearts which could unite
Like ours, or celebrate a bridal night
With such close sympathies, for they had sprung
From linked youth, and from the gentle might
Of earliest love, delayed and cherished long,
Which common hopes and fears made, like a tempest, strong.

XL

And such is Nature's law divine, that those
Who grow together cannot choose but love,
If faith or custom do not interpose,
Or common slavery mar what else might move

All gentlest thoughts ; as in the sacred grove
Which shades the springs of Æthiopian Nile,
That living tree, which, if the arrowy dove,
Strike with her shadow, shrinks in fear awhile,
But its own kindred leaves clasps while the sunbeams smile ;

XLI

And clings to them, when darkness may dissever
The close caresses of all duller plants
Which bloom on the wide earth—thus we for ever
Were linked, for love had nurst us in the haunts
Where knowledge from its secret source enchants
Young hearts with the fresh music of its springing,
Ere yet its gathered flood feeds human wants,
As the great Nile feeds Egypt ; ever flinging
Light on the woven boughs which o'er its waves are swinging.

XLII

The tones of Cythna's voice like echoes were
Of those far murmuring streams ; they rose and fell,
Mixed with mine own in the tempestuous air,—
And so we sate, until our talk befel
Of the late ruin, swift and horrible,
And how those seeds of hope might yet be sown,
Whose fruit is evil's mortal poison : well
For us, this ruin made a watch-tower lone,
But Cythna's eyes looked faint, and now two days were gone

XLIII

Since she had food :—therefore I did awaken
The Tartar steed, who, from his ebon mane,
Soon as the clinging slumbers he had shaken,
Bent his thin head to seek the brazen rein,
Following me obediently ; with pain
Of heart, so deep and dread, that one caress,
When lips and heart refuse to part again,
Till they have told their fill, could scarce express
The anguish of her mute and fearful tenderness.

XLIV

Cythna beheld me part, as I bestrode
That willing steed—the tempest and the night
Which gave my path its safety as I rode
Down the ravine of rocks, did soon unite
The darkness and the tumult of their might
Borne on all winds.—Far through the streaming rain
Floating at intervals the garments white
Of Cythna gleamed, and her voice once again
Came to me on the gust, and soon I reached the plain.

XLV

I dreaded not the tempest, nor did he
Who bore me, but his eyeballs wide and red
Turned on the lightning's cleft exultingly ;
And when the earth beneath his tameless tread,
Shook with the sullen thunder, he would spread

His nostrils to the blast, and joyously
Mock the fierce peal with neighings ; —thus we speu
O'er the lit plain, and soon I could descry
Where Death and Fire had gorged the spoil of victory.

XLVI

There was a desolate village in a wood,
Whose bloom-inwoven leaves now scattering fed
The hungry storm ; it was a place of blood,
A heap of heartless walls ;—the flames were dead
Within those dwellings now,—the life had fled
From all those corpses now,—but the wide sky
Flooded with lightning was ribbed overhead
By the black rafters, and around did lie
Women, and babes, and men, slaughtered confusedly.

XLVII

Beside the fountain in the market-place
Dismounting, I beheld those corpses stare
With horny eyes upon each other's face,
And on the earth, and on the vacant air,
And upon me, close to the waters where
I stooped to slake my thirst ;—I shrank to taste,
For the salt bitterness of blood was there !
But tied the steed beside, and sought in haste
If any yet survived amid that ghastly waste.

XLVIII

No living thing was there beside one woman,
Whom I found wandering in the streets, and she
Was withered from a likeness of aught human
Into a fiend, by some strange misery :
Soon as she heard my steps, she leaped on me,
And glued her burning lips to mine, and laughed
With a loud, long, and frantic laugh of glee,
And cried, " Now, Mortal, thou hast deeply quaffed
The Plague's blue kisses—soon millions shall pledge the draught !

XLIX

" My name is Pestilence—this bosom dry
Once fed two babes—a sister and a brother—
When I came home, one in the blood did lie
Of three death-wounds—the flames had ate the other !
Since then I have no longer been a mother,
But I am Pestilence ;—hither and thither
I flit about, that I may slay and smother ;—
All lips which I have kissed must surely wither,
But Death's—if thou art he, we'll go to work together !

L

" What seekest thou here ? the moonlight comes in flashes,—
The dew is rising dankly from the dell ;
'Twill moisten her ! and thou shalt see the gashes
In my sweet boy—now full of worms—but tell
First what thou seek'st."—" I seek for food."—" 'Tis well,
Thou shalt have food ; Famine, my paramour,
Waits for us at the feast—cruel and fell

Is Famine, but he drives not from his door
Those whom these lips have kissed, alone. No more, no more!"

LI

As thus she spake, she grasped me with the strength
Of madness, and by many a ruined hearth
She led, and over many a corpse :—at length
We came to a lone hut, where on the earth
Which made its floor, she in her ghastly mirth
Gathering from all those homes now desolate,
Had piled three heaps of loaves, making a dearth
Among the dead—round which she set in state
A ring of cold, stiff babes ; silent and stark they sate.

LII

She leaped upon a pile, and lifted high
Her mad looks to the lightning, and cried : " Eat !
Share the great feast—to-morrow we must die ! "
And then she spurned the loaves with her pale feet,
Towards her bloodless guests ;—that sight to meet,
Mine eyes and my heart ached, and but that she
Who loved me, did with absent looks defeat
Despair, I might have raved in sympathy ;
But now I took the food that woman offered me ;

LIII

And vainly having with her madness striven
If I might win her to return with me,
Departed. In the eastern beams of Heaven
The lightning now grew pallid—rapidly,
As by the shore of the tempestuous sea
The dark steed bore me, and the mountain grey
Soon echoed to his hoofs, and I could see
Cythna among the rocks, where she alway
Had sate, with anxious eyes fixed on the lingering day.

LIV

And joy was ours to meet : she was most pale,
Famished, and wet and weary, so I cast
My arms around her, lest her steps should fail
As to our home we went, and thus embraced,
Her full heart seemed a deeper joy to taste
Than e'er the prosperous know ; the steed behind
Trod peacefully along the mountain waste :
We reached our home ere morning could unbind
Night's latest veil, and on our bridal couch reclined.

LV

Her chilled heart having cherished in my bosom,
And sweetest kisses past, we two did share
Our peaceful meal :—as an autumnal blossom,
Which spreads its shrunk leaves in the sunny air,
After cold showers, like rainbows woven there,
Thus in her lips and cheeks the vital spirit
Mantled, and in her eyes, an atmosphere
Of health, and hope ; and sorrow languished near it,
And fear, and all that dark despondence doth inherit.

CANTO VII

I

So we sate joyous as the morning ray
Which fed upon the wrecks of night and storm
Now lingering on the winds ; light airs did play
Among the dewy weeds, the sun was warm,
And we sate linked in the inwoven charm
Of converse and caresses sweet and deep,
Speechless caresses, talk that might disarm
Time, though he wield the darts of death and sleep,
And those thrice mortal barbs in his own poison steep.

II

I told her of my sufferings and my madness,
And how, awakened from that dreamy mood
By Liberty's uprise, the strength of gladness
Came to my spirit in my solitude ;
And all that now I was, while tears pursued
Each other down her fair and listening cheek
Fast as the thoughts which fed them, like a flood
From sunbright dales ; and when I ceased to speak,
Her accents soft and sweet the pausing air did wake.

III

She told me a strange tale of strange endurance,
Like broken memories of many a heart
Woven into one ; to which no firm assurance,
So wild were they, could her own faith impart.
She said that not a tear did dare to start
From the swoln brain, and that her thoughts were firm
When from all mortal hope she did depart,
Borne by those slaves across the Ocean's term,
And that she reached the port without one fear infirm.

IV

One was she among many there, the thralls
Of the cold tyrant's cruel lust : and they
Laughed mournfully in those polluted halls ;
But she was calm and sad, musing alway
On loftiest enterprise, till on a day
The tyrant heard her singing to her lute
A wild and sad, and spirit-thrilling lay,
Like winds that die in wastes—one moment mute
The evil thoughts it made, which did his breast pollute.

V

Even when he saw her wondrous loveliness,
One moment to great Nature's sacred power
He bent and was no longer passionless ;
But when he bade her to his secret bower
Be borne a loveless victim, and she tore
Her locks in agony, and her words of flame
And mightier looks availed not ; then he bore
Again his load of slavery, and became
A king, a heartless beast, a pageant and a name.

VI

She told me what a loathsome agony
Is that when selfishness mocks love's delight,
Foul as in dreams most fearful imagery
To dally with the mowing dead—that night
All torture, fear, or horror, made seem light
Which the soul dreams or knows, and when the day
Shone on her awful frenzy, from the sight
Where like a Spirit in fleshy chains she lay
Struggling, aghast and pale the tyrant fled away.

VII

Her madness was a beam of light, a power
Which dawned through the rent soul; and words it gave,
Gestures and looks, such as in whirlwinds bore
Which might not be withstood, whence none could save
All who approached their sphere, like some calm wave
Vexed into whirlpools by the chasms beneath;
And sympathy made each attendant slave
Fearless and free, and they began to breathe
Deep curses, like the voice of flames far underneath.

VIII

The King felt pale upon his noon-day throne;
At night two slaves he to her chamber sent,
One was a green and wrinkled eunuch, grown
From human shape into an instrument
Of all things ill—distorted, bowed and bent.
The other was a wretch from infancy
Made dumb by poison; who nought knew or meant
But to obey: from the fire-isles came he,
A diver lean and strong, of Oman's coral sea.

IX

They bore her to a bark, and the swift stroke
Of silent rowers clove the blue moonlight seas,
Until upon their path the morning broke;
They anchored then, where, be there calm or breeze,
The gloomiest of the drear Symplegades
Shakes with the sleepless surge;—the Æthiop there
Wound his long arms around her, and with knees
Like iron clasped her feet, and plunged with her
Among the closing waves out of the boundless air.

X

" Swift as an eagle stooping from the plain
Of morning light, into some shadowy wood,
He plunged through the green silence of the main,
Through many a cavern which the eternal flood
Had scooped, as dark lairs for its monster brood;
And among mighty shapes which fled in wonder,
And among mightier shadows which pursued
His heels, he wound : until the dark rocks under
He touched a golden chain—a sound arose like thunder

XI

" A stunning clang of massive bolts redoubling
Beneath the deep—a burst of waters driven

As from the roots of the sea, raging and bubbling:
And in that roof of crags a space was riven
Thro' which there shone the emerald beams of heaven,
Shot through the lines of many waves inwoven,
Like sunlight through acacia woods at even,
Through which, his way the diver having cloven,
Past like a spark sent up out of a burning oven.

XII

" And then," she said, " he laid me in a cave
Above the waters, by that chasm of sea,
A fountain round and vast, in which the wave
Imprisoned, boiled and leaped perpetually,
Down which, one moment resting, he did flee,
Winning the adverse depth ; that spacious cell
Like an hupaithric temple wide and high,
Whose aëry dome is inaccessible,
Was pierced with one round cleft through which the sunbeams fell.

XIII

" Below, the fountain's brink was richly paven
With the deep wealth, coral, and pearl, and sand
Like spangling gold, and purple shells engraven
With mystic legends by no mortal hand,
Left there, when, thronging to the moon's command,
The gathering waves rent the Hesperian gate
Of mountains, and on such bright floor did stand
Columns, and shapes like statues, and the state
Of kingless thrones, which Earth did in her heart create.

XIV

" The fiend of madness which had made its prey
Of my poor heart, was lulled to sleep awhile :
There was an interval of many a day,
And a sea-eagle brought me food the while,
Whose nest was built in that untrodden isle,
And who, to be the jailor, had been taught,
Of that strange dungeon ; as a friend whose smile
Like light and rest at morn and even is sought,
That wild bird was to me, till madness misery brought.

XV

" The misery of a madness slow and creeping,
Which made the earth seem fire, the sea seem air,
And the white clouds of noon which oft were sleeping
In the blue heaven so beautiful and fair,
Like hosts of ghastly shadows hovering there ;
And the sea-eagle looked a fiend who bore
Thy mangled limbs for food !—Thus all things were
Transformed into the agony which I wore,
Even as a poisoned robe around my bosom's core.

XVI

" Again I knew the day and night fast fleeing,
The eagle and the fountain and the air ;
Another frenzy came—there seemed a being
Within me—a strange load my heart did bear,

As if some living thing had made its lair
Even in the fountains of my life :—a long
And wondrous vision wrought from my despair,
Then grew, like sweet reality among
Dim visionary woes, an unreposing throng.

XVII

" Methought I was about to be a mother—
Month after month went by, and still I dreamed
That we should soon be all to one another,
I and my child ; and still new pulses seemed
To beat beside my heart, and still I deemed
There was a babe within—and when the rain
Of winter through the rifted cavern streamed,
Methought, after a lapse of lingering pain,
I saw that lovely shape, which near my heart had lain.

XVIII

It was a babe, beautiful from its birth,—
It was like thee, dear love ! its eyes were thine,
Its brow, its lips, and so upon the earth
It laid its fingers, as now rest on mine
Thine own, beloved !—'twas a dream divine ;
Even to remember how it fled, how swift,
How utterly, might make the heart repine,—
Though 'twas a dream.''—Then Cythna did uplift
Her looks on mine, as if some doubt she sought to shift :

XIX

A doubt which would not flee, a tenderness
Of questioning grief, a source of thronging tears
Which, having past, as one whom sobs oppress,
She spoke : " Yes, in the wilderness of years
Her memory, aye, like a green home appears.
She sucked her fill even at this breast, sweet love,
For many months I had no mortal fears ;
Methought I felt her lips and breath approve,—
It was a human thing which to my bosom clove.

XX

" I watched the dawn of her first smiles, and soon
When zenith-stars were trembling on the wave,
Or when the beams of the invisible moon,
Or sun, from many a prism within the cave
Their gem-born shadows to the water gave,
Her looks would hunt them, and with outspread hand,
From the swift lights which might that fountain pave,
She would mark one, and laugh, when that command
Slighting, it lingered there, and could not understand.

XXI

" Methought her looks began to talk with me :
And no articulate sounds, but something sweet
Her lips would frame,—so sweet it could not be,
That it was meaningless ; her touch would meet
Mine, and our pulses calmly flow and beat
In response while we slept ; and on a day
When I was happiest in that strange retreat,

With heaps of golden shells we two did play,—
Both infants, weaving wings for time's perpetual way.

XXII

" Ere night, methought, her waning eyes were grown
Weary with joy, and tired with our delight,
We, on the earth, like sister twins lay down
On one fair mother's bosom :—from that night
She fled ;—like those illusions clear and bright,
Which dwell in lakes, when the red moon on high
Pause ere it wakens tempest ;—and her flight,
Though 'twas the death of brain'ess phantasy,
Yet smote my lonesome heart more than all misery.

XXIII

" It seemed that in the dreary night, the diver
Who brought me thither, came again, and bore
My child away. I saw the waters quiver,
When he so swiftly sunk, as once before :
Then morning came—it shone even as of yore,
But I was changed—the very life was gone
Out of my heart—I wasted more and more,
Day after day, and sitting there alone,
Vexed the inconstant waves with my perpetual moan.

XXIV

" I was no longer mad, and yet methought
My breasts were swoln and changed :—in every vein
The blood stood still one moment, while that thought
Was passing—with a gush of sickening pain
It ebbed even to its withered springs again :
When my wan eyes in stern resolve I turned
From that most strange delusion, which would fain
Have waked the dream for which my spirit yearned
With more than human love,—then left it unreturned.

XXV

" So now my reason was restored to me,
I struggled with that dream, which, like a beast
Most fierce and beauteous, in my memory
Had made its lair, and on my heart did feast ;
But all that cave and all its shapes possest
By thoughts which could not fade, renewed each one
Some smile, some look, some gesture which had blest
Me heretofore : I, sitting there alone,
Vexed the inconstant waves with my perpetual moan.

XXVI

" Time past, I know not whether months or years ;
For day, nor night, nor change of seasons made
Its note, but thoughts and unavailing tears :
And I became at last even as a shade,
A smoke, a cloud on which the winds have preyed,
Till it be thin as air ; until, one even,
A Nautilus upon the fountain played,
Spreading his azure sail where breath of Heaven
Descended not. among the waves and whirlpools driven.

XXVII

" And when the Eagle came, that lovely thing,
Oaring with rosy feet its silver boat,
Fled near me as for shelter ; on slow wing,
The Eagle, hovering o'er his prey, did float ;
But when he saw that I with fear did note
His purpose, proffering my own food to him,
The eager plumes subsided on his throat—
He came where that bright child of sea did swim,
And o'er it cast in peace his shadow broad and dim.

XXVIII

" This wakened me, it gave me human strength :
And hope, I know not whence or wherefore, rose,
But I resumed my ancient powers at length ;
My spirit felt again like one of those,
Like thine, whose fate it is to make the woes
Of humankind their prey—what was this cave ?
Its deep foundation no firm purpose knows
Immutable, resistless, strong to save,
Like mind while yet it mocks the all-devouring grave.

XXIX

" And where was Laon ? might my heart be dead,
While that far dearer heart could move and be ?
Or whilst over the earth the pall was spread,
Which I had sworn to rend ? I might be free,
Could I but win that friendly bird to me,
To bring me ropes ; and long in vain I sought
By intercourse of mutual imagery
Of objects, if such aid he could be taught ;
But fruit, and flowers, and boughs, yet never ropes he brought.

XXX

" We live in our own world, and mine was made
From glorious phantasies of hope departed :
Aye, we are darkened with their floating shade,
Or cast a lustre on them—time imparted
Such power to me, I became fearless-hearted ;
My eye and voice grew firm, calm was my mind,
And piercing, like the morn, now it has darted
Its lustre on all hidden things, behind
Yon dim and fading clouds which load the weary wind.

XXXI

" My mind became the book through which I grew
Wise in all human wisdom, and its cave,
Which like a mine I rifled through and through,
To me the keeping of its secrets gave—
One mind, the type of all, the moveless wave
Whose calm reflects all moving things that are,
Necessity, and love, and life, the grave,
And sympathy, fountains of hope and fear ;
Justice, and truth, and time, and the world's natural sphere.

XXXII

" And on the sand would I make signs to range
These woofs, as they were woven, of my thought ;

Clear elemental shapes, whose smallest change
A subtler language within language wrought :
The key of truths which once were dimly taught
In old Crotona ;—and sweet melodies
Of love, in that lone solitude I caught
From thine own voice in dream, when thy dear eyes
Shone through my sleep, and did that utterance harmonise.

XXXIII

" Thy songs were winds whereon I fled at will,
As in a winged chariot, o'er the plain
Of crystal youth ; and thou wert there to fill
My heart with joy, and there we sate again
On the grey margin of the glimmering main.
Happy as then but wiser far, for we
Smiled on the flowery grave in which were lain
Fear, Faith, and Slavery ; and mankind was free,
Equal, and pure, and wise, in wisdom's prophecy.

XXXIV

" For to my will my fancies were as slaves
To do their sweet and subtle ministries ;
And oft from that bright fountain's shadowy waves
They would make human throngs gather and rise
To combat with my overflowing eyes,
And voice made deep with passion—thus I grew
Familiar with the shock and the surprise
And war of earthly minds, from which I drew
The power which has been mine to frame their thoughts anew.

XXXV

" And thus my prison was the populous earth—
Where I saw—even as misery dreams of morn
Before the east has given its glory birth—
Religion's pomp made desolate by the scorn
Of Wisdom's faintest smile, and thrones uptorn,
And dwellings of mild people interspersed
With undivided fields of ripening corn,
And love made free,—a hope which we have nurst
Even with our blood and tears,—until its glory burst.

XXXVI

" All is not lost !   There is some recompense
For hope whose fountain can be thus profound,
Even throned Evil's splendid impotence,
Girt by its hell of power, the secret sound
Of hymns to truth and freedom,—the dread bound
Of life and death passed fearlessly and well,
Dungeons wherein the high resolve is found,
Racks which degraded woman's greatness tell,
And what may else be good and irresistible.

XXXVII

" Such are the thoughts which, like the fires that flare
In storm-encompassed isles, we cherish yet
In this dark ruin—such were mine even there ;
As in its sleep some odorous violet,
While yet its leaves with nightly dews are wet,

Breathes in prophetic dreams of day's uprise,
Or, as ere Scyth'an frost in fear has met
Spring's messengers descending from the skies,
The buds foreknow their life—this hope must ever rise.

XXXVIII

" So years had past, when sudden earthquake rent
The depth of ocean, and the cavern crackt
With sound, as if the world's wide continent
Had fallen in universal ruin wrackt ;
And through the cleft streamed in one cataract
The stifling waters :—when I woke, the flood,
Whose banded waves that crystal cave had sacked,
Was ebbing round me, and my bright abode
Before me yawned—a chasm desert, and bare, and broad.

XXXIX

" Above me was the sky, beneath the sea :
I stood upon a point of shattered stone,
And heard loose rocks rushing tumultuously
With splash and shock into the deep—anon
All ceased, and there was silence wide and lone.
I felt that I was free ! The Ocean spray
Quivered beneath my feet, the broad Heaven shone
Around, and in my hair the winds did play,
Lingering as they pursued their unimpeded way.

XL

" My spirit moved upon the sea like wind
Which round some thymy cape will lag and hover,
Though it can wake the still cloud, and unbind
The strength of tempest : day was almost over,
When through the fading light I could discover
A ship approaching—its white sails were fed
With the north wind—its moving shade did cover
The twilight deep ;—the mariners in dread
Cast anchor when they saw new rocks around them spread.

XLI

" And when they saw one sitting on a crag,
They sent a boat to me ;—the sailors rowed
In awe through many a new and fearful jag
Of overhanging rock, through which there flowed
The foam of streams that cannot make abode.
They came and questioned me, but, when they heard
My voice, they became silent, and they stood
And moved as men in whom new love had stirred
Deep thoughts : so to the ship we past without a word.

CANTO VIII

I

"I SATE beside the steersman then, and, gazing
Upon the west, cried, ' Spread the sails ! behold !
The sinking moon is like a watch-tower blazing

Over the mountains yet ;—the City of Gold
Yon Cape alone does from the sight withhold ;
The stream is fleet—the north breathes steadily
Beneath the stars ; they tremble with the cold !
Ye cannot rest upon the dreary sea ;—
Haste, haste to the warm home of happier destiny !

II

" The Mariners obeyed—the Captain stood
Aloof, and, whispering to the Pilot, said,
' Alas, alas ! I fear we are pursued
By wicked ghosts : a Phantom of the Dead,
The night before we sailed, came to my bed
In dream, like that ! ' The Pilot then replied,
' It cannot be—she is a human Maid—
Her low voice makes you weep—she is some bride,
Or daughter of high birth—she can be nought beside.'

III

" We past the islets, borne by wind and stream,
And as we sailed, the Mariners came near
And thronged around to listen ;—in the gleam
Of the pale moon I stood, as one whom fear
May not attaint, and my calm voice did rear :
' Ye are all human—yon broad moon gives light
To millions who the self-same likeness wear.
Even while I speak—beneath this very night,
Their thoughts flow on like ours, in sadness or delight.

IV

" ' What dream ye ? Your own hands have built a home,
Even for yourselves on a beloved shore :
For some, fond eyes are pining till they come,
How they will greet him when his toils are o'er,
And laughing babes rush from the well-known door !
Is this your care ? ye toil for your own good—
Ye feel and think—has some immortal power
Such purposes ? or in a human mood,
Dream ye some Power thus builds for man in solitude ?

V

" ' What is that Power ? Ye mock yourselves, and give
A human heart to what ye cannot know :
As if the cause of life could think and live !
'Twere as if man's own works should feel, and show
The hopes, and fears, and thoughts, from which they flow,
And he be like to them. Lo ! Plague is free
To waste, Blight, Poison, Earthquake, Hail, and Snow,
Disease, and Want, and worse necessity
Of hate and ill, and Pride, and Fear, and Tyranny.

VI

" ' What is that Power ? Some moonstruck sophist stood
Watching the shade from his own soul upthrown
Fill Heaven and darken Earth, and in such mood
The Form he saw and worshipped was his own,
His likeness in the world's vast mirror shown ;

And 'twere an innocent dream, but that a faith
Nursed by fear's dew of poison, grows thereon,
And that men say, that Power has chosen Death
On all who scorn its laws, to wreak immortal wrath.

VII

" ' Men say that they themselves have heard and seen,
Or known from others who have known such things,
A Shade, a Form, which Earth and Heaven between
Wields an invisible rod—that Priests and Kings,
Custom, domestic sway, ay, all that brings
Man's free-born soul beneath the oppressor's heel,
Are his strong ministers, and that the stings
Of death will make the wise his vengeance feel,
Though truth and virtue arm their hearts with tenfold steel.

VIII

" ' And it is said, this Power will punish wrong ;
Yes, add despair to crime, and pain to pain !
And deepest hell, and deathless snakes among,
Will bind the wretch on whom is fixed a stain,
Which, like a plague, a burthen, and a bane,
Clung to him while he lived ;—for love and hate,
Virtue and vice, they say are difference vain—
The will of strength is right—this human state
Tyrants, that they may rule, with lies thus desolate.

IX

" ' Alas, what strength ?   Opinion is more frail
Than yon dim cloud now fading on the moon
Even while we gaze, though it awhile avail
To hide the orb of truth—and every throne
Of Earth or Heaven, though shadow rests thereon,
One shape of many names :—for this ye plough
The barren waves of ocean ; hence each one
Is slave or tyrant ; all betray and bow,
Command, or kill, or fear, or wreak, or suffer woe.

X

" ' Its names are each a sign which maketh holy
All' power—ay, the ghost, the dream, the shade,
Of power—lust, falsehood, hate, and pride, and folly ;
The pattern whence all fraud and wrong is made,
A law to which mankind has been betrayed ;
And human love, is as the name well known
Of a dear mother, whom the murderer laid
In bloody grave, and, into darkness thrown,
Gathered her wildered babes around him as his own.

XI

" ' O love ! who to the hearts of wandering men
Art as the calm to Ocean's weary waves !
Justice, or truth, or joy ! thou only can
From slavery and religion's labyrinth caves
Guide us, as one clear star the seamen saves.
To give to all an equal share of good,
To track the steps of freedom, though through graves

She pass ; to suffer all in patient mood ;
To weep for crime, though stained with thy friend's dearest blood ;

XII

" ' To feel the peace of self-contentment's lot,
To own all sympathies, and outrage none ;
And, in the inmost bowers of sense and thought,
Until life's sunny day is quite gone down,
To sit and smile with Joy, or, not alone,
To kiss salt tears from the worn cheek of Woe ;
To live, as if to love and live were one ;—
This is not faith or law, nor those who bow
To thrones on Heaven or Earth such destiny may know.

XIII

" ' But children near their parents tremble now,
Because they must obey—one rules another,
And as one Power rules both high and low,
So man is made the captive of his brother,
And Hate is throned on high with Fear her mother,
Above the Highest—and those fountain-cells,
Whence love yet flowed when faith had choked all other,
Are darkened—Woman, as the bond-slave, dwells
Of man, a slave ; and life is poisoned in its wells.

XIV

" ' Man seeks for gold in mines, that he may weave
A lasting chain for his own slavery ;—
In fear and restless care that he may live
He toils for others, who must ever be
The joyless thralls of like captivity ;
He murders, for his chiefs delight in ruin ;
He builds the altar, that its idol's fee
May be his very blood ; he is pursuing,
O, blind and willing wretch ! his own obscure undoing.

XV

" ' Woman !—she is his slave, she has become
A thing I weep to speak—the child of scorn,
The outcast of a desolated home.
Falsehood, and fear, and toil, like waves have worn
Channels upon her cheek, which smiles adorn,
As calm decks the false Ocean :—well ye know
What Woman is, for none of Woman born
Can choose but drain the bitter dregs of woe,
Which ever from the oppressed to the oppressors flow.

XVI

" ' This need not be ; ye might arise, and will
That gold should lose its power, and thrones their glory ;
That love, which none may bind, be free to fill
The world, like light ; and evil faith, grown hoary
With crime, be quenched and die.—Yon promontory
Even now eclipses the descending moon !—
Dungeons and palaces are transitory—
High temples fade like vapour—Man alone
Remains, whose will has power when all beside is gone.

XVII

" ' Let all be free and equal !—From your hearts
I feel an echo ; through my inmost frame
Like sweetest sound, seeking its mate, it darts—
Whence come ye, friends ?   Alas, I cannot name
All that I read of sorrow, toil, and shame,
On your worn faces ; as in legends old
Which make immortal the disastrous fame
Of conquerors and impostors false and bold,
The discord of your hearts I in your looks behold.

XVIII

" ' Whence come ye, friends ? from pouring human blood
Forth on the earth ? or bring ye steel and gold,
That Kings may dupe and slay the multitude ?
Or from the famished poor, pale, weak, and cold,
Bear ye the earnings of their toil ? unfold !
Speak ! are your hands in slaughter's sanguine hue
Stain'd freshly ? have your hearts in guile grown old ?
Know yourselves thus ? ye shall be pure as dew,
And I will be a friend and sister unto you.

XIX

" ' Disguise it not—we have one human heart—
All mortal thoughts confess a common home :
Blush not for what may to thyself impart
Stains of inevitable crime : the doom
Is this, which has, or may, or must, become
Thine, and all humankind's.   Ye are the spoil
Which Time thus marks for the devouring tomb,
Thou and thy thoughts and they, and all the toil
Wherewith ye twine the rings of life's perpetual coil.

XX

" ' Disguise it not—ye blush for what ye hate,
And Enmity is sister unto Shame ;
Look on your mind—it is the book of fate—
Ah ! it is dark with many a blazoned name
Of misery—all are mirrors of the same ;
But the dark fiend who with his iron pen,
Dipped in scorn's fiery poison, makes his fame
Enduring there, would o'er the heads of men
Pass harmless, if they scorned to make their hearts his den.

XXI

" ' Yes, it is Hate, that shapeless fiendly thing
Of many names, all evil, some divine,
Whom self-contempt arms with a mortal sting ;
Which, when the heart its snaky folds entwine,
Is wasted quite, and when it doth repine
To gorge such bitter prey, on all beside
It turns with ninefold rage, as with its twine
When Amphisbæna some fair bird has tied,
Soon o'er the putrid mass he threats on every side.

XXII

" ' Reproach not thine own soul, but know thyself,
Nor hate another's crime, nor loathe thine own.
It is the dark idolatry of self,

Which, when our thoughts and actions once are gone,
Demands that man should weep, and bleed, and groan ;
O vacant expiation ! be at rest.—
The past is Death's, the future is thine own ;
And love and joy can make the foulest breast
A paradise of flowers, where peace might build her nest.'

XXIII

" ' Speak thou ! whence come ye ? '—A Youth made reply,
' Wearily, wearily o'er the boundless deep
We sail ;—thou readest well the misery
Told in these faded eyes, but much doth sleep
Within, which there the poor heart loves to keep,
Or dare not write on the dishonoured brow ;
Even from our childhood have we learned to steep
The bread of slavery in the tears of woe,
And never dreamed of hope or refuge until now.

XXIV

" ' Yes—I must speak—my secret would have perished
Even with the heart it wasted, as a brand
Fades in the dying flame whose life it cherished,
But that no human bosom can withstand
Thee, wondrous Lady, and the mild command
Of thy keen eyes :—yes, we are wretched slaves,
Who from their wonted loves and native land
Are reft, and bear o'er the dividing waves
The unregarded prey of calm and happy graves.

XXV

" ' We drag afar from pastoral vales the fairest
Among the daughters of those mountains lone,
We drag them there, where all things best and rarest
Are stained and trampled :—years have come and gone
Since, like the ship which bears me, I have known
No thought ;—but now the eyes of one dear Maid
On mine with light of mutual love have shone—
She is my life,—I am but as the shade
Of her,—a smoke sent up from ashes, soon to fade.

XXVI

" ' For she must perish in the tyrant's hall—
Alas, alas ! '—He ceased, and by the sail
Sate cowering—but his sobs were heard by all,
And still before the ocean and the gale
The ship fled fast till the stars 'gan to fail.
All round me gathered with mute countenance,
The Seamen gazed, the Pilot, worn and pale
With toil, the Captain with grey locks, whose glance
Met mine in restless awe—they stood as in a trance.

XXVII

" ' Recede not ! pause not now ! thou art grown old,
But Hope will make thee young, for Hope and Youth
Are children of one mother, even Love—behold !
The eternal stars gaze on us !—is the truth

Within your soul ? care for your own, or ruth
For other's sufferings ? do ye thirst to bear
A heart which not the serpent custom's tooth
May violate ?—Be free ! and even here,
Swear to be firm till death ! ' They cried, ' We swear ! we swear ! '

XXVIII

" The very darkness shook, as with a blast
Of subterranean thunder at the cry ;
The hollow shore its thousand echoes cast
Into the night, as if the sea, and sky,
And earth, rejoiced with new born liberty,
For in that name they swore ! Bolts were undrawn,
And on the deck, with unaccustomed eye
The captives gazing stood, and every one
Shrank as the inconstant torch upon her countenance shone.

XXIX

" They were earth's purest children, young and fair,
With eyes the shrines of unawakened thought,
And brows as bright as spring or morning, ere
Dark time had there its evil legend wrought
In characters of cloud which wither not.—
The change was like a dream to them ; but soon
They knew the glory of their altered lot,
In the bright wisdom of youth's breathless noon,
Sweet talk, and smiles, and sighs, all bosoms did attune.

XXX

" But one was mute, her cheeks and lips most fair,
Changing their hue like lilies newly blown,
Beneath a bright acacia's shadowy hair,
Waved by the wind amid the sunny noon,
Showed that her soul was quivering ; and full soon
That Youth arose, and breathlessly did look
On her and me, as for some speechless boon :
I smiled, and both their hands in mine I took,
And felt a soft delight from what their spirits shook.

CANTO IX

I

" THAT night we anchored in a woody bay,
And sleep no more around us dared to hover
Than, when all doubt and fear has passed away,
It shades the couch of some unresting lover,
Whose heart is now at rest : thus night passed over
In mutual joy :—around, a forest grew
Of poplars and dark oaks, whose shade did cover
The waning stars, prankt in the waters blue,
And trembled in the wind which from the morning flew.

II

" The joyous mariners, and each free maiden,
Now brought from the deep forest many a bough,
With woodland spoil most innocently laden ;

Soon wreaths of budding foliage seemed to flow
Over the mast and sails, the stern and prow
Were canopied with blooming boughs,—the while
On the slant sun's path o'er the waves we go
Rejoicing, like the dwellers of an isle
Doomed to pursue those waves that cannot cease to smile.

III

" The many ships spotting the dark blue deep
With snowy sails, fled fast as ours came nigh,
In fear and wonder ; and on every steep
Thousands did gaze, they heard the startling cry,
Like earth's own voice lifted unconquerably
To all her children, the unbounded mirth,
The glorious joy of thy name—Liberty !
They heard !—As o'er the mountains of the earth
From peak to peak leap on the beams of morning's birth :

IV

" So from that cry over the boundless hills,
Sudden was caught one universal sound,
Like a volcano's voice, whose thunder fills
Remotest skies,—such glorious madness found
A path through human hearts with stream which drowned
Its struggling fears and cares, dark custom's brood ;
They knew not whence it came, but felt around
A wide contagion poured—they called aloud
On Liberty—that name lived on the sunny flood.

V

" We reached the port—alas ! from many spirits
The wisdom which had waked that cry, was fled,
Like the brief glory which dark Heaven inherits
From the false dawn, which fades ere it is spread,
Upon the night's devouring darkness shed :
Yet soon bright day will burst—even like a chams
Of fire, to burn the shrouds outworn and dead,
Which wrap the world ; a wide enthusiasm,
To cleanse the fevered world as with an earthquake's spasm.

VI

" I walked through the great City then, but free
From shame or fear ; those toil-worn Mariners
And happy Maidens did encompass me ;
And like a subterranean wind that stirs
Some forest among caves, the hopes and fears
From every human soul, a murmur strange
Made as I past ; and many wept, with tears
Of joy and awe, and winged thoughts did range,
And half-extinguished words, which prophesied of change.

VII

" For, with strong speech I tore the veil that hid
Nature, and Truth, and Liberty, and Love,—
As one who from some mountain's pyramid,
Points to the unrisen sun !—the shades approve

His truth, and flee from every stream and grove.
Thus, gentle thoughts did many a bosom fill,—
Wisdom the mail of tried affections wove
For many a heart, and tameless scorn of ill
Thrice steeped in molten steel the unconquerable will.

VIII

" Some said I was a maniac wild and lost ;
Some, that I scarce had risen from the grave
The Prophet's virgin bride, a heavenly ghost :—
Some said I was a fiend from my weird cave,
Who had stolen human shape, and o'er the wave,
The forest, and the mountain, came ;—some said
I was the child of God, sent down to save
Women from bonds and death, and on my head
The burthen of their sins would frightfully be laid.

IX

" But soon my human words found sympathy
In human hearts : the purest and the best,
As friend with friend made common cause with me,
And they were few, but resolute ;—the rest,
Ere yet success the enterprise had blest,
Leagued with me in their hearts ;—their meals, their slumber,
Their hourly occupations, were possest
By hopes which I had armed to overnumber
Those hosts of meaner cares, which life's strong wings encumber.

X

" But chiefly women, whom my voice did waken
From their cold, careless, willing slavery,
Sought me : one truth their dreary prison has shaken,
They looked around, and lo ! they became free !
Their many tyrants sitting desolately
In slave-deserted halls, could none restrain ;
For wrath's red fire had withered in the eye,
Whose lightning once was death,—nor fear, nor gain
Could tempt one captive now to lock another's chain.

XI

" Those who were sent to bind me, wept, and felt
Their minds outsoar the bonds which clasped them round,
Even as a waxen shape may waste and melt
In the white furnace ; and a visioned swound,
A pause of hope and awe, the City bound,
Which, like the silence of a tempest's birth,
When in its awful shadow it has wound
The sun, the wind, the ocean, and the earth,
Hung terrible, ere yet the lightnings have leapt forth.

XII

" Like clouds inwoven in the silent sky,
By winds from distant regions meeting there,
In the high name of truth and liberty,
Around the City millions gathered were,
By hopes which sprang from many a hidden lair ;

Words, which the lore of truth in hues of grace
Arrayed, thine own wild songs which in the air
Like homeless odours floated, and the name
Of thee, and many a tongue which thou hadst dipped in flame.

XIII

" The Tyrant knew his power was gone, but Fear,
The nurse of Vengeance, bade him wait the event—
That perfidy and custom, gold and prayer,
And whatsoe'er, when force is impotent,
To fraud the sceptre of the world has lent,
Might as he judged, confirm his failing sway.
Therefore throughout the streets, the Priests he sent
To curse the rebels.—To their gods did they
For Earthquake, Plague, and Want, kneel in the public way.

XIV

" And grave and hoary men were bribed to tell
From seats where law is made the slave of wrong,
How glorious Athens in her splendour fell,
Because her sons were free,—and that among
Mankind, the many to the few belong,
By Heaven, and Nature, and Necessity.
They said, that age was truth, and that the young
Marred with wild hopes the peace of slavery,
With which old times and men had quelled the vain and free.

XV

" And with the falsehood of their poisonous lips
They breathed on the enduring memory
Of sages and of bards a brief eclipse ;
There was one teacher, whom necessity
Had armed with strength and wrong against mankind,
His slave and his avenger aye to be ;
That we were weak and sinful, frail and blind,
And that the will of one was peace, and we
Should seek for nought on earth but toil and misery.

XVI

" ' For thus we might avoid the hell hereafter.'
So spake the hypocrites, who cursed and lied ;
Alas, their sway was past and tears and laughter
Clung to their hoary hair, withering the pride
Which in their hollow hearts dared still abide ;
And yet obscener slaves with smoother brow,
And sneers on their strait lips, thin, blue, and wide,
Said, that the rule of men was over now,
And hence, the subject world to woman's will must bow ;

XVII

" And gold was scattered through the streets, and wine
Flowed at a hundred feasts within the wall.
In vain ! The steady towers in Heaven did shine
As they were wont, nor at the priestly call
Left Plague her banquet in the Æthiop's hall,

Nor Famine from the rich man's portal came,
Where at her ease she ever preys on all
Who throng to kneel for food : nor fear, nor shame,
Nor faith, nor discord, dimmed hope's newly kindled flame.

XVIII

" For gold was as a god whose faith began
To fade, so that its worshippers were few,
And Faith itself, which in the heart of man
Gives shape, voice, name, to spectral Terror, knew
Its downfall, as the altars lonelier grew,
Till the Priests stood alone within the fane
The shafts of falsehood unpolluting flew,
And the cold sneers of calumny were vain
The union of the free with discord's brand to stain.

XIX

" The rest thou knowest.—Lo !—we two are here—
We have survived a ruin wide and deep—
Strange thoughts are mine.—I cannot grieve nor fear,
Sitting with thee upon this lonely steep
I smile, though human love should make me weep.
We have survived a joy that knows no sorrow,
And I do feel a mighty calmness creep
Over my heart, which can no longer borrow
Its hues from chance or change, dark children of to-morrow.

XX

" We know not what will come—yet, Laon, dearest,
Cythna shall be the prophetess of love,
Her lips shall rob thee of the grace thou wearest,
To hide thy heart, and clothe the shapes which rove
Within the homeless future's wintry grove ;
For I now, sitting thus beside thee, seem
Even with thy breath and blood to live and move,
And violence and wrong are as a dream
Which rolls from steadfast truth, an unreturning stream.

XXI

" The blasts of autumn drive the winged seeds
Over the earth,—next come the snows, and rain,
And frosts, and storms, which dreary winter leads
Out of his Scythian cave, a savage train ;
Behold ! Spring sweeps over the world again,
Shedding soft dews from her ethereal wings ;
Flowers on the mountains, fruits over the plain,
And music on the waves and woods she flings,
And love on all that lives, and calm on lifeless things.

XXII

" O Spring ! of hope, and love, and youth, and gladness,
Wind-winged emblem ! brightest, best, and fairest !
Whence comest thou, when, with dark winter's sadness
The tears that fade in sunny smiles thou sharest ?
Sister of joy ! thou art the child who wearest

Thy mother's dying smile, tender and sweet ;
Thy mother Autumn, for whose grave thou bearest
Fresh flowers, and beams like flowers, with gentle feet,
Disturbing not the leaves which are her winding-sheet.

XXIII

" Virtue, and Hope, and Love, like light and Heaven,
Surround the world.—We are their chosen slaves.
Has not the whirlwind of our spirit driven
Truth's deathless germs to thought's remotest caves ?
Lo, Winter comes !—the grief of many graves,
The frost of death, the tempest of the sword,
The flood of tyranny, whose sanguine waves
Stagnate like ice at Faith, the enchanter's word,
And bind all human hearts in its repose abhorred.

XXIV

" The seeds are sleeping in the soil : meanwhile
The tyrant peoples dungeons with his prey ;
Pale victims on the guarded scaffold smile
Because they cannot speak ; and, day by day,
The moon of wasting Science wanes away
Among her stars, and in that darkness vast
The sons of earth to their foul idols pray,
And grey Priests triumph, and like blight or blast
A shade of selfish care o'er human looks is cast.

XXV

" This is the Winter of the world ;—and here
We die, even as the winds of Autumn fade,
Expiring in the frore and foggy air.—
Behold !   Spring comes, though we must pass, who made
The promise of its birth,—even as the shade
Which from our death, as from a mountain, flings
The future, a broad sunrise ; thus arrayed
As with the plumes of overshadowing wings,
From its dark gulf of chains, Earth like an eagle springs.

XXVI

" O dearest love ! we shall be dead and cold
Before this morn may on the world arise :
Wouldst thou the glory of its dawn behold ?
Alas ! gaze not on me, but turn thine eyes
On thine own heart—it is a paradise
Which everlasting spring has made its own,
And while drear winter fills the naked skies,
Sweet streams of sunny thought, and flowers fresh blown
Are there, and weave their sounds and odours into one.

XXVII

" In their own hearts the earnest of the hope
Which made them great, the good will ever find ;
And though some envious shade may interlope
Between the effect and it, one comes behind,
Who aye the future to the past will bind—

Necessity, whose sightless strength for ever
Evil with evil, good with good, must wind
In bands of union, which no power may sever :
They must bring forth their kind, and be divided never !

XXVIII

" The good and mighty of departed ages
Are in their graves, the innocent and free,
Heroes, and Poets, and prevailing Sages,
Who leave the vesture of their majesty
To adorn and clothe this naked world ;—and we
Are like to them—such perish, but they leave
All hope, or love, or truth, or liberty,
Whose forms their mighty spirits could conceive
To be a rule and law to ages that survive.

XXIX

" So be the turf heaped over our remains
Even in our happy youth, and that strange lot
Whate'er it be, when in these mingling veins
The blood is still, be ours ; let sense and thought
Pass from our being, or be numbered not
Among the things that are ; let those who come
Behind, for whom our steadfast will has bought
A calm inheritance, a glorious doom,
Insult with careless tread our undivided tomb.

XXX

" Our many thoughts and deeds, our life and love,
Our happiness, and all that we have been,
Immortally must live, and burn, and move,
When we shall be no more ; the world has seen
A type of peace ; and as some most serene
And lovely spot to a poor maniac's eye,
After long years, some sweet and moving scene
Of youthful hope returning suddenly,
Quells his long madness—thus man shall remember thee.

XXXI

" And calumny meanwhile shall feed on us,
As worms devour the dead, and near the throne
And at the altar, most accepted thus
Shall sneers and curses be ;—what we have done
None shall dare vouch, though it be truly known ;
That record shall remain, when they must pass
Who built their pride on its oblivion ;
And fame, in human hope which sculptured was,
Survive the perished scrolls of unenduring brass.

XXXII

" The while we two, beloved, must depart,
And Sense and Reason, those enchanters fair,
Whose wand of power is hope, would bid the heart
That gazed beyond the wormy grave despair :
These eyes, these lips, this blood, seems darkly there

To fade in hideous ruin ; no calm sleep
Peopling with golden dreams the stagnant air,
Seems our obscure and rotting eyes to steep
In joy ;—but senseless death—a ruin dark and deep !

XXXIII

" These are blind fancies.   Reason cannot know
What sense can neither feel, nor thought conceive ;
There is delusion in the world—and woe,
And fear, and pain—we know not whence we live,
Or why, or how, or what mute Power may give
Their being to each plant, and star, and beast,
Or even these thoughts.—Come near me !   I do weave
A chain I cannot break—I am possest
With thoughts too swift and strong for one lone human breast.

XXXIV

" Yes, yes—thy kiss is sweet, thy lips are warm—
O ! willingly, beloved, would these eyes,
Might they no more drink being from thy form,
Even as to sleep whence we again arise,
Close their faint orbs in death.   I fear nor prize
Aught that can now betide, unshared by thee—
Yes, Love, when wisdom fails, makes Cythna wise ;
Darkness and death, if death be true, must be
Dearer than life and hope, if unenjoyed with thee.

XXXV

" Alas ! our thoughts flow on with stream, whose waters
Return not to their fountain—Earth and Heaven,
The Ocean and the Sun, the clouds their daughters,
Winter, and Spring, and Morn, and Noon, and Even,
All that we are or know, is darkly driven
Towards one gulf.—Lo ! what a change is come
Since I first spake—but time shall be forgiven,
Though it change all but thee ! "   She ceased—night's gloom
Meanwhile had fallen on earth from the sky's sunless dome.

XXXVI

Though she had ceased, her countenance, uplifted
To heaven, still spake, with solemn glory bright ;
Her dark deep eyes, her lips, whose motions gifted
The air they breathed with love, her locks undight :
" Fair star of life and love," I cried, " my soul's delight,
Why lookest thou on the crystalline skies ?
O that my spirit were yon Heaven of night,
Which gazes on thee with its thousand eyes ! "
She turned to me and smiled—that smile was Paradise !

CANTO X

I

Was there a human spirit in the steed,
That thus with his proud voice, ere night was gone,
He broke our linked rest ? or do indeed
All living things a common nature own,

And thought erect a universal throne,
Where many shapes one tribute ever bear ?
And Earth, their mutual mother, does she groan
To see her sons contend ? and makes she bare
Her breast, that all in peace its drainless stores may share ?

II

I have heard friendly sounds from many a tongue
Which was not human—the lone Nightingale
Has answered me with her most soothing song,
Out of her ivy bower, when I sate pale
With grief, and sighed beneath ; from many a dale
The Antelopes who flocked for food have spoken
With happy sounds, and motions, that avail
Like man's own speech : and such was now the token
Of waning night, whose calm by that proud neigh was broken.

III

Each night, that mighty steed bore me abroad,
And I returned with food to our retreat,
And dark intelligence ; the blood which flowed
Over the fields, had stained the courser's feet ;—
Soon the dust drinks that bitter dew,—then meet
The vulture, and the wild-dog, and the snake,
The wolf, and the hyæna grey, and eat
The dead in horrid truce : their throngs did make
Behind the steed, a chasm like waves in a ship's wake.

IV

For, from the utmost realms of earth, came pouring
The banded slaves whom every despot sent
At that throned traitor's summons ; like the roaring
Of fire, whose floods the wild deer circumvent
In the scorched pastures of the South ; so bent
The armies of the leagued kings around
Their files of steel and flame ;—the continent
Trembled, as with a zone of ruin bound ;
Beneath their feet, the sea shook with their navies' sound.

V

From every nation of the earth they came,
The multitude of moving heartless things,
Whom slaves call men : obediently they came,
Like sheep whom from the fold the shepherd brings
To the stall, red with blood ; their many kings
Led them, thus erring, from their native home ;
Tartar and Frank, and millions whom the wings
Of Indian breezes lull, and many a band
The Arctic Anarch sent, and Idumea's sand,

VI

Fertile in prodigies and lies ;—so there
Strange natures made a brotherhood of ill.
The desert savage ceased to grasp in fear
His Asian shield and bow, when, at the will
Of Europe's subtler son, the bolt would kill

Some shepherd sitting on a rock secure ;
But smiles of wondering joy his face would fill,
And savage sympathy : those slaves impure,
Each one the other thus from ill to ill did lure.

VII

For traitorously did that foul Tyrant robe
His countenance in lies ;—even at the hour
When he was snatched from death, then o'er the globe,
With secret signs from many a mountain tower,
With smoke by day, and fire by night, the power
Of king and priests, those dark conspirators
He called :—they knew his cause their own, and swore
Like wolves and serpents to their mutual wars
Strange truce, with many a rite which Earth and Heaven abhors.

VIII

Myriads had come—millions were on their way ;
The Tyrant passed, surrounded by the steel
Of hired assassins, through the public way,
Choked with his country's dead ;—his footsteps reel
On the fresh blood—he smiles. " Ay, now I feel
I am a King in truth ! " he said, and took
His royal seat, and bade the torturing wheel
Be brought, and fire, and pincers, and the hook,
And scorpions ! that his soul on its revenge might look.

IX

" But first, go slay the rebels.—Why return
The victor bands ? " he said :. " millions yet live,
Of whom the weakest with one word might turn
The scales of victory yet ; let none survive
But those within the walls—each fifth shall give
The expiation for his brethren here.—
Go forth, and waste and kill ; "—" O king, forgive
My speech," a soldier answered ; " but we fear
The spirits of the night, and morn is drawing near ;

X

" For we were slaying still without remorse,
And now that dreadful chief beneath my hand
Defenceless lay, when on a hell-black horse,
An Angel bright as day, waving a brand
Which flashed among the stars, passed."—" Dost thou stand
Parleying with me, thou wretch ? " the king replied :
" Slaves, bind him to the wheel ; and of this band,
Whoso will drag that woman to his side
That scared him thus, may burn his dearest foe beside ;

XI

" And gold and glory shall be his.—Go forth ! "
They rushed into the plain.—Loud was the roar
Of their career : the horsemen shook the earth ;
The wheeled artillery's speed the pavement tore ;
The infantry, file after file, did pour

Their clouds on the utmost hills. Five days they slew
Among the wasted fields : the sixth saw gore
Stream through the city ; on the seventh, the dew
Of slaughter became stiff ; and there was peace anew :

XII

Peace in the desert fields and villages,
Between the glutted beasts and mangled dead !
Peace in the silent streets ! save when the cries
Of victims, to their fiery judgment led,
Made pale their voiceless lips, who seemed to dread
Even in their dearest kindred, lest some tongue
Be faithless to the fear yet unbetrayed ;
Peace in the Tyrant's palace, where the throng
Waste the triumphal hours in festival and song !

XIII

Day after day the burning Sun rolled on
Over the death-polluted land ;—it came
Out of the east like fire, and fiercely shone
A lamp of Autumn, ripening with its flame
The few lone ears of corn ;—the sky became
Stagnate with heat, so that each cloud and blast
Languished and died ; the thirsting air did claim
All moisture, and a rotting vapour past
From the unburied dead, invisible and fast.

XIV

First Want, then Plague, came on the beasts ; their food
Failed, and they drew the breath of its decay.
Millions on millions, whom the scent of blood
Had lured, or who, from regions far away,
Had tracked the hosts in festival array,
From their dark deserts ; gaunt and wasting now,
Stalked like fell shades among their perished prey ;
In their green eyes a strange disease did glow,
They sank in hideous spasm, or pains severe and slow.

XV

The fish were poisoned in the streams ; the birds
In the green woods perished ; the insect race
Was withered up ; the scattered flocks and herds
Who had survived the wild beasts' hungry chase
Died moaning, each upon the other's face
In helpless agony gazing ; round the City
All night, the lean hyænas their sad case
Like starving infants wailed—a woeful ditty !
And many a mother wept, pierced with unnatural pity.

XVI

Amid the aërial minarets on high,
The Æthiopian vultures fluttering fell
From their long line of brethren in the sky,
Startling the concourse of mankind.—Too well
These signs the coming mischief did foretell :—

Strange panic first, a deep and sickening dread
Within each heart, like ice, did sink and dwell,
A voiceless thought of evil, which did spread
With the quick glance of eyes, like withering lightnings shed.

XVII

Day after day, when the year wanes, the frosts
Strip its green crown of leaves, till all is bare;
So on those strange and congregated hosts
Came Famine, a swift shadow, and the air
Groaned with the burden of a new despair;
Famine, than whom Misrule no deadlier daughter
Feeds from her thousand breasts, though sleeping there
With lidless eyes, lie Faith, and Plague, and Slaughter,
A ghastly brood; conceived of Lethe's sullen water.

XVIII

There was no food; the corn was trampled down,
The flocks and herds had perished; on the shore
The dead and putrid fish were ever thrown:
The deeps were foodless, and the winds no more
Creaked with the weight of birds, but, as before
Those winged things sprang forth, were void of shade;
The vines and orchards, Autumn's golden store,
Were burned; so that the meanest food was weighed
With gold, and Avarice died before the god it made.

XIX

There was no corn—in the wide market-place
All loathliest things, even human flesh, was sold;
They weighed it in small scales—and many a face
Was fixed in eager horror then: his gold
The miser brought; the tender maid, grown bold
Through hunger, bared her scorned charms in vain;
The mother brought her eldest-born, controlled
By instinct blind as love, but turned again
And bade her infant suck, and died in silent pain.

XX

Then fell blue Plague upon the race of man.
" O, for the sheathed steel, so late which gave
Oblivion to the dead, when the streets ran
With brothers' blood! O, that the earthquake's grave
Would gape, or Ocean lift its stifling wave! "
Vain cries—throughout the streets, thousands pursued
Each by his fiery torture, howl and rave,
Or sit, in frenzy's unimagined mood,
Upon fresh heaps of dead—a ghastly multitude.

XXI

It was not hunger now, but thirst. Each well
Was choked with rotting corpses, and became
A cauldron of green mist made visible
At sunrise. Thither still the myriads came,
Seeking to quench the agony of the flame

Which raged like poison through their bursting veins ;
Naked they were from torture, without shame,
Spotted with nameless scars and lurid blains,
Childhood, and youth, and age, writhing in savage pains.

XXII

It was not thirst but madness ! Many saw
Their own lean image everywhere ; it went
A ghastlier self beside them, till the awe
Of that dread sight to self-destruction sent
Those shrieking victims ; some, ere life was spent,
Sought, with a horrid sympathy, to shed
Contagion on the sound ; and others rent
Their matted hair, and cried aloud, " We tread
On fire ! the avenging Power his hell on earth has spread."

XXIII

Sometimes the living by the dead were hid.
Near the great fountain in the public square,
Where corpses made a crumbling pyramid
Under the sun, was heard one stifled prayer
For life, in the hot silence of the air ;
And strange 'twas, amid that hideous heap to see
Some shrouded in their long and golden hair,
As if not dead, but slumbering quietly,
Like forms which sculptors carve, then love to agony.

XXIV

Famine had spared the palace of the king :—
He rioted in festival the while,
He and his guards and priests ; but Plague did fling
One shadow upon all. Famine can smile
On him who brings it food, and pass, with guile
Of thankful falsehood, like a courtier grey,
The house-dog of the throne ; but many a mile
Comes Plague, a winged wolf, who loathes alway
The garbage and the scum that strangers make her prey.

XXV

So, near the throne, amid the gorgeous feast,
Sheathed in resplendent arms, or loosely dight
To luxury, ere the mockery yet had ceased
That lingered on his lips, the warriors might
Was loosened, and a new and ghastlier night
In dreams of frenzy lapped his eyes ; he fell
Headlong, or with stiff eyeballs sate upright
Among the guests, or raving mad, did tell
Strange truths ; a dying seer of dark oppression's hell.

XXVI

The Princes and the Priests were pale with terror ;
That monstrous faith wherewith they ruled mankind
Fell, like a shaft loosed by the bowman's error,
On their own hearts : they sought and they could find
No refuge—'twas the blind who led the blind !

So, through the desolate streets to the high fane,
The many-tongued and endless armies wind
In sad procession : each among the train
To his own Idol lifts his supplications vain.

XXVII

" O God ! " they cried, " we know our secret pride
Has scorned thee, and thy worship, and thy name;
Secure in human power, we have defied
Thy fearful might ; we bend in fear and shame
Before thy presence ; with the dust we claim
Kindred.   Be merciful, O King of Heaven !
Most justly have we suffered for thy fame
Made dim, but be at length our sins forgiven,
Ere to despair and death thy worshippers be driven.

XXVIII

" O King of Glory !   Thou alone hast power !
Who can resist thy will ? who can restrain
Thy wrath, when on the guilty thou dost shower
The shafts of thy revenge,—a blistering rain ?
Greatest and best, be merciful again !
Have we not stabbed thine enemies, and made
The Earth an altar, and the Heavens a fane,
Where thou wert worshipped with their blood, and laid
Those hearts in dust which would thy searchless works have weighed ?

XXIX

" Well didst thou loosen on this impious City
Thine angels of revenge : recall them now ;
Thy worshippers abased, here kneel for pity,
And bind their souls by an immortal vow :
We swear by thee !   And to our oath do thou
Give sanction, from thine hell of fiends and flame,
That we will kill with fire and torments slow,
The last of those who mocked thy holy name,
And scorned the sacred laws thy prophets did proclaim."

XXX

Thus they with trembling limbs and pallid lips
Worshipped their own hearts' image, dim and vast,
Scared by the shade wherewith they would eclipse
The light of other minds ;—troubled they past
From the great Temple.   Fiercely still and fast
The arrows of the plague among them fell,
And they on one another gazed aghast,
And through the hosts contention wild befell,
As each of his own god the wondrous works did tell.

XXXI

And Oromaze, Joshua, and Mahomet,
Moses, and Buddh, Zerdusht, and Brahm, and Foh,
A tumult of strange names, which never met
Before, as watchwords of a single woe,
Arose.   Each raging votary 'gan to throw

Aloft his armed hands, and each did howl
" Our God alone is God ! " and slaughter now
Would have gone forth, when, from beneath a cowl,
A voice came forth, which pierced like ice through every soul.

XXXII

'Twas an Iberian Priest from whom it came,
A zealous man, who led the legioned west
With words which faith and pride had steeped in flame,
To quell the unbelievers ; a dire guest
Even to his friends was he, for in his breast
Did hate and guile lie watchful, intertwined,
Twin serpents in one deep and winding nest ;
He loathed all faith beside his own, and pined
To wreak his fear of Heaven in vengeance on mankind.

XXXIII

But more he loathed and hated the clear light
Of wisdom and free thought, and more did fear,
Lest, kindled once, its beams might pierce the night,
Even where his Idol stood ; for, far and near
Did many a heart in Europe leap to hear
That faith and tyranny were trampled down ;
Many a pale victim, doomed for truth to share
The murderer's cell, or see, with helpless groan,
The priests his children drag for slaves to serve their own.

XXXIV

He dared not kill the infidels with fire
Or steel, in Europe ; the slow agonies
Of legal torture mocked his keen desire :
So he made truce with those who did despise
The expiation, and the sacrifice,
That, though detested, Islam's kindred creed
Might crush for him those deadlier enemies ;
For fear of God did in his bosom breed,
A jealous hate of man, an unreposing need.

XXXV

" Peace ! Peace ! " he cried. " When we are dead, the Day
Of Judgment comes, and all shall surely know
Whose God is God, each fearfully shall pay
The errors of his faith in endless woe !
But there is sent a mortal vengeance now
On earth, because an impious race had spurned
Him whom we all adore,—a subtile foe,
By whom for ye this dread reward was earned,
And kingly thrones, which rest on faith, nigh overturned.

XXXVI

" Think ye, because we weep, and kneel, and pray,
That God will lull the pestilence ?   It rose
Even from beneath his throne, where, many a day
His mercy soothed it to a dark repose :
It walks upon the earth to judge his foes,

And what art thou and I, that he should deign
To curb his ghastly minister, or close
The gates of death, ere they receive the twain
Who shook with mortal spells his undefended reign ?

XXXVII

" Ay, there is famine in the gulf of hell,
Its giant worms of fire for ever yawn,—
Their lurid eyes are on us ! Those who fell
By the swift shafts of pestilence ere dawn,
Are in their jaws ! They hunger for the spawn
Of Satan, their own brethren, who were sent
To make our souls their spoil. See ! see ! they fawn
Like dogs, and they will sleep with luxury spent,
When those detested hearts their iron fangs have rent !

XXXVIII

" Our God may then lull Pestilence to sleep :—
Pile high the pyre of expiation now !
A forest's spoil of boughs, and on the heap
Pour venomous gums, which sullenly and slow,
When touched by flame, shall burn, and melt, and flow,
A stream of clinging fire,—and fix on high
A net of iron, and spread forth below
A couch of snakes, and scorpions, and the fry
Of centipedes and worms, earth's hellish progeny !

XXXIX

" Let Laon and Laone on that pyre,
Linked tight with burning brass, perish !—then pray
That, with this sacrifice, the withering ire
Of Heaven may be appeased." He ceased, and they
A space stood silent, as far, far away
The echoes of his voice among them died ;
And he knelt down upon the dust, alway
Muttering the curses of his speechless pride,
Whilst shame, and fear, and awe, the armies did divide.

XL

His voice was like a blast that burst the portal
Of fabled hell ; and as he spake, each one
Saw gape beneath the chasms of fire immortal,
And Heaven above seemed cloven, where, on a throne
Girt round with storms and shadows, sate alone
Their King and Judge. Fear killed in every breast
All natural pity then, a fear unknown
Before, and with an inward fire possest,
They raged like homeless beasts whom burning woods invest.

XLI

'Twas morn.—At noon the public crier went forth,
Proclaiming through the living and the dead,
" The Monarch saith, that his great empire's worth
Is set on Laon and Laone's head :
He who but one yet living here can lead,

Or who the life from both their hearts can wring,
Shall be the kingdom's heir,—a glorious meed !
But he who both alive can hither bring,
The Princess shall espouse, and reign an equal King."

XLII

Ere night the pyre was piled, the net of iron
Was spread above, the fearful couch below ;
It overtopped the towers that did environ
That spacious square ; for Fear is never slow,
To build the thrones of Hate, her mate and foe,
So, she scourged forth the maniac multitude
To rear this pyramid—tottering and slow.
Plague-stricken, foodless, like lean herds pursued
By gad-flies, they have piled the heath, and gums, and wood.

XLIII

Night came, a starless and a moonless gloom.
Until the dawn, those hosts of many a nation
Stood round that pile, as near one lover's tomb
Two gentle sisters mourn their desolation :
And in the silence of that expectation,
Was heard on high the reptiles' hiss and crawl——
It was so deep, save when the devastation
Of the swift pest with fearful interval,
Marking its path with shrieks, among the crowd would fall.

XLIV

Morn came.—Among those sleepless multitudes,
Madness, and Fear, and Plague, and Famine, still
Heaped corpse on corpse, as in autumnal woods
The frosts of many a wind with dead leaves fill
Earth's cold and sullen brooks. In silence still
The pale survivors stood ; ere noon, the fear
Of hell became a panic, which did kill
Like hunger or disease, with whispers drear,
As " Hush ! hark ! Come they yet ? Just Heaven ! thine hour is
   near ! "

XLV

And Priests rushed through their ranks, some counterfeiting
The rage they did inspire, some mad indeed
With their own lies. They said their god was waiting
To see his enemies writhe, and burn, and bleed,—
And that, till then, the snakes of Hell had need
Of human souls.—Three hundred furnaces
Soon blazed through the wide City. where, with speed,
Men brought their infidel kindred to appease
God's wrath, and while they burned, knelt round on quivering knees.

XLVI

The noontide sun was darkened with that smoke,
The winds of eve dispersed those ashes grey.
The madness which these rites had lulled, awoke
Again at sunset.—Who shall dare to say

The deeds which night and fear brought forth, or weigh
In balance just the good and evil there?
He might man's deep and searchless heart display,
And cast a light on those dim labyrinths, where
Hope, near imagined chasms, is struggling with despair.

XLVII

'Tis said, a mother dragged three children then,
To those fierce flames which roast the eyes in the head,
And laughed and died; and that unholy men,
Feasting like fiends upon the infidel dead,
Looked from their meal, and saw an Angel tread
The visible floor of Heaven, and it was she!
And, on that night, one without doubt or dread
Came to the fire and said, " Stop, I am he!
Kill me!"—They burned them both with hellish mockery.

XLVIII

And, one by one, that night, young maidens came,
Beauteous and calm, like shapes of living stone
Clothed in the light of dreams, and by the flame
Which shrank as overgorged, they laid them down,
And sung a low sweet song, of which alone
One word was heard, and that was Liberty;
And that some kissed their marble feet, with moan
Like love, and died, and then that they did die
With happy smiles, which sunk in white tranquillity.

CANTO XI

I

SHE saw me not—she heard me not—alone
Upon the mountain's dizzy brink she stood;
She spake not, breathed not, moved not—there was thrown
Over her look, the shadow of a mood
Which only clothes the heart in solitude,
A thought of voiceless death.—She stood alone,
Above, the Heavens were spread;—below, the flood
Was murmuring in its caves;—the wind had blown
Her hair apart, thro' which her eyes and forehead shone.

II

A cloud was hanging o'er the western mountains;
Before its blue and moveless depth were flying
Grey mists poured forth from the unresting fountains
Of darkness in the North:—the day was dying:—
Sudden, the sun shone forth; its beams were lying
Like boiling gold on Ocean, strange to see,
And on the shattered vapours, which, defying
The power of light in vain, tossed restlessly
In the red Heaven, like wrecks in a tempestuous sea.

III

It was a stream of living beams, whose bank
On either side by the cloud's cleft was made ;
And where its chasms that flood of glory drank,
Its waves gushed forth like fire, and, as if swayed
By some mute tempest, rolled on *her*.   The shade
Of her bright image floated on the river
Of liquid light, which then did end and fade—
Her radiant shape upon its verge did shiver ;
Aloft her flowing hair like strings of flame did quiver.

IV

I stood beside her, but she saw me not—
She looked upon the sea, and skies, and earth.
Rapture, and love, and admiration, wrought
A passion deeper far than tears, or mirth,
Or speech, or gesture, or whate'er has birth
From common joy ; which, with the speechless feeling
That led her there, united, and shot forth
From her far eyes, a light of deep revealing,
All but her dearest self from my regard concealing.

V

Her lips were parted, and the measured breath
Was now heard there ;—her dark and intricate eyes
Orb within orb, deeper than sleep or death,
Absorbed the glories of the burning skies,
Which, mingling with her heart's deep ecstasies,
Burst from her looks and gestures ;—and a light
Of liquid tenderness, like love, did rise
From her whole frame,—an atmosphere which quite
Arrayed her in its beams, tremulous and soft and bright.

VI

She would have clasped me to her glowing frame ;
Those warm and odorous lips might soon have shed
On mine the fragrance and the invisible flame
Which now the cold winds stole ;—she would have laid
Upon my languid heart her dearest head ;
I might have heard her voice, tender and sweet ;
Her eyes mingling with mine, might soon have fed
My soul with their own joy.—One moment yet
I gazed—we parted then, never again to meet !

VII

Never but once to meet on earth again !
She heard me as I fled—her eager tone
Sank on my heart, and almost wove a chain
Around my will to link it with her own,
So that my stern resolve was almost gone.
" I cannot reach thee ! whither dost thou fly ?
My steps are faint.—Come back, thou dearest one—
Return, ah me ! return ! "   The wind passed by
On which those accents died, faint, far, and lingeringly.

VIII

Woe! woe! that moonless midnight.—Want and Pest
Were horrible, but one more fell doth rear,
As in a hydra's swarming lair, its crest
Eminent among those victims—even the Fear
Of Hell: each girt by the hot atmosphere
Of his blind agony, like a scorpion stung
By his own rage upon his burning bier
Of circling coals of fire; but still there clung
One hope, like a keen sword on starting threads uphung:

IX

Not death—death was no more refuge or rest;
Not life—it was despair to be!—not sleep,
For fiends and chasms of fire had dispossessed
All natural dreams; to wake was not to weep,
But to gaze mad and pallid, at the leap
To which the Future, like a snaky scourge,
Or like some tyrant's eye, which aye doth keep
Its withering beam upon its slaves, did urge
Their steps:—they heard the roar of Hell's sulphureous surge.

X

Each of that multitude alone, and lost
To sense of outward things, one hope yet knew;
As on a foam-girt crag some seaman tost,
Stares at the rising tide, or like the crew
Whilst now the ship is splitting through and through;
Each, if the tramp of a far steed was heard,
Started from sick despair, or if there flew
One murmur on the wind, or if some word
Which none can gather yet, the distant crowd has stirred.

XI

Why became cheeks, wan with the kiss of death,
Paler from hope? they had sustained despair.
Why watched those myriads with suspended breath
Sleepless a second night? they are not here
The victims, and hour by hour, a vision drear,
Warm corpses fall upon the clay-cold dead;
And even in death their lips are writhed with fear.—
The crowd is mute and moveless—overhead
Silent Arcturus shines—Ha! hears't thou not the tread

XII

Of rushing feet? laughter? the shout, the scream,
Of triumph not to be contained? See! hark!
They come, they come! give way! Alas, ye deem
Falsely—'tis but a crowd of maniacs stark
Driven, like a troop of spectres, through the dark
From the choked well, whence a bright death-fire sprung,
A lurid earth-star, which dropped many a spark
From its blue train, and spreading widely, clung
To their wild hair, like mist the topmost pines among.

XIII

And many, from the crowd collected there,
Joined that strange dance in fearful sympathies;
There was the silence of a long despair,
When the last echo of those terrible cries
Came from a distant street, like agonies
Stifled afar.—Before the Tyrant's throne
All night his aged Senate sate, their eyes
In stony expectation fixed; when one
Sudden before them stood, a Stranger and alone.

XIV

Dark Priests and haughty Warriors gazed on him
With baffled wonder, for a hermit's vest
Concealed his face; but when he spake, his tone,
Ere yet the matter did their thoughts arrest,
Earnest, benignant, calm, as from a breast
Void of all hate or terror, made them start;
For as with gentle accents he addressed
His speech to them, on each unwilling heart
Unusual awe did fall—a spirit-quelling dart.

XV

" Ye Princes of the Earth, ye sit aghast
Amid the ruin which yourselves have made;
Yes, Desolation heard your trumpet's blast,
And sprang from sleep!—dark Terror has obeyed
Your bidding—Oh that I, whom ye have made
Your foe, could set my dearest enemy free
From pain and fear! but evil casts a shade
Which cannot pass so soon, and Hate must be
The nurse and parent still of an ill progeny.

XVI

" Ye turn to Heaven for aid in your distress;
Alas, that ye, the mighty and the wise,
Who, if ye dared, might not aspire to less
Than ye conceive of power, should fear the lies
Which thou, and thou, didst frame for mysteries
To blind your slaves :—consider your own thought,
An empty and a cruel sacrifice
Ye now prepare, for a vain idol wrought
Out of the fears and hate which vain desires have brought.

XVII

" Ye seek for happiness—alas the day!
Ye find it not in luxury nor in gold,
Nor in the fame, nor in the envied sway
For which, O willing slaves to Custom old,
Severe task-mistress! ye your hearts have sold.
Ye seek for peace, and when ye die, to dream
No evil dreams; all mortal things are cold
And senseless then. If aught survive, I deem
It must be love and joy, for they immortal seem.

XVIII

" Fear not the future, weep not for the past.
Oh, could I win your ears to dare be now
Glorious, and great, and calm ! that ye would cast
Into the dust those symbols of your woe,
Purple, and gold, and steel ! that ye would go
Proclaiming to the nations whence ye came,
That Want, and Plague, and Fear, from slavery flow ;
And that mankind is free, and that the shame
Of royalty and faith is lost in freedom's fame.

XIX

" If thus 'tis well—if not, I come to say
That Laon—." While the Stranger spoke, among
The Council sudden tumult and affray
Arose, for many of those warriors young
Had on his eloquent accents fed and hung
Like bees on mountain flowers ! they knew the truth,
And from their thrones in vindication sprung ;
The men of faith and law then without ruth
Drew forth their secret steel, and stabbed each ardent youth.

XX

They stabbed them in the back and sneered. A slave
Who stood behind the throne, those corpses drew
Each to its bloody, dark, and secret grave ;
And one more daring raised his steel anew
To pierce the Stranger : " What hast thou to do
With me, poor wretch ? "—Calm, solemn, and severe,
That voice unstrung his sinews, and he threw
His dagger on the ground, and pale with fear,
Sate silently—his voice then did the Stranger rear.

XXI

" It doth avail not that I weep for ye—
Ye cannot change, since ye are old and grey,
And ye have chosen your lot—your fame must be
A book of blood, whence in a milder day
Men shall learn truth, when ye are wrapt in clay :
Now ye shall triumph. I am Laon's friend,
And him to your revenge will I betray,
So ye concede one easy boon. Attend !
For now I speak of things which ye can apprehend.

XXII

" There is a People mighty in its youth,
A land beyond the Oceans of the West,
Where, though with rudest rites, Freedom and Truth
Are worshipped ; from a glorious mother's breast
Who, since high Athens fell, among the rest
Sate like the Queen of Nations, but in woe,
By inbred monsters outraged and oppressed,
Turns to her chainless child for succour now,
And draws the milk of power in Wisdom's fullest flow.

XXIII

" This land is like an Eagle, whose young gaze
Feeds on the noontide beam, whose golden plume
Floats moveless on the storm, and in the blaze
Of sunrise gleams when earth is wrapt in gloom ;
An epitaph of glory for the tomb
Of murdered Europe may thy fame be made,
Great People ! As the sands shalt thou become ;
Thy growth is swift as morn, when night must fade ;
The multitudinous Earth shall sleep beneath thy shade.

XXIV

" Yes, in the desert then is built a home
For Freedom. Genius is made strong to rear
The monuments of man beneath the dome
Of a new heaven ; myriads assemble there,
Whom the proud lords of man, in rage or fear,
Drive from their wasted homes. The boon I pray
Is this,—that Cythna shall be convoyed there,—
Nay, start not at the name—America !
And then to you this night Laon will I betray.

XXV

" With me do what ye will. I am your foe ! "
The light of such a joy as makes the stare
Of hungry snakes like living emeralds glow,
Shone in a hundred human eyes.—" Where, where
Is Laon ? haste ! fly ! drag him swiftly here !
We grant thy boon."—" I put no trust in ye,
Swear by the Power ye dread."—" We swear, we swear ! "
The Stranger threw his vest back suddenly,
And smiled in gentle pride, and said, " Lo ! I am he ! "

CANTO XII

I

THE transport of a fierce and monstrous gladness
Spread through the multitudinous streets, fast flying
Upon the winds of fear, from his dull madness
The starveling waked, and died in joy ; the dying,
Among the corpses in stark agony lying,
Just heard the happy tidings, and in hope
Closed their faint eyes ; from house to house replying
With loud acclaim, the living shook Heaven's cope,
And filled the startled Earth with echoes : morn did ope

II

Its pale eyes then ; and lo ! the long array
Of guards in golden arms, and priests beside,
Singing their bloody hymns, whose garbs betray
The blackness of the faith it seems to hide ;
And see, the Tyrant's gem-wrought chariot glide
Among the gloomy cowls and glittering spears—
A shape of light is sitting by his side,
A child most beautiful. I' the midst appears
Laon—exempt alone from mortal hopes and fears.

III

His head and feet are bare, his hands are bound
Behind with heavy chains, yet none do wreak
Their scoffs on him, though myriads throng around ;
There are no sneers upon his lip which speak
That scorn or hate has made him bold ; his cheek
Resolve has not turned pale,—his eyes are mild
And calm, and like the morn about to break,
Smile on mankind—his heart seems reconciled
To all things and itself, like a reposing child.

IV

Tumult was in the soul of all beside,
Ill joy, or doubt, or fear ; but those who saw
Their tranquil victim pass, felt wonder glide
Into their brain, and became calm with awe.—
See, the slow pageant near the pile doth draw.
A thousand torches in the spacious square,
Borne by the ready slaves of ruthless law,
Await the signal round : the morning fair
Is changed to a dim night by that unnatural glare.

V

And see ! beneath a sun-bright canopy,
Upon a platform level with the pile,
The anxious Tyrant sit, enthroned on high,
Girt by the chieftains of the host.   All smile
In expectation, but one child : the while
I, Laon, led by mutes, ascend my bier
Of fire, and look around.   Each distant isle
Is dark in the bright dawn ; towers far and near
Pierce like reposing flames the tremulous atmosphere.

VI

There was such silence through the host, as when
An earthquake, trampling on some populous town,
Has crushed ten thousand with one tread, and men
Expect the second ; all were mute but one,
That fairest child, who, bold with love, alone
Stood up before the king, without avail,
Pleading for Laon's life—her stifled groan
Was heard—she trembled like an aspen pale
Among the gloomy pines of a Norwegian vale.

VII

What were his thoughts linked in the morning sun,
Among those reptiles, stingless with delay,
Even like a tyrant's wrath ?—the signal-gun
Roared—hark, again !   In that dread pause he lay
As in a quiet dream—the slaves obey—
A thousand torches drop,—and hark, the last
Bursts on that awful silence.   Far away
Millions, with hearts that beat both loud and fast,
Watch for the springing flame expectant and aghast.

VIII

They fly—the torches fall—a cry of fear
Has startled the triumphant !—they recede !
For ere the cannon's roar has died, they hear
The tramp of hoofs like earthquake, and a steed
Dark and gigantic, with a tempest's speed,
Bursts through their ranks : a woman sits thereon,
Fairer it seems than aught that earth can breed,
Calm, radiant, like the phantom of the dawn,
A spirit from the caves of daylight wandering gone.

IX

All thought it was God's Angel come to sweep
The lingering guilty to their fiery grave ;
The tyrant from his throne in dread did leap,—
Her innocence his child from fear did save.
Scared by the faith they feigned, each priestly slave
Knelt for his mercy whom they served with blood,
And, like the refluence of a mighty wave
Sucked into the loud sea, the multitude
With crushing panic fled in terror's altered mood.

X

They pause, they blush, they gaze ; a gathering shout
Bursts like one sound from the ten thousand streams
Of a tempestuous sea : that sudden rout
One checked, who never in his mildest dreams
Felt awe from grace or loveliness, the seams
Of his rent heart so hard and cold a creed
Had seared with blistering ice—but he misdeems
That he is wise, whose wounds do only bleed
Inly for self ; thus thought the Iberian Priest indeed ;

XI

And others too, thought he was wise to see,
In pain, and fear, and hate, something divine ;
In love and beauty—no divinity.—
Now with a bitter smile, whose light did shine
Like a fiend's hope upon his lips and eyne,
He said, and the persuasion of that sneer
Rallied his trembling comrades—" Is it mine
To stand alone, when kings and soldiers fear
A woman ?   Heaven has sent its other victim here."

XII

" Were it not impious," said the King, " to break
Our holy oath ? "—" Impious to keep it, say ! "
Shrieked the exulting Priest :—" Slaves, to the stake
Bind her, and on my head the burthen lay
Of her just torments ;—at the Judgment Day
Will I stand up before the golden throne
Of Heaven, and cry, to thee I did betray
An infidel ! but for me she would have known
Another moment's joy !—the glory be thine own."

XIII

They trembled, but replied not, nor obeyed,
Pausing in breathless silence. Cythna sprung
From her gigantic steed, who, like a shade
Chased by the winds, those vacant streets among
Fled tameless, as the brazen rein she flung
Upon his neck, and kissed his moonèd brow.
A piteous sight, that one so fair and young,
The clasp of such a fearful death should woo
With smiles of tender joy as beamed from Cythna now.

XIV

The warm tears burst in spite of faith and fear,
From many a tremulous eye, but, like soft dews
Which feed spring's earliest buds, hung gathered there,
Frozen by doubt,—alas! they could not choose
But weep; for when her faint limbs did refuse
To climb the pyre, upon the mutes she smiled;
And with her eloquent gestures, and the hues
Of her quick lips, even as a weary child
Wins sleep from some fond nurse with its caresses mild,

XV

She won them, though unwilling, her to bind
Near me, among the stakes. When then had fled
One soft reproach that was most thrilling kind,
She smiled on me, and nothing then we said,
But each upon the other's countenance fed
Looks of insatiate love; the mighty veil
Which doth divide the living and the dead
Was almost rent, the world grew dim and pale,—
All light in Heaven or Earth beside our love did fail.—

XVI

Yet,—yet—one brief relapse, like the last beam
Of dying flames, the stainless air around
Hung silent and serene.—A blood-red gleam
Burst upwards, hurling fiercely from the ground
The globèd smoke.—I heard the mighty sound
Of its uprise, like a tempestuous ocean;
And, through its chasms I saw, as in a swound,
The tyrant's child fall without life or motion
Before his throne, subdued by some unseen emotion.

XVII

And is this death? The pyre has disappeared,
The Pestilence, the Tyrant, and the throng;
The flames grow silent—slowly there is heard
The music of a breath-suspending song,
Which, like the kiss of love when life is young,
Steeps the faint eyes in darkness sweet and deep;
With ever-changing notes it floats along,
Till on my passive soul there seemed to creep
A melody, like waves on wrinkled sands that leap.

XVIII

The warm touch of a soft and tremulous hand
Wakened me then ; lo, Cythna sate reclined
Beside me, on the waved and golden sand
Of a clear pool, upon a bank o'ertwined
With strange and star-bright flowers, which to the wind
Breathed divine odour ; high above, was spread
The emerald heaven of trees of unknown kind,
Whose moonlike blooms and bright fruit overhead
A shadow, which was light, upon the waters shed.

XIX

And round about sloped many a lawny mountain
With incense-bearing forests, and vast caves
Of marble radiance to that mighty fountain ;
And where the flood its own bright margin laves,
Their echoes talk with its eternal waves,
Which, from the depths whose jagged caverns breed
Their unreposing strife, it lifts and heaves,
Till through a chasm of hills they roll, and feed
A river deep, which flies with smooth but arrowy speed.

XX

As we sate gazing in a trance of wonder,
A boat approached, borne by the musical air
Along the waves, which sung and sparkled under
Its rapid keel—a winged shape sate there,
A child with silver-shining wings, so fair,
That as her bark did through the waters glide,
The shadow of the lingering waves did wear
Light, as from starry beams ; from side to side,
While veering to the wind, her plumes the bark did guide.

XXI

The boat was one curved shell of hollow pearl,
Almost translucent with the light divine
Of her within ; the prow and stern did curl,
Horned on high, like the young moon supine,
When, o'er dim twilight mountains dark with pine,
It floats upon the sunset's sea of beams,
Whose golden waves in many a purple line
Fade fast, till, borne on sunlight's ebbing streams,
Dilating, on earth's verge the sunken meteor gleams.

XXII

Its keel has struck the sands beside our feet ;—
Then Cythna turned to me, and from her eyes
Which swam with unshed tears, a look more sweet
Than happy love, a wild and glad surprise,
Glanced as she spake : " Ay, this is Paradise
And not a dream, and we are all united !
Lo, that is mine own child, who, in the guise
Of madness, came like day to one benighted
In lonesome woods : my heart is now too well requited ! "

XXIII

And then she wept aloud, and in her arms
Clasped that bright Shape, less marvellously fair
Than her own human hues and living charms;
Which, as she leaned in passion's silence there,
Breathed warmth on the cold bosom of the air,
Which seemed to blush and tremble with delight;
The glossy darkness of her streaming hair
Fell o'er that snowy child, and wrapt from sight
The fond and long embrace which did their hearts unite.

XXIV

Then the bright child, the plumed Seraph, came,
And fixed its blue and beaming eyes on mine,
And said, " I was disturbed by tremulous shame
When once we met, yet knew that I was thine
From the same hour in which thy lips divine
Kindled a clinging dream within my brain,
Which ever waked when I might sleep, to twine
Thine image with *her* memory dear—again
We meet; exempted now from mortal fear or pain.

XXV

" When the consuming flames had wrapt ye round,
The hope which I had cherished went away;
I fell in agony on the senseless ground,
And hid mine eyes in dust, and far astray
My mind was gone, when bright, like dawning day,
The Spectre of the Plague before me flew,
And breathed upon my lips, and seemed to say,
' They wait for thee, beloved!'—then I knew
The death-mark on my breast, and became calm anew.

XXVI

" It was the calm of love—for I was dying.
I saw the black and half-extinguished pyre
In its own grey and shrunken ashes lying;
The pitchy smoke of the departed fire
Still hung in many a hollow dome and spire
Above the towers, like night; beneath whose shade,
Awed by the ending of their own desire,
The armies stood; a vacancy was made
In expectation's depth, and so they stood dismayed.

XXVII

" The frightful silence of that altered mood,
The tortures of the dying clove alone,
Till one uprose among the multitude,
And said—' The flood' of time is rolling on,
We stand upon its brink, whilst *they* are gone
To glide in peace down death's mysterious stream.
Have ye done well? They moulder flesh and bone,
Who might have made this life's envenomed dream
A sweeter draught than ye will ever taste, I deem.

XXVIII

" ' These perish as the good and great of yore
Have perished, and their murderers will repent.
Yes, vain and barren tears shall flow before
Yon smoke has faded from the firmament
Even for this cause, that ye, who must lament
The death of those that made this world so fair,
Cannot recall them now ; but then is lent
To man the wisdom of a high despair,
When such can die, and he live on and linger here.

XXIX

" ' Ay, ye may fear not now the Pestilence,
From fabled hell as by a charm withdrawn ;
All power and faith must pass, since calmly hence
In pain and fire have unbelievers gone ;
And ye must sadly turn away, and moan
In secret, to his home each one returning ;
And to long ages shall this hour be known ;
And slowly shall its memory, ever burning,
Fill this dark night of things with an eternal morning.

XXX

" ' For me the world is grown too void and cold,
Since hope pursues immortal destiny
With steps thus slow—therefore shall ye behold
How those who love, yet fear not, dare to die ;
Tell to your children this ! ' then suddenly
He sheathed a dagger in his heart, and fell ;
My brain grew dark in death, and yet to me
There came a murmur from the crowd to tell
Of deep and mighty change which suddenly befell.

XXXI

" Then suddenly I stood a winged Thought
Before the immortal Senate, and the seat
Of that star-shining spirit, whence is wrought
The strength of its dominion, good and great,
The better Genius of this world's estate.
His realm around one mighty Fane is spread,
Elysian islands bright and fortunate,
Calm dwellings of the free and happy dead,
Where I am sent to lead ! "   These winged words she said,

XXXII

And with the silence of her eloquent smile,
Bade us embark in her divine canoe ;
Then at the helm we took our seat, the while
Above her head those plumes of dazzling hue
Into the wind's invisible stream she threw,
Sitting beside the prow : like gossamer,
On the swift breath of morn, the vessel flew
O'er the bright whirlpools of that fountain fair,
Whose shores receded fast, while we seemed lingering there ;

XXXIII

Till down that mighty stream dark, calm, and fleet,
Between a chasm of cedar mountains riven,
Chased by the thronging winds, whose viewless feet
As swift as twinkling beams, had, under Heaven,
From woods and waves wild sounds and odours driven,
The boat flew visibly—three nights and days,
Borne like a cloud through morn, and noon, and even,
We sailed along the winding watery ways
Of the vast stream, a long and labyrinthine maze.

XXXIV

A scene of joy and wonder to behold
That river's shapes and shadows changing ever,
Where the broad sunrise filled with deepening gold
Its whirlpools, where all hues did spread and quiver,
And where melodious falls did burst and shiver
Among rocks clad with flowers, the foam and spray
Sparkled like stars upon the sunny river,
Or when the moonlight poured a holier day,
One vast and glittering lake around green islands lay.

XXXV

Morn, noon, and even, that boat of pearl outran
The streams which bore it, like the arrowy cloud
Of tempest, or the speedier thought of man,
Which flieth forth and cannot make abode ;
Sometimes through forests, deep like night, we glode,
Between the walls of mighty mountains crowned
With Cyclopean piles, whose turrets proud,
The homes of the departed, dimly frowned
O'er the bright waves which girt their dark foundations round.

XXXVI

Sometimes between the wide and flowering meadows,
Mile after mile we sailed, and 'twas delight
To see far off the sunbeams chase the shadows
Over the grass ; sometimes beneath the night
Of wide and vaulted caves, whose roofs were bright
With starry gems, we fled, whilst from their deep
And dark green chasms, shades beautiful and white,
Amid sweet sounds across our path would sweep
Like swift and lovely dreams that walk the waves of sleep.

XXXVII

And ever as we sailed, our minds were full
Of love and wisdom, which would overflow
In converse wild, and sweet, and wonderful ;
And in quick smiles whose light would come and go,
Like music o'er wide waves, and in the flow
Of sudden tears, and in the mute caress—
For a deep shade was cleft, and we did know,
That virtue, though obscured on Earth, not less
Survives all mortal change in lasting loveliness.

XXXVIII

Three days and nights we sailed, as thought and feeling
Number delightful hours—for through the sky
The sphered lamps of day and night, revealing
New changes and new glories, rolled on high,
Sun, Moon, and moonlike lamps, the progeny
Of a diviner Heaven, serene and fair :
On the fourth day, wild as a wind-wrought sea,
The stream became, and fast and faster bare
The spirit-wingèd boat, steadily speeding there.

XXXIX

Steadily and swift, where the waves rolled like mountains
Within the vast ravine, whose rifts did pour
Tumultuous floods from their ten thousand fountains,
The thunder of whose earth-uplifting roar
Made the air sweep in whirlwinds from the shore,
Calm as a shade, the boat of that fair child
Securely fled, that rapid stress before,
Amid the topmost spray, and sunbows wild,
Wreathed in the silver mist : in joy and pride we smiled.

XL

The torrent of that wide and raging river
Is passed, and our aërial speed suspended.
We look behind ; a golden mist did quiver
When its wild surges with the lake were blended
Our bark hung there, as one line suspended
Between two heavens, that windless waveless lake ;
Which four great cataracts from four vales, attended
By mists, aye feed, from rocks and clouds they break,
And of that azure sea a silent refuge make.

XLI

Motionless resting on the lake awhile
I saw its marge of snow-bright mountains rear
Their peaks aloft, I saw each radiant isle,
And in the midst, afar, even like a sphere
Hung in one hollow sky, did there appear
The Temple of the Spirit ; on the sound
Which issued thence, drawn nearer and more near,
Like the swift moon this glorious earth around,
The charmed boat approached, and there its haven found.

PROMETHEUS UNBOUND

A LYRICAL DRAMA, IN FOUR ACTS

Audisne hæc Amphiarae, sub terram abdite ? —

[handwritten marginalia: from Aeschylus's tragedy Epigoni. Do you hear that, Amphiarus, hidden under the earth. Milto]

PREFACE

THE Greek tragic writers, in selecting as their subject any portion of their national history or mythology, employed in their treatment of it a certain arbitrary discretion. They by no means conceived themselves bound to adhere to the common interpretation, or to imitate in story, as in title, their rivals and predecessors. Such a system would have amounted to a resignation of those claims to preference over their competitors which incited the composition. The Agamemnonian story was exhibited on the Athenian theatre with as many variations as dramas.

I have presumed to employ a similar license. The "Prometheus Unbound" of Æschylus supposed the reconciliation of Jupiter with his victim as the price of the disclosure of the danger threatened to his empire by the consummation of his marriage with Thetis. Thetis, according to this view of the subject, was given in marriage to Peleus, and Prometheus, by the permission of Jupiter, delivered from his captivity by Hercules. Had I framed my story on this model, I should have done no more than have attempted to restore the lost drama of Æschylus; an ambition, which, if my preference to this mode of treating the subject had incited me to cherish, the recollection of the high comparison such an attempt would challenge, might well abate. But, in truth, I was averse from a catastrophe so feeble as that of reconciling the Champion with the Oppressor of mankind. The moral interest of the fable, which is so powerfully sustained by the sufferings and endurance of Prometheus, would be annihilated if we could conceive of him as unsaying his high language and quailing before his successful and perfidious adversary. The only imaginary being resembling in any degree Prometheus, is Satan: and Prometheus is, in my judgment, a more poetical character than Satan, because, in addition to courage, and majesty, and firm and patient opposition to omnipotent force, he is susceptible of being described as exempt from the taints of ambition, envy, revenge, and a desire for personal aggrandisement, which, in the Hero of Paradise Lost, interfere with the interest. The character of Satan engenders in the mind a pernicious casuistry, which leads us to weigh his faults with his wrongs, and to excuse the former because the latter exceed all measure. In the minds of those who consider that magnificent fiction with a religious feeling, it engenders something worse. But Prometheus is, as it were, the type of the highest perfection of moral and intellectual nature, impelled by the purest and the truest motives to the best and noblest ends.

This Poem was chiefly written upon the mountainous ruins of the Baths of Caracalla, among the flowery glades, and thickets of odoriferous blossoming trees, which are extending in everwinding labyrinths upon its immense platforms and dizzy arches suspended in the air. The bright blue sky of Rome, and the effect of the vigorous awakening of spring in that divinest climate, and the new life with which it drenches the spirits even to intoxication, were the inspiration of this drama.

The imagery which I have employed

will be found, in many instances, to have been drawn from the operations of the human mind, or from those external actions by which they are expressed. This is unusual in modern poetry, although Dante and Shakespeare are full of instances of the same kind : Dante indeed more than any other poet, and with greater success. But the Greek poets, as writers to whom no resource of awakening the sympathy of their contemporaries was unknown, were in the habitual use of this power ; and it is the study of their works (since a higher merit would probably be denied me), to which I am willing that my readers should impute this singularity.

One word is due in candour to the degree in which the study of contemporary writings may have tinged my composition, for such has been a topic of censure with regard to poems far more popular, and, indeed, more deservedly*popular, than mine. It is impossible that any one who inhabits the same age with such writers as those who stand in the foremost ranks of our own, can conscientiously assure himself that his language and tone of thought may not have been modified by the study of the productions of those extraordinary intellects. It is true, that, not the spirit of their genius, but the forms in which it has manifested itself, are due less to the peculiarities of their own minds than to the peculiarity of the moral and intellectual condition of the minds among which they have been produced. Thus a number of writers possess the form, whilst they want the spirit of those whom, it is alleged, they imitate : because the former is the endowment of the age in which they live, and the latter must be the uncommunicated lightning of their own mind.

The peculiar style of intense and comprehensive imagery which distinguishes the modern literature of England, has not been, as a general power, the product of the imitation of any particular writer. The mass of capabilities remains at every period materially the same ; the circumstances which awaken it to action perpetually change. If England were divided into forty republics, each equal in population and extent to Athens, there is no reason to suppose but that, under institutions not more perfect than those of Athens, each would produce philosophers and poets equal to those who (if we except Shakespeare) have never been surpassed. We owe the great writers of the golden age of our literature to that fervid awakening of the public mind which shook to dust the oldest and most oppressive form of the Christian religion. We owe Milton to the progress and development of the same spirit : the sacred Milton was, let it ever be remembered, a republican, and a bold inquirer into morals and religion. The great writers of our own age are, we have reason to suppose, the companions and forerunners of some unimagined change in our social condition, or the opinions which cement it. The cloud of mind is discharging its collected lightning, and the equilibrium between institutions and opinions is now restoring, or is about to be restored.

As to imitation, poetry is a mimetic art. It creates, but it creates by combination and representation. Poetical abstractions are beautiful and new, not because the portions of which they are composed had no previous existence in the mind of man, or in nature, but because the whole produced by their combination has some intelligible and beautiful analogy with those sources of emotion and thought, and with the contemporary condition of them : one great poet is a masterpiece of nature, which another not only ought to study but must study. He might as wisely and as easily determine that his mind should no longer be the mirror of all that is lovely in the visible universe, as exclude from his contemplation the beautiful which exists in the writings of a great contemporary. The pretence of doing it would be a presumption in any but the greatest ; the effect, even in him, would be strained, unnatural, and ineffectual. A poet

P.B's thoughts on poetry

is the combined product of such internal powers as modify the nature of others; and of such external influences as excite and sustain these powers: he is not one, but both. Every man's mind is, in this respect, modified by all the objects of nature and art; by every word and every suggestion which he ever admitted to act upon his consciousness; it is the mirror upon which all forms are reflected, and in which they compose one form. / Poets, not otherwise than philosophers, painters, sculptors, and musicians, are, in one sense, the creators, and, in another, the creations, of their age. | From this subjection the loftiest do not escape. There is a similarity between Homer and Hesiod, between Æschylus and Euripides, between Virgil and Horace, between Dante and Petrarch, between Shakespeare and Fletcher, between Dryden and Pope; each has a generic resemblance under which their specific distinctions are arranged. If this similarity be the result of imitation, I am willing to confess that I have imitated.

Let this opportunity be conceded to me of acknowledging that I have, what a Scotch philosopher characteristically terms, "a passion for reforming the world:" what passion incited him to write and publish his book, he omits to explain. For my part, I had rather be damned with Plato and Lord Bacon, than go to heaven with Paley and Malthus. But it is a mistake to suppose that I dedicate my poetical compositions solely to the direct enforcement of reform, or that I consider them in

any degree as containing a reasoned system on the theory of human life. Didactic poetry is my abhorrence; nothing can be equally well expressed in prose that is not tedious and supererogatory in verse. My purpose has hitherto been simply to familiarise the highly refined imagination of the more select classes of poetical readers with beautiful idealisms of moral excellence; aware that until the mind can love, and admire, and trust, and hope, and endure, reasoned principles of moral conduct are seeds cast upon the highway of life, which the unconscious passenger tramples into dust, although they would bear the harvest of his happiness. Should I live to accomplish what I purpose, that is, produce a systematical history of what appear to me to be the genuine elements of human society, let not the advocates of injustice and superstition flatter themselves that I should take Æschylus rather than Plato as my model.

The having spoken of myself with unaffected freedom will need little apology with the candid; and let the uncandid consider that they injure me less than their own hearts and minds by misrepresentation. Whatever talents a person may possess to amuse and instruct others, be they ever so inconsiderable, he is yet bound to exert them: if his attempt be ineffectual, let the punishment of an unaccomplished purpose have been sufficient; let none trouble themselves to heap the dust of oblivion upon his efforts; the pile they raise will betray his grave, which might otherwise have been unknown.

DRAMATIS PERSONÆ

PROMETHEUS
DEMOGORGON
JUPITER
The EARTH
OCEAN
APOLLO
MERCURY
HERCULES

ASIA
PANTHEA } Oceanïdes
IONE
The PHANTASM OF JUPITER
The SPIRIT OF THE EARTH
The SPIRIT OF THE MOON
SPIRITS OF THE HOURS
SPIRITS ECHOES FAUNS
FURIES

ACT I

SCENE.—*A Ravine of Icy Rocks in the Indian Caucasus.* PROMETHEUS *is discovered bound to the Precipice.* PANTHEA *and* IONE *are seated at his feet. Time, Night. During the Scene, Morning slowly breaks.*

Prometheus. Monarch of Gods and Dæmons, and all Spirits
But One, who throng those bright and rolling worlds
Which Thou and I alone of living things
Behold with sleepless eyes! regard this Earth
Made multitudinous with thy slaves, whom thou
Requitest for knee-worship, prayer, and praise,
And toil, and hecatombs of broken hearts,
With fear and self-contempt and barren hope.
Whilst me, who am thy foe, eyeless in hate,
Hast thou made reign and triumph, to thy scorn,
O'er mine own misery and thy vain revenge.
Three thousand years of sleep-unsheltered hours,
And moments aye divided by keen pangs
Till they seemed years, torture and solitude,
Scorn and despair,—these are mine empire.
More glorious far than that which thou surveyest
From thine unenvied throne, O Mighty God!
Almighty, had I deigned to share the shame
Of thine ill tyranny, and hung not here
Nailed to this wall of eagle-baffling mountain,
Black, wintry, dead, unmeasured; without herb,
Insect, or beast, or shape or sound of life.
Ah me, alas! pain, pain ever, for ever!

No change, no pause, no hope! Yet I endure.
I ask the Earth, have not the mountains felt?
I ask yon Heaven, the all-beholding Sun,
Has it not seen? The Sea, in storm or calm,
Heaven's ever-changing Shadow, spread below,
Have its deaf waves not heard my agony?
Ah me! alas, pain, pain ever, for ever!

The crawling glaciers pierce me with the spears
Of their moon-freezing crystals; the bright chains
Eat with their burning cold into my bones.
Heaven's winged hound, polluting from thy lips
His beak in poison not his own, tears up
My heart; and shapeless sights come wandering by,
The ghastly people of the realm of dream,
Mocking me: and the Earthquake-fiends are charged
To wrench the rivets from my quivering wounds
When the rocks split and close again behind:
While from their loud abysses howling throng
The genii of the storm, urging the rage
Of whirlwind, and afflict me with keen hail.
And yet to me welcome is day and night,
Whether one breaks the hoar frost of the morn,
Or starry, dim, and slow, the other climbs
The leaden-coloured east; for then they lead
The wingless, crawling hours, one among whom
—As some dark Priest hales the reluctant victim—
Shall drag thee, cruel King, to kiss the blood
From these pale feet, which then might trample thee
If they disdained not such a prostrate slave.

Disdain! Ah no! I pity thee. What
    ruin
Will hunt thee undefended through
    the wide Heaven!
How will thy soul, cloven to its depth
    with terror,
Gape like a hell within! I speak in
    grief, *milton reference*
Not exultation, for I hate no more,
As then ere misery made me wise.
    The curse
Once breathed on thee I would recall.
    Ye Mountains,
Whose many-voiced Echoes, through
    the mist
Of cataracts, flung the thunder of that
    spell!
Ye icy Springs, stagnant with wrinkl-
    ing frost,
Which vibrated to hear me, and then
    crept
Shuddering through India! Thou
    serenest Air,
Through which the Sun walks burn-
    ing without beams!
And ye swift Whirlwinds, who on
    poised wings
Hung mute and moveless o'er yon
    hushed abyss,
As thunder, louder than your own,
    made rock
The orbed world! If then my words
    had power,
Though I am changed so that aught
    evil wish
Is dead within; although no memory
    be
Of what is hate, let them not lose it
    now!
What was that curse? for ye all heard
    me speak.

FIRST VOICE: (*from the mountains*).
Thrice three hundred thousand years
    O'er the Earthquake's couch we
    stood
Oft, as men convulsed with fears,
    We trembled in our multitude.

SECOND VOICE: (*from the springs*).
Thunderbolts had parched our water,
    We had been stained with bitter
    blood,
And had run mute, 'mid shrieks of
    slaughter,
    Through a city and a solitude.

THIRD VOICE: (*from the air*).
I had clothed, since Earth uprose
    Its wastes in colours not their own;
And oft had my serene repose
    Been cloven by many a rending
    groan.

FOURTH VOICE: (*from the whirlwinds*).
We had soared beneath these moun-
    tains
Unresting ages; nor had thunder,
Nor yon volcano's flaming fountains,
Nor any power above or under,
    Ever made us mute with wonder.

FIRST VOICE.
But never bowed our snowy crest
    As at the voice of thine unrest.

SECOND VOICE.
Never such a sound before
To the Indian waves we bore.
A pilot asleep on the howling sea
Leaped up from the deck in agony,
And heard, and cried, " Ah, woe is
    me!"
And died as mad as the wild waves be.

THIRD VOICE.
By such dread words from Earth to
    Heaven
My still realm was never riven:
When its wound was closed, there
    stood
Darkness o'er the day like blood.

FOURTH VOICE.
And we shrank back: for dreams of
    ruin
To frozen caves our flight pursuing
Made us keep silence—thus—and
    thus—
Though silence is as hell to us.
    The Earth. The tongueless Caverns
    of the craggy hills
Cried, " Misery!" then; the hollow
    Heaven replied,
" Misery!" And the Ocean's purple
    waves,
Climbing the land, howled to the lash-
    ing winds,
And the pale nations heard it, " Mis-
    ery!"
    Prometheus. I hear a sound of
    voices: not the voice
Which I gave forth. Mother, thy
    sons and thou

Scorn him, without whose all-endur-
      ing will   [Jove,
Beneath the fierce omnipotence of
Both they and thou had vanished, like
      thin mist
Unrolled on the morning wind. Know
      ye not me,
The Titan ?   He who made his agony
The barrier to your else all-conquer-
      ing foe ?
Oh, rock-embosomed lawns, and
      snow-fed streams,
Now seen athwart frore vapours,
      deep below,
Through whose o'ershadowing woods
      I wandered once
With Asia, drinking life from her
      loved eyes ;
Why scorns the spirit which informs
      ye, now
To commune with me ? me alone,
      who checked,
As one who checks a fiend-drawn
      charioteer,
The falsehood and the force of him
      who reigns
Supreme, and with the groans of
      pining slaves
Fills your dim glens and liquid wilder-
      nesses :
Why answer ye not, still, Breth-
      ren ?
      The Earth.   They dare not.
      Prometheus. Who dares ? for I
      would hear that curse again.
Ha ! what an awful whisper rises up !
'Tis scarce like sound : it tingles
      through the frame
As lightning tingles, hovering ere it
      strike.
Speak, Spirit ! from thine inorganic
      voice
I only know that thou art moving
      near
And love.   How cursed I him ?
      The Earth. How canst thou hear,
Who knowest not the language of the
      dead ?
      Prometheus. Thou art a living
      spirit ; speak as they.
      The Earth. I dare not speak like
      life, lest Heaven's fell King
Should hear, and link me to some
      wheel of pain
More torturing than the one whereon
      I roll.

Subtle thou art and good ; and
      though the Gods
Hear not this voice, yet thou art more
      than God
Being wise and kind : earnestly
      hearken now.
      Prometheus. Obscurely through my
      brain, like shadows dim,
Sweep awful thoughts, rapid and
      thick.   I feel
Faint, like one mingled in entwining
      love ;
Yet 'tis not pleasure.
      The Earth. No, thou canst not
      hear :
Thou art immortal, and this tongue is
      known
Only to those who die.
      Prometheus.   And what art thou,
O melancholy Voice ?
      The Earth.   I am the Earth,
Thy mother ; she within those stony
      veins,
To the last fibre of the loftiest tree
Whose thin leaves trembled in the
      frozen air,
Joy ran, as blood within a living
      frame,
When thou didst from her bosom, like
      a cloud
Of glory, arise, a spirit of keen joy !
And at thy voice her pining sons up-
      lifted
Their prostrate brows from the pol-
      luting dust,
And our almighty Tyrant with fierce
      dread
Grew pale, until his thunder chained
      thee here.
Then, see those million worlds which
      burn and roll,
Around us : their inhabitants beheld
My sphered light wane in wide Hea-
      ven ; the sea
Was lifted by strange tempest, and
      new fire
From earthquake-rifted mountains
      of bright snow
Shook its portentous hair beneath
      Heaven's frown ;
Lightning and Inundation vexed the
      plains ;
Blue thistles bloomed in cities ; food-
      less toads
Within voluptuous chambers pant
      ing crawled ;

what's going on with the language of the dead and living here.

When Plague had fallen on man,
and beast, and worm,
And Famine ; and black blight on
herb and tree ;
And in the corn, and vines, and mea-
dow-grass,
Teemed ineradicable poisonous weeds
Draining their growth, for my wan
breast was dry
With grief ; and the thin air, my
breath, was stained
With the contagion of a mother's hate
Breathed on her child's destroyer ; ay,
I heard
Thy curse, the which, if thou remem-
berest not,
Yet my innumerable seas and streams,
Mountains and caves, and winds, and
yon wide air,
And the inarticulate people of the
dead,
Preserve, a treasured spell. We
meditate   [words
In secret joy and hope those dreadful
But dare not speak them.
   Prometheus. Venerable mother !
All else who live and suffer take from
thee
Some comfort ; flowers, and fruits,
and happy sounds,
And love, though fleeting ; these
may not be mine.
But mine own words, I pray, deny me
not.
   The Earth. They shall be told. Ere
Babylon was dust,
The Magus Zoroaster, my dear child,
Met his own image walking in the gar-
den.
That apparition, sole of men, he saw.
For know there are two worlds of life
and death :
One that which thou beholdest ; but
the other
Is underneath the grave, where do in-
habit
The shadows of all forms that think
and live
Till death unite them and they part
no more ;
Dreams and the light imaginings of
men,
And all that faith creates or love de-
sires,
Terrible, strange, sublime and beau-
teous shapes.

There thou art, and dost hang, a
writhing shade,
'Mid whirlwind-peopled mountains ;
all the gods
Are there, and all the powers of name-
less worlds,
Vast, sceptred phantoms ; heroes,
men, and beasts ;
And Demogorgon, a tremendous
gloom ;
And he, the supreme Tyrant, on his
throne
Of burning gold. Son, one of these
shall utter
The curse which all remember. Call
at will
Thine own ghost, or the ghost of
Jupiter,
Hades or Typhon, or what mightier
Gods
From all-prolific Evil, since thy ruin
Have sprung, and trampled on my
prostrate sons.
Ask, and they must reply : so the re-
venge
Of the Supreme may sweep through
vacant shades,
As rainy wind through the abandoned
gate
Of a fallen palace.
   Prometheus. Mother, let not aught
Of that which may be evil, pass again
My lips, or those of aught resembling
me.
Phantasm of Jupiter, arise, appear !

       IONE.

My wings are folded o'er mine ears :
   My wings are crossed o'er mine
   eyes :
Yet through their silver shade ap-
pears,
   And through their lulling plumes
   arise,
A Shape, a throng of sounds ;
   May it be no ill to thee
O thou of many wounds !
Near whom, for our sweet sister's
sake,
Ever thus we watch and wake.

      PANTHEA.

The sound is of whirlwind underground,
   Earthquake, and fire and mountains cloven
The shape is awful like the sound,

Clothed in dark purple, star-in-
woven.
A sceptre of pale gold
  To stay steps proud, o'er the slow
    cloud
His veined hand doth hold.
Cruel he looks, but calm and strong,
Like one who does, not suffers wrong.
  Phantasm of Jupiter. Why have
    the secret powers of this strange
    world
Driven me, a frail and empty phan-
    tom, hither
On direst storms? What unaccus-
    tomed sounds
Are hovering on my lips, unlike the
    voice
With which our pallid race hold
    ghastly talk
In darkness? And, proud sufferer,
    who art thou?
  Prometheus. Tremendous Image!
    as thou art must be
He whom thou shadowest forth. I
    am his foe,
The Titan. Speak the words which I
    would hear,
Although no thought inform thine
    empty voice.
  The Earth. Listen! And though
    your echoes must be mute.
Grey mountains, and old woods, and
    haunted springs,
Prophetic caves, and isle-surround-
    ing streams,
Rejoice to hear what yet ye cannot
    speak.
  Phantasm. A spirit seizes me and
    speaks within :   [cloud.
It tears me as fire tears a thunder-
  Panthea. See, how he lifts his
    mighty looks, the Heaven
Darkens above.
  Ione.   He speaks! O shelter me!
  Prometheus. I see the curse on ges-
    tures proud and cold,
And looks of firm defiance, and calm
    hate,
And such despair as mocks itself with
    smiles,
Written as on a scroll : yet speak :
    Oh speak!

PHANTASM.
Fiend, I defy thee! with a calm,
    fixed mind,

All that thou canst inflict I bid
    thee do ;
Foul Tyrant both of Gods and
    Human-kind,
  One only being shalt thou not
    subdue.
Rain then thy plagues upon me
    here,
  Ghastly disease, and frenzying
    fear ;
And let alternate frost and fire
Eat into me, and be thine ire
Lightning, and cutting hail, and
    legioned forms
Of furies, driving by upon the
    wounding storms.
Ay, do thy worst. Thou art omni-
    potent.
  O'er all things but thyself I
    gave thee power,
And my own will. Be thy swift
    mischiefs sent
  To blast mankind, from yon
    ethereal tower.
Let thy malignant spirit move
In darkness over those I love :
On me and mine I imprecate
The utmost torture of thy hate ;
And thus devote to sleepless agony,
This undeclining head while thou
    must reign on high.

But thou, who art the God and
    Lord : O thou
  Who fillest with thy soul this
    world of woe,
To whom all things of Earth and
    Heaven do bow
  In fear and worship : all-pre-
    vailing foe!
I curse thee! let a sufferer's curse
Clasp thee, his torturer, like re-
    morse ;
Till thine Infinity shall be
A robe of envenomed agony ;
And thine Omnipotence a crown of
    pain,
To cling like burning gold round thy
    dissolving brain.

Heap on thy soul, by virtue of this
    curse,
  Ill deeds, then be thou damned,
    beholding good ;
Both infinite as is the universe,
  And thou, and thy self-torturing
    solitude.

Prometheus's curse

An awful image of calm power
Though now thou sittest, let the
    hour
Come, when thou must appear to be
That which thou art internally.
And after many a false and fruitless
    crime,
Scorn track thy lagging fall through
    boundless space and time.

Prometheus. Were these my words,
    O Parent ?
The Earth. They were thine.
Prometheus. It doth repent me :
    words are quick and vain :
Grief for awhile is blind, and so was
    mine.
I wish no living thing to suffer pain.

THE EARTH.

Misery ! Oh misery to me,
That Jove at length should vanquish
    thee.
Wail, howl aloud, Land and Sea,
The Earth's rent heart shall answer ye.
Howl, Spirits of the living and the
    dead,
Your refuge, your defence lies fallen
    and vanquished.

FIRST ECHO.

Lies fallen and vanquished ?

SECOND ECHO.

Fallen and vanquished !

IONE.

Fear not : 'tis but some passing
    spasm,
The Titan is unvanquished still.
But see, where through the azure
    chasm
Of yon forked and snowy hill
Trampling the slant winds on high
    With golden-sandalled feet, that
    glow
Under plumes of purple dye,
Like rose-ensanguined ivory,
    A Shape comes now,
Stretching on high from his right
    hand
A serpent-cinctured wand.
Panthea. 'Tis Jove's world-wan-
    dering herald, Mercury.

IONE.

And who are those with hydra
    tresses

And iron wings that climb the wind,
Whom the frowning God represses
    Like vapours steaming up be-
    hind,
Clanging loud, an endless crowd—

PANTHEA.

These are Jove's tempest-walk-
    ing hounds,
Whom he gluts with groans and
    blood,
When charioted on sulphurous
    cloud
    He bursts Heaven's bounds.

IONE.

Are they now led, from the thin
    dead
On new pangs to be fed ?
Panthea. The Titan looks as ever,
    firm, not proud.
First Fury. Ha ! I scent life !
Second Fury. Let me but look
    into his eyes !
Third Fury. The hope of torturing
    him smells like a heap
Of corpses, to a death-bird after battle.
First Fury. Darest thou delay, O
    Herald ! take cheer, Hounds
Of Hell : what if the Son of Maia soon
Should make us food and sport—who
    can please long
The Omnipotent ?
Mercury.   Back to your towers
    of iron,
And gnash beside the streams of fire,
    and wail
Your foodless teeth.   Geryon, arise !
    and Gorgon,
Chimæra, and thou Sphinx, subtlest
    of fiends,
Who ministered to Thebes Heaven's
    poisoned wine,
Unnatural love, and more unnatural
    hate :
These shall perform your task.
First Fury. Oh, mercy ! mercy !
We die with our desire : drive us not
    back !
Mercury. Crouch then in silence.
                Awful Sufferer !
To thee unwilling, most unwillingly
I come, by the Great Father's will
    driven down,
To execute a doom of new revenge.
Alas ! I pity thee, and hate myself

That I can do no more : aye from thy
    sight
Returning, for a season, heaven seems
    hell,
So thy worn form pursues me night
    and day,
Smiling reproach. Wise art thou,
    firm and good,
But vainly wouldst stand forth alone
    in strife
Against the Omnipotent; as yon
    clear lamps
That measure and divide the weary
    years
From which there is no refuge, long
    have taught,
And long must teach. Even now
    thy Torturer arms
With the strange might of unim-
    agined pains
The powers who scheme slow agonies
    in Hell,
And my commission is to lead them
    here,
Or what more subtle, foul, or savage
    fiends
People the abyss, and leave them to
    their task.
Be it not so ! there is a secret known
To thee, and to none else of living
    things,
Which may transfer the sceptre of
    wide Heaven,
The fear of which perplexes the Su-
    preme ;   [throne
Clothe it in words, and bid it clasp his
In intercession ; bend thy soul in
    prayer,
And like a suppliant in some gorgeous
    fane,
Let the will kneel within thy haughty
    heart :
For benefits and meek submission
    tame
The fiercest and the mightiest.
    Prometheus.   Evil minds
Change good to their own nature. I
    gave all
He has ; and in return he chains me
    here
Years, ages, night and day ; whether
    the Sun
Split my parched skin, or in the
    moony night
The crystal-winged snow cling round
    my hair :

Whilst my beloved race is trampled
    down
By his thought-executing ministers.
Such is the tyrant's recompense : 'tis
    just :
He who is evil can receive no good ;
And for a world bestowed, or a friend
    lost,
He can feel hate, fear, shame ; not
    gratitude :
He but requites me for his own mis-
    deed.
Kindness to such is keen reproach
    which breaks
With bitter stings the light sleep of
    Revenge.
Submission, thou dost know I cannot
    try ;
For what submission but that fatal
    word,
The death-seal of mankind's capti-
    vity,
Like the Sicilian's hair-suspended
    sword,
Which trembles o'er his crown, would
    he accept,
Or could I yield ? Which yet I will
    not yield.
Let others flatter Crime, where it sits
    throned
In brief Omnipotence ; secure are
    they :
For Justice, when triumphant, will
    weep down
Pity, not punishment, on her own
    wrongs,
Too much avenged by those who err.
    I wait,
Enduring thus, the retributive hour
Which since we spake is even nearer
    now.
But hark, the hell-hounds clamour.
    Fear delay !
Behold ! Heaven lowers under thy
    father's frown.
    Mercury. Oh, that we might be
    spared : I to inflict,
And thou to suffer ! once more answer
    me :
Thou knowest not the period of Jove's
    power ?
    Prometheus. I know but this, that
    it must come.
    Mercury.   Alas !
Thou canst not count thy years to
    come of pain ?

Prometheus. They last while Jove
  must reign ; nor more, nor less
Do I desire or fear.
  Mercury.   Yet pause, and plunge
Into Eternity, where recorded time,
Even all that we imagine, age on age,
Seems but a point, and the reluctant
  mind
Flags, wearily in its unending flight,
Till it sink, dizzy, blind, lost, shelter-
  less ;
Perchance it has not numbered the
  slow years
Which thou must spend in torture,
  unreprieved ?
  Prometheus. Perchance no thought
  can count them, yet they pass.
  Mercury. If thou mightst dwell
  among the Gods the while,
Lapped in voluptuous joy ?
  Prometheus.   I would not quit
This bleak ravine, these unrepentant
  pains.
  Mercury. Alas ! I wonder at, yet
  pity thee.
  Prometheus. Pity the self-despising
  slaves of Heaven,
Not me, within whose mind sits peace
  serene,
As light in the sun, throned : how
  vain is talk !
Call up the fiends.
  Ione. O, sister, look ! White fire
Has cloven to the roots yon huge
  snow-loaded cedar ;
How fearfully God's thunder howls
  behind !
  Mercury. I must obey his words
  and thine : alas !
Most heavily remorse hangs at my
  heart !
  Panthea. See where the child of
  Heaven, with winged feet,
Runs down the slanted sunlight of the
  dawn.
  Ione. Dear sister, close thy plumes
  over thine eyes
Lest thou behold and die : they come :
  they come
Blackening the birth of day with
  countless wings,
And hollow underneath, like death.
  First Fury.   Prometheus !
  Second Fury. Immortal Titan !
  Third Fury. · Champion of Hea-
  ven's slaves !

  Prometheus. He whom some dread-
  ful voice invokes is here,
Prometheus, the chained Titan. Hor-
  rible forms,
What and who are ye ? Never yet
  there came
Phantasms so foul through monster-
  teeming Hell
From the all-miscreative brain of
  Jove ;
While I behold such execrable shapes,
Methinks I grow like what I contem-
  plate,
And laugh and stare in loathsome
  sympathy.
  First Fury. We are the ministers of
  pain and fear,
And disappointment, and mistrust,
  and hate,
And clinging crime ; and as lean dogs
  pursue
Through wood and lake some struck
  and sobbing fawn,
We track all things that weep, and
  bleed, and live,
When the great King betrays them to
  our will.
  Prometheus. Oh ! many fearful
  natures in one name,
I know ye ; and these lakes and
  echoes know
The darkness and the clangour of
  your wings.
But why more hideous than your
  loathed selves
Gather ye up in legions from the deep?
  Second Fury. We knew not that :
  Sisters, rejoice, rejoice !
  Prometheus. Can aught exult in its
  deformity ?
  Second Fury. The beauty of de-
  light makes lovers glad,
Gazing on one another : so are we.
As from the rose which the pale priest-
  ess kneels
To gather for her festal crown of
  flowers
The aërial crimson falls, flushing her
  cheek,
So from our victim's destined agony
The shade which is our form in-
  vests us round,
Else we are shapeless as our mother
  Night.
  Prometheus. I laugh your power,
  and his who sent you here,

To lowest scorn. Pour forth the cup of pain.

First Fury. Thou thinkest we will rend thee bone from bone,
And nerve from nerve, working like fire within ?

Prometheus. Pain is my element, as hate is thine ;
Ye rend me now : I care not.

Second Fury. Dost imagine
We will but laugh into thy lidless eyes ?

Prometheus. I weigh not what ye do, but what ye suffer,
Being evil. Cruel was the power which called
You, or aught else so wretched, into light.

Third Fury. Thou thinkst we will live through thee, one by one,
Like animal life, and though we can obscure not
The soul which burns within, that we will dwell
Beside it, like a vain loud multitude
Vexing the self-content of wisest men :
That we will be dread thought beneath thy brain,
And foul desire round thine astonished heart,
And blood within thy labyrinthine veins
Crawling like agony.

Prometheus. Why, ye are thus now ;
Yet am I king over myself, and rule
The torturing and conflicting throngs within,
As Jove rules you when Hell grows mutinous.

CHORUS OF FURIES.

From the ends of the earth, from the ends of the earth,
Where the night has its grave and the morning its birth,
Come, come, come !
Oh, ye who shake hills with the scream of your mirth,
When cities sink howling in ruin ; and ye
Who with wingless footsteps trample the sea,
And close upon Shipwreck and Famine's track,
Sit chattering with joy on the foodless wreck ;
Come, come, come !

Leave the bed, low, cold, and red,
Strewed beneath a nation dead ;
Leave the hatred, as in ashes
Fire is left for future burning :
It will burst in bloodier flashes
When ye stir it, soon returning :
Leave the self-contempt implanted
In young spirits, sense-enchanted,
Misery's yet unkindled fuel :
Leave Hell's secrets half unchanted,
To the maniac dreamer : cruel
More than ye can be with hate
Is he with fear.
Come, come, come !
We are steaming up from Hell's wide gate,
And we burthen the blasts of the atmosphere,
But vainly we toil till ye come here.

Ione. Sister, I hear the thunder of new wings.

Panthea. These solid mountains quiver with the sound
Even as the tremulous air : their shadows make
The space within my plumes more black than night.

FIRST FURY.

Your call was as a winged car,
Driven on whirlwinds fast and far ;
It rapt us from red gulfs of war.

SECOND FURY.

From wide cities, famine wasted ;
THIRD FURY.

Groans half-heard, and blood untasted,

FOURTH FURY.

Kingly conclaves, stern and cold,
Where blood with gold is bought and sold ;

FIFTH FURY.

From the furnace, white and hot,
In which—

A FURY.

Speak not ; whisper not :
I know all that ye would tell,

But to speak might break the spell
Which must bend the Invincible,
The stern of thought ;
He yet defies the deepest power
of Hell.
Fury. Tear the veil !
Another Fury.   It is torn.

CHORUS.
The pale stars of the morn
Shine on a misery, dire to be borne.
Dost thou faint, mighty Titan ?   We
laugh thee to scorn.
Dost thou boast the clear knowledge
thou waken'dst for man ?
Then was kindled within him a thirst
which outran
Those perishing waters ; a thirst of
fierce fever,
Hope, love, doubt, desire, which con-
sume him for ever.
One came forth of gentle worth
Smiling on the sanguine earth :
His words outlived him, like
swift poison
Withering up truth, peace,
and pity.
Look ! where round the wide ho-
rizon
Many a million-peopled city
Vomits smoke in the bright air.
Mark that outcry of despair !
'Tis his mild and gentle ghost
Wailing for the faith he kindled:
Look again ! the flames almost
To a glow-worm's lamp have
dwindled :
The survivors round the embers
Gather in dread.
Joy, joy, joy !
Past ages crowd on thee, but each one
remembers ;
And the future is dark, and the pres-
ent is spread
Like a pillow of thorns for thy slum-
berless head.

SEMICHORUS I.
Drops of bloody agony flow
From his white and quivering brow.
Grant a little respite now :
See ! a disenchanted nation
Springs like day from desolation ;
To Truth its state is dedicate,
And Freedom leads it forth, her
mate ;

A legioned band of linked brothers,
Whom Love calls children—

SEMICHORUS II.
'Tis another's.
See how kindred murder kin !
'Tis the vintage-time for death and
sin.
Blood, like new wine, bubbles with-
in :
Till Despair smothers
The struggling world, which slaves
and tyrants win.
[*All the* FURIES *vanish, except one.*
Ione. Hark, sister ! what a low yet
dreadful groan
Quite unsuppressed is tearing up the
heart
Of the good Titan, as storms tear the
deep,
And beasts hear the sea moan in in-
land caves.
Darest thou observe how the fiends
torture him ?
Panthea. Alas ! I looked forth
twice, but will no more.
Ione. What didst thou see ?
Panthea.   A woful sight : a youth
With patient looks nailed to a crucifix.
Ione. What next ?
Panthea. The heaven around, the
earth below
Was peopled with thick shapes of
human death,
All horrible, and wrought by human
hands,
And some appeared the work of
human hearts,
For men were slowly killed by frowns
and smiles :
And other sights too foul to speak
and live
Were wandering by. Let us not
tempt worse fear
By looking forth : those groans are
grief enough.
Fury. Behold an emblem : those
who do endure
Deep wrongs for man, and scorn, and
chains, but heap
Thousandfold torment on themselves
and him.
Prometheus. Remit the anguish of
that lighted stare ;
Close those wan lips ; let that thorn-
wounded brow

Stream not with blood; it mingles with thy tears!
Fix, fix those tortured orbs in peace and death,
So thy sick throes shake not that crucifix,
So those pale fingers play not with thy gore.
O, horrible! Thy name I will not speak,
It hath become a curse. I see, I see
The wise, the mild, the lofty, and the just,
Whom thy slaves hate for being like to thee,
Some hunted by foul lies from their heart's home,
An early-chosen, late-lamented home,
As hooded ounces cling to the driven hind;
Some linked to corpses in unwholesome cells:
Some—Hear I not the multitude laugh loud?—
Impaled in lingering fire: and mighty realms   [isles,
Float by my feet, like sea-uprooted
Whose sons are kneaded down in common blood
By the red light of their own burning homes.
    Fury. Blood thou canst see, and fire; and canst hear groans:
Worse things unheard, unseen, remain behind.
    Prometheus. Worse?
    Fury.   In each human heart terror survives
The ravin it has gorged: the loftiest fear
All that they would disdain to think were true:
Hypocrisy and custom make their minds
The fanes of many a worship, now outworn.
They dare not devise good for man's estate,
And yet they know not that they do not dare.
The good want power, but to weep barren tears.
The powerful goodness want: worse need for them.
The wise want love; and those who love want wisdom;

And all best things are thus confused to ill.
Many are strong and rich, and would be just,
But live among their suffering fellowmen
As if none felt: they know not what they do.
    Prometheus. Thy words are like a cloud of winged snakes;
And yet I pity those they torture not.
    Fury. Thou pitiest them? I speak no more!   [*Vanishes.*
    Prometheus.   Ah woe!
Ah woe! Alas! pain, pain ever, for ever!
I close my tearless eyes, but see more clear
Thy works within my woe-illumined mind,
Thou subtle tyrant! Peace is in the grave.
The grave hides all things beautiful and good:
I am a God and cannot find it there,
Nor would I seek it: for, though dread revenge,   tory.
This is defeat, fierce king! not victory.
The sights with which thou torturest gird my soul
With new endurance, till the hour arrives
When they shall be no types of things which are.
    Panthea. Alas! what sawest thou?
    Prometheus.   There are two woes:
To speak and to behold; thou spare me one.
Names are there, Nature's sacred watchwords, they
Were borne aloft in bright emblazonry;
The nations thronged around, and cried aloud,
As with one voice, Truth, liberty, and love!
Suddenly fierce confusion fell from heaven
Among them: there was strife, deceit, and fear:
Tyrants rushed in, and did divide the spoil.
This was the shadow of the truth I saw.
    The Earth. I felt thy torture, son, with such mixed joy

As pain and virtue give. To cheer
thy state
I bid ascend those subtle and fair
spirits,
Whose homes are the dim caves of
human thought,
And who inhabit, as birds wing the
wind,
Its world-surrounding ether: they
behold
Beyond that twilight realm, as in a
glass,
The future: may they speak com-
fort to thee!
Panthea. Look, sister, where a
troop of spirits gather,
Like flocks of clouds in spring's de-
lightful weather,
Thronging in the blue air!
Ione.   And see! more come,
Like fountain-vapours when the
winds are dumb,
That climb up the ravine in scattered
lines.
And hark! is it the music of the pines?
Is it the lake? Is it the waterfall?
Panthea. 'Tis something sadder,
sweeter far than all.

CHORUS OF SPIRITS.

From unremembered ages we
Gentle guides and guardians be
Of heaven-oppressed mortality!
And we breathe, and sicken not,
The atmosphere of human thought:
Be it dim, and dank, and grey,
Like a storm-extinguished day,
Travelled o'er by dying gleams:
Be it bright as all between
Cloudless skies and windless streams,
Silent, liquid, and serene;
As the birds within the wind,
As the fish within the wave,
As the thoughts of man's own mind
Float through all above the grave:
We make there our liquid lair,
Voyaging cloudlike and unpent
Through the boundless element:
Thence we bear the prophecy
Which begins and ends in thee!
Ione. More yet come, one by one:
the air around them
Looks radiant as the air around a star.

FIRST SPIRIT.

On a battle-trumpet's blast
I fled hither, fast, fast, fast,
'Mid the darkness upward cast.
From the dust of creeds outworn,
From the tyrant's banner torn,
Gathering round me, onward borne,
There was mingled many a cry—
Freedom! Hope! Death! Victory!
Till they faded through the sky;
And one sound above around,
One sound beneath, around, above,
Was moving; 'twas the soul of love;
'Twas the hope, the prophecy,
Which begins and ends in thee.

SECOND SPIRIT.

A rainbow's arch stood on the sea,
Which rocked beneath, immovably;
And the triumphant storm did flee,
Like a conqueror, swift and proud,
Between with many a captive cloud,
A shapeless, dark and rapid crowd,
Each by lightning riven in half:
I heard the thunder hoarsely laugh:
Mighty fleets were strewn like chaff
And spread beneath a hell of death
O'er the white waters. I alit
On a great ship lightning-split,
And speeded hither on the sigh
Of one who gave an enemy
His plank, then plunged aside to die.

THIRD SPIRIT.

I sate beside a sage's bed,
And the lamp was burning red
Near the book where he had fed,
When a Dream with plumes of flame,
To his pillow hovering came,
And I knew it was the same
Which had kindled long ago
Pity, eloquence, and woe;
And the world awhile below
Wore the shade its lustre made.
It has borne me here as fleet
As Desire's lightning feet:
I must ride it back ere morrow,
Or the sage will wake in sorrow.

FOURTH SPIRIT.

On a poet's lips I slept
Dreaming like a love-adept
In the sound his breathing kept;
Nor seeks nor finds he mortal blisses,
But feeds on the aërial kisses
Of shapes that haunt thought's
wildernesses.
He will watch from dawn to gloom
The lake-reflected sun illume

The yellow bees in the ivy-bloom,
Nor heed nor see, what things they be
But from these create he can
Forms more real than living man,
Nurslings of immortality !
One of these awakened me,
And I sped to succour thee.

Ione. Beholdst thou not two
shapes from the east and west
Come, as two doves to one beloved
nest,
Twin nurslings of the all-sustaining
air,
On swift still wings glide down the
atmosphere ?
And, hark ! their sweet sad voices !
'tis despair
Mingled with love and then dissolved
in sound.

Panthea. Canst thou speak, sister ?
all my words are drowned.

Ione. Their beauty gives me voice.
See how they float
On their sustaining wings of skyey
grain,
Orange and azure deepening into
gold :
Their soft smiles light the air like a
star's fire.

CHORUS OF SPIRITS.

Hast thou beheld the form of Love ?

FIFTH SPIRIT.

As over wide dominions
I sped, like some swift cloud that
wings the wide air's wildernesses,
That planet-crested shape swept by
on lightning-braided pinions,
Scattering the liquid joy of life from
his ambrosial tresses :
His footsteps paved the world with
light ; but as I past 'twas fading,
And hollow Ruin yawned behind :
great sages bound in madness,
And headless patriots, and pale youths
who perished, unupbraiding,
Gleamed in the night. I wandered
o'er, till thou, O King of sadness,
Turned by thy smile the worst I saw
to recollected gladness.

SIXTH SPIRIT.

Ah, sister ! Desolation is a delicate
thing :
It walks not on the earth, it floats not
on the air,

But treads with silent footstep, and
fans with silent wing
The tender hopes which in their
hearts the best and gentlest bear ;
Who, soothed to false repose by the
fanning plumes above,
And the music-stirring motion of its
soft and busy feet,
Dream visions of aërial joy, and call
the monster, Love,
And wake, and find the shadow Pain,
as he whom now we greet.

CHORUS.

Though Ruin now Love's shadow be,
Following him, destroyingly,
On Death's white and winged steed,
Which the fleetest cannot flee,
Trampling down both flower and
weed,
Man and beast, and foul and fair,
Like a tempest through the air ;
Thou shalt quell this horseman grim,
Woundless though in heart or limb.

Prometheus. Spirits ! how know ye
this shall be ?

CHORUS.

In the atmosphere we breathe,
As buds grow red when the snow-
storms flee,
From spring gathering up beneath,
Whose mild winds shake the elder-
brake,
And the wandering herdsmen know
That the white-thorn soon will blow :
Wisdom, Justice, Love, and Peace,
When they struggle to increase,
Are to us as soft winds be
To shepherd boys, the prophecy
Which begins and ends in thee.

Ione. Where are the Spirits fled ?

Panthea. Only a sense
Remains of them, like the omnipotence
Of music, when the inspired voice and
lute
Languish, ere yet the responses are
mute,
Which through the deep and labyrinthine soul,
Like echoes through long caverns,
wind and roll.

Prometheus. How fair these air-
born shapes ! and yet I feel
Most vain all hope but love ; and
thou art far,

Asia! who, when my being over-
flowed,
Wert like a golden chalice to bright
wine
Which else had sunk into the thirsty
dust.
All things are still: alas! how heav-
ily
This quiet morning weighs upon my
heart;
Though I should dream I could even
sleep with grief,
If slumber were denied not. I would
fain
Be what it is my destiny to be,
The saviour and the strength of
suffering man,
Or sink into the original gulf of things.
There is no agony, and no solace left;
Earth can console, Heaven can tor-
ment no more.
Panthea. Hast thou forgotten one
who watches thee
The cold dark night, and never sleeps
but when
The shadow of thy spirit falls on her?
Prometheus. I said all hope was
vain but love: thou lovest.
Panthea. Deeply in truth; but the
eastern star looks white,
And Asia waits in that far Indian vale
The scene of her sad exile; rugged
once
And desolate and frozen, like this
ravine;
But now invested with fair flowers
and herbs,
And haunted by sweet airs and
sounds, which flow
Among the woods and waters, from
the ether
Of her transforming presence, which
would fade
If it were mingled not with thine.
Farewell!

ACT II

SCENE I.—*Morning. A lonely Vale
in the Indian Caucasus.*

ASIA, *alone.*

Asia. From all the blasts of
heaven thou hast descended!
Yes, like a spirit, like a thought,
which makes

Unwonted tears throng to the horny
eyes,
And beatings haunt the desolated
heart,
Which should have learnt repose:
thou hast descended
Cradled in tempests; thou dost wake,
O Spring!
O child of many winds! As sud-
denly
Thou comest as the memory of a
dream,
Which now is sad because it hath been
sweet;
Like genius, or like joy, which riseth
up
As from the earth, clothing with
golden clouds
The desert of our life.
This is the season, this the day, the
hour;
At sunrise thou shouldst come, sweet
sister mine,
Too long desired, too long delaying,
come!
How like death-worms the wingless
moments crawl!
The point of one white star is quiver-
ing still
Deep in the orange light of widening
morn
Beyond the purple mountains:
through a chasm
Of wind-divided mist the darker lake
Reflects it; now it wanes: it gleams
again
As the waves fade, and as the burning
threads
Of woven cloud unravel in pale air:
'Tis lost! and through yon peaks of
cloud-like snow
The roseate sunlight quivers: hear
I not
The Æolian music of her sea-green
plumes
Winnowing the crimson dawn?
[PANTHEA *enters.*
I feel, I see
Those eyes which burn through smiles
that fade in tears,
Like stars half-quenched in mists of
silver dew.
Beloved and most beautiful, who
wearest
The shadow of that soul by which I
live.

How late thou art ! the sphered sun
  had climbed
The sea ; my heart was sick with
  hope, before
The printless air felt thy belated
  plumes.
    Panthea. Pardon, great Sister ! but
  my wings were faint
With the delight of a remembered
  dream,
As are the noontide plumes of sum-
  mer winds
Satiate with sweet flowers. I was
  wont to sleep
Peacefully, and awake refreshed and
  calm
Before the sacred Titan's fall, and thy
Unhappy love, had made, through
  use and pity,
Both love and woe familiar to my
  heart
As they had grown to thine : erewhile
  I slept
Under the glaucous caverns of old
  Ocean
Within dim bowers of green and
  purple moss,
Our young Ione's soft and milky arms
Locked then, as now, behind my dark,
  moist hair,
While my shut eyes and cheek were
  pressed within
The folded depth of her life-breathing
  bosom :   [wind
But not as now, since I am made the
Which fails beneath the music that I
  bear
Of thy most wordless converse ; since
  dissolved
Into the sense with which love talks,
  my rest
Was troubled and yet sweet ; my
  waking hours
Too full of care and pain.
    Asia.   Lift up thine eyes,
And let me read thy dream.
    Panthea.   As I have said,
With our sea-sister at his feet I slept.
The mountain mists, condensing at
  our voice
Under the moon had spread their
   snowy flakes,
From the keen ice shielding our linked
  sleep.
Then two dreams came. One, I
  remember not.

But in the other his pale wound-worn
  limbs
Fell from Prometheus, and the azure
  night
Grew radiant with the glory of that
  form
Which lives unchanged within, and
  his voice fell
Like music which makes giddy the
  dim brain,
Faint with intoxication of keen joy :
" Sister of her whose footsteps pave
  the world
With loveliness—more fair than
  aught but her,
Whose shadow thou art—lift thine
  eyes on me."
I lifted them : the overpowering light
Of that immortal shape was shadowed
  o'er
By love ; which, from his soft and
  flowing limbs,
And passion-parted lips, and keen,
  faint eyes,
Steamed forth like vaporous fire ; an
  atmosphere
Which wrapped me in its all-dissolv-
  ing power,
As the warm ether of the morning sun
Wraps ere it drinks some cloud of
  wandering dew.
I saw not, heard not, moved not, only
  felt
His presence flow and mingle through
  my blood
Till it became his life, and his grew
  mine,
And I was thus absorbed, until it
  passed,
And like the vapours when the sun
  sinks down,
Gathering again in drops upon the
  pines,
And tremulous as they, in the deep
  night
My being was condensed ; and as
  the rays
Of thought were slowly gathered, I
  could hear
His voice, whose accents lingered ere
  they died
Like footsteps of weak melody : thy
  name
Among the many sounds alone I heard
Of what might be articulate ; though
  still

I listened through the night when
sound was none.
Ione wakened then, and said to me :
" Canst thou divine what troubles me
to-nig'it ?
I always knew what I desired before,
Nor ever found delight to wish in
vain.
But now I cannot tell thee what I
seek ;
I know not ; something sweet, since
it is sweet
Even to desire ; it is thy sport, false
sister ;
Thou hast discovered some enchant-
ment old,
Whose spells have stolen my spirit
as I slept
And mingled it with thine : for when
just now
We kissed, I felt within thy parted lips
The sweet air that sustained me, and
the warmth
Of the life-blood, for loss of which
I faint,
Quivered between our intertwining
arms."
I answered not, for the Eastern star
grew pale,
But fled to thee.
　Asia.　Thou speakest, but thy
words　　　　　　　　　　[lift
Are as the air : I feel them not : Oh,
Thine eyes, that I may read his
written soul !
　Panthea. I lift them, though they
droop beneath the load
Of that they would express : what
canst thou see
But thine own fairest shadow imaged
there ?
　Asia. Thine eyes are like the deep,
blue, boundless heaven
Contracted to two circles underneath
Their long, fine lashes ; dark, far,
measureless
Orb within orb, and line through line
inwoven,
　Panthea. Why lookest thou as if
a spirit passed ?
　Asia.　There is a change ; beyond
their inmost depth
I see a shade, a shape : 'tis He,
arrayed
In the soft light of his own smiles,
which spread

Like radiance from the cloud-sur-
rounded morn.
Prometheus, it is thine ! depart not
yet !
Say not those smiles that we shall
meet again
Within that bright pavilion which
their beams
Shall build on the waste world ?　The
dream is told.
What shape is that between us ?　Its
rude hair
Roughens the wind that lifts it, its
regard
Is wild and quick, yet, 'tis a thing of
air,
For through its grey robe gleams the
golden dew
Whose stars the noon has quenched
not.
　Dream.　　Follow ! Follow !
　Panthea. It is mine other dream.
　Asia.　　　　　It disappears.
　Panthea. It passes now into my
mind.　Methought
As we sate here, the flower-enfolding
buds
Burst on yon lightning-blasted al-
mond tree,
When swift from the white Scythian
wilderness
A wind swept forth wrinkling the
Earth with frost :
I looked, and all the blossoms were
blown down ;
But on each leaf was stamped, as the
blue bells　　　　　　　　[grief,
Of Hyacinth tell Apollo's written
O, FOLLOW, FOLLOW !
　Asia.　　As you speak, your words
Fill, pause by pause, my own for-
gotten sleep
With shapes.　Methought among the
lawns together
We wandered, underneath the young
grey dawn,
And multitudes of dense white
fleecy clouds
Were wandering in thick flocks along
the mountains
Shepherded by the slow, unwilling
wind ;
And the white dew on the new-
bladed grass,
Just piercing the dark earth, hung
silently ;

And there was more which I remember not :
But on the shadows of the morning clouds,
Athwart the purple mountain slope, was written
FOLLOW, O FOLLOW ! As they vanished by,
And on each herb, from which Heaven's dew had fallen,
The like was stamped, as with a withering fire,
A wind arose among the pines ; it shook
The clinging music from their boughs, and then
Low, sweet, faint sounds, like the farewell of ghosts,
Were heard : O, FOLLOW, FOLLOW, FOLLOW ME !
And then I said, " Panthea, look on me."
But in the depth of those beloved eyes
Still I saw, FOLLOW, FOLLOW !
Echo.   Follow, follow !
Panthea. The crags, this clear spring morning, mock our voices,
As they were spirit-tongued.
Asia.   It is some being
Around the crags. What fine clear sounds ! O, list !

ECHOES (*unseen*).
Echoes we : listen !
   We cannot stay :
As dew-stars glisten
   Then fade away—
      Child of Ocean !

Asia. Hark ! Spirits, speak. The liquid responses
Of their aërial tongues yet sound.
Panthea.   I hear.

ECHOES.
O, follow, follow !
   As our voice recedeth
Through the caverns hollow,
   Where the forest spreadeth ;

(*More distant.*)

O, follow, follow,
Through the caverns hollow,
As the song floats thou pursue,
Where the wild bee never flew,

Through the noon-tide darkness deep,
By the odour-breathing sleep
Of faint night-flowers, and the waves
At the fountain-lighted caves,
While our music, wild and sweet,
Mocks thy gently falling feet,
      Child of Ocean !

Asia. Shall we pursue the sound ? It grows more faint
And distant.
Panthea. List ! the strain floats nearer now.

ECHOES.
In the world unknown
   Sleeps a voice unspoken ;
By thy step alone
   Can its rest be broken ;
      Child of Ocean !

Asia. How the notes sink upon the ebbing wind !

ECHOES.
O, follow, follow !
Through the caverns hollow,
As the song floats thou pursue,
By the woodland noon-tide dew ;
By the forests, lakes, and fountains,
Through the many-folded mountains ;
To the rents, and gulfs, and chasms,
Where the Earth reposed from spasms,
On the day when He and thou
Parted, to commingle now ;
      Child of Ocean !

Asia. Come, sweet Panthea, link thy hand in mine,
And follow, ere the voices fade away.

SCENE II.—*A Forest, intermingled with Rocks and Caverns.* ASIA *and* PANTHEA *pass into it. Two young Fauns are sitting on a Rock, listening.*

SEMICHORUS I. OF SPIRITS.
The path through which that lovely twain
   Have past, by cedar, pine, and yew,
   And each dark tree that ever grew,
Is curtained out from Heaven's wide blue ;
Nor sun, nor moon, nor wind, nor rain,

Can pierce its interwoven
bowers,
Nor aught, save where some cloud
of dew,
Drifted along the earth-creeping
breeze,
Between the trunks of the hoar trees,
Hangs each a pearl in the pale
flowers
Of the green laurel, blown anew;
And bends, and then fades silently,
One frail and fair anemone :
Or when some star of many a one
That climbs and wanders through
steep night,
Has found the cleft through which
alone
Beams fall from high those depths
upon
Ere it is borne away, away,
By the swift Heavens that cannot
stay,
It scatters drops of golden light,
Like lines of rain that ne'er unite :
And the gloom divine is all around ;
And underneath is the mossy ground.

SEMICHORUS II.
There the voluptuous nightingales,
Are awake through all the broad
noon-day,
When one with bliss or sadness fails,
And through the windless ivy
boughs,
Sick with sweet love, droops dying
away
On its mate's music-panting bosom ;
Another from the swinging blossom,
Watching to catch the languid
close
Of the last strain, then lifts on
high
The wings of the weak melody,
Till some new strain of feeling bear
The song, and all the woods are
mute ;
When there is heard through the dim
air
The rush of wings, and rising there
Like many a lake-surrounded flute,
Sounds overflow the listener's brain
So sweet, that joy is almost pain.

SEMICHORUS I.
There those enchanted eddies play
Of echoes, music-tongued, which
draw,

By Demogorgon's mighty law,
With melting rapture, or sweet awe,
All spirits on that secret way ;
As inland boats are driven to
Ocean
Down streams made strong with
mountain-thaw
And first there comes a gentle
sound
To those in talk or slumber
bound,
And wakes the destined, soft
emotion
Attracts, impels them ; those who
saw
Say from the breathing earth be-
hind
There streams a plume-uplifting
wind
Which drives them on their path,
while they
Believe their own swift wings and
feet
The sweet desires within obey :
And so they float upon their way,
Until, still sweet, but loud and
strong,
The storm of sound is driven along,
Sucked up and hurrying : as they
fleet
Behind, its gathering billows meet
And to the fatal mountain bear
Like clouds amid the yielding air.
First Faun. Canst thou imagine
where those spirits live
Which make such delicate music in
the woods ?   [caves
We haunt within the least frequented
And closest coverts, and we know
these wilds,
Yet never meet them, though we hear
them oft :
Where may they hide themselves ?
Second Faun.   'Tis hard to tell :
I have heard those more skilled in
spirits say,
The bubbles, which enchantment of
the sun
Sucks from the pale faint water-
flowers that pave
The oozy bottom of clear lakes and
pools,
Are the pavilions where such dwell
and float
Under the green and golden atmo-
sphere

Which noon-tide kindles through the
woven leaves ;
And when these burst, and the thin
fiery air,
The which they breathed within those
lucent domes,
Ascends to flow like meteors through
the night,
They ride on them, and rein their
headlong speed,
And bow their burning crests, and
glide in fire
Under the waters of the earth again.
    First Faun. If such live thus, have
others other lives,
Under pink blossoms or within the
bell;
Of meadow flowers, or folded violets
deep,
Or on their dying odours, when they
die,
Or on the sunlight of the sphered dew ?
    Second Faun. Ay, many more
which we may well divine.
But should we stay to speak, noon-
tide would come,
And thwart Silenus find his goats un-
drawn,
And grudge to sing those wise and
lovely songs
Of Fate, and Chance, and God, and
Chaos old,
And Love, and the chained Titan's
woeful doom.
And how he shall be loosed, and make
    the earth
One brotherhood : delightful strains
which cheer
Our solitary twilights, and which
charm
To silence the unenvying nightingales.

SCENE III.—*A Pinnacle of Rock
among Mountains.* ASIA *and*
PANTHEA.

    Panthea. Hither the sound has
borne us—to the realm
Of Demogorgon, and the mighty portal,
Like a volcano's meteor-breathing
chasm,
Whence the oracular vapour is hurled
up
Which lonely men drink wandering in
their youth,

And call truth, virtue, love, genius,
or joy,
That maddening wine of life, whose
dregs they drain
To deep intoxication ; and uplift,
Like Mænads who cry loud, Evoe !
Evoe !
The voice which is contagion to the
world.
    Asia. Fit throne for such a Power !
Magnificent !
How glorious art thou, Earth ! and if
thou be
The shadow of some spirit lovelier
still,
Though evil stain its work, and it
should be
Like its creation, weak yet beautiful,
I could fall down and worship that
and thee.
Even now my heart adoreth : Won-
derful !
Look, sister, ere the vapour dim thy
brain :
Beneath is a wide plain of billowy
mist,
As a lake, paving in the morning sky,
With azure waves which burst in sil-
ver light,
Some Indian vale.   Behold it, rolling
on
Under the curdling winds, and island-
ing
The peak whereon we stand, midway,
around,
Encinctured by the dark and bloom-
ing forests,
Dim twilight-lawns, and stream-illu-
mined caves,
And wind-enchanted shapes of wan-
dering mist ;
And far on high the keen sky-cleaving
mountains,
From icy spires of sunlike radiance
fling
The dawn, as lifted Ocean's dazzling
spray,
From some Atlantic islet scattered up,
Spangles the wind with lamp-like
water-drops.
The vale is girdled with their walls, a
howl
Of Cataracts from their thaw-cloven
ravines
Satiates the listening wind, continu-
ous, vast,

Awful as silence. Hark ! the rushing
  snow !
The sun-awakened avalanche ! whose
  mass,
Thrice sifted by the storm, had gath-
  ered there
Flake after flake, in heaven-defying
  minds
As thought by thought is piled, till
  some great truth
Is loosened, and the nations echo
  round,
Shaken to their roots, as do the moun-
  tains now.
  Panthea. Look how the gusty sea
    of mist is breaking
In crimson foam, even at our feet !
  it rises
As Ocean at the enchantment of the
  moon
Round foodless men wrecked on some
  oozy isle.
  Asia. The fragments of the cloud
    are scattered up ;
The wind that lifts them disentwines
  my hair ;
Its billows now sweep o'er mine eyes ;
  my brain
Grows dizzy ; I see shapes within the
  mist.
  Panthea. A countenance with beck-
    oning smiles : there burns
An azure fire within its golden locks !
Another and another : hark ! they
  speak !

SONG OF SPIRITS.
To the deep, to the deep,
    Down, down !
Through the shade of sleep,
Through the cloudy strife
Of Death and of Life ;
Through the veil and the bar
Of things which seem and are,
Even to the steps of the remotest
  throne,
    Down, down !

While the sound whirls around,
    Down, down !
As the fawn draws the hound,
As the lightning the vapour,
As a weak moth the taper ;
Death, despair ; love, sorrow ;
Time both ; to-day, to-morrow ;
As steel obeys the spirit of the stone,
    Down, down !

Through the grey, void abysm,
    Down, down !
Where the air is no prism,
And the moon and stars are not,
And the cavern-crags wear not
The radiance of Heaven,
Nor the gloom to Earth given,
Where there is one pervading, one
  alone,
    Down, down !

In the depth of the deep
    Down, down !
Like veiled lightning asleep,
Like the spark nursed in embers,
The last look Love remembers,
Like a diamond, which shines
On the dark wealth of mines.
A spell is treasured but for thee
  alone.
    Down, down !

We have bound thee, we guide thee ;
    Down, down !
With the bright form beside thee ;
Resist not the weakness,
Such strength is in meekness
That the Eternal, the Immortal,
Must unloose through life's portal
The snake-like Doom coiled under-
  neath his throne
    By that alone.

SCENE IV.—*The Cave of* DEMOGOR-
  GON. ASIA *and* PANTHEA.

  Panthea. What veiled form sits on
    that ebon throne ?
  Asia. The veil has fallen.
  Panthea.   I see a mighty dark-
    ness
Filling the seat of power, and rays of
  gloom
Dart round, as light from the merid-
  ian sun,
Ungazed upon and shapeless ; neith-
  er limb,
Nor form, nor outline ; yet we feel it
  is
A living spirit.
  Demogorgon. Ask   what   thou
    wouldst know.
  Asia. What canst thou tell ?
  Demogorgon.   All   things   thou
    dar'st demand.
  Asia. Who made the living world ?

Demogorgon.   GOD.
Asia.   Who made all
That it contains ? thought, passion,
    reason, will,
Imagination ?
    Demogorgon. God : Almighty God.
    Asia. Who made that sense which,
        when the winds of spring
In rarest visitation, or the voice
Of one beloved heard in youth alone,
Fills the faint eyes with falling tears
    which dim
The radiant looks of unbewailing
    flowers,
And leaves this peopled earth a soli-
    tude
When it returns no more ?
    Demogorgon.   Merciful God.
    Asia. And who made terror, mad-
        ness, crime, remorse,
Which from the links of the great
    chain of things,
To every thought within the mind of
    man
Sway and drag heavily, and each one
    reels
Under the load towards the pit of
    death ;
Abandoned hope, and love that turns
    to hate ;
And self-contempt, bitterer to drink
    than blood ;   [speech
Pain, whose unheeded and familiar
Is howling, and keen shrieks, day
    after day ;
And Hell, or the sharp fear of Hell ?
    Demogorgon.   He reigns.
    Asia. Utter his name : a world
        pining in pain
Asks but his name : curses shall drag
    him down.
    Demogorgon. He reigns.
    Asia. I feel, I know it : who ?
    Demogorgon.   He reigns.
    Asia. Who reigns ? There was the
        Heaven and Earth at first,
And Light and Love ; then Saturn,
    from whose throne
Time fell, an envious shadow : such
    the state
Of the earth's primal spirits beneath
    his sway,
As the calm joy of flowers and living
    leaves
Before the wind or sun has withered
    them

And semi-vital worms ; but he re-
    fused
The birthright of their being, know-
    ledge, power,
The skill which wields the elements,
    the thought
Which pierces this dim universe like
    light,
Self-empire, and the majesty of love ;
For thirst of which they fainted. Then
    Prometheus
Gave wisdom, which is strength, to
    Jupiter,
And with this law alone, " Let man
    be free,"
Clothed him with the dominion of
    wide Heaven.
To know nor faith, nor love, nor law ;
    to be
Omnipotent but friendless is to reign ;
And Jove now reigned ; for on the
    race of man
First famine, and then toil, and then
    disease,
Strife, wounds, and ghastly death un-
    seen before,
Fell ; and the unseasonable seasons
    drove,
With alternating shafts of frost and
    fire,
Their shelterless, pale tribes to moun-
    tain caves :
And in their desert hearts fierce wants
    he sent,
And mad disquietudes, and shadows
    idle
Of unreal good, which levied mutual
    war,
So ruining the lair wherein they raged.
Prometheus saw, and waked the le-
    gioned hopes
Which sleep within folded Elysian
    flowers,
Nepenthe, Moly, Amaranth, fadeless
    blooms,
That they might hide with thin and
    rainbow wings
The shape of Death ; and Love he
    sent to bind
The disunited tendrils of that vine
Which bears the wine of life, the hu-
    man heart ;
And he tamed fire which, like some
    beast of prey,
Most terrible, but lovely, played be-
    neath

The frown of man ; and tortured to
his will
Iron and gold, the slaves and signs of
power,
And gems and poisons and all subtlest
forms
Hidden beneath the mountains and
the waves.
He gave man speech, and speech cre-
ated thought,
Which is the measure of the universe ;
And Science struck the thrones of
earth and heaven,
Which shook, but fell not ; and the
harmonious mind
Poured itself forth in all-prophetic
song ;
And music lifted up the listening
spirit
Until it walked, exempt from mortal
care,
Godlike, o'er the clear billows of sweet
sound ;
And human hands first mimicked and
then mocked,
With moulded limbs more lovely
than its own,   [vine,
The human form, till marble grew di-
And mothers, gazing, drank the love
men see
Reflected in their race, behold, and
perish.
He told the hidden power of herbs and
springs,
And Disease drank and slept. Death
grew like sleep.
He taught the implicated orbits woven
Of the wide-wandering stars ; and
how the sun
Changes his lair, and by what secret
spell
The pale moon is transformed, when
her broad eye
Gazes not on the interlunar sea :
He taught to rule, as life directs the
limbs,
The tempest-winged chariots of the
Ocean,
And the Celt knew the Indian. Cities
then
Were built, and through their snow-
like columns flowed
The warm winds, and the azure
ether shone,
And the blue sea and shadowy hills
were seen.

Such, the alleviations of his state,
Prometheus gave to man, for which he
hangs
Withering in destined pain : but who
rains down
Evil, the immedicable plague, which,
while
Man looks on his creation like a God
And sees that it is glorious, drives him
on
The wreck of his own will, the scorn
of earth,
The outcast, the abandoned, the
alone ?
Not Jove : while yet his frown shook
heaven, ay, when
His adversary from adamantine
chains
Cursed him, he trembled like a slave.
Declare
Who is his master ? Is he too a
slave ?
   Demogorgon. All spirits are en-
slaved which serve things evil .
Thou knowest if Jupiter be such or no.
   Asia. Whom calledst thou God ?
   Demogorgon. I spoke but as ye
speak,
For Jove is the supreme of living
things.
   Asia. Who is the master of the
slave ?
   Demogorgon. If the abysm
Could vomit forth its secrets. But a
voice
Is wanting. the deep truth is image-
less ;
For what would it avail to bid thee
gaze
On the revolving world ? What to
bid speak
Fate. Time, Occasion, Chance and
Change ? To these
All things are subject but eternal
Love.
   Asia. So much I asked before, and
my heart gave
The response thou hast given ; and of
such truths
Each to itself must be the oracle.
One more demand ; and do thou
answer me
As my own soul would answer, did it
know
That which I ask. Prometheus shall
arise

Henceforth the sun of this rejoicing
　　world :
When shall the destined hour arrive !

Demogorgon.　　　　　　　Behold !

　Asia. The rocks are cloven, and
　　through the purple night
I see cars drawn by rainbow-winged
　　steeds
Which trample the dim winds : in
　　each there stands
A wild-eyed chariotcer urging their
　　flight.
Some look behind, as fiends pursued
　　them there,
And yet I see no shapes but the keen
　　stars :
Others, with burning eyes, lean forth,
　　and drink
With eager lips the wind of their own
　　speed,
As if the thing they loved fled on be-
　　fore,
And now, even now, they clasped it.
　　Their bright locks
Stream like a comet's flashing hair :
　　they all
Sweep onward.

　Demogorgon. These are the immor-
　　tal Hours,
Of whom thou didst demand. One
　　waits for thee.

　Asia. A spirit with a dreadful
　　countenance
Checks its dark chariot by the craggy
　　gulf.
Unlike thy brethren, ghastly chari-
　　oteer,
Who art thou ? Whither wouldst
　　thou bear me ? Speak !

　Spirit. I am the shadow of a des-
　　tiny
More dread than is my aspect : ere
　　yon planet
Has set, the darkness which ascends
　　with me
Shall wrap in lasting night heaven's
　　kingless throne.

　Asia. What meanest thou ?

　Panthea.　　　That terrible shadow
　　floats
Up from its throne, as may the lurid
　　smoke
Of earthquake-ruined cities o'er the
　　sea.
Lo ! it ascends the car ; the coursers
　　fly

Terrified : watch its path among the
　　stars
Blackening the night !

　Asia.　　　Thus I am answered :
　　strange !

　Panthea. See, near the verge, an-
　　other chariot stays ;
An ivory shell inlaid with crimson
　　fire,
Which comes and goes within its
　　sculptured rim
Of delicate strange tracery ;　the
　　young spirit
That guides it has the dove-like eyes
　　of hope ;
How its soft smiles attract the soul !
　　as light
Lures winged insects through the
　　lampless air.

SPIRIT.

My coursers are fed with the lightning,
　　They drink of the whirlwind's
　　　stream,
And when the red morning is bright-
　　'ning
　　They bathe in the fresh sunbeam ;
　　They have strength for their swift-
　　　ness, I deem,
Then ascend with me, daughter of
　　Ocean.

I desire : and their speed makes night
　　kindle ;
　　I fear : they outstrip the Typhoon ;
Ere the cloud piled on Atlas can
　　dwindle
　　We encircle the earth and the
　　　moon :
　　We shall rest from long labours at
　　　noon :
Then ascend with me, daughter of
　　Ocean.

SCENE V.—*The Car pauses within a
　　Cloud on the Top of a snowy
　　Mountain.* ASIA, PANTHEA, *and
　　the* SPIRIT OF THE HOUR

SPIRIT.

On the brink of the night and the
　　morning
　　My coursers are wont to respire ;
But the Earth has just whispered a
　　warning
　　That their flight must be swifter
　　　than fire :

They shall drink the hot speed of desire !

Asia. Thou breathest on their nostrils, but my breath
Would give them swifter speed.

Spirit.   Alas ! it could not.

Panthea. Oh Spirit ! pause, and tell whence is the light
Which fills the cloud ? the sun is yet unrisen.

Spirit. The sun will rise not until noon. Apollo
Is held in heaven by wonder ; and the light
Which fills this vapour, as the aërial hue
Of fountain-gazing roses fills the water,
Flows from thy mighty sister.

Panthea.   Yes, I feel—

Asia. What is it with thee, sister ? Thou art pale.

Panthea. How thou art changed ! I dare not look on thee ;
I feel but see thee not. I scarce endure
The radiance of thy beauty. Some good change
Is working in the elements, which suffer
Thy presence thus unveiled. The Nereids tell
That on the day when the clear hyaline
Was cloven at thy uprise, and thou didst stand
Within a veined shell, which floated on
Over the calm floor of the crystal sea,
Among the Egean isles, and by the shores
Which bear thy name ; love, like the atmosphere
Of the sun's fire filling the living world,
Burst from thee, and illumined earth and heaven
And the deep ocean and the sunless caves
And all that dwells within them ; till grief cast
Eclipse upon the soul from which it came :
Such art thou now ; nor is it I alone,
Thy sister, thy companion, thine own chosen one,

But the whole world which seeks thy sympathy.
Hearest thou not sounds i' the air which speak the love
Of all articulate beings ? Feelest thou not
The inanimate winds enamoured of thee ? List !   [*Music.*

Asia. Thy words are sweeter than aught else but his
Whose echoes they are : yet all love is sweet,
Given or returned. Common as light is love,   [ever,
And its familiar voice wearies not
Like the wide heaven, the all-sustaining air,
It makes the reptile equal to the God :
They who inspire it most are fortunate,
As I am now ; but those who feel it most
Are happier still, after long sufferings,
As I shall soon become.

Panthea. List ! Spirits, speak.

VOICE (*in the air, singing*).

Life of Life ! thy lips enkindle
      With their love the breath between them ;
And thy smiles before they dwindle
      Make the cold air fire ; then screen them
In those looks, where whoso gazes
Faints, entangled in their mazes.

Child of Light ! thy limbs are burning
      Through the vest which seems to hide them ;
As the radiant lines of morning
      Through the clouds, ere they divide them ;
And this atmosphere divinest
Shrouds thee wheresoe'er thou shinest.

Fair are others ; none beholds thee,
      But thy voice sounds low and tender
Like the fairest, for it folds thee
      From the sight, that liquid splendour,
And all feel, yet see thee never,
As I feel now, lost for ever !

Lamp of Earth ! where'er thou movest

Its dim shapes are clad with bright-
ness,
And the souls of whom thou lovest
Walk upon the winds with light-
ness,
Till they fail, as I am failing,
Dizzy, lost, yet unbewailing !

ASIA.

My soul is an enchanted boat,
Which, like a sleeping swan, doth
float
Upon the silver waves of thy sweet
singing ;
And thine doth like an angel sit
Beside the helm conducting it,
Whilst all the winds with melody are
ringing.
It seems to float ever, for ever,
Upon that many-winding river,
Between mountains, woods, abys-
ses,
A paradise of wildernesses !
Till, like one in slumber bound,
Borne to the ocean, I float down,
around,
Into a sea profound, of ever-spreading
sound.

Meanwhile thy spirit lifts its pinions
In music's most serene dominions ;
Catching the winds that fan that
happy heaven.
And we sail on, away, afar,
Without a course, without a star,
But, by the instinct of sweet music
driven ;
Till through Elysian garden islets
By thee, most beautiful of pilots,
Where never mortal pinnace glided,
The boat of my desire is guided :
Realms where the air we breathe is
love,
Which in the winds on the waves doth
move,
Harmonising this earth with what we
feel above

We have passed Age's icy caves,
And Manhood's dark and tossing
waves,
And Youth's smooth ocean, smiling to
betray :
Beyond the glassy gulfs we flee
Of shadow-peopled Infancy,
Through Death and Birth, to a di-
viner day :

A paradise of vaulted bowers
Lit by downward-gazing flowers,
And watery paths that wind be-
tween
Wildernesses calm and green,
Peopled by shapes too bright to see,
And rest, having beheld ; somewhat
like thee ;
Which walk upon the sea, and chant
melodiously !

ACT III

SCENE I.—*Heaven.* JUPITER *on his
Throne ;* THETIS *and the other
Deities assembled.*

Jupiter. Ye congregated powers of
heaven, who share
The glory and the strength of him
ye serve,
Rejoice ! henceforth I am omnipotent.
All else had been subdued to me ;
alone
The soul of man like unextinguished
fire,
Yet burns towards heaven with fierce
reproach, and doubt,
And lamentation, and reluctant
prayer,
Hurling up insurrection, which might
make
Our antique empire insecure, though
built
On eldest faith and hell's coeval, fear ;
And though my curses through the
pendulous air,
Like snow on herbless peaks, fall
flake by flake,
And cling to it ; though under my
wrath's night
It climb the crags of life, step after
step,
Which wound it, as ice wounds un-
sandalled feet,
It yet remains supreme o'er misery,
Aspiring, unrepressed, yet soon to fall:
Even now have I begotten a strange
wonder,
That fatal child, the terror of the
earth,
Who waits but till the destined hour
arrive,
Bearing from Demogorgon's vacant
throne

The dreadful might of ever-living
limbs
Which clothed that awful spirit un-
beheld,
To redescend, and trample out the
spark.
Pour forth heaven's wine, Idæan
Ganymede,
And let it fill the Dædal cups like fire,
And from the flower-inwoven soil
divine,
Ye all-triumphant harmonies arise,
As dew from earth under the twilight
stars :
Drink ! be the nectar circling through
your veins
The soul of joy, ye ever-living Gods,
Till exultation burst in one wide
voice
Like music from Elysian winds.
                                And thou
Ascend beside me, veiled in the light
Of the desire which makes thee one
with me,
Thetis, bright image of eternity !
When thou didst cry, " Insufferable
might !
God ! Spare me ! I sustain not the
quick flames,
The penetrating presence ; all my
being,
Like him whom the Numidian seps
did thaw
Into a dew with poison, is dissolved,
Sinking through its foundations : "
even then
Two mighty spirits, mingling made a
third
Mightier than either, which, unbodied
now,
Between us floats, felt, although un-
beheld,
Waiting the incarnation, which as-
cends,
(Hear ye the thunder of the fiery
wheels
Griding the winds ?) from Demogor-
gon's throne.
Victory ! victory ! Feelest thou not,
O world !
The earthquake of his chariot thun-
dering up
Olympus ?
[*The Car of the* HOUR *arrives.* DE-
MOGORGON *descends and moves
towards the Throne of* JUPITER.

Awful shape, what art thou ?
Speak !
Demogorgon. Eternity.   Demand
no direr name.
Descend, and follow me down the
abyss.
I am thy child, as thou wert Saturn's
child ;
Mightier than thee : and we must
dwell together
Henceforth in darkness. Lift thy
lightnings not.
The tyranny of heaven none may re-
tain,
Or reassume, or hold, succeeding
thee :
Yet if thou wilt, as 'tis the destiny
Of trodden worms to writhe till they
are dead,
Put forth thy might.
Jupiter.   Detested prodigy !
Even thus beneath the deep Titanian
prisons
I trample thee !   Thou lingerest ?
                                Mercy ! mercy !
No pity, no release, no respite ! Oh,
That thou wouldst make mine enemy
my judge,
Even where he hangs, seared by my
long revenge,
On Caucasus ! he would not doom me
thus.
Gentle, and just, and dreadless, is he
not
The monarch of the world ?   What
then art thou ?
No refuge ! no appeal !
                                Sink with me then,
We two will sink on the wide waves of
ruin,
Even as a vulture and a snake out-
spent
Drop, twisted in inextricable fight,
Into a shoreless sea.   Let hell un-
lock
Its mounded oceans of tempestuous
fire,
And whelm on them into the bottom-
less void
This desolated world, and thee, and
me,
The conqueror and the conquered,
and the wreck
Of that for which they combated.
                                Ai ! Ai !
The elements obey me not.   I sink

Dizzily down, ever, for ever, down.
And, like a cloud, mine enemy above
Darkens my fall with victory!   Ai!
  Ai!

Scene II.—*The Mouth of a great
    River in the Island Atlantis.
    Ocean is discovered reclining
    near the Shore;* Apollo *stands
    beside him.*

  Ocean. He fell, thou sayest, beneath
    his conqueror's frown?
  Apollo. Ay, when the strife was
    ended which made dim
The orb I rule, and shook the solid
    stars,
The terrors of his eye illumined
    heaven
With sanguine light, through the
    thick ragged skirts
Of the victorious darkness, as he fell:
Like the last glare of day's red agony,
Which, from a rent among the fiery
    clouds,
Burns far along the tempest-wrinkled
    deep.
  Ocean. He sunk to the abyss?   To
    the dark void?
  Apollo. An eagle so caught in
    some bursting cloud
On Caucasus, his thunder-baffled
    wings
Entangled in the whirlwind, and his
    eyes
Which gazed on the undazzling sun,
    now blinded
By the white lightning, while the
    ponderous hail
Beats on his struggling form, which
    sinks at length
Prone, and the aërial ice clings over it.
  Ocean. Henceforth the fields of
    Heaven-reflecting sea
Which are my realm, will heave, un-
    stained with blood,
Beneath the uplifting winds, like
    plains of corn
Swayed by the summer air; my
    streams will flow
Round many peopled continents, and
    round
Fortunate isles; and from their glassy
    thrones

Blue Proteus and his humid nymphs
    shall mark
The shadow of fair ships, as mortals
    see
The floating bark of the light laden
    moon
With that white star, its sightless
    pilot's crest,
Borne down the rapid sunset's ebbing
    sea;
Tracking their path no more by
    blood and groans,
And desolation, and the mingled
    voice
Of slavery and command; but by the
    light
Of wave-reflected flowers, and floating
    odours,
And music soft, and mild, free, gentle
    voices,
That sweetest music, such as spirits
    love.
  Apollo. And I shall gaze not on the
    deeds which make
My mind obscure with sorrow, as
    eclipse
Darkens the sphere I guide; but list,
    I hear
The small, clear, silver lute of the
    young Spirit
That sits i' the morning star.
  Ocean.   Thou must away;
Thy steeds will pause at even, till
    when farewell:
The loud deep calls me home even
    now to feed it
With azure calm out of the emerald
    urns
Which stand for ever full beside my
    throne.
Behold the Nereids under the green
    sea,
Their wavering limbs borne on the
    wind-like stream,
Their white arms lifted o'er their
    streaming hair
With garlands pied and starry sea-
    flower crowns,
Hastening to grace their mighty
    sister's joy.
            [*A sound of waves is heard.*
It is the unpastured sea hungering
    for calm.
Peace, monster; I come now.   Fare-
    well.
  Apollo. Farewell.

SCENE III.—*Caucasus*. PROME-
THEUS, HERCULES, IONE, *the*
EARTH, SPIRITS, ASIA, *and*
PANTHEA, *borne in the Car
with the* SPIRIT OF THE HOUR.

HERCULES *unbinds* PROMETHEUS,
who descends.

Hercules. Most glorious among
spirits! thus doth strength
To wisdom, courage, and long-suffer-
ing love,
And thee, who art the form they ani-
mate,
Minister like a slave.
Prometheus. Thy gentle words
Are sweeter even than freedom long
desired
And long delayed.
                Asia, thou light of life,
Shadow of beauty unbeheld; and ye,
Fair sister nymphs who made long
years of pain
Sweet to remember, through your love
and care;
Henceforth we will not part. There
is a cave
All overgrown with trailing odorous
plants,
Which curtain out the day with leaves
and flowers,
And paved with veined emerald, and
a fountain,
Leaps in the midst with an awaken-
ing sound.
From its curved roof the mountain's
frozen tears,
Like snow, or silver, or long diamond
spires,
Hang downward, raining forth a
doubtful light;
And there is heard the ever-moving
air,
Whispering without from tree to tree,
and birds,
And bees; and all around are mossy
seats,
And the rough walls are clothed with
long soft grass;
A simple dwelling, which shall be our
own;
Where we will sit and talk of time
and change,
As the world ebbs and flows, ourselves
unchanged.

What can hide man from mutability?
And if ye sigh, then I will smile; and
thou,
Ione, shalt chant fragments of sea-
music,
Until I weep, when ye shall smile
away
The tears she brought, which yet were
sweet to shed.
We will entangle buds and flowers and
beams
Which twinkle on the fountain's brim,
and make
Strange combinations out of common
things,
Like human babes in their brief inno-
cence;
And we will search with looks and
words of love,
For hidden thoughts, each lovelier
than the last,
Our unexhausted spirits; and like
lutes   [wind,
Touched by the skill of the enamoured
Weave harmonies divine, yet ever
new,
From difference sweet where discord
cannot be;
And hither come, sped on the charmed
winds,
Which meet from all the points of
heaven, as bees
From every flower aërial Enna feeds,
At their own island-homes in Himera,
The echoes of the human world which
tell
Of the low voice of love, almost un-
heard,
And dove-eyed pity's murmured pain,
and music,
Itself the echo of the heart, and all
That tempers or improves man's life,
now free;
And lovely apparitions, dim at first,
Then radiant as the mind, arising
bright
From the embrace of beauty, whence
the forms
Of which these are the phantoms,
casts on them
The gathered rays which are reality,
Shall visit us, the progeny immortal
Of Painting, Sculpture, and rapt
Poesy,
And arts, though unimagined, yet to
be.

The wandering voices and the shadows these
Of all that man becomes, the mediators
Of that best worship, love, by him and us
Given and returned; swift shapes and sounds, which grow
More fair and soft as man grows wise and kind,
And veil by veil, evil and error fall:
Such virtue has the cave and place around.

[*Turning to the* SPIRIT OF THE HOUR.

For thee, fair Spirit, one toil remains. Ione,
Give her that curved shell, which Proteus old,
Made Asia's nuptial boon, breathing within it
A voice to be accomplished, and which thou
Didst hide in grass under the hollow rock.

Ione. Thou most desired Hour, more loved and lovely
Than all thy sisters, this the mystic shell;
See the pale azure fading into silver
Lining it with a soft yet glowing light:
Looks it not like lulled music sleeping there?

Spirit. It seems in truth the fairest shell of Ocean;
Its sound must be at once both sweet and strange.

Prometheus. Go, borne over the cities of mankind
On whirlwind-footed coursers: once again
Outspeed the sun around the orbed world
And as thy chariot cleaves the kindling air,
Thou breathe into the many-folded shell,
Loosening its mighty music; it shall be
As thunder mingled with clear echoes: then
Return: and thou shalt dwell beside our cave.

And thou, O Mother Earth!—

The Earth.   I hear, I feel;
Thy lips are on me, and thy touch runs down
Even to the adamantine central gloom
Along these marble nerves; 'tis life, 'tis joy,
And, through my withered, old, and icy frame
The warmth of an immortal youth shoots down
Circling. Henceforth the many children fair
Folded in my sustaining arms; all plants,
And creeping forms, and insects rainbow-winged,
And birds, and beasts, and fish, and human shapes,
Which drew disease and pain from my wan bosom,
Draining the poison of despair, shall take
And interchange sweet nutriment; to me
Shall they become like sister-antelopes
By one fair dam, snow-white and swift as wind,
Nursed among lilies near a brimming stream.
The dew-mists of my sunless sleep shall float
Under the stars like balm: night-folded flowers
Shall suck unwithering hues in their repose:
And men and beasts in happy dreams shall gather
Strength for the coming day, and all its joy:
And death shall be the last embrace of her
Who takes the life she gave, even as a mother,
Folding her child, says, "Leave me not again."

Asia. Oh, mother! wherefore speak the name of death?
Cease they to love, and move, and breathe, and speak,
Who die?

The Earth. It would avail not to reply:
Thou art immortal, and this tongue is known
But to the uncommunicating dead.

Death is the veil which those who live
    call life :
They sleep, and it is lifted : and
    meanwhile
In mild variety the seasons mild
With rainbow-skirted showers, and
    odorous winds,
And long blue meteors cleansing the
    dull night,
And the life-kindling shafts of the
    keen sun's
All-piercing bow, and the dew-min-
    gled rain
Of the calm moonbeams, a soft in-
    fluence mild,
Shall clothe the forests and the fields,
    ay, even
The crag-built deserts of the barren
    deep,
With ever-living leaves, and fruits,
    and flowers.
And thou ! There is a cavern where
    my spirit
Was panted forth in anguish whilst
    thy pain
Made my heart mad, and those that
    did inhale it
Became mad too, and built a temple
    there,
And spoke, and were oracular, and
    lured
The erring nations round to mutual
    war,
And faithless faith, such as Jove kept
    with thee ;
Which breath now rises, as amongst
    tall weeds
A violet's exhalation, and it fills
With a serener light and crimson air
Intense, yet soft, the rocks and woods
    around ;
It feeds the quick growth of the ser-
    pent vine,
And the dark linked ivy tangling wild,
And budding, blown, or odour-faded
    blooms
Which star the winds with points of
    coloured light,
As they rain through them, and bright
    golden globes
Of fruit, suspended in their own green
    heaven,
And through their veined leaves and
    amber stems
The flowers whose purple and trans-
    lucid bowls

Stand ever mantling with aërial dew,
The drink of spirits ; and it circles
    round,
Like the soft waving wings of noonday
    dreams,
Inspiring calm and happy thoughts
    like mine,
Now thou art thus restored. This
    cave is thine,
Arise ! Appear !
    [A SPIRIT *rises in the likeness of a*
                  winged child.
          This is my torch-bearer ;
Who let his lamp out in old time with
    gazing
On eyes from which he kindled it
    anew,
With love, which is as fire, sweet
    daughter mine,
For such is that within thine own.
    Run, wayward,
And guide this company beyond the
    peak
Of Bacchic Nysa, Mænad-haunted
    mountain,
And beyond Indus and its tribute
    rivers,
Trampling the torrent streams and
    glassy lakes
With feet unwet, unwearied, undelay-
    ing,
And up the green ravine, across the
    vale,
Beside the windless and crystalline
    pool,
Where ever lies, on unerasing waves,
The image of a temple built above,
Distinct with column, arch, and
    architrave,
And palm-like capital, and over-
    wrought,
And populous most with living ima-
    gery,
Praxitelean shapes, whose marble
    smiles
Fill the hushed air with everlasting
    love.
It is deserted now, but once it bore
Thy name, Prometheus ; there the
    emulous youths
Bore to thy honour through the divine
    gloom
The lamp which was thine emblem ;
    even as those
Who bear the untransmitted torch of
    hope

Into the grave, across the night of life,
As thou hast borne it most triumphantly
To this far goal of Time.   Depart,
farewell.
Beside that temple is the destined
cave.

SCENE IV.—*A Forest.   In the Back-
ground   a   Cave.*   PROMETHEUS,
ASIA, PANTHEA, IONE, *and the*
SPIRIT OF THE EARTH.

Ione. Sister, it is not earthly : how
it glides
Under the leaves ! how on its head
there burns
A light, like a green star, whose emer-
ald beams
Are twined with its fair hair ! how, as
it moves,
The splendour drops in flakes upon the
grass !
Knowest thou it ?
  Panthea.   It is the delicate spirit
That guides the earth through heaven.
From afar
The populous constellations call that
light
The loveliest of the planets ;   and
sometimes
It floats along the spray of the salt sea,
Or makes its chariot of a foggy cloud,
Or walks through fields or cities while
men sleep,
Or o'er the mountain tops, or down
the rivers,
Or through the green waste wilderness,
as now,
Wondering at all it sees.   Before
Jove reigned
It loved our sister Asia, and it came
Each leisure hour to drink the liquid
light
Out of her eyes, for which it said it
thirsted
As one bit by a dipsas, and with her
It made its childish confidence, and
told her
All it had known or seen, for it saw
much,
Yet idly reasoned what it saw ; and
called her,
For whence it sprung it knew not, nor
do I,
Mother, dear Mother.

*The Spirit of the Earth (running
to Asia).* Mother, dearest mother,
May I then talk with thee as I was
wont ?
May I then hide my eyes in thy soft
arms,
After thy looks have made them tired
of joy ?
May I then play beside thee the long
noons,
When work is none in the bright silent
air ?
  Asia. I love thee, gentlest being !
and henceforth
Can cherish thee unenvied.   Speak, I
pray,
Thy simple talk once solaced, now delights.
  Spirit of the Earth. Mother, I am
grown wiser, though child
Cannot be wise like thee, within this
day ;
And happier too ; happier and wiser
both.
Thou knowest that toads, and snakes,
and loathly worms,
And venomous and malicious beasts,
and boughs
That bore ill berries in the woods, were
ever
A hindrance to my walks o'er the
green world :
And that, among the haunts of
humankind,
Hard-featured men, or with proud,
angry looks,
Of cold, staid gait, or false and hollow
smiles,
Or the dull sneer of self-loved ignor-
ance,
Or other such foul masks, with which
ill thoughts
Hide that fair being whom we spirits
call man ;
And women too, ugliest of all things
evil,
(Though fair, even in a world where
thou art fair,
When good and kind, free and sincere
like thee),
When false or frowning made me sick
at heart
To pass them, though they slept, and
I unseen.
Well, my path lately lay through a
great city

Into the woody hills surrounding it :
A sentinel was sleeping at the gate :
When there was heard a sound, so
  loud, it shook
The towers amid the moonlight, yet
  more sweet
Than any voice but thine, sweetest of
  all ;
A long, long sound, as it would never
  end :
And all the inhabitants leapt suddenly
Out of their rest, and gathered in the
  streets,
Locking in wonder up to Heaven,
  while yet
The music pealed along. I hid my-
  self
Within a fountain in the public square,
Where I lay like the reflex of the
  moon
Seen in a wave under green leaves ;
  and soon
Those ugly human shapes and visages
Of which I spoke as having wrought
  me pain,
Past floating through the air, and fad-
  ing still
Into the winds that scattered them ;
  and those
From whom they past seemed mild
  and lovely forms
After some foul disguise had fallen,
  and all
Were somewhat changed, and after
  brief surprise
And greetings of delighted wonder,
  all
Went to their sleep again : and when
  the dawn
Came, wouldst thou think that toads,
  and snakes, and efts,
Could e'er be beautiful ? yet so they
  were,
And that with little change of shape
  or hue :
All things had put their evil nature
  off :
I cannot tell my joy, when o'er a lake
Upon a drooping bough with nightshade twined,
I saw two azure halcyons clinging
  downward,
And thinning one bright bunch of
  amber berries,
With quick long beaks, and in the deep
  there lay

Those lovely forms imaged as in a
  sky ;
So with my thoughts full of these
  happy changes,
We meet again, the happiest change
  of a'l
  Asia. And never will we part, till
    thy chaste sister,
Who guides the frozen and inconstant
  moon,
Will look on thy more warm and equal
  light
Till her heart thaw like flakes of April
  snow,
And love thee.
  Spirit of the Earth. What ! as
    Asia loves Prometheus ?
  Asia. Peace, wanton ! thou art yet
    not old enough.
Think ye by gazing on each other's
  eyes
To multipy your lovely selves, and fill
With sphered fires the interlunar air ?
  Spirit of the Earth. Nay, mother,
    while my sister trims her lamp
  'Tis hard I should go darkling.
  Asia.   Listen ; look !
  [*The* SPIRIT OF THE HOUR *enters.*
  Prometheus. We feel what thou
    hast heard and seen : yet speak.
  Spirit of the Hour. Soon as the
    sound had ceased whose thunder
      filled
The abysses of the sky and the wide
  earth,
There was a change : the impalpable
  thin air
And the all-circling sunlight were
  transformed,
As if the sense of love, dissolved in
  them,
Had folded itself round the sphered
  world.
My vision then grew clear, and I could
  see
Into the mysteries of the universe :
Dizzy as with delight I floated down,
Winnowing the lightsome air with
  languid plumes,
My coursers sought their birth-place
  in the sun,
Where they henceforth will live ex-
  empt from toil,
Pasturing flowers of vegetable fire.
And where my moonlike car will stand
  within

A temple, gazed upon by Phidian
   forms
Of thee, and Asia, and the Earth, and
   me,
And you fair nymphs, looking the
   love we feel ;
In memory of the tidings it has borne ;
Beneath a dome fretted with graven
   flowers,
Poised on twelve columns of re-
   splendent stone,
And open to the bright and liquid sky.
Yoked to it by an amphisbænic snake
The likeness of those winged steeds
   will mock
The flight from which they find repose.
   Alas !
Whither has wandered now my partial
   tongue
When all remains untold which ye
   would hear ?
As I have said, I floated to the earth :
It was, as it is still, the pain of bliss
To move, to breathe, to be ; I wand-
   ering went
Among the haunts and dwellings of
   mankind,
And first was disappointed not to see
Such mighty change, as I had felt
   within,
Expressed in outward things ; but
   soon I looked,
And behold, thrones were kingless,
   and men walked
One with the other even as spirits do,
None fawned, none trampled ; hate,
   disdain, or fear,
Self-love or self-contempt, on human
   brows
No more inscribed, as o'er the gate of
   hell,
" All hope abandon, ye who enter
   here : "
None frowned, none trembled, none
   with eager fear
Gazed on another's eye of cold com-
   mand,
Until the subject of a tyrant's will
Became, worse fate, the abject of his
   own,
Which spurred him, like an outspent
   horse, to death.
None wrought his lips in truth-entang-
   ling lines
Which smiled the lie his tongue disdained to speak ;

None, with firm sneer, trod out in his
   own heart
The sparks of love and hope till there
   remained
Those bitter ashes, a soul self-con
   sumed,
And the wretch crept a vampire
   among men,
Infecting all with his own hideous ill ;
None talked that common, false, cold,
   hollow talk
Which makes the heart deny the *yes*
   it breathes,
Yet question that unmeant hypo-
   crisy
With such a self-mistrust as has no
   name.
And women, too, frank, beautiful,
   and kind
As the free heaven which rains fresh
   light and dew
On the wide earth, passed gentle radi-
   ant forms,
From custom's evil taint exempt and
   pure ;
Speaking the wisdom once they could
   not think,
Looking emotions once they feared to
   feel,
And changed to all which once they
   dared not be,
Yet being now, made earth like
   heaven. Nor pride,
Nor jealousy, nor envy, nor ill-shame,
The bitterest of those drops of treasured gall,
Spoilt the sweet taste of the nepenthe,
   love.

Thrones, altars, judgment-seats, and
   prisons—wherein,
And beside which, by wretched men
   were borne
Sceptres, tiaras, swords, and chains,
   and tomes
Of reasoned wrong, glozed on by ignorance—
Were like those monstrous and bar-
   baric shapes,
The ghosts of a no more-remembered
   fame,
Which, from their unworn obelisks,
   look forth
In triumph o'er the palaces and tombs
Of those who were their conquerors :
   mouldering round.

Those imaged to the pride of kings and
priests,
A dark yet mighty faith, a power as
wide
As is the world it wasted, and are now
But an astonishment; even so the
tools
And emblems of its last captivity,
Amid the dwellings of the peopled
earth,
Stand, not o'erthrown, but unregard-
ed now.
And those foul shapes, abhorred by
god and man,
Which, under many a name and many
a form,
Strange, savage, ghastly, dark, and
execrable,
Were Jupiter, the tyrant of the world;
And which the nations, panic-stricken,
served
With blood, and hearts broken by
long hope, and love
Dragged to his altars soiled and
garlandless,
And slain among men's unreclaiming
tears,
Flattering, the thing they feared,
which fear was hate,
Frown, mouldering fast, o'er their
abandoned shrines,
The painted veil, by those who were,
called life,
Which mimick'd, as with colours idly
spread,   [aside;
All men believed and hoped, is torn
The loathsome mask has fallen; the
man remains—
Sceptreless, free, uncircumscribed,
but man
Equal, unclassed, tribeless, and na-
tionless,
Exempt from awe, worship, degree,
the king
Over himself; just, gentle, wise:
but man.
Passionless? no, yet free from guilt or
pain,
Which were, for his will made or suffered them,
Nor yet exempt, though ruling them
like slaves,
From chance, and death, and mutability,
The clogs of that which else might
oversoar

The loftiest star of unascended heaven,
Pinnacled dim in the intense inane.

ACT IV

SCENE.—*A part of the Forest near the
Cave of* PROMETHEUS. PANTHEA
and IONE *are sleeping: they awaken
gradually during the first Song.*

VOICE OF UNSEEN SPIRITS.
The pale stars are gone!
For the sun, their swift shepherd,
To their folds them compelling,
In the depths of the dawn,
Hastes, in meteor-eclipsing array,
and they flee
Beyond his blue dwelling,
As fawns flee the leopard,
But where are ye?

*A train of dark Forms and Shadows
passes by confusedly singing.*
Here, oh! here:
We bear the bier
Of the Father of many a cancelled
year!
Spectres we
Of the dead Hours be,
We bear Time to his tomb in eternity.

Strew, oh! strew
Hair, not yew!
Wet the dusty pall with tears, not
dew!
Be the faded flowers
Of Death's bare bowers
Spread on the corpse of the King of
Hours!
Haste, oh, haste!
As shades are chased,
Trembling, by day, from heaven's
blue waste.
We melt away,
Like dissolving spray,
From the children of a diviner day,
With the lullaby
Of winds that die
On the bosom of their own harmony!

IONE.
What dark forms were they?

PANTHEA.
The past Hours weak and grey,
With the spoil which their toil
Raked together
From the conquest but One could foil.

IONE.
Have they past ?

PANTHEA.
                They have past ;
They outspeeded the blast,
While 'tis said, they are fled :

IONE.
Whither, oh ! whither ?

PANTHEA.
To the dark, to the past, to the
    dead.

VOICE OF UNSEEN SPIRITS.
Bright clouds float in heaven,
Dew-stars gleam on earth,
Waves assemble on ocean,
They are gathered and driven
By the storm of delight, by the panic
    of glee !
They shake with emotion,
They dance in their mirth.
        But where are ye ?

The pine boughs are singing
Old songs with new gladness,
The billows and fountains
Fresh music are flinging,
Like the notes of a spirit from land
    and from sea ;
The storms mock the mountains
With the thunder of gladness
        But where are ye ?

Ione. What charioteers are these ?
Panthea. Where are their chariots ?

SEMICHORUS OF HOURS.
The voice of the Spirits of Air and of
    Earth
Have drawn back the figured curtain
    of sleep,
Which covered our being and dark-
    ened our birth
In the deep.

A VOICE.
In the deep ?

SEMICHORUS II.
        Oh ! below the deep.

SEMICHORUS I.
A hundred ages we had been kept
Cradled in visions of hate and care,
And each one who waked as his
    brother slept,
Found the truth—

SEMICHORUS II.
Worse than his visions were !

SEMICHORUS I.
We have heard the lute of Hope in
    sleep ;
We have known the voice of Love in
    dreams,
We have felt the wand of Power, and
    leap—

SEMICHORUS II.
As the billows leap in the morning
    beams.

CHORUS.
Weave the dance on the floor of the
    breeze,
    Pierce with song heaven's silent
        light,
Enchant the day that too swiftly flees,
    To check its flight ere the cave of
        night.

Once the hungry Hours were hounds
    Which chased the day like a bleed-
        ing deer,
And it limped and stumbled with
    many wounds
    Through the nightly dells of the
        desert year.

But now, oh ! weave the mystic
    measure
    Of music, and dance, and shapes of
        light,
Let the Hours, and the spirits of
    might and pleasure,
    Like the clouds and sunbeams,
        unite.

A VOICE.
Unite.
Panthea. See, where the Spirits of
    the human mind
Wrapt in sweet sounds, as in bright
    veils, approach.

CHORUS OF SPIRITS.
We join the throng
Of the dance and the song,
By the whirlwind of gladness borne
    along ;
As the flying-fish leap
From the Indian deep,
And mix with the sea-birds half-
    asleep.

CHORUS OF HOURS.

Whence come ye, so wild and so fleet,
For sandals of lightning are on your
    feet,
And your wings are soft and swift as
    thought,
And your eyes are as love which is
    veiled not ?

CHORUS OF SPIRITS.

We come from the mind
Of human kind,
Which was late so dusk, and obscene,
    and blind;
    Now, 'tis an ocean
    Of clear emotion,
A heaven of serene and mighty mo-
    tion.

From that deep abyss
Of wonder and bliss,
Whose caverns are crystal palaces ;
    From those skyey towers
    Where   Thought's   crowned
        powers
Sit watching your dance, ye happy
    Hours !

From the dim recesses
Of woven caresses,
Where lovers catch ye by your loose
    tresses,
    From the azure isles,
    Where sweet Wisdom smiles,
Delaying your ships with her syren
    wiles.

From the temples high
Of man's ear and eye,
Roofed over Sculpture and Poesy ;
    From the murmurings
    Of the unsealed springs
Where Science bedews his Dædal
    wings.

    Years after years,
    Through blood, and tears,
And a thick hell of hatreds, and hopes,
    and fears ;
    We waded and flew,
    And the islets were few
Where the bud-blighted flowers of
    happiness grew.

    Our feet now, every palm,
    Are sandalled with calm,

And the dew of our wings is a rain of
    balm ;
    And, beyond our eyes,
    The human love lies,
Which makes all it gazes on, Paradise.

CHORUS OF SPIRITS AND HOURS.

Then weave the web of the mystic
    measure ;
From the depths of the sky and the
    ends of the earth,
    Come, swift Spirits of might and of
        pleasure,
Fill the dance and the music of mirth,
As the waves of a thousand streams
    rush by
To an ocean of splendour and har-
    mony !

CHORUS OF SPIRITS.

    Our spoil is won,
    Our task is done,
We are free to dive, or soar, or run ;
    Beyond and around,
    Or within the bound
Which clips the world with darkness
    round,

    We'll pass the eyes
    Of the starry skies
Into the hoar deep to colonise :
    Death, Chaos, and Night,
    From the sound of our flight,
Shall flee, like mist from a tempest's
    might.

    And Earth, Air, and Light,
    And the Spirit of Might,
Which drives round the stars in their
    fiery flight,
    And Love, Thought, and Breath,
    The powers that quell Death,
Wherever we soar shall assemble be-
    neath.

    And our singing shall build
    In the void's loose field
A world for the Spirit of Wisdom to
    wield ;
    We will take our plan
    From the new world of man
And our work shall be called the Pro-
    methean.

CHORUS OF HOURS.

Break the dance, and scatter the
    song ;
Let some depart, and some remain.

there is a lot of sound in this poem

SEMICHORUS I.

We, beyond heaven, are driven
  along :

SEMICHORUS II.

Us the enchantments of earth retain :

SEMICHORUS I.

Ceaseless, and rapid, and fierce, and
  free,
With the Spirits which build a new
  earth and sea
And a heaven where yet heaven could
  never be.

SEMICHORUS II.

Solemn, and slow, and serene, and
  bright,
Leading the Day, and outspeeding
  the Night,
With the powers of a world of perfect
  light.

SEMICHORUS I.

We whirl, singing loud, round the
  gathering sphere,
Till the trees, and the beasts, and the
  clouds appear
From its chaos made calm by love,
  not fear.

SEMICHORUS II.

We encircle the ocean and mountains
  of earth,
And the happy forms of its death and
  birth
Change to the music of our sweet
  mirth.

CHORUS OF HOURS AND SPIRITS.

Break the dance, and scatter the
  song,
   Let some depart and some re-
    main,
Wherever we fly we lead along
In leashes, like star-beams, soft, yet
  strong,
  The clouds that are heavy with
  love's sweet rain.

Panthea. Ha ! they are gone !
Ione.   Yet feel you no delight
From the past sweetness ?
Panthea. As the bare green hill
When some soft cloud vanishes into
  rain,

Laughs with a thousand drops of
  sunny water
To the unpavilioned sky !
  Ione.   Even whilst we speak
New notes arise. What is that awful
  sound ?
  Panthea. 'Tis the deep music of the
  rolling world,
Kindling within the strings of the
  waved air
Æolian modulations.
  Ione.   Listen too,
How every pause is filled with under-
  notes,
Clear, silver, icy, keen awakening
  tones,
Which pierce the sense, and live
  within the soul,
As the sharp stars pierce winter's
  crystal air
And gaze upon themselves within the
  sea.
  Panthea. But see where, through
  two openings in the forest
Which hanging branches overcanopy,
And where two runnels of a rivulet,
Between the close moss, violet in-
  woven,
Have made their path of melody, like
  sisters
Who part with sighs that they may
  meet in smiles,
Turning their dear disunion to an isle
Of lovely grief, a wood of sweet sad
  thoughts ;
Two visions of strange radiance float
  upon
The ocean-like enchantment of strong
  sound,
Which flows intenser, keener, deeper
  yet
Under the ground and through the
  windless air.
  Ione. I see a chariot like that thin-
  nest boat
In which the mother of the months is
  borne
By ebbing night into her western
  cave,
When she upsprings from interlunar
  dreams,
O'er which is curved an orblike
  canopy
Of gentle darkness, and the hills and
  woods

Distinctly seen through that dusk airy veil,
Regard like shapes in an enchanter's glass.
Its wheels are solid clouds, azure and gold,
Such as the genii of the thunder-storm
Pile on the floor of the illumined sea
When the sun rushes under it ; they roll
And move and grow as with an in-ward wind ;
Within it sits a winged infant, white
Its countenance, like the whiteness of bright snow,
Its plumes are as feathers of sunny frost,
Its limbs gleam white, through the wind-flowing folds
Of its white robe, woof of ethereal pearl.
Its hair is white, the brightness of white light
Scattered in strings ; yet its two eyes are heavens
Of liquid darkness, which the Deity
Within seems pouring, as a storm is poured
From jagged clouds, out of their arrowy lashes,
Tempering the cold and radiant air around,
With fire that is not brightness ; in its hand
It sways a quivering moonbeam, from whose point
A guiding power directs the chariot's prow
Over its wheeled clouds, which as they roll
Over the grass, and flowers, and waves, wake sounds,
Sweet as a singing rain of silver dew.
 Panthea. And from the other open-ing in the wood
Rushes, with loud and whirlwind har-mony,
A sphere, which is as many thousand spheres,
Solid as crystal, yet through all its mass
Flow, as through empty space, music and light :
Ten thousand orbs involving and in-volved,

Purple and azure, white, green and golden,
Sphere within sphere ; and every space between
Peopled with unimaginable shapes,
Such as ghosts dream dwell in the lampless deep,
Yet each inter-transpicuous, and they whirl
Over each other with a thousand mo-tions,
Upon a thousand sightless axles spin-ning,
And with the force of self-destroying swiftness,
Intensely, slowly, solemnly, roll on,
Kindling with mingled sounds, and many tones,
Intelligible words and music wild.
With mighty whirl the multitudinous orb
Grinds the bright brook into an azure mist
Of elemental subtlety, like light ;
And the wild odour of the forest flowers,
The music of the living grass and air,
The emerald light of leaf-entangled beams
Round its intense yet self-conflicting speed,
Seem kneaded into one aërial mass
Which drowns the sense. Within the orb itself,
Pillowed upon its alabaster arms,
Like to a child o'erwearied with sweet toil,
On its own folded wings, and wavy hair,
The Spirit of the Earth is laid asleep,
And you can see its little lips are moving,
Amid the changing light of their own smiles,
Like one who talks of what he loves in dream.
 Ione. 'Tis only mocking the orb's harmony.
 Panthea. And from a star upon its forehead, shoot,
Like swords of azure fire, or golden spears
With tyrant-quelling myrtle over-twined,
Embleming heaven and earth united now,

Vast beams like spokes of some in-
visible wheel
Which whirl as the orb whirls, swifter
than thought,
Filling the abyss with sunlike light-
nings,
And perpendicular now, and now
transverse,
Pierce the dark soil, and as they pierce
and pass,
Make bare the secrets of the earth's
deep heart ;
Infinite mine of adamant and gold,
Valueless stones, and unimagined
gems,
And caverns on crystalline columns
poised
With vegetable silver overspread ;
Wells of unfathomed fire, and water-
springs
Whence the great sea, even as a child
is fed,
Whose vapours clothe earth's mon-
arch-mountain tops
With kingly, ermine snow. The
beams flash on   [ruins
And make appear the melancholy
Of cancelled cycles ; anchors, beal s
of ships :
Planks turned to marble ; quivers,
helms, and spears,
And gorgon-headed targes, and the
wheels
Of scythed chariots, and the embla-
zonry
Of trophies, standards, and armorial
beasts,
Round which death laughed, sepul-
chred emblems
Of dead destruction, ruin within ruin !
The wrecks beside of many a city vast,
Whose population which the earth
grew over
Was mortal, but not human ; see,
they lie
Their monstrous works, and uncouth
skeletons,
Their statues, homes and fanes ; pro-
digious shapes
Huddled in grey annihilation, split,
Jammed in the hard, black deep :
and over these,
The anatomies of unknown winged
things,
And fishes which were isles of living
scale,

And serpents, bony chains, twisted
around
The iron crags, or within heaps of dust
To which the tortuous strength of
their last pangs
Had crushed the iron crags ; and
over these
The jagged alligator, and the might
Of earth-convulsing behemoth, which
once
Were monarch beasts, and on the
slimy shores,
And weed-overgrown continents of
earth,
Increased and multiplied like summer
worms
On an abandoned corpse, till the blue
globe
Wrapt deluge 'round it like a cloak,
and they
Yelled, gasped, and were abolished ;
or some God,
Whose throne was in a comet, passed
and cried,
"Be not !" And like my words they
were no more.

THE EARTH.

The joy, the triumph, the delight, the
madness !
The boundless, overflowing, bursting
gladness,
The vaporous exultation not to be
confined !
Ha ! ha ! the animation of delight
Which wraps me, like an atmosphere of light,
And bears me as a cloud is borne by
its own wind.

THE MOON.

Brother mine, calm wanderer,
Happy globe of land and air,
Some spirit is darted like a beam
from thee,
Which penetrates my frozen
frame,
And passes with the warmth of
flame,
With love, and odour, and deep
melody
Through me, through me !

THE EARTH.

Ha ! ha ! the caverns of my hollow
mountains,
My cloven fire-crags, sound-exulting
fountains,

Laugh with a vast and inextinguishable laughter.
The oceans, and the deserts, and
the abysses,
And the deep air's unmeasured wildernesses,
Answer from all their clouds and billows, echoing after.

They cry aloud as I do. Sceptred
curse,
Who all our green and azure universe
Threatenedst to muffle round with
black destruction, sending
A solid cloud to rain hot thunder-
stones,
And splinter and knead down my
children's bones,
All I bring forth, to one void mass
battering and blending.

Until each crag-like tower, and
storied column,
Palace, and obelisk, and temple
solemn,
My imperial mountains crowned with
cloud, and snow, and fire,
My sea-like forests, every blade
and blossom
Which finds a grave or cradle in my
bosom,
Were stamped by thy strong hate
into a lifeless mire.

How art thou sunk, withdrawn,
covered, drunk up
By thirsty nothing, as the brackish
cup
Drained by a desert-troop, a little
drop for all ;
And from beneath, around, within,
above,
Filling thy void annihilation, love
Bursts in like light on caves cloven by
the thunder-ball.

THE MOON.
The snow upon my lifeless moun-
tains
Is loosened into living fountains,
My solid oceans flow, and sing, and
shine :
A spirit from my heart bursts
forth,
It clothes with unexpected birth

My cold bare bosom ; Oh ! it must
be thine
On mine, on mine !

Gazing on thee I feel, I know,
Green stalks burst forth, and
bright flowers grow,
And living shapes upon my bosom
move :
Music is in the sea and air,
Winged clouds soar here and
there,
Dark with the rain new buds are
dreaming of :
'Tis love, all love !

THE EARTH.
It interpenetrates my granite mass :
Through tangled roots and trodden
clay doth pass,
Into the utmost leaves and delicatest
flowers ;
Upon the winds, among the clouds,
'tis spread :
It wakes a life in the forgotten dead,
They breathe a spirit up from their
obscurest bowers ;
And like a storm bursting its
cloudy prison
With thunder, and with whirlwind,
has arisen
Out of the lampless caves of unim-
agined being :
With earthquake shock and swift-
ness making shiver
Thought's stagnant chaos, unre-
moved for ever,
Till hate, and fear, and pain, light-
vanquished shadows, fleeing,

Leave Man, who was a many-sided
mirror,
Which could distort to many a
shape of error,
This true fair world of things, a sea
reflecting love ;
Which over all his kind, as the sun's
heaven
Gliding o'er ocean, smooth, serene,
and even
Darting from starry depths radiance
and light, doth move,

Leave Man, even as a leprous child
is left,
Who follows a sick beast to some
warm cleft

Of rocks, through which the might of
    healing springs is poured ;
  Then when it wanders home with
    rosy smile,
  Unconscious, and its mother fears
    awhile
It is a spirit, then, weeps on her child
    restored.

Man, oh, not men ! a chain of
    linked thought,
  Of love and might to be divided not,
Compelling the elements with ada-
    mantine stress ;
  As the sun rules, even with a ty-
    rant's gaze,
  The unquiet republic of the maze
Of planets, struggling fierce towards
    heaven's free wilderness.

Man, one harmonious soul of many
    a soul,
  Whose nature is its own divine
    control,
Where all things flow to all, as rivers
    to the sea ;
  Familiar acts are beautiful through
    love ;
  Labour, and pain, and grief, in life's
    green grove
Sport like tame beasts, none knew
    how gentle they could be !

  His will, with all mean passions,
    bad delights,
  And selfish cares, its trembling
    satellites,
A spirit ill to guide, but mighty to
    obey,
  Is as a tempest-winged ship, whose
    helm
  Love rules, through waves which
    dare not overwhelm,
Forcing life's wildest shores to own its
    sovereign sway.

  All things confess his strength.
    Through the cold mass
Of marble and of colour his dreams
    pass ;
Bright threads whence mothers weave
    the robes their children wear :
  Language is a perpetual Orphic
    song,
  Which rules with Dædal harmony a
    throng
Of thoughts and forms, which else
    senseless and shapeless were.

The lightning is his slave ; heaven's
    utmost deep
  Gives up her stars, and like a flock
    of sheep
They pass before his eye, are num-
    bered, and roll on !
  The tempest is his steed, he strides
    the air ;
  And the abyss shouts from her
    depth laid bare,
Heaven, hast thou secrets ? Man
    unveils me ; I have none.

THE MOON.

The shadow of white death has past
From my path in heaven at last,
A clinging shroud of solid frost and
    sleep ;
  And through my newly-woven
    bowers,
  Wander happy paramours,
Less mighty, but as mild as those
    who keep
          Thy vales more deep.

THE EARTH.

As the dissolving warmth of dawn
    may fold
A half unfrozen dew-globe, green and
    gold,
And crystalline, till it becomes a
    winged mist,
  And wanders up the vault of the
    blue day,
  Outlives the noon, and on the sun's
    last ray
Hangs o'er the sea, a fleece of fire
    and amethyst.

THE MOON.

  Thou art folded, thou art lying
  In the light which is undying
Of thine own joy, and heaven's
    smile divine ;
  All suns and constellations
    shower
  On thee a light, a life, a power
Which doth array thy sphere ; thou
    pourest thine
          On mine, on mine !

THE EARTH.

I spin beneath my pyramid of
    night,
Which points into the heavens
    dreaming delight,
Murmuring victorious joy in my en-
    chanted sleep ;

As a youth lulled in love-dreams
    faintly sighing,
Under the shadow of his beauty ly-
    ing,
Which round his rest a watch of light
    and warmth doth keep.

THE MOON.

As in the soft and sweet eclipse,
When soul meets soul on lovers'
    lips,
High hearts are calm, and brightest
    eyes are dull ;
So, when thy shadow falls on me,
Then am I mute and still, by thee
Covered ; of thy love, Orb most
    beautiful,
        Full, oh, too full !

Thou art speeding round the sun,
Brightest world of many a one ;
Green and azure sphere which
    shinest
With a light which is divinest
Among all the lamps of Heaven
To whom life and light is given ;
I, thy crystal paramour,
Borne beside thee by a power
Like the polar Paradise,
Magnet-like, of lover's eyes ;
I, a most enamoured maiden,
Whose weak brain is overladen
With the pleasure of her love,
Maniac-like around thee move
Gazing, an insatiate bride,
On thy form from every side,
Like a Mænad, round the cup
Which Agave lifted up
In the weird Cadmæan forest.
Brother, wheresoe'er thou soar-
    est
I must hurry, whirl and follow
Through the heavens wide and
    hollow,
Sheltered by the warm embrace
Of thy soul from hungry space,
Drinking from thy sense and
    sight
Beauty, majesty, and might,
As a lover or cameleon
Grows like what it looks upon,
As a violet's gentle eye
Gazes on the azure sky
Until its hue grows like what it
    beholds,
As a grey and watery mist

Glows like solid amethyst
Athwart the western mountain it
    enfolds
When the sunset sleeps
    Upon its snow.

THE EARTH.

And the weak day weeps
    That it should be so.
O gentle Moon, the voice of thy
    delight
Falls on me like thy clear and ten-
    der light
Soothing the seaman, borne the
    summer night
Through isles for ever calm ;
O gentle Moon, thy crystal accents
    pierce
The caverns of my pride's deep
    universe,
Charming the tiger joy, whose
    tramplings fierce
    Made wounds which need thy
        balm.
Panthea. I rise as from a bath of
    sparkling water,
A bath of azure light, among dark
    rocks,
Out of the stream of sound.
    Ione.   Ah me ! sweet sister,
The stream of sound has ebbed away
    from us,
And you pretend to rise out of its
    wave,
Because your words fall like the clear
    soft dew
Shaken from a bathing wood-nymph's
    limbs and hair.
    Panthea. Peace, peace ! a mighty
        power, which is as darkness,
Is rising out of Earth, and from the
    sky
Is showered like night, and from
    within the air
Bursts, like eclipse which had been
    gathered up
Into the pores of sunlight : the bright
    visions,
Wherein the singing spirits rode and
    shone,
Gleam like pale meteors through a
    watery night.
    Ione. There is a sense of words
        upon mine ear.
    Panthea. A universal sound like
        words : Oh I list.

DEMOGORGON.
Thou, Earth, calm empire of a happy
  soul,
  Sphere of divinest shapes and har-
    monies,
Beautiful orb ! gathering as thou dost
    roll
  The love which paves thy path
    along the skies.

THE EARTH.
I hear : I am as a drop of dew that
    dies.

DEMOGORGON.
Thou Moon, which gazest on the
    nightly Earth
  With wonder, as it gazes upon thee ;
Whilst each to men, and beasts, and
    the swift birth
  Of birds, is beauty, love, calm, har-
    mony :

THE MOON.
I hear : I am a leaf shaken by thee !

DEMOGORGON.
Ye kings of suns and stars ! Dæmons
    and Gods,
  Ethereal Dominations ! who pos-
    sess
Elysian, windless, fortunate abodes
  Beyond Heaven's constellated wil-
    derness.

A VOICE FROM ABOVE.
Our great Republic hears ; we are
    blest, and bless.

DEMOGORGON.
Ye happy dead ! whom beams of
    brightest verse
  Are clouds to hide, not colours to
    portray,
Whether your nature is that universe
  Which once ye saw and suffered—

A VOICE FROM BENEATH.
                        Or as they
Whom we have left, we change and
    pass away.

DEMOGORGON.
Ye elemental Genii, who have homes
  From man's high mind even to the
    central stone
Of sullen lead ; from Heaven's star-
    fretted domes

To the dull weed some sea-worm
    battens on :

A CONFUSED VOICE.
We hear : thy words waken Oblivion.

DEMOGORGON.
Spirits ! whose homes are flesh : ye
    beasts and birds,
  Ye worms and fish ; ye living
    leaves and buds ;
Lightning and wind ; and ye un-
    tameable herds,
  Meteors and mists, which throng
    air's solitudes.

A VOICE.
Thy voice to us is wind among still
    woods.

DEMOGORGON.
Man, who wert once a despot and a
    slave ;
A dupe and a deceiver ; a decay ;
A traveller from the cradle to the
    grave
  Through the dim night of this im-
    mortal day :

ALL.
Speak ! thy strong words may never
    pass away.

DEMOGORGON.
This the day, which down the void
    abysm
At the Earth-born's spell yawns for
    heaven's despotism,
  And conquest is dragged captive
    through the deep ;
Love, from its awful throne of patient
    power
In the wise heart, from the last giddy
    hour
  Of dread endurance, from the
    slippery steep,
And narrow verge of crag-like agony,
    springs
And folds over the world its healing
    wings.
Gentleness, Virtue, Wisdom, and En-
    durance,
These are the seals of that most firm
    assurance
  Which bars the pit over Destruc-
    tion's strength ;

And if, with infirm hand, Eternity,
Mother of many acts and hours,
  should free
  The serpent that would clasp her
    with his length,
These are the spells by which to re-
  assume
An empire o'er the disentangled
  doom.
To suffer woes which Hope thinks in-
  finite ;
To forgive wrongs darker than death
  or night ;

To defy Power, which seems omni-
  potent ;
To love, and bear ; to hope till Hope
  creates
From its own wreck the thing it con-
  templates
  Neither to change, nor falter, nor
  repent ;
This, like thy glory, Titan ! is to be
Good, great and joyous, beautiful
  and free ;
This is alone Life, Joy, Empire, and
  Victory !

THE CENCI

A TRAGEDY IN FIVE ACTS

DEDICATION
TO LEIGH HUNT, ESQ.

My dear Friend,

I inscribe with your name, from a distant country, and after an absence whose months have seemed years, this the latest of my literary efforts.

Those writings which I have hitherto published, have been little else than visions which impersonate my own apprehensions of the beautiful and the just. I can also perceive in them the literary defects incidental to youth and impatience ; they are dreams of what ought to be, or may be. The drama which I now present to you is a sad reality. I lay aside the presumptuous attitude of an instructor, and am content to paint, with such colours as my own heart furnishes, that which has been.

Had I known a person more highly endowed than yourself with all that it becomes a man to possess, I had solicited for this work the ornament of his name. One more gentle, honourable, innocent and brave; one of more exalted toleration for all who do and think evil, and yet himself more free from evil ; one who knows better how to receive, and how to confer a benefit, though he must ever confer far more than he can receive ; one of simpler, and, in the highest sense of the word, of purer life and manners, I never knew ; and I had already been fortunate in friendships when your name was added to the list.

In that patient and irreconcilable enmity with domestic and political tyranny and imposture which the tenor of your life has illustrated, and which, had I health and talents, should illustrate mine, let us, comforting each other in our task, live and die.

All happiness attend you !

Your affectionate friend,

PERCY B. SHELLEY.

ROME, *May* 29, 1819.

PREFACE

A manuscript was communicated to me during my travels in Italy, which was copied from the archives of the Cenci Palace at Rome, and contains a detailed account of the horrors which ended in the extinction of one of the noblest and richest families of that city during the Pontificate of Clement

VIII, in the year 1599. The story is that an old man, having spent his life in debauchery and wickedness, conceived at length an implacable hatred towards his children ; which showed itself towards one daughter under the form of an incestuous passion, aggravated by every circumstance of cruelty and violence. This daughter, after long and vain attempts to escape from what she considered a perpetual contamination both of body and mind, at length plotted with her mother-in-law and brother to murder their common tyrant. The young maiden, who was urged to this tremendous deed by an impulse which overpowered its horror, was evidently a most gentle and amiable being ; a creature formed to adorn and be admired, and thus violently thwarted from her nature by the necessity of circumstances and opinion. The deed was quickly discovered ; and, in spite of the most earnest prayers made to the Pope by the highest persons in Rome, the criminals were put to death. The old man had, during his life, repeatedly bought his pardon from the Pope for capital crimes of the most enormous and unspeakable kind, at the price of a hundred thousand crowns ; the death, therefore, of his victims can scarcely be accounted for by the love of justice. The Pope, among other motives for severity, probably felt that whosoever killed the Count Cenci deprived his treasury of a certain and copious source of revenue.[1] Such a story, if told so as to present to the reader all the feelings of those who once acted it, their hopes and fears, their confidences and misgivings, their various interests, passions, and opinions, acting upon and with each other, yet all conspiring to one tremendous end, would be as a light to make apparent some of

the most dark and secret caverns of the human heart.

On my arrival at Rome, I found that the story of the Cenci was a subject not to be mentioned in Italian society without awakening a deep and breathless interest : and that the feelings of the company never failed to incline to a romantic pity for the wrongs, and a passionate exculpation of the horrible deed to which they urged her, who has been mingled two centuries with the common dust. All ranks of people knew the outlines of this history, and participated in the overwhelming interest which it seems to have the magic of exciting in the human heart. I had a copy of Guido's picture of Beatrice, which is preserved in the Colonna Palace, and my servant instantly recognised it as the portrait of *La Cenci*.

This national and universal interest which the story produces and has produced for two centuries, and among all ranks of people in a great city, where the imagination is kept for ever active and awake, first suggested to me the conception of its fitness for a dramatic purpose. In fact, it is a tragedy which has already received, from its capacity of awakening and sustaining the sympathy of men, approbation and success. Nothing remained, as I imagined, but to clothe it to the apprehensions of my countrymen in such language and action as would bring it home to their hearts. The deepest and the sublimest tragic compositions, King Lear, and the two plays in which the tale of Œdipus is told, were stories which already existed in tradition, as matters of popular belief and interest, before Shakspeare and Sophocles made them familiar to the sympathy of all succeeding generations of mankind.

This story of the Cenci is indeed eminently fearful and monstrous: anything like a dry exhibition of it on the stage would be insupportable. The person who would treat such a subject must increase the ideal, and diminish the actual horror of the events, so that the pleasure which arises from the poetry which exists,

---

[1] The Papal Government formerly took the most extraordinary precautions against the publicity of facts which offer so tragical a demonstration of its own wickedness and weakness ; so that the communication of the MS. had become, until very lately, a matter of some difficulty.

in these tempestuous sufferings and crimes, may mitigate the pain of the contemplation of the moral deformity from which they spring. There must also be nothing attempted to make the exhibition subservient to what is vulgarly termed a moral purpose. The highest moral purpose aimed at in the highest species of the drama, is the teaching of the human heart, through its sympathies and antipathies, the knowledge of itself; in proportion to the possession of which knowledge every human being is wise, just, sincere, tolerant, and kind. If dogmas can do more, it is well : but a drama is no fit place for the enforcement of them. Undoubtedly no person can be truly dishonoured by the act of another; and the fit return to make to the most enormous injuries is kindness and forbearance, and a resolution to convert the injurer from his dark passions by peace and love. Revenge, retaliation, atonement, are pernicious mistakes. If Beatrice had thought in this manner, she would have been wiser and better; but she would never have been a tragic character : the few whom such an exhibition would have interested, could never have been sufficiently interested for a dramatic purpose, from the want of finding sympathy in their interest among the mass who surround them. It is in the restless and anatomising casuistry with which men seek the justification of Beatrice, yet feel that she has done what needs justification; it is in the superstitious horror with which they contemplate alike her wrongs and their revenge, that the dramatic character of what she did and suffered consists.

I have endeavoured as nearly as possible to represent the characters as they probably were, and have sought to avoid the error of making them actuated by my own conceptions of right or wrong, false or true : thus under a thin veil converting names and actions of the sixteenth century into cold impersonations of my own mind. They are represented as Catholics, and as Catholics deeply tinged with religion. To a Protestant apprehension there will appear something unnatural in the earnest and perpetual sentiment of the relations between God and man which pervade the tragedy of the Cenci. It will especially be startled at the combination of an undoubting persuasion of the truth of the popular religion, with a cool and determined perseverance in enormous guilt. But religion in Italy is not, as in Protestant countries, a cloak to be worn on particular days; or a passport which those who do not wish to be railed at carry with them to exhibit; or a gloomy passion for penetrating the impenetrable mysteries of our being, which terrifies its possessor at the darkness of the abyss to the brink of which it has conducted him. Religion co-exists, as it were, in the mind of an Italian Catholic with a faith in that of which all men have the most certain knowledge. It is interwoven with the whole fabric of life. It is adoration, faith, submission, penitence, blind admiration; not a rule for moral conduct. It has no necessary connexion with any one virtue. The most atrocious villain may be rigidly devout, and, without any shock to established faith, confess himself to be so. Religion pervades intensely the whole frame of society, and is, according to the temper of the mind which it inhabits, a passion, a persuasion, an excuse, a refuge; never a check. Cenci himself built a chapel in the court of his palace, and dedicated it to St. Thomas the Apostle, and established masses for the peace of his soul. Thus in the first scene of the fourth act, Lucretia's design in exposing herself to the consequences of an expostulation with Cenci after having administered the opiate, was to induce him by a feigned tale to confess himself before death; this being esteemed by Catholics as essential to salvation; and she only relinquishes her purpose when she perceives that her perseverance would expose Beatrice to new outrages.

I have avoided with great care in writing this play the introduction of what is commonly called mere poetry, and I imagine there will scarcely be found a detached simile or a single isolated description, unless Beatrice's description of the chasm appointed for her father's murder should be judged to be of that nature.[1]

In a dramatic composition the imagery and the passion should interpenetrate one another, the former being reserved simply for the full development and illustration of the latter. Imagination is as the immortal God which should assume flesh for the redemption of mortal passion. It is thus that the most remote and the most familiar imagery may alike be fit for dramatic purposes when employed in the illustration of strong feeling, which raises what is low, and levels to the apprehension that which is lofty, casting over all the shadow of its own greatness. In other respects I have written more carelessly ; that is, without an over-fastidious and learned choice of words. In this respect, I entirely agree with those modern critics who assert, that in order to move men to true sympathy, we must use the familiar language of men ; and that our great ancestors, the ancient English poets, are the writers a study of whom might incite us to do that for our own age which they have done for theirs. But it must be the real language of men in general, and not that of any particular class to whose society the writer happens to belong. So much for what I have attempted : I need not be assured that success is a very different matter ; particularly for one whose attention has but newly been awakened to the study of dramatic literature.

I endeavoured whilst at Rome to observe such monuments of this story as might be accessible to a stranger. The portrait of Beatrice at the Colonna Palace is most admirable as a work of art : it was taken by Guido during her confinement in prison. But it is most interesting as a just representation of one of the loveliest specimens

of the workmanship of Nature. There is a fixed and pale composure upon the features : she seems sad and stricken down in spirit, yet the despair thus expressed is lightened by the patience of gentleness. Her head is bound with folds of white drapery, from which the yellow strings of her golden hair escape, and fall about her neck. The moulding of her face is exquisitely delicate ; the eye-brows are distinct and arched ; the lips have that permanent meaning of imagination and sensibility which suffering has not repressed, and which it seems as if death scarcely could extinguish Her forehead is large and clear ; her eyes, which we are told were remarkable for their vivacity, are swollen with weeping and lustreless, but beautifully tender and serene. In the whole mien there is a simplicity and dignity which, united with her exquisite loveliness and deep sorrow, are inexpressibly pathetic. Beatrice Cenci appears to have been one of those rare, persons in whom energy and gentleness dwell together without destroying one another : her nature was simple and profound. The crimes and miseries in which she was an actor and a sufferer, are as the mask and the mantle in which circumstances clothed her for her impersonation on the scene of the world.

The Cenci Palace is of great extent ; and, though in part modernised, there yet remains a vast and gloomy pile of feudal architecture in the same state as during the dreadful scenes which are the subject of this tragedy. The palace is situated in an obscure corner of Rome, near the quarter of the Jews, and from the upper windows you see the immense ruins of Mount Palatine, half hidden under their profuse overgrowth of trees. There is a court in one part of the palace (perhaps that in which Cenci built the chapel to St. Thomas), supported by granite columns and adorned with antique friezes of fine workmanship, and built up, according to the ancient Italian fashion, with balcony over balcony of open work. One of the gates of the palace, formed of im-

[1] An idea in this speech was suggested by a most sublime passage in *El Purgatorio de San Patricio*, of Calderon : the only plagiarism which I have intentionally committed in the whole piece.

mense stones, and leading through a passage dark and lofty, and opening into gloomy subterranean chambers, struck me particularly.

Of the Castle of Petrella, I could obtain no further information than that which is to be found in the manuscript.

DRAMATIS PERSONÆ

COUNT FRANCESCO CENCI
GIACOMO ⎱ *his Sons*
BERNARDO ⎰
CARDINAL CAMILLO

ORSINO *a Prelate*
SAVELLA *the Pope's Legate*
OLIMPIO ⎱ *Assassins*
MARZIO ⎰

ANDREA, *Servant to* CENCI
Nobles, Judges, Guards, Servants
LUCRETIA, *Wife of* CENCI, *and stepmother of his children*
BEATRICE, *his daughter*

The SCENE *lies principally in Rome, but changes during the Fourth Act to Petrella, a Castle among the Apulian Apennines.*

TIME.—During the Pontificate of Clement VIII.

ACT I

SCENE I.—*An Apartment in the Cenci Palace.*

Enter COUNT CENCI *and* CARDINAL CAMILLO.

Camillo. That matter of the murder is hushed up
If you consent to yield his Holiness
Your fief that lies beyond the Pincian gate.—
It needed all my interest in the conclave
To bend him to this point : he said that you
Bought perilous impunity with your gold ;
That crimes like yours if once or twice compounded
Enriched the Church, and respited from hell
An erring soul which might repent and live :
But that the glory and the interest
Of the high throne he fills, little consist
With making it a daily mart of guilt
So manifold and hideous as the deeds
Which you scarce hide from men's revolted eyes.
    Cenci. The third of my possessions—let it go !
Ay, I once heard the nephew of the Pope
Had sent his architect to view the ground,

Meaning to build a villa on my vines
The next time I compounded with his uncle :
I little thought he should outwit me so !
Henceforth no witness—not the lamp—shall see
That which the vassal threatened to divulge.
Whose throat is choked with dust for his reward.
The deed he saw could not have rated higher
Than his most worthless life :—it angers me !   [Devil
Respited from Hell !—So may the
Respite their souls from Heaven.
    No doubt Pope Clement,
And his most charitable nephews, pray
That the Apostle Peter and the saints
Will grant for their sake that I long enjoy
Strength, wealth, and pride, and lust, and length of days,
Wherein to act the deeds which are the stewards
Of their revenue.—But much yet remains
To which they show no title.
    Camillo.   Oh, Count Cenci !
So much that thou mightst honourably live,
And reconcile thyself with thine own heart
And with thy God, and with the offended world.

How hideously look deeds of lust and
    blood
Through those snow-white and vener-
    able hairs !
Your children should be sitting round
    you now,
But that you fear to read upon their
    looks
The shame and misery you have
    written there.
Where is your wife ?   Where is your
    gentle daughter ?
Methinks her sweet looks, which
    make all things else
Beauteous and glad, might kill the
    fiend within you.
Why is she barred from all society
But her own strange and uncom-
    plaining wrongs ?
Talk with me, Count, you know I
    mean you well.
I stood beside your dark and fiery
    youth,
Watching its bold and bad career, as
    men
Watch meteors, but it vanished not—
    I marked
Your desperate and remorseless man-
    hood ; now
Do I behold you, in dishonoured age,
Charged with a thousand unrepented
    crimes.   [amend,
Yet I have ever hoped you would
And in that hope have saved your
    life three times.
    Cenci. For which Aldobrandino
    owes you now
My fief beyond the Pincian—Cardinal.
One thing, I pray you, recollect
    henceforth,
And so we shall converse with less
    restraint.
A man you knew spoke of my wife
    and daughter,
He was accustomed to frequent my
    house ;
So the next day *his* wife and daughter
    came
And asked if I had seen him ; and I
    smiled :
I think they never saw him any more.
    Camillo. Thou execrable man, be-
    ware !—
    Cenci.   Of thee ?
Nay, this is idle :—We should know
    each other.

As to my character for what men call
    crime,
Seeing I please my senses as I list,
And vindicate that right with force or
    guile,
It is a public matter, and I care not
If I discuss it with you.   I may speak
Alike to you and my own conscious
    heart,
For you give out that you have half
    reformed me,
Therefore strong vanity will keep you
    silent
If fear should not ; both will, I do not
    doubt.
All men delight in sensual luxury,
All men enjoy revenge ; and most
    exult
Over the tortures they can never feel ;
Flattering their secret peace with
    others' pain.
But I delight in nothing else.   I love
The sight of agony, and the sense of
    joy,
When this shall be another's, and
    that mine.
And I have no remorse, and little fear,
Which are, I think, the checks of
    other men.
This mood has grown upon me, until
    now
Any design my captious fancy makes
The picture of its wish, and it forms
    none
But such as men like you would start
    to know,
Is as my natural food and rest de-
    barred
Until it be accomplished.
    Camillo.   Art thou not
Most miserable ?
    Cenci.   Why miserable ?—
No.   I am what your theologians call
Hardened ; which they must be in
    impudence,
So to revile a man's peculiar taste.
True, I was happier than I am, while
    yet
Manhood remained to act the thing
    I thought ;
While lust was sweeter than revenge ;
    and now
Invention palls ; ay, we must all grow
    old :
But that there yet remains a deed to
    act

Whose horror might make sharp an
    appetite
Duller than mine—I'd do,—I know
    not what.
When I was young I thought of no-
    thing else
But pleasure ; and I fed on honey
    sweets :
Men, by St. Thomas ! cannot live like
    bees,
And I grew tired : yet, till I killed a
    foe,
And heard his groans, and heard his
    children's groans,
Knew I not what delight was else on
    earth,
Which now delights me little. I the
    rather   [ceals ;
Look on such pangs as terror ill con-
The dry, fixed eyeball ; the pale,
    quivering lip,
Which tell me that the spirit weeps
    within
Tears bitterer than the bloody sweat
    of Christ.
I rarely kill the body, which preserves,
Like a strong prison, the soul within
    my power,
Wherein I feed it with the breath of
    fear
For hourly pain.
    Camillo.   Hell's most aban-
    doned fiend
Did never, in the drunkenness of guilt,
Speak to his heart as now you speak
    to me ;
I thank my God that I believe you
    not.

Enter ANDREA.

    Andrea. My lord, a gentleman from
    Salamanca
Would speak with you.
    Cenci. Bid him attend me in the
    grand saloon.   [*Exit* ANDREA.
    Camillo. Farewell ; and I will pray
Almighty God that thy false impious
    words
Tempt not his spirit to abandon thee.
             [*Exit* CAMILLO.
    Cenci. The third of my possessions !
    I must use
Close husbandry, or gold. the old
    man's sword,
Falls from my withered hand. But
    yesterday

There came an order from the Pope to
    make
Fourfold provision for my cursed
    sons ;
Whom I have sent from Rome to
    Salamanca,
Hoping some accident might cut
    them off ;
And meaning, if I could, to starve
    them there.
I pray thee, God, send some quick
    death upon them !
Bernardo and my wife could not be
    worse
If dead and damned :—then, as to
    Beatrice—
    [*Looking around him suspiciously.*
I think they cannot hear me at that
    door ;
What if they should ? And yet I
    need not speak,
Though the heart triumphs with itself
    in words.
O, thou most silent air, that shalt not
    hear
What now I think ! Thou, pavement,
    which I tread
Towards her chamber,—let your
    echoes talk
Of my imperious step, scorning sur-
    prise,
But not of my intent !—Andrea !

Enter ANDREA.

    Andrea.   My lord !
    Cenci. Bid Beatrice attend me in
    her chamber
This evening :—no, at midnight, and
    alone.   [*Exeunt.*

SCENE II.—*A Garden of the Cenci
    Palace.*

Enter BEATRICE *and* ORSINO, *as in
    conversation.*

    Beatrice. Pervert not truth,
    Orsino. You remember where we
    held
That conversation ;—nay, we see the
    spot
Even from this cypress ;—two long
    years are past
Since, on an April midnight, under-
    neath
The moonlight-ruins of Mount Pala-
    tine,

I did confess to you my secret mind.

Orsino. You said you loved me
  then.

Beatrice.   You are a priest :
Speak to me not of love.

Orsino.   I may obtain
The dispensation of the Pope to
  marry.
Because I am a priest, do you believe
Your image, as the hunter some
  struck deer,
Follows me not whether I wake or
  sleep ?

Beatrice. As I have said, speak to
  me not of love ;
Had you a dispensation, I have not ;
Nor will I leave this home of misery
Whilst my poor Bernard, and that
  gentle lady
To whom I owe life, and these virtu-
  ous thoughts,
Must suffer what I still have strength
  to share.
Alas, Orsino ! All the love that once
I felt for you, is turned to bitter pain.
Ours was a youthful contract, which
  you first
Broke, by assuming vows no Pope
  will loose.
And thus I love you still, but holily,
Even as a sister or a spirit might ;
And so I swear a cold fidelity.
And it is well perhaps we shall not
  marry.
You have a sly, equivocating vein
That suits me not.—Ah, wretched
  that I am !
Where shall I turn ? Even now you
  look on me
As you were not my friend, and as if
  you
Discovered that I thought so, with
  false smiles   [wrong.
Making my true suspicion seem your
Ah ! No, forgive me ; sorrow makes
  me seem
Sterner than else my nature might
  have been ;
I have a weight of melancholy
  thoughts,
And they forebode,—but what can
  they forebode
Worse than I now endure ?

Orsino.   All will be well.
Is the petition yet prepared ? You
  know

My zeal for all you wish, sweet
  Beatrice ;
Doubt not but I will use my utmost
  skill
So that the Pope attend to your com-
  plaint.

Beatrice. Your zeal for all I wish ?
  —Ah me, you are cold !
Your utmost skill—speak but one
  word—(*Aside.*) Alas !
Weak and deserted creature that I am,
Here I stand bickering with my only
  friend !
(*To* ORSINO.) This night my father
  gives a sumptuous feast,
Orsino ; he has heard some happy
  news
From Salamanca, from my brothers
  there,
And with this outward show of love
  he mocks
His inward hate. 'Tis bold hypocrisy,
For he would gladlier celebrate their
  deaths,
Which I have heard him pray for on
  his knees :
Great God ! that such a father should
  be mine !—
But there is mighty preparation
  made,
And all our kin, the Cenci, will be
  there,
And all the chief nobility of Rome.
And he has bidden me and my pale
  mother
Attire ourselves in festival array.
Poor lady ! she expects some happy
  change
In his dark spirit from this act ; I
  none.
At supper I will give you the petition :
Till when—farewell.

Orsino. Farewell. [*Exit* BEATRICE.
                I know the Pope
Will ne'er absolve me from my
  priestly vow
But by absolving me from the revenue
Of many a wealthy see ; and, Bea-
  trice,
I think to win thee at an easier rate.
Nor shall he read her eloquent peti-
  tion :
He might bestow her on some poor
  relation
Of his sixth-cousin, as he did her
  sister,

THE CENCI

And I should be debarred from all access.

Then as to what she suffers from her father,

In all this there is much exaggeration :
Old men are testy, and will have their way,
A man may stab his enemy, or his vassal,
And live a free life as to wine or women,
And with a peevish temper may return
To a dull home, and rate his wife and children ;
Daughters and wives call this foul tyranny.
I shall be well content, if on my conscience
There rest no heavier sin than what they suffer
From the devices of my love—A net
From which she shall escape not. Yet I fear
Her subtle mind, her awe-inspiring gaze,
Whose beams anatomise me, nerve by nerve,
And lay me bare, and make me blush to see
My hidden thoughts.—Ah, no ! a friendless girl
Who clings to me, as to her only hope :—
I were a fool, not less than if a panther
Were panic-stricken by the antelope's eye,
If she escape me. [*Exit.*

SCENE III.—*A magnificent Hall in the Cenci Palace.*

A Banquet. Enter CENCI, LUCRETIA, BEATRICE, ORSINO, CAMILLO, NOBLES.

Cenci. Welcome, my friends and kinsmen ; welcome ye,
Princes and Cardinals, Pillars of the Church,
Whose presence honours our festivity.
I have too long lived like an anchorite,
And, in my absence from your merry meetings,
An evil word is gone abroad of me ;
But I do hope that you, my noble friends,

When you have shared the entertainment here,
And heard the pious cause for which 'tis given,
And we have pledged a health or two together,
Will think me flesh and blood as well as you ;
Sinful indeed, for Adam made all so,
But tender-hearted, meek and pitiful.
First Guest. In truth, my lord, you seem too light of heart,
Too sprightly and companionable a man,
To act the deeds that rumour pins on you. [*To his companion.*
I never saw such blithe and open cheer
In any eye !
Second Guest. Some most desired event,
In which we all demand a common joy,
Has brought us hither ; let us hear it, Count.
Cenci. It is indeed a most desired event.
If, when a parent, from a parent's heart,
Lifts from this earth to the great Father of all
A prayer, both when he lays him down to sleep,
And when he rises up from dreaming it ;
One supplication, one desire, one hope,
That he would grant a wish for his two sons,
Even all that he demands in their regard—
And suddenly, beyond his dearest hope,
It is accomplished, he should then rejoice,
And call his friends and kinsmen to a feast,
And task their love to grace his merriment,
Then honour me thus far—for I am he.
Beatrice (to LUCRETIA). Great God ! how horrible ! Some dreadful ill
Must have befallen my brothers.
Lucretia. Fear not, child,
He speaks too frankly.
Beatrice. Ah ! My blood runs cold.

I fear that wicked laughter round his eye,
Which wrinkles up the skin even to the hair.

Cenci. Here are the letters brought from Salan: **n** a;
Beatrice, read them to your mother. God,
I thank thee! In one night didst thou perform,
By ways inscrutable, the thing I sought.
My disobedient and rebellious sons
Are dead!—Why dead!—What means this change of cheer?
You hear me not, I tell you they are dead;
And they will need no food or raiment more:
The tapers that did light them the dark way
Are their last cost. The Pope, I think, will not
Expect I should maintain them in their coffins.
Rejoice with me—my heart is wondrous glad.

(LUCRETIA *sinks, half fainting;*
BEATRICE *supports her.*)

Beatrice. It is not true!—Dear lady, pray look up.
Had it been true, there is a God in Heaven,
He would not live to boast of such a boon.
Unnatural man, thou knowest that it is false.

Cenci. Ay, as the word of God; whom here I call
To witness that I speak the sober truth:—
And whose most favouring providence was shown
Even in the manner of their deaths. For Rocco
Was kneeling at the mass, with sixteen others,
When the Church fell and crushed him to a mummy;
The rest escaped unhurt. Cristofano   [man,
Was stabbed in error by a jealous
Whilst she he loved was sleeping with his rival;
All in the self-same hour of the same night;

Which shows that Heaven has special care of me.
I beg those friends who love me, that they mark
The day a feast upon their calendars.
It was the twenty-seventh of December:
Ay, read the letters if you doubt my oath.

[*The assembly appears confused;*
several of the guests rise.

First Guest. O, horrible! I will depart.—
Second Guest. And I.—
Third Guest.   No, stay!
I do believe it is some jest; though, faith, I
'Tis mocking us somewhat too solemnly.
I think his son has married the Infanta!
Or found a mine of gold in El Dorado:
'Tis but to season some such news; stay, stay!
I see 'tis only raillery by his smile.

Cenci (filling a bowl of wine, and
lifting it up).
Oh, thou bright wine, whose purple splendour leaps
And bubbles gaily in this golden bowl
Under the lamplight, as my spirits do,
To hear the death of my accursed sons!
Could I believe thou wert their mingled blood,
Then would I taste thee like a sacrament,
And pledge with thee the mighty Devil in Hell;
Who, if a father's curses, as men say,
Climb with swift wings after their children's souls,
And drag them from the very throne of Heaven,
Now triumphs in my triumph!—But thou art
Superfluous; I have drunken deep of joy,
And I will taste no other wine tonight.
Here, Andrea! Bear the bowl around.

A Guest (rising). Thou wretch!
Will none among this noble company
Check the abandoned villain?

Camillo.   For God's sake,
Let me dismiss the guests! You are
    insane,
Some ill will come of this.
  Second Guest.   Seize, silence him!
  First Guest. I will!
  Third Guest.   And I!
  *Cenci (addressing those who rise
    with a threatening gesture)*
Who moves? Who speaks?
    [*Turning to the company.*
                  'Tis nothing,
Enjoy yourselves.—Beware! for my
    revenge
Is as the sealed commission of a king,
That kills, and none dare name the
    murderer.
  [*The Banquet is broken up; several
    of the Guests are departing.*
  Beatrice. I do entreat you, go not,
    noble guests;
What although tyranny and impious
    hate
Stand sheltered by a father's hoary
    hair?
What if 'tis he who clothed us in these
    limbs
Who tortures them, and triumphs?
    What, if we,
The desolate and the dead, were his
    own flesh,
His children and his wife, whom he is
    bound
To love and shelter? Shall we
    therefore find
No refuge in this merciless wide world?
Oh, think what deep wrongs must
    have blotted out
First love, then reverence in a child's
    prone mind,
Till it thus vanquish shame and fear!
    Oh, think!
I have borne much, and kissed the
    sacred hand
Which crushed us to the earth, and
    thought its stroke
Was perhaps some paternal chastise-
    ment!
Have excused much, doubted; and
    when no doubt
Remained, have sought by patience,
    love and tears,
To soften him; and when this could
    not be,
I have knelt down through the long
    sleepless nights,

And lifted up to God, the father of all,
Passionate prayers: and when these
    were not heard,
I have still borne;—until I meet you
    here,
Princes and kinsmen, at this hideous
    feast
Given at my brothers' deaths. Two
    yet remain,
His wife remains and I, whom if ye
    save not,
Ye may soon share such merriment
    again
As fathers make over their children's
    graves.
Oh! Prince Colonna, thou art our
    near kinsman;
Cardinal, thou art the Pope's cham-
    berlain;
Camillo, thou art chief justiciary;
Take us away!
  *Cenci. (He has been conversing with
    CAMILLO during the first part of
    BEATRICE'S speech; he hears the
    conclusion, and now advances.)*
  I hope my good friends here
Will think of their own daughters—
    or perhaps
Of their own throats—before they
    lend an ear
To this wild girl.
  *Beatrice (not noticing the words of
    Cenci).*
                  Dare no one look on me?
None answer? Can one tyrant over-
    bear
The sense of many best and wisest
    men?
Or is it that I sue not in some form
Of scrupulous law, that ye deny my
    suit?
Oh, God! that I were buried with my
    brothers!
And that the flowers of this departed
    spring
Were fading on my grave! and that
    my father
Were celebrating now one feast for
    all!
  Camillo. A bitter wish for one so
    young and gentle;
Can we do nothing?—
  Colonna.   Nothing that I see.
Count Cenci were a dangerous enemy:
Yet I would second any one.
  A Cardinal.   And I.

Cenci. Retire to your chamber,
insolent girl !

Beatrice. Retire thou, impious man !
Ay, hide thyself
Where never eye can look upon thee
more !
Wouldst thou have honour and
obedience,
Who art a torturer ? Father, never
dream,
Though thou mayst overbear this
company,
But ill must come of ill.—Frown not
on me !
Haste, hide thyself, lest with aveng-
ing looks
My brothers' ghosts should hunt thee
from thy seat !
Cover thy face from every living eye,
And start if thou but hear a human
step :
Seek out some dark and silent corner,
there,   [God,
Bow thy white head before offended
And we will kneel around, and ferv-
ently
Pray that he pity both ourselves and
thee.

Cenci. My friends, I do lament this
insane girl
Has spoilt the mirth of our festivity.
Good night, farewell ; I will not make
you longer
Spectators of our dull domestic
quarrels.
Another time.—
          [Exeunt all but CENCI *and*
                    BEATRICE.
          My brain is swimming round ;
Give me a bowl of wine !
          (*To* BEATRICE). Thou painted
viper !
Beast that thou art ! Fair and yet
terrible !
I know a charm shall make thee meek
and tame,
Now get thee from my sight !
                    [Exit BEATRICE.
          Here, Andrea,
Fill up this goblet with Greek wine.
I said
I would not drink this evening, but I
must ;   [fail
For, strange to say, I feel my spirits
With thinking what I have decreed to
do.   *[Drinking the wine,*

Be thou the resolution of quick youth
Within my veins, and manhood's
purpose stern,
And age's firm, cold, subtle villainy ;
As if thou wert indeed my children's
blood
Which I did thirst to drink. The
charm works well ;
It must be done, it shall be done, I
swear !   *[Exit.*

ACT II

SCENE I.—*An Apartment in the Cenci
Palace.*

Enter LUCRETIA *and* BERNARDO.

Lucretia. Weep not, my gentle boy ;
he struck but me,
Who have borne deeper wrongs. In
truth, if he
Had killed me, he had done a kinder
deed.
Oh, God Almighty, do thou look upon
us,
We have no other friend but only
thee !
Yet weep not ; though I love you as
my own,
I am not your true mother.
Bernardo.   Oh, more, more
Than ever mother was to any child,
That have you been to me ! Had he
not been
My father, do you think that I should
weep ?
Lucretia. Alas ! poor boy, what else
couldst thou have done !

Enter BEATRICE.

Beatrice (*in a hurried voice*). Did
he pass this way ? Have you
seen him, brother ?
Ah ! no, that is his step upon the
stairs ;
'Tis nearer now ; his hand is on the
door ;
Mother, if I to thee have ever been
A duteous child, now save me ! Thou,
great God,
Whose image upon earth a father is,
Dost thou indeed abandon me ? He
comes ;
The door is opening now ; I see his
face ;

He frowns on others, but he smiles on
    me,
Even as he did after the feast last
    night.   [*Enter a Servant.*
Almighty God, how merciful thou art !
'Tis but Orsino's servant.—Well,
    what news ?
    Servant. My master bids me say,
    the Holy Father
Has sent back your petition thus un-
    opened.   [*Giving a paper.*
And he demands at what hour 'twere
    secure
To visit you again ?
    Lucretia.   At the Ave Mary.
               [*Exit Servant.*
So, daughter, our last hope has failed ;
    ah me,
How pale you look ! you tremble, and
    you stand
Wrapped in some fixed and fearful
    meditation,
As if one thought were overstrong
    for you :
Your eyes have a chill glare ; oh,
    dearest child !
Are you gone mad ? If not, pray
    speak to me.
    Beatrice. You see I am not mad ;
    I speak to you.
    Lucretia. You talked of something
    that your father did
After that dreadful feast ? Could it
    be worse
Than when he smiled and cried, " My
    sons are dead ! "
And everyone looked in his neigh-
    bour's face
To see if others were as white as he ?
At the first word he spoke I felt the
    blood
Rush to my heart, and fell into a
    trance ;   [wild ;
And when it passed I sat all weak and
Whilst you alone stood up, and with
    strong words
Check'd his unnatural pride ; and I
    could see
The devil was rebuked that lives in
    him.
Until this hour thus you have ever
    stood
Between us and your father's moody
    wrath
Like a protecting presence : your
    firm mind

Has been our only refuge and de-
    fence :
What can have thus subdued it ?
    What can now
Have given you that cold melancholy
    look,
Succeeding to your unaccustomed
    fear ?
    Beatrice. What is it that you say ?
    I was just thinking
'Twere better not to struggle any
    more.
Men, like my father, have been dark
    and bloody,
Yet never—O ! before worse comes of
    it,
'Twere wise to die : it ends in that at
    last.
    Lucretia. Oh, talk not so, dear
    child ! Tell me at once
What did your father do or say to
    you ?
He stayed not after that accursed
    feast
One moment in your chamber.—
    Speak to me.
    Bernardo. Oh, sister, sister, prithee,
    speak to us !
    Beatrice (*speaking very slowly with a
    forced calmness*). It was one
    word, mother, one little word ;
One look, one smile.   [*Wildly.*
           Oh ! he has trampled me
Under his feet, and made the blood
    stream down
My pallid cheeks. And he has given
    us all
Ditchwater, and the fever-stricken
    flesh
Of buffaloes, and bade us eat or
    starve,
And we have eaten. He has made
    me look
On my beloved Bernardo, when the
    rust
Of heavy chains has gangrened his
    sweet limbs,
And I have never yet despaired—but
    now !
What would I say ?
               [*Recovering herself.*
        Ah ! no, 'tis nothing new.
The sufferings we all share have made
    me wild :
He only struck and cursed me as he
    passed ;

He said, he looked, he did,— nothing at all
Beyond his wont, yet it disordered me.
Alas! I am forgetful of my duty,
I should preserve my senses for your sake.

Lucretia. Nay, Beatrice; have courage, my sweet girl.
If any one despairs it should be I,
Who loved him once, and now must live with him
Till God in pity call for him or me.
For you may, like your sister, find some husband,
And smile, years hence, with children round your knees
Whilst I, then dead, and all this hideous coil,
Shall be remembered only as a dream.

Beatrice. Talk not to me, dear lady, of a husband.
Did you not nurse me when my mother died?
Did you not shield me and that dearest boy?
And had we any other friend but you
In infancy, with gentle words and looks,
To win our father not to murder us?
And shall I now desert you? May the ghost
Of my dead mother plead against my soul,
If I abandon her who filled the place
She left, with more even than a mother's love!

Bernardo. And I am of my sister's mind. Indeed
I would not leave you in this wretchedness,
Even though the Pope should make me free to live
In some blithe place, like others of my age,
With sports, and delicate food, and the fresh air.
Oh, never think that I will leave you, mother!

Lucretia. My dear, dear children!

Enter CENCI, *suddenly.*

Cenci. What! Beatrice here?
Come hither!
She shrinks back, and covers her face.
      Nay, hide not your face, 'tis fair;

Look up! Why, yesternight you dared to look
With disobedient insolence upon me,
Bending a stern and an inquiring brow
On what I meant; whilst I then sought to hide
That which I came to tell you—but in vain.

Beatrice (*wildly staggering towards the door*). Oh, that the earth would gape! Hide me, oh God!

Cenci. Then it was I whose inarticulate words
Fell from my lips, who with tottering steps
Fled from your presence, as you now from mine.
Stay, I command you! From this day and hour
Never again, I think, with fearless eye,
And brow superior, and unaltered cheek,
And that lip made for tenderness or scorn,
Shalt thou strike dumb the meanest of mankind:
Me least of all. Now get thee to thy chamber,
Thou too, loathed image of thy cursed mother,   [*To* BERNARDO.
Thy milky, meek face makes me sick with hate!
      [*Exeunt* BEATRICE *and* BERNARDO.
(*Aside.*) So much has passed between us as must make
Me bold, her fearful.—'Tis an awful thing
To touch such mischief as I now conceive:
So men sit shivering on the dewy bank
And try the chill stream with their feet; once in—
How the delighted spirit pants for joy!

Lucretia (*advancing timidly towards him*). Oh, husband! Pray forgive poor Beatrice,
She meant not any ill.

Cenci.   Nor you perhaps?
Nor that young imp, whom you have taught by rote
Parricide with his alphabet? Nor Giacomo?
Nor those two most unnatural sons, who stirred

Enmity up against me with the Pope?
Whom in one night merciful God cut
  off :
Innocent lambs !   They thought not
  any ill.
_ou were not here conspiring ? you
  said nothing
Of how I might be dungeoned as a
  madman ;
Or be condemned to death for some
  offence,
And you would be the witnesses ?—
  This failing,
How just it were to hire assassins, or
Put sudden poison in my evening
  drink ?
Or smother me when overcome by
  wine ?
Seeing we had no other judge but
  God,
And he had sentenced me, and there
  were none
But you to be the executioners
Of his decree enregistered in heaven ?
Oh, no !   You said not this ?
  Lucretia.   So help me God,
I never thought the things you charge
  me with !
  Cenci. If you dare speak that
    wicked lie again,
I'll kill you.   What ! it was not by
  your counsel
That Beatrice disturbed the feast last
  night ?
You did not hope to stir some enemies
Against me, and escape, and laugh to
  scorn
What every nerve of you now trembles
  at ?
You judged that men were bolder
  than they are ;
Few dare to stand between their
  grave and me.
  Lucretia. Look not so dreadfully !
    By my salvation
I knew not aught that Beatrice de-
  signed ;
Nor do I think she designed any thing
Until she heard you talk of her dead
  brothers.
  Cenci. Blaspheming liar !   You are
    damned for this !
But I will take you where you may
  persuade
The stones you tread on to deliver
  you :

For men shall there be none but those
  who dare
All things ; not question that which I
  command.
On Wednesday next I shall set out :
  you know
That savage rock, the Castle of
  Petrella ?
'Tis safely walled, and moated round
  about :
Its dungeons under ground, and its
  thick towers
Never told tales ; though they have
  heard and seen
What might make dumb things speak.
  Why do you linger ?
Make speediest preparation for the
  journey !   [*Exit* LUCRETIA.
The all-beholding sun yet shines ; I
  hear
A busy stir of men about the streets ;
I see the bright sky through the win-
  dow panes :
It is a garish, broad, and peering
  day ;
Loud, light, suspicious, full of eyes
  and ears ;
And every little corner, nook, and
  hole,
Is penetrated with the insolent light.
Come, darkness !   Yet, what is the
  day to me ?
And wherefore should I wish for night,
  who do
A deed which shall confound both
  night and day ?
'Tis she shall grope through a be-
  wildering mist
Of horror : if there be a sun in heaven,
She shall not dare to look upon its
  beams ;
Nor feel its warmth.   Let her, then,
  wish for night ;
The act I think shall soon extinguish
  all
For me : I bear a darker, deadlier
  gloom
Than the earth's shade, or interlunar
  air.
Or constellations quenched in murki-
  est cloud,
In which l walk secure and unbeheld
Towards my purpose.—Would that it
  were done !
                              [*Exit.*

SCENE II. *A Chamber in the Vatican.*

Enter CAMILLO *and* GIACOMO, *in
conversation.*

Camillo. There is an obsolete and
doubtful law,
By which you might obtain a bare
provision
Of food and clothing.
  Giacomo.   Nothing more ? Alas !
Bare must be the provision which
strict law
Awards, and aged sullen avarice pays.
Why did my father not apprentice me
To some mechanic trade ?   I should
have then
Been trained in no high-born neces-
sities
Which I could meet not by my daily
toil.
The eldest son of a rich nobleman
Is heir to all his incapacities ;
He has wide wants, and narrow pow-
ers. If you,
Cardinal Camillo, were reduced at
once
From thrice-driven beds of down, and
delicate food,
An hundred servants, and six palaces,
To that which nature doth indeed re-
quire ?—
  Camillo. Nay, there is reason in
your plea ; 'twere hard.
  Giacomo. 'Tis hard for a firm man
to bear : but I
Have a dear wife, a lady of high birth,
Whose dowry in ill hour I lent my
father,
Without a bond or witness to the deed :
And children, who inherit her fine
senses,
The fairest creatures in this breathing
world ;
And she and they reproach me not.
Cardinal,
Do you not think the Pope would in-
terpose
And stretch authority beyond the
law ?
  Camillo. Though your peculiar
case is hard, I know
The Pope will not divert the course of
law.
After that impious feast the other
night

I spoke with him, and urged him then
to check
Your father's cruel hand ; he frowned,
and said,
" Children are disobedient, and they
sting
Their fathers' hearts to madness and
despair,
Requiting years of care with con-
tumely.
I pity the Count Cenci from my heart ;
His outraged love perhaps awakened
hate,
And thus he is exasperated to ill.
In the great war between the old and
young,
I, who have white hairs and a totter-
ing body,
Will keep at least blameless neutral-
ity."   [*Enter* ORSINO.
You, my good lord Orsino, heard
those words.
  Orsino. What words ?
  Giacomo.   Alas, repeat them not
again !
There then is no redress for me ; at
least
None but that which I may achieve
myself,
Since I am driven to the brink.   But,
say,
My innocent sister and my only
brother
Are dying underneath my father's
eye.
The memorable torturers of this land,
Galeaz Visconti, Borgia, Ezzelin,
Never inflicted on their meanest slave
What these endure ;   shall they have
no protection ?
  Camillo. Why, if they would peti-
tion to the Pope,
I see not how he could refuse it—yet
He holds it of most dangerous ex-
ample
In aught to weaken the paternal
power,
Being, as 'twere, the shadow of his
own.
I pray you now excuse me.   I have
business
That will not bear delay.
                         [*Exit* CAMILLO.
  Giacomo.   But you, Orsino,
Have the petition ; wherefore not
present it !

Orsino. I have presented it, and
    backed it with
My earnest prayers, and urgent inter-
    est ;
It was returned unanswered. I doubt
    not
But that the strange and execrable
    deeds
Alleged in it—in truth they might
    well baffle
Any belief—have turned the Pope's
    displeasure
Upon the accusers from the criminal :
So I should guess from what Camillo
    said.
    Giacomo. My friend, that palace-
    walking devil, Gold,
Has whispered silence to his Holiness :
And we are left, as scorpions ringed
    with fire.
What should we do but strike our-
    selves to death ?
For he who is our murderous perse-
    cutor
Is shielded by a father's holy name,
Or I would—   [*Stops abruptly.*
    Orsino. What ? Fear not to speak
    your thought.
Words are but holy as the deeds they
    cover :
A priest who has forsworn the God
    he serves ;
A judge who makes the truth weep at
    his decree ;
A friend who should weave counsel,
    as I now,   [guile ;
But as the mantle of some selfish
A father who is all a tyrant seems,
Were the profaner for his sacred
    name.
    Giacomo. Ask me not what I think ;
    the unwilling brain
Feigns often what it would not ; and
    we trust
Imagination with such phantasies
As the tongue dares not fashion into
    words ;
Which have no words, their horror
    makes them dim
To the mind's eye. My heart denies
    itself
To think what you demand.
    Orsino. But a friend's bosom
Is as the inmost cave of our own mind,
Where we sit shut rom the wide gaze
    of day,

And from the all-communicating air.
You look what I suspected—
    Giacomo. Spare me now !
I am as one lost in a midnight wood,
Who dares not ask some harmless
    passenger
The path across the wilderness, lest
    he,
As my thoughts are, should be—a
    murderer.
I know you are my friend, and all I
    dare
Speak to my soul that will I trust
    with thee.
But now my heart is heavy, and
    would take
Lone counsel from a night of sleepless
    care.
Pardon me, that I say farewell—fare-
    well !
I would that to my own suspected self
I could address a word so full of peace.
    Orsino. Farewell ! — Be your
    thoughts better or more bold.
I had disposed the Cardinal Camillo

                              [*Exit* GIACOMO·
To feed his hope with cold encourage-
    ment :
It fortunately serves my close designs
That 'tis a trick of this same family
To analyse their own and other
    minds.
Such self-anatomy shall teach the will
Dangerous secrets : for it tempts our
    powers,
Knowing what must be thought, and
    may be done,
Into the depth of darkest purposes :
So Cenci fell into the pit ; even I,
Since Beatrice unveiled me to myself,
And made me shrink from what I
    cannot shun,
Show a poor figure to my own esteem,
To which I grow half reconciled.
    I'll do
As little mischief as I can : that
    thought
Shall fee the accuser conscience.

                              [*After a pause.*
                    Now what harm
If Cenci should be murdered ?—yet, if
    murdered,
Wherefore by me ? And what if I
    could take
The profit, yet omit the sin and peril

THE CENCI

THE CENCI

THE CENCI

In such an action? Of all earthly
things
I fear a man whose blows outspeed his
words;
And such is Cenci : and while Cenci
lives
His daughter's dowry were a secret
grave
If a priest wins her.—Oh, fair Bea-
trice!
Would that I loved thee not, or, lov-
ing thee,
Could but despise danger, and gold,
and all
That frowns between my wish and its
effect,
Or smiles beyond it! There is no
escape :
Her bright form kneels beside me at
the altar,
And follows me to the resort of men,
And fills my slumber with tumultu-
ous dreams,
So when I wake my blood seems
liquid fire ;
And if I strike my damp and dizzy
head,
My hot palm scorches it : her very
name,
But spoken by a stranger, makes my
heart
Sicken and pant ; and thus unpro-
fitably
I clasp the phantom of unfelt delights,
Till weak imagination half possesses
The self-created shadow. Yet much
longer
Will I not nurse this life of feverous
hours :
From the unravelled hopes of Gia-
como
I must work out my own dear
purposes.
I see, as from a tower, the end of all :
Her father dead ; her brother bound
to me
By a dark secret, surer than the
grave ;
Her mother scared and unexpostulat-
ing
From the dread manner of her wish
achieved :
And she !—Once more take courage,
my faint heart ;
What dares a friendless maiden
matched with thee ?

I have such foresight as assures suc-
cess ;
Some unbeheld divinity doth ever,
When dread events are near, stir up
men's minds
To black suggestions ; and he prospers
best,
Not who becomes the instrument of
ill,
But who can flatter the dark spirit,
that makes
Its empire and its prey of other
hearts,
Till it become his slave—as I will do.
[*Exit.*

ACT III

Scene I.—*An Apartment in the
Cenci Palace.*

Lucretia ; *to her enter* Beatrice
(*she enters staggering, and speaks
wildly*).

Beatrice. Reach me that handker-
chief !—My brain is hurt,
My eyes are full of blood ; just wipe
them for me—
I see but indistinctly.—
    Lucretia.   My sweet child,
You have no wound ; 'tis only a
cold dew
That starts from your dear brow.—
        Alas ! Alas !
What has befallen ?
    Beatrice.   How comes this hair
undone ?
Its wandering strings must be what
blind me so,
And yet I tied it fast.—O horrible !
The pavement sinks under my feet !
    The walls
Spin round ! I see a woman weeping
there,
And standing calm and motionless,
whilst I
Slide giddily as the world reels.—My
God !
The beautiful blue heaven is flecked
with blood !
The sunshine on the floor is black !
    The air
Is changed to vapours such as the
dead breathe
In charnel-pits ! Pah ! I am choked !
    There creeps

A clinging, black, contaminating
  mist
About me—'tis substantial, heavy,
  thick ;
I cannot pluck it from me, for it glues
My fingers and my limbs to one an-
  other,
And eats into my sinews, and dis-
  solves
My flesh to a pollution, poisoning
The subtle, pure, and inmost spirit of
  life !
My God ! I never knew what the mad
  felt
Before ; for I am mad beyond all
  doubt !   [*More wildly.*
No, I am dead ! These putrefying
  limbs
Shut round and sepulchre the pant-
  ing soul,
Which would burst forth into the
  wandering air !   [*A pause.*
What hideous thought was that I
  had even now ?
'Tis gone ; and yet its burthen re-
  mains here
O'er these dull eyes—upon this weary
  heart !
O, world ! O life ! O, day ! O,
  misery !
  Lucretia. What ails thee, my poor
  child ? She answers not.
Her spirit apprehends the sense of
  pain,
But not its cause ; suffering has dried
  away
The source from which it sprung.—
  Beatrice (frantically). Like Parricide—
Misery has killed its father : yet its
  father
Never like mine—O, God ! What
  thing am I ?
  Lucretia. My dearest child, what
  has your father done ?
  Beatrice (doubtfully). Who art
  thou, questioner ? I have no
  father.   [*Aside.*
She is the madhouse nurse who tends
  on me,
It it a piteous office.
      [*To* LUCRETIA, *in a slow, subdued
      voice.*
      Do you know,
I thought I was that wretched Beatrice

Men speak of, whom her father some-
  times hales
From hall to hall by the entangled
  hair ;
At others, pens up naked in damp
  cells
Where scaly reptiles crawl, and
  starves her there,
Till she will eat strange flesh. This
  woeful story
So did I overact in my sick dreams,
That I imagined—no, it cannot be !
Horrible things have been in this wild
  world,
Prodigious mixtures, and confusions
  strange
Of good and ill ; and worse have been
  conceived
Than ever there was found a heart to
  do.
But never fancy imaged such a deed
As—
  [*Pauses, suddenly recollecting herself.*
      Who art thou ? Swear to
  me, ere I die
With fearful expectation, that indeed
Thou art not what thou seemest—
  Mother !
  Lucretia. Oh ! My sweet child,
  know you—
  Beatrice.   Yet speak it not :
For then if this be truth, that other
  too
Must be a truth, a firm enduring
  truth,
Linked with each lasting circum-
  stance of life,
Never to change, never to pass away.
Why so it is. This is the Cenci
  Palace ;
Thou art Lucretia ; I am Beatrice.
I have talked some wild words, but
  will no more.
Mother, come near me : from this
  point of time,
I am—
      [*Her voice dies away faintly*
  Lucretia. Alas ! what has befallen
  thee, child ?
What has thy father done ?
  Beatrice.   What have I done ?
Am I not innocent ? Is it my crime
That one with white hair, and imperi-
  ous brow,
Who tortured me from my forgotten
  years,

As parents only dare, should call him-
   self
My father, yet should be !—Oh, what
   am I ?
What name, what place, what
   memory shall be mine ?
What retrospects, outliving even des-
   pair ?
   Lucretia. He is a violent tyrant,
   surely, child :
We know that death alone can make
   us free ;
His death or ours. But what can he
   have done
Of deadlier outrage or worse injury ?
Thou art unlike thyself ; thine eyes
   shoot forth
A wandering and strange spirit.
   Speak to me,
Unlock those pallid hands whose fin-
   gers twine
With one another.
   Beatrice.   'Tis the restless life
Tortured within them. If I try to
   speak
I shall go mad. Ay, something must
   be done ;
What, yet I know not—something
   which shall make
The thing that I have suffered but a
   shadow   [it ;
In the dread lightning which avenges
Brief, rapid, irreversible, destroying
The consequence of what it cannot
   cure.
Some such thing is to be endured or
   done :
When I know what, I shall be still and
   calm,
And never anything will move me
   more.
But now !—Oh blood, which art my
   father's blood,
Circling through these contaminated
   veins,
If thou, poured forth on the pol-
   luted earth,
Could wash away the crime, and
   punishment
By which I suffer—no, that cannot
   be !
Many might doubt there were a God
   above
Who sees and permits evil, and so die :
That faith no agony shall obscure in
   me.

   Lucretia. It must indeed have been
   some bitter wrong,
Yet what, I dare not guess. Oh ! my
   lost child,
Hide not in proud impenetrable grief
Thy sufferings from my fear.
   Beatrice.   I hide them not.
What are the words which you would
   have me speak ?
I, who can feign no image in my mind
Of that which has transformed me ?
   I, whose though⁺
Is like a ghost shrouded and folded up
In its own formless horror ? Of all
   words,
That minister to mortal intercourse,
Which wouldst thou hear ? For
   there is none to tell
My misery : if another ever knew
Aught like to it, she died as I will die,
And left it, as I must, without a name.
Death ! Death ! Our law and our
   religion call thee
A punishment and a reward. Oh,
   which
Have I deserved ?
   Lucretia. The peace of innocence ;
Till in your season you be called to
   heaven.
Whate'er you may have suffered, you
   have done
No evil. Death must be the punish-
   ment
Of crime, or the reward of trampling
   down
The thorns which God has strewed
   upon the path
Which leads to immortality.
   Beatrice.   Ay, death—
The punishment of crime. I pray
   thee, God,
Let me not be bewildered while I
   judge.
If I must live day after day, and keep
These limbs, the unworthy temple of
   thy spirit,
As a foul den from which what thou
   abhorrest
May mock thee, unavenged—it shall
   not be !
Self-murder—no that might be no
   escape,
For thy decree yawns like a Hell
   between
Our will and it.—Oh ! in this mortal
   world

There is no vindication and no law,
Which can adjudge and execute the
    doom
Of that through which I suffer.

Enter ORSINO.

(*She approaches him solemnly.*) Wel-
    come, Friend !
I have to tell you that, since last we
    met,
I have endured a wrong so great and
    strange,
That neither life nor death can give
    me rest.
Ask me not what it is, for there are
    deeds
Which have no form, sufferings which
    have no tongue.
  Orsino. And what is he who has
    thus injured you ?
  Beatrice. The man they call my
    father : a dread name.
  Orsino. It cannot be—
  Beatrice. What it can be, or not,
Forbear to think. It is, and it has
    been ;
Advise me how it shall not be again.
I thought to die ; but a religious awe
Restrains me, and the dread lest
    death itself
Might be no refuge from the con-
    sciousness
Of what is yet unexpiated. Oh,
    speak !
  Orsino. Accuse him of the deed,
    and let the law
Avenge thee.
  Beatrice. Oh, ice-hearted coun-
    sellor !
If I could find a word that might
    make known
The crime of my destroyer ; and that
    done,
My tongue should like a knife tear out
    the secret
Which cankers my heart's core ; ay,
    lay all bare,
So that my unpolluted fame should be
With vilest gossips a stale mouthed
    story ;
A mock, a byword, an astonish-
    ment :—
If this were done, which never shall be
    done,
Think of the offender's gold, his
    dreaded hate,

And the strange horror of the
    accuser's tale,
Baffling belief, and overpowering
    speech ;
Scarce whispered, unimaginable-
    wrapt
In hideous hints—Oh, most assured
    redress !
  Orsino. You will endure it then ?
  Beatrice. Endure !—Orsino.
It seems your counsel is small profit.
[*Turns from him, and speaks half
    to herself.*
               Ay,
All must be suddenly resolved and
    done.
What is this undistinguishable mist
Of thoughts, which rise, like shadow
    after shadow,
Darkening each other ?
  Orsino. Should the offender live ?
Triumph in his misdeed ? and make,
    by use,
His crime, whate'er it is, dreadful no
    doubt,
Thine element ; until thou 'mayest
    become
Utterly lost ; subdued even to the hue
Of that which thou permittest ?
  Beatrice (*to herself*). Mighty
    death !
Thou double-visaged shadow ! Only
    judge !
Rightfullest arbiter !
    [*She retires, absorbed in thought.*
  Lucretia. If the lightning
Of God has e'er descended to
    avenge—
  Orsino. Blaspheme not ! His high
    providence commits
Its glory on this earth, and their own
    wrongs   [glect
Into the hands of men ; if they ne-
To punish crime—
  Lucretia. But if one, like this
    wretch,
Should mock, with gold, opinion, law,
    and power ?
If there be no appeal to that which
    makes
The guiltiest tremble ! If, because
    our wrongs,
For that they are unnatural, strange,
    and monstrous,
Exceed all measure of belief ? Oh,
    God !

If, for the very reasons which should
make
Redress most swift and sure, our
injurer triumphs?
And we, the victims, bear worse
punishment
Than that appointed for their tor-
turer?
  Orsino.   Think not
But that there is redress where there
is wrong,
So be bold enough to seize it.
  Lucretia.   How?
If there were any way to make all
sure,   [good
I know not—but I think it might be
To—
  Orsino. Why, his late outrage to
Beatrice;
For it is such, as I but faintly guess,
As makes remorse dishonour, and
leaves her
Only one duty, how she may avenge:
You, but one refuge from ills ill en-
dured;
Me, but one counsel—
  Lucretia.   For we cannot hope
That aid, or retribution, or resource
Will arise thence, where every other
one
Might find them with less need.
         [BEATRICE *advances.*
  Orsino. Then—
  Beatrice.   Peace, Orsino!
And, honoured Lady, while I speak,
I pray,
That you put off, as garments over-
worn,
Forbearance and respect, remorse and
fear,
And all the fit restraints of daily life,
Which have been borne from child-
hood, but which now
Would be a mockery to my holier
plea.
As I have said, I have endured a
wrong,
Which, though it be expressionless, is
such
As asks atonement, both for what is
past,
And lest I be reserved, day after day,
To load with crimes an overburthened
soul,
And be—what ye can dream not. I
have prayed

To God, and I have talked with my
own heart,
And have unravelled my entangled
will,
And have at length determined what
is right.
Art thou my friend, Orsino? False
or true?
Pledge thy salvation ere I speak.
  Orsino.   I swear
To dedicate my cunning, and my
strength,
My silence, and whatever else is mine,
To thy commands,   [vise
  Lucretia. You think we should de-
His death?
  Beatrice. And execute what is de-
vised,
And suddenly. We must be brief and
bold.
  Orsino. And yet most cautious.
  Lucretia.   For the jealous laws
Would punish us with death and in-
famy
For that which it became themselves
to do.
  Beatrice. Be cautious as ye may,
but prompt. Orsino,
What are the means?
  Orsino.   I know two dull, fierce
outlaws,
Who think man's spirit as a worm's,
and they
Would trample out, for any slight
caprice,
The meanest or the noblest life. This
mood
Is marketable here in Rome. They
sell
What we now want.
  Lucretia.   To-morrow, before
dawn,
Cenci will take us to that lonely rock,
Petrella, in the Apulian Apennines.
If he arrive there—
  Beatrice.   He must not arrive.
  Orsino. Will it be dark before you
reach the tower?
  Lucretia. The sun will scarce be set.
  Beatrice.   But I remember
Two miles on this side of the fort, the
road
Crosses a deep ravine; 'tis rough and
narrow,
And winds with short turns down the
precipice;

And in its depth there is a mighty
   rock,
Which has, from unimaginable years,
Sustained itself with terror and with
   toil
Over a gulf, and with the agony
With which it clings seems slowly
   coming down ;
Even as a wretched soul hour after
   hour
Clings to the mass of life ; yet, cling-
   ing, leans ;
And, leaning, makes more dark the
   dread abyss
In which it fears to fall : beneath
   this crag
Huge as despair, as if in weariness,
The melancholy mountain yawns—
   below,
You hear but see not an impetuous
   torrent
Raging among the caverns, and a
   bridge
Crosses the chasm ; and high above
   there grow,
With intersecting trunks, from crag to
   crag,
Cedars, and yews, and pines ; whose
   tangled hair
Is matted in one solid roof of shade
By the dark ivy's twine. At noon-day
   here
'Tis twilight, and at sunset blackest
   night.
  Orsino. Before you reach that
   bridge make some excuse
For spurring on your mules, or loiter-
   ing
Until—
  Beatrice. What sound is that ?
  Lucretia. Hark ! No, it cannot be
   a servant's step ;
It must be Cenci, unexpectedly
Returned—Make some excuse for be-
   ing here
  Beatrice (*to* ORSINO *as she goes out*).
That step we hear approach must
   never pass
The bridge of which we spoke.
    [*Exeunt* LUCRETIA *and* BEATRICE.
  Orsino.   What shall I do ?
Cenci must find me here, and I must
   bear
The imperious inquisition of his looks
As to what brought me hither : let me
   mask

Mine own in some inane and vacant
   smile.

Enter GIACOMO, *in a hurried manner.*

How ! Have you ventured thither ?
   know you then
That Cenci is from home ?
  Giacomo.   I sought him here ;
And now must wait till he returns.
  Orsino.   Great God !
Weigh you the danger of this rash-
   ness ?
  Giacomo.   Ay !
Does my destroyer know his danger ?
   We
Are now no more, as once, parent and
   child,
But man to man ; the oppressor to the
   oppressed ;
The slanderer to the slandered ; foe to
   foe.
He has cast Nature off, which was his
   shield,
And Nature casts him off, who is her
   shame ;
And I spurn both. Is it a father's
   throat
Which I will shake ? and say, I ask
   not gold ;
I ask not happy years ; nor memories
Of tranquil childhood ; nor home-
   sheltered love ;
Though all these hast thou torn from
   me, and more,   [hoard
But only my fair fame ; only one
Of peace, which I thought hidden
   from thy hate,
Under the penury heaped on me by
   thee ;
Or I will—God can understand and
   pardon,
Why should I speak with man ?
  Orsino.   Be calm, dear friend.
  Giacomo. Well, I will calmly tell
   you what he did.
This old Francesco Cenci, as you
   know,
Borrowed the dowry of my wife from
   me,
And then denied the loan ; and left
   me so
In poverty, the which I sought to
   mend
By holding a poor office in the state.
It had been promised to me, and al-
   ready

I bought new clothing for my ragged
  babes,
And my wife smiled ; and my heart
  knew repose ;
When Cenci's intercession, as I
  found,
Conferred this office on a wretch,
  whom thus
He paid for vilest service. I re-
  turned
With this ill news, and we sate sad to-
  gether
Solacing our despondency with tears
Of such affection and unbroken faith
As temper life's worst bitterness ;
  when he,
As he is wont, came to upbraid and
  curse,
Mocking our poverty, and telling us
Such was God's scourge for disobedi-
  ent sons,
And then, that I might strike him
  dumb with shame,
I spoke of my wife's dowry ; but he
  coined
A brief yet specious tale, how I had
  wasted
The sum in secret riot ; and he saw
My wife was touched, and he went
  smiling forth.
And when I knew the impression he
  had made,
And felt my wife insult with silent
  scorn
My ardent truth, and look averse and
  cold,
I went forth too ; but soon returned
  again ;
Yet not so soon but that my wife had
  taught
My children her harsh thoughts, and
  they all cried,
" Give us clothes, father ! Give us
  better food !
What you in one night squander were
  enough
For months ! " I looked and saw
  that home was hell.
And to that hell will I return no more,
Until mine enemy has rendered up
Atonement, or, as he gave life to me,
I will, reversing nature's law—
  Orsino.   Trust me,
The compensation which thou seekest
  here
Will be denied.

  Giacomo.   Then—Are you not my
    friend ?
Did you not hint at the alternative,
Upon the brink of which you see I
  stand,
The other day when we conversed to-
  gether ?   [parricide,
My wrongs were then less. That word
Although I am resolved, haunts me
  like fear.
  Orsino. It must be fear itself, for
    the bare word
Is hollow mockery. Mark, how wis-
  est God
Draws to one point the threads of a
  just doom,
So sanctifying it : what you devise
Is, as it were, accomplished.
  Giacomo.   Is he dead ?
  Orsino. His grave is ready. Know
    that since we met
Cenci has done an outrage to his
  daughter.
  Giacomo. What outrage ?
  Orsino.   That she speaks not,
    but you may
Conceive such half conjectures as I do,
From her fixed paleness, and the lofty
  grief
Of her stern brow, bent on the idle air,
And her severe unmodulated voice,
Drowning both tenderness and dread ;
  and last
From this ; that whilst her step-
  mother and I,
Bewildered in our horror, talk to-
  gether
With obscure hints ; both self-mis-
  understood,
And darkly guessing, stumbling, in
  our talk,
Over the truth, and yet to its re-
  venge,
She interrupted us, and with a look
Which told, before she spoke it, he
  must die—
  Giacomo. It is enough. My doubts
    are well appeased ;
There is a higher reason for the act
Than mine ; there is a holier judge
  than me,
A more unblamed avenger. Beatrice,
Who in the gentleness of thy sweet
  youth
Hast never trodden on a worm, or
  bruised

A living flower, but thou hast pitied it
With needless tears! Fair sister,
    thou in whom
Men wondered how such loveliness
    and wisdom
Did not destroy each other! Is there
    made
Ravage of thee? O, heart, I ask no
· more
Justification! Shall I wait, Orsino,
Till he return, and stab him at the
    door?

  Orsino. Not so; some accident
    might interpose
To rescue him from what is now most
    sure;
And you are unprovided where to fly,
How to excuse or to conceal. Nay,
    listen:
All is contrived; success is so assured
That—

        Enter BEATRICE.

  Beatrice. 'Tis my brother's voice!
    You know me not?
  Giacomo. My sister, my lost sister!
  Beatrice.   Lost indeed!
I see Orsino has talked with you, and
That you conjecture things too hor-
    rible
To speak, yet far less than the truth.
    Now, stay not,
He might return: yet kiss me; I
    shall know
That then thou hast consented to his
    death.
Farewell, farewell! Let piety to God,
Brotherly love, justice and clemency,
And all things that make tender hard-
    est hearts,
Make thine hard, brother. Answer
    not—farewell.
              [*Exeunt severally.*

SCENE II.—*A mean Apartment in*
    GIACOMO'S *House.*

    GIACOMO *alone.*

  Giacomo. 'Tis midnight, and Or-
sino comes not yet.
[*Thunder, and the sound of a storm.*
What! can the everlasting elements
Feel with a worm like man? If so,
    the shaft
Of mercy-winged lightning would not
    fall

On stones and trees. .My wife and
    children sleep:
They are now living in unmeaning
    dreams:
But I must wake, still doubting if
    that deed
Be just which was most necessary. O,
Thou unreplenished lamp! whose
    narrow fire
Is shaken by the wind, and on whose
    edge
Devouring darkness hovers! Thou
    small flame,
Which, as a dying pulse rises and falls,
Still flickerest up and down, how
    very soon,
Did I not feed thee, wouldst thou fail
    and be
As thou hadst never been! So wastes
    and sinks
Even now, perhaps, the life that kind-
    led mine:
But that no power can fill with vital
    oil
That broken lamp of flesh. Ha! 'tis
    the blood
Which fed these veins that ebbs till all
    is cold: [sinks
It is the form that moulded mine, that
Into the white and yellow spasms of
    death:
It is the soul by which mine was ar-
    rayed
In God's immortal likeness which now
    stands
Naked before Heaven's judgment-
    seat!   [*A bell strikes.*
          One! Two!
The hours crawl on; and when my
    hairs are white
My son will then perhaps be waiting
    thus,
Tortured between just hate and vain
    remorse;
Chiding the tardy messenger of news
Like those which I expect. I almost
    wish .
He be not dead, although my wrongs
    are great;
Yet—'tis Orsino's step.
              [*Enter* ORSINO.
         Speak!
  Orsino.   I am come
To say he has escaped.
  Giacomo.   Escaped!
  Orsino.   And safe

Within Petrella. He passed by the
  spot
Appointed for the deed an hour too
  soon.
  Giacomo. Are we the fools of such
    contingencies ?
And do we waste in blind misgivings
  thus
The hours when we should act ? Then
  wind and thunder,
Which seemed to howl his knell, is the
  loud laughter
With which Heaven mocks our weak-
  ness ! I henceforth
Will ne'er repent of aught designed or
  done,
But my repentance.
  Orsino.   See, the lamp is out.
  Giacomo. If no remorse is ours
    when the dim air
Has drank this innocent flame, why
  should we quail
When Cenci's life, that light by which
  ill spirits
See the worst deeds they prompt,
  shall sink for ever ?
No, I am hardened.
  Orsino.   Why, what need of
    this
Who feared the pale intrusion of re-
  morse
In a just deed ? Although our first
  plan failed,
Doubt not but he will soon be laid to
  rest.
But light the lamp ; let us not talk
  i' the dark.
  Giacomo (lighting the lamp.) And
    yet, once quenched, I cannot
    thus relume
My father's life : do you not think his
  ghost
Might plead that argument with God ?
  Orsino.   Once gone,
You cannot now recall your sister's
  peace ;
Your own extinguished years of youth
  and hope ;
Nor your wife's bitter words ; nor all
  the taunts
Which, from the prosperous, weak
  misfortune takes ;
Nor your dead mother ; nor—
  Giacomo.   O speak no more !
I am resolved, although this very
  hand

Must quench the life that animated
  it.
  Orsino. There is no need of that.
    Listen : you know
Olimpio, the castellan of Petrella
In old Colonna's time ; him whom
  your father
Degraded from his post ? And
  Marzio,
That desperate wretch, whom he de-
  prived last year
Of a reward of blood, well earned and
  due ?
  Giacomo. I knew Olimpio ; and
    they say he hated
Old Cenci so, that in his silent rage
His lips grew white only to see him
  pass.
Of Marzio I know nothing.
  Orsino.   Marzio's hate
Matches Olimpio's. I have sent
  these men,
But in your name, and as at your re-
  quest,
To talk with Beatrice and Lucretia.
  Giacomo. Only to talk ?
  Orsino.   The moments which
    even now
Pass onward to to-morrow's midnight
  hour,
May memorise their flight with death ;
  ere then
They must have talked, and may per-
  haps have done,
And made an end.
  Giacomo. Listen ! What sound
    is that ?
  Orsino. The house-dog moans, and
    the beams crack : nought else.
  Giacomo. It is my wife complaining
    in her sleep :
I doubt not she is saying bitter things
Of me ; and all my children round her
  dreaming
That I deny them sustenance.
  Orsino.   Whilst he
Who truly took it from them, and
  who fills
Their hungry rest with bitterness, now
  sleeps
Lapped in bad pleasures, and trium-
  phantly
Mocks thee in visions of successful
  hate
Too like the truth of day.
  Giacomo.   If e'er he wakes

Again, I will not trust to hireling
    hands—
    Orsino. Why, that were well. I
    must be gone ; good night !
When next we meet may all be done !
    Giacomo.   And all
Forgotten : Oh, that I had never
    been !   [*Exeunt*

ACT IV

SCENE I.—*An Apartment in the
    Castle of Petrella. Enter* CENCI.

    Cenci. She comes not ; yet I left
    her even now
Vanquished and faint. She knows
    the penalty
Of her delay ; yet what if threats are
    vain ?
Am I not now within Petrella's moat ?
Or fear I still the eyes and ears of
    Rome ?
Might I not drag her by the golden
    hair ?
Stamp on her ? Keep her sleepless,
    till her brain
Be overworn ? Tame her with chains
    and famine ?
Less would suffice. Yet so to leave
    undone
What I most seek ! No, 'tis her stub-
    born will,
Which, by its own consent, shall stoop
    as low
As that which drags it down.
                  [*Enter* LUCRETIA.
            Thou loathed wretch !
Hide thee from my abhorrence ; fly,
    begone !
Yet stay ! Bid Beatrice come hither.
    Lucretia.   Oh,
Husband ! I pray, for thine own
    wretched sake,
Heed what thou dost. A man who
    walks like thee
Through crimes, and through the
    danger of his crimes,
Each hour may stumble o'er a sudden
    grave.
And thou art old ; thy hairs are hoary
    grey ;
As thou wouldst save thyself from
    death and hell,

Pity thy daughter ; give her to some
    friend
In marriage ; so that she may tempt
    thee not,
To hatred, or worse thoughts, if worse
    there be.
    Cenci. What ! like her sister, who
    has found a home
To mock my hate from with prosper-
    ity ?
Strange ruin shall destroy both her and
    thee,
And all that yet remain. My death
    may be
Rapid, her destiny outspeeds it. Go,
Bid her come hither, and before my
    mood
Be changed, lest I should drag her by
    the hair.
    Lucretia She sent me to thee, hus-
    band. At thy presence
She fell, as thou dost know, into a
    trance ;
And in that trance she heard a voice
    which said,
" Cenci must die! Let him confess
    himself !
Even now the accusing angel waits to
    hear
If God, to punish his enormous crimes,
Harden his dying heart ! "
    Cenci.   Why—such things are :
No doubt divine revealings may be
    made
'Tis plain I have been favoured from
    above,
For when I cursed my sons, they died.
            —Ay—so—
As to the right or wrong, that's talk—
    repentance—
Repentance is an easy moment's
    work,
And more depends on God than me.
    Well—well—   !
I must give up the greater point,
    which was
To poison and corrupt her soul.
    [*A pause :* LUCRETIA *approaches
    anxiously, and then shrinks
    back as he speaks.*
                        One, two ;
Ay—Rocco and Cristofano my curse
Strangled : and Giacomo, I think,
    will find
Life a worse Hell than that beyond
    the grave :

Beatrice shall, if there be skill in hate,
Die in despair, blaspheming ; to
  Bernardo,
He is so innocent, I will bequeath
The memory of these deeds, and make
  his youth
The sepulchre of hope, where evil
  thoughts
Shall grow like weeds on a neglected
  tomb.
When all is done, out in the wide
  Campagna,
I will pile up my silver and my gold ;
My costly robes, paintings, and tapes-
  tries ;
My parchments, and all records of my
  wealth ;
And make a bonfire in my joy, and
  leave
Of my possessions nothing but my
  name ;
Which shall be an inheritance to strip
Its wearer bare as infamy. That done,
My soul, which is a scourge, will I re-
  sign
Into the hands of him who wielded it ;
Be it for its own punishment or theirs,
He will not ask it of me till the lash
Be broken in its last and deepest
  wound ;
Until its hate be all inflicted. Yet,
Lest death outspeed my purpose, let
  me make
Short work and sure.
                                    [Going.
    Lucretia (stops him). Oh, stay !
  It was a feint :
She had no vision, and she heard no
  voice.
I said it but to awe thee.
    Cenci.   That is well.
Vile palterer with the sacred truth of
  God,
Be thy soul choked with that blas-
  pheming lie !
For Beatrice, worse terrors are in
  store,
To bend her to my will.
    Lucretia.   Oh ! to what will ?
What cruel sufferings, more than she
  has known,
Canst thou inflict ?
    Cenci.   Andrea ! go, call my
  daughter,
And if she comes not, tell her that I
  come.

What sufferings ? I will drag her,
  step by step,
Through infamies unheard of among
  men ;
She shall stand shelterless in the broad
  noon
Of public scorn, for acts blazoned
  abroad,
One among which shall be—What ?
  Canst thou guess ?
She shall become (for what she most
  abhors
Shall have a fascination to entrap
Her loathing will,) to her own con-
  scious self
All she appears to others ; and when
  dead,
As she shall die unshrived and unfor-
  given,
A rebel to her father and her God,
Her corpse shall be abandoned to the
  hounds ;
Her name shall be the terror of the
  earth ;
Her spirit shall approach the throne
  of God
Plague-spotted with my curses. I
  will make
Body and soul a monstrous lump of
  ruin.

                  Enter ANDREA.

    Andrea. The lady Beatrice—
    Cenci.   Speak, pale slave ! What
Said she ?
    Andrea. My lord, 'twas what she
  looked ; she said :
" Go tell my father that I see the gulf
Of Hell between us two, which he may
  pass ;
I will not."   [*Exit* ANDREA.
    Cenci.   Go thou quick, Lucretia,
Tell her to come ; yet let her under-
  stand
Her coming is consent : and say,
  moreover,
That if she come not I will curse her.
                            [*Exit* LUCRETIA.
                                        Ha !
With what but with a father's curse
  doth God
Panic-strike armed victory, and make
  pale
Cities in their prosperity ? The
  world's Father

Must grant a parent's prayer against
  his child,
Be he who asks even what men call me.
Will not the deaths of her rebellious
  brothers
Awe her before I speak ? For I on
  them
Did imprecate quick ruin, and it
  came.   [*Enter* LUCRETIA.
Well ; what ? Speak, wretch !
  Lucretia.   She said, " I cannot
  come ;
Go tell my father that I see a torrent
Of his own blood raging between us."
  Cenci (*kneeling*)   God !
Hear me ! If this most specious mass
  of flesh,
Which thou hast made my daughter ;
  this my blood,
This particle of my divided being ;
Or rather, this my bane and my dis-
  ease,
Whose sight infects and poisons me ;
  this devil,
Which sprung from me as from a hell,
  was meant
To aught good use ; if her bright
  loveliness
Was kindled to illumine this dark
  world ;
If nursed by thy selectest dew of love,
Such virtues blossom in her as should
  make
The peace of life, I pray thee for my
  sake,
As thou the common God and Father
  art
Of her, and me, and all ; reverse that
  doom !
Earth, in the name of God, let her
  food be
Poison, until she be encrusted round
With leprous stains ! Heaven, rain
  upon her head
The blistering drops of the Maremma's
  dew,
Till she be speckled like a toad ; parch
  up
Those love-enkindled lips, warp those
  fine limbs
To loathed lameness ! All-beholding
  sun,
Strike in thine envy those life-darting
  eyes
With thine own blinding beams !
  Lucretia.   Peace ! peace !

For thine own sake unsay those dread-
  ful words.
When high God grants, he punishes
  such prayers.
  Cenci (*leaping up, and throwing
  his right hand towards Heaven*).
  He does his will, I mine ! This
  in addition,
That if she have a child——
  Lucretia.   Horrible thought !
  Cenci. That if she ever have a
  child ; and thou,
Quick Nature ! I adjure thee by thy
  God,
That thou be fruitful in her, and in-
  crease
And multiply, fulfilling his command,
And my deep imprecation ! May it
  be
A hideous likeness of herself ; that as
From a distorting mirror, she may see
Her image mixed with what she most
  abhors,
Smiling upon her from her nursing
  breast.
And that the child may from its in-
  fancy
Grow, day by day, more wicked and
  deformed,
Turning her mother's love to misery :
And that both she and it may live,
  until
It shall repay her care and pain with
  hate,
Of what may else be more unnatural.
So he may hunt her through the
  clamorous scoffs
Of the loud world to a dishonoured
  grave.
Shall I revoke this curse ? Go, bid
  her come.
Before my words are chronicled in
  heaven.   [*Exit* LUCRETIA.
I do not feel as if I were a man,
But like a fiend appointed to chastise
The offences of some unremembered
  world.
My blood is running up and down my
  veins !
A fearful pleasure makes it prick and
  tingle :
I feel a giddy sickness of strange awe;
My heart is beating with an expect-
  ation
Of horrid joy.   [*Enter* LUCRETIA.
          What ? Speak !

Lucretia.   She bids thee curse ;
And if thy curses, as they cannot do,
Could kill her soul—
    Cenci.   She would not come. 'Tis well,
I can do both ; first take what I demand,
And then extort concession. To thy chamber !
Fly ere I spurn thee : and beware this night
That thou cross not my footsteps. It were safer
To come between the tiger and his prey.   [*Exit* LUCRETIA.
It must be late ; mine eyes grow weary dim
With unaccustomed heaviness of sleep.
Conscience ! Oh, thou most insolent of lies !
They say that sleep, that healing dew of heaven,
Steeps not in balm the foldings of the brain
Which thinks thee an impostor. I will go,   [rest,
First to belie thee with an hour of
Which will be deep and calm, I feel ; and then—
O, multitudinous Hell, the fiends will shake
Thine arches with the laughter of their joy !
There shall be lamentation heard in Heaven
As o'er an angel fallen ; and upon Earth
All good shall droop and sicken, and ill things
Shall, with a spirit of unnatural life,
Stir and be quickened—even as I am now.   [*Exit.*

SCENE II.—*Before the Castle of Petrella.*

Enter BEATRICE *and* LUCRETIA, *above on the ramparts.*

Beatrice. They come not yet.
Lucretia.   'Tis scarce midnight.
Beatrice.   How slow
Behind the course of thought, even sick with speed,
Lags leaden-footed Time !
Lucretia.   The minutes pass—

If he should wake before the deed is done ?
    Beatrice. O, Mother ! He must never wake again.
What thou hast said persuades me that our act
Will but dislodge a spirit of deep hell
Out of a human form.
    Lucretia.   'Tis true he spoke
Of death and judgment with strange confidence
For one so wicked ; as a man believing
In God, yet recking not of good or ill.
And yet to die without confession !—
    Beatrice.   Oh
Believe that Heaven is merciful and just,
And will not add our dread necessity
To the amount of his offences.
    [*Enter* OLIMPIO *and* MARZIO, *below.*
Lucretia.   See,
They come.
    Beatrice. All mortal things must hasten thus
To their dark end. Let us go down.
    [*Exeunt* LUCRETIA *and* BEATRICE
                from above.
Olimpio. How feel you to this work ?
    Marzio.   As one who thinks
A thousand crowns excellent market price
For an old murderer's life. Your cheeks are pale.
    Olimpio. It is the white reflection of your own,
Which you call pale.
    Marzio. Is that their natural hue ?
    Olimpio. Or 'tis my hate, and the deferred desire
To wreak it, which extinguishes their blood.
    Marzio. You are inclined then to this business ?
    Olimpio.   Ay,
If one should bribe me with a thousand crowns
To kill a serpent which had stung my child,
I could not be more willing.
    [*Enter* BEATRICE *and* LUCRETIA
                below.
                Noble ladies !
    Beatrice. Are ye resolved ?
    Olimpio.   Is he asleep ?

Marzio.   Is all
Quiet ?
  Lucretia. I mixed an opiate with
his drink :
He sleeps so soundly—
  Beatrice. That his death will be
But as a change of sin-chastising
  dreams,
A dark continuance of the Hell within
  him,
Which God extinguish ! But ye are
  resolved ?
Ye know it is a high and holy deed ?
  Olimpio. We are resolved.
  Marzio.   As to the how this act
Be warranted, it rests with you.
  Beatrice.   Well, follow !
  Olimpio. Hush ! Hark ! What noise
  is that ?
  Marzio.   Ha ! someone comes !
  Beatrice. Ye   conscience-stricken
  cravens, rock to rest
Your baby hearts. It is the iron gate,
Which ye left open, swinging to the
  wind,
That enters whistling as in scorn.
  Come, follow !
And be your steps like mine, light,
  quick, and bold.   [*Exeunt.*

SCENE III.—*An Apartment in the
        Castle.*

Enter BEATRICE *and* LUCRETIA.

  Lucretia. They are about it now.
  Beatrice.   Nay, it is done.
  Lucretia. I have not heard him
  groan.
  Beatrice.   He will not groan.
  Lucretia. What sound is that ?
  Beatrice. List ! 'tis the tread of
  feet
About his bed.
  Lucretia.   My God !
If he be now a cold stiff corpse—
  Beatrice.   O, fear not
What may be done, but what is left
  undone :
The act seals all.
      [*Enter* OLIMPIO *and* MARZIO.
      Is it accomplished ?
  Marzio.   What ?
  Olimpio. Did you not call ?
  Beatrice.   When ?
  Olimpio.   Now.

  Beatrice.   I ask if all is over ?
  Olimpio. We dare not kill an old
  and sleeping man ;
His thin grey hair, his stern and
  reverent brow,
His veined hands crossed on his heav-
  ing breast,
And the calm innocent sleep in which
  he lay,
Quelled me. Indeed, indeed, I can-
  not do it.
  Marzio. But I was bolder ; for I
  chid Olimpio,
And bade him bear his wrongs to his
  own grave,
And leave me the reward. And now
  my knife
Touched the loose wrinkled throat,
  when the old man
Stirred in his sleep, and said, " God !
  hear, O hear,
A father's curse ! What, art thou not
  our father ? "
And then he laughed. I knew it was
  the ghost
Of my dead father speaking through
  his lips,
And could not kill him.
  Beatrice.   Miserable slaves !
Where, if ye dare not kill a sleeping
  man,
Found ye the boldness to return to me
With such a deed undone ? Base
  palterers !
Cowards and traitors ! Why, the
  very conscience
Which ye would sell for gold and for
  revenge
Is an equivocation : it sleeps over
A thousand daily acts disgracing
  men ;
And when a deed, where mercy insults
  Heaven—
Why do I talk ?
      [*Snatching a dagger from one of
         them, and raising it.*
     Hadst thou a tongue to say,
She murdered her own father, I must
  do it !
But never dream ye shall outlive him
  long !
  Olimpio. Stop, for God's sake !
  Marzio. I will go back and kill
  him.
  Olimpio. Give me the weapon, we
  must do thy will.

Beatrice. Take it! Depart! Return!

[*Exeunt* OLIMPIO *and* MARZIO.

How pale thou art!
We do but that which 'twere a deadly crime
To leave undone.

Lucretia. Would it were done!

Beatrice. Even whilst
That doubt is passing through your mind, the world
Is conscious of a change. Darkness and hell
Have swallowed up the vapour they sent forth
To blacken the sweet light of life. My breath
Comes, methinks, lighter, and the jellied blood
Runs freely through my veins. Hark!

[*Enter* OLIMPIO *and* MARZIO.

He is—

Olimbio. Dead!

Marzio. We strangled him, that there might be no blood;
And then we threw his heavy corpse i' the garden
Under the balcony; 'twill seem it fell.

Beatrice (*giving them a bag of coin*). Here, take this gold, and hasten to your homes.
And, Marzio, because thou wast only awed
By that which made me tremble, wear thou this!

[*Clothes him in a rich mantle.*

It was the mantle which my grandfather
Wore in his high prosperity, and men
Envied his state: so may they envy thine. [God
Thou wert a weapon in the hand of
To a just use. Live long and thrive!
And, mark,
If thou hast crimes, repent: this deed is none. [*A horn is sounded.*

Lucretia. Hark, 'tis the castle horn: my God! it sounds
Like the last trump.

Beatrice. Some tedious guest is coming.

Lucretia. The drawbridge is let down; there is a tramp
Of horses in the court! fly, hide yourselves!

[*Exeunt* OLIMPIO *and* MARZIO.

Beatrice. Let us retire to counterfeit deep rest;
I scarcely need to counterfeit it now;
The spirit which doth reign within these limbs
Seems strangely undisturbed. I could even sleep
Fearless and calm: all ill is surely past. [*Exeunt.*

SCENE IV.—*Another Apartment in the Castle.*

Enter on one side the Legate SAVELLA, *introduced by a Servant, and on the other* LUCRETIA *and* BERNARDO.

Savella. Lady, my duty to his Holiness
Be my excuse that thus unseasonably
I break upon your rest. I must speak with
Count Cenci; doth he sleep?

Lucretia (*in a hurried and confused manner*). I think he sleeps;
Yet, wake him not, I pray, spare me awhile,
He is a wicked and a wrathful man;
Should he be roused out of his sleep to-night,
Which is, I know, a hell of angry dreams,
It were not well; indeed it were not well.
Wait till daybreak,— (*Aside.*) O, I am deadly sick!

Savella. I grieve thus to distress you, but the Count
Must answer charges of the gravest import,
And suddenly; such my commission is.

Lucretia (*with increased agitation*). I dare not rouse him, I know none who dare;
'Twere perilous;—you might as safely waken
A serpent; or a corpse in which some fiend
Were laid to sleep.

Savella. Lady, my moments here
Are counted. I must rouse him from his sleep,
Since none else dare.

Lucretia (*aside*). O, terror! O, despair!

[*To* BERNARDO.] Bernardo, conduct you the Lord Legate to
Your father's chamber.
[*Exeunt* SAVELLA *and* BERNARDO.

Enter BEATRICE.

Beatrice.   'Tis a messenger
Come to arrest the culprit who now stands
Before the throne of unappealable God.
Both Earth and Heaven, consenting arbiters,
Acquit our deed.
Lucretia.   Oh, agony of fear !
Would that he yet might live ! Even now I heard
The legate's followers whisper as they passed
They had a warrant for his instant death.
All was prepared by unforbidden means,
Which we must pay so dearly, having done.
Even now they search the tower, and find the body ;
Now they suspect the truth ; now they consult,
Before they come to tax us with the fact ;
O horrible, 'tis all discovered !
Beatrice.   Mother,
What is done wisely, is done well. Be bold
As thou art just. 'Tis like a truant child,
To fear that others know what thou hast done,
Even from thine own strong consciousness, and thus
Write on unsteady eyes and altered cheeks
All thou wouldst hide. Be faithful to thyself,
And fear no other witness but thy fear.
For if, as cannot be, some circumstance
Should rise in accusation, we can blind
Suspicion with such cheap astonishment,
Or overbear it with such guiltless pride,

As murderers cannot feign. The deed is done,
And what may follow now regards not me.
I am as universal as the light ;
Free as the earth-surrounding air ; as firm
As the world's centre. Consequence, to me,
Is as the wind which strikes the solid rock,
But shakes it not.
               [*A cry within and tumult.*
Voices. Murder ! Murder ! Murder !

Enter BERNARDO *and* SAVELLA.

Savella (*to his followers*). Go, search the castle round ; sound the alarm ;
Look to the gates, that none escape !
Beatrice.   What now ?
Bernardo. I know not what to say —my father's dead.
Beatrice. How, dead ? he only sleeps ; you mistake, brother.
His sleep is very calm, very like death;
'Tis wonderful how well a tyrant sleeps.
He is not *dead ?*
Bernàrdo.   Dead ; murdered !
Lucretia (*with extreme agitation*). Oh, no, no,
He is not murdered, though he may be dead ;
I have alone the keys of those apartments.
Savella. Ha ! Is it so ?
Beatrice. My lord, I pray excuse us ;
We will retire ; my mother is not well ;
She seems quite overcome with this strange horror.
[*Exeunt* LUCRETIA *and* BEATRICE.
Savella. Can you suspect who may have murdered him ?
Bernardo. I know not what to think.
Savella. Can you name any
Who had an interest in his death ?
Bernardo.   Alas !
I can name none who had not, and those most
Who most lament that such a deed is done ;
My mother, and my sister, and myself.

Savella. 'Tis strange ! There were
    clear marks of violence.
I found the old man's body in the
    moonlight,
Hanging beneath the window of his
    chamber
Among the branches of a pine : he
    could not
Have fallen there, for all his limbs lay
    heaped
And effortless ; 'tis true there was no
    blood.—
Favour me, sir—it much imports
    your house
That all should be made clear—to tell
    the ladies
That I request their presence.

                    [*Exit* BERNARDO.

Enter Guards, bringing in MARZIO.

  Guard.   We have one.
  Officer. My lord, we found this ruf-
    fian and another
Lurking among the rocks ; there is no
    doubt
But that they are the murderers of
    Count Cenci :
Each had a bag of coin ; this fellow
    wore
A gold-inwoven robe, which, shining
    bright
Under the dark rocks to the glimmer-
    ing moon,
Betrayed them to our notice : the
    other fell
Desperately fighting.
  Savella. What does he confess ?
  Officer. He keeps firm silence ; but
    these lines found on him
May speak.
  Savella. Their language is at least
    sincere.   [*Reads.*

  " To THE LADY BEATRICE.

  " That the atonement of what my
nature sickens to conjecture may soon
arrive, I send thee, at thy brother's
desire, those who will speak and do
more than I dare write.
        " Thy devoted servant,
                    " ORSINO."

Enter LUCRETIA, BEATRICE, *and*
            BERNARDO.

Knowest thou this writing, lady ?
  Beatrice.   No.

  Savella.   Nor thou ?
  Lucretia (*her conduct throughout the
    scene is marked by extreme agita-
    tion*).
Where was it found ? What is it ?
    It should be
Orsino's hand ! It speaks of that
    strange horror
Which never yet found utterance, but
    which made
Between that hapless child and her
    dead father
A gulf of obscure hatred.
  Savella.   Is it so ?
Is it true, lady, that thy father did
Such outrages as to awaken in thee
Unfilial hate ?
  Beatrice. Not hate, 'twas more
    than hate :
This is most true, yet wherefore ques-
    tion me ?
  Savella. There is a deed demanding
    question done ;   [not.
Thou hast a secret which will answer
  Beatrice. What sayest ? My lord,
    your words are bold and rash.
  Savella. I do arrest all present in
    the name
Of the Pope's Holiness. You must
    to Rome.
  Lucretia. O, not to Rome ! In-
    deed we are not guilty.
  Beatrice. Guilty ! Who dares talk
    of guilt ? My lord,
I am more innocent of parricide
Than is a child born fatherless. Dear
    mother,
Your gentleness and patience are no
    shield
For this keen-judging world, this two-
    edged lie,
Which seems, but is not. What ! will human laws,
Rather will ye who are their ministers,
Bar all access to retribution first,
And then, when Heaven doth inter-
    pose to do
What ye neglect, arming familiar
    things
To the redress of an unwonted crime,
Make ye the victims who demanded it
Culprits ? 'Tis ye are culprits ! That
    poor wretch
Who stands so pale, and trembling,
    and amazed,
If it be true he murdered Cenci, was

A sword in the right hand of justest God.
Wherefore should I have wielded it? unless
The crimes which mortal tongue dare never name,
God therefore scruples to avenge.

Savella. You own
That you desired his death?

Beatrice. It would have been
A crime no less than his, if for one moment
That fierce desire had faded in my heart.
'Tis true I did believe, and hope, and pray,
Ay, I even knew—for God is wise and just,
That some strange sudden death hung over him.
'Tis true that this did happen, and most true, [earth,
There was no other rest for me on No other hope in Heaven;—now what of this?

Savella. Strange thoughts beget strange deeds; and here are both:
I judge thee not.

Beatrice. And yet, if you arrest me,
You are the judge and executioner
Of that which is the life of life: the breath
Of accusation kills an innocent name,
And leaves for lame acquittal the poor life,
Which is a mask without it. 'Tis most false
That I am guilty of foul parricide;
Although I must rejoice, for justest cause,
That other hands have sent my father's soul
To ask the mercy he denied to me.
Now leave us free: stain not a noble house
With vague surmises of rejected crime;
Add to our sufferings and your own neglect
No heavier sum; let them have been enough:
Leave us the wreck we have.

Savella. I dare not, lady.
I pray that you prepare yourselves for Rome:

There the Pope's further pleasure will be known.

Lucretia. O, not to Rome! O, take us not to Rome!

Beatrice. Why not to Rome, dear mother? There, as here,
Our innocence is as an armed heel
To trample accusation. God is there,
As here, and with his shadow ever clothes
The innocent, the injured and the weak;
And such are we. Cheer up, dear lady! lean
On me; collect your wandering thoughts. My lord,
As soon as you have taken some refreshment,
And had all such examinations made
Upon the spot, as may be necessary
To the full understanding of this matter,
We shall be ready. Mother, will you come?

Lucretia. Ha! they will bind us to the rack, and wrest
Self-accusation from our agony!
Will Giacomo be there? Orsino? Marzio?
All present; all confronted; all demanding
Each from the other's countenance the thing*
Which is in every heart! O, misery!
[*She faints, and is borne out.*

Savella. She faints; an ill appearance this.

Beatrice. My lord,
She knows not yet the uses of the world.
She fears that power is as a beast which grasps
And loosens not: a snake whose look transmutes
All things to guilt, which is its nutriment.
She cannot know how well the supine slaves
Of blind authority read the truth of things
When written on a brow of guilelessness:
She sees not yet triumphant Innocence
Stand at the judgment-seat of mortal man,

A judge and an accuser of the wrong
Which drags it there.   Prepare yourself, my lord ;
Our suite will join yours in the court
below.   [*Exeunt.*

ACT V

SCENE I.—*An Apartment in* ORSINO'S
Palace.

Enter ORSINO *and* GIACOMO.

Giacomo. Do evil deeds thus
quickly come to end ?
O that the vain remorse which must
chastise
Crimes done, had but as loud a voice
to warn,
As its keen sting is mortal to avenge !
O that the hour when present had
cast off
The mantle of its mystery, and shown
The ghastly form with which it now
returns
When its scared game is roused,
cheering the hounds
Of conscience to their prey ! Alas,
alas !
It was a wicked thought, a piteous
deed,
To kill an old and hoary-headed
father.
Orsino. It has turned out unluckily,
in truth.
Giacomo. To violate the sacred
doors of sleep ;
To cheat kind nature of the placid
death
Which she prepares for overwearied
age ;
To drag from Heaven an unrepentant
soul,
Which might have quenched in recon-
ciling prayers
A life of burning crimes—
Orsino.   You cannot say
I urged you to the deed.
Giacomo.   O, had I never
Found in thy smooth and ready
countenance
The mirror of my darkest thoughts ;
hadst thou
Never with hints and questions made
me look

Upon the monster of my thought,
until
It grew familiar to desire—
Orsino.   'Tis thus
Men cast the blame of their unpros-
perous acts
Upon the abettors of their own re-
solve ;
Or any thing but their weak, guilty
selves.
And yet, confess the truth, it is the
peril
In which you stand that gives you
this pale sickness
Of penitence ; confess, 'tis fear dis-
guised
From its own shame that takes the
mantle now
Of thin remorse.   What if we yet
were safe ?
Giacomo. How can that be ? Al-
ready Beatrice,
Lucretia, and the murderer, are in
prison.   [speak,
I doubt not officers are, whilst we
Sent to arrest us.
Orsino.   I have all prepared
For instant flight. We can escape
even now,
So we take fleet occasion by the hair.
Giacomo. Rather expire in tor-
tures, as I may.
What ! will you cast by self-accusing
flight
Assured conviction upon Beatrice ?
She who alone, in this unnatural
work,
Stands like God's angel ministered
upon
By fiends ; avenging such a nameless
wrong
As turns black parricide to piety ;
Whilst we for basest ends—I fear, Or-
sino,
While I consider all your words and
looks,
Comparing them with your proposal
now,
That you must be a villain.   For
what end
Could you engage in such a perilous
crime,
Training me on with hints, and signs,
and smiles,
Even to this gulf ?   Thou art no liar ?
No.

Thou art a lie! Traitor and mur-
derer!
Coward and slave! But no—defend
thyself; [*Drawing.*
Let the sword speak what the indig-
nant tongue
Disdains to brand thee with.
Orsino.　　　Put up your weapon.
Is it the desperation of your fear
Makes you thus rash and sudden with
your friend,
Now ruined for your sake? If honest
anger
Have moved you, know, that what I
just proposed
Was but to try you. As for me, I
think
Thankless affection led me to this
point,
From which, if my firm temper could
repent,
I cannot now recede. Even whilst
we speak,
The ministers of justice wait below:
They grant me these brief moments.
Now, if you
Have any word of melancholy com-
fort
To speak to your pale wife, 'twere
best to pass
Out at the postern, and avoid them so.
Giacomo. Oh, generous friend!
How canst thou pardon me?
Would that my life could purchase
thine!
Orsino.　　　　　That wish
Now comes a day too late. Haste;
fare thee well!
Hear'st thou not steps along the cor-
ridor? [*Exit* GIACOMO.
I'm sorry for it; but the guards are
waiting
At his own gate, and such was my
contrivance
That I might rid me both of him and
them.
I thought to act a solemn comedy
Upon the painted scene of this new
world,
And to attain my own peculiar ends
By some such plot of mingled good
and ill
As others weave; but there arose a
Power
Which grasped and snapped the
threads of my device,

And turned it to a net of ruin—Ha!
[*A shout is heard.*
Is that my name I hear proclaimed
abroad?
But I will pass, wrapt in a vile dis-
guise;
Rags on my back, and a false inno-
cence
Upon my face, through the misdeem-
ing crowd,
Which judges by what seems. 'Tis
easy then,
For a new name, and for a country
new,
And a new life, fashioned on old
desires,
To change the honours of abandoned
Rome.
And these must be the masks of that
within,
Which must remain unaltered.—Oh,
I fear
That what is past will never let me
rest!
Why, when none else is conscious, but
myself,
Of my misdeeds, should my own
heart's contempt
Trouble me? Have I not the power
to fly
My own reproaches? Shall I be the
slave
Of—what? A word! which those
of this false world
Employ against each other, not
themselves;
As men wear daggers not for self-
offence.
But if I am mistaken, where shall I
Find the disguise to hide me from my-
self,
As now I skulk from every other eye?
[*Exit.*

SCENE II.—*A Hall of Justice.*

CAMILLO, JUDGES, *etc., are discovered
seated;* MARZIO *is led in.*

First Judge. Accused, do you per-
sist in your denial?
I ask you, are you innocent, or guilty?
I demand who were the participators
In your offence? Speak truth, and
the whole truth.
Marzio. My God! I did not kill
him; I know nothing;

Olimpio sold the robe to me from which
You would infer my guilt.

Second Judge. Away with him!

First Judge. Dare you, with lips yet white from the rack's kiss,
Speak false? Is it so soft a questioner,
That you would bandy lover's talk with it,
Till it wind out your life and soul? Away!

Marzio. Spare me! O, spare! I will confess.

First Judge. Then speak.

Marzio. I strangled him in his sleep.

First Judge. Who urged you to it?

Marzio. His own son Giacomo and the young prelate
Orsino sent me to Petrella; there
The ladies Beatrice and Lucretia
Tempted me with a thousand crowns, and I
And my companion forthwith murdered him.
Now let me die.

First Judge. This sounds as bad as truth. Guards, there,
Lead forth the prisoners.

[*Enter* LUCRETIA, BEATRICE, *and* GIACOMO, *guarded.*
Look upon this man;
When did you see him last?

Beatrice. We never saw him.

Marzio. You know me too well, Lady Beatrice.

Beatrice. I know thee! How! where? when?

Marzio. You know 'twas I
Whom you did urge with menaces and bribes
To kill your father. When the thing was done, [gold,
You clothed me in a robe of woven
And bade me thrive: how I have thriven, you see.
You, my Lord Giacomo, Lady Lucretia,
You know that what I speak is true.

[BEATRICE *advances towards him; he covers his face, and shrinks back.*
Oh, dart
The terrible resentment of those eyes
On the dread earth! Turn them away from me!

They wound: 'twas torture forced the truth. My lords,
Having said this, let me be led to death.

Beatrice. Poor wretch, I pity thee: yet stay awhile.

Camillo. Guards, lead him not away.

Beatrice. Cardinal Camillo,
You have a good repute for gentleness
And wisdom: can it be that you sit here
To countenance a wicked farce like this?
When some obscure and trembling slave is dragged
From sufferings which might shake the sternest heart,
And bade to answer, not as he believes,
But as those may suspect or do desire,
Whose questions thence suggest their own reply: [ments
And that in peril of such hideous tor-
As merciful God spares even the damned. Speak now
The thing you surely know, which is, that you,
If your fine frame were stretched upon that wheel,
And you were told, " Confess that you did poison
Your little nephew: that fair blue-eyed child
Who was the lodestar of your life:"
and though
All see, since his most swift and piteous death,
That day and night, and heaven and earth, and time,
And all the things hoped for or done therein,
Are changed to you, through your exceeding grief,
Yet you would say, " I confess any-thing "—
And beg from your tormentors, like that slave,
The refuge of dishonourable death.
I pray thee, Cardinal, that thou assert
My innocence.

Camillo (*much moved*). What shall we think, my lords?
Shame on these tears! I thought the heart was frozen
Which is their fountain. I would pledge my soul

That she is guiltless.

Judge. Yet she must be tortured.

Camillo. I would as soon have tortured mine own nephew
(If he now lived, he would be just her age ;
His hair, too, was her colour, and his eyes
Like hers in shape, but blue, and not so deep :)
As that most perfect image of God's love
That ever came sorrowing upon the earth.
She is as pure as speechless infancy !

Judge. Well, be her purity on your head, my lord,
If you forbid the rack. His Holiness   [crime
Enjoined us to pursue this monstrous
By the severest forms of law ; nay, even
To stretch a point against the criminals.
The prisoners stand accused of parricide,
Upon such evidence as justifies
Torture.

Beatrice. What evidence ?   This man's ?

Judge.   Even so.

Beatrice (*to* MARZIO). Come near.
And who art thou, thus chosen forth
Out of the multitude of living men,
To kill the innocent ?

Marzio.   I am Marzio,
Thy father's vassal.

Beatrice.   Fix thine eyes on mine ;
Answer to what I ask.
            [*Turning to the Judges.*
            I prithee mark
His countenance : unlike bold calumny,
Which sometimes dares not speak the thing it looks,
He dares not look the thing he speaks, but bends
His gaze on the blind earth.
(*To* MARZIO.) What ! wilt thou say
That I did murder my own father ?

Marzio.   Oh !
Spare me ! My brain swims round—
            I cannot speak—
It was that horrid torture forced the truth.

Take me away !   Let her not look on me !
I am a guilty miserable wretch !
I have said all I know ; now, let me die !

Beatrice. My lords, if by my nature I had been
So stern, as to have planned the crime alleged,
Which your suspicions dictate to this slave,
And the rack makes him utter, do you think
I should have left this two-edged instrument
Of my misdeed ; this man ; this bloody knife,
With my own name engraven on the heft,
Lying unsheathed amid a world of foes,
For my own death ?   That with such horrible need
For deepest silence, I should have neglected
So trivial a precaution, as the making
His tomb the keeper of a secret written
On a thief's memory ?   What is his poor life ?   [cide
What are a thousand lives ?   A parricide
Had trampled them like dust ; and see, he lives !
            [*Turning to* MARZIO.
And thou—

Marzio. Oh, spare me ! Speak to me no more !
That stern yet piteous look, those solemn tones,
Wound worse than torture.
(*To the Judges.*)   I have told it all ;
For pity's sake lead me away to death.

Camillo. Guards, lead him nearer the Lady Beatrice,
He shrinks from her regard like autumn's leaf
From the keen breath of the serenest north.

Beatrice. Oh, thou who tremblest on the giddy verge
Of life and death, pause ere thou answerest me ;
So mayst thou answer God with less dismay :
What evil have we done thee ?   I, alas !

Have lived but on this earth a few sad years,
And so my lot was ordered, that a father
First turned the moments of awakening life
To drops, each poisoning youth's sweet hope ; and then
Stabbed with one blow my everlasting soul,
And my untainted fame ; and even that peace
Which sleeps within the core of the heart's heart.
But the wound was not mortal ; so my hate
Became the only worship I could lift
To our great Father, who in pity and love,
Armed thee, as thou dost say, to cut him off ;
And thus his wrong becomes my accusation :
And art thou the accuser ? If thou hopest
Mercy in heaven, show justice upon earth :
Worse than a bloody hand is a hard heart.
If thou hast done murders, made thy life's path
Over the trampled laws of God and man,
Rush not before thy Judge, and say : " My Maker,
I have done this and more ; for there was one
Who was most pure and innocent on earth ;
And because she endured what never any,
Guilty or innocent, endured before ;
Because her wrongs could not be told, nor thought ;
Because thy hand at length did rescue her ;
I with my words killed her and all her kin."
Think, I adjure you, what it is to slay
The reverence living in the minds of men
Towards our ancient house, and stainless fame !
Think what it is to strangle infant pity,
Cradled in the belief of guileless looks,

Till it become a crime to suffer. Think
What 'tis to blot with infamy and blood
All that which shows like innocence, and is,—
Hear me, great God ! I swear, most innocent,—
So that the world lose all discrimination
Between the sly, fierce, wild regard of guilt,
And that which now compels thee to reply
To what I ask : Am I, or am I not
A parricide ?
  Marzio.   Thou art not !
  Judge.   What is this ?
  Marzio. I here declare those whom I did accuse
Are innocent. 'Tis I alone am guilty.
  Judge. Drag him away to torments ; let them be
Subtle and long drawn out, to tear the folds
Of the heart's inmost cell. Unbind him not
Till he confess.
  Marzio. Torture me as ye will :
A keener pain has wrung a higher truth
From my last breath. She is most innocent !
Bloodhounds, not men, glut yourselves well with me !
I will not give you that fine piece of nature
To rend and ruin.
                    [*Exit* Marzio, *guarded.*
  Camillo. What say ye now, my lords ?
  Judge. Let tortures strain the truth till it be white
As snow thrice-sifted by the frozen wind.
  Camillo. Yet stained with blood.
  Judge (*to* Beatrice). Know you this paper, lady ?
  Beatrice. Entrap me not with questions. Who stands here
As my accuser ! Ha ! wilt thou be he,
Who art my judge ? Accuser, witness, judge,
What, all in one ? Here is Orsino's name ;
Where is Orsino ? Let his eye meet mine.

What means this scrawl ?   Alas ! ye
 know not what,
And therefore on the chance that it
 may be
Some evil, will ye kill us ?

   Enter an Officer.

Officer.   Marzio's dead.
Judge. What did he say ?
Officer. Nothing.   As soon as we
Had bound him on the wheel, he
 smiled on us,
As one who baffles a deep adversary ;
And, holding his breath, died.
 Judge.   There remains nothing
But to apply the question to those
 prisoners,
Who yet remain stubborn.
 Camillo.   I overrule
Further proceedings, and in the be-
 half
Of these most innocent and noble
 persons
Will use my interest with the Holy
 Father.
 Judge. Let the Pope's pleasure
 then be done.   Meanwhile
Conduct these culprits each to separ-
 ate cells ;
And be the engines ready : for this
 night,
If the Pope's resolution be as grave,
Pious, and just as once, I'll wring the
 truth
Out of those nerves and sinews, groan
 by groan.   *[Exeunt.*

SCENE III.—*The Cell of a Prison.*
BEATRICE *is discovered asleep on a*
couch.

   Enter BERNARDO.

Bernardo. How gently slumber
 rests upon her face,
Like the last thoughts of some day
 sweetly spent,
Closing in night and dreams, and so
 prolonged.
After such torments as she bore last
 night,
How light and soft her breathing
 comes.   Ah, me !
Methinks that I shall never sleep
 again.
But I must shake the heavenly dew of
 rest

From this sweet folded flower, thus—
 wake ; awake ;
What, sister, canst thou sleep ?
 Beatrice (awaking).   I was just
 dreaming
That we were all in Paradise.   Thou
 knowest
This cell seems like a kind of Paradise
After our father's presence.
 Bernardo.   Dear, dear sister,
Would that thy dream were not a
 dream !   O, God !
How shall I tell ?
 Beatrice.   What wouldst thou tell,
 sweet brother ?
 Bernardo. Look not so calm and
 happy, or, even whilst
I stand considering what I have to
 say,
My heart will break.
 Beatrice.   See now, thou mak'st
 me weep :
How very friendless thou wouldst be,
 dear child,
If I were dead.   Say what thou hast
 to say.
 Bernardo. They have confessed ;
 they could endure no more
The tortures—
 Beatrice.   Ha !   What was there
 to confess ?
They must have told some weak and
 wicked lie
To flatter their tormentors.   Have
 they said
That they were guilty ?   O white in-
 nocence,
That thou shouldst wear the mask of
 guilt to hide
Thine awful and serenest countenance
From those who know thee not !

Enter JUDGE, *with* LUCRETIA *and*
  GIACOMO, *guarded.*

      Ignoble hearts !
For some brief spasms of pain, which
 are at least
As mortal as the limbs through which
 they pass,
Are centuries of high splendour laid in
 dust ?
And that eternal honour which should
 live
Sunlike, above the reek of mortal
 fame,

Changed to a mockery and a byword? What !
Will you give up these bodies to be dragged
At horses' heels, so that our hair should sweep
The footsteps of the vain and senseless crowd,
Who, that they may make our calamity
Their worship and their spectacle, will leave
The churches and the theatres as void
As their own hearts ? Shall the light multitude
Fling, at their choice, curses or faded pity,
Sad funeral flowers to deck a living corpse,
Upon us as we pass, to pass away,
And leave—what memory of our having been ? thou,
Infamy, blood, terror, despair ? O
Who wert a mother to the parentless,
Kill not thy child ! Let not her wrongs kill thee !
Brother, lie down with me upon the rack,
And let us each be silent as a corpse ;
It soon will be as soft as any grave.
'Tis but the falsehood it can wring from fear
Makes the rack cruel.
  Giacomo. They will tear the truth
Even from thee at last, those cruel pains :
For pity's sake say thou art guilty now.
  Lucretia. O, speak the truth ! Let us all quickly die :
And after death, God is our judge, not they ;
He will have mercy on us.
  Bernardo. If indeed
It can be true, say so, dear sister mine ;
And then the Pope will surely pardon you,
And all be well.
  Judge. Confess, or I will warp
Your limbs with such keen tortures—
  Beatrice. Tortures ! Turn
The rack henceforth into a spinning-wheel !
Torture your dog, that he may tell when last
He lapped the blood his master shed —not me !
My pangs are of the mind, and of the heart
And of the soul ; ay, of the inmost soul,
Which weeps within tears as of burning gall
To see, in this ill world where none are true,
My kindred false to their deserted selves,
And with considering all the wretched life
Which I have lived, and its now wretched end ;
And the small justice shown by Heaven and Earth
To me or mine ; and what a tyrant thou art,
And what slaves these ; and what a world we make,
The oppressor and the oppressed—such pangs compel
My answer. What is it thou wouldst with me ?
  Judge. Art thou not guilty of thy father's death ?
  Beatrice. Or wilt thou rather tax high-judging God
That he permitted such an act as that
Which I have suffered, and which he beheld ;
Made it unutterable, and took from it
All refuge, all revenge, all consequence,
But that which thou hast called my father's death ?
Which is or is not what men call a crime,
Which either I have done, or have not done ;
Say what ye will. I shall deny no more.
If ye desire it thus, thus let it be,
And so an end of all. Now do your will ;
No other pains shall force another word.
  Judge. She is convicted, but has not confessed.
Be it enough. Until their final sentence
Let none have converse with them. You, young lord,

Linger not here !

Beatrice. O, tear him not away !

Judge. Guards ! do your duty.

Bernardo (*embracing* BEATRICE). Oh ! would ye divide

Body from soul ?

Officer. That is the headsman's business.

[*Exeunt all but* LUCRETIA, BEATRICE, *and* GIACOMO.

Giacomo. Have I confessed ? Is it all over now ?

No hope ? no refuge ? O weak, wicked tongue,

Which hast destroyed me, would that thou hadst been

Cut out and thrown to dogs first ! To have killed

My father first, and then betrayed my sister ;

Ay, thee ! the one thing innocent and pure

In this black, guilty world, to that which I

So well deserve ! My wife ! my little ones !

Destitute, helpless ; and I—Father ! God !

Canst thou forgive even the unforgiving,

When their full hearts break thus, thus ?—

[*Covers his face and weeps.*

Lucretia. O, my child !

To what a dreadful end are we all come !

Why did I yield ? Why did I not sustain

Those torments ? Oh ! that I were all dissolved

Into these fast and unavailing tears,

Which flow and feel not !

Beatrice. What 'twas weak to do,

'Tis weaker to lament, once being done ;

Take cheer ! The God who knew my wrong, and made

Our speedy act the angel of his wrath,

Seems, and but seems, to have abandoned us.

Let us not think that we shall die for this.

Brother, sit near me ; give me your firm hand,

You had a manly heart. Bear up ! bear up !

Oh ! dearest lady, put your gentle head

Upon my lap, and try to sleep awhile :

Your eyes look pale, hollow, and overworn,

With heaviness of watching and slow grief.

Come, I will sing you some low, sleepy tune,

Not cheerful, nor yet sad ; some dull old thing,

Some outworn and unused monotony,

Such as our country gossips sing and spin,

Till they almost forget they live : lie down !

So ; that will do. Have I forgot the words ?

Faith ! they are sadder than I thought they were.

SONG.

False friend, wilt thou smile or weep
When my life is laid asleep ?
Little cares for a smile or a tear,
The clay-cold corpse upon the bier ;
  Farewell ! Heigh ho !
  What is this whispers low ?
There is a snake in thy smile, my dear ;
And bitter poison within thy tear.

Sweet sleep ! were death like to thee,
Or if thou couldst mortal be,
I would close these eyes of pain ;
When to wake ? Never again.
  O World ! farewell !
  Listen to the passing bell !
It says, thou and I must part,
With a light and a heavy heart.

[*The scene closes.*

SCENE IV.—*A Hall of the Prison.*

Enter CAMILLO *and* BERNARDO.

Camillo. The Pope is stern ; not to be moved or bent.

He looked as calm and keen as is the engine

Which tortures and which kills, exempt itself

From aught that it inflicts ; a marble form,

A rite, a law, a custom ; not a man.

He frowned, as if to frown had been the trick

Of his machinery, on the advocates

Presenting the defences, which he tore

And threw behind, muttering with
hoarse, harsh voice :
" Which among ye defended their old
father
Killed in his sleep ? "   Then to an-
other : " Thou
Dost this in virtue of thy place ; 'tis
well."
He turned to me then, looking depre-
cation,
And said these three words, coldly :
" They must die."
   Bernardo.   And yet you left him
not ?
   Camillo.   I urged him still ;
Pleading, as I could guess, the devil-
ish wrong
Which prompted your unnatural
parent's death.
And he replied, " Paolo Santa Croce
Murdered his mother yester evening,
And he is fled. Parricide grows so
rife,
That soon, for some just cause no
doubt the young
Will strangle us all, dozing in our
chairs.
Authority, and power, and hoary hair
Are grown crimes capital. You are
my nephew,
You come to ask their pardon ; stay
a moment ;
Here is their sentence ; never see me
more
Till, to the letter, it be all fulfilled."
   Bernardo. O, God, not so ! I did
believe indeed
That all you said was but sad prepara-
tion
For happy news.   O, there are words
and looks
To bend the sternest purpose ! Once
I knew them,
Now I forget them at my dearest
need.
What think you if I seek him out, and
bathe
His feet and robe with hot and bitter
tears ?
Importune him with prayers, vexing
his brain
With my perpetual cries, until in rage
He strike me with his pastoral cross,
and trample
Upon my prostrate head, so that my
blood

May stain the senseless dust on which
he treads,
And remorse waken mercy ? I will
do it !
O, wait till I return ! [*Rushes out.*
   Camillo.   Alas ! poor boy !
A wreck-devoted seaman thus might
pray
To the deaf sea.

Enter LUCRETIA, BEATRICE, *and*
    GIACOMO, *guarded.*

   Beatrice.   I hardly dare to fear
That thou bring'st other news than a
just pardon.
   Camillo. May God in heaven be
less inexorable
To the Pope's prayers, than he has
been to mine.
Here is the sentence and the warrant.
   Beatrice (*wildly*).   Oh,
My God ! Can it be possible I have
To die so suddenly ? So young to go
Under the obscure, cold, rotting,
wormy ground !
To be nailed down into a narrow
place ;
To see no more sweet sunshine ; hear
no more
Blithe voice of living thing ; muse
not again
Upon familiar thoughts, sad, yet thus
lost !
How fearful ! to be nothing ! Or to
be—
What ?   O, where am I ? Let me
not go mad !
Sweet   Heaven,   forgive   weak
thoughts ! If there should be
No God, no Heaven, no Earth in the
void world ;
The wide, grey, lampless, deep, unpeopled world !
If all things then should be—my
father's spirit,
His eye, his voice, his touch surrounding me ;
The atmosphere and breath of my
dead life !
If sometimes, as a shape more like
himself,
Even the form which tortured me on
earth,
Masked in grey hairs and wrinkles, he
should come,

And wind me in his hellish arms, and fix
His eyes on mine, and drag me down, down, down !
For was he not alone omnipotent
On Earth, and ever present ? even though dead,
Does not his spirit live in all that breathe,
And work for me and mine still the same ruin,
Scorn, pain, despair ?   Who ever yet returned
To teach the laws of death's untrodden realm ?
Unjust perhaps as those which drive us now,
O, whither, whither ?
   Lucretia.   Trust in God's sweet love,
The tender promises of Christ : ere night
Think we shall be in Paradise.
   Beatrice.   'Tis past !
Whatever comes, my heart shall sink no more.
And yet, I know not why, your words strike chill :
How tedious, false and cold seem all things !   I
Have met with much injustice in this world ;
No difference has been made by God or man,
Or any power moulding my wretched lot,
'Twixt good or evil, as regarded me.
I am cut off from the only world I know,
From light and life, and love, in youth's sweet prime.
You do well telling me to trust in God ;
I hope I do trust in him.   In whom else
Can any trust ?   And yet my heart is cold.
   [*During the latter speeches* GIACOMO *has retired conversing with* CAMILLO, *who now goes out :* GIACOMO *advances.*
   Giacomo. Know you not, mother— sister, know you not ?
Bernardo even now is gone to implore
The Pope to grant our pardon.
   Lucretia.   Child, perhaps

It will be granted.   We may all then live
To make these woes a tale for distant years :
O, what a thought !   It gushes to my heart
Like the warm blood.
   Beatrice.   Yet both will soon be cold :
O, trample out that thought !   Worse than despair,
Worse than the bitterness of death, is hope :
It is the only ill which can find place
Upon the giddy, sharp, and narrow hour
Tottering beneath us.   Plead with the swift frost
That it should spare the eldest flower of spring :
Plead with awakening earthquake, o'er whose couch
Even now a city stands, strong, fair and free ;
Now stench and blackness yawns, like death.   O, plead
With famine, or wind-walking pestilence,
Blind lightning, or the deaf sea, not with man !
Cruel, cold, formal man ; righteous in words,
In deeds a Cain.   No, mother, we must die :
Since such is the reward of innocent lives,
Such the alleviation of worst wrongs.
And whilst our murderers live, and hard, cold men,
Smiling and slow, walk through a world of tears
To death as to life's sleep ; 'twere just the grave
Were some strange joy for us.   Come, obscure Death,
And wind me in thine all-embracing arms !
Like a fond mother hide me in thy bosom,
And rock me to the sleep from which none wake.
Live ye, who live, subject to one another
As we were once, who now—
               [BERNARDO *rushes in.*
   Bernardo.   O, horrible !

That tears, that looks, that hope
    poured forth in prayer,
Even till the heart is vacant and
    despairs,
Should all be vain! The ministers
    of death
Are waiting round the doors. I
    thought I saw
Blood on the face of one—what if
    'twere fancy?
Soon the heart's blood of all I love on
    earth
Will sprinkle him, and he will wipe it
    off
As if 'twere only rain. O life! O
    world!
Cover me! let me be no more! To
    see
That perfect mirror of pure innocence
Wherein I gazed, and grew happy
    and good,
Shivered to dust! To see thee,
    Beatrice,
Who made all lovely thou didst look
    upon—
Thee, light of life—dead, dark! while
    I say, sister,
To hear I have no sister; and thou,
    mother,
Whose love was a bond to all our
    loves—
Dead! The sweet bond broken.

      Enter CAMILLO *and Guards.*

            They come! Let me
Kiss those warm lips before their
    crimson leaves
Are blighted — white — cold. Say
    farewell, before
Death chokes that gentle voice! O
    let me hear
You speak!
   Beatrice.   Farewell, my tender
    brother. Think
Of our sad fate with gentleness, as
    now:

And let mild, pitying thoughts
    lighten for thee
Thy sorrow's load. Err not in harsh
    despair,
But tears and patience. One thing
    more, my child:
For thine own sake be constant to the
    love
Thou bearest us; and to the faith
    that I,
Though wrapt in a strange cloud of
    crime and shame,
Lived ever holy and unstained. And
    though
Ill tongues shall wound me, and our
    common name
Be as a mark stamped on thine inno-
    cent brow
For men to point at as they pass, do
    thou
Forbear, and never think a thought
    unkind
Of those who perhaps love thee in
    their graves.
So mayst thou die as I do; fear and
    pain
Being subdued. Farewell! Farewell!
    Farewell!
   Bernardo. I cannot say farewell!
   Camillo.   O, Lady Beatrice!
   Beatrice. Give yourself no un-
    necessary pain.
My dear Lord Cardinal. Here,
    mother, tie
My girdle for me, and bind up this
    hair
In any simple knot: ay, that does
    well.
And yours I see is coming down. How
    often
Have we done this for one another!
    now
We shall not do it any more. My
    lord,
We are quite ready. Well, 'tis very
    well.

HELLAS

A LYRICAL DRAMA

ΜΑΝΤΙΣ' ΕΙΜ' 'ΕΣΘΛΩΝ 'ΑΓΩΝΩΝ.

ŒDIP. COLON.

TO HIS EXCELLENCY

PRINCE ALEXANDER MAVROCORDATO,

LATE SECRETARY FOR FOREIGN AFFAIRS TO THE HOSPODAR OF WALLACHIA.

THE DRAMA OF HELLAS IS INSCRIBED,

AS AN IMPERFECT TOKEN OF THE ADMIRATION, SYMPATHY, AND FRIENDSHIP OF

THE AUTHOR.

PISA, *November* 1, 1821.

PREFACE

THE poem of "Hellas," written at the suggestion of the events of the moment, is a mere improvise, and derives its interest (should it be found to possess any) solely from the intense sympathy which the Author feels with the cause he would celebrate.

The subject, in its present state, is insusceptible of being treated otherwise than lyrically, and if I have called this poem a drama, from the circumstance of its being composed in dialogue, the licence is not greater than that which has been assumed by other poets, who have called their productions epics, only because they have been divided into twelve or twenty-four books.

The "Persæ" of Æschylus afforded me the first model of my conception, although the decision of the glorious contest now waging in Greece being yet suspended, forbids a catastrophe parallel to the return of Xerxes and the desolation of the Persians. I have, therefore, contented myself with exhibiting a series of lyric pictures, and with having wrought upon the curtain of futurity, which falls upon the unfinished scene, such figures of indistinct and visionary delineation as suggest the final triumph of the Greek cause as a portion of the cause of civilisation and social improvement.

The drama (if drama it must be called) is, however, so inartificial that I doubt whether, if recited on the Thespian waggon to an Athenian village at the Dionysiaca, it would have obtained the prize of the goat. I shall bear with equanimity any punishment greater than the loss of such a reward which the Aristarchi of the hour may think fit to inflict.

The only *goat-song* which I have yet attempted has, I confess, in spite of the unfavourable nature of the subject, received a greater and a more valuable portion of applause than I expected, or than it deserved.

Common fame is the only authority which I can allege for the details which form the basis of the poem, and I must trespass upon the forgiveness of my readers for the display of newspaper erudition to which I have been reduced. Undoubtedly, until the conclusion of the war, it will be impossible to obtain an account of it sufficiently authentic for historical materials; but poets have their privilege, and it is unquestionable that actions of the most exalted courage have been performed by the Greeks—that they have gained more than one naval victory, and that their defeat in Wallachia was signalised by circumstances of heroism more glorious even than victory.

The apathy of the rulers of the civilised world, to the astonishing circumstances of the descendants of that nation to which they owe their civilisation—rising as it were from the ashes of their ruin, is something perfectly inexplicable to a mere spectator of the shows of this mortal scene. We are all Greeks. Our laws, our literature, our religion, our arts, have their root in Greece. But for Greece —Rome the instructor, the conqueror, or the metropolis of our ancestors, would have spread no illumination with her arms, and we might still have been savages and idolators ; or, what is worse, might have arrived at such a stagnant and miserable state of social institutions as China and Japan possess.

The human form and the human mind attained to a perfection in Greece which has impressed its image on those faultless productions, whose very fragments are the despair of modern art, and has propagated impulses which cannot cease, through a thousand channels of manifest or imperceptible operation, to ennoble and delight mankind until the extinction of the race.

The modern Greek is the descendant of those glorious beings whom the imagination almost refuses to figure to itself as belonging to our kind ; and he inherits much of their sensibility, their rapidity of conception, their enthusiasm, and their courage. If in many instances he is degraded by moral and political slavery to the practice of the basest vices it engenders, and that below the level of ordinary degradation ; let us reflect that the corruption of the best produces the worst, and that habits which subsist only in relation to a peculiar state of social institution may be expected to cease, as soon as that relation is dissolved. In fact, the Greeks, since the admirable novel of " Anastatius " could have been a faithful picture of their manners, have undergone most important changes ; the flower of their youth, returning to their country from the universities of Italy, Germany, and France, have communicated to their fellow-citizens the latest results of that social perfection of which their ancestors were the original source. The university of Chios contained before the breaking out of the revolution, eight hundred students, and among them several Germans and Americans. The munificence and energy of many of the Greek princes and merchants, directed to the renovation of their country, with a spirit and a wisdom which has few examples, is above all praise.

The English permit their own oppressors to act according to their natural sympathy with the Turkish tyrant, and to brand upon their name the indelible blot of an alliance with the enemies of domestic happiness, of Christianity, and civilisation.

Russia desires to possess, not to liberate Greece ; and is contented to see the Turks, its natural enemies, and the Greeks, its intended slaves, enfeeble each other, until one or both fall into its net. The wise and generous policy of England would have consisted in establishing the independence of Greece, and in maintaining it both against Russia and the Turks ;—but when was the oppressor generous or just ?

The Spanish Peninsula is already free. France is tranquil in the enjoyment of a partial exemption from the abuses which its unnatural and feeble government are vainly attempting to revive. The seed of blood and misery has been sown in Italy, and a more vigorous race is arising to go forth to the harvest. The world waits only the news of a revolution of Germany, to see the tyrants who have pinnacled themselves on its supineness, precipitated into the ruin from which they shall never rise. Well do these destroyers of mankind know their enemy, when they impute the insurrection in Greece to the same spirit before which they tremble throughout the rest of Europe ; and that enemy well knows the power and cunning of its opponents, and watches the moment of their approaching weakness and inevitable division, to wrest the bloody sceptres from their grasp.

DRAMATIS PERSONÆ

MAHMUD	DAOOD
HASSAN	AHASUERUS, *a Jew*
CHORUS *of Greek Captive Women.*	*Messengers, Slaves, and Attendants*

SCENE—*Constantinople*   TIME—*Sunset*

SCENE, *a Terrace, on the Seraglio.*

MAHMUD (*sleeping*), *an Indian slave sitting beside his Couch.*

CHORUS OF GREEK CAPTIVE WOMEN.

WE strew these opiate flowers
  On thy restless pillow,—
They were stript from Orient bowers,
  By the Indian billow.
    Be thy sleep
    Calm and deep,
Like theirs who fell—not ours who
  weep!

INDIAN.

Away, unlovely dreams!
  Away, false shapes of sleep!
Be his, as Heaven seems,
  Clear, and bright, and deep!
Soft as love, and calm as death,
Sweet as a summer night without a
  breath.

CHORUS.

Sleep, sleep! our song is laden
  With the soul of slumber;
It was sung by a Samian maiden,
  Whose lover was of the number
    Who now keep
    That calm sleep
Whence none may wake, where none
  shall weep.

INDIAN.

I touch thy temples pale!
  I breathe my soul on thee!
And could my prayers avail,
  All my joy should be
Dead, and I would live to weep,
So thou mightst win one hour of quiet
  sleep.

CHORUS.

  Breath low, low,
The spell of the mighty mistress
  now!
When Conscience lulls her sated
  snake,
And Tyrants sleep, let Freedom
  wake.
    Breathe low, low,

The words, which, like secret fire,
  shall flow
Through the veins of the frozen earth
    —low, low!

SEMICHORUS I.

Life may change, but it may fly
  not;
Hope may vanish, but can die not
Truth be veiled, but still it burneth
Love repulsed,—but it returneth

SEMICHORUS II.

Yet were life a charnel, where
Hope lay coffined with Despair;
Yet were truth a sacred lie,
Love were lust—

SEMICHORUS I.

        If Liberty
Lent not life its soul of Light,
Hope its iris of delight,
Truth its prophet's robe to wear,
Love its power to give and bear.

CHORUS.

In the great morning of the world,
The spirit of God with might un-
  furled
The flag of Freedom over Chaos,
  And all its banded anarchs fled,
Like vultures frighted from Imaus,
  Before an earthquake's tread.—
So from Time's tempestuous dawn
Freedom's splendour burst and
  shone:—
Thermopylæ and Marathon
Caught, like mountains beacon-
  lighted,
  The springing Fire.—The winged
  glory
On Philippi half-alighted,
  Like an eagle on a promontory.
Its unwearied wings could fan
The quenchless ashes of Milan.
From age to age, from man to man
  It lived; and lit from land to land
  Florence, Albion, Switzerland.
Then night fell; and, as from night,
Re-assuming fiery flight,

From the West swift Freedom came,
   Against the course of heaven and
     doom,
A second sun arrayed in flame,
   To burn, to kindle, to illume.
From far Atlantis its young beams
Chased the shadows and the dreams.
France, with all her sanguine steams,
   Hid, but quenched it not ; again
     Through clouds its shafts of glory
     rain
From utmost Germany to Spain.
As an eagle fed with morning
Scorns the embattled tempest's warn-
    ing,
When she seeks her aerie hanging
   In the mountain-cedar's hair,
And her brood expect the clanging
   Of her wings through the wild air,
Sick with famine ;—Freedom, so
To what of Greece remaineth now
Returns ; her hoary ruins glow
Like orient mountains lost in day ;
   Beneath the safety of her wings
Her renovated nurslings play,
   And in the naked lightnings
Of truth they purge their dazzled
    eyes.
Let Freedom leave, where'er she flies,
A Desert, or a Paradise ;
   Let the beautiful and the brave
   Share her glory, or a grave.

SEMICHORUS I.
With the gifts of gladness
   Greece did thy cradle strew ;

SEMICHORUS II.
With the tears of sadness
   Greece did thy shroud bedew ;

SEMICHORUS I
With an orphan's affection
   She followed thy bier through
    time !

SEMICHORUS II.
And at thy resurrection
   Re-appeareth, like thou, sub-
    lime !

SEMICHORUS I.
If Heaven should resume thee,
   To Heaven shall her spirit
    ascend ;

SEMICHORUS II.
If Hell should entomb thee,

To Hell shall her high hearts
   bend.

SEMICHORUS I.
If Annihilation—

SEMICHORUS II.
Dust let her glories be ;
And a name and a nation
   Be forgotten, Freedom with thee !

INDIAN.
His brow grows darker—breathe not
   —move not !
He starts—he shudders ;—ye that
   love not,
With your panting loud and fast
Have awakened him at last.
   Mahmud (*starting from his sleep*).
   Man the Seraglio-guard ! make
    fast the gate.
What ! from a cannonade of three
   short hours ?
'Tis false ! that breach towards the
   Bosphorus
Cannot be practicable yet—Who
   stirs ?
Stand to the match ; that when the
   foe prevails,
One spark may mix in reconciling
   ruin
The conqueror and the conquered !
   Heave the tower
Into the gap—wrench off the roof.
          [*Enter* HASSAN.
               Ha ! what !
The truth of day lightens upon my
   dream,
And I am Mahmud still.
   Hassan.   Your Sublime Highness
Is strangely moved.
   Mahmud.   The times do cast
   strange shadows
On those who watch and who must
   rule their course,
Lest they, being first in peril as in
   glory,
Be whelmed in the fierce ebb :—and
   these are of them.
Thrice has a gloomy vision hunted me
As thus from sleep into the troubled
   day ;
It shakes me as the tempest shakes
   the sea,
Leaving no figure upon memory's
   glass.
Would that—no matter. Thou didst
   say thou knewest

A Jew, whose spirit is a chronicle
Of strange and secret and forgotten
   things.
I bade thee summon him :—'tis said
   his tribe
Dream, and are wise interpreters of
   dreams.
   Hassan. The Jew of whom I spake
      is old,—so old
He seems to have outlived a world's
   decay ;
The hoary mountains and the wrink-
   led ocean
Seem younger still than he ; his hair
   and beard
Are whiter than the tempest-sifted
   snow ;
His cold pale limbs and pulseless
   arteries
Are like the fibres of a cloud.instinct
With light, and to the soul that
   quickens them
Are as the atoms of the mountain-
   drift
To the winter wind ;—but from his
   eye looks forth
A life of unconsumed thought, which
   pierces   [come.
The present, and the past, and the to-
Some say that this is he whom the
   great prophet
Jesus, the son of Joseph, for his
   mockery,
Mocked with the curse of immortality.
Some feign that he is Enoch ; others
   dream
He was pre-Adamite, and has survived
Cycles of generation and of ruin.
The sage, in truth, by dreadful
   abstinence,
And conquering penance of the
   mutinous flesh,
Deep contemplation, and unwearied
   study,
In years outstretched beyond the date
   of man,
May have attained to sovereignty
   and science
Over those strong and secret things
   and thoughts
Which others fear and know not.
   Mahmud.   I would talk
With this old Jew.
   Hassan.   Thy will is even now
Made known to him, where he dwells
   in a sea-cavern

'Mid the Demonesi, less accessible
Than thou or God ! He who would
   question him
Must sail alone at sunset, where the
   stream
Of ocean sleeps around those foamless
   isles
When the young moon is westering as
   now,
And evening airs wander upon the
   wave ;
And when the pines of that bee-
   pasturing isle,
Green Erebinthus, quench the fiery
   shadow
Of his gilt prow within the sapphire
   water,
Then must the lonely helmsman cry
   aloud,
"Ahasuerus!" and the caverns round
Will answer, Ahasuerus ! If his prayer
Be granted, a faint meteor will arise,
Lighting him over Marmora, and a
   wind
Will rush out of the sighing pine
   forest,
And with the wind a storm of har-
   mony
Unutterably sweet, and pilot him
Through the soft twilight to the
   Bosphorus :
Thence, at the hour and place and
   circumstance
Fit for the matter of their conference,
The Jew appears. Few dare, and few
   who dare,
Win the desired communion—but
   that shout
Bodes—   [*A shout within.*
   Mahmud. Evil, doubtless ; like all
      human sounds.
Let me converse with spirits.
   Hassan.   That shout again.
   Mahmud. This Jew whom thou
      hast summoned—
   Hassan.   Will be here—
   Mahmud. When the omnipotent
      hour, to which are yoked
He, I, and all things, shall compel—
   enough.
Silence those mutineers—that
   drunken crew
That crowd about the pilot in the
   storm.
Ay ! strike the foremost shorter by a
   head !

They weary me, and I have need of rest.
Kings are like stars—they rise and set, they have
The worship of the world, but no repose.   [*Exeunt severally.*

CHORUS.

Worlds on worlds are rolling ever
From creation to decay,
Like the bubbles on a river,
  Sparkling, bursting, borne away.
    But they are still immortal
Who, through birth's orient portal,
And death's dark chasm hurrying to and fro,
  Clothe their unceasing flight
  In the brief dust and light
Gathered around their chariots as they go;
    New shapes they still may weave,
    New gods, new laws receive,
Bright or dim are they, as the robes they last
  On Death's bare ribs had cast.

A power from the unknown God;
A Promethean conqueror came;
Like a triumphal path he trod
  The thorns of death and shame.
    A mortal shape to him
    Was like the vapour dim
Which the orient planet animates with light;
  Hell, Sin, and Slavery came,
  Like bloodhounds mild and tame,
Nor preyed until their lord had taken flight.
    The moon of Mahomet
    Arose, and it shall set:
While blazoned as on heaven's immortal noon
  The Cross leads generations on

Swift as the radiant shapes of sleep
  From one whose dreams are Paradise,
Fly, when the fond wretch wakes to weep,
  And day peers forth with her blank eyes:
    So fleet, so faint, so fair,

    The Powers of earth and air
Fled from the folding star of Bethlehem:
    Apollo, Pan, and Love,
    And even Olympian Jove
Grew weak, for killing Truth had glared on them.
    Our hills, and seas, and streams,
    Dispeopled of their dreams,
Their waters turned to blood, their dew to tears,
  Wailed for the golden years.

Enter MAHMUD, HASSAN, DAOOD, *and others.*

  Mahmud. More gold? our ancestors bought gold with victory,
And shall I sell it for defeat?
  Daood.   The Janizars
Clamour for pay.
  Mahmud.   Go! bid them pay themselves
With Christian blood! Are there no Grecian virgins
Whose shrieks and spasms and tears they may enjoy?
No infidel children to impale on spears?
No hoary priests after that Patriarch
Who bent the curse against his country's heart,
Which clove his own at last? Go! bid them kill:
Blood is the seed of gold.
  Daood.   It has been sown,
And yet the harvest to the sickle-men
Is as a grain to each.
  Mahmud.   Then take this signet,
Unlock the seventh chamber, in which lie
The treasures of victorious Solyman.
An empire's spoils stored for a day of ruin.
O spirit of my sires! is it not come?
The prey-birds and the wolves are gorged and sleep;
But these, who spread their feast on the red earth,
Hunger for gold, which fills not.—See them fed;
Then lead them to the rivers of fresh death.   [*Exit* DAOOD.
Oh! miserable dawn, after a night
More glorious than the day which it usurped!

O faith in God ! O power on earth !
O word
Of the great Prophet, whose over-
shadowing wings
Darkened the thrones and idols of the
west,
Now bright !—For thy sake cursed be
the hour,
Even as a father by an evil child,
When the orient moon of Islam rolled
in triumph
From Caucasus to white Ceraunia !
Ruin above, and anarchy below ;
Terror without, and treachery within ;
The chalice of destruction full, and all
Thirsting to drink ; and who among
us dares
To dash it from his lips ? and where is
Hope ?
  Hassan. The lamp of our dominion
still rides high ;
One God is God—Mahomet is his
Prophet.
Four hundred thousand Moslems,
from the limits
Of utmost Asia, irresistibly
Throng, like full clouds at the
sirocco's cry,
But not like them to weep their
strength in tears ;
They have destroying lightning, and
their step
Wakes earthquake, to consume and
overwhelm,   [pus,
And reign in ruin. Phrygian Olym-
Tmolus, and Latmos, and Mycale,
roughen
With horrent arms, and lofty ships,
even now,
Like vapours anchored to a moun-
tain's edge,
Freighted with fire and whirlwind,
wait at Scala
The convoy of the ever-veering wind.
Samos is drunk with blood ;—the
Greek has paid
Brief victory with swift loss and long
despair.
The false Moldavian serfs fled fast and
far
When the fierce shout of "Allah-illa-
Allah ! "
Rose like the war-cry of the northern
wind,
Which kills the sluggish clouds, and
leaves a flock

Of wild swans struggling with the
naked storm.
So were the lost Greeks on the
Danube's day !
If night is mute, yet the returning
sun
Kindles the voices of the morning
birds ;
Nor at thy bidding less exultingly
Than birds rejoicing in the golden
day,
The Anarchies of Africa unleash
Their tempest-winged cities of the
sea,
To speak in thunder to the rebel
world.
Like sulphureous clouds half-shat-
tered by the storm,
They sweep the pale Ægean, while the
Queen
Of Ocean, bound upon her island
throne,
Far in the West, sits mourning that
her sons,
Who frown on Freedom, spare a smile
for thee.
Russia still hovers, as an eagle might
Within a cloud, near which a kite and
crane
Hang tangled in inextricable fight,
To stoop upon the victor ; for she
fears
The name of Freedom, even as she
hates thine :
But recreant Austria loves thee as the
Grave
Loves Pestilence, and her slow dogs
of war,
Fleshed with the chase, come up from
Italy,
And howl upon their limits : for they
see
The panther Freedom fled to her old
cover,
Amid seas and mountains, and a
mightier brood
Crouch around. What Anarch wears
a crown or mitre,
Or bears the sword, or grasps the key
of gold,
Whose friends are not thy friends,
whose foes thy foes ?
Our arsenals and our armouries are
full ;
Our forts defy assaults ; ten thous-
and cannon

Lie ranged upon the beach, and hour
  by hour
Their earth-convulsing wheels affright
  the city
The galloping of fiery steeds makes
  pale
The Christian merchant, and the
  yellow Jew
Hides his hoard deeper in the faithless
  earth.
Like clouds, and like the shadows of
  the clouds,
Over the hills of Anatolia,
Swift in wide troops the Tartar
  chivalry
Sweep ;—the far-flashing of their
  starry lances
Reverberates the dying light of day.
We have one God, one King, one
  Hope, one Law ;
But many-headed Insurrection stands
Divided in itself, and soon must fall.
  Mahmud. Proud words, when deeds
  come short, are seasonable :
Look, Hassan, on yon crescent moon,
  emblazoned
Upon that shattered flag of fiery cloud
Which leads the rear of the depart-
  ing day,
Wan emblem of an empire fading
  now !
See how it trembles in the blood-red
  air,   [spent,
And like a mighty lamp whose oil is
Shrinks on the horizon's edge, while,
  from above,
One star with insolent and victorious
  light
Hovers above its fall, and with keen
  beams,
Like arrows through a fainting ante-
  lope,
Strikes its weak form to death.
  Hassan.   Even as that moon
Renews itself——
  Mahmud. Shall we be not renewed !
Far other bark than ours were needed
  now
To stem the torrent of descending
  time :
The spirit that lifts the slave before
  its lord
Stalks through the capitals of armed
  kings,
And spreads his ensign in the wilder-
  ness ;

Exults in chains ; and when the rebel
  falls,
Cries like the blood of Abel from the
  dust ;
And the inheritors of earth, like
  beasts
When earthquake is unleashed, with
  idiot fear
Cower in their kingly dens—as I do
  now.
What were defeat, when Victory
  must appal ?
Or Danger, when Security looks pale?
How said the messenger—who from
  the fort
Islanded in the Danube, saw the
  battle
Of Bucharest ?—that—
  Hassan.   Ibrahim's scimitar
Drew with its gleam swift victory
  from heaven,
To burn before him in the night of
  battle—
A light and a destruction.
  Mahmud.   Ay ! the day
Was ours ; but how ?—
  Hassan.   The light Wallachians,
The Arnaut, Servian, and Albanian
  allies,
Fled from the glance of our artillery
Almost before the thunder-stone alit;
One half the Grecian army made a
  bridge
Of safe and slow retreat, with Moslem
  dead ;
The other—
  Mahmud. Speak—tremble not—
  Hassan.   Islanded
By victor myriads, formed in hollow
  square
With rough and steadfast front, and
  thrice flung back
The deluge of our foaming cavalry ;
Thrice their keen wedge of battle
  pierced our lines.
Our baffled army trembled like one
  man
Before a host, and gave them space
  but soon,
From the surrounding hills, the
  batteries blazed,
Kneading them down with fire and
  iron rain.
Yet none approached ; till, like a field
  of corn

Under the hook of the swart sickle-
man,
The bands, entrenched in mounds of
Turkish dead,
Grew weak and few.   Then said the
Pacha, " Slaves,
Render yourselves—they have aban-
doned you—
What hope of refuge, or retreat, or
aid ?
We grant your lives."—" Grant that
which is thine own,"
Cried one, and fell upon his sword and
died !
Another—" God, and man, and hope
abandon me ;
But I to them and to myself remain
Constant ; " he bowed his head, and
his heart burst.
A third exclaimed, " There is a refuge,
tyrant,
Where thou darest not pursue, and
canst not harm,
Shouldst thou pursue ; there we shall
meet again."
Then held his breath, and, after a
brief spasm,
The indignant spirit cast its mortal
garment
Among the slain—dead earth upon
the earth !   [ways,
So these survivors, each by different
Some strange, all sudden, none dis-
honourable.
Met in triumphant death ; and when
our army
Closed in, while yet wonder, and awe,
and shame
Held back the base hyænas of the
battle
That feed upon the dead and fly the
living,
One rose out of the chaos of the slain ;
And if it were a corpse which some
dread spirit
Of the old saviours of the land we rule
Had lifted in its anger, wandering by ;
Or if there burned within the dying
man
Unquenchable disdain of death, and
faith
Creating what it feigned ;—I cannot
tell :
But he cried, " Phantoms of the free,
we come !

Armies of the Eternal, ye who strike
To dust the citadels of sanguine kings,
And shake the souls throned on their
stony hearts,
And thaw their frost-work diadems
like dew ;—
O ye who float around this clime, and
weave
The garment of the glory which it
wears ;
Whose fame, though earth betray the
dust it clasped,
Lies sepulchred in monumental
thought ;—
Progenitors of all that yet is great,
Ascribe to your bright senate, O ac-
cept
In your high ministrations, us, your
sons—
Us first, and the more glorious yet to
come !
And ye, weak conquerors ! giants who
look pale
When the crushed worm rebels be-
neath your tread—
The vultures, and the dogs, your pen-
sioners tame,
Are overgorged ; but, like oppressors,
still
They crave the relic of Destruction's
feast.
The exhalations and the thirsty winds
Are sick with blood ; the dew is foul
with death—
Heaven's light is quenched in slaugh-
ter :   Thus where'er
Upon your camps, cities, or towers,
or fleets,
The obscene birds the reeking rem-
nants cast
Of these dead limbs, upon your
streams and mountains,
Upon your fields, your gardens, and
your house-tops,
Where'er the winds shall creep, or the
clouds fly,
Or the dews fall, or the angry sun look
down
With poisoned light—Famine, and
Pestilence,
And Panic, shall wage war upon our
side !
Nature from all her boundaries is
moved
Against ye : Time has found ye light
as foam.

The earth rebels ; and Good and Evil stake
Their empire o'er the unborn world of men
On this one cast—but ere the die be thrown,
The renovated genius of our race,
Proud umpire of the impious game, descends
A seraph-winged Victory, bestriding
The tempest of the Omnipotence of God,
Which sweeps all things to their appointed doom,
And you to oblivion ! "—More he would have said,
But—

    Mahmud. Died—as thou shouldst ere thy lips had painted
Their ruin in the hues of our success.
A rebel's crime, gilt with a rebels tongue ?
Your heart is Greek, Hassan.

    Hassan. It may be so :
A spirit not my own wrenched me within,
And I have spoken words I fear and hate ;
Yet would I die for—

    Mahmud. Live ! O live ! outlive
Me and this sinking empire :—but the fleet—

    Hassan. Alas !

    Mahmud. The fleet which, like a flock of clouds
Chased by the wind, flies the insurgent banner.
Our winged castles from their merchant ships !
Our myriads before their weak pirate bands !
Our arms before their chains ! Our years of empire
Before their centuries of servile fear !
Death is awake ! Repulsed on the waters,
They own no more the thunder-bearing banner
Of Mahmud ; but like hounds of a base breed,
Gorge from a stranger's hand, and rend their master.

    Hassan. Latmos, and Ampelos, and Phanae, saw
The wreck—

    Mahmud. The caves of the Icarian isles
Hold each to the other in loud mockery,
And with the tongue as of a thousand echoes
First of the sea-convulsing fight—and then—
Thou darest to speak—senseless are the mountains,
Interpret thou their voice !

    Hassan. My presence bore
A part in that day's shame. The Grecian fleet
Bore down at day-break from the North, and hung
As multitudinous on the ocean line
As cranes upon the cloudless Thracian wind.
Our squadron, convoying ten thousand men,
Was stretching towards Nauplia when the battle
Was kindled.—
First through the hail of our artillery
The agile Hydriote barks with press of sail
Dashed :—ship to ship, cannon to cannon, man
To man, were grappled in the embrace of war,
Inextricable but by death or victory.
The tempest of the raging fight convulsed
To its crystalline depths that stainless sea,
And shook heaven's roof of golden morning clouds
Poised on an hundred azure mountain-isles.
In the brief trances of the artillery,
One cry from the destroyed and the destroyer
Rose, and a cloud of desolation wrapt
The unforeseen event, till the north wind
Sprung from the sea, lifting the heavy veil
Of battle-smoke—then victory—victory !
For, as we thought, three frigates from Algiers
Bore down from Naxos to our aid, but soon
The abhorred Cross glimmered behind, before,

Among, around us : and that fatal
 sign
Dried with its beams the strength of
 Moslem hearts,
As the sun drinks the dew.—What
 more ? We fled !
Our noonday path over the sanguine
 foam
Was beaconed, and the glare struck
 the sun pale,
By our consuming transports ; the
 fierce light
Made all the shadows of our sails
 blood-red,
And every countenance blank. Some
 ships lay feeding
The ravening fire even to the water's
 level :
Some were blown up ; some, settling
 heavily,
Sunk ; and the shrieks of our com-
 panions died
Upon the wind, that bore us fast and
 far,
Even after they were dead. Nine
 thousand perished !
We met the vultures legioned in the
 air,
Stemming the torrent of the tainted
 wind :
They, screaming from their cloudy
 mountain peaks,
Stooped through the sulphureous
 battle-smoke, and perched
Each on the weltering carcase that we
 loved,
Like its ill angel or its damned soul.
Riding upon the bosom of the sea,
We saw the dog-fish hastening to their
 feast.
Joy waked the voiceless people of the
 sea,
And ravening famine left his ocean-
 cave
To dwell with war, with us, and with
 despair.
We met night three hours to the west
 of Patmos,   Cease !
As with night, tempest—
 Mahmud.

Enter a Messenger.

 Messenger.   Your Sublime Highness,
That Christian hound, the Muscovite
 ambassador.

Has left the city.   If the rebel fleet
Had anchored in the port, had victory
Crowned the Greek legions in the
 Hippodrome,
Panic were tamer.—Obedience and
 Mutiny,
Like giants in contention planet-
 struck,
Stand gazing on each other.—There is
 peace
In Stamboul.—
 Mahmud.   Is the grave not calmer
 still ?
Its ruin shall be mine.
 Hassan.   Fear not the Russian ;
The tiger leagues not with the stag at
 bay
Against the hunter.—Cunning, base
 and cruel,
He crouches, watching till the spoil be
 won,
And must be paid for his reserve in
 blood.
After the war is fought, yield the sleek
 Russian
That which thou canst not keep, his
 deserved portion
Of blood, which shall not flow through
 streets and fields,
Rivers and seas, like that which we
 may win,
But stagnate in the veins of Christian
 slaves !

Enter Second Messenger.

 Second Messenger. Nauplia, Tri-
 polizza, Mothon, Athens,
Navarin, Artas, Monembasia,
Corinth and Theles, are carried by
 assault ;
And every Islamite who made his
 dogs
Fat with the flesh of Galilean slaves,
Passed at the edge of the sword : the
 lust of blood,
Which made our warriors drunk, is
 quenched in death ;
But like a fiery plague breaks out
 anew
In deeds which make the Christian
 cause look pale
In its own light. The garrison of
 Patras
Has store but for ten days, nor is there
 hope

But from the Briton ; at once slave
and tyrant,
His wishes still are weaker than his
fears ;
Or he would sell what faith may yet
remain
From the oaths broke in Genoa and
in Norway ;
And if you buy him not, your trea-
sury
Is empty even of promises—his own
coin.
The freeman of a western poet chief
Holds Attica with seven thousand
rebels,
And has beat back the pacha of Negro-
pont ;
The aged Ali sits in Yanina,
A crownless metaphor of empire ;
His name, that shadow of his withered
might,
Holds our besieging army like a spell
In prey to famine, pest, and mutiny :
He, bastioned in his citadel, looks
forth
Joyless upon the sapphire lake that
mirrors
The ruins of the city where he reigned
Childless and sceptreless.   The Greek
has reaped
The costly harvest his own blood
matured,
Not the sower, Ali—who has bought
a truce
From Ypsilanti, with ten camel-loads
Of Indian gold.

Enter a Third Messenger.

Mahmud.   What more ?
Third Messenger.   The Christian
tribes
Of Lebanon and the Syrian wilderness
Are in revolt—Damascus, Hems,
Aleppo,
Tremble ; — the Arab menaces Me-
dina ;
The Ethiop has entrenched himself
in Sennaar,
And keeps the Egyptian rebel well
employed,
Who denies homage, claims investi-
ture
As price of tardy aid.   Persia de-
mands
The cities on the Tigris, and the Geor-
gians

Refuse their living tribute. Crete and
Cyprus,
Like mountain-twins that from each
other's veins
Catch the volcano-fire and earthquake
spasm,
Shake in the general fever.   Through
the city,
Like birds before a storm, the San-
tons shriek,
And prophesyings horrible and new
Are heard among the crowd ; that sea
of men
Sleeps on the wrecks it made, breath-
less and still.
A Dervise, learned in the Koran,
preaches
That it is written how the sins of
Islam
Must raise up a destroyer even now.
The Greeks expect a Saviour from the
west ;
Who shall not come, men say, in
clouds and glory,
But in the omnipresence of that spirit
In which all live and are.   Ominous
signs
Are blazoned broadly on the noon-
day sky ;
One saw a red cross stamped upon the
sun ;
It has rained blood ; and monstrous
births declare
The secret wrath of Nature and her
Lord.
The army encamped upon the Cydaris
Was roused last night by the alarm of
battle,
And saw two hosts conflicting in the
air,—
The shadows doubtless of the unborn
time,
Cast on the mirror of the night. While
yet
The fight hung balanced, there arose
a storm
Which swept the phantoms from
among the stars.
At the third watch the spirit of the
plague
Was heard abroad flapping among
the tents :
Those who relieved watch found the
sentinels dead.
The last news from the camp is, that a
thousand

Have sickened, and—

Enter a Fourth Messenger.

Mahmud. And thou, pale ghost, dim shadow
Of some untimely rumour, speak!
Fourth Messenger. One comes
Fainting with toil, covered with foam and blood ;
He stood, he says, upon Clelonit's
Promontory, which o'erlooks the isles that groan
Under the Briton's frown, and all their waters
Then trembling in the splendour of the moon ;
When, as the wandering clouds unveiled or hid
Her boundless light, he saw two adverse fleets
Stalk through the night in the horizon's glimmer,
Mingling fierce thunders and sulphureous gleams,
And smoke which strangled every infant wind
That soothed the silver clouds through the deep air.
At length the battle slept, but the sirocco
Awoke, and drove his flock of thunder-clouds
Over the sea-horizon, blotting out
All objects—save that in the faint moon-glimpse
He saw, or dreamed he saw the Turkish admiral
And two, the loftiest, of our ships of war,
With the bright image of that Queen of Heaven,
Who hid, perhaps, her face for grief, reversed ;
And the abhorred Cross—

Enter an Attendant.

Attendant. Your sublime Highness,
The Jew, who——
Mahmud. Could not come more seasonably :
Bid him attend. I'll hear no more ! too long
We gaze on danger through the mist of fear.

And multiply upon our shattered hopes
The images of ruin. Come what will !
To-morrow and to-morrow are as lamps
Set in our path to light us to the edge,
Through rough and smooth ; nor can we suffer aught
Which he inflicts not in whose hand we are. [*Exeunt.*

SEMICHORUS I.
Would I were the winged cloud
Of a tempest swift and loud '
    I would scorn
    The smile of morn,
And the wave where the moon-rise is born !
    I would leave
    The spirits of eve
A shroud for the corpse of the day to weave
From other threads than mine !
Bask in the blue noon divine
    Who would, not I.

SEMICHORUS II.
    Whither to fly ?

SEMICHORUS I.
Where the rocks that gird th' Ægean
Echo to the battle pæan
    Of the free—
    I would flee
A tempestuous herald of victory !
    My golden rain
    For the Grecian slain
Should mingle in tears with the bloody main ;
And my solemn thunder-knell
Should ring to the world the passing-bell
    Of tyranny !

SEMICHORUS.
    Ah king ! wilt thou chain
    The rack and the rain ?
Wilt thou fetter the lightning and hurricane ?
    The storms are free,
    But we——

CHORUS.
O Slavery ! thou frost of the world's prime,
  Killing its flowers and leaving its thorns bare,

Thy touch has stamped these limbs
    with crime,
These brows thy branding garland
    bear ;
    But the free heart, the impassive
        soul,
    Scorn thy control !

SEMICHORUS I.

"Let there be light ! " said Liberty ;
And like sunrise from the sea,
Athens arose !—Around her born,
Shone like mountains in the morn,
Glorious states ;—and are they
    now
Ashes, wrecks, oblivion ?

SEMICHORUS II.
                             Go
Where Thermæ and Asopus swal-
    lowed
    Persia, as the sand does foam.
Deluge upon deluge followed,
    Discord, Macedon, and Rome :
And, lastly, thou !

SEMICHORUS I.
            Temples and towers,
Citadels and marts, and they
    Who live and die there, have been
        ours,
And may be thine, and must decay ;
    But Greece and her foundations are
Built below the tide of war,
Based on the crystalline sea
Of thought and its eternity ;
Her citizens, imperial spirits,
Rule the present from the past,
On all this world of men inherits
    Their seal is set.

SEMICHORUS II.
            Hear ye the blast,
Whose Orphic thunder thrilling
    calls
From ruin her Titanian walls ?
Whose spirit shakes the sapless
    bones
    Of Slavery ? Argos, Corinth,
        Crete,
Hear, and from their mountain
    thrones
    The dæmons and the nymphs
        repeat
        The harmony.

SEMICHORUS I.
        I hear ! I hear !

SEMICHORUS II.
The world's eyeless charioteer,
    Destiny, is hurrying by !
What faith is crushed, what empire
    bleeds
Beneath her earthquake - footed
    steeds ?
What eagle-winged victory sits
At her right hand ? what shadow flits
Before ? what splendour rolls be-
    hind ?
    Ruin and Renovation cry,
"Who but we ? "

SEMICHORUS I.
        I hear ! I hear !
The hiss as of a rushing wind,
The roar as of an ocean foaming,
The thunder as of earthquake coming
        I hear ! I hear !
The crash as of an empire falling,
The shrieks as of a people calling
"Mercy ! Mercy ! "—How they thrill !
Then a shout of " Kill ! kill ! kill ! "
And then a small still voice, thus—

SEMICHORUS II.
                For
Revenge and wrong bring forth their
    kind,
    The foul cubs like their parents are,
Their den is in their guilty mind,
    And Conscience feeds them with
        despair.

SEMICHORUS I.
In sacred Athens, near the fane
    Of wisdom, Pity's altar stood ;
Serve not the unknown God in vain,
But pay that broken shrine again
    Love for hate, and tears for blood.

Enter MAHMUD *and* AHASUERUS.

Mahmud. Thou art a man, thou
    sayest, even as we—
Ahasuerus. No more !
Mahmud.   But raised above thy
    fellow-men
By thought, as I by power.
    Ahasuerus.   Thou sayest so.
Mahmud. Thou art an adept in the
    difficult lore

Of Greek and Frank philosophy ; thou numberest
The flowers, and thou measurest the stars ;
Thou severest element from element ;
Thy spirit is present in the past, and sees
The birth of this old world through all its cycles
Of desolation and of loveliness ;
And when man was not, and how man became
The monarch and the slave of this low sphere,
And all its narrow circles—it is much.
I honour thee, and would be what thou art
Were I not what I am ; but the unborn hour,
Cradled in fear and hope, conflicting storms,
Who shall unveil ? Nor thou, nor I, nor any
Mighty or wise. I apprehend not
What thou hast taught me, but I now perceive
That thou art no interpreter of dreams ;   [God,
Thou dost not own that art, device, or
Can make the future present—let it come !
Moreover thou disdainest us and ours !
Thou art as God, whom thou contemplatest.
   Ahasuerus. Disdain thee ?— not the worm beneath my feet !
The Fathomless has care for meaner things
Than thou canst dream, and has made pride for those
Who would be what they may not, or would seem
That which they are not. Sultan ! talk no more
Of thee and me, the future and the past ;
But look on that which cannot change —the One
The unborn, and the undying. Earth and ocean,
Space, and the isles of life or light that gem
The sapphire floods of interstellar air,
This firmament pavilioned upon chaos,

With all its cressets of immortal fire,
Whose outwall, bastioned impregnably
Against the escape of boldest thoughts, repels them
As Calpe the Atlantic clouds—this whole
Of suns, and worlds, and men, and beasts, and flowers,
With all the silent or tempestuous workings
By which they have been, are, or cease to be,
Is but a vision ;—all that it inherits
Are motes of a sick eye, bubbles, and dreams ;
Thought is its cradle and its grave, nor less
The future and the past are idle shadows
Of thought's eternal flight—they have no being ;
Nought is but that it feels itself to be.
   Mahmud. What meanest thou ? thy words stream like a tempest
Of dazzling mist within my brain— they shake
The earth on which I stand, and hang like night
On Heaven above me. What can they avail ?
They cast on all things, surest, brightest, best,
Doubt, insecurity, astonishment.
   Ahasuerus. Mistake me not ! All is contained in each.
Dodona's forest to an acorn's cup
Is that which has been or will be, to that
Which is—the absent to the present. Thought
Alone, and its quick elements, Will, Passion,
Reason, Imagination, cannot die ;
They are what that which they regard appears,
The stuff whence mutability can weave
All that it hath dominion o'er,—worlds, worms,
Empires, and superstitions. What has thought
To do with time, or place, or circumstance ?
Wouldst thou behold the future ?—ask and have !

Knock and it shall be opened—look, and lo !

The coming age is shadowed on the past,

As on a glass.

 Mahmud.   Wild, wilder thoughts convulse

My spirit—Did not Mahomet the Second

Win Stamboul ?

 Ahasuerus. Thou wouldst ask that giant spirit

The written fortunes of thy house and faith.

Thou wouldst cite one out of the grave to tell

How what was born in blood must die.

 Mahmud.   Thy words

Have power on me ! I see——

 Ahasuerus.   What hearest thou?

 Mahmud. A far whisper——

Terrible silence.

 Ahasuerus. What succeeds ?

 Mahmud.   The sound

As of the assault of an imperial city,

The hiss of inextinguishable fire,

The roar of giant cannon ;—the earth-quaking

Fall of vast bastions and precipitous towers,

The shock of crags shot from strange engin'ry,

The clash of wheels, and clang of armed hoofs,

And crash of brazen mail, as of the wreck

Of adamantine mountains—the mad blast

Of trumpets, and the neigh of raging steeds,

And shrieks of women whose thrill ja s the blood,

And one sweet laugh, most horrible to hear,

As of a joyous infant waked, and playing

With its dead mother's breast ; and now more loud

The mingled battle-cry—ha ! hear I not

'Εν τούτῳ νίκη. Allah-illah-Allah !

 Ahasuerus. The sulphureous mist is raised—thou seest—

 Mahmud.   A chasm,

As of two mountains, in the wall of Stamboul ;

And in that ghastly breach the Islam-ites,

Like giants on the ruins of a world,

Stand in the light of sunrise. In the dust

Glimmers a kingless diadem, and one

Of regal port has cast himself beneath

The stream of war. Another, proud-ly clad

In golden arms, spurs a Tartarian barb

Into the gap, and with his iron mace

Directs the torrent of that tide of men,

And seems—he is—Mahomet !

 Ahasuerus.   What thou seest

Is but the ghost of thy forgotten dream ;

A dream itself, yet less, perhaps than that

Thou call'st reality. Thou mayst be-hold

How cities, on which empire sleeps enthroned,

Bow their towered crests to muta-bility.

Poised by the flood, e'en on the height thou holdest,

Thou mayst now learn how the full tide of power

Ebbs to its depths.—Inheritor of glory,

Conceived in darkness, born in blood, and nourished

With tears and toil, thou seest the mortal throes

Of that whose birth was but the same. The Past

Now stands before thee like an Incar-nation

Of the To-come ; yet wouldst thou commune with

That portion of thyself which was ere thou

Didst start for this brief race whose crown is death ;

Dissolve with that strong faith and fervent passion

Which called it from the uncreated deep,

Yon cloud of war with its tempestu-ous phantoms

Of raging death ; and draw with mighty will

The imperial shade hither.

     [*Exit* AHASUERUS.

 Mahmud.   Approach !

 Phantom.   I come

Thence whither thou must go ! The grave is fitter
To take the living, than give up the dead ;
Yet has thy faith prevailed, and I am here.
The heavy fragments of the power which fell
When I arose, like shapeless crags and clouds,
Hang round my throne on the abyss, and voices
Of strange lament soothe my supreme repose,
Wailing for glory never to return.—
  A later Empire nods in its decay ;
The autumn of a greener faith is come,
And wolfish change, like winter, howls to strip
The foliage in which Fame, the eagle, built
Her aërie, while Dominion whelped below.
The storm is in its branches, and the frost
Is on its leaves, and the blank deep expects
Oblivion on oblivion, spoil on spoil,
Ruin on ruin : thou art slow, my son ;
The Anarchs of the world of darkness keep
A throne for thee, round which thine empire lies
Boundless and mute ; and for thy subjects thou,
Like us, shall rule the ghosts of murdered life,
The phantoms of the powers who rule thee now—
Mutinous passions and conflicting fears,
And hopes that sate themselves on dust and die,
Stript of their mortal strength, as thou of thine.
Islam must fall, but we will reign together
Over its ruins in the world of death :—
And if the trunk be dry, yet shall the seed
Unfold itself even in the shape of that
Which gathers birth in its decay. Woe ! woe !
To the weak people tangled in the grasp
Of its last spasms.

Mahmud.   Spirit, woe to all !
Woe to the wronged and the avenger ! Woe
To the destroyer, woe to the destroyed !
Woe to the dupe, and woe to the deceiver !
Woe to the oppressed and woe to the oppressor !
Woe both to those that suffer and inflict ;
Those who are born, and those who die ! But say,
Imperial shadow of the thing I am,
When, how, by whom, Destruction must accomplish
Her consummation ?
  Phantom.   Ask the cold pale Hour,
Rich in reversion of impending death,
When *he* shall fall upon whose ripe grey hairs
Sit care, and sorrow, and infirmity—
The weight which Crime, whose wings are plumed with years,
Leaves in his flight from ravaged heart to heart
Over the heads of men, under which burthen
They bow themselves unto the grave : fond wretch !
He leans upon his crutch, and talks of years
To come, and how in hours of youth renewed
He will renew lost joys, and——
  Voice without.   Victory ! victory !
             [*The Phantom vanishes.*
  Mahmud. What sound of the importunate earth has broken
My mighty trance ?
  Voice without.   Victory ! victory !
  Mahmud. Weak lightning before darkness ! poor faint smile
Of dying Islam ! Voice which art the response
Of hollow weakness ! Do I wake and live ?
Were there such things ? or may the unquiet brain,
Vexed by the wise mad talk of the old Jew,
Have shaped itself these shadows of its fear ?
It matters not !—for nought we see or dream,

Possess, or lose, or grasp at, can be
    worth
More than it gives or teaches.   Come
    what may,
The future must become the past, and
    I
As they were, to whom once this
    present hour,
This gloomy crag of time to which I
    cling,
Seemed an Elysian isle of peace and
    joy
Never to be attained.—I must rebuke
This drunkenness of triumph ere it die,
And dying, bring despair.—Victory !
    —poor slaves !

                              [*Exit* MAHMUD.

Voice without. Shout in the jubilee
    of death !   The Greeks
Are as a brood of lions in the net,
Round which the kingly hunters of
    the earth
Stand smiling.   Anarchs, ye whose
    daily food
Are curses, groans, and gold, the fruit
    of death,
From Thule to the girdle of the world,
Come, feast ! the board groans with
    the flesh of men—
The cup is foaming with a nation's
    blood,
Famine and thirst await : eat, drink,
    and die !

SEMICHORUS I.
Victorious Wrong, with vulture
    scream,
Salutes the risen sun, pursues the fly-
    ing day !
  I saw her ghastly as a tyrant's
    dream,
Perch on the trembling pyramid of
    night,
Beneath which earth and all her
    realms pavilioned lay
In visions of the dawning undelight.
      Who shall impede her flight ?
      Who rob her of her prey ?

Voice without. Victory ! victory !
    Russia's famished eagles
Dare not to prey beneath the Cres-
    cent's light.
Impale the remnant of the Greeks !
    despoil !

Violate ! make their flesh cheaper
    than dust !

SEMICHORUS II.
    Thou voice which art
The herald of the ill in splendour
    hid !
    Thou echo of the hollow heart
Of monarchy, bear me to thine
    abode
    When desolation flashes o'er a
    world destroyed,
Oh ! bear me to those isles of jagged
    cloud
    Which float like mountains on
    the earthquakes, 'mid
The momentary oceans of the light-
    ning ;
    Or to some toppling promon-
    tory proud
    Of solid tempest, whose black
    pyramid,
Riven, overhangs the founts in-
    tensely brightening
    Of those dawn-tinted deluges
    of fire
    Before their waves expire,
When heaven and earth are light,
    and only light
    In the thunder-night !

Voice without. Victory ! victory !
    Austria, Russia, England,
And that tame serpent, that poor
    shadow, France,
Cry peace, and that means death when
    monarchs speak.
Ho, there ! bring torches, sharpen
    those red stakes !
These chains are light, fitter for slaves
    and poisoners
Than Greeks.   Kill ! plunder ! burn !
    let none remain.

SEMICHORUS I.
    Alas for Liberty !
If numbers, wealth, or unfulfill-
    ing years,
    Or fate, can quell the free ;
    Alas for Virtue ! when
Torments, or contumely, or the
    sneers
    Of erring judging men
    Can break the heart where it
    abides.

Alas! if Love, whose smile makes
    this obscure world splendid
    Can change, with its false
      times and tides,
    Like hope and terror—
      Alas for Love!
And Truth, who wanderest lone and
    unbefriended,
    If thou canst veil thy lie-consum-
      ing mirror
      Before the dazzled eyes of
      Error.
      Alas for thee! Image of the
      Above.

SEMICHORUS II.

Repulse, with plumes from conquest
    torn,
Led the ten thousand from the limits
    of the morn
    Through many an hostile Anarchy!
At length they wept aloud and cried,
    " The sea! the sea!"
    Through exile, persecution, and
    despair,
      Rome was, and young Atlantis
      shall become
      The wonder, or the terror, or the
      tomb
Of all whose step wakes power lulled
    in her savage lair
    But Greece was as a hermit child,
      Whose fairest thoughts and limbs
      were built
    To woman's growth, by dreams so
    mild
      She knew not pain or guilt;
And now, O Victory, blush! and Em-
    pire, tremble,
    When ye desert the free!
    If Greece must be
A wreck, yet shall its fragments re-
    assemble,
And build themselves again impreg-
    nably
    In a diviner clime,
To Amphionic music, on some Cape
    sublime,
Which frowns above the idle foam of
    Time.

SEMICHORUS I.

Let the tyrants rule the desert they
    have made;
    Let the free possess the paradise
    they claim;

Be the fortune of our fierce oppressors
    weighed
    With our ruin, our resistance, and
    our name!

SEMICHORUS II.

Our dead shall be the seed of their
    decay,
    Our survivors be the shadows of
    their pride,
Our adversity a dream to pass away—
    Their dishonour a remembrance to
    abide!

Voice without. Victory! Victory!
    The bought Briton sends
The keys of ocean to the Islamite.
Now shall the blazon of the Cross be
    veiled,
And British skill directing Othman
    might,
Thunder-strike rebel victory. O
    keep holy
This jubilee of unrevenged blood!
Kill! crush! despoil! Let not a
    Greek escape!

SEMICHORUS I.

Darkness has dawned in the East
    On the noon of time:
    The death-birds descend to their
    feast,
    From the hungry clime.
Let Freedom and Peace flee far
    To a sunnier strand,
And follow Love's folding star!
    To the Evening land!

SEMICHORUS II.

The young moon has fed
    Her exhausted horn
With the sunset's fire:
    The weak day is dead,
      But the night is not born;
And, like loveliness panting with
    wild desire,
While it trembles with fear and de-
    light,
Hesperus flies from awakening
    night,
And pants in its beauty and speed
    with light
Fast-flashing, soft and bright.
Thou beacon of love! thou lamp of
    the free!
    Guide us far, far away,

To climes where now, veiled by the
        ardour of day,
    Thou art hidden
From waves on which weary noon
Faints in her summer swoon,
Between kingless continents, sin-
        less as Eden,
Around mountains and islands invio-
        lably
    Pranked on the sapphire sea.

SEMICHORUS I.
    Through the sunset of hope,
Like the shapes of a dream,
What Paradise islands of glory
        gleam
    Beneath Heaven's cope.
Their shadows more clear float by—
The sound of their oceans, the light of
        their sky,
The music and fragrance their soli-
        tudes breathe,
Burst like morning on dreams, or like
        Heaven on death,
    Through the walls of our prison ;
    And Greece, which was dead, is
        arisen !

CHORUS.
The world's great age begins anew,
    The golden years return,
The earth doth like a snake renew
    Her winter weeds outworn :
Heaven smiles, and faiths and em-
        pires gleam
Like wrecks of a dissolving dream.

A brighter Hellas rears its moun-
        tains
    From waves serener far ;
A new Peneus rolls its fountains
    Against the Morning Star.
Where fairer Tempes bloom, there
        sleep
Young Cyclads on a sunnier deep.

A loftier Argo cleaves the main,
    Fraught with a later prize ;
Another Orpheus sings again,
    And loves, and weeps, and dies;
A new Ulysses leaves once more
Calypso for his native shore.

O write no more the tale of Troy,
    If earth Death's scroll must be !
Nor mix with Laian rage the joy
    Which dawns upon the free :
Although a subtler Sphinx renew
Riddles of death Thebes never knew.

Another Athens shall arise,
    And to remoter time
Bequeath, like sunset to the skies,
    The splendour of its prime ;
And leave, if nought so bright may
        live,
All earth can take or heaven can
        give.

Saturn and Love their long repose
    Shall burst, more bright and good
Than all who fell, than One who
        rose,
    Than many unsubdued :
Not gold, not blood, their altar
        dowers,
But votive tears, and symbol flow-
        ers.

O cease ! must hate and death
        return ?
    Cease ! must men kill and die ?
Cease ! drain not to its dregs the
        urn
    Of bitter prophecy.
The world is weary of the past,
O might it die or rest at last !

[1] See Notes at the end of the volume.

ŒDIPUS TYRANNUS

or, SWELLFOOT THE TYRANT

A TRAGEDY IN TWO ACTS

Translated from the Original Doric

————Choose Reform or Civil War,
When through thy streets, instead of hare with dogs,
A CONSORT-QUEEN shall hunt a KING with hogs,
Riding on the IONIAN MINOTAUR.

ADVERTISEMENT

THIS Tragedy is one of a triad, or system of three Plays (an arrangement according to which the Greeks were accustomed to connect their Dramatic representations), elucidating the wonderful and appalling fortunes of the SWELLFOOT dynasty. It was evidently written by some *learned Theban*, and from its characteristic dulness, apparently before the duties on the importation of *Attic salt* had been repealed by the Bœotarchs. The tenderness with which he beats the PIGS proves him to have been a *sus Bœotiæ ;* possibly *Epicuri de grege Porcus ;* for, as the poet observes,

" A fellow feeling makes us wond'rous kind."

No liberty has been taken with the translation of this remarkable piece of antiquity, except the suppressing a seditious and blasphemous chorus of the Pigs and Bulls at the last act. The word Hoydipouse (or more properly Œdipus) has been rendered literally SWELLFOOT, without its having been conceived necessary to determine whether a swelling of the hind or the fore feet of the Swinish Monarch is particularly indicated.

Should the remaining portions of this Tragedy be found, entitled, " *Swellfoot in Angaria*," and "*Charité*," the Translator might be tempted to give them to the reading Public.

DRAMATIS PERSONÆ

TYRANT SWELLFOOT, *King of Thebes*
IONA TAURINA, *his Queen*
MAMMON, *Arch-Priest of Famine*
PURGANAX
DAKRY   } *Wizards, Ministers of*
LAOCTONOS }   SWELLFOOT

The GADFLY
The LEECH
The RAT
The MINOTAUR
MOSES, *the Sow-gelder*
SOLOMON, *the Porkman*

ZEPHANIAH, *Pig-butcher*
CHORUS *of the Swinish Multitude.—Guards, Attendants, Priests, etc., etc.*
SCENE—*Thebes*

ACT I

SCENE I.—*A magnificent Temple, built of thigh-bones and death's-heads, and tiled with scalps. Over the Altar the statue of Famine, veiled ; a number of boars, sows, and sucking-pigs, crowned with thistle, shamrock, and oak, sitting on the steps,* and clinging round the Altar of the Temple.

Enter SWELLFOOT, *in his royal robes, without perceiving the* PIGS.

Swellfoot. Thou supreme Goddess ! by whose power divine
These graceful limbs are clothed in proud array

[He contemplates himself with satisfaction.

Of gold and purple, and this kingly
   paunch
Swells like a sail before a favouring
   breeze,
And these most sacred nether promon-
   tories
Lie satisfied with layers of fat ; and
   these
Bœotian cheeks, like Egypt's Pyra-
   mid,
(Nor with less toil were their founda-
   tions laid, ')
Sustain the cone of my untroubled
   brain,
That point, the emblem of a point-
   less nothing !
Thou to whom Kings and laurelled
   Emperors,
Radical butchers, Paper-money-mil-
   lers,
Bishops and deacons, and the entire
   army
Of those fat martyrs to the persecu-
   tion
Of stifling turtle-soup, and brandy-
   devils,
Offer their secret vows ! Thou plen-
   teous Ceres
Of their Eleusis, hail !　　　[eigh !
  The Swine. Eigh ! eigh ! eigh !
  Swellfoot.　Ha ! what are ye,
Who, crowned with leaves devoted to
   the Furies,
Cling round this sacred shrine ?
  Swine. Aigh ! aigh ! aigh !
  Swellfoot.　　　What, ye that are
The very beasts that offered at her
   altar
With blood and groans, salt-cake, and
   fat, and inwards,
Ever propitiate her reluctant will
When taxes are withheld ?
  Swine. Ugh ! ugh ! ugh !
  Swellfoot.　　What ! ye who grub
With filthy snouts my red potatoes up
In Allan's rushy bog ? Who eat the
   oats
Up, from my cavalry in the Hebrides?
Who swill the hog-wash soup my
   cooks digest

  ¹ See universal history for an account of the
number of people who died and the immense
consumption of garlic by the wretched Egyp-
tians, who made a sepulcher for the name as well
as the bodies of their tyrants.

From bones, and rags, and scraps of
   shoe-leather,
Which should be given to cleaner pigs
   than you ?

  The Swine.—Semichorus I.
   The same, alas ! the same ;
   Though only now the name
    Of pig remains to me.

   Semichorus II.
  If 'twere your kingly will
  Us wretched swine to kill,
   What should we yield to
    thee ?
Swellfoot. Why skin and bones, and
  some few hairs for mortar.

   Chorus of Swine.
I have heard your Laureate sing,
That pity was a royal thing ;
Under your mighty ancestors, we
   pigs
Were bless'd as nightingales on
   myrtle sprigs,
Or grasshoppers that live on noon-
   day dew,
And sung, old annals tell, as sweetly
   too :
But now our sties are fallen in, we
   catch
   The murrain and the mange, the
    scab and itch ;
Sometimes your royal dogs tear
   down our thatch,
   And then we seek the shelter of a
    ditch ;
Hog-wash or grains, or ruta-baga,
   none
Has yet been ours since your reign
   begun.

   First Sow.
My pigs, 'tis in vain to tug !

   Second Sow.
I could almost eat my litter !

   First Pig.
I suck, but no milk will come
  from the dug.

   Second Pig.
Our skin and our bones would be
  bitter.

   The Boars.
We fight for this rag of greasy rug,
Though a trough of wash would be
  fitter.

SEMICHORUS.

Happier swine were they than we,
Drowned in the Gadarean sea—
I wish that pity would drive out the
    devils
Which in your royal bosom hold
    their revels,
And sink us in the waves of your com
    passion !
Alas ! the pigs are an unhappy
    nation !
Now if your majesty would have
    our bristles
  To bind your mortar with, or fill
    our colons
With rich blood, or make brawn
    out of our gristles,
  In policy—ask else your royal
    Solons—
You ought to give us hog-wash and
    clean straw,
And sties well thatched ; besides,
    it is the law !
Swellfoot. This is sedition, and rank
    blasphemy !
Ho ! there, my guards !

Enter a GUARD.

Guard.   Your sacred Majesty ?
Swellfoot. Call in the Jews, Solo-
    mon the court porkman,
Moses the sow-gelder, and Zephaniah
    the hog-butcher.
Guard. They are in waiting, sire.

Enter SOLOMON, MOSES, *and*
    ZEPHANIAH.

Swellfoot. Out with your knife, old
    Moses, and spay those sows,
  [*The* PIGS *run about in consternation.*
That load the earth with pigs ; cut
    close and deep.
Moral restraint I see has no effect,
Nor prostitution, nor our own example,
Starvation, typhus fever, war, nor
    prison—
This was the art which the arch-priest
    of Famine
Hinted at in his charge to the Theban
    clergy—
Cut close and deep, good Moses.
  Moses.   Let your majesty
Keep the boars quiet, else—
  Swellfoot.   Zephaniah, cut

That fat hog's throat, the brute seems
    overfed ;
Seditious hunks ! to whine for want
    of grains.
  Zephaniah. Your sacred majesty,
    he has the dropsy ;—
We shall find pints of hydatids in's
    liver,
He has not half an inch of wholesome
    fat
Upon his carious ribs—
  Swellfoot.   'Tis all the same,
He'll serve instead of riot-money,
    when
Our murmuring troops bivouac in
    Thebes' streets ;
And January winds, after a day
Of butchering, will make them relish
    carrion.
Now, Solomon, I'll sell you in a lump
The whole kit of them.
  Solomon.   Why, your majesty,
I could not give——
  Swellfoot.   Kill them out of the
    way,
That shall be price enough, and let me
    hear
Their everlasting grunts and whines
    no more !
  [*Exeunt, driving in the* SWINE.

Enter MAMMON, *the Arch-Priest ; and*
    PURGANAX, *Chief of the Council
    of Wizards.*

  Purganax. The future looks as
    black as death, a cloud,
Dark as the frown of Hell, hangs over
    it—
The troops grow mutinous—the re-
    venue fails—
There's something rotten in us—for
    the level
Of the State slopes, its very bases
    topple ;
The boldest turn their backs upon
    themselves !
  Mammon. Why what's the matter,
    my dear fellow, now ?
Do the troops mutiny ?—decimate
    some regiments ;
Does money fail ?—come to my mint
    —coin paper,
Till gold be at a discount, and,
    ashamed
To show his bilious face, go purge him-
    self,

In emulation of her vestal whiteness.

Purganax. Oh, would that this
   were all ! The oracle !

Mammon. Why it was I who
   spoke that oracle,

And whether I was dead drunk or
   inspired,

I cannot well remember ; nor, in truth,

The oracle itself !

Purganax.   The words went
   thus :—

" Bœotia, choose reform or civil war !

When through the streets, instead of
   hare with dogs,

A Consort-Queen shall hunt a King
   with hogs,

Riding on the Ionian Minotaur."

Mammon. Now if the oracle had
   ne'er foretold

This sad alternative, it must arrive,

Or not, and so it must now that it has ;

And whether I was urged by grace
   divine,

Or Lesbian liquor to declare these
   words,

Which must, as all words must, be
   false or true ;

It matters not : for the same power
   made all,

Oracle, wine, and me and you—or
   none—

'Tis the same thing. If you knew as
   much

Of oracles as I do——

Purganax.   You arch-priests

Believe in nothing ; if you were to
   dream

Of a particular number in the lottery,

You would not buy the ticket !

Mammon.   Yet our tickets

Are seldom blanks. But what steps
   have you taken ?

For prophecies, when once they get
   abroad,

Like liars who tell the truth to serve
   their ends,

Or hypocrites, who, from assuming
   virtue,

Do the same actions that the virtuous do,

Contrive their own fulfilment. This
   Iona—

Well—you know what the chaste
   Pasiphae did,

Wife to that most religious King of
   Crete,

And still how popular the tale is here;

And these dull swine of Thebes boast
   their descent

From the free Minotaur. You know
   they still

Call themselves bulls, though thus
   degenerate ;

And everything relating to a bull

Is popular and respectable in Thebes :

Their arms are seven bulls in a field
   gules.

They think their strength consists in
   eating beef,—

Now there were danger in the precedent

If Queen Iona——

Purganax.   I have taken good
   care

That shall not be. I struck the crust
   o' the earth

With this enchanted rod, and Hell lay
   bare !

And from a cavern full of ugly shapes,

I chose a LEECH, a GADFLY, and a RAT.

The gadfly was the same which Juno
   sent

To agitate Io,[1] and which Ezechiel [2]
   mentions

That the Lord whistled for out of the
   mountains

Of utmost Ethiopia, to torment

Mesopotamian Babylon. The beast

Has a loud trumpet like the scarabee;

His crooked tail is barbed with many
   stings,

Each able to make a thousand wounds,
   and each

Immedicable ; from his convex eyes

He sees fair things in many hideous
   shapes,

And trumpets all his falsehood to the
   world.

Like other beetles he is fed on dung—

He has eleven feet with which he
   crawls,

Trailing a blistering slime ; and this
   foul beast

Has tracked Iona from the Theban
   limits,

From isle to isle, from city unto city,

Urging her flight from the far Cher-
   sonese

---

[1] The Prometheus Bound of Æschylus.

[2] And the Lord whistled for the gadfly out of
Æthiopia, and for the bee out of Egypt, etc.—
EZECHIEL.

To fabulous Solyma, and the Ætnean
    Isle,
Ortygia, Melite, and Calypso's Rock,
And the swart tribes of Garamant
    and Fez,
Æolia and Elysium, and thy shores,
Parthenope, which now, alas! are
    free!
And through the fortunate Saturnian
    land,
Into the darkness of the West.
    Mammon.   But if
This Gadfly should drive Iona hither?
    Purganax. Gods! what an *if!* but
    there is my grey RAT;   [out
So thin with want, he can crawl in and
Of any narrow chink and filthy hole,
And he shall creep into her dressing-
    room,
And—
    Mammon. My dear friend, where
    are your wits? as if
She does not always toast a piece of
    cheese,
And bait the trap? and rats, when
    lean enough
To crawl through *such* chinks——
    Purganax. But my LEECH—a leech
Fit to suck blood, with lubricous
    round rings,
Capaciously expatiative, which make
His little body like a red balloon,
As full of blood as that of hydrogen,
Sucked from men's hearts; insati-
    ably he sucks
And clings and pulls—a horse-leech,
    whose deep maw
The plethoric King Swellfoot could
    not fill,
And who, till full, will cling for ever.
    Mammon.   This
For Queen Iona might suffice, and
    less;
But 'tis the swinish multitude I fear,
And in that fear I have——
    Purganax.   Done what?
    Mammon.   Disinherited
My eldest son Chrysaor, because he
Attended public meetings, and would
    always
Stand prating there of commerce,
    public faith,
Economy, and unadulterate coin,
And other topics, ultra-Radical;
And have entailed my estate, called
    the Fool's Paradise,

And funds, in fairy money, bonds and
    bills,
Upon my accomplished daughter
    Banknotina,
And married her to the Gallows.[1]
    Purganax.   A good match!
    Mammon. A high connection, Pur-
    ganax. The bridegroom
Is of a very ancient family
Of Hounslow Heath, Tyburn, and the
    New Drop,
And has great influence in both
    Houses;—Oh!
He makes the fondest husband; nay
    too fond :—
New-married people should not kiss
    in public ;—
But the poor souls love one another
    so!
And then my little grandchildren,
    the Gibbets,
Promising children as you ever saw,—
The young playing at hanging, the
    elder learning
How to hold Radicals. They are well
    taught too,
For every Gibbet says its catechism,
And reads a select chapter in the
    Bible
Before it goes to play.
    [*A most tremendous humming is heard.*
    Purganax.   Ha! what do I hear?

Enter GADFLY.

Mammon. Your Gadfly, as it seems,
    is tired of gadding.

GADFLY.
Hum! hum! hum!
From the lakes of the Alps, and the
    cold grey scalps
    Of the mountains, I come!
Hum! hum! hum!
From Morocco and Fez, and the high
    palaces
    Of golden Byzantium;
From the temples divine of old
    Palestine,
    From Athens and Rome,
    With a ha! and a hum!
    I come! I come!

All inn-doors and windows
    Were open to me!

[1] " If one should marry a gallows, and beget
young gibbets, I never saw one so prone."—
CYMBELINE.

I saw all that sin does,
　　Which lamps hardly see
That burn in the night by the cur-
　　tained bed,—
The impudent lamps! for they
　　blushed not red.
　　Dinging and singing,
　　From slumber I rung her,
　　Loud as the clank of an iron-
　　　monger!
　　Hum! hum! hum!

　　Far, far, far,
With the trump of my lips, and the
　　sting at my hips,
　　I drove her—afar!
　　Far far, far,
From city to city, abandoned of pity,
A ship without needle or star;—
Homeless she past, like a cloud on the
　　blast,
　　Seeking peace, finding war;—
　　She is here in her car,
　　From afar, and afar;—
　　Hum! hum!

I have stung her and wrung her!
　　The venom is working;—
　　And if you had hung her
　　With canting and quirking,
She could not be deader than she will
　　be soon;—
I have driven her close to you under
　　the moon,
Night and day, hum! hum! ha!
I have hummed her and drummed her
From place to place, till at last I have
　　dumbed her.
　　Hum! hum! hum!

Leech.
　　I will suck
　　Blood or muck!
The disease of the state is a
　　plethory,
Who so fit to reduce it as I?

Rat.
　　I'll slily seize and
Let blood from her weasand,—
Creeping through crevice, and chink,
　　and cranny,
With my snaky tail, and my sides so
　　scranny.
Purganax. Aroint ye! thou unpro-
　　fitable worm!
　　　　　　　　　　　　[To the Leech.

And thou, dull beetle, get thee back
　　to hell!　　　　[To the Gadfly.
To sting the ghosts of Babylonian
　　kings,
And the ox-headed Io.——

Swine (within).
　　Ugh, ugh, ugh!
　　Hail Iona the divine,
　　We will be no longer swine,
　　But bulls with horns and dewlaps.

Rat.
　　　　　　　　　　　　　　For,
You know, my lord, the Minotaur—
Purganax (fiercely). Be silent!
　　get to hell! or I will call
The cat out of the kitchen. Well,
　　Lord Mammon,
This is a pretty business!
　　　　　　　　　　　　[Exit the Rat.
Mammon. 　　　　　　　I will go
And spell some scheme to make it
　　ugly then. 　　　　　　[Exit.

Enter Swellfoot.

Swellfoot. She is returned! Taurina
　　is in Thebes
When Swellfoot wishes that she were
　　in hell!
Oh, Hymen! clothed in yellow
　　jealousy,
And waving o'er the couch of wedded
　　kings
The torch of Discord with its fiery
　　hair;
This is thy work, thou patron saint of
　　queens!
Swellfoot is wived! though parted
　　by the sea,
The very name of wife had conjugal
　　rights;
Her cursed image ate, drank, slept
　　with me,
And in the arms of Adiposa oft
Her memory has received a hus-
　　band's—
　　[A loud tumult, and cries of " Iona
　　　　for ever!— No Swellfoot!"
　　　　　　　　　　　　　　Hark!
How the swine cry "Iona Taurina!"
I suffer the real presence: Purganax,
Off with her head!
Purganax. 　　　But I must first
　　impanel
A jury of the pigs.
Swellfoot. 　　　Pack them then.

Purganax. Or fattening some few
  in two separate sties,
And giving them clean straw, tying
  some bits
Of ribbon round their legs—giving
  their sows
Some tawdry lace, and bits of lustre
  glass,
And their young boars white and red
  rags, and tails
Of cows, and jay feathers, and stick-
  ing cauliflowers
Between the ears of the old ones ; and
  when
They are persuaded, that by the
  inherent virtue
Of these things, they are all imperial
  pigs,
Good Lord ! they'd rip each other's
  bellies up,
Not to say help us in destroying her.
  Swellfoot. This plan might be tried
  too ;—where's General Laoctonos ?

Enter LAOCTONOS *and* DAKRY.

It is my royal pleasure
That you, Lord General, bring the
  head and body,
If separate it would please me better,
  hither
Of Queen Iona.
  Laoctonos. That pleasure I well
  knew,
And made a charge with those
  battalions bold,
Called, from their dress and grin, the
  royal apes,
Upon the swine, who in a hollow
  square
Enclosed her, and received the first
  attack
Like so many rhinoceroses, and then
Retreating in good order, with bare
  tusks
And wrinkled snouts presented to the
  foe,
Bore her in triumph to the public sty.
What is still worse, some sows upon
  the ground
Have given the ape-guards apples,
  nuts, and gin,
And they all whisk their tails aloft,
  and cry,
" Long live Iona ! down with Swell-
  foot ! "

Purganax.   Hark !
The Swine (without). Long live
  Iona ! down with Swellfoot !
Dakry. I went to the garret of the
  swineherd's tower,
Which overlooks the sty, and made a
  long
Harangue (all words) to the assembled
  swine,
Of delicacy, mercy, judgment, law,
Morals, and precedents, and purity,
Adultery, destitution, and divorce,
Piety, faith, and state necessity,
And how I loved the queen !—and
  then I wept,
With the pathos of my own eloquence,
And every tear turned to a millstone,
  which
Brained many a gaping pig, and there
  was made
A slough of blood and brains upon
  the place,
Greased with the pounded bacon ;
  round and round
The millstones rolled, ploughing the
  pavement up,
And hurling sucking-pigs into the air,
With dust and stones.——

Enter MAMMON.

Mammon.   I wonder that grey
  wizards
Like you should be so beardless in
  their schemes ;
It had been but a point of policy
To keep Iona and the swine apart.
Divide and rule ! but ye have made a
  junction
Between two parties who will govern
  you,
But for my art.—Behold this BAG ! it
  is
The poison-BAG of that Green Spider
  huge,
On which our spies skulked in ovation
  through
The streets of Thebes, when they were
  paved with dead
A bane so much the deadlier fills it
  now,
As calumny is worse than death,—for
  here
The Gadfly's venom, fifty times dis-
  tilled,
Is mingled with the vomit of the
  Leech,

In due proportion, and black rats-
bane, which
That very Rat, who like the Pontic
tyrant,
Nurtures himself on poison, dare not
touch :—
All is sealed up with the broad seal of
Fraud,
Who is the Devil's Lord High Chan-
cellor,
And over it the primate of all Hell
Murmured this pious baptism :—
" Be thou called
The GREEN BAG ; and this power and
grace be thine
That thy contents, on whomsoever
poured,
Turn innocence to guilt, and gentlest
looks
To savage, foul, and fierce deformity.
Let all, baptised by thy infernal dew,
Be called adulterer, drunkard, liar,
wretch !
No name left out which orthodoxy
loves,
Court Journal or legitimate Re-
view !
Be they called tyrant, beast, fool,
glutton, lover
Of other wives and husbands than
their own—
The heaviest sin on this side of the
Alps !
Wither they to a ghastly caricature
Of what was human !—let not man
nor beast
Behold their face with unaverted
eyes !
Or hear their names with ears that
tingle not
With blood of indignation, rage, and
shame ! "
This is a perilous liquor ;—good my
lords.

[SWELLFOOT *approaches to touch
the* GREEN BAG.

Beware ! for God's sake, beware !—
if you should break
The seal, and touch the fatal
liquor——
Purganax.   There !
Give it to me. I have been used to
handle
All sorts of poisons. His dread
majesty
Only desires to see the colour of it.

Mammon. Now, with a little com-
mon sense, my lords,
Only undoing all that has been done
(Yet so as it may seem we but con-
firm it,)
Our victory is assured. We must
entice
Her majesty from the sty, and make
the pigs
Believe that the contents of the
GREEN BAG
Are the true test of guilt or innocence.
And that, if she be guilty, 'twill trans-
form her .
To manifest deformity like guilt.
If innocent, she will become trans-
figured
Into an angel, such as they say she
is ;
And they will see her flying through
the air,
So bright that she will dim the noon-
day sun ;
Showering down blessings in the
shape of comfits.
This, trust a priest, is just the sort
of thing
Swine will believe. I'll wager you
will see them
Climbing upon the thatch of their low
sties ;
With pieces of smoked glass, to watch
her sail
Among the clouds, and some will
hold the flaps
Of one another's ears between their
teeth,
To catch the coming hail of comfits in.
You, Purganax, who have the gift o'
the gab,
Make them a solemn speech to this
effect :
I go to put in readiness the feast
Kept to the honour of our goddess
Famine,
Where, for more glory, let the cere-
mony
Take place of the uglification of the
Queen.
Dakry (to SWELLFOOT). I, as the
keeper of your sacred conscience,
Humbly remind your majesty that
the care
Of your high office, as man-milliner
To red Bellona, should not be de-
ferred.

Purganax. All part, in happier plight to meet again. [*Exeunt.*

ACT II

SCENE I.—*The Public Sty. The* BOARS *in full Assembly.*

Enter PURGANAX.

Purganax. Grant me your patience, gentlemen and boars,
Ye, by whose patience under public burthens
The glorious constitution of these sties
Subsists, and shall subsist. The lean pig-rates
Grow with the growing populace of swine,
The taxes, that true source of piggish-ness,
(How can I find a more appropriate term
To include religion, morals, peace, and plenty,
And all that fit Bœotia as a nation
To teach the other nations how to live ?)
Increase with piggishness itself ; and still
Does the revenue, that great spring of all
The patronage, and pensions, and by-payments,
Which freeborn pigs regard with jealous eyes,
Diminish, till at length, by glorious steps,
All the land's produce will be merged in taxes,
And the revenue will amount to——nothing !
The failure of a foreign market for
Sausages, bristles, and blood-pud-dings,
And such home manufactures, is but partial ;
And, that the population of the pigs,
Instead of hog-wash, has been fed on straw
And water, is a fact which is—you know—
That is—it is a state necessity—
Temporary, of course. Those im-pious pigs,

Who, by frequent squeaks, have dared impugn
The settled Swellfoot system, or to make
Irreverent mockery of the genu-flexions
Inculcated by the arch-priest, have been whipt
Into a loyal and an orthodox whine.
Things being in this happy state, the Queen
Iona——

A loud cry from the Pigs. She is innocent ! most innocent !
Purganax. That is the very thing that I was saying,
Gentlemen swine ; the Queen Iona being
Most innocent, no doubt, returns to Thebes,
And the lean sows and boars collect about her,
Wishing to make her think that *we* believe
(I mean those more substantial pigs, who swill
Rich hog-wash, while the others mouth damp straw)
That she is guilty ; thus, the lean pig faction
Seeks to obtain that hog-wash, which has been
Your immemorial right, and which I will
Maintain you in to the last drop of——
A Boar (interrupting him). What
Does any one accuse her of ?
Purganax. Why, no one
Makes *any* positive accusation ;—but
There were hints dropped, and so the privy wizards
Conceived that it became them to advise
His majesty to investigate their truth ;—
Not for his own sake ; he could be content
To let his wife play any pranks she pleased,
If, by that sufferance, *he* could please the pigs ;
But then he fears the morals of the swine,
The sows especially, and what effect
It might produce upon the purity and

Religion of the rising generation
Of sucking-pigs, if it could be sus-
pected
That Queen Iona—   [*A pause.*
   First Boar.   Well, go on ; we long
To hear what she can possibly have
done.
   Purganax. Why, it is hinted, that a
certain bull—
Thus much is *known* :—the milk-
white bulls that feed
Beside Clitumnus and the crystal
lakes
Of the Cisalpine mountains, in fresh
dews
Of lotus-grass and blossoming
asphodel,
Sleeking their silken hair, and with
sweet breath
Loading the morning winds until they
faint
With living fragrance, are so beauti-
ful !——   [rode
Well, *I* say nothing ;—but Europa
On such a one from Asia into Crete,
And the enamoured sea grew calm
beneath
His gliding beauty. And Pasiphaë,
Iona's grandmother,——but *she* is
innocent !
And that both you and I, and all
assert.
   First Boar. Most innocent !
   Purganax.   Behold this BAG ;
a bag—
   Second Boar. Oh! no GREEN
BAGS !! Jealousy's eyes are
green,
Scorpions are green, and water-
snakes, and efts,
And verdigris, and—
   Purganax.   Honourable swine.
In piggish souls can prepossessions
reign ?
Allow me to remind you, grass is
green—
All flesh is grass ;—no bacon but is
flesh—
Ye are but bacon. This divining
BAG
(Which is not green, but only bacon
colour)
Is filled with liquor, which if sprinkled
o'er
A woman guilty of—we all know
what—

Makes her so hideous, till she finds
one blind,
She never can commit the like again.
If innocent, she will turn into an
angel,
And rain down blessings in the shape
of comfits
As she flies up to heaven. Now, my
proposal
Is to convert her sacred majesty
Into an angel, (as I am sure we shall
do,)
By pouring on her head this mystic
water.   [*Showing the Bag.*
I know that she is innocent ; I wish
Only to prove her so to all the world.
   First Boar. Excellent, just, and
noble Purganax !
   Second Boar. How glorious it will
be to see her majesty
Flying above our heads, her petti-
coats
Streaming like—like—like——
   Third Boar.   Anything.
   Purganax.   Oh, no !
But like a standard of an admiral's
ship,
Or like the banner of a conquering
host,
Or like a cloud dyed in the dying day,
Unravelled on the blast from a white
mountain ;
Or like a meteor, or a war-steed's
mane,
Or waterfall from a dizzy precipice
Scattered upon the wind.
   First Boar.   Or a cow's tail,—
   Second Boar. Or *anything*, as the
learned boar observed.
   Purganax. Gentlemen boars, I
move a resolution,
That her most sacred majesty should
be
Invited to attend the feast of Famine,
And to receive upon her chaste white
body
Dews of Apotheosis from this BAG.
   [*A great confusion is heard of the
Pigs out of Doors, which com-
municates itself to those within.
During the first Strophe, the doors
of the Sty are staved in, and a
number of exceedingly lean Pigs
and Sows and Boars rush in.*

SEMICHORUS I.
No ! Yes !

SEMICHORUS II.
Yes! No!

SEMICHORUS I.
A law!

SEMICHORUS II.
A flaw!

SEMICHORUS I.
Porkers, we shall lose our wash,
Or must share it with the lean pigs!

FIRST BOAR.
Order! order! be not rash!
Was there ever such a scene, pigs!

AN OLD SOW (*rushing in*).
I never saw so fine a dash
Since I first began to wean pigs.

SECOND BOAR (*solemnly*).
The Queen will be an angel time
enough.
I vote, in form of an amendment, that
Purganax rub a little of that stuff
Upon his face—
  Purganax.   [*His heart is seen to
        beat through his waistcoat.*
Gods! What would ye be at?

SEMICHORUS I.
Purganax has plainly shown a
Cloven foot and jackdaw feather.

SEMICHORUS II.
I vote Swellfoot and Iona
Try the magic test together;
Whenever royal spouses bicker,
Both should try the magic liquor.

AN OLD BOAR (*aside*).
A miserable state is that of pigs,
For if their drivers would tear caps
  and wigs,
  The swine must bite each other's ear
    therefore.

AN OLD SOW (*aside*).
A wretched lot Jove has assigned to
  swine,
Squabbling makes pig-herds hungry,
  and they dine
  On bacon, and whip sucking-pigs
    the more.

CHORUS.
Hog-wash has been ta'en away:
  If the Bull-Queen is divested,

We shall be in every way
  Hunted, stript, exposed, mo-
    lested;
Let us do whate'er we may,
  That she shall not be arrested.
QUEEN, we entrench you with walls
  of brawn,
And palisades of tusks, sharp as a
  bayonet:
Place your most sacred person here.
  We pawn
Our lives that none a finger dare to
  lay on it.
  Those who wrong you, wrong
    us;
  Those who hate you, hate us;
  Those who sting you, sting us;
  Those who bait you, bait us;
  The *oracle* is now about to be
  Fulfilled by circumvolving
    destiny;
Which says: " Thebes, choose *reform*
  or *civil war*,
When through your streets, instead
  of hare with dogs,
A CONSORT-QUEEN shall hunt a
  KING with hogs,
Riding upon the IONIAN MINO-
  TAUR."

Enter IONA TAURINA.

Iona Taurina (*coming forward*).
  Gentlemen swine, and gentle
    lady-pigs,
The tender heart of every boar acquits
Their QUEEN, of any act incongruous
With native piggishness, and she
  reposing
With confidence upon the grunting
  nation,
Has thrown herself, her cause, her life,
  her all,
Her innocence, into their hoggish
  arms;
Nor has the expectation been de-
  ceived
Of finding shelter there.   Yet know,
  great boars,
(For such who ever lives among you
  finds you,
And so do I) the innocent are proud!
I have accepted your protection only
In compliment of your kind love and
  care,
Not for necessity.   The innocent

Are safest there where trials and
    dangers wait ;
Innocent Queens o'er white-hot
    plough-shares tread
Unsinged ; and ladies, Erin's laure-
    ate sings it,[1]
Decked with rare gems, and beauty
    rarer still,
Walked from Killarney to the Giant's
    Causeway,
Through rebels, smugglers, troops of
    yeomanry,
White-boys, and orange-boys, and
    constables,
Tithe-proctors, and excise-people,
    uninjured !
Thus I !—
Lord PURGANAX, I do commit myself
Into your custody, and am prepared
To stand the test, whatever it may
    be !
    Purganax. This magnanimity in
    your sacred majesty
Must please the pigs. You cannot
    fail of being
A heavenly angel. Smoke your bits
    of glass,
Ye loyal swine, or her transfiguration
Will blind your wondering eyes.
    An Old Boar (*aside*). Take care,
    my lord,
They do not smoke you first.
    Purganax. At the approaching
    feast
Of Famine, let the expiation be.
    Swine. Content ! content !
    Iona Taurina (*aside*). I, most con-
    tent of all,
Know that my foes even thus prepare
    their fall !
                   [*Exeunt omnes.*

SCENE II.—*The interior of the Temple
of* FAMINE. *The statue of the
Goddess, a skeleton clothed in party-
coloured rags, seated upon a heap
of skulls and loaves intermingled.
A number of exceedingly fat Priests
in black garments arrayed on each
side, with marrow-bones and cleavers
in their hands. A flourish of
trumpets.*

Enter MAMMON *as Arch-priest,* SWELL-

[1] " Rich and rare were the gems she wore."
        See Moore's Irish Melodies.

FOOT, DAKRY, PURGANAX, LAOC-
TONOS, *followed by* IONA TAURINA
*guarded. On the other side enter the
Swine.*

CHORUS OF PRIESTS.
*Accompanied by the Court Porkman on
marrow-bones and cleavers.*

Goddess bare, and gaunt, and pale,
Empress of the world, all hail !
What though Cretans old called thee
    City-crested Cybele ?
We call thee FAMINE !
Goddess of fasts and feasts, starving
    and cramming ;
Through thee, for emperors, kings,
    and priests and lords,
Who rule by viziers, sceptres, bank-
    notes, words,
The earth pours forth its plenteous
    fruits,
Corn, wool, linen, flesh, and roots—
Those who consume these fruits
    through thee grow fat
Those who produce these fruits
    through thee grow lean,
Whatever change takes place, oh,
    stick to that !
And let things be as they have
    ever been;
At least while we remain thy priests,
And proclaim thy fasts and feasts !
Through thee the sacred SWELLFOOT
    dynasty
Is based upon a rock amid that sea
Whose waves are swine—so let it ever
    be !
    [SWELLFOOT, *etc., seat themselves
    at a table magnificently covered
    at the upper end of the temple.
    Attendants pass over the stage with
    hog-wash in pails. A number of
    Pigs, exceedingly lean, follow
    them licking up the wash.*
    Mammon. I fear your sacred
    majesty has lost
The appetite which you were used to
    have.
Allow me now to recommend this
    dish—
A simple kickshaw by your Persian
    cook,
Such as is served at the great King's
    second table.
The price and pains which its ingredi-
    ents cost,

Might have maintained some dozen families
A winter or two—not more—so plain a dish
Could scarcely disagree.—
Swellfoot.   After the trial,
And these fastidious pigs are gone, perhaps
I may recover my lost appetite,—
I feel the gout flying about my stomach—
Give me a glass of Maraschino punch.
Purganax (filling his glass and standing up).
The Glorious Constitution of the pigs!
All. A toast! a toast! stand up, and three times three!
Dakry. No heel-taps—darken daylights!
Laoctonos.   Claret, somehow,
Puts me in mind of blood, and blood of claret!
Swellfoot. Laoctonos is fishing for a compliment,
But 'tis his due. Yes, you have drunk more wine,
And shed more blood, than any man in Thebes.
                                    [*To* PURGANAX.
For God's sake stop the grunting of those pigs.
Purganax. We dare not, sire! 'tis Famine's privilege.

CHORUS OF SWINE.

Hail to thee, hail to thee, Famine!
Thy throne is on blood, and thy robe is of rags;
Thou devil which livest on damning;
Saint of new churches, and cant, and GREEN BAGS;
Till in pity and terror thou risest,
Confounding the schemes of the wisest.
When thou liftest thy skeleton form,
When the loaves and the skulls roll about,
We will greet thee—the voice of a storm
Would be lost in our terrible shout!

Then hail to thee, hail to thee, Famine!
Hail to thee, Empress of Earth!

When thou risest, dividing possessions;
When thou risest, uprooting oppressions;
In the pride of thy ghastly mirth.
Over palaces, temples, and graves,
We will rush as thy minister-slaves,
Trampling behind in thy train,
Till all be made level again!

Mammon. I hear a crackling of the giant bones
Of the dread image, and in the black pits
Which once were eyes, I see two livid flames:
These prodigies are oracular, and show
The presence of the unseen Deity.
Mighty events are hastening to their doom!
Swellfoot. I only hear the lean and mutinous swine
Grunting about the temple.
Dakry.   In a crisis
Of such exceeding delicacy, I think
We ought to put her majesty, the QUEEN,
Upon her trial without delay.
Mammon.   The BAG
Is here.
Purganax. I have rehearsed the entire scene
With an ox-bladder and some ditch-water,
On Lady P.—it cannot fail.
                        [*Taking up the bag.*
Your majesty (*to* SWELLFOOT)
In such a filthy business had better
Stand on one side, lest it should sprinkle you.
A spot or two on me would do no harm;
Nay, it might hide the blood, which the sad genius
Of the Green Isle has fixed, as by a spell,
Upon my brow—which would stain all its seas
But which those seas could never wash away!
Iona Taurina. My lord, I am ready, —nay, I am impatient,
To undergo the test.
    [*A graceful figure in a semi-transparent veil passes unnoticed*

through the temple : the word LIBERTY *is seen through the veil, as if it were written in fire upon its forehead. Its words are almost drowned in the furious grunting of the* Pigs, *and the business of the trial. She kneels on the steps of the Altar, and speaks in tones at first faint and low, but which ever become louder and louder.*

Mighty Empress ! Death's white wife !
Ghastly mother-in-law of life !
By the God who made thee such,
By the magic of thy touch,
By the starving and thy cramming,
Of fasts and feasts !—by thy dread self, O Famine !
I charge thee ! when thou wake the multitude,
Thou lead them not upon the paths of blood.
The earth did never mean her foison
For those who crown life's cup with poison
Of fanatic rage and meaningless revenge—
    But for those radiant spirits, who are still
The standard-bearers in the van of Change.
    Be they th' appointed stewards, to fill
The lap of Pain, and Toil, and Age !—
Remit, O Queen ! thy accustom'd rage !
Be what thou art not ! In voice faint and low
FREEDOM calls *Famine*,—her eternal foe—
To brief alliance, hollow truce.—Rise now !

[*Whilst the veiled figure has been chanting this strophe,* MAMMON, DAKRY, LAOCTONOS, *and* SWELLFOOT, *have surrounded* IONA TAURINA, *who, with her hands folded on her breast, and her eyes lifted to Heaven, stands, as with saint-like resignation, to wait the issue of the business, in perfect confidence of her innocence.*

[PURGANAX, *after unsealing the*

GREEN BAG, *is gravely about to pour the liquor upon her head, when suddenly the whole expression of her figure and countenance changes ; she snatches it from his hand with a loud laugh of triumph, and empties it over* SWELLFOOT *and his whole Court, who are instantly changed into a number of filthy and ugly animals, and rush out of the temple. The image of* FAMINE *then arises with a tremendous sound, the* PIGS *begin scrambling for the loaves, and are tripped up by the skulls; all those who eat the loaves are turned into* BULLS, *and arrange themselves quietly behind the altar. The image of* FAMINE *sinks through a chasm in the earth, and a* MINOTAUR *rises.*

Minotaur. I am the Ionian Minotaur, the mightiest
Of all Europa's taurine progeny—
I am the old traditional man bull ;
And from my ancestors having been Ionian,
I am called Ion, which, by interpretation,
Is JOHN ; in plain Theban, that is to say,
My name's JOHN BULL ; I am a famous hunter,
And can leap any gate in all Bœotia,
Even the palings of the royal park,
Or double ditch about the new enclosures ;
And if your majesty will deign to mount me,
At least till you have hunted down your game,
I will not throw you.

Iona Taurina.
[*During this speech she has been putting on boots and spurs, and a hunting-cap, buckishly cocked on one side, and tucking up her hair, she leaps nimbly on his back.*

Hoa ! hoa ! tallyho ! tallyho ! ho ! ho !
Come, let us hunt these ugly badgers down,
These stinking foxes, these devouring otters,

These hares, these wolves, these any-
    thing but men.
Hey, for a whipper-in ! my loyal pigs,
Now let your noses be as keen as
    beagles',   [and your cries
Your steps as swift as greyhounds',
More dulcet and symphonious than
    the bells   [day ;
Of village towers, on sunshine holi-
Wake all the dewy woods with jang-
    ling music.
Give them no law (are they not beasts
    of blood ?)
But such as they gave you. Tallyho !
    ho !
Through forest, furze, and bog, and
    den, and desert,
Pursue the ugly beasts ! tallyho ! ho !

FULL CHORUS OF IONA AND THE
    SWINE.

    Tallyho ! tallyho .
Through rain, hail, and snow,
Through brake, gorse, and briar,
Through fen, flood, and mire,
    We go ! we go !

    Tallyho ! tallyho !
Through pond, ditch, and slough,
Wind them, and find them,
Like the devil behind them,
    Tallyho ! tallyho !

[*Exeunt, in full cry ;* IONA *driving
on the* SWINE, *with the empty*
GREEN BAG.

EARLY POEMS

A SUMMER-EVENING CHURCH-
YARD

LECHDALE, GLOUCESTERSHIRE.

THE wind has swept from the wide
    atmosphere
    Each vapour that obscured the sun-
      set's ray ;
And pallid evening twines its beaming
    hair
    In duskier braids around the lan-
      guid eyes of day :
Silence and twilight, unbeloved of
    men,
Creep hand in hand from yon obscur-
    est glen.

They breathe their spells towards the
    departing day,
    Encompassing the earth, air, stars,
      and sea ;
Light, sound, and motion own the
    potent sway,
    Responding to the charm with its
      own mystery.

The winds are still, or the dry church-
    tower grass
Knows not their gentle motions as
    they pass.

Thou too, aërial Pile ! whose pin-
    nacles
    Point from one shrine like pyramids
      of fire,
Obeyest in silence their sweet solemn
    spells,
    Clothing in hues of heaven thy dim
      and distant spire,
Around whose lessening and invisible
    height
Gather among the stars the clouds of
    night.

The dead are sleeping in their sepul-
    chres :
    And, mouldering as they sleep, a
      thrilling sound,
Half sense, half thought, among the
    darkness stirs,
    Breathed from their wormy beds all
      living things around.

And mingling with the still night and
    mute sky
Its awful hush is felt inaudibly.

Thus solemnised and softened, death
    is mild
    And terrorless as this serenest
       night :
Here could I hope, like some inquiring
    child
    Sporting on graves, that death did
       hide from human sight
Sweet secrets, or beside its breathless
    sleep
That loveliest dreams perpetual
    watch did keep.

MUTABILITY

We are as clouds that veil the mid-
    night moon ;
    How restlessly they speed, and
       gleam, and quiver,
Streaking the darkness radiantly !—
    yet soon
    Night closes round, and they are
       lost for ever ;

Or like forgotten lyres, whose disson-
    ant strings
    Give various response to each vary-
       ing blast,
To whose frail frame no second mo-
    tion brings
    One mood or modulation like the
       last.

We rest—a dream has power to poi-
    son sleep ;
    We rise—one wandering thought
       pollutes the day ;
We feel, conceive or reason, laugh or
    weep ;
    Embrace fond woe, or cast our
       cares away :

It is the same !—For, be it joy or sor-
    row,
    The path of its departure still is
       free ;
Man's yesterday may ne'er be like his
    morrow ;
    Nought may endure but Mutability.

ON DEATH

*There is no work, nor device, nor know-
ledge, nor wisdom, in the grave,
whither thou goest.*—ECCLESIASTES.

The pale, the cold, and the moony
    smile
    Which the meteor beam of a star-
       less night
Sheds on a lonely and sea-girt isle,
    Ere the dawning of morn's un-
       doubted light,
Is the flame of life so fickle and wan
That flits round our steps till their
    strength is gone.

O man ! hold thee on in courage of
    soul
    Through the stormy shades of thy
       worldly way.
And the billows of cloud that around
    thee roll
    Shall sleep in the light of a wondrous
       day,
Where hell and heaven shall leave
    thee free
To the universe of destiny.

This world is the nurse of all we know,
    This world is the mother of all we
       feel,
And the coming of death is a fearful
    blow,
    To a brain unencompassed with
       nerves of steel ;
When all that we know, or feel, or see,
Shall pass like an unreal mystery.

The secret things of the grave are
    there,
    Where all but this frame must surely
       be,
Though the fine-wrought eye and the
    wrondrous ear
    No longer will live to hear or to see
All that is great and all that is strange
In the boundless realm of unending
    change.

Who telleth a tale of unspeaking
    death ?
    Who lifteth the veil of what is to
       come ?
Who painteth the shadows that are
    beneath

The wide-winding caves of the peopled tomb ?
Or uniteth the hopes of what shall be
With the fears and the love for that which we see ?

TO COLERIDGE

ΔΑΚΡΤΕΙ ΔΙΟΙΣΩ ΠΟΤΜΟΝ ΑΠΟΤΜΟΝ

Oh ! there are spirits in the air,
  And genii of the evening breeze,
And gentle ghosts, with eyes as fair
  As starbeams among twilight
    trees :—
Such lovely ministers to meet
Oft hast thou turned from men thy lonely feet.

With mountain winds, and bab-
    bling springs,
  And mountain seas, that are the voice
Of these inexplicable things,
  Thou didst hold commune, and rejoice
When they did answer thee ; but they
Cast, like a worthless boon, thy love away.

And thou hast sought in starry eyes
  Beams that were never meant for thine,
Another's wealth ;—tame sacrifice
  To a fond faith ! still dost thou pine ?
Still dost thou hope that ungreeting hands,
Voice, looks, or lips, may answer thy demands ?

Ah ! wherefore didst thou build thine hope
  On the false earth's inconstancy?
Did thine own mind afford no scope
  Of love, or moving thoughts to thee ?
That natural scenes or human smiles
Could steal the power to wind thee in their wiles.

Yes, all the faithless smiles are fled
  Whose falsehood left thee broken-hearted ;

The glory of the moon is dead ;
  Night's ghosts and dreams have now departed ;
Thine own soul still is true to thee,
But changed to a foul fiend through misery.

This fiend, whose ghastly presence ever
  Beside thee like thy shadow hangs,
Dream not to chase ;—the mad endeavour
  Would scourge thee to severer pangs.
Be as thou art. Thy settled fate,
Dark as it is, all change would aggra-vate.

TO WORDSWORTH

Poet of Nature, thou hast wept to know
That things depart which never may return ;
Childhood and youth, friendship and love's first glow,
Have fled like sweet dreams, leaving thee to mourn.
These common woes I feel. One loss is mine,
Which thou too feel'st ; yet I alone deplore.
Thou wert as a lone star, whose light did shine
On some frail bark in winter's mid-night roar :
Thou hast like to a rock-built refuge stood
Above the blind and battling multi-tude :
In honoured poverty thy voice did weave
Songs consecrate to truth and liberty,—
Deserting these, thou leavest me to grieve,
Thus having been, that thou shouldst cease to be.

LINES

The cold earth slept below,
  Above the cold sky shone,
    And all around
    With a chilling sound,

From caves of ice and fields of snow,
The breath of night like death did
    flow
    Beneath the sinking moon.

The wintry hedge was black,
    The green grass was not seen,
      The birds did rest
      On the bare thorn's breast,
Whose roots beside the pathway
    track,
Had bound their folds o'er many a
    crack
      Which the frost had made be-
      tween.

Thine eyes glowed in the glare
    Of the moon's dying light,
      As a fen-fire's beam
      On a sluggish stream
Gleams dimly—so the moon shone
    there,
And it yellowed the strings of thy
    tangled hair,
      That shook in the wind of night.

The moon made thy lips pale, beloved;
    The wind made thy bosom chill ;
      The night did shed
      On thy dear head
Its frozen dew, and thou didst lie
Where the bitter breath of the naked
    sky
      Might visit thee at will.

STANZAS.—APRIL, 1814

AWAY ! the moor is dark beneath the
    moon,
    Rapid clouds have drunk the last
    pale beam of even :
Away ! the gathering winds will call
    the darkness soon,
    And profoundest midnight shroud
    the serene lights of heaven.
Pause not ! The time is past ! Every
    voice cries, " Away ! "
    Tempt not with one last glance thy
    friend's ungentle mood :
Thy lover's eye, so glazed and cold,
    dares not entreat thy stay
    Duty and dereliction guide thee
    back to solitude.

Away, away ! to thy sad and silent
    home ;
    Pour bitter tears on its desolated
    hearth ;
Watch the dim shades as like ghosts
    they go and come,
    And complicate strange webs of
    melancholy mirth.
The leaves of wasted autumn woods
    shall float around thine head,
    The blooms of dewy spring shall
    gleam beneath thy feet :
But thy soul or this world must fade
    in the frost that binds the dead,
    Ere midnight's frown and morn-
    ing's smile, ere thou and peace
    may meet.

The cloud shadows of midnight pos-
    sess their own repose,
    For the weary winds are silent, or
    the moon is in the deep ;
Some respite to its turbulence unrest-
    ing ocean knows ;
    Whatever moves, or toils, or grieves
    hath its appointed sleep.
Thou in the grave shalt rest—yet till
    the phantoms flee
    Which that house and heath and
    garden made dear to thee ere-
    while,
Thy remembrance, and repentance,
    and deep musings, are not free
    From the music of two voices, and
    the light of one sweet smile.

FEELINGS OF A REPUBLICAN ON THE FALL OF BONAPARTE

I HATED thee, fallen tyrant ! I did
    groan
To think that a most unambitious
    slave,
Like thou, shouldst dance and revel on
    the grave
Of Liberty. Thou mightst have
    built thy throne
Where it had stood even now : thou
    didst prefer
A frail and bloody pomp, which time
    has swept
In fragments towards oblivion. Mas-
    sacre,
For this I prayed, would on thy sleep
    have crept,

Treason and Slavery, Rapine, Fear
and Lust, [know
And stifled thee, their minister. I
Too late, since thou and France are
in the dust,

That Virtue owns a more eternal foe
Than force or fraud : old Custom,
legal Crime,
And bloody Faith, the foulest birth of
time.

POEMS WRITTEN IN 1816

THE SUNSET

THERE late was One, within whose
subtle being,
As light and wind within some deli-
cate cloud
That fades amid the blue noon's burn-
ing sky,
Genius and death contended. None
may know
The sweetness of the joy which made
his breath
Fail, like the trances of the summer
air,
When, with the Lady of his love, who
then
First knew the unreserve of mingled
being,
He walked along the pathway of a
field,
Which to the east a hoar wood
shadowed o'er,
But to the west was open to the sky.
There now the sun had sunk, but lines
of gold
Hung on the ashen clouds, and on the
points
Of the far level grass and nodding
flowers,
And the old dandelion's hoary beard,
And, mingled with the shades of twi-
light, lay
On the brown massy woods—and in
the east
The broad and burning moon linger-
ingly rose
Between the black trunks of the
crowded trees,
While the faint stars were gathering
overhead.—
" Is it not strange, Isabel," said the
youth,

" I never saw the sun ? We will walk
here
To-morrow ; thou shalt look on it
with me."
That night the youth and lady min-
gled lay
In love and sleep—but when the
morning came
The lady found her lover dead and
cold.
Let none believe that God in mercy
gave
That stroke. The lady died not, nor
grew wild,
But year by year lived on—in truth
I think
Her gentleness and patience and sad
smiles,
And that she did not die, but lived to
tend
Her aged father, were a kind of mad-
ness,
If madness 'tis to be unlike the world.
For but to see her were to read the
tale
Woven by some subtlest bard, to
make hard hearts
Dissolve away in wisdom-working
grief ;—
Her eyelashes were torn away with
tears,
Her lips and cheeks were like things
dead—so pale ;
Her hands were thin, and through
their wandering veins
And weak articulations might be seen
Day's ruddy light. The tomb of thy
dead self
Which one vexed ghost inhabits,
night and day,
Is all, lost child, that now remains of
thee !

" Inheritor of more than earth can give,
Passionless calm, and silence unre-
proved,
Whether the dead find, oh, not sleep !
but rest,
And are the uncomplaining things
they seem,
Or live, or drop in the deep sea of
Love ;
Oh, that like thine, mine epitaph were
—Peace ! "
This was the only moan she ever
made.

HYMN TO INTELLECTUAL BEAUTY

The awful shadow of some unseen
Power
Floats tho' unseen among us ;
visiting
This various world with as incon-
stant wing
As summer winds that creep from
flower to flower :
Like moonbeams that behind some
piny mountain shower,
It visits with inconstant glance
Each human heart and counten-
ance ;
Like hues and harmonies of evening,
Like clouds in starlight widely
spread,
Like memory of music fled,
Like aught that for its grace may
be
Dear and yet dearer for its mystery.—

Spirit of BEAUTY, that dost consecrate
With thine own hues all thou dost
shine upon
Of human thought or form, where
art thou gone ?
Why dost thou pass away and leave
our state,
This dim vast vale of tears, vacant
and desolate ?
Ask why the sunlight not for ever
Weaves rainbows o'er yon mountain river ;
Why aught should fail and fade that
once is shown ;

Why fear and dream and death
and birth
Cast on the daylight of this earth
Such gloom ; why man has such
a scope
For love and hate, despondency and
hope ;

No voice from some sublimer world
hath ever
To sage or poet these responses
given :
Therefore the names of Demon,
Ghost, and Heaven,
Remain the records of their vain
endeavour ;
Frail spells, whose uttered charm
might not avail to sever,
From all we hear and all we see,
Doubt, chance, and mutability.
Thy light alone, like mist o'er moun-
tains driven,
Or music by the night wind sent
Through strings of some still in-
strument,
Or moonlight on a midnight
stream,
Gives grace and truth to life's unquiet
dream.

Love, Hope, and Self-esteem, like
clouds depart
And come, for some uncertain mo-
ments lent.
Man were immortal and omnipo-
tent,
Didst thou, unknown and awful as
thou art,
Keep with thy glorious train firm
state within his heart.
Thou messenger of sympathies
That wax and wane in lovers'
eyes ;
Thou, that to human thought art
nourishment,
Like darkness to a dying flame !
Depart not as thy shadow came :
Depart not, lest the grave should
be,
Like life and fear, a dark reality.

While yet a boy I sought for ghosts,
and sped
Thro' many a listening chamber,
cave, and ruin,

And starlight wood, with fearful
    steps pursuing
Hopes of high talk with the departed
    dead.
I called on poisonous names with
    which our youth is fed
    I was not heard, I saw them not ;
    When musing deeply on the lot
Of life, at that sweet time when winds
    are wooing
    All vital things that wake to
      bring
    News of birds and blossoming,
    Sudden, thy shadow fell on me ;
I shrieked, and clasped my hands in
    ecstasy !

I vowed that I would dedicate my
    powers
    To thee and thine : have I not kept
    the vow ?
    With beating heart and streaming
    eyes, even now
I call the phantoms of a thousand
    hours
Each from his voiceless grave : they
    have in visioned bowers
    Of studious zeal or love's delight
    Outwatched with me the envious
    night :
They know that never joy illumed
    my brow,
    Unlinked with hope that thou
    wouldst free
    This world from its dark slavery,
    That thou, O awful LOVELINESS,
Wouldst give whate'er these words
    cannot express.

The day becomes more solemn and
    serene
    When noon is past : there is a har-
    mony
    In autumn, and a lustre in its sky,
Which thro' the summer is not heard
    nor seen,
As if it could not be, as if it had not
    been !
    Thus let thy power, which like
    the truth
    Of nature on my passive youth
Descended, to my onward life supply
    Its calm, to one who worships
    thee,
    And every form containing thee,

Whom, SPIRIT fair, thy spells did
    bind
To fear himself, and love all human-
    kind.

MONT BLANC

LINES WRITTEN IN THE VALE OF
CHAMOUNI

I

THE everlasting universe of things
Flows through the mind, and rolls its
    rapid waves,
Now dark—now glittering—now re-
    flecting gloom—
Now lending splendour, where from
    secret springs
The source of human thought its
    tribute brings
Of waters,—with a sound but half its
    own,
Such as a feeble brook will oft assume
In the wild woods, among the moun-
    tains lone,
Where waterfalls around it leap for
    ever,
Where woods and winds contend, and
    a vast river
Over its rocks ceaselessly bursts and
    raves.

II

Thus thou, Ravine of Arve—dark,
    deep Ravine—
Thou many-coloured, many-voiced
    vale,
Over whose pines and crags and cav-
    erns sail
Fast clouds, shadows, and sunbeams ;
    awful scene,
Where Power in likeness of the Arve
    comes down
From the ice-gulfs that gird his secret
    throne,
Bursting through these dark moun-
    tains like the flame
Of lightning through the tempest ;
    thou dost lie,
The giant brood of pines around thee
    clinging,
Children of elder time, in whose devo-
    tion,
The chainless winds still come and
    ever came

To drink their odours, and their
    mighty swinging
To hear—an old and solemn har-
    mony:
Thine earthly rainbows stretched
    across the sweep
Of the ethereal waterfall, whose veil
Robes some unsculptured image ; the
    strange sleep
Which, when the voices of the desert
    fail,
Wraps all in its own deep eternity ;—
Thy caverns echoing to the Arve's
    commotion
A loud, lone sound, no other sound
    can tame ;
Thou art pervaded with that cease-
    less motion,
Thou art the path of that unresting
    sound—
Dizzy Ravine ! and when I gaze on
    thee,
I seem as in a trance sublime and
    strange
To muse on my own separate fantasy,
My own, my human mind, which pas-
    sively,
Now renders and receives fast influ-
    encings,
Holding an unremitting interchange
With the clear universe of things
    around ;
One legion of wild thoughts, whose
    wandering wings
Now float above thy darkness, and
    now rest
Where that or thou art no unbidden
    guest,
In the still cave of the witch Poesy,
Seeking among the shadows that pass
    by
Ghosts of all things that are, some
    shade of thee,
Some phantom, some faint image ;
    till the breast
From which they fled recalls them,
    thou art there !

III

Some say that gleams of a remoter
    world
Visit the soul in sleep,—that death is
    slumber,
And that its shapes the busy thoughts
    outnumber

Of those who wake and live. I look
    on high ;
Has some unknown omnipotence un-
    furled
The veil of life and death ? or do I lie
In dream, and does the mightier world
    of sleep
Speed far around and inaccessibly
Its circles ? For the very spirit fails,
Driven like a homeless cloud from
    steep to steep
That vanishes among the viewless
    gales !
Far, far above, piercing the infinite
    sky,
Mont Blanc appears,—still, snowy,
    and serene—   [forms
Its subject mountains their unearthly
Pile around it, ice and rock ; broad
    vales between
Of frozen flood, unfathomable deeps,
Blue as the overhanging heaven, that
    spread   [steeps ;
And wind among the accumulated
A desert peopled by the storms alone,
Save when the eagle brings some hun-
    ter's bone,
And the wolf tracks her there—how
    hideously
Its shapes are heaped around ! rude,
    bare, and high,
Ghastly, and scarred, and riven.—Is
    this the scene
Where the old Earthquake-demon
    taught her young
Ruin ? Were these their toys ? or
    did a sea
Of fire envelope once this silent snow ?
None can reply—all seems eternal
    now.
The wilderness has a mysterious
    tongue
Which teaches awful doubt, or faith
    so mild,
So solemn, so serene, that man may
    be
But for such faith with nature recon-
    ciled ;
Thou hast a voice, great Mountain,
    to repeal
Large codes of fraud and woe ; not
    understood,
By all, but which the wise, and great,
    and good,
Interpret or make felt, or deeply feel.

IV

The fields, the lakes, the forests, and
the streams,
Ocean, and all the living things that
dwell
Within the dædal earth ; lightning,
and rain,
Earthquake, and fiery flood, and
hurricane,
The torpor of the year when feeble
dreams
Visit the hidden buds, or dreamless
sleep
Holds every future leaf and flower,—
the bound
With which from that detested trance
they leap ;
The works and ways of man, their
death and birth,
And that of him, and all that his may
be ;
All things that move and breathe with
toil and sound
Are born and die, revolve, subside,
and swell.
Power dwells apart in its tranquillity,
Remote, serene, and inaccessible :
And *this*, the naked countenance of
earth,
On which I gaze, even these primæval
mountains,
Teach the adverting mind. The gla-
ciers creep,
Like snakes that watch their prey,
from their far fountains,
Slowly rolling on ; there, many a
precipice
Frost and the Sun in scorn of mortal
power
Have piled—dome, pyramid, and
pinnacle,
A city of death, distinct with many a
tower
And wall impregnable of beaming ice.
Yet not a city, but a flood of ruin
Is there, that from the boundaries of
the sky
Rolls its perpetual stream ; vast
pines are strewing
Its destined path, or in the mangled
soil
Branchless and shattered stand ; the
rocks, drawn down
From yon remotest waste, have over-
thrown

The limits of the dead and living
world,
Never to be reclaimed. The dwelling-
place
Of insects, beasts, and birds, becomes
its spoil ;
Their food and their retreat for ever
gone,
So much of life and joy is lost. The
race
Of man flies far in dread ; his work
and dwelling
Vanish, like smoke before the tem-
pest's stream,
And their place is not known. Below,
vast caves
Shine in the rushing torrent's restless
gleam,
Which from those secret chasms in
tumult welling
Meet in the Vale, and one majestic
River,
The breath and blood of distant lands,
for ever
Rolls its loud waters to the ocean
waves,
Breathes its swift vapours to the cir-
cling air.

V

Mont Blanc yet gleams on high : the
power is there,
The still and solemn power of many
sights
And many sounds, and much of life
and death.
In the calm darkness of the moonless
nights,
In the long glare of day, the snows
descend
Upon that Mountain ; none beholds
them there,
Nor when the flakes burn in the sink-
ing sun,
Or the starbeams dart through them :
—Winds contend
Silently there, and heap the snow,
with breath
Rapid and strong, but silently! Its
home
The voiceless lightning in these soli-
tudes
Keeps innocently, and like vapour
broods

Over the snow.   The secret strength
of things,
Which governs thought, and to the
infinite dome
Of heaven is as a law, inhabits thee !

And what were thou, and earth, and
stars, and sea,
If to the human mind's imaginings
Silence and solitude were vacancy ?

SWITZERLAND, *June* 23, 1816.

POEMS WRITTEN IN 1817

PRINCE ATHANASE

A FRAGMENT

PART I

THERE was a youth, who, as with toil
and travel,
Had grown quite weak and grey before his time ;
Nor any could the restless griefs unravel

Which burned within him, withering
up his prime
And goading him, like fiends, from
land to land.
Not his the load of any secret crime,

For nought of ill his heart could
understand,
But pity and wild sorrow for the
same ;
Not his the thirst for glory or command,

Baffled with blast of hope-consuming
shame ;
Nor evil joys which fire the vulgar
breast,
And quench in speedy smoke its feeble
flame,

Had left within his soul the dark unrest :
Nor what religion fables of the grave
Feared he,—Philosophy's accepted
guest.

For none than he a purer heart could
have,
Or that loved good more for itself
alone ;
Of nought in heaven or earth was he
the slave.

What sorrow, strange, and shadowy,
and unknown,

Sent him, a hopeless wanderer,
through mankind ?—
If with a human sadness he did groan,

He had a gentle yet aspiring mind ;
Just, innocent, with varied learning
fed ;
And such a glorious consolation find

In others' joy, when all their own is
dead :
He loved, and laboured for his kind
in grief,
And yet, unlike all others, it is said

That from such toil he never found
relief.
Although a child of fortune and of
power,   [chief,
Of an ancestral name the orphan

His soul had wedded wisdom, and her
dower
Is love and justice, clothed in which
he sate
Apart from men, as in a lonely tower,

Pitying the tumult of their dark
estate.—
Yet even in youth did he not e'er
abuse
The strength of wealth or thought, to
consecrate

Those false opinions which the harsh
rich use
To blind the world they famish for
their pride ;
Nor did he hold from any man his
dues,

But, like a steward in honest dealings
tried,
With those who toiled and wept, the
poor and wise,
His riches and his cares he did divide.

Fearless he was, and scorning all disguise,
What he dared do or think, though
men might start,
He spoke with mild yet unaverted
eyes ;

Liberal he was of soul, and frank of
heart,
And to his many friends—all loved
him well—
Whate'er he knew or felt he would
impart,

If words he found those inmost
thoughts to tell ;
If not, he smiled or wept ; and his
weak foes
He neither spurned nor hated—
though with fell

And mortal hate their thousand
voices rose,
They passed like aimless arrows from
his ear.—
Nor did his heart or mind its portal
close

To those, or them, or any, whom life's
sphere
May comprehend within its wide
array.
What sadness made that vernal spirit
sere ?

He knew not. Though his life day
after day,
Was failing, like an unreplenished
stream ;
Though in his eyes a cloud and burthen lay,

Through which his soul, like Vesper's
serene beam
Piercing the chasms of ever rising
clouds,
Shone, softly burning ; though his
lips did seem

Like reeds which quiver in impetuous
floods ;
And through his sleep, and o'er each
waking hour,
Thoughts after thoughts, unresting
multitudes,

Were driven within him by some
secret power,
Which bade them blaze, and live, and
roll afar,

Like lights and sounds, from haunted
tower to tower,

O'er castled mountains borne, when
tempest's war
Is levied by the night-contending
winds,
And the pale dalesmen watch with
eager ear ;—

Though such were in his spirit, as the
fiends
Which wake and feed on everliving
woe,—
What was this grief, which ne'er in
other minds

A mirror found, he knew not,
none could know ;
But on whoe'er might question him he
turned
The light of his frank eyes, as if to
show

He knew not of the grief within that
burned,
But asked forbearance with a mournful look ;
Or spoke in words from which none
ever learned

The cause of his disquietude ; or
shook
With spasms of silent passion ; or
turned pale :
So that his friends soon rarely under-
took

To stir his secret pain without
avail ;—
For all who knew and loved him then
perceived
That there was drawn an adamantine
veil

Between his heart and mind,—both
unrelieved
Wrought in his brain and bosom
separate strife.
Some said that he was mad, others
believed

That memories of an antenatal life
Made this, where now he dwelt, a
penal hell :
And others said that such mysterious
grief

From God's displeasure, like a darkness, fell

On souls like his, which owned no
    higher law
Than love—love, calm, steadfast, in-
    vincible

By mortal fear or supernatural awe ;
And others,—" 'Tis the shadow of a
    dream
Which the veiled eye of memory never
    saw,

" But through the soul's abyss, like
    some dark stream
Through shattered mines and caverns
    underground
Rolls, shaking its foundations ; and no
    beam

" Of joy may rise, but it is quenched
    and drowned
In the dim whirlpools of this dream
    obscure.
Soon its exhausted waters will have
    found

" A lair of rest beneath thy spirit pure,
O Athanase !—in one so good and
    great,
Evil or tumult cannot long endure."

So spake they : idly of another's state
Babbling vain words and fond philo-
    sophy :
This was their consolation ; such de-
    bate

Men held with one another ; nor did
    he,
Like one who labours with a human
    woe,
Decline this talk ; as if its theme
    might be

Another, not himself, he to and fro
Questioned and canvassed it with
    subtlest wit ;
And none but those who loved him
    best could know

That which he knew not, how it galled
    and bit
His weary mind, this converse vain
    and cold ;
For like an eyeless nightmare grief
    did sit

Upon his being ; a snake which fold
    by fold
Pressed out the life of life, a clinging
    fiend

Which clenched him if he stirred with
    deadlier hold ;—
And so his grief remained—let it re-
    main—untold.[1]

FRAGMENTS OF PRINCE ATHANASE [2]

PART II

FRAGMENT I

PRINCE ATHANASE had one beloved
    friend,
An old, old man, with hair of silver
    white,
And lips where heavenly smiles would
    hang and blend

With his wise words ; and eyes whose
    arrowy light
Shone like the reflex of a thousand
    minds.
He was the last whom superstition's
    blight

Had spared in Greece—the blight that
    cramps and blinds,—
And in his olive bower at Œnoe
Had sate from earliest youth.   Like
    one who finds

[1] The Author was pursuing a fuller development of the ideal character of Athanase, when
it struck him that in an attempt at extreme
refinement and analysis, his conceptions might
be betrayed into the assuming a morbid character. The reader will judge whether he is a
loser or gainer by this difference.—*Author's Note.*

[2] The idea Shelley had formed of Prince Athanase was a good deal modelled on Alastor. In the
first sketch of the Poem he named it Pandemos
and Urania. Athanase seeks through the
world the One whom he may love. He meets,
in the ship in which he is embarked, a lady, who
appears to him to embody his ideal of love and
beauty. But she proves to be Pandemos, or
the earthly and unworthy Venus, who, after
disappointing his cherished dreams and hopes,
deserts him. Athanase, crushed by sorrow,
pines and dies. " On his death bed the lady,
who can really reply to his soul, comes and kisses
his lips."—*The Death bed of Athanase.*   The poet
describes her—

Her hair was brown, her sphered eyes were brown,
And in their dark and liquid moisture swam,
Like the dim orb of the eclipsed moon ;

Yet when the spirit flashed beneath, there came
The light from them, as when tears of delight
Double the western planet's serene flame.

This slender note is all we have to aid our imagination in shaping out the form of the poem,
such as its author imaged.—*M.S.*

A fertile island in the barren sea,
One mariner who has survived his
  mates
Many a drear month in a great ship—
  so he

With soul-sustaining songs, and sweet
  debates
Of ancient lore, there fed his lonely
  being :
" The mind becomes that which it
  contemplates,"—

And thus Zonoras, by for ever seeing
Their bright creations, grew like wisest men ;
And when he heard the crash of nations fleeing

A bloodier power than ruled thy ruins
  then,
O sacred Hellas ! many weary years
He wandered, till the path of Laian's
  glen

Was grass-grown—and the unremembered tears
Were dry in Laian for their honoured
  chief,
Who fell in Byzant, pierced by Moslem spears :—

And as the lady looked with faithful
  grief
From her high lattice o'er the rugged
  path,
Where she once saw that horseman
  toil, with brief

And blighting hope, who with the
  news of death
Struck body and soul as with a mortal
  blight,
She saw beneath the chestnuts far beneath,

An old man toiling up, a weary wight ;
And soon within her hospitable hall
She saw his white hairs glittering in
  the light

Of the wood fire, and round his shoulders fall,
And his wan visage and his withered
  mien,
Yet calm and gentle and majestical.

And Athanase, her child, who must
  have been

Then three years old, sate opposite
  and gazed
In patient silence.

SUCH was Zonoras ; and as daylight
  finds
One amaranth glittering on the path
  of frost,
When autumn nights have nipt all
  weaker kinds,

Thus through his age, dark, cold, and
  tempest-tost,
Shone truth upon Zonoras ; and he
  filled
From fountains pure, nigh overgrown
  and lost,

The spirit of Prince Athanase, a child,
With soul-sustaining songs of ancient
  lore
And philosophic wisdom, clear and
  mild.

And sweet and subtle talk now ever-
  more,
The pupil and the master shared ;
  until,
Sharing that undiminishable store,

The youth, as shadows on a grassy
  hill
Outrun the winds that chase them,
  soon outran
His teacher, and did teach with native skill

Strange truths and new to that experienced man.
Still they were friends, as few have
  ever been
Who mark the extremes of life's discordant span.

So in the caverns of the forest green,
Or by the rocks of echoing ocean hoar,
Zonoras and Prince Athanase were
  seen

By summer woodmen ; and when
  winter's roar
Sounded o'er earth and sea its blast
  of war,
The Balearic fisher, driven from
  shore,

Hanging upon the peaked wave afar,
Then saw their lamp from Laian's
  turret gleam,

Piercing the stormy darkness, like a star

Which pours beyond the sea one steadfast beam,
Whilst all the constellations of the sky
Seemed reeling through the storm ; they did but seem—

For, lo ! the wintry clouds are all gone by,
And bright Arcturus through yon pines is glowing,
And far o'er southern waves, immovably

Belted Orion hangs—warm light is flowing
From the young moon into the sunset's chasm.—

" O summer eve ! with power divine, bestowing

" On thine own bird the sweet enthusiasm
Which overflows in notes of liquid gladness,
Filling the sky like light ! How many a spasm

" Of fevered brains, oppressed with grief and madness,
Were lulled by thee, delightful nightingale !
And these soft waves, murmuring a gentle sadness,

" And the far sighings of yon piny dale
Made vocal by some wind, we feel not here.—
I bear alone what nothing may avail

" To lighten—a strange load ! "—No human ear
Heard this lament ; but o'er the visage wan
Of Athanase, a ruffling atmosphere

Of dark emotion, a swift shadow ran,
Like wind upon some forest-bosomed lake,
Glassy and dark.—And that divine old man

Beheld his mystic friend's whole being shake,
Even where its inmost depths were gloomiest—
And with a calm and measured voice he spake,

And, with a soft and equal pressure, prest
That cold lean hand :—" Dost thou remember yet
When the curved moon then lingering in the west

" Paused, in yon waves her mighty horns to wet,
How in those beams we walked, half resting on the sea ?
'Tis just one year—sure thou dost not forget—

" Then Plato's words of light in thee and me
Lingered like moonlight in the moonless east,
For we had just then read—thy memory

" Is faithful now—the story of the feast ;
And Agathon and Diotima seemed
From death and dark forgetfulness released."

FRAGMENT III

'TWAS at the season when the Earth upsprings
From slumber, as a sphered angel's child,
Shadowing its eyes with green and golden wings,

Stands up before its mother bright and mild,
Of whose soft voice the air expectant seems—
So stood before the sun, which shone and smiled

To see it rise thus joyous from its dreams,
The fresh and radiant Earth. The hoary grove
Waxed green—the flowers burst forth like starry beams ;—

The grass in the warm sun did start and move,
And sea-buds burst beneath the waves serene :—
How many a one, though none be near to love,

Loves then the shade of his own soul, half seen

In any mirror—or the spring's young
    minions,
The winged leaves amid the copses
    green ;—

How many a spirit then puts on the
    pinions
Of fancy, and outstrips the lagging
    blast,
And his own steps—and over wide
    dominions

Sweeps in his dream-drawn chariot,
    far and fast,
More fleet than storms—the wide
    world shrinks below,
When winter and despondency are
    past.

'Twas at this season that Prince
    Athanase
Pass'd the white Alps—those eagle-
    baffling mountains
Slept in their shrouds of snow ;—be-
    side the ways

The waterfalls were voiceless—for
    their fountains
Were changed to mines of sunless
    crystal now,
Or by the curdling winds—like brazen
    wings

Which clanged along the mountain's
    marble brow—
Warped into adamantine fretwork,
    hung
And filled with frozen light the
    chasm below.

FRAGMENT IV

THOU art the wine whose drunkenness
    is all
We can desire, O Love ! and happy
    souls,
Ere from thy vine the leaves of au-
    tumn fall,

Catch thee, and feed from their o'er-
    flowing bowls
Thousands who thirst for thy am-
    brosial dew ;
Thou art the radiance which where
    ocean rolls

Investest it ; and when the heavens
    are blue

Thou fillest them ; and when the
    earth is fair,
The shadow of thy moving wings im-
    bue

Its deserts and its mountains, till they
    wear
Beauty like some bright robe ;—thou
    ever soarest
Among the towers of men, and as soft
    air

In spring, which moves the un-
    awakened forest,
Clothing with leaves its branches bare
    and bleak,
Thou floatest among men ; and aye
    implorest

That which from thee they should
    implore :—the weak
Alone kneel to thee, offering up the
    hearts
The strong have broken—yet where
    shall any seek

A garment whom thou clothest not ?

MARLOW, 1817.

MARIANNE'S DREAM

A PALE dream came to a Lady fair,
    And said, "A boon, a boon, I pray !
I know the secrets of the air ;
    And things are lost in the glare of
    day,
Which I can make the sleeping see,
If they will put their trust in me.

"And thou shalt know of things un-
    known,
    If thou wilt let me rest between
The veiny lids, whose fringe is thrown
    Over thine eyes so dark and sheen":
And half in hope, and half in fright,
The Lady closed her eyes so bright.

At first all deadly shapes were driven
    Tumultuously across her sleep,
And o'er the vast cope of bending
    heaven
    All ghastly-visaged clouds did
    sweep;
And the Lady ever looked to spy
If the gold sun shone forth on high.

And as towards the east she turned,
    She saw aloft in the morning air,

Which now with hues of sunrise
burned,
  A great black Anchor rising there ;
And wherever the Lady turned her
eyes
It hung before her in the skies.

The sky was blue as the summer sea,
  The depths were cloudless over-
head.
The air was calm as it could be,
  There was no sight nor sound of
dread,
But that black Anchor floating still
Over the piny eastern hill.

The Lady grew sick with a weight of
fear,
  To see that Anchor ever hanging,
And veiled her eyes ; she then did
hear
  The sound as of a dim low clanging,
And looked abroad if she might know
Was it aught else, or but the flow
Of the blood in her own veins, to and
fro.

There was a mist in the sunless air,
  Which shook as it were with an
earthquake shock,
But the very weeds that blossomed
there
  Were moveless, and each mighty
rock
Stood on its basis steadfastly ;
The Anchor was seen no more on high.

But piled around with summits hid
  In lines of cloud at intervals,
Stood many a mountain pyramid
  Among whose everlasting walls
Two mighty cities shone, and ever
Through the red mists their domes did
quiver.

On two dread mountains, from whose
crest,
  Might seem, the eagle for her brood
Would ne'er have hung her dizzy nest
  Those tower-encircled cities stood.
A vision strange such towers to see,
Sculptured and wrought so gor-
geously,
Where human art could never be.

And columns framed of marble white,
  And giant fanes, dome over dome

Piled, and triumphant gates, all
bright
  With workmanship, which could
not come
From touch of mortal instrument,
Shot o'er the vales, or lustre lent
From its own shapes magnificent.

But still the Lady heard that clang
  Filling the wide air far away ;
And still the mist whose light did
hang
  Among the mountains shook alway,
So that the Lady's heart beat fast,
As half in joy and half aghast,
On those high domes her look she
cast.

Sudden from out that city sprung
  A light that made the earth grow
red ;
Two flames that each with quivering
tongue
Licked its high domes, and overhead
Among those mighty towers and
fanes
Dropped fire, as a volcano rains
Its sulphurous ruin on the plains.

And hark ! a rush, as if the deep
  Had burst its bonds ; she looked
behind
And saw over the western steep
  A raging flood descend, and wind
Through that wide vale : she felt no
fear,
But said within herself, " 'Tis clear
These towers are Nature's own, and
she
To save them has sent forth the sea."

And now those raging billows came
  Where that fair Lady sate, and she
Was borne towards the showering
flame
  By the wild waves heaped tumultu-
ously,
And, on a little plank, the flow
Of the whirlpool bore her to and fro.

The waves were fiercely vomited
  From every tower and every dome,
And dreary light did widely shed
  O'er that vast flood's suspended
foam,
Beneath the smoke which hung its
night
On the stained cope of heaven's light.

The plank whereon that Lady sate
  Was driven through the chasms
    about and about,
Between the peaks so desolate
  Of the drowning mountain, in and
    out,
As the thistle-beard on a whirlwind
    sails—
While the flood was filling those hol-
    low vales.

At last her plank an eddy crost,
  And bore her to the city's wall,
Which now the flood had reached al-
    most;
  It might the stoutest heart appall
To hear the fire roar and hiss
Through the domes of those mighty
    palaces.

The eddy whirled her round and round
  Before a gorgeous gate, which stood
Piercing the clouds of smoke which
    bound
  Its aëry arch with light like blood;
She looked on that gate of marble
    clear
With wonder that extinguished fear.

For it was filled with sculptures rarest
  Of forms most beautiful and
    strange,
Like nothing human, but the fairest
  Of winged shapes, whose legions
    range
Throughout the sleep of those who are,
Like this same Lady, good and fair.

And as she looked, still lovelier grew
  Those marble forms; the sculptor
    sure
Was a strong spirit, and the hue
  Of his own mind did there endure
After the touch, whose power had
    braided
Such grace, was in some sad change
    faded.

She looked, the flames were dim, the
    flood
  Grew tranquil as a woodland river
Winding through hills in solitude;
  Those marble shapes then seemed to
    quiver
And their fair limbs to float in motion,
Like weeds unfolding in the ocean.

And their lips moved; one seemed to
    speak,
  When suddenly the mountain
    crackt,
And through the chasm the floor did
    break
  With an earth-uplifting cataract:
The statues gave a joyous scream,
And on its wings the pale thin dream
Lifted the Lady from the stream.

The dizzy flight of that phantom pale
  Waked the fair Lady from her sleep,
And she arose, while from the veil
  Of her dark eyes the dream did
    creep;
And she walked about as one who
    knew
That sleep has sights as clear and true
As any waking eyes can view.

DEATH

THEY die—the dead return not.—
    Misery
  Sits near an open grave and calls
    them over,
A youth with hoary hair and haggard
    eye—
  They are names of kindred, friend
    and lover,
Which he so feebly calls—they all are
    gone!
Fond wretch, all dead, those vacant
    names alone,
  This most familiar scene, my
    pain—
  These tombs alone remain.

Misery, my sweetest friend—oh!
    weep no more!
  Thou wilt not be consoled—I
    wonder not:
For I have seen thee from thy dwell-
    ing's door
  Watch the calm sunset with
    them, and this spot
Was even as bright and calm, but
    transitory,
And now thy hopes are gone, thy
    hair is hoary;
  This most familiar scene, my
    pain—
  These tombs alone remain.

TO CONSTANTIA

SINGING

Thus to be lost and thus to sink and
die,
  Perchance were death indeed !—
  Constantia, turn !
In thy dark eyes a power like light
doth lie,
  Even though the sounds which were
  thy voice, which burn
Between thy lips, are laid to sleep ;
  Within thy breath, and on thy hair,
  like odour, it is yet,
And from thy touch like fire doth leap.
  Even while I write, my burning
  cheeks are wet,
  Alas, that the torn heart can bleed,
  but not forget !

A breathless awe, like the swift change
  Unseen but felt in youthful slum-
  bers,
Wild, sweet, but uncommunicably
  strange,
  Thou breathest now in fast ascend-
  ing numbers.
The cope of heaven seems rent and
  cloven
  By the enchantment of thy strain,
And on my shoulders wings are woven,
  To follow its sublime career,
Beyond the mighty moons that wane
  Upon the verge of nature's utmost
  sphere,
  Till the world's shadowy walls are
  passed and disappear.

Her voice is hovering o'er my soul—
  it lingers
  O'ershadowing it with soft and
  lulling wings,
The blood and life within those snowy
  fingers
  Teach witchcraft to the instru-
  mental strings.
My brain is wild, my breath comes
  quick—
  The blood is listening in my frame,
And thronging shadows, fast and
  thick,
  Fall on my overflowing eyes ;
My heart is quivering like a flame ;
  As morning dew, that in the sun-
  beam dies,
  I am dissolved in these consuming
  ecstasies.

I have no life, Constantia, now, but
  thee,
  Whilst, like the world-surrounding
  air, thy song
Flows on, and fills all things with
  melody.—
  Now is thy voice a tempest swift
  and strong,
On which, like one in trance upborne,
  Secure o'er rocks and waves I
  sweep,
Rejoicing like a cloud of morn.
  Now 'tis the breath of summer
  night,
Which, when the starry waters sleep,
  Round western isles, with incense-
  blossoms bright
  Lingering, suspends my soul in its
  voluptuous flight.

TO CONSTANTIA

The rose that drinks the fountain dew
  In the pleasant air of noon,
Grows pale and blue with altered
  hue—
  In the gaze of the nightly moon ;
For the planet of frost, so cold and
  bright,
Makes it wan with her borrowed light.

Such is my heart—roses are fair,
  And that at best a withered
  blossom ;
But thy false care did idly wear
  Its withered leaves in a faithless
  bosom !
And fed with love, like air and dew,
Its growth——

SONNET.—OZYMANDIAS

I met a traveller from an antique land
Who said : Two vast and trunkless
  legs of stone
Stand in the desert. Near them, on
  the sand,
Half sunk, a shattered visage lies,
  whose frown,
And wrinkled lip, and sneer of cold
  command,
Tell that its sculptor well those passions read
Which yet survive, stamped on these
  lifeless things.

The hand that mocked them and the heart that fed ;
And on the pedestal these words appear :
" My name is Ozymandias, king of kings :
Look on my works, ye mighty, and despair ! "
Nothing beside remains. Round the decay
Of that colossal wreck, boundless and bare,
The lone and level sands stretch far away.

TO THE LORD CHANCELLOR

THY country's curse is on thee, darkest crest
  Of that foul, knotted, many-headed worm
Which rends our Mother's bosom—priestly pest !
  Masked resurrection of a buried form !

Thy country's curse is on thee ! Justice sold,
  Truth trampled, Nature's landmarks overthrown,
And heaps of fraud-accumulated gold,
  Plead, loud as thunder, at Destruction's throne.

And, whilst that slow sure Angel which aye stands
  Watching the beck of Mutability
Delays to execute her high commands,
  And, though a nation weeps, spares thine and thee ;

Oh let a father's curse be on thy soul,
  And let a daughter's hope be on thy tomb,
And both on thy grey head a leaden cowl
  To weigh thee down to thine approaching doom !

I curse thee by a parent's outraged love ;
  By hopes long cherished and too lately lost ;
By gentle feelings thou couldst never prove ;
  By griefs which thy stern nature never crossed ;

By those infantine smiles of happy light
  Which were a fire within a stranger's hearth,
Quenched even when kindled, in untimely night
  Hiding the promise of a lovely birth ;

By those unpractised accents of young speech,
  Which he who is a father thought to frame
To gentlest lore such as the wisest teach.
  Thou strike the lyre of mind ! Oh grief and shame !

By all the happy see in children's growth,
  That undeveloped flower of budding years,
Sweetness and sadness interwoven both,
  Source of the sweetest hopes and saddest fears ;

By all the days, under a hireling's care,
  Of dull constraint and bitter heaviness,—
Oh wretched ye if ever any were,
  Sadder than orphans yet not fatherless !—

By the false cant which on their innocent lips
  Must hang like poison on an opening bloom ;
By the dark creeds which cover with eclipse
  Their pathway from the cradle to the tomb ;

By thy most impious hell, and all its terrors ;
  By all the grief, the madness, and the guilt
Of thine impostures, which must be their errors,
  That sand on which thy crumbling power is built ;

By thy complicity with lust and hate,
  Thy thirst for tears, thy hunger after gold,
The ready frauds which ever on thee wait,

The servile arts in which thou hast
　grown old ;

By thy most killing sneer, and by thy
　smile,
　By all the acts and snares of thy
　　black den,
And—for thou canst outweep the
　crocodile—
　By thy false tears, those millstones
　　braining men ;

By all the hate which checks a father's
　love ;
　By all the scorn which kills a
　　father's care ;
By those most impious hands that
　dared remove
　Nature's high bounds ; by thee ;
　　and by despair ;—

Yes, the despair which bids a father
　groan,
　And cry, " My children are no
　　longer mine ;
The blood within those veins may be
　mine own,
　But, tyrant, their polluted souls are
　　thine ! "—

I curse thee, though I hate thee not.
　O slave !
　If thou couldst quench the earth-
　　consuming hell
Of which thou art a demon, on thy
　grave
　This curse should be a blessing.
　　Fare thee well !

LINES TO A CRITIC

HONEY from silkworms who can
　gather,
　Or silk from the yellow bee ?
The grass may grow in winter weather
　As soon as hate in me,

Hate men who cant, and men who
　pray,
　And men who rail like thee ;
An equal passion to repay
　They are not coy like me.

Or seek some slave of power and gold,
　To be thy dear heart's mate ;
Thy love will move that bigot cold,
　Sooner than me thy hate.

A passion like the one I prove
　Cannot divided be ;
I hate thy want of truth and love—
　How should I then hate thee ?

LINES

THAT time is dead for ever, child,
Drowned, frozen, dead for ever !
　We look on the past,
　And stare aghast
At the spectres wailing, pale, and
　ghast,
Of hopes which thou and I beguiled
　To death on life's dark river.

The stream we gazed on then rolled
　by;
Its waves are unreturning ;
　But we yet stand
　In a lone land,
Like tombs to mark the memory
Of hopes and fears, which fade and flee
　In the light of life's dim morning.

ON FANNY GODWIN

HER voice did quiver as we parted,
　Yet knew I not that heart was
　　broken
From which it came, and I departed
　Heeding not the words then spoken,
　　Misery—O Misery,
　　　This world is all too wide for
　　　thee.

POEMS WRITTEN IN 1818

ADVERTISEMENT

TO ROSALIND AND HELEN, AND LINES WRITTEN AMONG THE EUGANEAN HILLS.

NAPLES, *Dec.* 20, 1818.

THE story of ROSALIND AND HELEN is, undoubtedly, not an attempt in the highest style of poetry. It is in no degree calculated to excite profound meditation ; and if, by interesting the affections and amusing the imagination, it awaken a certain ideal melancholy favourable to the reception of more important impressions, it will produce in the reader all that the writer experienced in the composition. I resigned myself, as I wrote, to the impulse of the feelings which moulded the conception of the story ; and this impulse determined the pauses of a measure, which only pretends to be regular, inasmuch as it corresponds with, and expresses, the irregularity of the imaginations which inspire it.

I do not know which of the few scattered poems I left in England will be selected by my bookseller to add to this collection. One, which I sent from Italy, was written after a day's excursion among those lovely mountains which surround what was once the retreat, and where is now the sepulchre, of Petrarch. If any-one is inclined to condemn the insertion of the introductory lines, which image forth the sudden relief of a state of deep despondency by the radiant visions disclosed by the sudden burst of an Italian sunrise in autumn, on the highest peak of those delightful mountains, I can only offer as my excuse, that they were not erased at the request of a dear friend, with whom added years of intercourse only add to my apprehension of its value, and who would have had more right than anyone to complain, that she has not been able to extinguish in me the very power of delineating sadness.

ROSALIND AND HELEN

SCENE.—*The Shore of the Lake of Como.*

ROSALIND, HELEN, *and her Child.*

HELEN.

Come hither, my sweet Rosalind.
'Tis long since thou and I have met :
And yet methinks it were unkind
Those moments to forget.
Come, sit by me. I see thee stand
By this lone lake, in this far land,
Thy loose hair in the light wind flying,
Thy sweet voice to each tone of even
United, and thine eyes replying
To the hues of yon fair heaven.
Come, gentle friend ! wilt sit by me ?
And be as thou wert wont to be
Ere we were disunited ?
None doth behold us now : the power
That led us forth at this lone hour
Will be but ill requited
If thou depart in scorn : oh ! come
And talk of our abandoned home.
Remember, this is Italy,
And we are exiles. Talk with me
Of that our land, whose wilds and floods,
Barren and dark although they be,
Were dearer than these chestnut woods ;
Those heathy paths, that inland stream,
And the blue mountains, shapes which seem
Like wrecks of childhood's sunny dream :
Which that we have abandoned now,
Weighs on the heart like that remorse
Which altered friendship leaves. I seek
No more our youthful intercourse.

That cannot be !   Rosalind, speak,
Speak to me.   Leave me not.—When
    morn did come,
When evening fell upon our common
    home,
When for one hour we parted,—do
    not frown ;
I would not chide thee, though thy
    faith is broken ;
But turn to me.   Oh ! by this cher-
    ished token
Of woven hair, which thou wilt not
    disown,
Turn, as 'twere but the memory of me,
And not my scorned self who prayed
    to thee.

ROSALIND.

Is it a dream, or do I see
And hear frail Helen ?   I would flee
Thy tain'ing touch ; but former years
Arise, and bring forbidden tears ;
And my o'erburthened memory
Seeks yet its lost repose in thee.
I share thy crime.   I cannot choose
But weep for thee : mine own strange
    grief
But seldom stoops to such relief ;
Nor ever did I love thee less,
Though mourning o'er thy wickedness
Even with a sister's woe.   I knew
What to the evil world is due,
And therefore sternly did refuse
To link me with the infamy
Of one so lost as Helen.   Now
Bewildered by my dire despair,
Wondering I blush and weep that
    thou
Shouldst love me still,—thou only !—
    There,
Let us sit on that grey stone,
Till our mournful talk be done.

HELEN.

Alas ! not there ; I cannot bear
The murmur of this lake to hear.
A sound from thee, Rosalind dear,
Which never yet I heard elsewhere
But in our native land, recurs,
Even here where now we meet.   It
    stirs
Too much of suffocating sorrow !
In the dell of yon dark chestnut wood
Is a stone seat, a solitude
Less like our own.   The ghost of peace
Will not desert this spot.   To-mor-
    row,

If thy kind feelings should not cease,
We may sit here.

ROSALIND.
            Thou lead, my sweet,
And I will follow.

HENRY.
                'Tis Fenici's seat
Where you are going ?—This is not
    the way,
Mamma ; it leads behind those trees
    that grow
Close to the little river.

HELEN.
            Yes ; I know ;
I was bewildered.   Kiss me, and be
    gay,
Dear boy, why do you sob ?

HENRY.
            I do not know :
But it might break anyone's heart to
    see
You and the lady cry so bitterly.

HELEN.
It is a gentle child, my friend.   Go
    home,
Henry, and play with Lilla till I
    come.
We only cried with joy to see each
    other ;
We are quite merry now—Good
    night.
            The boy
Lifted a sudden look upon his mother,
And in the gleam of forced and hollow
    joy
Which lightened o'er her face
    laughed with the glee
Of light and unsuspecting infancy,
And whispered in her ear, " Bring
    home with you
That sweet, strange lady-friend."
    Then off he flew,
But stopped, and beckoned with a
    meaning smile,
Where the road turned.   Pale Rosa-
    lind the while,
Hiding her face, stood weeping
    silently.

In silence then they took the way
Beneath the forest's solitude.
It was a vast and antique wood,
Through which they took their way ;
And the grey shades of evening

O'er that green wilderness did fling
Still deeper solitude.
Pursuing still the path that wound
The vast and knotted trees around,
Through which slow shades were
    wandering,
To a deep lawny dell they came,
To a stone seat beside a spring,
O'er which the columned wood did
    frame
A roofless temple, like the fane
Where, ere new creeds could faith
    obtain,
Man's early race once knelt beneath
The overhanging deity.
O'er this fair fountain hung the sky,
Now spangled with rare stars. The
    snake,
The pale snake, that with eager
    breath
Creeps here his noontide thirst to
    slake,
Is beaming with many a mingled hue,
Shed from yon dome's eternal blue,
When he floats on that dark and lucid
    flood
In the light of his own loveliness ;
And the birds that in the fountain dip
Their plumes, with fearless fellow-
    ship
Above and round him wheel and
    hover.
The fitful wind is heard to stir
One solitary leaf on high ;
The chirping of the grasshopper
Fills every pause. There is emotion
In all that dwells at noontide here :
Then, through the intricate wild
    wood,
A maze of life and light and motion
Is woven. But there is stillness now ;
Gloom, and the trance of Nature now;
The snake is in his cave asleep ;
The birds are on the branches dream-
    ing ;
Only the shadows creep ;
Only the glow worm is gleaming :
Only the owls and the nightingales
Wake in this dell when daylight fails,
And grey shades gather in the woods;
And the owls have all fled far away
In a merrier glen to hoot and play,
For the moon is veiled and sleeping
    now.
The accustomed nightingale still
    broods

On her accustomed bough,
But she is mute ; for her false mate
Has fled and left her desolate.

This silent spot tradition old
Had peopled with the spectral dead.
For the roots of the speaker's hair
    felt cold
And stiff, as with tremulous lips he
    told
That a hellish shape at midnight led
The ghost of a youth with hoary hair,
And sate on the seat beside him there,
Till a naked child came wandering by,
When the fiend would change to a
    lady fair !
A fearful tale ! The truth was worse :
For here a sister and a brother
Had solemnised a monstrous curse,
Meeting in this fair solitude :
For beneath yon very sky,
Had they resigned to one another
Body and soul. The multitude,
Tracking them to the secret wood,
Tore limb from limb their innocent
    child,
And stabbed and trampled on its
    mother ;
But the youth, for God's most holy
    grace,
A priest saved to burn in the market-
    place.
Duly at evening Helen came
To this lone silent spot,
From the wrecks of a tale of wilder
    sorrow
So much of sympathy to borrow
As soothed her own dark lot.
Duly each evening from her home,
With her fair child would Helen come
To sit upon that antique seat,
While the hues of day were pale ;
And the bright boy beside her feet
Now lay, lifting at intervals
His broad blue eyes on her ;
Now, where some sudden impulse
    calls
Following. He was a gentle boy
And in all gentle sports took joy;
Oft in a dry leaf for a boat,
With a small feather for a sail,
His fancy on that spring would float,
If some invisible breeze might stir
Its marble calm : and Helen smiled
Through tears of awe on the gay child,
To think that a boy as fair as he,

In years which never more may be,
By that same fount, in that same
    wood,
The like sweet fancies had pursued ;
And that a mother, lost like her,
Had mournfully sate watching him.
Then all the scene was wont to swim
Through the mist of a burning tear.

For many months had Helen known
This scene ; and now she thither
    turned
Her footsteps, not alone.
The friend whose falsehood she had
    mourned,
Sate with her on that seat of stone.
Silent they sate ; for evening,
And the power its glimpses bring
Had, with one awful shadow, quelled
The passion of their grief. They sate
With linked hands, for unrepelled
Had Helen taken Rosalind's.
Like the autumn wind, when it un-
    binds
The tangled locks of the nightshade's
    hair,
Which is twined in the sultry summer
    air
Round the walls of an outworn sepul-
    chre,
Did the voice of Helen, sad and sweet,
And the sound of her heart that ever
    beat,
As with sighs and words she breathed
    on her,
Unbind the knots of her friend's
    despair,
Till her thoughts were free to float and
    flow ;
And from her labouring bosom now,
Like the bursting of a prisoned flame,
The voice of a long-pent sorrow came.

ROSALIND.

I saw the dark earth fall upon
The coffin ; and I saw the stone
Laid over him whom this cold breast
Had pillowed to his nightly rest !
Thou knowest not, thou canst not
    know
My agony. Oh ! I could not weep :
The sources whence such blessings
    flow
Were not to be approached by me !
But I could smile, and I could sleep,
Though with a self-accusing heart.
In morning's light, in evening's gloom,

I watched,—and would not thence
    depart,
My husband's unlamented tomb.
My children knew their sire was gone ;
But when I told them, " he is dead,"
They laughed aloud in frantic glee,
They clapped their hands and leaped
    about,
Answering each other's ecstasy
With many a prank and merry shout ;
But I sat silent and alone,
Wrapped in the mock of mourning
    weed.

They laughed, for he was dead ; but I
Sate with a hard and tearless eye,
And with a heart which would deny
The secret joy it could not quell,
Low muttering o'er his loathed name ;
Till from that self-contention came
Remorse where sin was none ; a hell
Which in pure spirits should not
    dwell.

I'll tell the truth.   He was a man
Hard, selfish, loving only gold,
Yet full of guile ; his pale eyes ran
With tears, which each some false-
    hood told,
And oft his smooth and bridled tongue
Would give the lie to his flushing
    cheek :
He was a coward to the strong ;
He was a tyrant to the weak,
On whom his vengeance he would
    wreak :
For scorn, whose arrows search the
    heart,
From many a stranger's eye would
    dart,
And on his memory cling, and follow
His soul to its home so cold and
    hollow.
He was a tyrant to the weak,
And we were such, alas the day !
Oft, when my little ones at play,
Were in youth's natural lightness
    gay,
Or if they listened to some tale
Of travellers, or of fairy land,—
When the light from the wood fire's
    dying brand
Flashed on their faces,—if they heard
Or thought they heard upon the stair
His footstep, the suspended word
Died on my lips : we all grew pale ;

The babe at my bosom was hushed
    with fear
If it thought it heard its father near;
And my two wild boys would near my
    knee
Cling, cowed and cowering fearfully.
I'll tell the truth: I loved another.
His name in my ear was ever ringing,
His form to my brain was ever cling-
    ing;
Yet if some stranger breathed that
    name,
My lips turned white, and my heart
    beat fast;
My nights were once haunted by
    dreams of flame,
My days were dim in the shadow cast,
By the memory of the same!
Day and night, day and night,
He was my breath and life and light,
For three short years, which soon
    were past.
On the fourth, my gentle mother
Led me to the shrine, to be
His sworn bride eternally.
And now we stood on the altar stair,
When my father came from a distant
    land,
And with a loud and fearful cry,
Rushed between us suddenly.
I saw the stream of his thin grey hair,
I saw his lean and lifted hand,
And heard his words,—and live! O
    God!
Wherefore do I live?—"Hold, hold!"
He cried,—"I tell thee 'tis her bro-
    ther!
Thy mother, boy, beneath the sod
Of yon churchyard rests in her
    shroud so cold.
I am now weak, and pale, and old:
We were once dear to one another,
I and that corpse! Thou art our
    child!"
Then with a laugh both long and wild
The youth upon the pavement fell:
They found him dead! All looked
    on me,
The spasms of my despair to see;
But I was calm. I went away;
I was clammy-cold like clay!
I did not weep—I did not speak;
But day by day, week after week,
I walked about like a corpse alive!
Alas! sweet friend, you must believe
This heart is stone—it did not break.

My father lived a little while,
But all might see that he was dying,
He smiled with such a woeful smile!
When he was in the churchyard lying
Among the worms, we grew quite
    poor,
So that no one would give us bread;
My mother looked at me, and said
Faint words of cheer, which only
    meant
That she could die and be content;
So I went forth from the same church
    door
To another husband's bed.
And this was he who died at last,
When weeks and months and years
    had past,
Through which I firmly did fulfil
My duties, a devoted wife,
With the stern step of vanquish'd
    will,
Walking beneath the night of life,
Whose hours extinguished, like slow
    rain
Falling for ever, pain by pain,
The very hope of death's dear rest;
Which, since the heart within my
    breast
Of natural life was dispossest,
Its strange sustainer there had been.

When flowers were dead, and grass
    was green
Upon my mother's grave,—that
    mother
Whom to outlive, and cheer, and
    make
My wan eyes glitter for her sake,
Was my vowed task, the single care
Which once gave life to my despair,—
When she was a thing that did not
    stir,
And the crawling worms were cradling
    her
To a sleep more deep and so more
    sweet
Than a baby's rocked on its nurse's
    knee,
I lived; a living pulse then beat
Beneath my heart that awakened
    me.
What was this pulse so warm and
    free?
Alas! I knew it could not be
My own dull blood: 'twas like a
    thought

Of liquid love, that spread and
    wrought
Under my bosom and in my brain,
And crept with the blood through
    every vein,
And hour by hour, day after day,
The wonder could not charm away,
But laid in sleep my wakeful pain,
Until I knew it was a child,
And then I wept. For long, long
    years
These frozen eyes had shed no tears :
But now—'twas the season fair and
    mild
When April has wept itself to May :
I saté through the sweet sunny day
By my window bowered round with
    leaves
And down my cheeks the quick tears
    ran   [eaves,
Like twinkling rain-drops from the
When warm spring showers are pass-
    ing o'er :
O Helen, none can ever tell
The joy it was to weep once more !

I wept to think how hard it were
To kill my babe, and take from it
The sense of light, and the warm air,
And my own fond and tender care,
And love and smiles ; ere I knew yet
That these for it might, as for me,
Be the masks of a grinning mockery.
And haply, I would dream, 'twere
    sweet
To feed it from my faded breast,
Or mark my own heart's restless beat
Rock it to its untroubled rest ;
And watch the growing soul beneath
Dawn in faint smiles ; and hear its
    breath,
Half interrupted by calm sighs ;
And search the depth of its fair eyes
For long departed memories !
And so I lived till that sweet load
Was lightened. Darkly forward
    flowed
The stream of years, and on it bore
Two shapes of gladness to my sight ;
Two other babes, delightful more
In my lost soul's abandoned night,
Than their own country ships may be
Sailing towards wrecked mariners,
Who cling to the rock of a wintry sea.
For each, as it came, brought sooth-
    ing tears,

And a loosening warmth, as each one
    lay
Sucking the sullen milk away,
About my frozen heart did play,
And weaned it, oh how painfully !—
As they themselves were weaned each
    one
From that sweet food,—even from
    the thirst
Of death, and nothingness, and rest,
Strange inmate of a living breast !
Which all that I had undergone
Of grief and shame, since she, who
    first
The gates of that dark refuge closed,
Came to my sight, and almost burst
The seal of that Lethean spring ;
But these fair shadows interposed :
For all delights are shadows now !
And from my brain to my dull brow
The heavy tears gather and flow :
I cannot speak—Oh let me weep !

The tears which fell from her wan eyes
Glimmered among the moonlight
    dew !
Her deep hard sobs and heavy sighs
Their echoes in the darkness threw.
When she grew calm, she thus did
    keep
The tenor of her tale :—
                                He died,
I know not how. He was not old,
If age be numbered by its years ;
But he was bowed and bent with fears.
Pale with the quenchless thirst of gold,
Which, like fierce fever, left him
    weak ;
And his strait lip and bloated cheek
Were warped in spasms by hollow
    sneers ;
And selfish cares with barren plough,
Not age, had lined his narrow brow,
And foul and cruel thoughts, which
    feed
Upon the withering life within,
Like vipers on some poisonous weed.
Whether his ill were death or sin
None knew, until he died indeed,
And then men owned they were the
    same.

Seven days within my chamber lay
That corse, and my babes made holi-
    day :
At last. I told them what is death :

The eldest with a kind of shame,
Came to my knees with silent breath,
And sate awe-stricken at my feet ;
And soon the others left their play,
And sate there too.   It is unmeet
To shed on the brief flower of youth
The withering knowledge of the
      grave ;
From me remorse then wrung that
      truth.
I could not bear the joy which gave
Too just a response to mine own.
In vain.   I dared not feign a groan ;
And in their artless looks I saw,
Between the mists, of fear and awe,
That my own thought was theirs ;
      and they
Expressed it not in words, but said,
Each in its heart, how every day
Will pass in happy work and play,
Now he is dead and gone away !

After the funeral all our kin
Assembled, and the will was read.
My friend, I tell thee, even the dead
Have strength, their putrid shrouds
      within,
To blast and torture.   Those who
      live
Still fear the living, but a corse
Is merciless, and power doth give
To such pale tyrants half the spoil
He rends from those who groan and
      toil,
Because they blush not with remorse
Among their crawling worms.   Be-
      hold,
I have no child ! my tale grows old
With grief, and staggers : let it reach
The limits of my feeble speech,
And languidly at length recline
On the brink of its own grave and
      mine.

Thou knowest what a thing is
      Poverty
Among the fallen on evil days :
'Tis Crime, and Fear, and Infamy,
And houseless Want in frozen ways
Wandering ungarmented, and Pain,
And, worse than all, that inward
      stain,
Foul Self-contempt, which drowns in
      sneers
Youth's starlight smile, and makes
      its tears
First like hot gall, then dry for ever !

And well thou knowest a mother
      never
Could doom her children to this ill,
And well he knew the same.   The will
Imported, that if e'er again
I sought my children to behold,
Or in my birthplace did remain
Beyond three days, whose hours were
      told,
They should inherit nought : and he,
To whom next came their patrimony,
A sallow lawyer, cruel and cold,
Aye watched me, as the will was read,
With eyes askance, which sought to
      see
The secrets of my agony ;
And with close lips and anxious brow
Stood canvassing still to and fro
The chance of my resolve, and all
The dead man's caution just did call ;
For in that killing lie 'twas said—
" She is adulterous, and doth hold
In secret that the Christian creed
Is false, and therefore is much need
That I should have a care to save
My children from eternal fire."
Friend, he was sheltered by the grave,
And therefore dared to be a liar !
In truth, the Indian on the pyre
Of her dead husband, half-consumed,
As well might there be false, as I
To those abhorred embraces doomed,
Far worse than fire's brief agony.
As to the Christian creed, if true
Or false, I never questioned it :
I took it as the vulgar do :
Nor my vext soul had leisure yet
To doubt the things men say, or deem
That they are other than they seem.

All present who those crimes did hear
In feigned or actual scorn and fear,
Men, women, children, slunk away,
Whispering with self-contented pride,
Which half suspects its own base lie.
I spoke to none, nor did abide,
But silently I went my way,
Nor noticed I where joyously
Sate my two younger babes at play,
In the courtyard through which I
      past :
But went with footsteps firm and fast
Till I came to the brink of the ocean
      green,
And there, a woman with grey hairs,
Who had my mother's servant been,

Kneeling, with many tears and prayers,
Made me accept a purse of gold,
Half of the earnings she had kept
To refuge her when weak and old.

With woe, which never sleeps or slept,
I wander now.   'Tis a vain thought—
But on yon Alp, whose snowy head
'Mid the azure air is islanded
(We see it o'er the flood of cloud,
Which sunrise from its eastern caves
Drives, wrinkling into golden waves,
Hung with its precipices proud,
From that grey stone where first we
met),
There, now who knows the dead feel
nought,
Should be my grave ; for he who yet
Is my soul's soul, once said : " 'Twere
sweet
'Mid stars and lightnings to abide,
And winds and lulling snows, that
beat
With their soft flakes the mountain
wide,
When weary meteor lamps repose,
And languid storms their pinions
close :
And all things strong and bright and
pure,
And ever during, aye endure :
Who knows, if one were buried there,
But these things might our spirits
make,
Amid the all-surrounding air,
Their own eternity partake ? "
Then 'twas a wild and playful saying
At which I laughed or seemed to
laugh :
They were his words : now heed my
praying,
And let them be my epitaph.
Thy memory for a term may be
My monument.   Wilt remember me ?
I know thou wilt, and canst forgive
Whilst in this erring world to live
My soul disdained not, that I thought
Its lying forms were worthy aught,
And much less thee.

HELEN.
        O speak not so,
But come to me and pour thy woe
Into this heart, full though it be,
Aye overflowing with its own :

I thought that grief had severed me
From all beside who weep and groan ;
Its likeness upon earth to be,
Its express image ; but thou art
More wretched.   Sweet ! we will not
part
Henceforth, if death be not division ;
If so, the dead feel no contrition.
But wilt thou hear, since last we
parted
All that has left me broken-hearted ?

ROSALIND.
Yes, speak.   The faintest stars are
scarcely shorn
Of their thin beams, by that delusive
morn
Which sinks again in darkness, like
the light
Of early love, soon lost in total night.

HELEN.
Alas ! Italian winds are mild,
But my bosom is cold—wintry cold—
When the warm air weaves, among
the fresh leaves,
Soft music, my poor brain is wild,
And I am weak like a nursling child,
Though my soul with grief is grey and
old.

ROSALIND.
Weep not at thine own words, tho'
they must make
Me weep.   What is thy tale ?

HELEN.
        I fear 'twill shake
Thy gentle heart with tears.   Thou
well
Rememberest when we met no more,
And, though I dwelt with Lionel,
That friendless caution pierced me
sore
With grief—a wound my spirit bore
Indignantly ; but when he died,
With him lay dead both hope and
pride.

Alas ! all hope is buried now.
But then men dreamed the aged earth
Was labouring in that mighty birth,
Which many a poet and a sage
Has aye foreseen—the happy age
When truth and love shall dwell below
Among the works and ways of men ;
Which on this world not power but
will

Even now is wanting to fulfil.
Among mankind what thence befel
Of strife, how vain, is known too well ;
When Liberty's dear pæan fell
'Mid murderous howls. To Lionel,
Though of great wealth and lineage
  high,
Yet through those dungeon walls there
  came
Thy thrilling light, O Liberty !
And as the meteor's midnight flame
Startles the dreamer, sunlight truth
Flashed on his visionary youth,
And filled him, not with love, but
  faith,
And hope, and courage mute in
  death;
For love and life in him were twins,
Born at one birth : in every other
First life, then love its course begins,
Though they be children of one
  mother ;
And so through this dark world they
  fleet
Divided, till in death they meet :
But he loved all things ever. Then
He passed amid the strife of men,
And stood at the throne of armed
  power
Pleading for a world of woe :
Secure as one on a rock-built tower
O'er the wrecks which the surge trails
  to and fro,
'Mid the passions wild of humankind
He stood, like a spirit calming them ;
For, it was said, his words could bind
Like music the lulled crowd, and stem
That torrent of unquiet dream
Which mortals truth and reason
  deem,
But is revenge, and fear, and pride.
Joyous he was ; and hope and peace
On all who heard him did abide,
Raining like dew from his sweet talk,
As where the evening star may walk
Along the brink of the gloomy seas,
Liquid mists of splendour quiver.
His very gestures touched to tears
The unpersuaded tyrant, never
So moved before : his presence stung
The torturers with their victims' pain,
And none knew how ; and through
  their ears,
The subtle witchcraft of his tongue
Unlocked the hearts of those who
  keep

Gold, the world's bond of slavery.
Men wondered and some sneered to
  see
One sow what he could never reap :
For he is rich, they said, and young,
And might drink from the depths of
  luxury.
If he seeks fame, fame never crowned
The champion of a trampled creed :
If he seeks power, power is enthroned
'Mid ancient rights and wrongs, to
  feed
Which hungry wolves with praise and
  spoil,
Those who would sit near power must
  toil ;
And such, there sitting, all may see.
What seeks he ? All that others
  seek
He casts away, like a vile weed
Which the sea casts unreturningly.

That poor and hungry men should
  break
The laws which wreak them toil and
  scorn,
We understand ; but Lionel
We know is rich and nobly born.
So wondered they ; yet all men loved
Young Lionel, though few approved ;
All but the priests, whose hatred fell
Like the unseen blight of a smiling
  day,
The withering honey-dew, which
  clings
Under the bright green buds of May,
Whilst they unfold their emerald
  wings :
For he made verses wild and queer
On the strange creeds priests hold so
  dear,
Because they bring them land and
  gold.
Of devils and saints, and all such gear,
He made tales which whoso heard or
  read
Would laugh till he were almost dead.
So this grew a proverb : " Don't get
  old
Till Lionel's ' Banquet in Hell ' you
  hear,
And then you will laugh yourself
  young again."
So the priests hated him, and he
Repaid their hate with cheerful glee.
Ah ! smiles and joyance quickly died,

For public hope grew pale and dim
In an altered time and tide,
And in its wasting withered him,
As a summer flower that blows too
    soon
Droops in the smile of the waning
    moon,
When it scatters through an April
    night
The frozen dews of wrinkling blight.
None now hoped more. Grey Power
    was seated
Safely on her ancestral throne ;
And Faith, the Python, undefeated
Even to its blood-stained steps
    dragged on
Her foul and wounded train ; and
    men
Were trampled and deceived again,
And words and shows again could
    bind
The wailing tribes of humankind
In scorn and famine. Fire and blood
Raged round the raging multitude,
To fields remote by tyrants sent
To be the scorned instrument,
With which they drag from mines of
    gore
The chains their slaves yet ever wore ;
And in the streets men met each
    other,
And by old altars and in halls,
And smiled again at festivals.
But each man found in his heart's
    brother
Cold cheer ; for all, though half
    deceived,
The outworn creeds again believed,
And the same round anew began,
Which the weary world yet ever ran.

Many then wept, not tears, but gall,
Within their hearts, like drops which
    fall
Wasting the fountain-stone away.
And in that dark and evil day
Did all desires and thoughts, that
    claim
Men's care—ambition, friendship,
    fame,
Love, hope, though hope was now
    despair—
Indue the colours of this change,
As from the all-surrounding air
The earth takes hues obscure and
    strange,

When storm and earthquake linger
    there.

And so, my friend, it then befel
To many, most to Lionel,
Whose hope was like the life of youth
Within him, and when dead, became
A spirit of unresting flame,
Which goaded him in his distress
Over the world's vast wilderness.
Three years he left his native land,
And on the fourth, when he returned,
None knew him : he was stricken
    deep
With some disease of mind, and
    turned
Into aught unlike Lionel.
On him—on whom, did he pause in
    sleep,
Serenest smiles were wont to keep,
And, did he wake, a winged band
Of bright persuasions, which had fed
On his sweet lips and liquid eyes,
Kept their swift pinions half out-
    spread
To do on men his least command—
On him, whom once 'twas Paradise
Even to behold, now misery lay :
In his own heart 'twas merciless,
To all things else none may express
Its innocence and tenderness.

'Twas said that he had refuge sought
In love from his unquiet thought
In distant lands, and been deceived
By some strange show ; for there were
    found,
Blotted with tears, as those relieved
By their own words are wont to do,
These mournful verses on the ground,
By all who read them blotted too.
" How am I changed ! my hopes were
    once like fire :
I loved, and I believed that life was
    love.
How am I lost ! on wings of swift
    desire
Among Heaven's winds my spirit
    once did move.
I slept, and silver dreams did aye
    inspire
My liquid sleep. I woke, and did
    approve
All nature to my heart, and thought
    to make
A Paradise of earth for one sweet sake

I love, but I believe in love no more :
I feel desire, but hope not.   O, from
    sleep
Most vainly must my weary brain
    implore
Its long-lost flattery now.   I wake to
    weep,
And sit through the long day gnawing
    the core
Of my bitter heart, and, like a miser,
    keep,
Since none in what I feel take pain or
    pleasure,
To my own soul its self-consuming
    treasure.''

He dwelt beside me near the sea ;
And oft in evening did we meet,
When the waves, beneath the star-
    light, flee
O'er the yellow sands with silver feet,
And talked.   Our talk was sad and
    sweet,
Till slowly from his mien there passed
The desolation which it spoke ;
And smiles,—as when the lightning's
    blast
Has parched some heaven-delighting
    oak,
The next spring shows leaves pale and
    rare,
But like flowers delicate and fair,
On its rent boughs—again arrayed
His countenance in tender light :
His words grew subtle fire, which
    made
The air his hearers breathed delight :
His motions, like the winds, were free,
Which bend the bright grass grace-
    fully,
Then fade away in circlets faint :
And winged Hope, on which upborne
His soul seemed hovering in his eyes,
Like some bright spirit newly-born
Floating amid the sunny skies,
Sprang forth from his rent heart anew.
Yet o'er his talk, and looks, and mien,
Tempering their loveliness too keen,
Past woe its shadow backward threw,
Till like an exhalation, spread
From flowers half drunk with evening
    dew,
They did become infectious : sweet
And subtle mists of sense and thought
Which wrapt us soon, when we might
    meet,

Almost from our own looks, and
    aught
The wide world holds.   And so, his
    mind
Was healed, while mine grew sick
    with fear :
For ever now his health declined,
Like some frail bark which cannot
    bear
The impulse of an altered wind,
Though prosperous ; and my heart
    grew full
'Mid its new joy of a new care :
For his cheek became, not pale, but
    fair,
As rose-o'ershadowed lilies are ;
And soon his deep and sunny hair,
In this alone less beautiful,
Like grass in tombs grew wild and
    rare.
The blood in his translucent veins
Beat, not like animal life, but love
Seemed now its sullen springs to
    move,
When life had failed, and all its
    pains ;
And sudden sleep would seize him oft
Like death, so calm, but that a tear,
His pointed eyelashes between,
Would gather in the light serene
Of smiles, whose lustre bright and
    soft
Beneath lay undulating there.
His breath was like inconstant flame,
As eagerly it went and came ;
And I hung o'er him in his sleep,
Till, like an image in the lake
Which rains disturb, my tears would
    break
The shadow of that slumber deep ;
Then he would bid me not to weep,
And say, with flattery false, yet sweet,
That death and he could never meet,
If I would never part with him.
And so we loved, and did unite
All that in us was yet divided :
For when he said, that many a rite,
By men to bind but once provided,
Could not be shared by him and me,
Or they would kill him in their glee,
I shuddered, and then laughing said,
'' We will have rites our faith to bind,
But our church shall be the starry
    night,
Our altar the grassy earth outspread,
And our priest the muttering wind.''

'Twas sunset as I spoke : one star
Had scarce burst forth, when from
    afar
The ministers of misrule sent,
Seized upon Lionel, and bore
His chained limbs to a dreary tower
In the midst of a city vast and wide
For he, they said, from his mind had
    bent
Against their gods keen blasphemy,
For which, though his soul must
    roasted be
In hell's red lakes immortally,
Yet even on earth must he abide
The vengeance of their slaves—a trial,
I think, men call it. What avail
Are prayers and tears, which chase
    denial
From the fierce savage, nursed in
    hate ?
What the knit soul that pleading and
    pale
Makes wan the quivering cheek,
    which late
It painted with its own delight ?
We were divided. As I could,
I stilled the tingling of my blood,
And followed him in their despite,
As a widow follows, pale and wild,
The murderers and corse of her only
    child :
And when we came to the prison door,
And I prayed to share his dungeon
    floor
With prayers which rarely have been
    spurned,
And when men drove me forth and I
Stared with blank frenzy on the sky,
A farewell look of love he turned,
Half-calming me ; then gazed awhile,
As if through that black and massy
    pile,
And through the crowd around him
    there,
And through the dense and murky air,
And the thronged streets, he did espy
What poets knew and prophesy ;
And said, with voice that made them
    shiver,
And clung like music in my brain,
And which the mute walls spoke
    again
Prolonging it with deepened strain—
" Fear not the tyrants shall rule for
    ever,
Or the priests of the bloody faith ;

They stand on the brink of that
    mighty river,
Whose waves they have tainted with
    death :
It is fed from the depths of a thous-
    and dells,
Around them it foams, and rages, and
    swells,
And their swords and their sceptres I
    floating see,
Like wrecks, in the surge of eternity.''

I dwelt beside the prison gate,
And the strange crowd that out and
    in
Passed, some, no doubt, with mine
    own fate,
Might have fretted me with its cease-
    less din,
But the fever of care was louder
    within.
Soon, but too late, in penitence
Or fear, his foes released him thence :
I saw his thin and languid form,
As leaning on the jailer's arm,
Whose hardened eyes grew moist the
    while,
To meet his mute and faded smile,
And hear his words of kind farewell,
He tottered forth from his damp cell.
Many had never wept before,
From whom fast tears then gushed
    and fell ;
Many will relent no more,
Who sobbed like infants then ; ay,
    all
Who thronged the prison's stony hall,
The rulers or the slaves of law
Felt with a new surprise and awe
That they were human, till strong
    shame
Made them again become the same.
The prison bloodhounds, huge and
    grim,
From human looks the infection
    caught,
And fondly crouched and fawned on
    him ;
And men have heard the prisoners
    say,
Who in their rotting dungeons lay,
That from that hour, throughout one
    day,
The fierce despair and hate, which
    kept
Their trampled bosoms, almost slept :

When, like twin vultures, they hung
  feeding
On each heart's wound, wide torn
  and bleeding,
Because their jailer's rule, they
  thought,
Grew merciful, like a parent's sway.

I know not how, but we were free:
And Lionel sate alone with me,
As the carriage drove through the
  streets apace ;
And we looked upon each other's face;
And the blood in our fingers inter-
  twined
Ran like the thoughts of a single mind,
As the swift emotions went and came
Through the veins of each united
  frame.
So through the long long streets we
  past
Of the million-peopled city vast ;
Which is that desert, where each one
Seeks his mate yet is alone,
Beloved and sought and mourned of
  none ;
Until the clear blue sky was seen,
And the grassy meadows bright and
  green,
And then I sunk in his embrace,
Enclosing there a mighty space
Of love : and so we travelled on
By woods, and fields of yellow flowers,
And towns, and villages, and towers,
Day after day of happy hours.
It was the azure time of June,
When the skies are deep in the stain-
  less noon,
And the warm and fitful breezes
  shake
The fresh green leaves of the hedge-
  row brier ;
And there were odours then to make
The very breath we did respire
A liquid element, whereon
Our spirits, like delighted things
That walk the air on subtle wings,
Floated and mingled far away,
'Mid the warm winds of the sunny day.
And when the Evening Star came forth
Above the curve of the new bent
  moon,
And light and sound ebbed from the
  earth,
Like the tide of the full and weary sea
To the depths of its own tranquillity,

Our natures to its own repose
Did the earth's breathless sleep
  attune :
Like flowers, which on each other
  close
Their languid leaves when daylight's
  gone,
We lay, till new emotions came,
Which seemed to make each mortal
  frame
One soul of interwoven flame,
A life in life, a second birth,
In worlds diviner far than earth,
Which, like two strains of harmony
That mingle in the silent sky,
Then slowly disunite, passed by
And left the tenderness of tears,
A soft oblivion of all fears,
A sweet sleep : so we travelled on
Till we came to the home of Lionel,
Among the mountains wild and lone,
Beside the hoary western sea,
Which near the verge of the echoing
  shore
The massy forest shadowed o'er.

The ancient steward, with hair all
  hoar,
As we alighted, wept to see,
His master changed so fearfully ;
And the old man's sobs did waken me
From my dream of unremaining
  gladness ;
The truth flashed o'er me like quick
  madness
When I looked, and saw that there
  was death
On Lionel : yet day by day
He lived, till fear grew hope and faith,
And in my soul I dared to say,
" Nothing so bright can pass away :
Death is dark, and foul, and dull,
But he is—O how beautiful ! "
Yet day by day he grew more weak,
And his sweet voice, when he might
  speak,
Which ne'er was loud, became more
  low ;
And the light which flashed through
  his waxen cheek
Grew faint, as the rose-like hues
  which flow
From sunset o'er the Alpine snow :
And death seemed not like death in
  him,
For the spirit of life o'er every limb

Lingered, a mist of sense and thought.
When the summer wind faint odours
    brought
From mountain flowers, even as it
    passed,
His cheek would change, as the noon-
    day sea
Which the dying breeze sweeps fit-
    fully.
If but a cloud the sky o'ercast,
You might see his colour come and
    go,
And the softest strain of music made
Sweet smiles, yet sad, arise and fade
Amid the dew of his tender eyes :
And the breath, with intermitting
    flow,
Made his pale lips quiver and part.
You might hear the beatings of his
    heart,
Quick, but not strong ; and with my
    tresses
When oft he playfully would bind
In the bowers of mossy lonelinesses
His neck, and win me so to mingle
In the sweet depth of woven caresses,
And our faint limbs were intertwined,
Alas ! the unquiet life did tingle
From mine own heart through every
    vein,
Like a captive in dreams of liberty,
Who beats the walls of his stony cell.
But his, it seemed already free,
Like the shadow of fire surrounding
    me !
On my faint eyes and limbs did dwell
That spirit as it passed, till soon,
As a frail cloud wandering o'er the
    moon,
Beneath its light invisible,
Is seen when it folds its grey wings
    again
To alight on midnight's dusky plain,
I lived and saw, and the gathering
    soul
Passed from beneath that strong
    control,
And I fell on a life which was sick
    with fear
Of all the woe that now I bear.
Amid a bloomless myrtle wood,
On a green and sea-girt promontory,
Not far from where we dwelt, there
    stood
In record of a sweet sad story,
An altar and a temple bright

Circled by steps, and o'er the gate
Was sculptured, " To Fidelity" ;
And in the shrine an image sate,
All veiled : but there was seen the
    light
Of smiles, which faintly could express
A mingled pain and tenderness,
Through that ethereal drapery.
The left hand held the head, the
    right—
Beyond the veil, beneath the skin,
You might see the nerves quivering
    within—
Was forcing the point of a barbed dart.
Into its side-convulsing heart.
An unskilled hand, yet one informed
With genius, had the marble warmed
With that pathetic life. This tale
It told : A dog had from the sea,
When the tide was raging fearfully,
Dragged Lionel's mother, weak and
    pale,
Then died beside her on the sand,
And she that temple thence had
    planned ;
But it was Lionel's own hand
Had wrought the image. Each new
    moon
That lady did, in this lone fane,
The rites of a religion sweet,
Whose god was in her heart and
    brain :
The seasons' loveliest flowers were
    strewn
On the marble floor beneath her feet,
And she brought crowns of sea-buds
    white,
Whose odour is so sweet and faint,
And weeds, like branching chrysolite,
Woven in devices fine and quaint,
And tears from her brown eyes did
    stain
The altar : need but look upon
That dying statue, fair and wan,
If tears should cease, to weep again :
And rare Arabian odours came,
Through the myrtle copses, steaming
    thence
From the hissing frankincense,
Whose smoke, wool-white as ocean
    foam,
Hung in dense flocks beneath the
    dome,
That ivory dome, whose azure night
With golden stars, like heaven, was
    bright

O'er the split cedars' pointed flame ;
And the lady's harp would kindle
    there
The melody of an old air,
Softer than sleep ; the villagers
Mixed their religion up with hers,
And as they listened round, shed tears.

One eve he led me to this fane :
Daylight on its last purple cloud
Was lingering grey, and soon her
    strain
The nightingale began ; now loud,
Climbing in circles the windless sky,
Now dying music ; suddenly
'Tis scattered in a thousand notes,
And now to the hushed ear it floats
Like field-smells known in infancy,
Then failing, soothes the air again.
We sate within that temple lone,
Pavilioned round with Parian stone :
His mother's harp stood near, and oft
I had awakened music soft
Amid its wires : the nightingale
Was pausing in her heaven-taught
    tale :
" Now drain the cup," said Lionel,
" Which the poet-bird has crowned
    so well
With the wine of her bright and
    liquid song !
Heardst thou not sweet words among
That heaven-resounding minstrelsy !
Heardst thou not, that those who die
Awake in a world of ecstasy ?
That love, when limbs are interwoven,
And sleep when the night of life is
    cloven,
And thought, to the world's dim
    boundaries clinging,
And music, when one beloved is
    singing,
Is death ? Let us drain right joy-
    ously
The cup which the sweet bird fills for
    me."

He paused, and to my lips he bent
His own : like spirit his words went
Through all my limbs with the speed
    of fire ;
And his keen eyes, glittering through
    mine,
Filled me with the flame divine,
Which in their orbs was burning far,
Like the light of an unmeasured star.

In the sky of midnight dark and deep:
Yes, 'twas his soul that did inspire
Sounds, which my skill could ne'er
    awaken ;
And first, I felt my fingers sweep
The harp, and a long quivering cry
Burst from my lips in symphony :
The dusk and solid air was shaken,
As swift and swifter the notes came
From my touch, that wandered like
    quick flame,
And from my bosom, labouring
With some unutterable thing :
The awful sound of my own voice
    made
My faint lips tremble ; in some mood
Of wordless thought Lionel stood
So pale, that even beside his cheek
The snowy column from its shade
Caught whiteness : yet his counten-
    ance
Raised upward, burned with radiance
Of spirit-piercing joy, whose light,
Like the moon struggling through the
    night
Of whirlwind-rifted clouds, did break
With beams that might not be con-
    fined.

I paused, but soon his gestures
    kindled
New power, as by the moving wind
The waves are lifted, and my song
To low soft notes now changed and
    dwindled
And from the twinkling wires among,
My languid fingers drew and flung
Circles of life-dissolving sound,
Yet faint : in aëry rings they bound
My Lionel, who, as every strain
Grew fainter but more sweet, his mien
Sunk with the sound relaxedly ;
And slowly now he turned to me,
As slowly faded from his face
That awful joy : with looks serene
He was soon drawn to my embrace,
And my wild song then died away
In murmurs : words, I dare not say,
We mixed, and on his lips mine
    fed
Till they methought felt still and cold:
" What is it with thee, love ? " I said ;
No word, no look, no motion ! yes,
There was a change, but spare to
    guess,
Nor let that moment's hope be told.

I looked, and knew that he was dead,
And fell, as the eagle on the plain
Falls when life deserts her brain,
And the mortal lightning is veiled
     again.
O that I were now dead ! but such,
Did they not, love, demand too much.
Those dying murmurs ?   He forbad.
O that I once again were mad !
And yet, dear Rosalind, not so,
For I would live to share thy woe.
Sweet boy ! did I forget thee too ?
Alas, we know not what we do
When we speak words.
                    No memory more
Is in my mind of that seashore.
Madness came on me, and a troop
Of misty shapes did seem to sit
Beside me, on a vessel's poop,
And the clear north wind was driving
     it.
Then I heard strange tongues, and
     saw strange flowers;
And the stars methought grew unlike
     ours,
And the azure sky and the stormless
     sea
Made me believe that I had died,
And waked in a world which was to
     me
Drear hell, though heaven to all be-
     side.
Then a dead sleep fell on my mind,
Whilst animal life many long years
Had rescued from a chasm of tears ;
And when I woke, I wept to find
That the same lady, bright and wise,
With silver locks and quick brown
     eyes,
The mother of my Lionel,
Had tended me in my distress,
And died some months before.   Nor
     less
Wonder, but far more peace and joy,
Brought in that hour my lovely boy ;
For through that trance my soul had
     well
The impress of thy being kept ;
And if I waked, or if I slept,
No doubt; though memory faithless
     be,
Thy image ever dwelt on me ;
And thus, O Lionel ! like thee
Is our sweet child.   'Tis sure most
     strange
I knew not of so great a change,

As that which gave him birth, who
     now
Is all the solace of my woe.

That Lionel great wealth had left
By will to me, and that of all
The ready lies of law bereft,
My child and me might well befall.
But let me think not of the scorn,
Which from the meanest I have borne.
When, for my child's beloved sake,
I mixed with slaves, to vindicate
The very laws themselves do make :
Let me not say scorn is my fate,
Lest I be proud, suffering the same
With those who live in deathless fame.

She ceased.—" Lo, where red morn-
     ing thro' the woods
Is burning o'er the dew ! " said Rosa-
     lind.
And with these words they rose, and
     towards the flood
Of the blue lake, beneath the leaves
     now wind
With equal steps and fingers inter-
     twined :
Thence to a lonely dwelling, where
     the shore
Is shadowed with rocks, and cypresses
Cleave with their dark green cones the
     silent skies,
And with their shadows the clear
     depths below,
And where a little terrace from its
     bowers,
Of blooming myrtle and faint lemon-
     flowers,
Scatters its sense-dissolving fragrance
     o'er
The liquid marble of the windless
     lake;
And where the aged forest's limbs
     look hoar,
Under the leaves which their green
     garments make,
They come : 'tis Helen's home, and
     clean and white,
Like one which tyrants spare on our
     own land
In some such solitude, its casements
     bright
Shone through their vine leaves in
     the morning sun,
And even within 'twas scarce like
     Italy.

And when she saw how all things
  there were planned.
As in an English home, dim memory
Disturbed poor Rosalind : she
  stood as one
Whose mind is where his body cannot
  be,
Till Helen led her where her child yet
  slept,
And said, " Observe, that brow was
  Lionel's,
Those lips were his, and so he ever
  kept
One arm in sleep, pillowing his head
  with it.
You cannot see his eyes, they are two
  wells
Of liquid love : let us not wake him
  yet."
But Rosalind could bear no more, and
  wept
A shower of burning tears, which fell
  upon
His face, and so his opening lashes
  shone
With tears unlike his own, as he did
  leap
In sudden wonder from his innocent
  sleep.

So Rosalind and Helen lived together
Thenceforth, changed in all else, yet
  friends again,
Such as they were, when o'er the
  mountain heather
They wandered in their youth,
  through sun and rain.
And after many years, for human
  things
Change even like the ocean and the
  wind,
Her daughter was restored to Rosa-
  lind,
And in their circle thence some visit-
  ings
Of joy 'mid their new calm would
  intervene :
A lovely child she was, of looks serene,
And motions which o'er things indif-
  ferent shed
The grace and gentleness from
  whence they came.
And Helen's boy grew with ier, and
  they fed
From the same flowers of thought,
  until each mind

Like springs which mingle in one
  flood became,
And in their union soon their parents
  saw
The shadow of the peace denied to
  them.
And Rosalind,—for when the living
  stem
Is cankered in its heart, the tree must
  fall,—
Died ere her time ; and with deep grief
  and awe
The pale survivors followed her re-
  mains
Beyond the region of dissolving rains,
Up the cold mountain she was wont
  to call
Her tomb ; and on Chiavenna's preci-
  pice
They raised a pyramid of lasting ice,
Whose polished sides, ere day had yet
  begun,
Caught the first glow of the unrisen
  sun,
The last, when it had sunk ; and
  through the night
The charioteers of Arctos wheeled
  round
Its glittering point, as seen from
  Helen's home,
Whose sad inhabitants each year
  would come,
With willing steps climbing that
  rugged height,
And hang long locks of hair, and gar-
  lands bound
With amaranth flowers, which, in the
  clime's despite,
Filled the frore air with unaccus-
  . tomed light :
Such flowers, as in the wintry memory
  bloom
Of one friend left, adorned that frozen
  tomb.

Helen, whose spirit was of softer
  mould,
Whose sufferings too were less, death
  slowlier led
Into the peace of his dominion cold :
She died among her kindred, being
  old ;
And know, that if love die not in the
  dead
As in the living, none of mortal kind
Are blest, as now Helen and Rosalind.

LINES WRITTEN AMONG THE EUGANEAN HILLS

Many a green isle needs must be
In the deep wide sea of misery,
Or the mariner, worn and wan,
Never thus could voyage on
Day and night, and night and day,
Drifting on his dreary way,
With the solid darkness black
Closing round his vessel's track ;
Whilst above, the sunless sky,
Big with clouds, hangs heavily,
And behind the tempest fleet
Hurries on with lightning feet,
Riving sail, and cord, and plank,
Till the ship has almost drank
Death from the o'er-brimming deep ;
And sinks down, down, like that sleep
When the dreamer seems to be
Weltering through eternity ;
And the dim low line before
Of a dark and distant shore
Still recedes, as ever still
Longing with divided will ;
But no power to seek or shun,
He is ever drifted on
O'er the unreposing wave
To the haven of the grave.
What, if there no friends will greet ;
What, if there no heart will meet
His with love's impatient beat ;
Wander wheresoe'er he may,
Can he dream before that day
To find refuge from distress
In friendship's smile, in love's caress ?
Then 'twill wreak him little woe
Whether such there be or no :
Senseless is the breast, and cold,
Which relenting love would fold ,
Bloodless are the veins and chill
Which the pulse of pain did fill :
Every little living nerve
That from bitter words did swerve
Round the tortured lips and brow,
Are like sapless leaflets now
Frozen upon December's bough.

On the beach of a northern sea
Which tempests shake eternally,
As once the wretch there lay to sleep,
Lies a solitary heap,
One white skull and seven dry bones,
On the margin of the stones,
Where a few grey rushes stand,
Boundaries of the sea and land :
Nor is heard one voice of wail
But the sea-mews, as they sail
O'er the billows of the gale ;
Or the whirlwind up and down
Howling like a slaughtered town,
When a king in glory rides
Through the pomp of fratricides :
Those unburied bones around
There is many a mournful sound ;
There is no lament for him,
Like a sunless vapour, dim,
Who once clothed with life and
        thought
What now moves nor murmurs not.

Ay, many flowering islands lie
In the waters of wide Agony :
To such a one this morn was led
My bark, by soft winds piloted.
'Mid the mountains Euganean,
I stood listening to the pæan
With which the legioned rooks did
        hail
The sun's uprise majestical ;
Gathering round with wings all hoar,
Through the dewy mist they soar
Like grey shades, till the eastern
        heaven
Bursts, and then, as clouds of even,
Flecked with fire and azure, lie
In the unfathomable sky,
So their plumes of purple grain,
Starred with drops of golden rain,
Gleam above the sunlight woods,
As in silent multitudes
On the morning's fitful gale
Through the broken mist they sail ;
And the vapours cloven and gleaming
Follow down the dark steep stream-
        ing,
Till all is bright, and clear and still,
Round the solitary hill.
Beneath is spread like a green sea
The waveless plain of Lombardy,
Bounded by the vaporous air,
Islanded by cities fair ;
Underneath day's azure eyes,
Ocean's nursling, Venice lies,—
A peopled labyrinth of walls,
Amphitrite's destined halls,
Which her hoary sire now paves
With his blue and beaming waves.
Lo ! the sun upsprings behind,
Broad, red, radiant, half-reclined
On the level quivering line
Of the waters crystalline ;
And before that chasm of light,

As within a furnace bright,
Column, tower, and dome, and spire,
Shine like obelisks of fire,
Pointing with inconstant motion
From the altar of dark ocean
To the sapphire-tinted skies;
As the flames of sacrifice
From the marbled shrines did rise,
As to pierce the dome of gold
Where Apollo spoke of old.

Sun-girt City! thou hast been
Ocean's child, and then his queen
Now is come a darker day,
And thou soon must be his prey,
If the power that raised thee here
Hallow so thy watery bier.
A less drear ruin then than now,
With thy conquest-branded brow
Stooping to the slave of slaves
From thy throne among the waves,
Wilt thou be, when the sea-mew
Flies, as once before it flew,
O'er thine isles depopulate,
And all is in its ancient state,
Save where many a palace-gate
With green sea-flowers overgrown
Like a rock of ocean's own,
Topples o'er the abandon'd sea
As the tides change sullenly.
The fisher on his watery way,
Wandering at the close of day,
Will spread his sail and seize his oar,
Till he pass the gloomy shore,
Lest thy dead should, from their sleep
Bursting o'er the starlight deep,
Lead a rapid masque of death
O'er the waters of his path.

Those who alone thy towers behold
Quivering through aërial gold,
As I now behold them here,
Would imagine not they were
Sepulchres, where human forms,
Like pollution-nourish'd worms,
To the corpse of greatness cling,
Murdered and now mouldering:
But if Freedom should awake
In her omnipotence, and shake
From the Celtic Anarch's hold
All the keys of dungeons cold,
Where a hundred cities lie
Chained like thee, ingloriously,
Thou and all thy sister band
Might adorn this sunny land,
Twining memories of old time

With new virtues more sublime;
If not, perish thou and they;
Clouds which stain truth's rising day
By her sun consumed away,
Earth can spare ye; while like flowers,
In the waste of years and hours,
From your dust new nations spring
With more kindly blossoming.

Perish! let there only be
Floating o'er thy heartless sea,
As the garment of thy sky
Clothes the world immortally,
One remembrance, more sublime
Than the tattered pall of Time,
Which scarce hides thy visage wan:
That a tempest-cleaving swan
Of the songs of Albion,
Driven from his ancestral streams,
By the might of evil dreams,
Found a nest in thee: and Ocean
Welcomed him with such emotion
That its joy grew his, and sprung
From his lips like music flung
O'er a mighty thunder-fit,
Chastening terror: what though yet
Poesy's unfailing river,
Which through Albion winds for ever,
Lashing with melodious wave
Many a sacred poet's grave,
Mourn its latest nursling fled!
What though thou with all thy dead
Scarce can for this fame repay
Aught thine own,—oh, rather say,
Though thy sins and slaveries foul
Overcloud a sunlike soul!
As the ghost of Homer clings
Round Scamander's wasting springs;
As divinest Shakespeare's might
Fills Avon and the world with light,
Like omniscient power, which he
Imaged 'mid mortality;
As the love from Petrarch's urn,
Yet amid yon hills doth burn, [heart
A quenchless lamp, by which the
Sees things unearthly; so thou art,
Mighty spirit: so shall be
The city that did refuge thee.

Lo, the sun floats up the sky,
Like thought-winged Liberty,
Till the universal light
Seems to level plain and height;
From the sea a mist has spread,
And the beams of morn lie dead
On the towers of Venice now,

Like its glory of long ago.
By the skirts of that grey cloud
Many-domed Padua proud
Stands, a peopled solitude,
'Mid the harvest-shining plain,
Where the peasant heaps his grain
In the garner of his foe,
And the milk-white oxen slow
With the purple vintage strain,
Heaped upon the creaking wain,
That the brutal Celt may swill
Drunken sleep with savage will;
And the sickle to the sword
Lies unchanged, though many a lord
Like a weed whose shade is poison,
Overgrows this region's foison,
Sheaves of whom are ripe to come
To destruction's harvest-home:
Men must reap the things they sow,
Force from force must ever flow,
Or worse; but 'tis a bitter woe
That love or reason cannot change
The despot's rage, the slave's revenge.
Padua, thou within whose walls
Those mute guests at festivals,
Son and Mother, Death and Sin,
Played at dice for Ezzelin,
Till Death cried, " I win, I win !"
And Sin cursed to lose the wager,
But Death promised, to assuage her
That he would petition for
Her to be made Vice-Emperor,
When the destined years were o'er,
Over all between the Po
And the eastern Alpine snow,
Under the mighty Austrian.
Sin smiled so as Sin only can,
And since that time, ay, long before,
Both have ruled from shore to shore.
That incestuous pair, who follow
Tyrants as the sun the swallow,
As Repentance follows Crime,
And as changes follow Time.
In thine halls the lamp of learning,
Padua, now no more is burning;
Like a meteor, whose wild way
Is lost over the grave of day,
It gleams betrayed and to betray:
Once remotest nations came
To adore that sacred flame,
When it lit not many a hearth
On this cold and gloomy earth;
Now new fires from Antique light
Spring beneath the wide world's
    might :
But their spark lies dead in thee,

Trampled out by tyranny.
As the Norway woodman quells,
In the depth of piny dells,
One light flame among the brakes,
While the boundless forest shakes,
And its mighty trunks are torn
By the fire thus lowly born ;
The spark beneath his feet is dead,
He starts to see the flames it fed
Howling through the darkened sky
With myriad tongues victoriously,
And sinks down in fear : so thou,
O tyranny ! beholdest now
Light around thee, and thou hearest
The loud flames ascend, and fearest :
Grovel on the earth ; ay, hide
In the dust thy purple pride !
Noon descends around me now :
'Tis the noon of autumn's glow
When a soft and purple mist
Like a vaporous amethyst,
Of an air-dissolved star
Mingling light and fragrance, far
From the curved horizon's bound
To the point of heaven's profound,
Fills the overflowing sky ;
And the plains that silent lie
Underneath ; the leaves unsodden
Where the infant frost has trodden
With his morning-winged feet,
Whose bright print is gleaming yet ;
And the red and golden vines,
Piercing with their trellised lines
The rough, dark-skirted wilderness ;
The dun and bladed grass no less,
Pointing from this hoary tower
In the windless air ; the flower
Glimmering at my feet ; the line
Of the olive-sandalled Apennine
In the south dimly islanded ;
And the Alps, whose snows are spread
High between the clouds and sun ;
And of living things each one ;
And my spirit, which so long
Darkened this swift stream of song,
Interpenetrated lie
By the glory of the sky ;
Be it love, light, harmony,
Odour, or the soul of all
Which from heaven like dew doth fall,
Or the mind which feeds this verse
Peopling the lone universe.
Noon descends, and after noon
Autumn's evening meets me soon,
Leading the infantine moon,
And that one star, which to her

Almost seems to minister
Half the crimson light she brings
From the sunset's radiant springs ;
And the soft dreams of the morn
(Which like winged winds had borne
To that silent isle, which lies
'Mid remembered agonies,
The frail bark of this lone being),
Pass, to other sufferers fleeing,
And its ancient pilot, Pain,
Sits beside the helm again.
Other flowering isles must be
In the sea of life and agony :
Other spirits float and flee
O'er that gulf : even now, perhaps,
On some rock the wild wave wraps,
With folding wings they waiting sit
For my bark, to pilot it
To some calm and blooming cove,
Where for me, and those I love,
May a windless bower be built,
Far from passion, pain, and guilt,
In a dell 'mid lawny hills,
Which the wild sea-murmur fills,
And soft sunshine, and the sound

Of old forests echoing round,
And the light and smell divine
Of all flowers that breathe and shine.
We may live so happy there,
That the spirits of the air,
Envying us, may even entice
To our healing paradise
The polluting multitude ;
But their rage would be subdued
By that clime divine and calm,
And the winds whose wings rain balm
On the uplifted soul, and leaves
Under which the bright sea heaves ;
While each breathless interval
In their whisperings musical
The inspired soul supplies
With its own deep melodies ;
And the love which heals all strife
Circling, like the breath of life,
All things in that sweet abode
With its own mild brotherhood.
They, not it, would change ; and soon
Every sprite beneath the moon
Would repent its envy vain,
And the earth grow young again.

JULIAN AND MADDALO

A CONVERSATION

Count Maddalo is a Venetian noble-man of ancient family and of great fortune, who, without mixing much in the society of his countrymen, re-sides chiefly at his magnificent palace in that city. He is a person of the most consummate genius ; and cap-able, if he would direct his energies to such an end, of becoming the re-deemer of his degraded country. But it is his weakness to be proud : he derives, from a comparison of his own extraordinary mind with the dwarfish intellects that surround him, an intense apprehension of the no-thingness of human life. His pas-sions and his powers are incomparably greater than those of other men, and, instead of the latter having been employed in curbing the former, they have mutually lent each other strength. His ambition preys upon itself, for want of objects which it can consider worthy of exertion. I say that Maddalo is proud, because I can find no other word to express the con-

centered and impatient feelings which consume him ; but it is on his own hopes and affections only that he seems to trample, for in social life no human being can be more gentle, patient, and unassuming than Mad-dalo. He is cheerful, frank, and witty. His more serious conversa-tion is a sort of intoxication ; men are held by it as by a spell. He has tra-velled much ; and there is an inex-pressible charm in his relation of his adventures in different countries.

Julian is an Englishman of good family, passionately attached to those philosophical notions which assert the power of man over his own mind, and the immense improvements of which, by the extinction of certain moral superstitions, human society may yet be susceptible. Without concealing the evil in the world, he is for ever speculating how good may be made superior. He is a complete infidel, and a scoffer at all things reputed holy ; and Maddalo takes a wicked pleasure in drawing out his taunts against religion. What Maddalo thinks on these matters is not exactly known. Julian, in spite of his heterodox opinions, is conjectured by his friends to possess some good qualities. How far this is possible the pious reader will determine. Julian is rather serious.

Of the Maniac I can give no information. He seems by his own account to have been disappointed in love. He was evidently a very cultivated and amiable person when in his right senses. His story, told at length, might be, like many other stories of the same kind : the unconnected exclamations of his agony will perhaps be found a sufficient comment for the text of every heart.

The meadows with fresh streams, the bees
    with thyme,
The goats with the green leaves of bud-
    ding spring,
Are saturated not—nor Love with tears.
                    VIRGIL'S GALLUS.

I RODE one evening with Count Mad-
    dalo
Upon the bank of land which breaks
    the flow
Of Adria towards Venice : a bare
    strand
Of hillocks, heaped from ever-shifting
    sand,
Matted with thistles and amphibious
    weeds,
Such as from earth's embrace the salt
    ooze breeds,
Is this, an uninhabited seaside,
Which the lone fisher, when his nets
    are dried,
Abandons : and no other object breaks
The waste, but one dwarf tree and
    some few stakes
Broken and unrepaired, and the tide
    makes
A narrow space of level sand thereon,
Where 'twas our wont to ride while
    day went down.   [waste
This ride was my delight. I love all
And solitary places ; where we taste
The pleasure of believing what we see
Is boundless, as we wish our souls to
    be :
And such was this wide ocean, and
    this shore

More barren than its billows : and yet
    more   [I love
Than all, with a remembered friend
To ride as then I rode ;—for the winds
    drove
The living spray along the sunny air
Into our faces ; the blue heavens were
    bare,
Stripped to their depths by the
    awakening north ;
And, from the waves, sound like de-
    light broke forth
Harmonizing with solitude, and sent
Into our hearts aërial merriment.

So, as we rode, we talked ; and the
    swift thought,   [not,
Winging itself with laughter, lingered
But flew from brain to brain ; such
    glee was ours,
Charged with light memories of re-
    membered hours,
None slow enough for sadness, till we
    came
Homeward, which always makes the
    spirit tame.
This day had been cheerful but cold,
    and now
The sun was sinking, and the wind
    also.
Our talk grew somewhat serious, as
    may be
Talk interrupted with such raillery
As mocks itself, because it cannot
    scorn
The thoughts it would extinguish :—
    'twas forlorn,   [tell,
Yet pleasing ; such as once, so poets
The devils held within the dales of
    hell,
Concerning God, freewill, and destiny.
Of all that Earth has been, or yet may
    be ;
All that vain men imagine or believe,
Or hope can paint, or suffering can
    achieve,
We descanted ; and I (for ever still
Is it not wise to make the best of ill ?
Argued against despondency ; but
    pride   [side.
Made my companion take the darker
The sense that he was greater than his
    kind
Had struck, methinks, his eagle spirit
    blind
By gazing on its own exceeding light.

Meanwhile the sun paused ere it
    should alight
Over the horizon of the mountains—
    Oh !
How beautiful is sunset, when the
    glow
Of heaven descends upon a land like
    thee,
Thou paradise of exiles, Italy !
Thy mountains, seas, and vineyards,
    and the towers,
Of cities they encircle !—It was ours
To stand on thee, beholding it : and
    then,
Just where we had dismounted, the
    Count's men
Were waiting for us with the gondola.
As those who pause on some delightful
    way,
Though bent on pleasant pilgrimage,
    we stood
Looking upon the evening, and the
    flood
Which lay between the city and the
    shore,
Paved with the image of the sky : the
    hoar
And airy Alps, towards the north,
    appeared,
Thro' mist a heaven-sustaining bul-
    wark, reared
Between the east and west ; and half
    the sky
Was roofed with clouds of rich em-
    blazonry,
Dark purple at the zenith, which still
    grew
Down the steep west into a wondrous
    hue
Brighter than burning gold, even to
    the rent
Where the swift sun yet paused in his
    descent
Among the many-folded hills—they
    were
Those famous Euganean hills, which
    bear,
As seen from Lido through the har-
    bour piles,
The likeness of a clump of peaked
    isles—
And then, as if the earth and sea had
    been
Dissolved into one lake of fire, were
    seen

Those mountains towering, as from
    waves of flame,
Around the vaporous sun, from which
    there came
The inmost purple spirit of light, and
    made
Their very peaks transparent. " Ere
    it fade,"
Said my companion, " I will show you
    soon
A better station."   So, o'er the lagune
We glided ; and from that funereal
    bark
I leaned, and saw the city, and could
    mark
How from their many isles, in even-
    ing's gleam,
Its temples and its palaces did seem
Like fabrics of enchantment piled to
    heaven.
I was about to speak, when—" We are
    even
Now at the point I meant," said Mad-
    dalo,
And bade the gondolieri cease to row.
" Look, Julian, on the west, and listen
    well
If you hear not a deep and heavy
    bell."   [sun
I looked, and saw between us and the
A building on an island, such a one
As age to age might add, for uses
    vile,—
A windowless, deformed, and dreary
    pile ;
And on the top an open tower, where
    hung
A bell, which in the radiance swayed
    and swung,
We could just hear its coarse and iron
    tongue :
The broad sun sank behind it, and it
    tolled
In strong and black relief—" What
    we behold
Shall be the madhouse and its belfry
    tower,"—
Said Maddalo ; " and even at this
    hour,
Those who may cross the water hear
    that bell,
Which calls the maniacs, each one
    from his cell,
To vespers."—" As much skill as need
    to pray,

In thanks or hope for their dark lot
  have they,
To their stern maker," I replied.—" O,
  ho !
You talk as in years past," said Mad-
  dalo.
" 'Tis strange men change not. You
  were ever still
Among Christ's flock a perilous infidel,
A wolf for the meek lambs : if you
  can't swim,
Beware of providence."   I looked on
  him,
But the gay smile had faded from his
  eye.
" And such," he cried, " is our mor-
  tality ;
And this must be the emblem and the
  sign
Of what should be eternal and divine ;
And like that black and dreary bell,
  the soul,
Hung in a heaven-illumined tower,
  must toll
Our thoughts and our desires to meet
  below
Round the rent heart, and pray—as
  madmen do ;
For what ? they know not, till the
  night of death,
As sunset that strange vision, severeth
Our memory from itself, and us from
  all
We sought, and yet were baffled."   I
  recall   [mar
The sense of what he said, although I
The force of his expressions.   The
  broad star
Of day meanwhile had sunk behind
  the hill ;
And the black bell became invisible ;
And the red tower looked grey ; and
  all between,
The churches, ships, and palaces,
  were seen
Huddled in gloom ; into the purple
  sea
The orange hues of heaven sunk si-
  lently.
We hardly spoke, and soon the gon-
  dola
Conveyed me to my lodging by the
  way.
The following morn was rainy, cold,
  and dim :

Ere Maddalo arose I called on him,
And whilst I waited with his child I
  played ;
A lovelier toy sweet Nature never
  made ;
A serious, subtle, wild, yet gentle be
  ing ;
Graceful without design, and unfore-
  seeing ; ▾
With eyes—Oh ! speak not of her
  eyes ! which seem
Twin mirrors of Italian Heaven, yet
  gleam
With such deep meaning as we never
  see
But in the human countenance.
  With me
She was a special favourite : I had
  nursed
Her fine and feeble limbs, when she
  came first
To this bleak world ; and yet she
  seemed to know
On second sight her ancient play-
  fellow,
Less changed than she was by six
  months or so.
For, after her first shyness was worn
  out,   [about,
We sate there, rolling billiard balls
When the Count entered.   Salutations
  passed :
" The words you spoke last night
  might well have cast
A darkness on my spirit :—if man be
The passive thing you say, I should
  not see
Much harm in the religions and old
  saws,
(Tho' I may never own such leaden
  laws)
Which break a teachless nature to the
  yoke :
Mine is another faith."—Thus much
  I spoke,
And, noting he replied not, added—
  " See
This lovely child ; blithe, innocent,
  and free ;
She spends a happy time, with little
  care ;
While we to such sick thoughts sub-
  jected are,
As came on you last night.   It is our
  will

Which thus enchains us to permitted
  ill.
We might be otherwise ; we might be
  all
We dream of, happy, high, majestical.
Where is the beauty, love, and truth,
  we seek,
But in our minds ?   And, if we were
  not weak,
Should we be less in deed than in de-
  sire ? ''—
—'' Ay, if we were not weak,—and we
  aspire,
How vainly ! to be strong,'' said Mad-
  dalo :
'' You talk Utopian ''—
        '' It remains to know,''
I then rejoined, '' and those who try,
  may find
How strong the chains are which our
  spirit bind :
Brittle perchance as straw.   We are
  assured
Much may be conquered, much may
  be endured,
Of what degrades and crushes us.
  We know
That we have power over ourselves to
  do
And suffer—*what*, we know not till
  we try ;
But something nobler than to live
  and die :
So taught the kings of old philosophy,
Who reigned before religion made
  men blind ;
And those who suffer with their suf-
  fering kind,
Yet feel this faith, religion.''
        '' My dear friend.''
Said Maddalo, '' my judgment will
  not bend
To your opinion, though I think you
  might
Make such a system refutation-tight,
As far as words go.   I knew one like
  you,
Who to this city came some months
  ago,
With whom I argued in this sort,—
  and he
Is now gone mad—and so he an-
  swered me,
Poor fellow !—But if you would like
  to go,

We'll visit him, and his wild talk will
  show
How   vain   are   such   aspiring
  theories.''—

'' I hope to prove the induction other-
  wise,
And that a want of that true theory
  still,
Which seeks a soul of goodness in
  things ill,
Or in himself or others, has thus
  bowed
His being :—there are some by nature
  proud,
Who, patient in all else, demand but
  this—
To love and be beloved with gentle-
  ness :—
And being scorned, what wonder if
  they die
Some living death ?   This is not
  destiny,
But man's own wilful ill.''
             As thus I spoke,
Servants announced the gondola, and
  we
Through the fast-falling rain and
  high-wrought sea
Sailed to the island where the mad-
  house stands.
We disembarked.   The clap of tor-
  tured hands,
Fierce yells and howlings, and lam-
  entings keen,
And laughter where complaint had
  merrier been,
Accosted us.   We climbed the oozy
  stairs
Into an old courtyard.   I heard on
  high,
Then, fragments of most touching
  melody,
But looking up saw not the singer
  there.—
Thro' the black bars in the tempestuous air
I saw, like weeds on a wrecked palace
  growing,
Long tangled locks flung wildly forth
  and flowing,
Of those on a sudden who were beguiled
Into strange silence, and looked forth
  and smiled.

Hearing sweet sounds.   Then I :
    " Methinks there were
A cure of these with patience and kind
  care,
If music can thus move.   But what
  is he,
Whom we seek here ? "
    " Of his sad history
I know but this," said Maddalo : " he
  came
To Venice a dejected man, and fame
Said he was wealthy, or he had been
  so.
Some thought the loss of fortune
  wrought him woe ;
But he was ever talking in such sort
As you do,—but more sadly ;—he
  seemed hurt.
Even as a man with his peculiar
  wrong,
To hear but of the oppression of the
  strong,
Or those absurd deceits (I think with
  you
In some respects, you know) which
  carry through
The excellent impostors of this earth
When they outface detection.   He
  had worth,
Poor fellow ! but a humorist in his
  way."

—" Alas, what drove him mad ? "
    " I cannot say :
A lady came with him from France,
  and when
She left him and returned, he wan-
  dered then
About yon lonely isles of desert sand,
Till he grew wild.   He had no cash
  nor land
Remaining :—the police had brought
  him here—
Some fancy took him, and he would
  not bear
Removal, so I fitted up for him
Those rooms beside the sea, to please
  his whim ;
And sent him busts, and books, and
  urns for flowers,
Which had adorned his life in happier
  hours,
And instruments of music.   You may
  guess
A stranger could do little more or less
For one so gentle and unfortunate—

And those are his sweet strains which
  charm the weight
From madmen's chains, and make
  this hell appear
A heaven of sacred silence, hushed to
  hear."

" Nay, this was kind of you,—he had
  no claim,
As the world says."
    " None but the very same
Which I on all mankind, were I, as he,
Fallen to such deep reverse.   His
  melody
Is interrupted now : we hear the din
Of madmen, shriek on shriek, again
  begin :
Let us now visit him : after this
  strain,
He ever communes with himself
  again,
And sees and hears not any."
    Having said
These words, we called the keeper,
  and he led
To an apartment opening on the sea—
There the poor wretch was sitting
  mournfully
Near a piano, his pale fingers twined
One with the other ; and the ooze
  and wind
Rushed through an open casement,
  and did sway
His hair, and starred it with the
  brackish spray.
His head was leaning on a music-book,
And he was muttering ; and his
  lean limbs shook.
His lips were pressed against a folded
  leaf,
In hue too beautiful for health, and
  grief
Smiled in their motions as they lay
  apart,
As one who wrought from his own fer-
  vid heart
The eloquence of passion : soon he
  raised
His sad meek face, and eyes lustrous
  and glazed,
And spoke,—sometimes as one who
  wrote, and thought
His words might move some heart
  that heeded not,
If sent to distant lands ;—and then as
  one

Reproaching deeds never to be undone,
With wondering self-compassion ;—
then his speech
Was lost in grief, and then his words
came each
Unmodulated and expressionless,—
But that from one jarred accent you
might guess
It was despair made them so uniform :
And all the while the loud and gusty
storm
Hissed through the window, and we
stood behind,
Stealing his accents from the envious
wind,
Unseen. I yet remember what he
said
Distinctly, such impression his words
made.

" Month after month," he cried, " to
bear this load,
And, as a jade urged by the whip and
goad,
To drag life on—which like a heavy
chain
Lengthens behind with many a link
of pain,
And not to speak my grief—O, not
to dare
To give a human voice to my despair ;
But live, and move, and, wretched
thing ! smile on,
As if I never went aside to groan,
And wear this mask of falsehood even
to those
Who are most dear—not for my own
repose.
Alas ! no scorn, nor pain, nor hate,
could be
So heavy as that falsehood is to me—
But that I cannot bear more altered
faces
Than needs must be, more changed
and cold embraces,
More misery, disappointment, and
mistrust,
To own me for their father. Would
the dust
Were covered in upon my body now !
That the life ceased to toil within my
brow !
And then these thoughts would at the
last be fled :

Let us not fear such pain can vex the
dead.

" What Power delights to torture us ?
I know
That to myself I do not wholly owe
What now I suffer, though in part I
may.
Alas ! none strewed fresh flowers upon
the way
Where, wandering heedlessly, I met
pale Pain,
My shadow, which will leave me not
again.
If I have erred, there was no joy in
error,
But pain, and insult, and unrest, and
terror.
I have not, as some do, bought peni-
tence
With pleasure, and a dark yet sweet
offence ;
For then if love, and tenderness, and
truth,
Had overlived Hope's momentary
youth,
My creed should have redeemed me
from repenting.
But loathed scorn and outrage un-
relenting
Met love excited by far other seeming
Until the end was gained :—as one
from dreaming
Of sweetest peace, I woke, and found
my state
Such as it is.—

" O thou, my spirit's mate
Who, for thou art compassionate and
wise,
Wouldst pity me from thy most gentle
eyes
If this sad writing thou shouldst ever
see ;
My secret groans must be unheard by
thee ;
Thou wouldst weep tears, bitter as
blood, to know
Thy lost friend's incommunicabl
woe.
Ye few by whom my nature has been
weighed
In friendship, let me not that name
degrade,
By placing on your hearts the secret
load

Which crushes mine to dust.   There
    is one road
To peace, and that is truth, which fol-
    low ye !
Love sometimes leads astray to
    misery.
Yet think not,though subdued (and I
    may well
Say that I am subdued)—that the full
    hell
Within me would infect the untainted
    breast
Of sacred nature with its own unrest;
As some perverted beings think to
    find
In scorn or hate a medicine for the
    mind
Which scorn or hate hath wounded.
    —O, how vain !
The dagger heals not, but may rend
    again.
Believe that I am ever still the same
In creed as in resolve ; and what may
    tame
My heart, must leave the understand-
    ing free,
Or all would sink under this agony.—
Nor dream that I will join the vulgar
    lie,
Or with my silence sanction tyranny,
Or seek a moment's shelter from my
    pain
In any madness which the world calls
    gain ;
Ambition, or revenge, or thoughts as
    stern
As those which make me what I am,
    or turn
To avarice, or misanthropy, or lust :
Heap on me soon, O grave, thy wel-
    come dust !
Till then the dungeon may demand
    its prey ;
And Poverty and Shame may meet
    and say,
Halting beside me in the public way,—
' That love-devoted youth is ours :
    let's sit
Beside him : he may live some six
    months yet.'—
Cr the red scaffold, as our country
    bends,
May ask some willing victim ; or ye,
    friends,
May fall under some sorrow, which
    this heart

Or hand may share, or vanquish, or
    avert ;
I am prepared, in truth, with no proud
    joy,
To do or suffer aught, as when a boy
I did devote to justice and to love,
My nature, worthless now.
                    " I must remove
A veil from my pent mind.   'Tis torn
    aside !
O ! pallid as death's dedicated bride,
Thou mockery which art sitting by
    my side,
Am I not wan like thee ? At the
    grave's call
I haste, invited to thy wedding-ball,
To meet the ghastly paramour, for
    whom
Thou hast deserted me,—and made
    the tomb
Thy bridal bed.   But I beside thy
    feet
Will lie, and watch ye from my wind-
    ing-sheet
Thus—wide awake though dead—
    Yet stay, O, stay
Go not so soon—I know not what I
    say—
Hear but my reasons—I am mad, I
    fear,
My fancy is o'erwrought—thou art
    not here,
Pale art thou 'tis most true——but
    thou art gone—
Thy work is finished ; I am left alone.

        *   *   *

" Nay was it I who woo'd thee to this
    breast,
Which like a serpent thou envenomest
As in repayment of the warmth it
    lent ?
Didst thou not seek me for thine own
    content ?
Did not thy love awaken mine ? I
    thought
That thou wert she who said ' You
    kiss me not
Ever ; I fear you do not love me now,'
In truth I loved even to my over-
    throw
Her who would fain forget these
    words, but they
Cling to her mind, and cannot pass
    away.

        *   *   *

" You say that I am proud ; that
  when I speak,
My lip is tortured with the wrongs
  which break
The spirit it expresses.—Never one
Humbled himself before, as I have
  done ;
Even the instinctive worm on which
  we tread
Turns, though it wound not—then,
  with prostrate head,
Sinks in the dust, and writhes like me
  —and dies :
——No — wears a living death of
  agonies ;
As the slow shadows of the pointed
  grass
Mark the eternal periods, its pangs
  pass,
Slow, ever-moving, making moments
  be
As mine seem,—each an immortality !

* * *

" That you had never seen me ! never
  heard
My voice ! and more than all had
  ne'er endured
The deep pollution of my loathed embrace ;
That your eyes ne'er had lied love in
  my face !
That, like some maniac monk, I had
  torn out
The nerves of manhood by their bleeding root
With mine own quivering fingers ! so
  that ne'er
Our hearts had for a moment mingled
  there,
To disunite in horror ! These were
  not
With thee like some suppressed and
  hideous thought,
Which flits athwart our musings, but
  can find
No rest within a pure and gentle
  mind—
Thou sealedst them with many a bare
  broad word,
And sear'dst my memory o'er them,
  —for I heard
And can forget not—they were ministered,
One after one, those curses. Mix
  them up

Like self-destroying poisons in one
  cup ;
And they will make one blessing,
  which thou ne'er
Didst imprecate for on me——death !
                             " It were
A cruel punishment for one most cruel,
If such can love, to make that love the
  fuel
Of the mind's hell—hate, scorn, re-
  morse, despair :
But *me*, whose heart a stranger's tear
  might wear
As water-drops the sandy fountain
  stone ;
Who loved and pitied all things, and
  could moan
For woes which others hear not, and
  could see
The absent with a glass of phantasy,
And near the poor and trampled sit
  and weep,
Following the captive to his dungeon
  deep ;
Me, who am as a nerve o'er which do
  creep
The else-unfelt oppressions of this
  earth,
And was to thee the flame upon thy
  hearth,
When all beside was cold :—that thou
  on me
Should rain these plagues of blister-
  ing agony—
Such curses are from lips once elo-
  quent
With love's too partial praise ! Let
  none relent
Who intend deeds too dreadful for a
  name
Henceforth, if an example for the same
They seek :—for thou on me lookedst
  so and so,
And didst speak thus and thus. I
  live to show
How much men bear, and die not.

* * *

                            " Thou wilt tell,
With the grimace of hate, how horrible
It was to meet my love when thine
  grew less ;
Thou wilt admire how I could e'er
  address
Such features to love's work . . .
    This taunt, though true,

(For indeed Nature nor in form nor
      hue
Bestowed on me her choicest work-
      manship)
Shall not be thy defence : for since
      thy lip
Met mine first, years long past,—since
      thine eye kindled
With soft fire under mine,—I have not
      dwindled,
Nor changed in mind, or body, or in
      aught
But as love changes what it loveth not
After long years and many trials.

*   *   *

                    " How vain
Are words ; I thought never to speak
      again,
Not even in secret, not to my own
      heart—
But from my lips the unwilling ac-
      cents start,
And from my pen the words flow as I
      write,
Dazzling my eyes with scalding tears
      —my sight
Is dim to see that (charactered in vain
On this unfeeling leaf) which burns
      the brain
And eats into it, blotting all things
      fair,
And wise and good, which time had
      written there.
Those who inflict must suffer, for they
      see
The work of their own hearts, and
      that must be
Our chastisement,or recompense.—O
      child !
I would that thine were like to be more
      mild
For both our wretched sakes,—for
      thine t' e most,
Who feel'st already all that thou hast
      lost,
Without the power to wish it thine
      again.
And, as slow years pass, a funereal
      train,
Each with the ghost of some lost hope
      or friend
Following it like its shadow, wilt thou
      bend
No thought on my dead memory ?

*   *   *

                    " Alas, love !
Fear me not : against thee I'd not
      move
A finger in despite. Do I not live
That thou mayst have less bitter cause
      to grieve ?
I give thee tears for scorn, and love for
      hate ;
And, that thy lot may be less desolate
Than his on whom thou tramplest, I
      refrain
From that sweet sleep which medi-
      cines all pain.
Then—when thou speakest of me—
      never say,
' He could forgive not.'—Here I cast
      away
All human passions, all revenge, all
      pride ;
I think, speak, act no ill; I do but hide
Under these words, like embers, every
      spark
Of that which has consumed me.
      Quick and dark
The grave is yawning :—as its roof
      shall cover
My limbs with dust and worms, under
      and over,
So let oblivion hide this grief.—The
      air
Closes upon my accents as despair
Upon my heart—let death upon my
      care ! "

He ceased and, overcome, leant back
      awhile ;
Then rising, with a melancholy smile,
Went to a sofa, and lay down, and
      slept
A heavy sleep, and in his dreams he
      wept,
And muttered some familiar name,
      and we
Wept without shame in his society.
I think I never was impressed so
      much !
The man who was not, must have
      lacked a touch
Of human nature.—Then we lingered
      not,
Although our argument was quite
      forgot ;
But, calling the attendants, went to
      dine
At Maddalo's ; yet neither cheer nor
      wine

Could give us spirits, for we talked of him,
And nothing else, till daylight made stars dim.
And we agreed it was some dreadful ill
Wrought on him boldly, yet unspeakable,
By a dear friend ; some deadly change in love
Of one vowed deeply which he dreamed not of ;
For whose sake he, it seemed, had fixed a blot
Of falsehood in his mind, which flourished not
But in the light of all-beholding truth ;
And having stamped this canker on his youth,
She had abandoned him :—and how much more
Might be his woe, we guessed not :—he had store
Of friends and fortune once, as we could guess
From his nice habits and his gentleness :
These now were lost—it were a grief indeed
If he had changed one unsustaining reed
For all that such a man might else adorn.
The colours of his mind seemed yet unworn ;
For the wild language of his grief was high—
Such as in measure were called poetry.
And I remember one remark, which then
Maddalo made : he said—" Most wretched men
Are cradled into poetry by wrong :
They learn in suffering what they teach in song."

If I had been an unconnected man,
I, from the moment, should have formed some plan
Never to leave sweet Venice : for to me
It was delight to ride by the lone sea :
And then the town is silent—one may write
Or read in gondolas, by day or night,
Having the little brazen lamp alight,
Unseen, uninterrupted :—books are there,
Pictures, and casts from all those statues fair
Which were twin-born with poetry ! —and all
We seek in towns, with little to recall
Regret for the green country :—I might sit
In Maddalo's great palace, and his wit
And subtle talk would cheer the winter night,
And make me know myself :—and the fire light
Would flash upon our faces, till the day
Might dawn, and make me wonder at my stay.
But I had friends in London too. The chief
Attraction here was that I sought relief
From the deep tenderness that maniac wrought
Within me—'twas perhaps an idle thought,
But I imagined that if, day by day,
I watched him, and seldom went away,
And studied all the beatings of his heart
With zeal, as men study some stubborn art
For their own good, and could by patience find
An entrance to the caverns of his mind,
I might reclaim him from his dark estate.
In friendships I had been most fortunate,
Yet never saw I one whom I would call
More willingly my friend :—and this was all
Accomplished not ;—such dreams of baseless good
Oft come and go, in crowds or solitude,
And leave no trace !—but what I now designed
Made, for long years, impression on my mind.
The following morning, urged by my affairs,

I left bright Venice.
        After many years,
And many changes, I returned : the
   name
Of Venice, and its aspect, was the
   same ;
But Maddalo was travelling, far away,
Among the mountains of Armenia.
His dog was dead : his child had now
   become
A woman, such as it has been my
   doom   [earth,
To meet with few ; a wonder of this
Where there is little of transcendent
   worth,—
Like one of Shakspeare's women.
   Kindly she,
And with a manner beyond courtesy,
Received her father's friend ; and,
   when I asked,
Of the lorn maniac, she her memory
   tasked,
And told, as she had heard, the mourn-
  · ful tale :
" That the poor sufferer's health be-
   gan to fail
Two years from my departure : but
   that then
The lady, who had left him, came
   again :
Her mien had been imperious, but she
   now
Looked meek ; perhaps remorse had
   brought her low.
Her coming made him better ; and
   they stayed
Together at my father's,—for I
   played,
As I remember, with the lady's shawl ;
I might be six years old.—But, after
   all,
She left him."
        " Why, her heart must have
   been tough ;
How did it end ? "
        " And was not this enough ?
They met, they parted."
        " Child, is there no more ? "

" Something within that interval
   which bore
The stamp of *why* they parted, *how*
   they met ;—
Yet, if thine aged eyes disdain to wet
Those wrinkled cheeks with youth's
   remembered tears.

Ask me no more ; but let the silent
   years
Be closed and cered over their
   memory,
As yon mute marble where their
   corpses lie."

I urged and questioned still : she told
   me how
All happened—but the cold world
   shall not know.

THE WOODMAN AND THE NIGHTINGALE

A WOODMAN whose rough heart was
   out of tune
(I think such hearts yet never came
   to good),
Hated to hear, under the stars or
   moon,

One nightingale in an interfluous
   wood
Satiate the hungry dark with melody.
And, as a vale is watered by a flood,

Or as the moonlight fills the open sky
Struggling with darkness—as a tuberose
Peoples some Indian dell with scents
   which lie

Like clouds above the flower from
   which they rose,
The singing of that happy nightingale
In this sweet forest, from the golden
   close

Of evening till the star of dawn may
   fail,
Was interfused upon the silentness.
The folded roses and the violets pale

Heard her within their slumbers ; the
   abyss
Of heaven with all its planets ; the
   dull ear
Of the night-cradled earth ; the loneliness

Of the circumfluous waters ; every
   sphere
And every flower and beam and cloud
   and wave,
And every wind of the mute atmosphere,

And every beast stretched in its rugged cave,

And every bird lulled on its mossy bough,

And every silver moth fresh from the grave,

Which is its cradle—ever from below
Aspiring like one who loves too fair, too far,

To be consumed within the purest glow

Of one serene and unapproached star,
As if it were a lamp of earthly light,
Unconscious as some human lovers are,

Itself how low, how high, beyond all height
The heaven where it would perish !— and every form
That worshipped in the temple of the night

Was awed into delight, and by the charm
Girt as with an interminable zone ;
Whilst that sweet bird, whose music was a storm

Of sound, shook forth the dull oblivion
Out of their dreams ; harmony became love
In every soul but one. . . .

—————

And so this man returned with axe and saw
At evening close from killing the tall treen,
The soul of whom by nature's gentle law

Was each a wood nymph, and kept ever green
The pavement and the roof of the wild copse,
Chequering the sunlight of the blue serene

With jagged leaves,—and from the forest tops
Singing the winds to sleep—or weeping oft
Fast showers of aërial water drops

Into their mother's bosom, sweet and soft,

Nature's pure tears which have no bitterness.
Around the cradles of the birds aloft

They spread themselves into the loveliness
Of fan-like leaves, and over pallid flowers
Hang like moist clouds : or, where high branches kiss,

Make a green space among the silent bowers—
Like a vast fane in a metropolis,
Surrounded by the columns and the towers

All overwrought with branch-like traceries—
In which there is religion, and the mute
Persuasion of unkindled melodies,

Odours and gleams and murmurs, which the lute
Of the blind pilot-spirit of the blast
Stirs as it sails, now grave and now acute,

Wakening the leaves and waves ere it has past
To such brief unison as on the brain
One tone, which never can recur, has cast,

One accent never to return again.

MISERY—A FRAGMENT

Come, be happy !—sit near me,
Shadow-vested Misery :
Coy, unwilling, silent bride,
Mourning in thy robe of pride,
Desolation—deified !

Come, be happy !—sit near me :
Sad as I may seem to thee,
I am happier far than thou,
Lady, whose imperial brow
Is endiademed with woe.

Misery ! we have known each other,
Like a sister and a brother
Living in the same lone home,
Many years—we must live some
Hours or ages yet to come.

'Tis an evil lot, and yet
Let us make the best of it ;

If love can live when pleasure dies,
We two will love, till in our eyes
This heart's Hell seem Paradise.

Come, be happy !—lie thee down
On the fresh grass newly mown,
Where the grasshopper doth sing
Merrily—one joyous thing
In a world of sorrowing !

There our tent shall be the willow,
And mine arm shall be thy pillow :
Sounds and odours, sorrowful
Because they once were sweet, shall
    lull
Us to slumber deep and dull.

Ha ! thy frozen pulses flutter
With a love thou dar'st not utter.
Thou art murmuring—thou art weep-
    ing—
Is thine icy bosom leaping
While my burning heart lies sleeping ?

Kiss me ;—oh ! thy lips are cold ;
Round my neck thine arms enfold—
They are soft, but chill and dead ;
And thy tears upon my head
Burn like points of frozen lead.

Hasten to the bridal bed—
Underneath the grave 'tis spread :
In darkness may our love be hid,
Oblivion be our coverlid—
We may rest, and none forbid.

Clasp me, till our hearts be grown
Like two shadows into one ;
Till this dreadful transport may
Like a vapour fade away
In the sleep that lasts alway.

We may dream in that long sleep,
That we are not those who weep ;
Even as Pleasure dreams of thee,
Life-deserting Misery,
Thou mayst dream of her with me.

Let us laugh, and make our mirth,
At the shadows of the earth,
As dogs bay the moonlight clouds,
Which, like spectres wrapt in shrouds,
Pass o'er night in multitudes.

All the wide world, beside us
Show like multitudinous
Puppets passing from a scene ;
What but mockery can they mean,
Where I am—where thou hast been ?

TO MARY ——

O Mary dear, that you were here
With your brown eyes bright and
    clear,
And your sweet voice, like a bird
Singing love to its lone mate
In the ivy bower disconsolate ;
Voice the sweetest ever heard !
And your brow more * * *
Than the * * * sky
Of this azure Italy.

Mary dear, come to me soon,
I am not well whilst thou art far ;
As sunset to the sphered moon,
As twilight to the western star,
Thou, beloved, art to me.

O Mary dear, that you were here !
The Castle echo whispers "Here !"

Este, *September*, 1818.

PASSAGE OF THE APENNINES

Listen, listen, Mary mine,
To the whisper of the Apennine,
It bursts on the roof like the thunder's
    roar,
Or like the sea on a northern shore,
Heard in its raging ebb and flow
By the captives pent in the cave
    below.
The Apennine in the light of day
Is a mighty mountain dim and grey,
Which between the earth and sky
    doth lay ;
But when night comes, a chaos dread
On the dim starlight then is spread,
And the Apennine walks abroad with
    the storm.

ON A FADED VIOLET

The colour from the flower is gone,
    Which like thy sweet eyes smiled
    on me ;
The odour from the flower is flown,
    Which breathed of thee and only
    thee !

A withered, lifeless, vacant form,
    It lies on my abandoned breast,
And mocks the heart which yet is
    warm
    With cold and silent rest.

I weep—my tears revive it not ;
I sigh—it breathes no more on me ;
Its mute and uncomplaining lot
Is such as mine should be.

STANZAS

WRITTEN IN DEJECTION, NEAR NAPLES

THE sun is warm, the sky is clear,
    The waves are dancing fast and
    bright,
Blue isles and snowy mountains
    wear
    The purple noon's transparent
    light :
The breath of the moist air is light,
    Around its unexpanded buds ;
Like many a voice of one delight,
    The winds, the birds, the ocean
    floods,
The City's voice itself is soft like
    Solitude's.

I see the Deep's untrampled floor
    With green and purple seaweeds
    strown ;
I see the waves upon the shore,
    Like light dissolved in star show-
    ers, thrown :
I sit upon the sands alone,
    The lightning of the noontide
    ocean
Is flashing round me, and a tone
    Arises from its measured motion,
How sweet ! did any heart now share
    in my emotion.

Alas ! I have nor hope nor health,
    Nor peace within nor calm
    around,
Nor that content surpassing wealth
    The sage in meditation found,
And walked with inward glory
    crowned—
    Nor fame, nor power, nor love,
    nor leisure.
Others I see whom these sur-
    round—
    Smiling they live, and call life
    pleasure ;—
To me that cup has been dealt in
    another measure.

Yet now despair itself is mild,
    Even as the winds and waters
    are :

I could lie down like a tired child,
    And weep away the life of care
Which I have borne, and yet must
    bear,
Till death like sleep might steal
    on me,
And I might feel in the warm air
    My cheek grow cold, and hear
    the sea
Breathe o'er my dying brain its last
    monotony.

Some might lament that I were
    cold,
    As I when this sweet day is gone,
Which my lost heart, too soon
    grown old,
    Insults with this untimely moan ;
They might lament—for I am one
    Whom men love not,—and yet
    regret,
Unlike this day, which, when the
    sun
    Shall on its stainless glory set,
Will linger, though enjoyed, like joy
    in memory yet.

SONG FOR TASSO

I *loved*—alas ! our life is love ;
But when we cease to breathe and
    move,
I do suppose love ceases too.
I *thought*, but not as now I do,
Keen thoughts and bright of linked
    lore,
Of all that men had thought before,
And all that Nature shows, and more.

And still I love, and still I think,
But strangely, for my heart can drink
The dregs of such despair, and live,
And love ;
And if I think, my thoughts come
    fast ;
I mix the present with the past,
And each seems uglier than the last.

Sometimes I see before me flee
A silver spirit's form, like thee,
O Leonora, and I sit
[   ] still watching it,
Till by the grated casement's ledge
It fades, with such a sigh, as sedge
Breathes o'er the breezy streamlet's
    edge.

THE PAST

WILT thou forget the happy hours
Which we buried in 'Love's sweet
　　bowers,
Heaping over their corpses cold
'Blossoms and leaves instead of
　　mould?　　·
Blossoms which were the joys that
　　fell,
And leaves, the hopes that yet
　　remain.

Forget the dead, the past? O yet
There are ghosts that may take re-
　　venge for it;
Memories that make the heart a tomb,
Regrets which glide through the
　　spirit's gloom,
And with ghastly whispers tell
That joy, once lost, is pain.

MAZENGHI [1]

O! FOSTER-NURSE of man's aban-
　　doned glory
Since Athens, its great mother, sunk
　　in splendour,
Thou shadowest forth that mighty
　　shape in story,
As ocean its wrecked fanes, severe yet
　　tender:
The light invested angel Poesy
Was drawn from the dim world to
　　welcome thee.

And thou in painting didst transcribe
　　all taught
By loftiest meditations; marble knew
The sculptor's fearless soul—and, as
　　he wrought,
The grace of his own power and free-
　　dom grew.
And more than all, heroic, just, sub-
　　lime,
Thou wert among the false—was this
　　thy crime?

Yes; and on Pisa's marble walls the
　　twine
Of direst weed hangs garlanded—the
　　snake

Inhabits its wrecked palaces;—in
　　thine
A beast of subtler venom now doth
　　make
Its lair, and sits amid their glories
　　overthrown,
And thus thy victim's fate is as thine
　　own.

The sweetest flowers are ever frail
　　and rare,
And love and freedom blossom but to
　　wither;
And good and ill like vines entangled
　　are,
So that their grapes may oft be
　　plucked together;
Divide the vintage ere thou drink,
　　then make
Thy heart rejoice for dead Mazenghi's
　　sake.

No record of his crime remains in
　　story,
But if the morning bright as evening
　　shone,
It was some high and holy deed, by
　　glory
Pursued into forgetfulness, which won
From the blind crowd he made secure
　　and free
The Patriot's meed, toil, death, and
　　infamy.

For when by sound of trumpet was de-
　　clared
A price upon his life, and there was set
A penalty of blood on all who shared
So much of water with him as might
　　wet
His lips, which speech divided not—
　　he went
Alone, as you may guess, to banish-
　　ment.

Amid the mountains, like a hunted
　　beast,
He hid himself, and hunger, toil, and
　　cold,
Month after month endured; it was
　　a feast
Whene'er he found those globes of
　　deep red gold
Which in the woods the strawberry-
　　tree doth bear,
Suspended in their emerald atmo-
　　sphere.

---

[1] This fragment refers to an event, told in
Sismondi's *Histoire des Républiques Italiennes*,
which occurred during the war when Florence
finally subdued Pisa, and reduced it to a
province. The opening stanzas are addressed to
the conquering city.—*M. S.*

And in the roofless huts of vast mo-
    rasses,
Deserted by the fever-stricken serf,
All overgrown with reeds and long
    rank grasses,
And hillocks heaped of moss-inwoven
    turf,   [made,
And where the huge and speckled aloe
Rooted in stones, a broad and pointed
    shade,

He housed himself. There is a point
    of strand
Near Vada's tower and town ; and on
    one side
The treacherous marsh divides it from
    the land,
Shadowed by pine and ilex forests
    wide ;
And on the other creeps eternally,
Through muddy weeds, the shallow
    sullen sea.

NAPLES, 1818.

SONNET

LIFT not the painted veil which those
    who live

Call life ; though unreal shapes be
    pictured there,
And it but mimic all we would be-
    lieve
With colours idly spread,—behind,
    lurk Fear
And Hope, twin Destinies ; who ever
    weave
Their shadows, o'er the chasm, sight-
    less and drear.

I knew one who had lifted it—he
    sought,
For his lost heart was tender, things
    to love,
But found them not, alas ! nor was
    there aught
The world contains, the which he
    could approve.
Through the unheeding many he did
    move,
A splendour among shadows, a bright
    blot
Upon this gloomy scene, a Spirit
    that strove
For truth, and like the Preacher
    found it not.

POEMS WRITTEN IN 1819

THE MASQUE OF ANARCHY

I

As I lay asleep in Italy,
There came a voice from over the sea,
And with great power it forth led me
To walk in the visions of Poesy.

II

I met Murder on the way—
He had a mask like Castlereagh—
Very smooth he looked, yet grim ;
Seven bloodhounds followed him :

III

All were fat ; and well they might
Be in admirable plight,
For one by one, and two by two,
He tossed them human hearts to
    chew,
Which from his white cloak he drew.

IV

Next came Fraud, and he had on
Like Lord E——, an ermine gown ;
His big tears, for he wept well,
Turned to millstones as they fell ;

V

And the little children, who
Round his feet played to and fro,
Thinking every tear a gem,
Had their brains knocked out by
    them.

VI

Clothed with the Bible as with light,
And the shadow of the night,
Like S * * * next, Hypocrisy,
On a crocodile came by.

VII

And many more Destructions played
In this ghastly masquerade,
All disguised, even to the eyes,
Like bishops, lawyers, peers, or spies.

VIII

Last came Anarchy; he rode
On a white horse splashed with blood;
He was pale even to the lips,
Like Death in the Apocalypse.

IX

And he wore a kingly crown;
In his hand a sceptre shone;
On his brow this mark I saw—
" I am God, and King, and Law ! "

X

With a pace stately and fast,
Over English land he past,
Trampling to a mire of blood
The adoring multitude.

XI

And a mighty troop around,
With their trampling shook the
    ground,
Waving each a bloody sword,
For the service of their Lord.

XII

And, with glorious triumph, they
Rode through England, proud and
    gay,
Drunk as with intoxication,
Of the wine of desolation.

XIII

O'er fields and towns, from sea to sea,
Passed the pageant swift and free,
Tearing up, and trampling down,
Till they came to London town.

XIV

And each dweller, panic-stricken,
Felt his heart with terror sicken,
Hearing the tremendous cry
Of the triumph of Anarchy.

XV

For with pomp to meet him came,
Clothed in arms like blood and flame,
The hired murderers who did sing,
" Thou art God, and Law, and King.

XVI

" We have waited, weak and lone,
For thy coming, Mighty One !

Our purses are empty, our swords are
    cold,
Give us glory, and blood, and gold."

XVII

Lawyers and priests, a motley crowd,
To the earth their pale brows bowed;
Like a bad prayer not over loud,
Whispering—" Thou art Law and
    God ! "

XVIII

Then all cried with one accord,
" Thou art King, and Law, and Lord:
Anarchy, to thee we bow,
Be thy name made holy now ! "

XIX

And Anarchy, the skeleton,
Bowed and grinned to every one,
As well as if his education
Had cost ten millions to the nation.

XX

For he knew the palaces
Of our kings were nightly his;
His the sceptre, crown, and globe,
And the gold-inwoven robe.

XXI

So he sent his slaves before
To seize upon the Bank and Tower,
And was proceeding with intent
To meet his pensioned Parliament,

XXII

When one fled past, a maniac maid,
And her name was Hope, she said:
But she looked more like Despair;
And she cried out in the air:

XXIII

" My father Time is weak and grey
With waiting for a better day;
See how idiot-like he stands,
Trembling with his palsied hands!

XXIV

" He has had child after child,
And the dust of death is piled
Over every one but me—
Misery ! oh, Misery ! "

XXV

Then she lay down in the street,
Right before the horses' feet,
Expecting, with a patient eye,
Murder, Fraud, and Anarchy.

XXVI

When between her and her foes
A mist, a light, an image rose,

Small at first, and weak and frail
Like the vapour of the vale :

XXVII

Till as clouds grow on the blast,
Like tower-crowned giants striding
    fast,
And glare with lightnings as they fly,
And speak in thunder to the sky,

XXVIII

It grew—a shape arrayed in mail
Brighter than the viper's scale,
And upborne on wings whose grain
Was like the light of sunny rain.

XXIX

On its helm, seen far away,
A planet, like the morning's, lay ;
And those plumes it light rained
    through,
Like a shower of crimson dew.

XXX

With step as soft as wind it passed
O'er the heads of men—so fast
That they knew the presence there,
And looked—and all was empty air.

XXXI

As flowers beneath May's footsteps
    waken,
As stars from night's loose hair are
    shaken,
As waves arise when loud winds call,
Thoughts sprung where'er that step
    did fall.

XXXII

And the prostrate multitude
Looked—and ankle-deep in blood,
Hope, that maiden most serene,
Was walking with a quiet mien :

XXXIII

And Anarchy, the ghastly birth,
Lay dead earth upon the earth ;
The Horse of Death, tameless as wind,
Fled, and with his hoofs did grind
To dust the murderers thronged be-
    hind.

XXXIV

A rushing light of clouds and splend-
    our,
A sense, awakening and yet tender,
Was heard and felt—and at its close
These words of joy and fear arose ;

XXXV

As if their own indignant earth,
Which gave the sons of England birth,
Had felt their blood upon her brow,
And shuddering with a mother's
    throe,

XXXVI

Had turned every drop of blood,
By which her face had been bedewed,
To an accent unwithstood,
As if her heart had cried aloud—

XXXVII

" Men of England, Heirs of Glory,
Heroes of unwritten story,
Nurslings of one mighty mother,
Hopes of her, and one another !

XXXVIII

" Rise, like lions after slumber,
In unvanquishable number,
Shake your chains to earth like dew,
Which in sleep had fall'n on you !
Ye are many, they are few.

XXXIX

" What is freedom ?   Ye can tell
That which Slavery is too well,
For its very name has grown
To an echo of your own.

XL

" 'Tis to work, and have such pay
As just keeps life from day to day
In your limbs as in a cell
For the tyrants' use to dwell :

XLI

" So that ye for them are made,
Loom, and plough, and sword, and
    spade ;
With or without your own will, bent
To their defence and nourishment.

XLII

" 'Tis to see your children weak
With their mothers pine and peak,
When the winter winds are bleak :—
They are dying whilst I speak.

XLIII

" 'Tis to hunger for such diet,
As the rich man in his riot
Casts to the fat dogs that lie
Surfeiting beneath his eye.

XLIV

" 'Tis to let the Ghost of Gold
Take from toil a thousandfold

More than e'er his substance could
In the tyrannies of old :

XLV

" Paper coin—that forgery
Of the title-deeds, which ye
Hold to something of the worth
Of the inheritance of Earth.

XLVI

" 'Tis to be a slave in soul,
And to hold no strong controul
Over your own wills, but be
All that others make of ye.

XLVII

" And at length when ye complain,
With a murmur weak and vain,
'Tis to see the tyrant's crew
Ride over your wives and you :—
Blood is on the grass like dew !

XLVIII

" Then it is to feel revenge,
Fiercely thirsting to exchange
Blood for blood—and wrong for
    wrong :
Do not thus when ye are strong !

XLIX

" Birds find rest in narrow nest,
When weary of their winged quest ;
Beasts find fare in woody lair,
When storm and snow are in the air.

L

" Horses, oxen, have a home,
When from daily toil they come ;
Household dogs, when the wind roars,
Find a home within warm doors.

LI

" Asses, swine, have litter spread,
And with fitting food are fed ;
All things have a home but one :
Thou, O Englishman, hast none !

LII

" This is slavery—savage men,
Or wild beasts within a den,
Would endure not as ye do :
But such ills they never knew.

LIII

" What are thou, Freedom ? Oh !
    could slaves
Answer from their living graves
This demand, tyrants would flee
Like a dream's dim imagery.

LIV

" Thou art not, as impostors say,
A shadow soon to pass away,
A superstition, and a name
Echoing from the cave of Fame.

LV

" For the labourer thou art bread
And a comely table spread,
From his daily labour come,
In a neat and happy home.

LVI

" Thou art clothes, and fire, and
    food
For the trampled multitude :
No—in countries that are free
Such starvation cannot be,
As in England now we see.

LVII

" To the rich thou art a check ;
When his foot is on the neck
Of his victim, thou dost make
That he treads upon a snake.

LVIII

" Thou art Justice—ne'er for gold
May thy righteous laws be sold,
As laws are in England :—thou
Shieldest alike the high and low.

LIX

" Thou art Wisdom—freemen never
Dream that God will doom for ever
All who think those things untrue
Of which priests make such ado.

LX

" Thou art Peace—never by thee
Would blood and treasure wasted be,
As tyrants wasted them, when all
Leagued to quench thy flame in
    Gaul.

LXI

" What if English toil and blood
Was poured forth, even as a flood ?
It availed,—O Liberty !
To dim—but not extinguish thee.

LXII

"Thou art Love—the rich have kissed
Thy feet ; and like him following
    Christ,
Given their substance to the free,
And through the rough world fol-
    lowed thee.

LXIII

" Oh! turn their wealth to arms, and make
War for thy beloved sake,
On wealth and war and fraud; whence they
Drew the power which is their prey.

LXIV

" Science, and Poetry, and Thought,
Are thy Lamps; they make the lot
Of the dwellers in a cot
Such, they curse their maker not.

LXV

" Spirit, Patience, Gentleness,
All that can adorn and bless,
Art thou: let deeds, not words, express
Thine exceeding loveliness.

LXVI

" Let a great assembly be
Of the fearless and the free,
On some spot of English ground,
Where the plains stretch wide around.

LXVII

" Let the blue sky overhead,
The green earth on which ye tread,
All that must eternal be,
Witness the solemnity.

LXVIII

" From the corners uttermost
Of the bounds of English coast;
From every hut, village, and town,
Where those who live and suffer, moan
For others' misery, or their own:

LXIX

" From the workhouse and the prison,
Where pale as corpses newly risen,
Women, children, young and old,
Groan for pain, and weep for cold;

LXX

" From the haunts of daily life,
Where is waged the daily strife
With common wants and common cares,
Which sow the human heart with tares;

LXXI

" Lastly, from the palaces,
Where the murmur of distress
Echoes, like the distant sound
Of a wind, alive around;

LXXII

" Those prison-halls of wealth and fashion,
Where some few feel such compassion
For those who groan, and toil, and wail,
As must make their brethren pale;

LXXIII

" Ye who suffer woes untold,
Or to feel, or to behold
Your lost country bought and sold
With a price of blood and gold!

LXXIV

" Let a vast assembly be,
And with great solemnity
Declare with ne'er said words, that ye
Are, as God has made ye, free.

LXXV

" Be your strong and simple words
Keen to wound as sharpened swords,
And wide as targes let them be,
With their shade to cover ye.

LXXVI

" Let the tyrants pour around
With a quick and startling sound,
Like the loosening of a sea,
Troops of armed emblazonry.

LXXVII

" Let the charged artillery drive,
Till the dead air seems alive
With the clash of clanging wheels
And the tramp of horses' heels.

LXXVIII

" Let the fixed bayonet
Gleam with sharp desire to wet
Its bright point in English blood,
Looking keen as one for food.

LXXIX

" Let the horsemen's scimitars
Wheel and flash, like sphereless stars
Thirsting to eclipse their burning
In a sea of death and mourning.

LXXX

" Stand ye calm and resolute,
Like a forest close and mute,
With folded arms, and looks which are
Weapons of an unvanquished war.

LXXXI

" And let Panic, who outspeeds
The career of armed steeds,

Pass, a disregarded shade,
Through your phalanx undismayed.

LXXXII

" Let the laws of your own land,
Good or ill, between ye stand,
Hand to hand, and foot to foot,
Arbiters of the dispute.

LXXXIII

" The old laws of England—they
Whose reverend heads with age are
    grey,
Children of a wiser day ;
And whose solemn voice must be
Thine own echo—Liberty !

LXXXIV

" On those who first should violate
Such sacred heralds in their state,
Rest the blood that must ensue ;
And it will not rest on you.

LXXXV

" And if then the tyrants dare,
Let them ride among you there ;
Slash, and stab, and maim, and hew
What they like, that let them do.

LXXXVI

" With folded arms and steady eyes,
And little fear, and less surprise,
Look upon them as they slay,
Till their rage has died away :

LXXXVII

" Then they will return with shame,
To the place from which they came,
And the blood thus shed will speak
In hot blushes on their cheek :

LXXXVIII

" Every woman in the land
Will point at them as they stand—
They will hardly dare to greet
Their acquaintance in the street :

LXXXIX

" And the bold true warriors,
Who have hugged danger in the wars,
Will turn to those who would be free
Ashamed of such base company :

XC

" And that slaughter to the nation
Shall steam up like inspiration,
Eloquent, oracular,
A volcano heard afar :

XCI

"And these words shall then become,
Like Oppression's thundered doom,
Ringing through each heart and brain
Heard again—again—again !

XCII

" Rise, like lions after slumber
In unvanquishable number !
Shake your chains to earth, like dew
Which in sleep had fallen on you :
Ye are many—they are few ! "

PETER BELL THE THIRD
By MICHING MALLECHO, Esq.

Is it a party in a parlour,
Crammed just as they on earth were
    crammed,
Some sipping punch—some sipping tea,
But, as you by their faces see,
All silent, and all——damned !
    Peter Bell, by W. WORDSWORTH.

OPHELIA.—What means this, my lord ?
HAMLET.—Marry, this is Miching Mal-
    lecho ; it means mischief.
                        SHAKSPEARE

DEDICATION.

To THOMAS BROWN, ESQ., THE
    YOUNGER, H.F.

DEAR TOM,—Allow me to request
you to introduce Mr. Peter Bell to
the respectable family of the Fudges ;
although he may fall short of those
very considerable personages in the
more active properties which charac-
terize the Rat and the Apostate, I
suspect that even you, their historian,
will confess that he surpasses them
in the more peculiarly legitimate
qualification of intolerable dulness. .

You know Mr. Examiner Hunt ;
well—it was he who presented me to
two of the Mr. Bells. My intimacy
with the younger Mr. Bell naturally
sprung from this introduction to his
brothers. And in presenting him to
you, I have the satisfaction of being
able to assure you that he is considerably the dullest of the three.

There is this particular advantage
in an acquaintance with any one of
the Peter Bells, that if you know one
Peter Bell, you know three Peter

Bells; they are not one, but three; not three, but one. An awful mystery, which, after having caused torrents of blood, and having been hymned by groans enough to deafen the music of the spheres, is at length illustrated to the satisfaction of all parties in the theological world, by the nature of Mr. Peter Bell.

Peter is a polyhedric Peter, or a Peter with many sides. He changes colours like a chameleon, and his coat like a snake. He is a Proteus of a Peter. He was at first sublime, pathetic, impressive, profound; then dull; then prosy and dull; and now dull—O, so very dull! it is an ultra-legitimate dulness.

You will perceive that it is not necessary to consider Hell and the Devil as supernatural machinery. The whole scene of my epic is in "this world which is"—so Peter informed us before his conversion to *White Obi*——

——The world of all of us, *and where We find our happiness, or not at all.*

Let me observe that I have spent six or seven days in composing this sublime piece; the orb of my moonlight genius has made the fourth part of its revolution round the dull earth which you inhabit, driving you mad, while it has retained its calmness and its splendour, and I have been fitting this its last phase "to occupy a permanent station in the literature of my country."

Your works, indeed, dear Tom, sell better; but mine are far superior. The public is no judge; posterity sets all to rights.

Allow me to observe that so much has been written of Peter Bell, that the present history can be considered only, like the Iliad, as a continuation of that series of cyclic poems, which have already been candidates for bestowing immortality upon, at the same time that they receive it from, his character and adventures. In this point of view, I have violated no rule of Syntax in beginning my composition with a conjunction; the full stop which closes the poem continued by me, being, like the full stops at the end of the Iliad and Odyssey, a full stop of a very qualified import.

Hoping that the immortality which you have given to the Fudges, you will receive from them; and in the firm expectation, that when London shall be an habitation of bitterns, when St. Paul's and Westminster Abbey shall stand, shapeless and nameless ruins, in the midst of an unpeopled marsh; when the piers of Waterloo Bridge shall become the nuclei of islets of reeds and osiers and cast the jagged shadows of their broken arches on the solitary stream, some transatlantic commentator will be weighing in the scales of some new and now unimagined system of criticism, the respective merits of the Bells and the Fudges, and their historians,

I remain, dear Tom,
Yours sincerely,
MICHING MALLECHO.

December 1, 1819.

P.S.—Pray excuse the date of place; so soon as the profits of the publication come in, I mean to hire lodgings in a more respectable street.

PROLOGUE

PETER BELLS, one, two and three,
O'er the wide world wandering be.—
First, the antenatal Peter,
Wrapt in weeds of the same metre,
The so long predestined raiment
Clothed, in which to walk his way
   meant
The second Peter; whose ambition
Is to link the proposition,
As the mean of two extremes—
(This was learnt from Aldrich's
   themes)
Shielding from the guilt of schism
The orthodoxal syllogism;
The First Peter—he who was
Like the shadow in the glass
Of the second, yet unripe,
His substantial antitype.—
Then came Peter Bell the Second,
Who henceforward must be reckoned
The body of a double soul,
And that portion of the whole
Without which the rest would seem

Ends of a disjointed dream.—
And the Third is he who has
O'er the grave been forced to pass
To the other side, which is,—
Go and try else,—just like this.

Peter Bell the First was Peter
Smugger, milder, softer, neater,
Like the soul before it is
Born from *that* world into *this*.
The next Peter Bell was he
Predevote, like you and me,
To good or evil as may come ;
His was the severer doom,—
For he was an evil Cotter
And a polygamic Potter.[1]

And the last is Peter Bell,
Damned since our first parents fell,
Damned eternally to Hell—
Surely he deserves it well !

PART THE FIRST

DEATH

AND Peter Bell, when he had been
    With   fresh-imported   hell-fire
        warmed,
Grew serious—from his dress and
    mien
'Twas very plainly to be seen
    Peter was quite reformed.

His eyes turned up, his mouth turned
    down,
    His accent caught a nasal twang ;
He oiled his hair,[2] there might be
    heard
The grace of God in every word
    Which Peter said or sang.

But Peter now grew old, and had
    An ill no doctor could unravel ;
His torments almost drove him
    mad ;—

[1] The oldest scholiasts read—
    A *dodecagamic* Potter.
This is at once more descriptive and more
megalophonous,—but the alliteration of the text
had captivated the vulgar ear of the herd of
later commentators.

[2] To those who have not duly appreciated the
distinction between *Whale* and *Russia* oil, this
attribute might rather seem to belong to the
Dandy than the Evangelic. The effect, when
to the windward, is indeed so similar, that it
requires a subtle naturalist to discriminate the
animals. They belong, however, to distinct
genera.

Some said it was a fever bad—
    Some swore it was the gravel.

His holy friends then came about,
    And with long preaching and per-
        suasion,
Convinced the patient that, withou',
    The smallest shadow of a doubt
    He was predestined to damnation.

They said—" Thy name is Peter Bell,
    Thy skin is of a brimstone hue ;
Alive or dead—ay, sick or well—
The one God made to rhyme with
    hell ;
    The other, I think, rhymes with
        you."

Then Peter set up such a yell !—
    The nurse, who with some water
        gruel
Was climbing up the stairs, as well
As her old legs could climb them—fell
    And broke them both—the fall
        was cruel.

The Parson from the casement lept
    Into the lake of Windermere—
And many an eel—though no adept
In God's right reason for it—kept
    Gnawing his kidneys half a year.

And all the rest rushed through the
    door,
    And tumbled over one another,
And broke their skulls.—Upon the
    floor
Meanwhile sat Peter Bell, and swore,
    And cursed his father and his
        mother ;

And raved of God, and sin, and
    death,
Blaspheming like an infidel ;
And said, that with his clenched
    teeth,
He'd seize the earth from underneath,
    And drag it with him down to hell.

As he was speaking came a spasm,
    And wrenched his gnashing teeth
        asunder
Like one who sees a strange phantasm
He lay,—there was a silent chasm
    Betwixt his upper jaw and under.

And yellow death lay on his face ;
    And a fixed smile that was not
        human

Told, as I understand the case,
That he was gone to the wrong
    place :—
    I heard all this from the old woman.

Then there came down from Lang-
    dale Pike
    A cloud, with lightning, wind and
    hail ;
It swept over the mountains like
An ocean,—and I heard it strike
    The woods and crags of Grasmere
    vale.

And I saw the black storm come
    Nearer, minute after minute ;
Its thunder made the cataracts
    dumb ;
With hiss, and clash, and hollow
    hum,
    It neared as if the Devil was in it.

The Devil *was* in it :—he had bought
    Peter for half-a-crown ; and when
The storm which bore him vanished.
    nought
That in the house that storm had
    caught
    Was ever seen again.

The gaping neighbours came next
    day—
They found all vanished from the
    shore :
The Bible, whence he used to pray,
Half scorched under a hencoop lay :
    Smashed glass—and nothing more !

PART THE SECOND

THE DEVIL

THE DEVIL, I safely can aver,
    Has neither hoof, nor tail, nor
    sting ;
Nor is he, as some sages swear,
A spirit, neither here nor there,
    In nothing—yet in everything.

He is—what we are ; for sometimes
    The Devil is a gentleman ;
At others a bard bartering rhymes
For sack ; a statesman spinning
    crimes ;
    A swindler, living as he can ;

A thief, who cometh in the night,
    With whole boots and net panta-
    loons,

Like someone whom it were not
    right
To mention ;—or the luckless wight,
    From whom he steals nine silver
    spoons.

But in this case he did appear
    Like a slop-merchant from Wap-
    ping,
And with smug face, and eye severe,
On every side did perk and peer
    Till he saw Peter dead or napping.

He had on an upper Benjamin
    (For he was of the driving schism)
In the which he wrapt his skin
From the storm he travelled in,
    For fear of rheumatism.

He called the ghost out of the
    corse ;—
    It was exceedingly like Peter,—
Only its voice was hollow and
    hoarse—
It had a queerish look of course—
    Its dress too was a little neater.

The Devil knew not his name and lot,
    Peter knew not that he was Bell :
Each had an upper stream of thought,
Which made all seem as it was not ;
    Fitting itself to all things well.

Peter thought he had parents dear,
    Brothers, sisters, cousins, cronies,
In the fens of Lincolnshire ;
He perhaps had found them there
    Had he gone and boldly shown his

Solemn phiz in his own village ;
    Where he thought oft when a boy
He'd clomb the orchard walls to
    pillage
The produce of his neighbour's
    tillage,
    With marvellous pride and joy.

And the Devil thought he had,
    'Mid the misery and confusion
Of an unjust war, just made
A fortune by the gainful trade
Of giving soldiers rations bad—
    The world is full of strange delu-
    sion.

That he had a mansion planned
    In a square like Grosvenor Square,
That he was aping fashion, and
That he now came to Westmoreland
    To see what was romantic there.

And all this, though quite ideal,—
Ready at a breath to vanish,—
Was a state not more unreal
Than the peace he could not feel,
    Or the care he could not banish.

After a little conversation,
    The Devil told Peter, if he chose,
He'd bring him to the world of
    fashion
By giving him a situation
    In his own service—and new
    clothes.

And Peter bowed, quite pleased and
    proud,
    And after waiting some few days
For a new livery—dirty yellow
Turned up with black—the wretched
    fellow
    Was bowled to Hell in the Devil's
    chaise.

PART THE THIRD

HELL

Hell is a city much like London—
    A populous and a smoky city;
There are all sorts of people undone,
And there is little or no fun done ;
    Small justice shown, and still
    less pity.

There is a Castles, and a Canning,
    A Cobbett and a Castlereagh ;
All sorts of caitiff corpses planning,
All sorts of cozening for trepanning
    Corpses less corrupt than they.

There is a * * *, who has lost
    His wits, or sold them, none knows
    which ;
He walks about a double ghost,
And though as thin as Fraud almost—
    Ever grows more grim and rich.

There is a Chancery Court ; a King ;
    A manufacturing mob ; a set
Of thieves who by themselves are
    sent
Similar thieves to represent ;
    An army ; and a public debt.

Which last is a scheme of paper
    money,
    And means—being interpreted—
" Bees, keep your wax—give us the
    honey,

And we will plant, while skies are
    sunny,
    Flowers, which in winter serve
    instead."

There is great talk of revolution—
    And a great chance of despotism—
German soldiers — camps — confu-
    sion—   [sion—
Tumults — lotteries — rage — delu-
Gin—suicide—and Methodism.

Taxes too, on wine and bread,
    And meat, and beer, and tea, and
    cheese,
From which those patriots pure are
    fed,
Who gorge before they reel to bed,
    The tenfold essence of all these.

There are mincing women, mewing,
    (Like cats, who *amant miserè*,[1])
Of their own virtue, and pursuing
Their gentler sisters to that ruin,
    Without which—what were chas-
    tity ?[2]

Lawyers—judges—old hobnobbers
    Are there—bailiffs—chancellors—
Bishops—great and little robbers—
Rhymesters — pamphleteers—stock-
    jobbers—
    Men of glory in the wars,—

Things whose trade is, over ladies
    To lean, and flirt, and stare, and
    simper,
Till all that is divine in woman
Grows cruel, courteous, smooth, in-
    human,
    Crucified 'twixt a smile and whim-
    per.

Thrusting, toiling, wailing, moiling,
    Frowning, preaching—such a riot !
Each with never-ceasing labour,

---

[1] One of the attributes in Linnæus's description of the Cat. To a similar cause the cater-
wauling of more than one species of this genus
is to be referred ; except, indeed, that the poor
quadruped is compelled to quarrel with its own
pleasures, whilst the biped is supposed only to
quarrel with those of others.
[2] What would this husk and excuse for a
virtue be without its kernel prostitution, or the
kernel prostitution without this husk of a
virtue ? I wonder the women of the town do
not form an association, like the Society for the
Suppression of Vice, for the support of what
may be called the " King, Church, and Constitution " of their order. But this subject is almost
too horrible for a joke.

Whilst he thinks he cheats his
neighbour,
Cheating his own heart of quiet.

And all these meet at levèes ;—
Dinners convivial and political ;—
Suppers of epic poets ;—teas,
Where small-talk dies in agonies ;—
Breakfasts professional and criti-
cal ;

Lunches and snacks so aldermanic
That one would furnish forth ten
dinners,
Where reigns a Cretan-tongued panic,
Lest news Russ, Dutch, or Alemannic,
Should make some losers, and
some winners,

At conversazioni—balls—
Conventicles — and drawing-
rooms—
Courts of law—committees—calls
Of a morning—clubs—book-stalls—
Churches — masquerades — and
tombs.

And this is Hell—and in this smother
All are damnable and damned ;
Each one damning, damns the other ;
They are damned by one another,
By none other are they damned.

'Tis a lie to say, " God damns ! " [1]
Where was Heaven's Attorney-
General
When they first gave out such flams ?
Let there be an end of shams,
They are mines of poisonous
mineral.

Statesmen damn themselves to be
Cursed ; and lawyers damn their
souls
To the auction of a fee ;
Churchmen damn themselves to see
God's sweet love in burning coals.

The rich are damned beyond all cure,
To taunt, and starve, and trample
on
The weak and wretched ; and the
poor

[1] This libel on our national oath, and this
accusation of all our countrymen of being in the
daily practice of solemnly asseverating the most
enormous falsehood, I fear deserves the notice
of a more active Attorney-General than that here
alluded to,

Damn their broken hearts to endure
Stripe on stripe, with groan on
groan.

Sometimes the poor are damned
indeed
To take,—not means for being
blest,—
But Cobbett's snuff, revenge ; that
weed
From which the worms that it doth
feed
Squeeze less than they before
possessed.

And some few, like we know who,
Damned—but God alone knows
why—
To believe their minds are given
To make this ugly Hell a Heaven ;
In which faith they live and die.

Thus, as in a town plague-stricken,
Each man be he sound or no
Must indifferently sicken ;
As when day begins to thicken,
None knows a pigeon from a
crow,—

So good and bad, sane and mad,
The oppressor and the oppressed ;
Those who weep to see what others
Smile to inflict upon their brothers ;
Lovers, haters, worst and best ;

All are damned—they breathe an air,
Thick, infected, joy-dispelling ;
Each pursues what seems most fair,
Mining like moles, through mind, and
there
Scoop palace-caverns vast, where Care
In throned state is ever dwelling.

PART THE FOURTH

SIN

Lo, Peter in Hell's Grosvenor Square,
A footman in the Devil's service !
And the misjudging world would
swear
That every man in service there
To virtue would prefer vice.

But Peter, though now damned, was
not
What Peter was before damnation,
Men oftentimes prepare a lot

Which ere it finds them, is not what
   Suits with their genuine station.

All things that Peter saw and felt
   Had a peculiar aspect to him ;
And when they came within the belt
Of his own nature, seemed to melt,
   Like cloud to cloud, into him.

And so the outward world uniting
   To that within him, he became
Considerably uninviting
To those, whose meditation slighting,
   Were moulded in a different frame.

And he scorned them, and they
    scorned him :
   And he scorned all they did ; and
    t ey
Did all that men of their own trim
Are wont to do to please their whim,
   Drinking, lying, swearing, play.

Such were his fellow-servants ; thus
   His virtue, like our own, was built
Too much on that indignant fuss
Hypocrite Pride stirs up in us
   To bully out another's guilt.

He had a mind which was somehow
   At once circumference and centre
Of all he might or feel or know ;
Nothing went ever out, although
   Something did ever enter.

He had as much imagination
   As a pint-pot ;—he never could
Fancy another situation,
From which to dart his contempla-
    tion,
   Than that wherein he stood.

Yet his was individual mind,
   And new created all he saw
In a new manner, and refined
Those new creations, and combined
   Them, by a master-spirit's law.

Thus—though unimaginative—
   An apprehension clear, intense,
Of his mind's work, had made alive
The things it wrought on ; I believe
   Wakening a sort of thought in sense.

But from the first 'twas Peter's drift
   To be a kind of moral eunuch,
He touched the hem of Nature's shift,
Felt faint—and never dared uplift
   The closest, all-concealing tunic.

She laughed the while, with an arch
    smile,
   And kissed him with a sister's kiss,
And said—" My best Diogenes,
I love you well—but, if you please,
   Tempt not again my deepest bliss.

" 'Tis you are cold—for I, not coy,
   Yield love for love, frank, warm and
    true ;
And Burns, a Scottish peasant boy—
His errors prove it—knew my joy
   More, learned friend, than you.

" ' *Bocca bacciata non perde ventura*
   Anzi rinnuova come fa la luna ' :—
So thought Boccaccio, whose sweet
   words might cure a
Male prude, like you, from what you
   now endure, a
Low-tide in soul, like a stagnant
   laguna."

Then Peter rubbed his eyes severe,
   And smoothed his spacious fore-
    head down
With his broad palm ;—'twixt love
    and fear,
He looked, as he no doubt felt, queer,
   And in his dream sate down.

The Devil was no uncommon crea-
    ture ;
   A leaden-witted thief—just hud-
    dled
Out of the dross and scum of Nature ;
A toad-like lump of limb and feature,
   With mind, and heart, and fancy
    muddled.

He was that heavy, dull, cold thing,
   The spirit of evil well may be :
A drone too base to have a sting ;
Who gluts, and grimes his lazy wing,
   And calls lust, luxury.

Now he was quite the kind of wight
   Round whom collect, at a fixed era,
Venison, turtle, hock, and claret,—
Good cheer—and those who come to
    share it—
   And best East Indian madeira !

It was his fancy to invite
   Men of science, wit, and learning,
Who came to lend each other light ;
He proudly thought that his gold's
    might
   Had set those spirits burning.

And men of learning, science, wit,
  Considered him as you and I
Think of some rotten tree, and sit
Lounging and dining under it,
  Exposed to the wide sky.

And all the while, with loose fat smile,
  The willing wretch sat winking
    there,
Believing 'twas his power that made
That jovial scene—and that all paid
  Homage to his unnoticed chair.

Though to be sure this place was Hell;
  He was the Devil—and all they—
What though the claret circled well,
And wit, like ocean, rose and fell ?—
  Were damned eternally.

PART THE FIFTH

Grace

AMONG the guests who often stayed
  Till the Devil's *petits-soupers*,
A man there came, fair as a maid,
And Peter noted what he said,
  Standing behind his master's chair.

He was a mighty poet—and
  A subtle-souled psychologist;
All things he seemed to understand,
Of old or new—of sea or land—
  But his own mind—which was a
    mist.

This was a man who might have
    turned
  Hell into Heaven—and so in glad-
    ness
A Heaven unto himself have earned:
But he in shadows undiscerned
  Trusted,—and damned himself to
    madness.

He spoke of poetry, and how
  " Divine it was—a light—a love—
A spirit which like wind doth blow
As it listeth, to and fro :
  A dew rained down from God
    above.

" A power which comes and goes like
    dream,
  And which none can ever trace—
Heaven's light on earth—Truth's
    brightest beam."

And when he ceased there lay the
    gleam
  Of those words upon his face.

Now Peter, when he heard such talk,
  Would, heedless of a broken pate,
Stand like a man asleep, or baulk
Some wishing guest of knife or fork,
  Or drop and break his master's
    plate.

At night he oft would start and wake
  Like a lover, and began
In a wild measure songs to make
On moor, and glen, and rocky lake,
  And on the heart of man,

And on the universal sky—
  And the wide earth's bosom green,
And the sweet, strange mystery
Of what beyond these things may lie,
  And yet remain unseen.

For in his thought he visited
  The spots in which, ere dead and
    damned,
He his wayward life had led ;
Yet knew not whence the thoughts
    were fed,
  Which thus his fancy crammed.

And these obscure remembrances
  Stirred such harmony in Peter,
That whensoever he should please,
He could speak of rocks and trees
  In poetic metre.

For though it was without a sense
  Of memory, yet he remembered
    well
Many a ditch and quickset fence ;
Of lakes he had intelligence,
  He knew something of heath and
    fell.

He had also dim recollections
  Of pedlars tramping on their
    rounds ;
Milkpans and pails ; and odd collec-
    tions
Of saws, and proverbs ; and reflec-
    tions
  Old parsons make in burying-
    grounds.

But Peter's verse was clear, and
    came
  Announcing from the frozen hearth
Of a cold age, that none might tame

The soul of that diviner flame
  It augured to the Earth.

Like gentle rains, on the dry plains,
  Making that green which late was
    grey,
Or like the sudden moon, that stains
Some gloomy chamber's window
    panes
  With a broad light like day.

For language was in Peter's hand,
  Like clay, while he was yet a potter;
And he made songs for all the land,
Sweet both to feel and understand,
  As pipkins late to mountain Cotter.

And Mr. ——, the bookseller,
  Gave twenty pounds for some ;—
    then scorning
A footman's yellow coat to wear,
Peter, too proud of heart, I fear,
  Instantly gave the Devil warning.

Whereat the Devil took offence,
  And swore in his soul a great oath
    then,
" That for his damned impertinence
He'd bring him to a proper sense
  Of what was due to gentlemen ! "—

PART THE SIXTH
DAMNATION

" O THAT mine enemy had written
  A book ! " — cried Job, a fearful
    curse ;
If to the Arab, as the Briton,
'Twas galling to be critic-bitten—
  The Devil to Peter wished no worse.

When Peter's next new book found
    vent,
  The Devil to all the first Reviews
A copy of it slily sent,
With five-pound note as compliment,
  And this short notice—" Pray
    abuse."

Then *seriatim*, month and quarter,
  Appeared such mad tirades.—One
    said—
" Peter seduced Mrs. Foy's daughter,
Then drowned the mother in Ulls-
    water,
  The last thing as he went to bed."

Another—" Let him shave his head !
  Where's Dr. Willis ?—Or is he jok-
    ing ?
What does the rascal mean or hope,
No longer imitating Pope,
  In that barbarian Snakspeare pok-
    ing ? "

One more, " Is incest not enough ?
  And must there be adultery too ?
Grace after meat ? Miscreant and
    Liar !
Thief ! Blackguard ! Scoundrel !
  Fool ! Hell fire
  Is twenty times too good for you.

" By that last book of yours WE think
  You've double-damned yourself to
    scorn ;
We warned you whilst yet on the
    brink
You stood. From your black name
    will shrink
  The babe that is unborn."

All these Reviews the Devil made
  Up in a parcel, which he had
Safely to Peter's house conveyed.
For carriage, tenpence Peter paid—
  Untied them—read them—went
    half mad.

" What ! " cried he, " this is my re-
    ward
  For nights of thought, and days of
    toil ?
Do poets, but to be abhorred
By men of whom they never heard,
  Consume their spirits' oil ?

" What have I done to them ?—and
    who
  Is Mrs. Foy ? 'Tis very cruel
To speak of me and Emma so !
Adultery ! God defend me ! Oh !
  I've half a mind to fight a duel.

" Or," cried he, a grave look collect-
    ing,
  " Is it my genius, like the moon,
Sets those who stand her face inspect-
    ing,
That face within their brain reflect-
    ing,
  Like a crazed bell-chime, out of
    tune ? "

For Peter did not know the town,
 But thought, as country readers do,
For half-a-guinea or a crown,
 He bought oblivion or renown
  From God's own voice [1] in a review.

All Peter did on this occasion
Was, writing some sad stuff in prose.
It is a dangerous invasion
When poets criticise ; their station
 Is to delight, not pose.

The Devil then sent to Leipsic fair,
 For Born's translation of Kant's
  book ;
A world of words, tail foremost, where
Right — wrong — false — true — and
  foul—and fair,
 As in a lottery-wheel are shook.

Five thousand crammed octavo pages
 Of German psychologics,—he
Who his *furor verborum* assuages
Thereon, deserves just seven months'
  wages
 More than will e'er be due to me.

I looked on them nine several days,
 And then I saw that they were bad;
A friend, too, spoke in their dis-
  praise,—
He never read them ;—with amaze
 I found Sir William Drummond
  had.

When the book came, the Devil sent
It to P. Verbovale,[2] Esquire,
With a brief note of compliment,
By that night's Carlisle mail. It
 went,
 And set his soul on fire.

Fire, which *ex luce præbens fumum,*
 Made him beyond the bottom see
Of truth's clear well—when I and
 you, Ma'am,

Go, as we shall do, *subter humum,*
 We may know more than he.

Now Peter ran to seed in soul
 Into a walking paradox ;
For he was neither part nor whole,
Nor good, nor bad—nor knave nor
 fool,
 —Among the woods and rocks.

Furious he rode, where late he ran,
 Lashing and spurring his tame
  hobby ;
Turned to a formal puritan,
A solemn and unsexual man,—
 He half believed *White Obi.*

This steed in vision he would ride,
 High trotting over nine-inch
  bridges,
With Flibbertigibbet, imp of pride,
Mocking and mowing by his side—
A mad-brained goblin for a guide—
 Over corn-fields, gates, and hedges.

After these ghastly rides, he came
 Home to his heart, and found
  from thence
Much stolen of its accustomed flame ;
His thoughts grew weak, drowsy, and
 lame
 Of their intelligence.

To Peter's view, all seemed one hue ;
 He was no Whig, he was no Tory ;
No Deist and no Christian he ;—
He got so subtle, that to be
 Nothing, was all his glory.

One single point in his belief
 From his organization sprung,
The heart-enrooted faith, the chief
Ear in his doctrines' blighted sheaf,
 That " happiness is wrong ; "

So thought Calvin and Dominic ;
 So think their fierce successors, who
Even now would neither stint nor
  stick
Our flesh from off our bones to pick,
 If they might " do their do."

His morals thus were undermined :—
 The old Peter—the hard, old Potter
Was born anew within his mind ;

[1] *Vox populi vox Dei.* As Mr. Godwin truly
observes of a more famous saying, *of some merit
as a popular maxim, but totally destitute of
philosophical accuracy.*
[2] Quasi, *Qui valet verba :*—*i. e.,* all the words
which have been, are, or may be expended by,
for, against, with, or on him. A sufficient proof
of the utility of this history. Peter's progenitor
who selected this name seems to have possessed
a *pure anticipated cognition* of the nature and
modesty of this ornament of his posterity.

He grew dull, harsh, sly, unrefined,
    As when he tramped beside the
        Otter.[1]

In the death hues of agony
    Lambently flashing from a fish,
Now Peter felt amused to see
Shades like a rainbow's rise and flee,
    Mixed with a certain hungry wish.[2]

So in his Country's dying face
    He looked—and lovely as she lay,
Seeking in vain his last embrace,
Wailing her own abandoned case,
    With hardened sneer he turned
        away :

And coolly to his own soul said ;—
    " Do you not think that we might
        make
A poem on her when she's dead ?
Or, no—a thought is in my head—
    Her shroud for a new sheet I'll take.

" My wife wants one.—Let who will
        bury
    This mangled corpse !   And I and
        you,
My dearest soul, will then make merry,
As the Prince Regent did with
        Sherry,—
    Ay—and at last desert me too."

And so his Soul would not be gay,
    But moaned within him ; like a
        fawn
Moaning within a cave, it lay
Wounded and wasting, day by day,
    Till all its life of life was gone.

[1] A famous river in the new Atlantis of the Dynastophylic Pantisocratists.

[2] See the description of the beautiful colours produced during the agonizing death of a number of trout, in the fourth part of a long poem in blank verse, published within a few years. That poem contains curious evidence of the gradual hardening of a strong but circumscribed sensibility, of the perversion of a penetrating but panic-stricken understanding. The author might have derived a lesson which he had probably forgotten from these sweet and sublime verses.
This lesson, Shepherd, let us two divide,
Taught both by what she * shows and what conceals,
Never to blend our pleasure or our pride
With sorrow of the meanest thing that feels.
    * Nature.

As troubled skies stain waters clear,
    The storm in Peter's heart and
        mind
Now made his verses dark and queer :
They were the ghosts of what they
        were,
    Shaking dim grave-clothes in the
        wind.

For he now raved enormous folly,
    Of Baptisms, Sunday-schools, and
        Graves,
'Twould make George Colman melan-
        choly,
To have heard him, like a male Molly,
    Chaunting those stupid staves.

Yet the Reviews, who heaped abuse
    On Peter while he wrote for free-
        dom,
So soon as in his song they spy
The folly which soothes tyranny,
    Praise him, for those who feed 'em.

" He was a man, too great to scan ;—
    A planet lost in truth's keen rays —
His virtue, awful and prodigious ;—
He was the most sublime, religious,
    Pure-minded Poet of these days."

As soon as he read that, cried Peter,
    " Eureka ! I have found the way
To make a better thing of metre
Than e'er was made by living crea-
        ture
    Up to this blessed day."

Then Peter wrote odes to the Devil —
    In one of which he meekly said :
" May Carnage and Slaughter,
Thy niece and thy daughter,
May Rapine and Famine,
Thy gorge ever cramming,
    Glut thee with living and dead !

" May death and damnation,
    And consternation,
Flit up from hell with pure intent !
    Slash them at Manchester,
    Glasgow, Leeds, and Chester ;
Drench all with blood from Avon to
        Trent.

" Let thy bodyguard yeomen
    Hew down babes and women,

And laugh with bold triumph till
    Heaven be rent,
  When Moloch in Jewry,
  Munched children with fury,
It was thou, Devil, dining with pure
    intent." [1]

PART THE SEVENTH

DOUBLE DAMNATION

THE Devil now knew his proper cue.-
  Soon as he read the ode, he drove
To his friend Lord Mac Murder-
    chouse's,
A man of interest in both Houses,
  And said :—" For money or for
    love,

" Pray find some cure or sinecure ;
  To feed from the superfluous taxes,
A friend of ours—a poet—fewer
Have fluttered tamer to the lure
  Than he." His lordship stands
    and racks his

Stupid brains, while one might count
  As many beads as he had bor-
    oughs,—
At length replies ; from his mean
    front,
Like one who rubs out an account,
  Smoothing away the unmeaning
    furrows :

" It happens fortunately, dear Sir,
  I can. I hope I need require
No pledge from you, that he will stir
In our affairs ;—like Oliver,
  That he'll be worthy of his hire."

These words exchanged, the news
    sent off
  To Peter, home the Devil hied,—
Took to his bed ; he had no cough,

[1] It is curious to observe how often extremes
meet. Cobbett and Peter use the same language
for a different purpose : Peter is indeed a sort of
metrical Cobbett. Cobbett is, however, more
mischievous than Peter, because he pollutes a
holy and now unconquerable cause with the
principles of legitimate murder ; whilst the other
only makes a bad one ridiculous and odious.
    If either Peter or Cobbett should see this note,
each will feel more indignation at being compared
to the other than at any censure implied in the
moral perversion laid to their charge.

No doctor, — meat and drink
    enough,—
  Yet that same night he died.

The Devil's corpse was leaded down ;
  His decent heirs enjoyed his pelf,
Mourning-coaches, many a one,
Followed his hearse along the town :—
  Where was the Devil himself ?

When Peter heard of his promotion,
  His eyes grew like two stars for bliss,
There was a bow of sleek devotion,
Engendering in his back ; each mo-
    tion
  Seemed a Lord's shoe to kiss.

He hired a house, bought plate, and
    made
  A genteel drive up to his door,
With sifted gravel neatly laid,—
As if defying all who said,
  Peter was ever poor.

But a disease soon struck into
  The very life and soul of Peter—
He walked about—slept—had the hue
Of health upon his cheeks—and few
  Dug better—none a heartier eater.

And yet a strange and horrid curse
  Clung upon Peter, night and day,
Month after month the thing grew
    worse,
And deadlier than in this my verse,
  I can find strength to say.

Peter was dull—he was at first
  Dull—O, so dull—so very dull !
Whether he talked, wrote, or re-
    hearsed—
Still with this dulness was he cursed—
  Dull—beyond all conception—dull.

No one could read his books—no mor-
    tal,
  But a few natural friends, would
    hear him ;
The parson came not near his portal ;
His state was like that of the immor-
    tal
  Described by Swift—no man could
    bear him.

His sister, wife, and children yawned,
  With a long, slow, and drear ennui,

All human patience far beyond ;
Their hopes of Heaven each would
      have pawned,
      Anywhere else to be.

But in his verse, and in his prose,
   The essence of his dulness was
Concentred and compressed so close,
'Twould have made Guatimozin doze
   On his red gridiron of brass.

A printer's boy, folding those pages,
   Fell slumbrously upon one side ;
Like those famed Seven who slept
      three ages.
To wakeful frenzy's vigil rages,
   As opiates, were the same applied.

Even the Reviewers who were hired
   To do the work of his reviewing,
With   adamantine   nerves,   grew
      tired ;—
Gaping and torpid they retired,
   To dream of what they should be
      doing.

And worse and worse, the drowsy
      curse
   Yawned in him till it grew a pest—
A wide contagious atmosphere,
Creeping like cold through all things
      near ;
   A power to infect and to infest.

His servant-maids and dogs grew dull ;
   His kitten, late a sportive elf ;
The woods and lakes, so beautiful,
Of dim stupidity were full,
   All grew dull as Peter's self.

The earth under his feet—the springs,
   Which lived within it a quick life,
The air, the winds of many wings,
That fan it with new murmurings,
   Were dead to their harmonious
      strife.

The birds and beasts within the wood,
   The insects, and each creeping
      thing,
Were now a silent multitude ;
Love's work was left unwrought—no
      brood
   Near Peter's house took wing.

And every neighbouring cottager
   Stupidly yawned upon the other :
No jackass brayed ; no little cur
Cocked up his ears ;—no man would
      stir
   To save a dying mother.

Yet all from that charmed district
      went
   But some half-idiot and half-knave.
Who rather than pay any rent,
Would live with marvellous content,
   Over his father's grave.

No bailiff dared within that space,
   For fear of the dull charm, to enter ;
A man would bear upon his face,
For fifteen months, in any case,
   The yawn of such a venture.

Seven miles above—below—around—
   This pest of dulness holds its sway ;
A ghastly life without a sound ;
To Peter's soul the spell is bound—
   How should it ever pass away ?

LINES

WRITTEN DURING THE CASTLEREAGH
ADMINISTRATION

CORPSES are cold in the tomb,
Stones on the pavement are dumb,
Abortions are dead in the womb,
And their mothers look pale—like the
      white shore
   Of Albion. free no more.

Her sons are as stones in the way—
They are masses of senseless clay—
They are trodden and move not
      away,—
The abortion, with which she tra-
      vaileth,
   Is Liberty—smitten to death.

Then trample and dance, thou Op-
      pressor,
For thy Victim is no redressor,
Thou art sole lord and possessor
Of her corpses, and clods, and abor-
      tions—they pave
   Thy path to the grave.

Hearest thou the festival din,
Of death, and destruction, and sin,

And wealth, crying " Havoc !"
    within ?
'Tis the Bacchanal triumph, which
    makes truth dumb,
Thine Epithalamium.

Ay, marry thy ghastly wife l
Let fear, and disquiet, and strife
Spread thy couch in the chamber of
    life,
Marry Ruin, thou tyrant ! and God
    be thy guide
To the bed of the bride.

SONG

TO THE MEN OF ENGLAND

MEN of England, wherefore plough
For the lords who lay ye low ?
Wherefore weave with toil and care,
The rich robes your tyrants wear ?

Wherefore feed, and clothe, and save,
From the cradle to the grave,
Those ungrateful drones who would
Drain your sweat—nay, drink your
    blood !

Wherefore, Bees of England, forge
Many a weapon, chain, and scourge,
That these stingless drones may spoil
The forced produce of your toil ?

Have ye leisure, comfort, calm,
Shelter, food, love's gentle balm ?
Or what is it ye buy so dear
With your pain and with your fear ?

The seed ye sow another reaps ;
The wealth ye find, another keeps ;
The robes ye weave, another wears ;
The arms ye forge, another bears.

Sow seed,—but let no tyrant reap ;
Find wealth,—let no impostor heap ;
Weave robes,—let not the idle wear ;
Forge arms,—in your defence to bear.

Shrink to your cellars, holes, and cells;
In halls ye deck, another dwells.
Why shake the chains ye wrought ?
    Ye see
The steel ye tempered glance on ye.

With plough and spade, and hoe and
    loom,
Trace your grave, and build your
    tomb,

And weave your winding-sheet, till
    fair
England be your sepulchre.

ENGLAND IN 1819

AN old, mad, blind, despised, and
    dying king,—
Princes, the dregs of their dull race,
    who flow
Through public scorn—mud from a
    muddy spring,—
Rulers, who neither see, nor feel, nor
    know,
But leech-like to their fainting coun-
    try cling,
Till they drop, blind in blood, without
    a blow,—
A people starved and stabbed in the
    untilled field,
An army, which liberticide and prey
Makes as a two-edged sword to all
    who wield,
Golden and sanguine laws which
    tempt and slay,—
Religion Christless, Godless—a book
    sealed ;
A Senate—Time's worst statute un-
    repealed,—
Are graves, from which a glorious
    Phantom may
Burst, to illumine our tempestuous
    day.

SIMILES

FOR TWO POLITICAL CHARACTERS OF 1819

As from an ancestral oak
    Two empty ravens sound their
        clarion,
Yell by yell, and croak by croak,
When they scent the noonday smoke
    Of fresh human carrion :—

As two gibbering night-birds flit,
    From their bowers of deadly hue,
Through the night to frighten it,
When the morn is in a fit,
    And the stars are none or few :—

As a shark and dogfish wait
    Under an Atlantic isle,
For the negro-ship whose freight
Is the theme of their debate,
    Wrinkling their red gills the while—

Are ye, two vultures sick for battle,
   Two scorpions under one wet stone,
Two bloodless wolves whose dry
   throats rattle,
Two crows perched on the murrained
   cattle,
Two vipers tangled into one.

GOD SAVE THE QUEEN

God prosper, speed, and save,
God raise from England's grave,
   Her murdered Queen !
Pave with swift victory
The steps of Liberty,
Whom Britons own to be
     Immortal Queen !

See, she comes throned on **high**,
On swift Eternity !
    God save the Queen !
Millions on millions wait,
Firm, rapid, and elate,
On her majestic state—
    God save the Queen !

She is Thine own pure soul
Moulding the mighty whole.
    God save the Queen !
She is Thine own deep love
Rained down from heaven above,
Wherever she rest or move,
    God save our Queen !

'Wilder her enemies
In their own dark disguise !
    God save our Queen !
All earthly things that dare
Her sacred name to bear,
Strip them, as kings are, bare :
    God save the Queen !

Be her eternal throne
Built in our hearts alone—
    God save the Queen !
Let the oppressor hold
Canopied seats of gold ;
She sits enthroned of old
    O'er our hearts Queen.

Lips touched by seraphim
Breathe out the choral hymn
    " God save the Queen ! "
Sweet as if angels sang,
Loud as that trumpet's clang
Wakening the world's dead gang,—
    God save the Queen !

AN ODE

TO THE ASSERTERS OF LIBERTY

   Arise, arise, arise !
There is blood on the earth that de-
   nies ye bread
   Be your wounds like eyes
To weep for the dead, the dead, the
    dead.
What other grief were it just to pay ?
Your sons, your wives, your brethren,
   were they ;
Who said they were slain on the battle
   day ?

   Awaken, awaken, awaken !
   The slave and the tyrant are twin-
    born foes ;
   Be the cold chains shaken
To the dust, where your kindred
   repose, repose :
Their bones in the grave will start
   and move,
When they hear the voices of those
   they love,
Most loud in the holy combat above.

   Wave, wave high the banner !
   When Freedom is riding to con-
    quest by :
   Though the slaves that fan her
   Be famine and toil, giving sigh for
   sigh.
And ye who attend her imperial car,
Lift not your hands in the banded
   war,
But in her defence whose children ye
   are.

   Glory, glory, glory,
   To those who have greatly suffered
    and done !
   Never name in story
   Was greater than that which ye
    shall have won.
Conquerors have conquered their foes
   alone,
Whose revenge, pride, and power,
   they have overthrown ;
Ride ye, more victorious, over your
   own.

   Bind, bind every brow
   With crownals of violet, ivy and
    pine :
   Hide the blood-stains now
   With hues which sweet Nature has
    made divine,

Green strength, azure hope, and eter-
    nity.
But let not the pansy among them be;
Ye were injured, and that means
    memory.

ODE TO HEAVEN

CHORUS OF SPIRITS

FIRST SPIRIT.

PALACE-ROOF of cloudless nights !
Paradise of golden lights !
    Deep, immeasurable, vast,
Which art now, and which wert then !
Of the present and the past,
Of the eternal where and when,
    Presence-chamber, temple, home,
    Ever-canopying dome,
    Of acts and ages yet to come !

Glorious shapes have life in thee,
Earth, and all earth's company ;
    Living globes which ever throng
Thy deep chasms and wildernesses ;
    And green worlds that glide along ;
And swift stars with flashing tresses ;
    And icy moons most cold and
        bright,
    And mighty suns beyond the night,
    Atoms of intensest light.

Even thy name is as a god,
Heaven ! for thou art the abode
    Of that power which is the glass
Wherein man his nature sees.
    Generations as they pass
Worship thee with bended knees.
    Their unremaining gods and they
    Like a river roll away ;
    Thou remainest such alway.

SECOND SPIRIT.

Thou art but the mind's first chamber,
Round which its young fancies clam-
    ber,
    Like weak insects in a cave,
Lighted up by stalactites ;
    But the portal of the grave,
Where a world of new delights
    Will make thy best glories seem
    But a dim and noonday gleam
    From the shadow of a dream !

THIRD SPIRIT.

Peace ! the abyss is wreathed with
    scorn

At your presumption, atom-born !
    What is heaven ? and what are ye
Who its brief expanse inherit ?
    What are suns and spheres which
        flee
With the instinct of that spirit
    Of which ye are but a part ?
    Drops which Nature's mighty heart
    Drives through thinnest veins.
        Depart !

What is heaven ? a globe of dew,
Filling in the morning new
    Some eyed flower, whose young
        leaves waken
On an unimagined world :
    Constellated suns unshaken,
Orbits measureless, are furled
    In that frail and fading sphere,
    With ten millions gathered there,
    To tremble, gleam, and disappear.

ODE TO THE WEST WIND [1]

O WILD West Wind, thou breath of
    Autumn's being,
Thou, from whose unseen presence
    the leaves dead
Are driven, like ghosts from an en-
    chanter fleeing,

Yellow, and black, and pale, and
    hectic red,
Pestilence-stricken multitudes : O
    thou,
Who chariotest to their dark wintry
    bed

The winged seeds, where they lie cold
    and low,
Each like a corpse within its grave,
    until

[1] This poem was conceived and chiefly written
in a wood that skirts the Arno, near Florence,
and on a day when that tempestuous wind,
whose temperature is at once mild and animating,
was collecting the vapours which pour down the
autumnal rains. They began, as I foresaw, at
sunset, with a violent tempest of hail and rain,
attended by that magnificent thunder and
lightning peculiar to the Cisalpine regions.

The phenomenon alluded to at the conclusion
of the third stanza is well known to naturalists.
The vegetation at the bottom of the sea, of
rivers, and of lakes, sympathizes with that
of the land in the change of seasons, and is con-
sequently influenced by the winds which an-
nounce it.

Thine azure sister of the spring shall
    blow
Her clarion o'er the dreaming earth,
    and fill
(Driving sweet birds like flocks to
    feed in air)
With living hues and odours plain
    and hill :
Wild Spirit, which art moving every-
    where ;
Destroyer and preserver ; hear, oh
    hear !

II

Thou on whose stream, 'mid the
    steep sky's commotion,
Loose clouds like earth's decaying
    leaves are shed,
Shook from the tangled boughs of
    Heaven and Ocean,

Angels of rain and lightning : there
    are spread
On the blue surface of thine airy surge,
Like the bright hair uplifted from the
    head

Of some fierce Mænad, even from the
    dim verge
Of the horizon to the zenith's height,
The locks of the approaching storm.
    Thou dirge

Of the dying year, to which this clos-
    ing night
Will be the dome of a vast sepulchre,
Vaulted with all thy congregated
    might

Of vapours, from whose solid atmo-
    sphere
Black rain, and fire, and hail, will
    burst : Oh hear !

III

Thou who didst waken from his sum-
    mer dreams
The blue Mediterranean, where he lay
Lulled by the coil of his crystalline
    streams,

Beside a pumice isle in Baiæ's bay,
And saw in sleep old palaces and
    towers
Quivering within the wave's intenser
    day,

All overgrown with azure moss and
    flowers

So sweet, the sense faints picturing
    them ! Thou
For whose path the Atlantic's level
    powers
Cleave themselves into chasms, while
    far below
The sea-blooms and the oozy woods
    which wear
The sapless foliage of the ocean, know

Thy voice, and suddenly grow grey
    with fear,
And tremble and despoil themselves :
    Oh hear !

IV

If I were a dead leaf thou mightest
    bear ;
If I were a swift cloud to fly with thee ;
A wave to pant beneath thy power,
    and share

The impulse of thy strength, only less
    free
Than thou, O uncontrollable ! If
    even
I were as in my boyhood, and could be

The comrade of thy wanderings over
    heaven,
As then, when to outstrip the skyey
    speed
Scarce seemed a vision, I would ne'er
    have striven

As thus with thee in prayer in my sore
    need.
Oh ! lift me as a wave, a leaf, a cloud !
I fall upon the thorns of life ! I bleed !

A heavy weight of hours has chained
    and bowed
One too like thee : tameless, and
    swift, and proud.

V

Make me thy lyre, even as the forest
    is :
What if my leaves are falling like its
    own !
The tumult of thy mighty harmonies

Will take from both a deep autumnal
    tone,
Sweet though in sadness. Be thou,
    spirit fierce
My spirit ! Be thou me, impetuous
    one !

Drive my dead thoughts over the universe
Like withered leaves to quicken a new birth ;
And, by the incantation of this verse,

Scatter, as from an unextinguished hearth
Ashes and sparks, my words among mankind !
Be through my lips to unawakened earth

The trumpet of a prophecy ! O wind,
    Winter comes, can Spring be far behind ?

AN EXHORTATION

CHAMELEONS feed on light and air :
    Poets' food is love and fame :
If in this wide world of care
    Poets could but find the same
With as little toil as they,
    Would they ever change their hue
    As the light chameleons do,
Suiting it to every ray
Twenty times a day ?

Poets are on this cold earth,
    As chameleons might be,
Hidden from their early birth
    In a cave beneath the sea ;
Where light is, chameleons change !
    Where love is not, poets do :
    Fame is love disguised : if few
Find either, never think it strange
That poets range.

Yet dare not stain with wealth or power
    A poet's free and heavenly mind :
If bright chameleons should devour
    Any food but beams and wind,
They would grow as earthly soon
    As their brother lizards are.
    Children of a sunnier star,
Spirits from beyond the moon,
Oh, refuse the boon !

LINES WRITTEN FOR MISS SOPHIA STACEY

THOU art fair, and few are fairer
    Of the nymphs of earth or ocean.
They are robes that fit the wearer—

Those soft limbs of thine, whose motion
Ever falls and shifts and glances,
As the life within them dances.

Thy deep eyes, a double planet,
    Gaze the wisest into madness
With soft clear fire.   The winds that fan it
    Are those thoughts of gentle gladness
Which, like zephyrs on the billow,
Make thy gentle soul their pillow.

If whatever face thou paintest
    In those eyes grows pale with pleasure,
If the fainting soul is faintest
    When it hears thy harp's wild measure,
Wonder not that, when thou speakest,
Of the weak my heart is weakest.

As dew beneath the wind of morning,
    As the sea which whirlwinds waken,
As the birds at thunder's warning,
    As aught mute but deeply shaken,
As one who feels an unseen spirit,
Is my heart when thine is near it.

VIA VAL FONDA, FLORENCE.

ON

THE "MEDUSA" OF LEONARDO DA VINCI

IN THE FLORENTINE GALLERY

IT lieth, gazing on the midnight sky,
    Upon the cloudy mountain peak supine ;
Below, far lands are seen tremblingly ;
    Its horror and its beauty are divine.
Upon its lips and eyelids seems to lie
    Loveliness like a shadow, from which shine,
Fiery and lurid, struggling underneath,
The agonies of anguish and of death.

Yet it is less the horror than the grace
    Which turns the gazer's spirit into stone
Whereon the lineaments of that dead face
    Are graven, till the characters be grown

Into itself, and thought no more can
   trace ;
   'Tis the melodious hues of beauty
      thrown
Athwart the darkness and the glare
   of pain,
Which humanised and harmonize the
   strain.

And from its head as from one body
   grow,
   As [   ] grass out of a watery
      rock,
Hairs which are vipers, and they curl
   and flow,
   And their long tangles in each other
      lock,
And with unending involutions show
   Their mailed radiance, as it were to
      mock
The torture and the death within,
   and saw
The solid air with many a ragged jaw.

And from a stone beside, a poisonous
   eft
   Peeps idly into these Gorgonian
      eyes ;
Whilst in the air a ghastly bat, bereft
   Of sense, has flitted with a mad sur-
      prise
Out of the cave this hideous light hath
   cleft,
   And he comes hastening like a
      moth that hies
After a taper ; and the midnight sky
Flares, a light more dread than ob-
   scurity.

'Tis the tempestuous loveliness of
   terror ;
   For from the serpents gleams a
      brazen glare

Kindled by that inextricable error,
   Which makes a thrilling vapour of
      the air
Become a [   ] and ever-shift-
      ing mirror
   Of all the beauty and the terro
      there—
A woman's countenance, with serpen
      locks,
Gazing in death on heaven from those
      wet rocks.

FLORENCE, 1819.

TO WILLIAM SHELLEY

(With what truth I may say—
      Roma ! Roma ! Roma !
Non è piu come era prima !)

MY lost William, thou in whom
   Some bright spirit lived, and did
That decaying robe consume
   Which its lustre faintly hid,
Here its ashes find a tomb,
   But beneath this pyramid
Thou art not—if a thing ivine
Like thee can die, thy funeral shrine
Is thy mother's grief and mine.

Where art thou, my gentle child ?
   Let me think thy spirit feeds,
With its life intense and mild,
   The love of living leaves and weeds,
Among these tombs and ruins wild ;—
   Let me think that through low
      seeds
Of the sweet flowers and sunny grass,
Into their hues and scents may pass,
A portion ————

June, 1819.

POEMS WRITTEN IN 1820

THE SENSITIVE PLANT

PART I

A SENSITIVE Plant in a garden grew,
And the young winds fed it with
silver dew,
And it opened its fan-like leaves to
the light,
And closed them beneath the kisses of
night.

And the spring arose on the garden
fair,
And the Spirit of Love fell everywhere ;
And each flower and herb on Earth's
dark breast
Rose from the dreams of its wintry
rest.

But none ever trembled and panted
with bliss
In the garden, the field, or the wilderness,
Like a doe in the noon-tide with love's
sweet want,
As the companionless Sensitive Plant.

The snowdrop, and then the violet,
Arose from the ground with warm
rain wet,
And their breath was mixed with
fresh odour, sent
From the turf, like the voice and the
instrument.

Then the pied wind-flowers and the
tulip tall,
And narcissi, the fairest among them
all,
Who gaze on their eyes in the stream's
recess,
Till they die of their own dear loveliness.

And the Naiad-like lily of the vale,
Whom youth makes so fair and passion so pale,
That the light of its tremulous bells
is seen
Through their pavilions of tender
green ;

And the hyacinth purple, and white,
and blue,
Which flung from its bells a sweet peal
anew
Of music so delicate, soft, and intense,
It was felt like an odour within the
sense ;

And the rose like a nymph to the bath
addrest,
Which unveiled the depth of her
glowing breast,
Till, fold after fold, to the fainting air
The soul of her beauty and love lay
bare ;

And the wand-like lily, which lifted
up,
As a Mænad, its moonlight-coloured
cup,
Till the fiery star, which is its eye,
Gazed through the clear dew on the
tender sky ;

And the jessamine faint, and the
sweet tuberose,
The sweetest flower for scent that
blows ;
And all rare blossoms from every
clime
Grew in that garden in perfect prime.

And on the stream whose inconstant
bosom
Was pranked, under boughs of embowering blossom,
With golden and green light, slanting
through
Their heaven of many a tangled hue,

Broad water-lilies lay tremulously,
And starry river-buds glimmered by,
And around them the soft stream did
glide and dance
With a motion of sweet sound and
radiance.

And the sinuous paths of lawn and of
moss,
Which led through the garden along
and across,
Some open at once to the sun and the
breeze,

Some lost among bowers of blossoming trees,

Were all paved with daisies and delicate bells,
As fair as the fabulous asphodels,
And flowerets which drooping as day drooped too,
Fell into pavilions, white, purple, and blue,
To roof the glow-worm from the evening dew.

And from this undefiled Paradise
The flowers (as an infant's awakening eyes
Smile on its mother, whose singing sweet
Can first lull, and at last must awaken it),

When Heaven's blithe winds had unfolded them,
As mine-lamps enkindle a hidden gem,
Shone smiling to heaven, and every one
Shared joy in the light of the gentle sun ;

For each one was interpenetrated
With the light and the odour its neighbour shed,
Like young lovers whom youth and love make dear,
Wrapped and filled by their mutual atmosphere.

But the Sensitive Plant, which could give small fruit
Of the love which it felt from the leaf to the root,
Received more than all, it loved more than ever,
Where none wanted but it, could belong to the giver—

For the Sensitive Plant has no bright flower ;
Radiance and odour are not its dower ;
It loves, even like Love, its deep heart is full,
It desires what it has not, the beautiful !

The light winds, which from unsustaining wings
Shed the music of many murmurings ;

The beams which dart from many a star
Of the flowers whose hues they bear afar ;
The plumed insects swift and free,
Like golden boats on a sunny sea,
Laden with light and odour, which pass
Over the gleam of the living grass ;

The unseen clouds of the dew, which lie
Like fire in the flowers till the sun rides high,
Then wander like spirits among the spheres,
Each cloud faint with the fragrance it bears ;
The quivering vapours of dim noontide,
Which, like a sea, o'er the warm earth glide,
In which every sound, and odour, and beam,
Move, as reeds in a single stream ;

Each and all like ministering angels were
For the Sensitive Plant sweet joy to bear,
Whilst the lagging hours of the day went by
Like windless clouds o'er a tender sky.

And when evening descended from heaven above,
And the earth was all rest, and the air was all love,
And delight, though less bright, was far more deep,
And the day's veil fell from the world of sleep,

And the beasts, and the birds, and the insects were drowned
In an ocean of dreams without a sound ;
Whose waves never mark, though they ever impress
The light sand which paves it, consciousness ;

(Only overhead the sweet nightingale
Ever sang more sweet as the day might fail,
And snatches of its Elysian chant
Were mixed with the dreams of the Sensitive Plant.)

The Sensitive Plant was the earliest
Up-gathered into the bosom of rest ;
A sweet child weary of its delight,
The feeblest and yet the favourite,
Cradled within the embrace of night.

PART II

THERE was a power in this sweet
place,
An Eve in this Eden ; a ruling grace
Which to the flowers, did they waken
or dream,
Was as God is to the starry scheme.

A Lady, the wonder of her kind,
Whose form was upborne by a lovely
mind,
Which, dilating, had moulded her
mien and motion
Like a sea-flower unfolded beneath
the ocean,

Tended the garden from morn to
even :
And the meteors of that sublunar heaven,
Like the lamps of the air when night
walks forth,
Laughed round her footsteps up from
the Earth !

She had no companion of mortal race,
But her tremulous breath and her
flushing face
Told whilst the morn kissed the sleep
from her eyes,
That her dreams were less slumber
than Paradise :

As if some bright Spirit for her sweet
sake
Had deserted heaven while the stars
were awake,
As if yet around her he lingering were,
Though the veil of daylight concealed
him from her.

Her step seemed to pity the grass it
pressed :
You might hear, by the heaving of
her breast,
That the coming and the going of the
wind
Brought pleasure there and left passion behind.

And wherever her airy footstep trod,
Her trailing hair from the grassy sod

Erased its light vestige, with shadowy
sweep,
Like a sunny storm o'er the dark
green deep.

I doubt not the flowers of that garden
sweet
Rejoiced in the sound of her gentle
feet ;
I doubt not they felt the spirit that
came
From her glowing fingers through all
their frame.

She sprinkled bright water from the
stream
On those that were faint with the
sunny beam ;
And out of the cups of the heavy
flowers
She emptied the rain of the thunder
showers.

She lifted their heads with her tender
hands,
And sustained them with rods and
osier bands ;
If the flowers had been her own infants, she
Could never have nursed them more
tenderly.

And all killing insects and gnawing
worms,
And things of obscene and unlovely
forms,
She bore in a basket of Indian woof,
Into the rough woods far aloof,

In a basket, of grasses and wild
flowers full,
The freshest her gentle hands could
pull
For the poor banished insects, whose
intent,
Although they did ill, was innocent.

But the bee and the beamlike ephe-
meris,
Whose path is the lightning's, and
soft moths that kiss
The sweet lips of the flowers, and
harm not, did she
Make her attendant angels be.

And many an antenatal tomb,
Where butterflies dream of the life
to come,

She left clinging round the smooth
   and dark
Edge of the odorous cedar bark.

This fairest creature from earliest
   spring
Thus moved through the garden
   ministering
All the sweet season of summer tide,
And ere the first leaf looked brown
   —she died !

PART III

THREE days the flowers of the garden
   fair,
Like stars when the moon is awa-
   kened, were,
Or the waves of the Baiæ, ere lumi-
   nous
She floats up through the smoke of
   Vesuvius.

And on the fourth, the Sensitive
   Plant
Felt the sound of the funeral chant,
And the steps of the bearers, heavy
   and slow,
And the sobs of the mourners, deep
   and low ;

The weary sound and the heavy
   breath,
And the silent motions of passing
   death,
And the smell, cold, oppressive, and
   dank,
Sent through the pores of the coffin
   plank ;

The dark grass, and the flowers
   among the grass,
Were bright with tears as the crowd
   did pass ;
From their sighs the wind caught a
   mournful tone,
And sate in the pines and gave groan
   for groan.

The garden, once fair, became cold
   and foul,
Like the corpse of her who had been
   its soul :
Which at first was lovely as if in sleep,
Then slowly changed, till it grew a
   heap
To make men tremble who never
   weep.

Swift summer into the autumn flowed,
And frost in the mist of the morning
   rode,
Though the noonday sun looked
   clear and bright,
Mocking the spoil of the secret night.

The rose-leaves, like flakes of crimson
   snow,
Paved the turf and the moss below.
The lilies were drooping, and white,
   and wan,
Like the head and the skin of a dying
   man,

And Indian plants, of scent and hue
The sweetest that ever were fed on
   dew,
Leaf after leaf, day by day,
Were massed into the common clay.

And the leaves, brown, yellow, and
   grey, and red,
And white with the whiteness of what
   is dead,
Like troops of ghosts on the dry wind
   passed ;
Their whistling noise made the birds
   aghast.

And the gusty winds waked the
   winged seeds
Out of their birthplace of ugly weeds,
Till they clung round many a sweet
   flower's stem,
Which rotted into the earth with
   them.

The water-blooms under the rivulet
Fell from the stalks on which they
   were set ;
And the eddies drove them here and
   there,
As the winds did those of the upper
   air.

Then the rain came down, and the
   broken stalks
Were bent and tangled across the
   walks ;
And the leafless net-work of parasite
   bowers
Massed into ruin, and all sweet
   flowers.

Between the time of the wind and the
   snow,
All loathliest weeds began to grow,

Whose coarse leaves were splashed
  with many a speck,
Like the water-snake's belly and the
  toad's back.

And thistles, and nettles, and darnels
  rank,
And the dock, and henbane, and hem-
  lock dank,
Stretch'd out its long and hollow
  shank,
And stifled the air till the dead wind
  stank.

And plants, at whose names the verse
  feels loath,
Filled the place with a monstrous
  undergrowth,
Prickly, and pulpous, and blistering,
  and blue,
Livid, and starred with a lurid dew.

And agarics and fungi, with mildew
  and mould,
Started like mist from the wet ground
  cold ;
Pale, fleshy, as if the decaying dead
With a spirit of growth had been animated !

Spawn, weeds, and filth, a leprous
  scum,
Made the running rivulet thick and
  dumb,
And at its outlet, flags huge as stakes
Dammed it up with roots knotted
  like water-snakes.

And hour by hour, when the air was
  still,
The vapours arose which have
  strength to kill :
At morn they were seen, at noon they
  were felt,
At night they were darkness no star
  could melt.

And unctuous meteors from spray to
  spray
Crept and flitted in broad noonday
Unseen ; every branch on which they
  alit
By a venomous blight was burned and
  bit.

The Sensitive Plant, like one forbid,
Wept, and the tears within each lid
Of its folded leaves which together
  grew,

Were changed to a blight of frozen
  glue.

For the leaves soon fell, and the
  branches soon
By the heavy axe of the blast were
  hewn ;
The sap shrank to the root through
  every pore,
As blood to a heart that will beat no
  more.

For Winter came : the wind was his
  whip ;
One choppy finger was on his lip :
He had torn the cataracts from the
  hills,
And they clanked at his girdle like
  manacles ;

His breath was a chain which without
  a sound
The earth, and the air, and the water
  bound ;
He came, fiercely driven in' his
  chariot-throne
By the tenfold blasts of the Arctic
  zone.

Then the weeds which were forms of
  living death,
Fled from the frost to the earth beneath :
Their decay and sudden flight from
  frost
Was but like the vanishing of a ghost !

And under the roots of the Sensitive
  Plant
The moles and the dormice died for
  want :
The birds dropped stiff from the
  frozen air,
And were caught in the branches
  naked and bare.

First there came down a thawing rain,
And its dull drops froze on the boughs
  again,
Then there steamed up a freezing dew
Which to the drops of the thaw-rain
  grew ;

And a northern whirlwind, wandering
  about
Like a wolf that had smelt a dead
  child out,
Shook the boughs thus laden, and
  heavy and stiff,

And snapped them off with his rigid
griff.

When winter had gone and spring
came back,
The Sensitive Plant was a leafless
wreck ;
But the mandrakes, and toadstools,
and docks, and darnels,
Rose like the dead from their ruined
charnels.

CONCLUSION

WHETHER the Sensitive Plant, or that
Which within its boughs like a spirit
sat,
Ere its outward form had known
decay,
Now felt this change, I cannot say.

Whether that lady's gentle mind,
No longer with the form combined
Which scattered love, as stars do
light,
Found sadness, where it left delight,

I dare not guess ; but in this life
Of error, ignorance and strife,
Where nothing is, but all things seem,
And we the shadows of the dream,

It is a modest creed, and yet
Pleasant, if one considers it,
To own that death itself must be,
Like all the rest, a mockery.

That garden sweet, that lady fair,
And all sweet shapes and odours
there,
In truth have never passed away :
'Tis we, 'tis ours, are changed ! not
they.

For love, and beauty, and delight,
There is no death nor change ; their
might
Exceeds our organs, which endure
No light, being themselves obscure.

A VISION OF THE SEA

'TIS the terror of tempest. The rags
of the sail
Are flickering in ribbons within the
fierce gale :
From the stark night of vapours the
dim rain is driven,
And when lightning is loosed like a
deluge from heaven,
She sees the black trunks of the
water-spouts spin,
And bend, as if heaven was ruining in,
Which they seemed to sustain with
their terrible mass
As if ocean had sunk from beneath
them : they pass
To their graves in the deep with an
earthquake of sound,
And the waves and the thunders,
made silent around,
Leave the wind to its echo. The ves-
sel, now tossed
Through the low trailing rack of the
tempest, is lost
In the skirts of the thunder-cloud :
now down the sweep
Of the wind-cloven wave to the chasm
of the deep
It sinks, and the walls of the watery
vale
Whose depths of dread calm are unmoved by the gale,
Dim mirrors of ruin, hang gleaming
about ;
While the surf, like a chaos of stars,
like a rout
Of death flames, like whirlpools of
fire-flowing iron,
With splendour and terror the black
ship environ ;
Or like sulphur-flakes hurled from a
mine of pale fire,
In fountains spout o'er it. In many
a spire
The pyramid-billows, with white
points of brine,
In the cope of the lightning incon-
stantly shine,
As piercing the sky from the floor of
the sea.

The great ship seems splitting ! it
cracks as a tree,
While an earthquake is splintering its
root, ere the blast
Of the whirlwind that stript it of
branches has passed.
The intense thunder-balls which are
raining from heaven
Have shattered its mast, and it stands
black and riven.
The chinks suck destruction. The
heavy dead hulk

On the living sea rolls an inanimate
    bulk,
Like a corpse on the clay which is
    hung'ring to fold
Its corruption around it. Mean-
    while, from the hold,
One deck is burst up from the waters
    below,
And it splits like the ice when the
    thaw-breezes blow
O'er the lakes of the desert !   Who sit
    on the other ?
Is that all the crew that lie burying
    each other,
Like the dead in a breach, round the
    foremast ?   Are those
Twin tigers, who burst, when the
    waters arose,   [the hold
In the agony of terror, their chains in
(What now makes them tame, is what
    then made them bold)
Who crouch, side by side, and have
    driven, like a crank,
The deep grip of their claws through
    the vibrating plank ?
Are these all ?
             Nine weeks the tall
    vessel had lain
On the windless expanse of the
    watery plain,
Where the death-darting sun cast no
    shadow at noon,
And there seemed to be fire in the
    beams of the moon,
Till a lead-coloured fog gathered up
    from the deep,
Whose breath was quick pestilence ;
    then, the cold sleep
Crept, like blight through the ears of
    a thick field of corn,
O'er the populous vessel.   And even
    and morn,
With their hammocks for coffins the
    seamen aghast
Like dead men the dead limbs of
    their comrades cast
Down the deep, which closed on them
    above and around,
And the sharks and the dogfish their
    grave-clothes unbound,
And were glutted like Jews with this
    manna rained down
From God on their wilderness.   One
    after one
The mariners died ; on the eve of this
    day,

When the tempest was gathering in
    cloudy array,
But seven remained.   Six the thun-
    der had smitten,
And they lie black as mummies on
    which Time has written
His scorn of the embalmer ;   the
    seventh, from the deck
An oak splinter pierced through his
    breast and his back,
And hung out to the tempest, a wreck
    on the wreck.

No more ?   At the helm sits a woman
    more fair
Than heaven, when, unbinding its
    star-braided hair,
It sinks with the sun on the earth and
    the sea.
She clasps a bright child on her up-
    gathered knee,
It laughs at the lightning, it mocks
    the mixed thunder
Of the air and the sea, with desire and
    with wonder
It is beckoning the tigers to rise and
    come near,
It would play with those eyes where
    the radiance of fear
Is outshining the meteors ; its bosom
    beats high,
The heart-fire of pleasure has kindled
    its eye ;
Whilst its mother's is lustreless.
    " Smile not, my child,
But sleep deeply and sweetly, and so
    be beguiled
Of the pang that awaits us, whatever
    that be,
So dreadful since thou must divide it
    with me !
Dream, sleep !   This pale bosom, thy
    cradle and bed,
Will it rock thee not, infant ?   'Tis
    beating with dread !
Alas ! what is life, what is death, what
    are we,
That when the ship sinks we no longer
    may be ?
What ! to see thee no more, and to
    feel thee no more ?   [before ?
To be after life what we have been
Not to touch those sweet hands, not
    to look on those eyes,
Those lips, and that hair, all that
    smiling disguise

Thou yet wearest, sweet spirit, which
    I, day by day,
Have so long called my child, but
    which now fades away
Like a rainbow, and I the fallen
    shower ? "
                 Lo ! the ship
Is settling, it topples, the leeward
    ports dip ;
The tigers leap up when they feel the
    slow brine
Crawling inch by inch on them ; hair,
    ears, limbs, and eyne,
Stand rigid with horror ; a loud, long,
    hoarse cry
Burst at once from their vitals tre-
    mendously,
And 'tis borne down the mountainous
    vale of the wave,
Rebounding, like thunder, from crag
    to cave,
Mixed with the clash of the lashing
    rain,
Hurried on by the might of the hurri-
    cane :
The hurricane came from the west,
    and passed on
By the path of the gate of the eastern
    sun,
Transversely dividing the stream of
    the storm ;   [form
As an arrowy serpent, pursuing the
Of an elephant, bursts through the
    brakes of the waste.
Black as a cormorant the screaming
    blast,
Between ocean and heaven, like an
    ocean, passed,
Till it came to the clouds on the verge
    of the world
Which, based on the sea and to hea-
    ven upcurled,
Like columns and walls did surround
    and sustain
The dome of the tempest ; it rent
    them in twain,
As a flood rends its barriers of moun-
    tainous crag ;
And the dense clouds in many a ruin
    and rag,
Like the stones of a temple ere earth-
    quake has passed,
Like the dust of its fall, on the whirl-
    wind are cast ;
They are scattered like foam on the
    torrent ; and where

The wind has burst out through the
    chasm, from the air
Of clear morning, the beams of the
    sunrise flow in,
Unimpeded, keen, golden, and crys-
    talline,
Banded armies of light and of air ; at
    one gate
They encounter, but interpenetrate.
And that breach in the tempest is
    widening away,
And the caverns of cloud are torn up
    by the day,
And the fierce winds are sinking with
    weary wings,
Lulled by the motion and murmur-
    ings,
And the long glassy heave of the rock-
    ing sea,
And over head glorious, but dreadful
    to see,
The wrecks of the tempest, like va-
    pours of gold,
Are consuming in sunrise.   The
    heaped waves behold,
The deep calm of blue heaven dilating
    above,
And, like passions made still by the
    presence of Love,
Beneath the clear surface reflecting it
    slide
Tremulous with soft influence ; ex-
    tending its tide
From the Andes to Atlas, round
    mountain and isle,
Round sea-birds and wrecks, paved
    with heaven's azure smile,
The wide world of waters is vibrating.
                   Where
Is the ship ? On the verge of the
    wave where it lay
One tiger is mingled in ghastly affray
With a sea-snake. The foam and the
    smoke of the battle
Stain the clear air with sunbows ; the
    jar, and the rattle
Of solid bones crushed by the in-
    finite stress
Of the snake's adamantine volumi-
    nousness ;
And the hum of the hot blood that
    spouts and rains
Where the gripe of the tiger has
    wounded the veins,
Swollen with rage, strength, and
    effort ; the whirl and the splash

As of some hideous engine whose
   brazen teeth smash
The thin winds and soft waves into
   thunder ! the screams
And hissings crawl fast o'er the
   smooth ocean-streams,
Each sound like a centipede.   Near
   this commotion,
A blue shark is hanging within the
   blue ocean,
The fin-winged tomb of the victor.
   The other
Is winning his way from the fate of
   his brother,
To his own with the speed of despair.
   Lo ! a boat
Advances ;   twelve rowers with the
   impulse of thought
Urge on the keen keel, the brine
   foams.   At the stern
Three marksmen stand levelling.
   Hot bullets burn
In the breast of the tiger, which yet
   bears him on
To his refuge and ruin.   One frag-
   ment alone,
'Tis dwindling and sinking, 'tis now
   almost gone,
Of the wreck of the vessel peers out
   of the sea.
With her left hand she grasps it im-
   petuously,
With her right she sustains her fair
   infant.   Death, Fear,
Love, Beauty, are mixed in the atmo-
   sphere,
Which trembles and burns with the
   fervour of dread
Around her wild eyes, her bright hand,
   and her head,
Like a meteor of light o'er the waters !
   her child
Is yet smiling,and playing, and murmuring :   so smiled
The false deep ere the storm.   Like a
   sister and brother
The child and the ocean still smile on
   each other,
Whilst ———

THE CLOUD

I

I BRING fresh showers for the thirsting
   flowers,
   From the seas and the streams ;

I bear light shades for the leaves when
   laid
   In their noonday dreams.
From my wings are shaken the dews
   that waken
   The sweet buds every one,
When rocked to rest on their mother's
   breast,
   As she dances about the sun.
I wield the flail of the lashing hail,
   And whiten the green plains under,
And then again I dissolve it in rain,
   And laugh as I pass in thunder.

II

I sift the snow on the mountains be-
   low,
   And their great pines groan aghast ;
And all the night 'tis my pillow white,
   While I sleep in the arms of the
   blast.
Sublime on the towers of my skyey
   bowers,
   Lightning my pilot sits,
In a cavern under is fettered the
   thunder,
   It struggles and howls at fits ;
Over earth and ocean with gentle
   motion,
   This pilot is guiding me,
Lured by the love of the genii that
   move
   In the depths of the purple sea ;
Over the rills, and the crags, and the
   hills,
   Over the lakes and the plains,
Wherever he dream, under mountain
   or stream,
   The Spirit he loves remains ;
And I all the while bask in heaven's
   blue smile,
   Whilst he is dissolving in rains.

III

The sanguine sunrise, with his meteor
   eyes,
   And his burning plumes outspread,
Leaps on the back of my sailing rack,
   When the morning star shines dead.
As on the jag of a mountain crag,
   Which an earthquake rocks and
   swings,
An eagle alit one moment may sit
   In the light of its golden wings.
And when sunset may breathe, from
   the lit sea beneath,
   Its ardours of rest and of love,

And the crimson pall of eve may fall
  From the depth of heaven above,
With wings folded I rest, on mine airy
    nest,
  As still as a brooding dove.

IV

That orbed maiden, with white fire
    laden,
  Whom mortals call the moon,
Glides glimmering o'er my fleece-like
    floor,
  By the midnight breezes strewn :
And wherever the beat of her unseen
    feet,
  Which only the angels hear,
May have broken the woof of my
    tent's thin roof,
  The stars peep behind her and
    peer ;
And I laugh to see them whirl and
    flee,
  Like a swarm of golden bees,
When I widen the rent in my wind-
    built tent,
Till the calm rivers, lakes, and seas,
Like strips of the sky fallen through
    me on high,
  Are each paved with the moon
    and these.

V

I bind the sun's throne with the
    burning zone,
  And the moon's with a girdle of
    pearl ;
The volcanoes are dim, and the stars
    reel and swim,
  When the whirlwinds my banner
    unfurl.
From cape to cape, with a bridge-like
    shape,
  Over a torrent sea,
Sunbeam-proof, I hang like a roof,
  The mountains its columns be.
The triumphal arch through which
    I march,
  With hurricane, fire, and snow,
When the powers of the air are
    chained to my chair,
  Is the million-coloured bow ;
The sphere-fire above its soft colours
    wove,
  While the moist earth was laughing
    below.

VI

I am the daughter of earth and water,
  And the nursling of the sky :
I pass through the pores of the ocean
    and shores ;
  I change, but I cannot die.
For after the rain, when with never
    a stain,
  The pavilion of heaven is bare,
And the winds and sunbeams with
    their convex gleams,
Build up the blue dome of air,
I silently laugh at my own cenotaph,
  And out of the caverns of rain,
Like a child from the womb, like a
    ghost from the tomb,
  I arise and unbuild it again.

TO A SKYLARK

I

Hail to thee, blithe spirit !
  Bird thou never wert,
That from heaven, or near it,
  Pourest thy full heart
In profuse strains of unpremeditated
    art.

II

Higher still and higher,
  From the earth thou springest
Like a cloud of fire ;
  The blue deep thou wingest,
And singing still dost soar, and
    soaring ever singest.

III

In the golden lightning
  Of the sunken sun,
O'er which clouds are brighten
    ing,
  Thou dost float and run ;
Like an unbodied joy whose race is
    just begun.

IV

The pale purple even
  Melts around thy flight ;
Like a star of heaven,
  In the broad daylight
Thou art unseen, but yet I hear thy
    shrill delight.

V

Keen as are the arrows
  Of that silver sphere,

Whose intense lamp narrows
In the white dawn clear,
Until we hardly see, we feel that it
is there.

VI

All the earth and air
With thy voice is loud,
As, when night is bare,
From one lonely cloud
The moon rains out her beams, and
heaven is overflowed.

VII

What thou art we know not;
What is most like thee?
From rainbow clouds there flow
not
Drops so bright to see,
As from thy presence showers a rain
of melody.

VIII

Like a poet hidden
In the light of thought,
Singing hymns unbidden,
Till the world is wrought
To sympathy with hopes and fears
it heeded not:

IX

Like a high-born maiden
In a palace tower,
Soothing her love-laden
Soul in secret hour
With music sweet as love, which
overflows her bower:

X

Like a glow-worm golden
In a dell of dew,
Scattering unbeholden
Its aërial hue
Among the flowers and grass, which
screen it from the view:

XI

Like a rose embowered
In its own green leaves,
By warm winds deflowered,
Till the scent it gives
Makes faint with too much sweet
these heavy-winged thieves.

XII

Sound of vernal showers
On the twinkling grass,

Rain-awakened flowers,
All that ever was
Joyous and clear, and fresh, thy
music doth surpass.

XIII

Teach us, sprite or bird,
What sweet thoughts are
thine:
I have never heard
Praise of love or wine
That panted forth a flood of rapture
so divine.

XIV

Chorus hymeneal,
Or triumphal chaunt,
Matched with thine would be all
But an empty vaunt—
A thing wherein we feel there is some
hidden want.

XV

What objects are the fountains
Of thy happy strain?
What fields, or waves, or moun-
tains?
What shapes of sky or plain?
What love of thine own kind? what
ignorance of pain?

XVI

With thy clear keen joyance
Languor cannot be:
Shadow of annoyance
Never came near thee:
Thou lovest: but ne'er knew love's
sad satiety.

XVII

Waking or asleep,
Thou of death must deem
Things more true and deep
. Than we mortals dream,
Or how could thy notes flow in such
a crystal stream?

XVIII

We look before and after,
And pine for what is not:
Our sincerest laughter
With some pain is fraught;
Our sweetest songs are those that
tell of saddest thought,

XIX

Yet if we could scorn
Hate, and pride, and fear ;
If we were things born
Not to shed a tear,
I know not how thy joy we ever
should come near.

XX

Better than all measures
Of delightful sound,
Better than all treasures
That in books are found,
Thy skill to poet were, thou scorner
of the ground !

XXI

Teach me half the gladness
That thy brain must know,
Such harmonious madness
From my lips would flow,
The world should listen then, as I am
listening now.

TO ———

I FEAR thy kisses, gentle maiden,
Thou needest not fear mine ;
My spirit is too deeply laden
Ever to burthen thine.

I fear thy mien, thy tones, thy
motion,
Thou needest not fear mine ;
Innocent is the heart's devotion
With which I worship thine.

LOVE'S PHILOSOPHY

THE fountains mingle with the river,
And the rivers with the ocean,
The winds of heaven mix for ever
With a sweet emotion ;
Nothing in the world is single ;
All things by a law divine
In one another's being mingle—
Why not I with thine ?

See the mountains kiss high heaven,
And the waves clasp one another ;
No sister flower would be forgiven
If it disdained its brother :
And the sunlight clasps the earth,
And the moonbeams kiss the sea ;—
What are all these kissings worth,
If thou kiss not me ?

ODE TO LIBERTY

Yet freedom, yet, thy banner torn but
flying,
Streams like a thunder-storm against the
wind.—BYRON.

I

A GLORIOUS people vibrated again
The lightning of the nations:
Liberty,
From heart to heart, from tower to
tower, o'er Spain,
Scattering contagious fire into the
sky,
Gleamed. My soul spurned the
chains of its dismay,
And, in the rapid plumes of
song,
Clothed itself sublime and
strong ;
As a young eagle soars the morning
clouds among,
Hovering inverse o'er its accus-
tomed prey ;
Till from its station in the
heaven of fame
The Spirit's whirlwind rapt it, and
the ray
Of the remotest sphere of living
flame
Which paves the void, was from
behind it flung,
As foam from a ship's swiftness,
when there came
A voice out of the deep ; I will
record the same.

II

"The Sun and the serenest Moon
sprang forth ;
The burning stars of the abyss were
hurl'd
Into the depths of heaven. The
dædal earth,
That island in the ocean of the
world,
Hung in its cloud of all-sustaining
air :
But this divinest universe
Was yet a chaos and a curse,
For thou wert not : but power from
worst producing worse,
The spirit of the beasts was kindled
there,
And of the birds, and of the
watery forms,

And there was war among them
   and despair
   Within them, raging without
      truce or terms :
The bosom of their violated nurse
   Groaned, for beasts warred on
      beasts, and worms on
      worms,
And men on men ; each heart was
   as a hell of storms.

III

" Man, the imperial shape, then multi-
   plied
His generations under the pavilion
Of the Sun's throne : palace and
      pyramid,
   Temple and prison, to many a
      swarming million,
Were, as to mountain-wolves their
   ragged caves.
   This human living multitude
      Was savage, cunning, blind,
      and rude,
For thou wert not ; but o'er the
   populous solitude,
   Like one fierce cloud over a waste
      of waves,
   Hung tyranny ; beneath, sate
      deified
   The sister-pest, congregator of
      slaves :
      Into the shadow of her pinions
      wide,
Anarchs and priests who feed on gold
   and blood,
   Till with the stain their inmost
      souls are dyed,
   Drove the astonished herds of men
      from every side.

IV

" The nodding promontories, and blue
      isles,
   And cloud-like mountains, and
      dividuous waves
Of Greece, basked glorious in the
   open smiles
   Of favouring heaven : from their
   enchanted caves
Prophetic echoes flung dim melody
   On the unapprehensive wild.
      The vine, the corn, the olive
      mild,
Grew, savage yet, to human use
   unreconciled ;

And like unfolded flowers beneath
      the sea,
   Like the man's thought dark in
      the infant's brain,
Like' aught that is which wraps
      what is to be,
   Art's deathless dreams lay
      veiled by many a vein
Of Parian stone ; and yet a speechless
      child,
   Verse murmured, and Philosophy
      did strain
   Her lidless eyes for thee ; when
      o'er the Ægean main

V

" Athens arose : a city such as vision
   Builds from the purple crags and
      silver towers
Of battlemented cloud, as in derision
   Of kingliest masonry : the ocean
      floors
Pave it ; the evening sky pavilions it ;
   Its portals are inhabited
      By thunder-zoned winds, each
      head
Within its cloudy wings with sun-fire
   garlanded,
   A divine work ! Athens diviner yet
      Gleamed with its crest of
      columns, on the will
Of man, as on a mount of diamond,
   set ;
   For thou wert, and thine all-
      creative skill
Peopled, with forms that mock the
      eternal dead
   In marble immortality, that hill
   Which was thine earliest throne
      and latest oracle.

VI

" Within the surface of Time's fleeting
      river
   Its wrinkled image lies, as then it
      lay
Immovably unquiet, and for ever
   It trembles, but it cannot pass
      away !
The voices of thy bards and sages
      thunder
      With an earth-awakening
      blast
      Through the caverns of the
      past :
Religion veils her eyes ; Oppression
   shrinks aghast :

A winged sound of joy and love,
    and wonder,
    Which soars where Expectation
        never flew,
    Rending the veil of space and time
        asunder !
    One ocean feeds the clouds, and
        streams, and dew ;
One sun illumines heaven ; one spirit
        vast
    With life and love makes chaos ever
        new,
    As Athens doth the world with
        thy delight renew.

VII

" Then Rome was, and from thy deep
    bosom fairest,
    Like a wolf-cub from a Cadmæan
        Mænad,[1]
She drew the milk of greatness,
        though thy dearest
    From that Elysian food was yet
        unweaned ;
And many a deed of terrible upright-
        ness
    By thy sweet love was sancti-
        fied ;
    And in thy smile, and by thy
        side,
Saintly Camillus lived, and firm
        Atilius died.
    But when tears stained thy robe of
        vestal whiteness,
    And gold profaned thy Capitolian
        throne,
    Thou didst desert, with spirit-
        winged lightness,
    The senate of the tyrants : they
        sunk prone
Slaves of one tyrant. Palatinus
        sighed
    Faint echoes of Iónian song ; that
        tone
    Thou didst delay to hear, lament-
        ing to disown.

VIII

" From what Hyrcanian glen or frozen
    hill,
    Or piny promontory of the Arctic
        main,
Or utmost islet inaccessible,

---

1 See the " Bacchæ " of Euripides.

Didst thou lament the ruin of thy
        reign,
Teaching the woods and waves, and
        desert rocks,
    And every Naiad's ice-cold
        urn,
    To talk in echoes sad and
        stern,
Of that sublimest lore which man
        had dared unlearn
For neither didst thou watch the
        wizard flocks
    Of the Scald's dreams, nor haunt
        the Druid's sleep.
What if the tears rained through
        thy shattered locks,
    Were quickly dried ? for thou
        didst groan, not weep,
When from its sea of death to kill
        and burn,
    The Galilean serpent forth did
        creep,
And made thy world an undistin-
        guishable heap.

IX

" A thousand years the Earth cried
        ' Where art thou ? '
And then the shadow of thy coming
        fell
On Saxon Alfred's olive-cinctured
        brow :
    And many a warrior-peopled cita-
        del,
Like rocks, which fire lifts out of the
        flat deep,
    Arose in sacred Italy,
    Frowning o'er the tempestuous
        sea
Of kings, and priests, and slaves, in
        tower-crowned majesty :
    That multitudinous anarchy did
        sweep,
    And burst around their walls.
        like idle foam,
    Whilst from the human spirit's
        deepest deep,
    Strange melody with love and
        awe struck dumb
Dissonant arms ; and Art which
        cannot die,
    With divine want traced on our
        earthly home
    Fit imagery to pave heaven's ever-
        lasting dome.

X

"Thou huntress swifter than the Moon! thou terror
Of the world's wolves! thou bearer of the quiver,
Whose sunlike shafts pierce tempest-winged Error,
As light may pierce the clouds when they discover
In the calm regions of the orient day!
Luther caught thy wakening glance:
Like lightning from his leaden lance
Reflected, it dissolved the visions of the trance
In which, as in a tomb, the nations lay;
And England's prophets hailed thee as their queen,
In songs whose music cannot pass away,
Though it must flow for ever: not unseen
Before the spirit-sighted countenance
Of Milton didst thou pass, from the sad scene
Beyond whose night he saw, with a dejected mien.

XI

"The eager hours and unreluctant years
As on a dawn-illumined mountain stood,
Trampling to silence their loud hopes and fears,
Darkening each other with their multitude,
And cried aloud, 'Liberty!' Indignation
Answered Pity from her cave;
Death grew pale within the grave,
And desolation howled to the destroyer, 'Save!'
When, like heaven's sun, girt by the exhalation
Of its own glorious light, thou didst arise,
Chasing thy foes from nation unto nation
Like shadows: as if day had cloven the skies
At dreaming midnight o'er the Western wave,

Men started, staggering with a glad surprise,
Under the lightnings of thine familiar eyes.

XII

"Thou heaven of earth! what spells could pall thee then,
In ominous eclipse? A thousand years,
Bred from the slime of deep oppression's den,
Dyed all thy liquid light with blood and tears,
Till thy sweet stars could weep the stain away;
How like Bacchanals of blood
Round France, the ghastly vintage, stood
Destruction's sceptred slaves, and Folly's mitred brood!
When one, like them, but mightier far than they,
The Anarch of thine own bewildered powers,
Rose: armies mingled in obscure array,
Like clouds with clouds, darkening the sacred bowers
Of serene heaven. He, by the past pursued,
Rests with those dead but unforgotten hours,
Whose ghosts scare victor kings in their ancestral towers.

XIII

"England yet sleeps: was she not called of old?
Spain calls her now, as with its thrilling thunder
Vesuvius wakens Ætna, and the cold
Snow-crags by its reply are cloven in sunder:
O'er the lit waves every Æolian isle
From Pithecusa to Pelorus
Howls, and leaps, and glares in chorus:
They cry, 'Be dim, ye lamps of heaven suspended o'er us,'
Her chains are threads of gold, she need but smile
And they dissolve; but Spain's were links of steel,
Till bit to dust by virtue's keenest file.

Twins of a single destiny ! appeal
To the eternal years enthroned
    before us,
In the dim West ; impress us from
    a seal,
All ye have thought and done !
    Time cannot dare conceal.

XIV

"Tomb of Arminius ! render up thy
    dead
Till, like a standard from a watch-
    tower's staff,
His soul may stream over the tyrant's
    head !
Thy victory shall be his epitaph,
Wild Bacchanal of truth's mysterious
    wine,
        King-deluded Germany,
        His dead spirit lives in thee.
Why do we fear or hope ? thou art
    already free !
And thou, lost Paradise of this
    divine
    And   glorious   world !   thou
        flowery wilderness !
Thou island of eternity ! thou
    shrine
    Where desolation, clothed with
        loveliness,
Worships the thing thou wert ! O
    Italy,
Gather thy blood into thy heart ;
    repress
The beasts who make their dens
    thy sacred palaces.

XV

"O that the free would stamp the
    impious name
Of 'King' into the dust ; or write
    it there,
So that this blot upon the page of
    fame
Were as the serpent's path, which
    the light air
Erases, and the flat sands close be-
    hind !
    Ye the oracle have heard :
    Lift the victory-flashing sword,
And cut the snaky knots of this foul
    Gordian word,
    Which, weak itself as stubble, yet
        can bind
    Into a mass, irrefragably firm,

The axes and the rods which awe
    mankind :
    The sound has poison in it, 'tis
        the sperm
Of what makes life foul, cankerous,
    and abhorred ;
    Disdain not thou, at thine ap-
        pointed term,
    To set thine armed heel on this
        reluctant worm.

XVI

"O that the wise from their bright
    minds would kindle
    Such lamps within the dome of this
        dim world,
That the pale name of PRIEST might
    shrink and dwindle
    Into the hell from which it first
        was hurled,
A scoff of impious pride from fiends
    impure,
        Till human thoughts might
            kneel alone,
        Each before the judgment-
            throne
Of its own aweless soul, or of the
    power unknown !
    O that the words which make the
        thoughts obscure
    From which they spring, as
        clouds of glimmering dew
    From a white lake blot heaven's
        blue portraiture,
    Were stript of their thin masks
        and various hue,
And frowns and smiles and splen-
    dours not their own,
    Till in the nakedness of false and
        true
    They stand before their Lord, each
        to receive its due.

XVII

"He who taught man to vanquish
    whatsoever
Can be between the cradle and the
    grave,
Crowned him the King of Life.   O
    vain endeavour !
If on his own high will, a willing
    slave,
He has enthroned the oppression and
    the oppressor.
        What if earth can clothe and
            feed

Amplest millions at their need,
And power in thought be as the tree
    within the seed ?
Or what if Art, an ardent inter-
    cessor,
    Diving on fiery wings to Nature's
      throne,
Checks the great mother stooping
    to caress her,
    And cries, 'Give me, thy child,
      dominion
Over all height and depth ?' if Life
    can breed
New wants, and wealth from those
    who toil and groan,
    Rend of thy gifts and hers a
      thousandfold for one.

XVIII

"Come thou, but lead out of the
    inmost cave
Of man's deep spirit, as the Morn-
    ing Star
Beckons the Sun from the Eoan wave,
    Wisdom. I hear the pennons of
    her car
Self-moving like cloud charioted by
    flame ;
      Comes she not, and come ye
      not,
      Rulers of eternal thought,
To judge with solemn truth life's ill-
    apportioned lot ?
    Blind Love, and equal Justice, and
      the Fame
    Of what has been, the Hope of
      what will be ?
O, Liberty ! if such could be thy
    name
    Wert thou disjoined from these,
      or they from thee :
If thine or theirs were treasures to
    be bought
By blood or tears, have not the
    wise and free
Wept tears, and blood like tears ?"
    The solemn harmony

XIX

Paused, and the spirit of that mighty
    singing
    To its abyss was suddenly with-
    drawn ;
Then as a wild swan, when sublimely
    winging

Its path athwart the thunder-
    smoke of dawn,
Sinks headlong through the aërial
    golden light
    On the heavy sounding plain,
    When the bolt has pierced its
      brain ;
As summer clouds dissolve unbur-
    thened of their rain ;
As a far taper fades with fading
    night ;
    As a brief insect dies with dying
      day,
My song, its pinions disarrayed of
    might,
    Drooped ; o'er it closed the
      echoes far away
Of the great voice which did its flight
    sustain,
    As waves which lately paved his
      watery way
    Hiss round a drowner's head in
      their tempestuous play.

ARETHUSA

ARETHUSA arose
From her couch of snows
In the Acroceraunian mountains,—
    From cloud and from crag
    With many a jag,
Shepherding her bright fountains.
    She leapt down the rocks
    With her rainbow locks
Streaming among the streams ;—
    Her steps paved with green
    The downward ravine
Which slopes to the western gleams :
    And gliding and springing,
    She went, ever singing,
In murmurs, as soft as sleep ;
    The Earth seemed to love her,
    And Heaven smiled above her,
As she lingered towards the deep.

    Then Alpheus bold,
    On his glacier cold,
With his trident the mountains
    strook ;
    And opened a chasm
    In the rocks :—with the spasm
All Erymanthus shook.
    And the black south wind
    It concealed behind

The urns of the silent snow,
    And earthquake and thunder
    Did render in sunder
The bars of the springs below :
    The beard and the hair
    Of the river God were
Seen through the torrent's sweep,
    As he followed the light
    Of the fleet nymph's flight
To the brink of the Dorian deep.

    " Oh, save me ! Oh, guide me !
    And bid the deep hide me !
For he grasps me now by the hair ! "
    The loud Ocean heard,
    To its blue depth stirred,
And divided at her prayer ;
    And under the water
    The Earth's white daughter
Fled like a sunny beam ;
    Behind her descended
    Her billows, unblended
With the brackish Dorian stream :
    Like a gloomy stain
    On the emerald main
Alpheus rushed behind,—
    As an eagle pursuing
    A dove to its ruin
Down the streams of the cloudy wind.

    Under the bowers
    Where the Ocean Powers
Sit on their pearled thrones :
    Through the coral woods
    Of the weltering floods
Over heaps of unvalued stones ;
    Through the dim beams
    Which amid the streams
Weave a network of coloured light ;
    And under the caves,
    Where the shadowy waves
Are as green as the forest's night :—
    Outspeeding the shark,
    And the swordfish dark,
Under the ocean foam,
    And up through the rifts
    Of the mountain clifts
They passed to their Dorian home.

    And now from their fountains
    In Enna's mountains,
Down one vale where the morning basks,
    Like friends once parted
    Grown single-hearted,
They ply their watery tasks.

    At sunrise they leap
    From their cradles steep
In the cave of the shelving hill ;
    At noontide they flow
    Through the woods below
And the meadows of Asphodel ;
    And at night they sleep
    In the rocking deep
Beneath the Ortygian shore ;—
    Like spirits that lie
    In the azure sky
When they love but live no more.

PISA.

HYMN OF APOLLO

THE sleepless Hours who watch me as I lie,
    Curtained with star-inwoven tapestries
From the broad moonlight of the sky,
    Fanning the busy dreams from my dim eyes,—
Waken me when their Mother, the grey Dawn,
Tells them that dreams and that the moon is gone.

Then I arise, and climbing Heaven's blue dome,
    I walk over the mountains and the waves,
Leaving my robe upon the ocean foam ;
    My footsteps pave the clouds with fire ; the caves
Are filled with my bright presence, and the air
Leaves the green earth to my embraces bare.

The sunbeams are my shafts, with which I kill
    Deceit, that loves the night and fears the day ;
All men who do or even imagine ill
    Fly me, and from the glory of my ray
Good minds and open actions take new might,
Until diminished by the reign of night.

I feed the clouds, the rainbows, and the flowers,

With their ethereal colours; the
  Moon's globe
And the pure stars in their eternal
  bowers
  Are tinctured with my power as
    with a robe;
Whatever lamps on Earth or Heaven
  may shine
Are portions of one power, which is
  mine.

I stand at noon upon the peak of
  Heaven,
  Then with unwilling steps I wander
    down
Into the clouds of the Atlantic even;
  For grief that I depart they weep
    and frown:
What look is more delightful than the
  smile
With which I soothe them from the
  western isle?

I am the eye with which the Universe
  Beholds itself and knows itself
    divine;
All harmony of instrument or verse,
  All prophecy, all medicine are
    mine,
All light of Art or Nature;—to my
  song
Victory and praise in their own right
  belong.

HYMN OF PAN

FROM the forests and highlands
  We come, we come;
From the river-girt islands,
    Where loud waves are dumb
      Listening to my sweet pipings.
The wind in the reeds and the rushes,
  The bees on the bells of thyme,
  The birds on the myrtle bushes,
  The cicale above in the lime,
And the lizards below in the grass,
Were as silent as ever old Tmolus [1]
    was,
      Listening to my sweet pipings.

[1] This and the former poem were written at the
request of a friend, to be inserted in a drama
on the subject of Midas. Apollo and Pan contended before Tmolus for the prize in music.

Liquid Peneus was flowing,
  . And all dark Tempe lay
In Pelion's shadow, outgrowing
    The light of the dying day,
      Speeded   with   my   sweet
        pipings.
The Sileni, and Sylvans, and Fauns,
  And the Nymphs of the woods and
    .   waves,
To the edge of the moist river lawns,
  And the brink of the dewy caves,
And all that did then attend and fol-
  low,
Were silent with love, as you now,
  Apollo,
    With envy of my sweet pipings.

I sang of the dancing stars,
    I sang of the dædal Earth,
And of Heaven—and the giant wars,
    And Love, and Death, and
      Birth,—
        And then I changed my pip-
          ings,—
Singing how down the vale of Menalus
  I pursued a maiden and clasped a
    reed:
Gods and men, we are all deluded
    thus!
  It breaks in our bosom and then we
    bleed:
All wept, as I think both ye now
  would,
If envy or age had not frozen your
  blood,
    At the sorrow of my sweet pip-
      ings.

THE QUESTION

I DREAMED that, as I wandered by
  the way,
  Bare winter suddenly was changed
    to spring,
And gentle odours led my steps astray,
  Mixed with a sound of waters mur-
    muring
Along a shelving bank of turf, which
  lay
    Under a copse, and hardly dared to
      fling
Its green arms round the bosom of
  the stream,
But kissed it and then fled, as thou
  mightest in dream.

There grew pied wind-flowers and
violets,
Daisies, those pearled Arcturi of
the earth,
The constellated flower that never
sets ;
Faint oxlips ; tender bluebells, at
whose birth
The sod scarce heaved ; and that tall
flower that wets
Its mother's face with heaven-col-
lected tears,
When the low wind, its playmate's
voice, it hears.

And in the warm hedge grew lush
eglantine,
Green cowbind and the moonlight-
coloured May,
And cherry-blossoms, and white cups,
whose wine
Was the bright dew yet drained not
by the day ;
And wild roses, and ivy serpentine,
With its dark buds and leaves, wan-
dering astray ;
And flowers azure, black, and streaked
with gold,
Fairer than any wakened eyes behold.

And nearer to the river's trembling
edge
There grew broad flag-flowers, purple pranked with white,
And starry river-buds among the
sedge,
And floating water-lilies, broad and
bright,
Which lit the oak that overhung the
hedge
With moonlight beams of their own
watery light ;
And bulrushes, and reeds of such deep
green
As soothed the dazzled eye with sober
sheen.

Methought that of these visionary
flowers
I made a nosegay, bound in such a
way
That the same hues, which in their
natural bowers
Were mingled or opposed, the like
array

Kept these imprisoned children of the
Hours
Within my hand,—and then, elate
and gay,
I hastened to the spot whence I had
come,
That I might there present it !—Oh !
to whom ?

THE TWO SPIRITS

AN ALLEGORY

FIRST SPIRIT.

O THOU, who plumed with strong de-
sire
Wouldst float above the earth, be-
ware !
A shadow tracks thy flight of fire—
Night is coming !
Bright are the regions of the air,
And among the winds and beams
It were delight to wander there—
Night is coming !

SECOND SPIRIT.

The deathless stars are bright above :
If I would cross the shade at night,
Within my heart is the lamp of love,
And that is day !
And the moon will smile with gentle
light
On my golden plumes where'er they
move ;
The meteors will linger round my
flight,
And make night day.

FIRST SPIRIT.

But if the whirlwinds of darkness
waken
Hail, and lightning, and stormy
rain ;
See the bounds of the air are shaken—
Night is coming !
The red swift clouds of the hurricane
Yon declining sun have o'ertaken,
The clash of the hail sweeps over the
plain—
Night is coming !

SECOND SPIRIT.

I see the light, and I hear the sound ;
I'll sail on the flood of the tempest
dark,

With the calm within and the light
around
   Which makes night day :
And thou, when the gloom is deep and
stark,
   Look from thy dull earth, slumber-
bound,
My moonlight flight thou then mayst
mark
   On high, far away.

Some say there is a precipice
   Where one vast pine is frozen to
ruin
O'er piles of snow and chasms of ice
   'Mid Alpine mountains ;
And that the languid storm, pursuing
   That winged shape, for ever flies
Round those hoar branches, aye re-
newing
   Its aëry fountains.

Some say when nights are dry and
clear,
   And the death-dews sleep on the
morass,
Sweet whispers are heard by the
traveller,
   Which make night day :
And a silver shape like his early love
doth pass
   Upborne by her wild and glittering
hair,
And when he awakes on the fragrant
grass,
   He finds night day.

THE WANING MOON

AND like a dying lady, lean and pale,
Who totters forth, wrapt in a gauzy
veil,
Out of her chamber, led by the insane
And feeble wanderings of her fading
brain,
The moon arose upon the murky earth,
A white and shapeless mass.

SONG OF PROSERPINE,

WHILST GATHERING FLOWERS ON THE
PLAIN OF ENNA

SACRED Goddess, Mother Earth,
   Thou from whose immortal bosom,

Gods, and men, and beasts have birth,
   Leaf and blade, and bud and blos-
som,
Breathe thine influence most divine
On thine own child, Proserpine.

If with mists of evening dew
   Thou dost nourish these young
flowers
Till they grow, in scent and hue,
   Fairest children of the Hours,
Breathe thine influence most divine
On thine own child, Proserpine.

LETTER TO MARIA GISBORNE

LEGHORN, *July* 1, 1820.

THE spider spreads her webs, whether
she be
In poet's tower, cellar, or barn, or
tree ;
The silkworm in the dark-green mul-
berry leaves
His winding-sheet and cradle ever
weaves !
So I, a thing whom moralists call
worm,
Sit spinning still round this decaying
form,
From the fine threads of rare and
subtle thought—
No net of words in garish colours
wrought,
To catch the idle buzzers of the day—
But a soft cell, where, when that fades
away,
Memory may clothe in wings my liv-
ing name
And feed it with the asphodels of fame,
Which in those hearts which most re-
member me
Grow, making love an immortality.

Whoever should behold me now, I
wist,
Would think I were a mighty mechan-
ist,
Bent with sublime Archimedean art
To breathe a soul into the iron heart
Of some machine portentous, or
strange gin,
Which by the force of figured spells
might win
Its way over the sea, and sport there-
in ;

For round the walls are hung dread
engines, such
As Vulcan never wrought for Jove to
clutch
Ixion or the Titan :—or the quick
Wit of that man of God, St. Dominic,
To convince Atheist, Turk, or Heretic;
Or those in philosophic councils met,
Who thought to pay some interest for
the debt
They owed to Jesus Christ for their
salvation,
By giving a faint foretaste of damna-
tion
To Shakespeare, Sidney, Spenser, and
the rest
Who made our land an island of the
blest,
When lamp-like Spain, who now re-
lumes her fire
On Freedom's hearth, grew dim with
empire :—
With thumbscrews, wheels, with
tooth and spike and jag,
With fishes found under the utmost
crag
Of Cornwall, and the storm-encom-
passed isles, [smiles
Where to the sky the rude sea seldom
Unless in treacherous wrath, as on the
morn
When the exulting elements in scorn,
Satiated with destroyed destruction,
lay
Sleeping in beauty on their mangled
prey,
As panthers sleep : and other strange
and dread
Magical forms the brick-floor over-
spread—
Proteus transformed to metal did not
make
More figures, or more strange ; nor
did he take
Such shapes of unintelligible brass,
Or heap himself in such a horrid mass
Of tin and iron not to be understood,
And forms of unimaginable wood,
To puzzle Tubal Cain and all his
brood :
Great screws, and cones, and wheels,
and grooved blocks,
The elements of what will stand the
shocks
Of wave and wind and time.—Upon
the table

More knacks and quips there be than
I am able
To cataloguise in this verse of mine :
A pretty bowl of wood—not full of
wine,
But quicksilver ; that dew which the
gnomes drink
When at their subterranean toil they
swink,
Pledging the demons of the earth-
quake who
Reply to them in lava—cry, "Halloo!"
And call out to the cities o'er their
head,—
Roofs, towns, and shrines,—the dying
and the dead
Crash through the chinks of earth—
and then all quaff
Another rouse, and hold their sides
and laugh.
This quicksilver no gnome has drunk
—within
The walnut-bowl it lies, veined and
thin,   [stains
In colour like the wake of light that
The Tuscan deep, when from the
moist moon rains
The inmost shower of its white fire—
the breeze
Is still—blue heaven smiles over the
pale seas.
And in this bowl of quicksilver—for I
Yield to the impulse of an infancy
Outlasting manhood—I have made to
float
A rude idealism of a paper boat—
A hollow screw with cogs—Henry
will know
The thing I mean, and laugh at me,—
if so
He fears not I should do more mis-
chief.—Next
Lie bills and calculations much per-
plext,
With steamboats, frigates, and ma-
chinery quaint,
Traced over them in blue and yellow
paint.
Then comes a range of mathematical
Instruments, for plans nautical and
statical,
A heap of rosin, a green broken glass
With ink in it ;—a china cup that was
What it will never be again, I think,
A thing from which sweet lips were
wont to drink

The liquor doctors rail at—and which I
Will quaff in spite of them—and when we die
We'll toss up who died first of drinking tea,
And cry out, "Heads or tails?" where'er we be.
Near that a dusty paint-box, some old hooks,
A half-burnt match, an ivory block, three books,
Where conic sections, spherics, logarithms,
To great Laplace, from Saunderson and Sims,
Lie heaped in their harmonious disarray
Of figures,—disentangle them who may.
Baron de Tott's Memoirs beside them lie,
And some odd volumes of old chemistry.
Near them a most inexplicable thing.
With least in the middle—I'm conjecturing
How to make Henry understand;—but—no,
I'll leave, as Spenser says, with many mo,
This secret in the pregnant womb of time,
Too vast a matter for so weak a rhyme.

And here like some weird Archimage sit I,
Plotting dark spells, and devilish enginery,
The self-impelling steam-wheels of the mind
Which pump up oaths from clergymen, and grind
The gentle spirit of our meek reviews
Into a powdery foam of salt abuse,
Ruffling the ocean of their self-content:—
I sit—and smile or sigh as is my bent,
But not for them—Libeccio rushes round
With an inconstant and an idle sound,
I heed him more than them—the thunder-smoke

Is gathering on the mountains, like a cloak
Folded athwart their shoulders broad and bare;
The ripe corn under the undulating air
Undulates like an ocean;—and the vines
Are trembling wide in all their trellised lines;
The murmur of the awakening sea doth fill
The empty pauses of the blast;—the hill
Looks hoary through the white electric rain [strain
And from the glens beyond, in sullen
The interrupted thunder howls; above
One chasm of heaven smiles, like the eye of love
On the unquiet world;—while such things are.
How could one worth your friendship heed the war
Of worms? The shriek of the world's carrion jays,
Their censure, or their wonder, or their praise?
You are not here! The quaint witch Memory sees
In vacant chairs your absent images,
And points where once you sat, and now should be,
But are not.—I demand if ever we
Shall meet as then we met;—and she replies,
Veiling in awe her second-sighted eyes,
" I know the past alone—but summon home
My sister Hope, she speaks of all to come."
But I, an old diviner, who know well
Every false verse of that sweet oracle,
Turned to the sad enchantress once again,
And sought a respite from my gentle pain,
In acting every passage o'er and o'er
Of our communion.—How on the seashore
We watched the ocean and the sky together,
Under the roof of blue Italian weather;
How I ran home through last year's thunderstorm,

And felt the transverse lightning linger warm
Upon my cheek : and how we often made
Treats for each other, where good will outweighed   [cheer,
The frugal luxury of our country
As it well might, were it less firm and clear
Than ours must ever be ;—and how we spun   [sun
A shroud of talk to hide us from the
Of this familiar life, which seems to be
But is not,—or is but quaint mockery
Of all we would believe ; or sadly blame
The jarring and inexplicable frame
Of this wrong world :—and then anatomize
The purposes and thoughts of men whose eyes
Were closed in distant years ;—or widely guess
The issue of the earth's great business,
When we shall be as we no longer are;
Like babbling gossips safe, who hear the war
Of winds, and sigh, but tremble not ; or how
You listened to some interrupted flow
Of visionary rhyme ;—in joy and pain
Struck from the inmost fountains of my brain,
With little skill perhaps ;—or how we sought
Those deepest wells of passion or of thought
Wrought by wise poets in the waste of years,
Staining the sacred waters with our tears ;
Quenching a thirst ever to be renewed !
Or how I, wisest lady ! then induced
The language of a land which now is free,
And winged with thoughts of truth and majesty,
Flits round the tyrant's sceptre like a cloud,
And bursts the peopled prisons, and cries aloud,
" My name is Legion ! "—-that majestic tongue
Which Calderon over the desert flung
Of ages and of nations ; and which found

An echo in our hearts, and with the sound
Startled oblivion ;—thou wert then to me
As is a nurse—when inarticulately
A child would talk as its grown parents do.
If living winds the rapid clouds pursue,
If hawks chase doves through the aërial way,
Huntsmen the innocent deer, and beasts their prey,
Why should not we rouse with the spirit's blast
Out of the forest of the pathless past
These recollected pleasures ?
                                   You are now
In London, that great sea, whose ebb and flow
At once is deaf and loud, and on the shore
Vomits its wrecks, and still howls on for more.
Yet in its depth what treasures ! You will see
Your old friend Godwin, greater none than he ;
Though fallen on evil times, yet will he stand,
Among the spirits of our age and land,
Before the dread tribunal of To-come
The foremost, whilst rebuke stands pale and dumb.
You will see Coleridge ; he who sits obscure
In the exceeding lustre and the pure
Intense irradiation of a mind,
Which, with its own internal lustre blind,
Flags wearily through darkness and despair—
A cloud-encircled meteor of the air,
A hooded eagle among blinking owls.
You will see Hunt ; one of those happy souls
Which are the salt of the earth, and without whom
This world would smell like what it is —a tomb ;
Who is, what others seem :—his room no doubt
Is still adorned by many a cast from Shout,
With graceful flowers, tastefully placed about ;

And coronals of bay from ribbons
hung,
And brighter wreaths in neat dis-
order flung,
The gifts of the most learned among
some dozens
Of female friends, sisters-in-law, and
cousins.
And there is he with his eternal puns,
Which beat the dullest brain for
smiles, like duns
Thundering for money at a poet's
door ;
Alas ! it is no use to say, " I'm poor ! "
Or oft in graver mood, when he will
look
Things wiser than were ever said in
book,
Except in Shakspeare's wisest ten-
derness.
You will see Hogg and I cannot ex-
press
His virtues, though I know that they
are great,
Because he locks, then barricades, the
gate
Within which they inhabit ;—of his
wit,
And wisdom, you'll cry out when you
are bit.
He is a pearl within an oyster-shell,
One of the richest of the deep. And
there
Is English Peacock with his mountain
Fair
Turned into a Flamingo,—that shy
bird
That gleams i' the Indian air. Have
you not heard
When a man marries, dies, or turns
Hindoo,
His best friends hear no more of him ?
but you
Will see him, and will like him too, I
hope,
With the milk-white Snowdonian
antelope
Matched with his camelopard ; his
fine wit
Makes such a wound, the knife is lost
in it ;
A strain too learned for a shallow age,
Too wise for selfish bigots ;—let his
page,
Which charms the chosen spirits of
the age,

Fold itself up for a serener clime
Of years to come, and find its recom-
pense
In that just expectation. Wit and
sense,
Virtue and human knowledge—all
that might
Make this dull world a business of de-
light,
Are all combined in Horace Smith.—
And these,
With some exceptions, which I need
not tease
Your patience by descanting on, are
all
You and I know in London.
                                        I recall
My thoughts, and bid you look upon
the night :
As water does a sponge, so the moon-
light
Fills the void, hollow, universal air.
What see you ?—Unpavilioned hea-
ven is fair,
Whether the moon, into her chamber
gone,
Leaves midnight to the golden stars,
or wan
Climbs with diminished beams the
azure steep ;
Or whether clouds sail o'er the inverse
deep,
Piloted by the many-wandering blast,
And the rare stars rush through them,
dim and fast.
All this is beautiful in every land.
But what see you beside ?   A shabby
stand
Of hackney-coaches—a brick house or
wall
Fencing some lonely court, white with
the scrawl
Of our unhappy politics ;—or worse—
A wretched woman reeling by, whose
curse
Mixed with the watchman's, partner
of her trade,
You must accept in place of serenade—
Or yellow-haired Pollonia murmuring
To Henry, some unutterable thing.

I see a chaos of green leaves and fruit
Built round dark caverns, even to the
root
Of the living stems who feed them ;
in whose bowers

There sleep in their dark dew the fold-
    ed flowers :
Beyond, the surface of the unsickled
    corn
Trembles not in the slumbering air,
    and borne
In circles quaint, and ever-changing
    dance,
Like winged stars the fireflies flash
    and glance
Pale in the open moonshine ; but each
    one
Under the dark trees seems a little
    sun,
A meteor tamed ; a fixed star gone
    astray
From the silver regions of the Milky
    Way.
Afar the Contadino's song is heard,
Rude, but made sweet by distance ;
    —and a bird
Which cannot be a nightingale, and
    yet
I know none else that sings so sweet
    as it
At this late hour ;—and then all is
    still :—
Now Italy or London, which you will !

Next winter you must pass with me ;
    I'll have
My house by that time turned into a
    grave
Of dead despondence and low-
    thoughted care,
And all the dreams which our tor-
    menters are.
Oh ! that Hunt, Hogg, Peacock, and
    Smith were there,
With everything belonging to them
    fair !—
We will have books ; Spanish, Italian,
    Greek,
And ask one week to make another
    week
As like his father, as I'm unlike mine.
Though we eat little flesh and drink
    no wine,
Yet let's be merry ; we'll have tea
    and toast ;
Custards for supper, and an endless
    host
Of syllabubs and jellies, and mince-
    pies,
And other such ladylike luxuries,—

Feasting on which we will philoso-
    phise.
And we'll have fires out of the Grand
    Duke's wood,
To thaw the six weeks' winter in our
    blood.
And then we'll talk ;—what shall we
    talk about ?
Oh ! there are themes enough for
    many a bout
Of thought-entangled descant ; as
    to nerves—
With cones and parallelograms and
    curves
I've sworn to strangle them if once
    they dare
To bother me,—when you are with me
    there.
And they shall never more sip lauda-
    num
From Helicon or Himeros [1] ;—well,
    come,
And in spite of * * * and of the devil,
We'll make our friendly philosophic
    revel
Outlast the leafless time ;—till buds
    and flowers
Warn the obscure inevitable hours
Sweet meeting by sad parting to re-
    new :—
" To-morrow to fresh woods and pas-
    tures new."

TO MARY

(ON HER OBJECTING TO THE FOLLOW-
ING POEM, UPON THE SCORE OF ITS
CONTAINING NO HUMAN INTEREST)

I

How, my dear Mary, are you critic-
    bitten,
  (For vipers kill, though dead,) by
    some review,
That you condemn these verses I have
    written,
  Because they tell no story, false or
    true !
What, though no mice are caught by
    a young kitten.
  May it not leap and play as grown
    cats do,

[1] Ἵμερος, from which the river Himera was
named, is, with some slight shade of difference,
synonym of Love.

Till its claws come ?   Prithee, for this
  one time,
Content thee with a visionary rhyme.

II

What hand would crush the silken-
  winged fly,
  The youngest of inconstant April's
    minions,
Because it cannot climb the purest
  sky,
  Where the swan sings, amid the
    sun's dominions ?
Not thine.   Thou knowest 'tis its
  doom to die,
  When day shall hide within her twi-
    light pinions,
The lucent eyes, and the eternal smile,
Serene as thine, which lent it life
  awhile.

III

To thy fair feet a winged Vision came,
  Whose date should have been long-
    er than a day,
And o'er thy head did beat its wings
  for fame,
  And in thy sight its fading plumes
    display ;
The watery bow burned in the even-
  ing flame,
  But the shower fell, the swift Sun
    went his way—
And that is dead.—O, let me not be-
  lieve
That anything of mine is fit to live !

IV

Wordsworth informs us he was nine-
  teen years
  Considering and re-touching Peter
    Bell ;
Watering his laurels with the killing
  tears
  Of slow, dull care, so that their roots
    to hell
Might pierce, and their wide branches
  blot their spheres
  Of heaven, with dewy leaves and
    flowers ; this well
May be, for Heaven and Earth con-
  spire to foil
The over-busy gardener's blundering
  toil.

v

My Witch indeed is not so sweet a
  creature
  As Ruth or Lucy, whom his grace-
    ful praise
Clothes for our grandsons—but she
  matches Peter,
  Though he took nineteen years, and
    she three days
In dressing.   Light the vest of flow-
  ing metre
  She wears ; he, proud as dandy
    with his stays,
Has hung upon his wiry limbs a dress
Like King Lear's " looped and win-
  dowed raggedness."

VI

If you strip Peter, you will see a fel-
  low,
  Scorched by Hell's hyperequatorial
    climate
Into a kind of a sulphureous yellow :
  A lean mark, hardly fit to fling a
    rhyme at ;
In shape a Scaramouch, in hue
  Othello,
  If you unveil my Witch, no priest
    nor primate
Can shrive you of that sin,—if sin
  there be
In love, when it becomes idolatry.

THE WITCH OF ATLAS

i

BEFORE those cruel twins, whom at
  one birth
  Incestuous Change bore to her
    father Time,
Error and Truth, had hunted from the
  earth
  All those bright natures which
    adorned its prime,
And left us nothing to believe in, worth
  The pains of putting into learned
    rhyme,
A lady-witch there lived on Atlas'
  mountain
Within a cavern by a secret fountain.

II

Her mother was one of the Atlantides :
  The all-beholding Sun had ne'er be-
    holden

In his wide voyage o'er continents and
   seas
  So fair a creature, as she lay en-
    folden
In the warm shadow of her loveliness;
  He kissed her with his beams, and
   made all golden
The chamber of grey rock in which she
   lay—
She, in that dream of joy, dissolved
   away.

III

'Tis said, she was first changed into a
   vapour,
  And then into a cloud, such clouds
   as flit,
Like splendour-winged moths about a
   taper,
  Round the red west when the sun
   dies in it:
And then into a meteor, such as caper
  On hill-tops when the moon is in a
   fit;
Then, into one of those mysterious
   stars
Which hide themselves between the
   Earth and Mars.

IV

Ten times the Mother of the Months
   had bent
  Her bow beside the folding-star,
   and bidden
With that bright sign the billows to
   indent
  The sea-deserted sand: like children
   chidden,
At her command they ever came and
   went:—
  Since in that cave a dewy splendour
   hidden,
Took shape and motion: with the living form
Of this embodied Power, the cave
   grew warm.

V

A lovely lady garmented in light
  From her own beauty—deep her
   eyes, as are
Two openings of unfathomable night
  Seen through a tempest's cloven
   roof;—her hair
Dark—the dim brain whirls dizzy
   with delight,

Picturing her form;—her soft smiles
   shone afar,
And her low voice was heard like love,
   and drew
All living things towards this wonder
   new.

VI

And first the, spotted camelopard
   came,
  And then the wise and fearless ele-
    phant;
Then the sly serpent, in the golden
   flame
  Of his own volumes intervolved;—
   all gaunt
And sanguine beasts her gentle looks
   made tame. .
  They drank before her at her sacred fount;
And every beast of beating heart grew
   bold,
Such gentleness and power even to
   behold.

VII

The brinded lioness led forth her
   young,
  That she might teach them how
   they should forego
Their inborn thirst of death; the pard
   unstrung
  His sinews at her feet, and sought
   to know,
With looks whose motions spoke with-
   out a tongue,
  How he might be as gentle as the
   doe.
The magic circle of her voice and eyes
All savage natures did imparadise.

VIII

And old Silenus, shaking a green stick
  Of lilies, and the wood-gods in a
   crew
Came, blithe, as in the olive copses
   thick
  Cicadæ are, drunk with the noon-
   day 'dew:
And Driope and Faunus followed
   quick,
  Teasing the God to sing them some-
   thing new,
Till in this cave they found the lady
   lone,
Sitting upon a seat of emerald stone.

IX

And universal Pan, 'tis said, was there,
  And though none saw him,—
    through the adamant
Of the deep mountains, through the
    trackless air,
  And through those living spirits,
    like a want,
He passed out of his everlasting lair
  Where the quick heart of the great
    world doth pant,
And felt that wondrous lady all
    alone,
And she felt him upon her emerald
    throne.

X

And every nymph of stream and
    spreading tree,
  And every shepherdess of Ocean's
    flocks,
Who drives her white waves over the
    green sea ;
  And Ocean, with the brine on his
    grey locks,
And quaint Priapus with his com-
    pany,
  All came, much wondering how the
    enwombed rocks
Could have brought forth so beauti-
    ful a birth ;—
Her love subdued their wonder and
    their mirth.

XI

The herdsmen and the mountain
    maidens came,
  And the rude kings of pastoral
    Garamant—
Their spirits shook within them, as a
    flame
  Stirred by the air under a cavern
    gaunt :
Pigmies, and Polyphemes, by many a
    name,
  Centaurs and Satyrs, and such
    shapes as haunt
Wet clefts,—and lumps, neither alive
    nor dead,
Dog-headed, bosom-eyed, and bird-
    footed.

XII

For she was beautiful : her beauty
    made

The bright world dim, and every-
    thing beside
Seemed like the fleeting image of a
    shade :
  No thought of living spirit could
    abide
(Which to her looks had ever been be-
    trayed)
  On any object in the world so wide,
On any hope within the circling skies,
But on her form, and in her inmost
    eyes.

XIII

Which when the lady knew, she took
    her spindle
  And twined three threads of fleecy
    mist, and three
Long lines of light, such as the dawn
    may kindle
  The clouds and waves and moun-
    tains with, and she
As many starbeams, ere their lamps
    could dwindle
  In the belated moon, wound skil-
    fully ;
And with these threads a subtle veil
    she wove—
A shadow for the splendour of her
    love.

XIV

The deep recesses of her odorous
    dwelling
  Were stored with magic treasures—
    sounds of air,
Which had the power all spirits of
    compelling,
  Folded in cells of crystal silence
    there ;
Such as we hear in youth, and think
    the feeling
  Will never die—yet ere we are
    aware,
The feeling and the sound are fled and
    gone,
And the regret they leave remains
    alone.

XV

And there lay visions swift, and sweet,
    and quaint,
  Each in its thin sheath like a chry-
    salis ;
Some eager to burst forth, some weak
    and faint

With the soft burthen of intensest
    bliss
It is its work to bear to many a saint
    Whose heart adores the shrine
        which holiest is,
Even Love's—and others white, green,
    grey, and black,
And of all shapes—and each was at
    her beck.

XVI

And odours in a kind of aviary
    Of ever-blooming Eden trees she
        kept,
Clipt in a floating net, a lovesick
    Fairy
    Had woven from dew-beams while
        the moon yet slept ;
As bats at the wired window of a dairy,
    They beat their vans ; and each
        was an adept,
When loosed and missioned, making
    wings of winds,
To stir sweet thoughts or sad, in des-
    tined minds.

XVII

And liquors clear and sweet, whose
    healthful might
    Could medicine the sick soul to
        happy sleep,
And change eternal death into a night
    Of glorious dreams — or if eyes
        needs must weep
Could make their tears all wonder and
    delight,
    She in her crystal vials did closely
        keep :
If men could drink of those clear vials,
    'tis said
The living were not envied of the
    dead.

XVIII

Her cave was stored with scrolls of
    strange device,
    The works of some Saturnian Archi-
        mage,
Which taught the expiations at whose
    price
    Men from the Gods might win that
        happy age
Too lightly lost, redeeming native
    vice ;
    And which might quench the earth-
        consuming rage

Of gold and blood—till men should
    live and move
Ha   onious as the sacred stars above.

XIX

And how all things that seem untam-
    able,
    Not to be checked and not to be
        confined,
Obey the spells of wisdom's wizard
    skill ;
    Time, Earth and Fire—the Ocean
        and the Wind,
And all their shapes—and man's im-
    perial will ;
    And other scrolls whose writings did
        unbind
The inmost lore of Love—let the
    profane
Tremble to ask what secrets they
    contain.

XX

And wondrous works of substances
    unknown,
    To which the enchantment of her
        father's power
Had changed those ragged blocks of
    savage stone,
    Were heaped in the recesses of her
        bower ;
Carved lamps and chalices, and phials
    which shone
    In their own golden beams—each
        like a flower,
Out of whose depth a firefly shakes
    his light
Under a cypress in a starless night.

XXI

At first she lived alone in this wild
    home,
    And her thoughts were each a min-
        ister,
Clothing themselves or with the ocean
    foam,
    Or with the wind, or with the speed
        of fire,
To work whatever purposes might
    come
    Into her mind : such power her
        mighty Sire
Had girt them with, whether to fly or
    run,
Through all the regions which he
    shines upon.

XXII

The Ocean nymphs and Hamadry-
ades,
   Oreads and Naiads with long weedy
   locks,
Offered to do her bidding through the
   seas,
   Under the earth, and in the hollow
   rocks,
And far beneath the matted roots of
   trees,
   And in the gnarled heart of stubborn oaks,
So they might live for ever in the light
Of her sweet presence—each a satel-
   lite.

XXIII

" This may not be," the wizard maid
   replied ;
   " The fountains where the Naiades
   bedew
Their shining hair, at length are
   drained and dried ;
   The solid oaks forget their strength,
   and strew.
Their latest leaf upon the mountains
   wide ;
   The boundless ocean, like a drop of
   dew
Will be consumed—the stubborn centre must
Be scattered, like a cloud of summer
   dust.

XXIV

" And ye with them will perish one
   by one :
   If I must sigh to think that this
   shall be,
If I must weep when the surviving
   Sun
   Shall smile on your decay—Oh,
   ask not me
To love you till your little race is run ;
I cannot die as ye must—over me
Your leaves shall glance—the streams
   in which ye dwell
Shall be my paths henceforth, and so
   farewell ! "

XXV

She spoke and wept : the dark and
   azure well
   Sparkled beneath the shower of her
   bright tears,

And every little circlet where they fell,
   Flung to the cavern roof inconstant
   spheres
And intertangled lines of light :—a
   knell
   Of sobbing voices came upon her
   ears
From those departing Forms, o'er the
   serene
Of the white streams and of the forest
   green.

XXVI

All day the wizard lady sat aloof,
   Spelling out scrolls of dread anti-
   quity,
Under the cavern's fountain-lighted
   roof ;
   Or broidering the pictured poesy
Of some high tale upon her growing.
   woof,
   Which the sweet splendour of her
   smiles could dye
In hues outshining heaven—and ever
   she
Added some grace to the wrought
   poesy.

XXVII

While on her hearth lay blazing many
   a piece
   Of sandal wood, rare gums, and cin-
   namon ;
Men scarcely know how beautiful fire
   is ;
   Each flame of it is as a precious.
   stone
Dissolved in ever-moving light, and
   this
   Belongs to each and all who gaze
   upon.
The Witch beheld it not, for in her
   hand
She held a woof that dimmed the
   burning brand.

XXVIII

This lady never slept, but lay in trance
   All night within the fountain—as in
   sleep.
Its emerald crags glowed in her
   beauty's glance :
   Through the green splendour of the
   water deep
She saw the constellations reel and
   dance

Like fireflies—and withal did ever
  keep
The tenour of her contemplations
  calm,
With open eyes, closed feet, and
  folded palm.

XXIX

And when the whirlwinds and the
  clouds descended
    From the white pinnacles of that
    cold hill,
She passed at dewfall to a space ex-
  tended,
    Where, in a lawn of flowering
    asphodel
Amid a wood of pines and cedars
  blended,
    There yawned an inextinguishable
    well
Of crimson fire, full even to the brim,
And overflowing all the margin trim.

XXX

Within the which she lay when the
  fierce war
    Of wintry winds shook that innocu-
    ous liquor
In many a mimic moon and bearded
  star,
    O'er woods and lawns—the serpent
    heard it flicker
In sleep, and dreaming still, he crept
  afar—
    And when the windless snow de-
    scended thicker
Than autumn leaves, she watched it
  as it came
Melt on the surface of the level flame.

XXXI

She had a Boat which some say Vulcan wrought
    For Venus, as the chariot of her
    star ;
But it was found too feeble to be
  fraught
    With all the ardours in that sphere
    which are,
And so she sold it, and Apollo bought
  And gave it to this daughter : from
  a car
Changed to the fairest and the lightest
  boat
Which ever upon mortal stream did
  float.

XXXII

And others say, that, when but three
  hours old,
    The firstborn Love out of his cradle
    leapt,
And clove dun Chaos with his wings of
  gold
    And like a horticultural adept,
Stole a strange seed, and wrapt it up
  in mould,
    And sewed it in his mother's star,
    and kept
Watering it all the summer with sweet
  dew,
And with his wings fanning it as it
  grew.

XXXIII

The plant grew strong and green—the
  snowy flower
    Fell, and the long and gourd-like
    fruit began
To turn the light and dew by inward
  power
    To its own substance : woven tra-
    cery ran
Of light firm texture, ribbed and
  branching, o'er
    The solid rind, like a leaf's veined
    fan,
Of which Love scooped this boat, and
  with soft motion
Piloted it round the circumfluous
  ocean.

XXXIV

This boat she moored upon her fount,
  and lit
    A living spirit within all its frame,
Breathing the soul of swiftness into it.
    Couched on the fountain like a
    panther tame,
One of the twain at Evan's feet that
  sit ;
    Or as on Vesta's sceptre a swift
    flame,
Or on blind Homer's heart a winged
  thought,—
In joyous expectation lay the boat.

XXXV

Then by strange art she kneaded fire
  and snow
    Together, tempering the repugnant
    mass

With liquid love—all things together
        grow
    Through which the harmony of love
        can pass ;
And a fair Shape out of her hands did
        flow
    A living image, which did far sur-
        pass
In beauty that bright shape of vital
        stone
Which drew the heart out of Pygma-
        lion.

XXXVI

A sexless thing it was, and in its
        growth
    It seemed to have developed no
        defect
Of either sex, yet all the grace of
        both,—
    In gentleness and strength its limbs
        were decked ;
The bosom lightly swelled with its full
        youth,
    The countenance was such as might
        select
Some artist that his skill should never
        die,
Imaging forth such perfect purity.

XXXVII

From its smooth shoulders hung two
        rapid wings,
Fit to have borne it to the seventh
        sphere,
Tipt with the speed of liquid lighten-
        ings,
    Dyed in the ardours of the atmo-
        sphere :
She led her creature to the boiling
        springs
    Where the light boat was moored,
        and said—" Sit here ! "
And pointed to the prow, and took
        her seat
Beside the rudder with opposing feet.

XXXVIII

And down the streams which clove
        those mountains vast
    Around their inland islets, and amid
The panther-peopled forests, whose
        shade cast
    Darkness and odours, aud a plea-
        sure hid

In melancholy gloom, the pinnace
        passed ;
    By many a star-surrounded pyra-
        mid
Of icy crag cleaving the purple sky,
And caverns yawning round un-
        fathomably.

XXXIX

The silver moon into that winding
        dell,
    With slanted gleam athwart the
        forest tops,
Tempered like golden evening, feebly
        fell ;
    A green and glowing light, like that
        which drops
From folded lilies in which glow-
        worms dwell,
    When earth over her face night's
        mantle wraps ;
Between the severed mountains lay
        on high
Over the stream, a narrow rift of sky.

XL

And ever as she went, the Image lay
    With folded wings and unawakened
        eyes ;
And o'er its gentle countenance did
        play
    The busy dreams, as thick as sum-
        mer flies
Chasing the rapid smiles that would
        not stay,
    And drinking the warm tears, and
        the sweet sighs
Inhaling, which, with busy murmur
        vain,
They had aroused from that full heart
        and brain.

XLI

And ever down the prone vale, like a
        cloud
    Upon a stream of wind, the pin-
        nace went :
Now lingering on the pools, in which
        abode
    The calm and darkness of the deep,
        content
In which they paused ; now o'er the
        shallow road
    Of white and dancing waters, all
        besprent

With sand and polished pebbles :—
   mortal boat
In such a shallow rapid could not
   float.

XLII

And down the earthquaking cata-
   racts, which shiver
   Their snowlike waters into golden
     air,
Or under chasms unfathomable ever
   Sepulchre them, till in their rage
     they tear
A subterranean portal for the river,
   It fled—the circling sunbows did
     upbear
Its fall down the hoar precipice of
   spray,
Lighting it far upon its lampless way.

XLIII

And when the wizard lady would
   ascend
   The labyrinths of some many-wind-
     ing vale,
Which to the inmost mountain up-
     ward tend—
   She called " Hermaphroditus ! "
     and the pale
And heavy hue which slumber could
     extend
   Over its lips and eyes, as on the gale
A rapid shadow from a slope of grass,
Into the darkness of the stream did
   pass.

XLIV

And it unfurled its heaven-coloured
   pinions ;
   With stars of fire spotting the
     stream below
And from above into the Sun's
     dominions
   Flinging a glory, like the golden
     glow
In which spring clothes her emerald-
     winged minions,
   All interwoven with fine feathery
     snow
And moonlight splendour of intensest
   rime,
With which frost paints the pines in
   winter time.

XLV

And then it winnowed the Elysian
     air
   Which ever hung about that lady
     bright,
With its ethereal vans—and speeding
     there,
   Like a star up the torrent of the
     night,
Or a swift eagle in the morning glare
   Breasting the whirlwind with im-
     petuous flight,
The pinnace, oared by those en-
     chanted wings,
Clove the fierce streams towards their
   upper springs.

XLVI

The water flashed like sunlight by the
   prow
   Of a noon-wandering meteor flung
     to Heaven ;
The still air seemed as if its waves did
   flow
   In tempest down the mountains,—
     loosely driven
The lady's radiant hair streamed to
   and fro ;
   Beneath, the billows having vainly
     striven
Indignant and impetuous, roared to
   feel
The swift and steady motion of the
   keel.

XLVII

Or, when the weary moon was in the
   wane,
   Or in the noon of interlunar night,
The lady-witch in visions could not
   chain
   Her spirit ; but sailed forth under
     the light
Of shooting stars, and bade extend
     amain
   His storm outspeeding wings, th
     Hermaphrodite ;
She to the Austral waters took her
   way,
Beyond the fabulous Thamondocona.

XLVIII

Where, like a meadow which no scythe
   has shaven,

Which rain could never bend, or
 whirl-blast shake,
With the Antarctic constellations
 paven,
 Canopus and his crew, lay th' Austral lake—
There she would build herself a windless haven
 Out of the clouds whose moving
 turrets make
The bastions of the storm, when
 through the sky
The spirits of the tempest thundered
 by.

XLIX

A haven, beneath whose translucent
 floor
 The tremulous stars sparkled un-
 fathomably,
And around which the solid vapours
 hoar,
 Based on the level waters, to the
 sky
Lifted their dreadful crags ; and like
 a shore
 Of wintry mountains, inaccessibly
Hemmed in with rifts and precipices
 grey
And hanging crags, many a cove and
 bay.

L

And whilst the outer lake beneath the
 lash
 Of the wind's scourge, foamed like
 a wounded thing
And the incessant hail with stony
 clash
 Ploughed up the waters, and the
 flagging wing
Of the roused cormorant in the lightning flash
 Looked like the wreck of some wind-
 wandering
Fragment of inky thunder-smoke—
 this haven
Was as a gem to copy Heaven engraven.

LI

On which that lady played her many
 pranks,
 Circling the image of a shooting
 star,
Even as a tiger on Hydaspes' banks

Outspeeds the antelopes which
 speediest are,
In her light boat ; and many quips
 and cranks
 She played upon the water ; till the
 car
Of the late moon, like a sick matron
 wan,
To journey from the misty east
 began.

LII

And then she called out of the hollow
 turrets
 Of those high clouds, white, golden,
 and vermilion,
The armies of her ministering
 spirits—
 In mighty legions million after million
They came, each troop emblazoning
 its merits
 On meteor flags ; and many a proud
 pavilion,
Of the intertexture of the atmosphere,
They pitched upon the plain of the
 calm mere.

LIII

They framed the imperial tent of their
 great queen
 Of woven exhalations, underlaid
With lambent lightning-fire, as may
 be seen
 A dome of thin and open ivory inlaid
With crimson silk—cressets from the
 serene
 Hung there, and on the water for
 her tread,
A tapestry of fleece-like mist was
 strewn,
Dyed in the beams of the ascending
 moon.

LIV

And on a throne o'erlaid with starlight, caught
 Upon those wandering isles of aëry
 dew,
Which highest shoals of mountain
 shipwreck not,
 She sate, and heard all that had
 happened new
Between the earth and moon since
 they had brought

The last intelligence—and now she
 grew
Pale as that moon, lost in the watery
 night—
And now she wept, and now she
 laughed outright.

LV

These were tame pleasures.—She
 would often climb
  The steepest ladder of the crudded
  rack
Up to some beaked cape of cloud sub-
 lime,
  And like Arion on the dolphin's
  back
Ride singing through the shoreless air.
 Oft time
  Following the serpent lightning's
  winding track,
She ran upon the platforms of the
 wind,
And laughed to hear the fireballs
 roar behind.

LVI

And sometimes to those streams of
 upper air,
  Which whirl the earth in its diurnal
  round,
She would ascend, and win the spirits
 there
  To let her join their chorus. Mortals found
That on those days the sky was calm
 and fair,
  And mystic snatches of harmonious
  sound
Wandered upon the earth where'er
 she passed,
And happy thoughts of hope, too
 sweet to last.

LVII

But her choice sport was, in the hour
 of sleep,
  To glide adown old Nilus, when he
  threads
Egypt and Æthiopia, from the steep
  Of utmost Axumé, until he spreads
Like a calm flock of silver-fleeced
 sheep,
  His waters on the plain : and
  crested heads
Of cities and proud temples gleam
 amid,
And many a vapour-belted pyramid.

LVIII

By Mœris and the Mareotid lakes,
  Strewn with faint blooms like
  bridal-chamber floors ;
Where naked boys bridling tame
 water-snakes,
  Or charioteering ghastly alligators,
Had left on the sweet waters mighty
 wakes
  Of those huge forms :—within the
  brazen doors
Of the great Labyrinth slept both boy
 and beast,
Tired with the pomp of their Osirian
 feast.

LIX

And where within the surface of the
 river
  The shadows of the massy temples
  lie,
And never are erased—but tremble
 ever
  Like things which every cloud can
  doom to die,
Through lotus-pav'n canals, and
 wheresoever
  The works of man pierced that
  serenest sky
With tombs, and towers, and fane,
 'twas her delight
To wander in the shadow of the
 night.

LX

With motion like the spirit of that .
 wind
  Whose soft step deepens slumber,
  her light feet
Passed through the peopled haunts of
 humankind,
Scattering sweet visions from her
 presence sweet,
Through fane and palace-court and
 labyrinth mined
  With many a dark and subterranean street
Under the Nile ; through chambers
 high and deep
She passed, observing mortals in their
 sleep.

LXI

A pleasure sweet doubtless it was to
 see

Mortals subdued in all the shapes
    of sleep.
Here lay two sister-twins in infancy ;
    There a lone youth who in his
        dreams did weep ;
Within, two lovers linked innocently
    In their loose locks which over both
        did creep
Like ivy from one stem ;—and there
    lay calm,
Old age with snow-bright hair and
    folded palm.

LXII

But other troubled forms of sleep
    she saw,
    Not to be mirrored in a holy song,
Distortions foul of supernatural awe,
    And pale imaginings of visioned
        wrong,
And all the code of custom's lawless
    law
    Written upon the brows of old and
        young :
" This," said the wizard maiden, " is
    the strife
Which stirs the liquid surface of
    man's life."

LXIII

And little did the sight disturb her
    soul—
    We, the weak mariners of that wide
        lake,
    Where'er its shores extend or billows
        roll,
    Our course unpiloted and starless
        make
O'er its wide surface to an unknown
    goal,—
    But she in the calm depths her way
        could take,
Where in bright bowers immortal
    forms abide,
Beneath the weltering of the restless
    tide.

LXIV

And she saw princes couched under
    the glow
    Of sunlike gems ; and round each
        temple-court
In dormitories ranged, row after row,
    She saw the priests asleep,—all of
        one sort,
Fo all were educated to be so.

The peasants in their huts, and in
    the port
The sailors she saw cradled on the
    waves,
And the dead lulled within their
    dreamless graves.

LXV

And all the forms in which those
    spirits lay,
    Were to her sight like the diaphan-
        ous
Veils, in which those sweet ladies oft
    array
    Their delicate limbs, who would
        conceal from us
Only their scorn of all concealment :
    they
    Move in the light of their own
        beauty thus.
But these and all now lay with sleep
    upon them,
And little thought a Witch was look-
    ing on them.

LXVI

She all those human figures breathing
    there
    Beheld as living spirits—to her
        eyes
The naked beauty of the soul lay
    bare,
    And often through a rude and worn
        disguise
She saw the inner form most bright
    and fair—
    And then,—she had a charm of
        strange device,
Which, murmured on mute lips with
    tender tone,
Could make that spirit mingle with
    her own.

LXVII

Alas, Aurora ! what wouldst thou
    have given
    For such a charm, when Tithon
        became grey ?
Or how much, Venus, of thy silver
    heaven
    Wouldst thou have yielded, ere
        Proserpina
Had half (oh ! why not all ?) the debt
    forgiven
    Which dear Adonis had been
        doomed to pay,

To any witch who would have taught
  you it ?
The Heliad doth not know its value
  yet.

LXVIII

'Tis said in after times her spirit free
  Knew what love was, and felt itself
    alone—
But holy Dian could not chaster be
  Before she stooped to kiss Endy-
    mion,
Than now this lady—like a sexless bee
  Tasting all blossoms, and confined
    to none—
Among those mortal forms, the wiz-
  ard maiden
Passed with an eye serene and heart
  unladen.

LXIX

To those she saw most beautiful, she
  gave
  Strange panacea in a crystal bowl.
They drank in their deep sleep of that
  sweet wave,
And lived thenceforth as if some con-
  trol,
Mightier than life, were in them ; and
  the grave
  Of such, when death oppressed the
    weary soul,
Was a green and over-arching bower
Lit by the gems of many a starry
  flower.

LXX

For on the night that they were
  buried, she
  Restored the embalmers' ruining,
  and shook
The light out of the funeral lamps,
  to be
  A mimic day within that deathy
    nook ;
And she unwound the woven imagery
  Of second childhood's swaddling
    bands, and took
The coffin, its last cradle, from its
  niche,
And threw it with contempt into a
  ditch.

LXXI

And there the body lay, age after
  age,

Mute, breathing, beating, warm,
  and undecaying,
Like one asleep in a green hermitage,
  With gentle sleep about its eyelids
    playing,
And living in its dreams beyond the
  rage
  Of death or life ; while they were
    still arraying
In liveries ever new the rapid, blind,
And fleeting generations of mankind.

LXXII

And she would write strange dreams
  upon the brain
  Of those who were less beautiful,
  and make
All harsh and crooked purposes more
  vain
  Than in the desert is the serpent's
    wake
Which the sand covers,—all his evil
  gain
  The miser in such dreams would
    rise and shake
Into a beggar's lap ;—the lying scribe
Would his own lies betray without a
  bribe.

LXXIII

The priests would write an explana-
  tion full,
  Translating hieroglyphics into
    Greek,
How the god Apis really was a bull,
  And nothing more ; and bid the
    herald stick
The same against the temple doors,
  and pull
  The old cant down ; they licensed
    all to speak
Whate'er they thought of hawks, and
  cats, and geese,
By pastoral letters to each diocese.

LXXIV

The king would dress an ape up in his
  crown
  And robes, and seat him on his
    glorious seat,
And on the right hand of the sunlike
  throne
  Would place a gaudy mock-bird to
    repeat
The chatterings of the monkey.—
  Every one

Of the prone courtiers crawled to
kiss the feet
Of their great Emperor when the
morning came ;
And kissed—alas, how many kiss the
same !

LXXV

The soldiers dreamed that they were
blacksmiths, and
Walked out of quarters in somnam-
bulism,
Round the red anvils you might see
them stand
Like Cyclopses in Vulcan's sooty
abysm,
Beating their swords to ploughshares ;
—in a band
The gaolers sent those of the liberal
schism
Free through the streets of Memphis ;
much, I wis,
To the annoyance of king Amasis.

LXXVI

And timid lovers who had been so
coy,
They hardly knew whether they
loved or not,
Would rise out of their rest, and take
sweet joy,
To the fulfilment of their inmost
thought ;
And when next day the maiden and
the boy
Met one another, both, like sinners
caught,
Blushed at the thing which each believed was done
Only in fancy—till the tenth moon
shone ;

LXXVII

And then the Witch would let them
take no ill :
Of many thousand schemes which
lovers find
The Witch found one,—and so they
took their fill
Of happiness in marriage warm and
kind.
Friends who, by practice of some envious skill,
Were torn apart, a wide wound,
mind from mind !

She did unite again with visions clear
Of deep affection and of truth sincere.

LXXVIII

These were the pranks she played
among the cities
Of mortal men, and what she did
to sprites
And Gods, entangling them in her
sweet ditties,
To do her will, and show their
subtle slights,
I will declare another time ; for it is
A tale more fit for the weird winter
nights—
Than for these garish summer days,
when we
Scarcely believe much more than we
can see.

DEATH

DEATH is here, and death is there
Death is busy everywhere,
All around, within, beneath,
Above is death—and we are death.

Death has set his mark and seal
On all we are and all we feel,
On all we know and all we fear,

*   *   *   *

First our pleasures die—and then
Our hopes, and then our fears—and
when
These are dead, the debt is due,
Dust claims dust—and we die too.

All things that we love and cherish,
Like ourselves, must fade and perish ;
Such is our rude mortal lot—
Love itself would, did they not.

TO THE MOON

ART thou pale for weariness
Of climbing heaven, and gazing on
the earth,
Wandering companionless
Among the stars that have a differ-
ent birth,—
And ever-changing, like a joyless eye
That finds no object worth its con-
stancy ?

ODE TO NAPLES

EPODE I. *a.*

I STOOD within the city disinterred ; [2]
  And heard the autumnal leaves like
    light footfalls
Of spirits passing through the streets ;
  and heard
    The Mountain's slumberous voice
      at intervals
      Thrill through those roofless
        halls ;
The oracular thunder penetrating
  shook
  .The listening soul in my suspended
    blood ;
I felt that Earth out of her deep heart
  spoke—
    I felt, but heard not :—through
      white columns glowed
    The isle-sustaining Ocean flood,
A plane of light between two heavens
  of azure :
    Around me gleamed many a bright
      sepulchre
Of whose pure beauty, Time, as if his
  pleasure
    Were to spare Death, had never
      made erasure ;
      But every living lineament was
      clear
        As in the sculptor's thought ;
        and there
The wreaths of stony myrtle, ivy and
  pine,
    Like winter leaves o'ergrown by
      moulded snow,
    Seemed only not to move and grow
    Because the crystal silence of the
    air
Weighed on their life ; even as the
  Power divine,
Which then lulled all things, brooded
  upon mine.

[1] The Author has connected many recollections
of his visit to Pompeii and Baiæ with the enthusiasm excited by the intelligence of the
proclamation of a Constitutional Government at
Naples. This has given a tinge of picturesque
and descriptive imagery to the introductory
Epodes, which depicture the scenes and some of
the majestic feelings permanently connected with
the scene of this animating event.—*Author's
note.*

[2] Pompeii.

EPODE II. *a.*

Then gentle winds arose,
  With many a mingled close
Of wild Æolian sound and mountain
  odour keen ;
  And where the Baian ocean
  Welters with air-like motion,
Within, above, around its bowers of
  starry green,
  Moving the sea-flowers in those
    purple caves,
  Even as the ever stormless atmo-
    sphere
  Floats o'er the Elysian realm,
It bore me (like an Angel, o'er the
  waves
  Of sunlight, whose swift pinnace of
    dewy air
  No storm can overwhelm ;)
  I sailed where ever flows
  Under the calm Serene
  A spirit of deep emotion,
  From the unknown graves
  Of the dead kings of Melody. [3]
Shadowy Aornos darkened o'er the
  helm
The horizontal ether ; heaven stript
  bare
Its depths over Elysium, where the
  prow
Made the invisible water white as
  snow ;
From that Typhæan mount, Inarimé,
There streamed a sunlit vapour, like
  the standard
  Of some ethereal host ;
  Whilst from all the coast,
Louder and louder, gathering round,
  there wandered
Over the oracular woods and divine
  sea
Prophesyings which grew articulate—
They seize me—I must speak them ;
  —be they fate !

STROPHE *a.* I.

NAPLES ! thou Heart of men, which
  ever pantest
  Naked, beneath the lidless eye of
    heaven !
Elysian City, which to calm enchant-
  est
  The mutinous air and sea ! They
    round thee, even
  As sleep round Love, are driven !
Metropolis of a ruined Paradise

[3] Homer and Virgil.

Long lost, late won, and yet but
half regained !
Bright Altar of the bloodless sacri-
fice,
Which armed Victory offers up
unstained
To Love, the flower-enchained !
Thou which wert once, and then didst
cease to be,
Now art, and henceforth ever shall be,
free,
If Hope, and Truth, and Justice
can avail.
Hail, hail, all hail !

STROPHE β. 2.

Thou youngest giant birth,
Which from the groaning earth
Leap'st, clothed in armour of impene-
trable scale !
Last of the Intercessors
Who 'gainst the Crowned Trans-
gressors
Pleadest before God's love ! Arrayed
in Wisdom's mail,
Wave thy lightning lance in
mirth ;
Nor let thy high heart fail,
Though from their hundred gates the
leagued Oppressors,
With hurried legions move ! Hail,
hail, all hail !

ANTISTROPHE α. 1.

What though Cimmerian Anarchs
dare blaspheme
Freedom and thee ? Thy shield is as
a mirror
To make their blind slaves see, and
with fierce gleam
To turn his hungry sword upon the
wearer ;
A new Actæon's error
Shall theirs have been—devoured by
their own hounds !
Be thou like the imperial Basilisk,
Killing thy foe with unapparent
wounds !
Gaze on oppression, till, at that
dread risk
Aghast, she pass from the Earth's
disk ;
Fear not, but gaze—for freemen
mightier grow,
And slaves more feeble, gazing on
their foe.

If Hope, and Truth, and Justice
may avail,
Thou shalt be great.—All hail !

ANTISTROPHE β. 2.

From Freedom's form divine,
From Nature's inmost shrine.
Strip every impious gawd, rend error
veil by veil :
O'er ruin desolate,
O'er Falsehood's fallen state,
Sit thou sublime, unawed ; be the
Destroyer pale !
And equal laws be thine,
And winged words let sail,
Freighted with truth even from the
throne of God
That wealth, surviving fate, be thine.
—All hail !

ANTISTROPHE α.γ.

Didst thou not start to hear Spain's
thrilling pæan
From land to land re-echoed sol-
emnly,
Till silence became music ? From
the Æææan [1]
To the cold Alps, eternal Italy
Starts to hear thine ! The Sea
Which paves the desert streets of Ven-
ice, laughs
In light and music ; widowed Genoa
wan,
By moonlight spells ancestral epi-
taphs,
Murmuring, where is Doria ? fair
Milan,
Within whose veins long ran
The viper's [2] palsying venom, lifts
her heel
To bruise his head. The signal and
the seal
(If Hope, and Truth, and Justice
can avail)
Art thou of all these hopes.—O
hail !

ANTISTROPHE β.γ.

Florence ! beneath the sun,
Of cities fairest one,
Blushes within her bower for Free-
dom's expectation :

[1] Æææa, the Island of Circe.
[2] The viper was the armorial device of the
Visconti, tyrants of Milan.

From eyes of quenchless hope
Rome tears the priestly cope,
As ruling once by power, so now by
      admiration,—
    An athlete stript to run
    From a remoter station
For the high prize lost on Philippi's
      shore :—
    As then Hope, Truth, and Justice
      did avail,
    So now may Fraud and Wrong !
      O hail !

EPODE I. β.

Hear ye the march as of the Earth-
      born Forms
    Arrayed against the ever-living
      Gods ?
The crash and darkness of a thousand
      storms
    Bursting their inaccessible abodes
    Of crags and thunder clouds ?
See ye the banners blazoned to the
      day,
    Inwrought with emblems of bar-
      baric pride ?
Dissonant threats kill Silence far
      away,
    The Serene Heaven which wraps
      our Eden wide
With iron light is dyed,
The Anarchs of the North lead forth
      their legions
    Like Chaos o'er creation, un-
      creating ;
An hundred tribes nourished on
      strange religions
And lawless slaveries,—down the
      aërial regions
    Of the white Alps, desolating,
    Famished wolves that bide no
      waiting,
Blotting the glowing footsteps of old
      glory,
Trampling our columned cities into
      dust,
    Their dull and savage lust
    On Beauty's corse to sickness sati-
      ating—
They come ! The fields they tread
      look black and hoary
With fire—from their red feet the
      streams run gory !

EPODE II. β.

Great Spirit, deepest Love !
Which rulest and dost move

All things which live and are, within
      the Italian shore ;
    Who spreadest heaven around it,
    Whose woods, rocks, waves, sur-
      round it ;
Who sittest in thy star, o'er Ocean's
      western floor,
    Spirit of beauty ! at whose soft
      command
The sunbeams and the showers distil
      its foison !
    From the Earth's bosom chill ;
    O bid those beams be each a blind-
      ing brand
Of lightning ! bid those showers be
      dews of poison !
    Bid the Earth's plenty kill !
    Bid thy bright Heaven above
    Whilst light and darkness bound
      it,
    Be their tomb who planned
    To make it ours and thine !
Or, with thine harmonizing ardours
      fill
And raise thy sons, as o'er the prone
      horizon
Thy lamp feeds every twilight wave
      with fire—
Be man's high hope and unextinct
      desire
The instrument to work thy will
      divine !
Then clouds from sunbeams, ante-
      lopes from leopards
    And frowns and fears from Thee,
    Would not more swiftly flee,
Than Celtic wolves from the Ausonian
      shepherds.—
    Whatever, Spirit, from thy starry
      shrine
    Thou yieldest or withholdest, Oh !
      let be
    This City of thy worship, ever
      free !

SUMMER AND WINTER

It was a bright and cheerful after-
      noon,
Towards the end of the sunny month
      of June,
When the north wind congregates in
      crowds
The floating mountains of the silver
      clouds

From the horizon—and the stainless
    sky
Opens beyond them like eternity.
All things rejoiced beneath the sun,
    the weeds,
The river, and the cornfields, and
    the reeds ;
The willow leaves that glanced in the
    light breeze,
And the firm foliage of the larger
    trees.

It was a winter such as when birds die
In the deep forests ; and the fishes lie
Stiffened in the translucent ice, which
    makes
Even the mud and slime of the warm
    lakes
A wrinkled clod, as hard as brick ;
    and when,
Among their children, comfortable
    men
Gather about great fires, and yet feel
    cold :
Alas ! then for the homeless beggar
    old !

LINES TO A REVIEWER

ALAS ! good friend, what profit can
    you see
In hating such a hateless thing as me?
There is no sport in hate where all the
    rage
Is on one side. In vain would you
    assuage
Your frowns upon an unresisting
    smile,
In which not even contempt lurks, to
    beguile
Your heart, by some faint sympathy
    of hate.
Oh ! conquer what you cannot satiate !
For to your passion I am far more coy
Than ever yet was coldest maid or
    boy
In winter noon. Of your antipathy
If I am the Narcissus you are free
To pine into a sound with hating me.

AUTUMN

A DIRGE

THE warm sun is failing, the bleak
    wind is wailing,

The bare boughs are sighing, the pale
    flowers are dying,
    And the year
On the earth her deathbed, in a
    shroud of leaves dead,
    Is lying,
Come, months, come away,
From November to May,
In your saddest array ;
Follow the bier
Of the dead cold year,
And like dim shadows watch by her
    sepulchre.

The chill rain is falling, the nipt worm
    is crawling,
The rivers are swelling, the thunder
    is knelling
    For the year ;
The blithe swallows are flown, and the
    lizards each gone
    To his dwelling ;
Come, months, come away ;
Put on white, black, and grey,
Let your light sisters play—
Ye, follow the bier
Of the dead cold year,
And make her grave green with tear
    on tear.

THE WORLD'S WANDERERS

TELL me, thou star, whose wings of
    light
Speed thee in thy fiery flight,
In what cavern of the night
    Will thy pinions close now ?

Tell me, moon, thou pale and grey
Pilgrim of heaven's homeless way,
In what depth of night or day
    Seekest thou repose now ?

Weary wind, who wanderest
Like the world's rejected guest,
Hast thou still some secret nest
    On the tree or billow ?

LIBERTY

THE fiery mountains answer each
    other ;
Their thunderings are echoed from
    zone to zone ;
The tempestuous oceans awake one
    another,

And the ice-rocks are shaken round
    winter's throne,
  When the clarion of the Typhoon is
    blown.

From a single cloud the lightning
    flashes,
Whilst a thousand isles are illumined
    around ;
Earthquake is trampling one city to
    ashes,
An hundred are shuddering and tot-
    tering ; the sound
  Is bellowing underground.

But keener thy gaze than the light-
    ning's glare,
And swifter thy step than the earth-
    quake's tramp ;
Thou deafenest the rage of the ocean ;
    thy stare
Makes blind the volcanoes ; the sun's
    bright lamp
  To thine is a fen-fire damp.

From billow and mountain and
    exhalation
The sunlight is darted through va-
    pour and blast ;
From spirit to spirit, from nation to
    nation,
From city to hamlet, thy dawning is
    cast,—
  And tyrants and slaves are like sha-
    dows of night
    In the van of the morning light.

AN ALLEGORY

A PORTAL as of shadowy adamant
    Stands yawning on the highway of
      the life
Which we all tread, a cavern huge
    and gaunt ;
    Around it rages an unceasing strife
Of shadows, like the restless clouds
    that haunt
The gap of some cleft mountain, lifted
    high
Into the whirlwinds of the upper sky.

And many passed it by with careless
    tread,
    Not knowing that a shadowy
      [   ]
Tracks every traveller even to where
    the dead

Wait peacefully for their com-
    panion new ;
But others, by more curious humour
    led,
    Pause to examine,—these are very
      few,
And they learn little there, except to
    know
That shadows follow them where'er
    they go.

THE TOWER OF FAMINE [1]

AMID the desolation of a city,
Which was the cradle, and is now the
    grave,
Of an extinguished people ; so that
    pity
Weeps o'er the shipwrecks of obli-
    vion's wave,
There stands the Tower of Famine.
    It is built
Upon some prison-homes, whose
    dwellers rave
For bread, and gold, and blood : pain,
    linked to guilt,
Agitates the light flame of their hours,
Until its vital oil is spent or spilt :
There stands the pile, a tower amid
    the towers
And sacred domes ; each marble-
    ribbed roof,
The brazen-gated temples, and the
    bowers
Of solitary wealth ! the tempest-proof
Pavilions of the dark Italian air
Are by its presence dimmed—they
    stand aloof,
And are withdrawn—so that the
    world is bare,
As if a spectre, wrapt in shapeless
    terror,
Amid a company of ladies fair
Should glide and glow, till it became
    a mirror
Of all their beauty, and their hair and
    hue,
The life of their sweet eyes, with all
    its error,
Should be absorbed, till they to
    marble grew.

[1] At Pisa there still exists the prison of Ugo-
lino, which goes by the name of " La Torre della
Fame " : in the adjoining building the galley-
slaves are confined. It is situated near the
Ponte al Mare on the Arno.

SONNET

YE hasten to the dead ! What seek
    ye there,
Ye restless thoughts and busy pur-
    poses
Of the idle brain, which the world's
    livery wear ?
O thou quick Heart, which pantest to
    possess
All that anticipation feigneth fair !
Thou vainly curious Mind which
    wouldest guess
Whence thou didst come, and
    whither thou mayest go,
And that which never yet was known
    wouldst know—   press
Oh, whither hasten ye, that thus ye
With such swift feet life's green and
    pleasant path,
Seeking alike from happiness and woe
A refuge in the cavern of grey death ?
O heart, and mind, and thoughts !
    What thing do you
Hope to inherit in the grave below ?

TIME LONG PAST

LIKE the ghost of a dear friend dead
    Is time long past.
A tone which is now forever fled,
A hope which is now forever past,
A lover so sweet it could not last,
    Was time long past.

There were sweet dreams in the night
    Of time long past :
And, was it sadness or delight,
Each day a shadow onward cast
Which made us wish it yet might
    last—
    That time long past.

There is regret, almost remorse,
    For time long past.
'Tis like a child's belovèd corse
A father watches, till at last
Beauty is like remembrance cast
    From time long past.

POEMS WRITTEN IN 1821

EPIPSYCHIDION :

VERSES ADDRESSED TO THE NOBLE
AND UNFORTUNATE

LADY EMILIA VIVIANI,

NOW IMPRISONED IN THE CONVENT
OF ST. ANNE, PISA

" L'anima amante si slancia furio del
creato, e si crea nel infinito un Mondo
tutto per essa, diverso assai da questo
oscuro e pauroso baratro."—*Her own
words.*

My Song, I fear that thou wilt find but
    few
Who fitly shall conceive thy reasoning,
Of such hard matter dost thou entertain ;
Whence, if by misadventure, chance
    should bring
Thee to base company (as chance may do),
Quite unaware of what thou dost contain,
I prithee comfort thy sweet self again,
My last delight ! tell them that they are
    dull,
And bid them own that thou art beauti-
    ful,

ADVERTISEMENT

THE writer of the following lines died
at Florence, as he was preparing for a
voyage to one of the wildest of the
Sporades, which he had bought, and
where he had fitted up the ruins of an
old building, and where it was his
hope to have realised a scheme of life,
suited perhaps to that happier and
better world of which he is now an
inhabitant, but hardly practicable in
this. His life was singular ; less on
account of the romantic vicissitudes
which diversified it, than the ideal
tinge which it received from his own
character and feelings. The present
Poem, like the "Vita Nuova" of Dante,
is sufficiently intelligible to a certain
class of readers without a matter-of-
fact history of the circumstances to
which it relates ; and to a certain
other class it must ever remain in-
comprehensible, from a defect of a

common organ of perception for the
ideas of which it treats. Not but
that, *gran vergogna sarebbe a colui, che
rimasse cosa sotto veste di figura, o di
colore rettorico ; e domandato non
sapesse denudare le sue parole da cotal
veste, in guisa che avessero verace
intendimento.*

The present poem appears to have
been intended by the writer as the
dedication to some longer one. The
stanza on the preceding page is almost a literal translation from Dante's
famous canzone

Voi ch' intendendo, il terzo ciel movete,
etc.

The presumptuous application of
the concluding lines to his own composition will raise a smile at the ex-
pense of my unfortunate friend : be
it a smile not of contempt, but pity.
                S.

EPIPSYCHIDION

Sweet Spirit ! Sister of that orphan
    one,
Whose empire is the name thou weep-
    est on
In my heart's temple I suspend to
    thee
These votive wreaths of withered
    memory.

Poor captive bird ! who, from thy
    narrow cage,
Pourest such music, that it might
    assuage
The rugged hearts of those who pris-
    oned thee,
•Were they not deaf to all sweet mel-
    ody ;
This song shall be thy rose : its petals
    pale
Are dead, indeed, my adored Night-
    ingale !
But soft and fragrant is the faded
    blossom,
And it has no thorn left to wound thy
    bosom.

High, spirit-winged Heart ! who
    dost for ever
Beat thine unfeeling bars with vain
    endeavour,
Till those bright plumes of thought,
    in which arrayed

It over-soared this low and worldly
    shade,
Lie shattered ; and thy panting
    wounded breast
Stains with dear blood its unmaternal
    nest !
I weep vain tears : blood would less
    bitter be,
Yet poured forth gladlier, could it
    profit thee.

Seraph of Heaven ! too gentle to be
    human,
Veiling beneath that radiant form of
    Woman
All that is insupportable in thee
Of light, and love, and immortality !
Sweet Benediction in the eternal
    Curse !
Veiled Glory of this lampless Uni-
    verse !
Thou Moon beyond the clouds ! Thou
    living Form
Among the Dead ! thou Star above
    the Storm !
Thou Wonder, and thou Beauty, and
    thou Terror,
Thou Harmony of Nature's art ! Thou
    Mirror
In whom, as in the splendour of the
    Sun,
All shapes look glorious which thou
    gazest on !
Ay, even the dim words which ob-
    scure thee now
Flash, lightning-like, with unaccus-
    tomed glow ;
I pray thee that thou blot from this
    sad song
All of its much mortality and wrong,
With those clear drops, which start
    like sacred dew
From the twin lights thy sweet soul
    darkens through,
Weeping, till sorrow becomes ecstasy :
Then smile on it, so that it may not
    die.

I never thought before my death
    to see
Youth's vision thus made perfect :
    Emily,
I love thee ; though the world by no
    thin name
Will hide that love from its unvalued
    shame,

Would we two had been twins of the
  same mother!
Or, that the name my heart lent to
  another
Could be a sister's bond for her and
  thee,
Blending two beams of one eternity!
Yet were one lawful and the other
  true,
These names, though dear, could paint
  not, as is due,
How beyond refuge I am thine. Ah
  me!
I am not thine: I am a part of *thee*.

  Sweet Lamp! my moth-like Muse
  has burnt its wings,
Or, like a dying swan who soars and
  sings,
Young Love should teach Time, in his
  own grey style,
All that thou art. Art thou not void
  of guile,
A lovely soul formed to be blest and
  bless?
A well of sealed and secret happiness,
Whose waters like blithe light and
  music are,
Vanquishing dissonance and gloom?
  A Star
Which moves not in the moving Hea-
  vens, alone?
A smile amid dark frowns? a gentle
  tone
Amid rude voices? a beloved light?
A Solitude, a Refuge, a Delight?
A lute, which those whom love has
  taught to play
Make music on, to soothe the rough-
  est day
And lull fond grief asleep? a buried
  treasure?
A cradle of young thoughts of wing-
  less pleasure?
A violet-shrouded grave of Woe?—I
  measure
The world of fancies, seeking one like
  thee,
And find—alas! mine own infirmity.

  She met me, Stranger, upon life's
  rough way
And lured me towards sweet Death;
  as Night by Day,
Winter by Spring, or Sorrow by swift
  Hope,

Led into light, life, peace. An ante-
  lope,
In the suspended impulse of its light-
  ness,
Were less ethereally light: the bright-
  ness
Of her divinest presence trembles
  through
Her limbs, as underneath a cloud of
  dew
Embodied in the windless heaven of
  June,
Amid the splendour-winged stars, the
  Moon
Burns inextinguishably beautiful:
And from her lips, as from a hyacinth
  full
Of honey-dew, a liquid murmur drops,
Killing the sense with passion: sweet
  as stops
Of planetary music heard in trance.
In her mild lights the starry spirits
  dance,
The sunbeams of those wells which
  ever leap
Under the lightnings of the soul—too
  deep
For the brief fathom-line of thought
  or sense.
The glory of her being, issuing thence,
Stains the dead, blank, cold air with a
  warm shade
Of unentangled intermixture, made
By Love, of light and motion; one in-
  tense
Diffusion, one serene Omnipresence,
Whose flowing outlines mingle in
  their flowing
Around her cheeks and utmost fingers
  glowing   [there
With the unintermitted blood, which
Quivers (as in a fleece of snow-like air
The crimson pulse of living morning
  quiver),
Continuously prolonged, and ending
  never,
Till they are lost, and in that Beauty
  furled
Which penetrates and clasps and fills
  the world;
Scarce visible from extreme loveli-
  ness.
Warm fragrance seems to fall from
  her light dress,
And her loose hair; and where some
  heavy tress

The air of her own speed has disen-
   twined,
The sweetness seems to satiate the
   faint wind ;
And in the soul a wild odour is felt,
Beyond the sense, like fiery dews that
   melt
Into the bosom of a frozen bud.
See where she stands ! a mortal shape
   induced
With love and life and light and deity,
And motion which may change but
   cannot die ;
An image of some bright Eternity ;
A shadow of some golden dream ; a
   Splendour
Leaving the third sphere pilotless ;
   a tender
Reflection on the eternal Moon of
   Love,
Under whose motions life's dull bil-
   lows move ;
A Metaphor of Spring and Youth and
   Morning ;
A vision like incarnate April, warning
With smiles and tears, Frost the
   Anatomy
Into his summer grave.
               Ah ! woe is me !
What have I dared ? where am I
   lifted ? how
Shall I descend, and perish not ? I
   know
That Love makes all things equal : I
   have heard
By mine own heart this joyous truth
   averred :
The spirit of the worm beneath the
   sod,   [God.
In love and worship, blends itself with

  Spouse ! Sister ! Angel ! Pilot of the
   Fate
Whose course has been so starless ! O
   too late
Beloved !   O too soon adored, by me !
For in the fields of immortality
My spirit should at first have wor-
   shipped thine,
A divine presence in a place divine ;
Or should have moved beside it on
   this earth,
A shadow of that substance, from its
   birth ;
But not as now :—I love thee ; yes, I
   feel

That on the fountain of my heart a
   seal
Is set, to keep its waters pure and
   bright
For thee, since in those *tears* thou
   hast delight.
We—are we not formed, as notes of
   music are,
For one another, though dissimilar ;
Such difference without discord, as
   can make
Those sweetest sounds, in which all
   spirits shake,
As trembling leaves in a continuous
   air ?

  Thy wisdom speaks in me, and bids
   me dare
Beacon the rocks on which high hearts
   are wrecked.
I never was attached to that great
   sect,
Whose doctrine is, that each one
   should select
Out of the crowd a mistress or a
   friend,
And all the rest, though fair and wise,
   commend
To cold oblivion, though it is in the
   code
Of modern morals, and the beaten
   road
Which those poor slaves with weary
   footsteps tread,
Who travel to their home among the
   dead
By the broad highway of the world,
   and so
With one chained friend, perhaps a
   jealous foe,
The dreariest and the longest journey
   go.

  True Love in this differs from gold
   and clay,
That to divide is not to take away.
Love is like understanding, that grows
   bright,
Gazing on many truths ; 'tis like thy
   light,
Imagination ! which, from earth and
   sky,
And from the depths of human phantasy,
As from a thousand prisms and mirrors, fills

The Universe with glorious beams,
  and kills
Error, the worm, with many a sun-
  like arrow
Of its reverberated lightning. Narrow
The heart that loves, the brain that
  contemplates,
The life that wears, the spirit that
  creates
One object, and one form, and builds
  thereby
A sepulchre for its eternity.

  Mind from its object differs most in
    this :
Evil from good ; misery from happi-
  ness ;
The baser from the nobler ; the im-
  pure
And frail, from what is clear and must
  endure.
If you divide suffering and dross, you
  may
Diminish till it is consumed away ;
If you divide pleasure and love and
  thought,
Each part exceeds the whole ; and we
  know not
How much, while any yet remains
  unshared,
Of pleasure may be gained, of sorrow
  spared :
This truth is that deep well, whence
  sages draw
The unenvied light of hope ; the
  eternal law
By which those live, to whom this
  world of life
Is as a garden ravaged, and whose
  strife
Tills for the promise of a later birth
The wilderness of this Elysian earth.

  There was a Being whom my spirit
    oft
Met on its visioned wanderings, far
  aloft,
In the clear golden prime of my
  youth's dawn,
Upon the fairy isles of sunny lawn,
Amid the enchanted mountains, and
  the caves
Of divine sleep, and on the air-like
  waves
Of wonder-level dream, whose tremu-
  lous floor

Paved her light steps ;—on an imagined shore,
Under the grey beak of some promontory
She met me, robed in such exceeding
  glory,
That I beheld her not. In solitudes
Her voice came to me through the
  whispering woods,
And from the fountains, and the
  odours deep
Of flowers, which, like lips murmuring
  in their sleep
Of the sweet kisses which had lulled
  them there
Breathed but of *her* to the enamoured
  air ;
And from the breezes whether low or
  loud,
And from the rain of every passing
  cloud,
And from the singing of the summer
  birds,
And from all sounds, all silence. In
  the words
Of antique verse and high romance,—
  in form,
Sound, colour—in whatever checks
  that Storm
Which with the shattered present
  chokes the past ;
And in that best philosophy, whose
  taste
Makes this cold common hell, our
  life, a doom
As glorious as a fiery martyrdom ;
Her Spirit was the harmony of
  truth.—

  Then, from the caverns of my
    dreamy youth
I sprang, as one sandalled with plumes
  of fire,
And towards the lodestar of my one
  desire,
I flitted, like a dizzy moth, whose
  flight
Is as a dead leaf's in the owlet light,
When it would seek in Hesper's set-
  ting sphere
A radiant death, a fiery sepulchre,
As if it were a lamp of earthly
  flame.—
But She, whom prayers or tears then
  could not tame,

Passed, like a God throned on a winged
  planet,
Whose burning plumes to tenfold
  swiftness fan it,
Into the dreary cone of our life's
  shade ;
And as a man with mighty loss dis-
  mayed,
I would have followed, though the
  grave between
Yawned like a gulf whose spectres are
  unseen :
When a voice said :—" O Thou of
  hearts the weakest,
The phantom is beside thee whom
  thou seekest."
Then I—" Where ? " the world's
  echo answered " where ! "
And in that silence, and in my despair,
I questioned every tongueless wind
  that flew
Over my tower of mourning, if it
  knew
Whither 'twas fled, this soul out of
  my soul ;
And murmured names and spells
  which have control
Over the sightless tyrants of our fate ;
But neither prayer nor verse could
  dissipate
The night which closed on her ; nor
  uncreate
That world within this Chaos, mine
  and me,
Of which she was the veiled Divinity,
The world I say of thoughts that wor-
  shipped her :
And therefore I went forth, with hope
  and fear,
And every gentle passion sick to
  death,
Feeding my course with expectation's
  breath,
Into the wintry forest of our life ;
And struggling through its error with
  vain strife,
And stumbling in my weakness and
  my haste,
And half bewildered by new forms, I
  passed
Seeking among those untaught fores-
  ters
If I could find one form resembling
  hers,
In which she might have masked her-
  self from me.

There,—One, whose voice was ven-
  omed melody
Sate by a well, under blue night-
  shade bowers ;
The breath of her false mouth was
  like faint flowers,
Her touch was as electric poison,—
  flame
Out of her looks into my vitals came,
And from her living cheeks and bosom
  flew
A killing air, which pierced like honey-
  dew
Into the core of my green heart, and
  lay
Upon its leaves ; until, as hair grown
  grey
O'er a young brow, they hid its un-
  blown prime
With ruins of unseasonable time.

In many mortal forms I rashly
  sought
The shadow of that idol of my
  thought.
And some were fair—but beauty dies
  away :
Others were wise—but honeyed words
  betray :
And One was true—oh ! why not
  true to me ?
Then, as a hunted deer, that could
  not flee,
I turned upon my thoughts, and stood
  at bay,
Wounded, and weak, and panting ;
  the cold day
Trembled, for pity of my strife and
  pain,
When, like a noonday dawn, there
  shone again
Deliverance. One stood on my path
  who seemed
As like the glorious shape which I had
  dreamed,
As is the Moon, whose changes ever
  run
Into themselves, to the eternal Sun ;
The cold chaste Moon, the Queen of
  Heaven's bright isles,
Who makes all beautiful on which she
  smiles.
That wandering shrine of soft yet icy
  flame
Which ever is transformed, yet still
  the same,

And warms not but illumines. Young
   and fair
As the descended Spirit of that sphere,
She hid me, as the Moon may hide the
   night
From its own darkness, until all was
   bright
Between the Heaven and Earth of my
   calm mind,
And, as a cloud charioted by the wind,
She led me to a cave in that wild
   place,
And sat beside me, with her downward
   face
Illumining my slumbers, like the
   Moon
Waxing and waning o'er Endymion.
And I was laid asleep, spirit and limb,
And all my being became bright or
   dim
As the Moon's image in a summer sea,
According as she smiled or frowned
   on me ;
And there I lay, within a chaste cold
   bed :
Alas ! I then was nor alive nor dead:—
For at her silver voice came Death
   and Life,
Unmindful each of their accustomed
   strife,
Masked like twin babes, a sister and a
   brother,
The wandering hopes of one aban-
   doned mother,
And through the cavern without
   wings they flew,
And cried, " Away ! he is not of our
   crew."
I wept, and, though it be a dream, I
   weep.

   What storms then shook the ocean
   of my sleep,
Blotting that Moon, whose pale and
   waning lips
Then shrank as in the sickness of
   eclipse ;—
And how my soul was as a lampless
   sea,
And who was then its Tempest ; and
   when She,
The Planet of that hour, was
   quenched, what frost
Crept o'er those waters, till from coast
   to coast
The moving billows of my being fell

Into a death of ice, immovable ;—
And then—what earthquakes made
   it gape and split,
The white Moon smiling all the while
   on it,
These words conceal :—If not, each
   word would be
The key of staunchless tears.   Weep
   not for me !

   At length, into the obscure forest
   came
The vision I had sought through
   grief and shame.
Athwart that wintry wilderness of
   thorns
Flashed from her motion splendour
   like the Morn's,
And from her presence life was radi-
   ated
Through the grey earth and branches
   bare and dead ;
So that her way was paved, and
   roofed above
With flowers as soft as thoughts of
   budding love ;
And music from her respiration spread
Like light,—all other sounds were
   penetrated
By the small, still, sweet spirit of that
   sound,
So that the savage winds hung mute
   around ;
And odours warm and fresh fell from
   her hair
Dissolving the dull cold in the froze
   air :
Soft as an Incarnation of the Sun,
When light is changed to love, this
   glorious One
Floated into the cavern where I lay,
And called my Spirit, and the dream-
   ing clay
Was lifted by the thing that dreamed
   below
As smoke by fire, and in her beauty's
   glow
I stood, and felt the dawn of my long
   night
Was penetrating me with living light :
I knew it was the Vision veiled from
   me
So many years—that it was Emily.

   Thin Spheres of light who rule this
   passive Earth,

This world of love, this *me*; and into
  birth
Awaken all its fruits and flowers, and
  dart
Magnetic might into its central heart;
And lift its billows and its mists, and
  guide
By everlasting laws each wind and
  tide
To its fit cloud, and its appointed
  cave;
And lull its storms, each in the craggy
  grave
Which was its cradle, luring to faint
  bowers
The armies of the rainbow-winged
  showers;
And, as those married lights, which
  from the towers
Of Heaven look forth and fold the
  wandering globe
In liquid sleep and splendour, as a
  robe;
And all their many-mingled influence
  blend,
If equal, yet unlike, to one sweet
  end;—
So ye, bright regents, with alternate
  sway,   [day!
Govern my sphere of being, night and
Thou, not disdaining even a borrowed
  might;
Thou, not eclipsing a remoter light;
And, through the shadow of the sea-
  sons three,
From Spring to Autumn's sere ma-
  turity,
Light it into the Winter of the tomb,
Where it may ripen to a brighter
  bloom.
Thou too, O Comet, beautiful and
  fierce,
Who drew the heart of this frail Uni-
  verse
Towards thine own; till, wrecked in
  that convulsion,
Alternating attraction and repulsion,
Thine went astray, and that was rent
  in twain;
Oh, float into our azure heaven again!
Be there love's folding-star at thy
  return;
The living Sun will feed thee from its
  urn
Of golden fire; the Moon will veil her
  horn

In thy last smiles; adoring Even and
  Morn
Will worship thee with incense of
  calm breath
And lights and shadows; as the star
  of Death
And Birth is worshipped by those
  sisters wild
Called Hope and Fear—upon the
  heart are piled
Their offerings,—of this sacrifice
  divine
A World shall be the altar.
                          Lady mine,
Scorn not these flowers of thought,
  the fading birth
Which from its heart of hearts that
  plant puts forth,
Whose fruit, made perfect by thy
  sunny eyes,
Will be as of the trees of Paradise.

The day is come, and thou wilt fly
  with me.
To whatsoe'er of dull mortality
Is mine, remain a vestal sister still;
To the intense, the deep, the im-
  perishable,
Not mine, but me, henceforth be thou
  united
Even as a bride, delighting and de-
  lighted.
The hour is come:—the destined
  Star has risen
Which shall descend upon a vacant
  prison.
The walls are high, the gates are
  strong, thick set
The sentinels—but true love never
  yet
Was thus constrained: it overleaps
  all fence:
Like lightning, with invisible vio-
  lence
Piercing its continents; like Heaven's
  free breath,
Which he who grasps can hold not;
  liker Death,
Who rides upon a thought, and makes
  his way
Through temple, tower, and palace,
  and the array
Of arms: more strength has Love
  than he or they;
For he can burst his charnel, and
  make free

The limbs in chains, the heart in agony,
The soul in dust and chaos.
                    Emily,
A ship is floating in the harbour now,
A wind is hovering o'er the mountain's brow ;
There is a path on the sea's azure floor,
No keel has ever ploughed that path before ;
The halcyons brood around the foamless isles ;
The treacherous Ocean has forsworn its wiles ;
The merry mariners are bold and free :
Say, my heart's sister, wilt thou sail with me ?
Our bark is as an albatross, whose nest
Is a far Eden of the purple East ;
And we between her wings will sit, while Night,
And Day, and Storm, and Calm, pursue their flight,
Our ministers, along the boundless Sea,
Treading each other's heels, unheededly.
It is an isle under Ionian skies,
Beautiful as a wreck of Paradise,
And, for the harbours are not safe and good,
This land would have remained a solitude
But for some pastoral people native there,
Who from the Elysian, clear, and golden air
Draw the last spirit of the age of gold,
Simple and spirited ; innocent and bold.
The blue Ægean girds this chosen home,
With ever-changing sound and light and foam,
Kissing the sifted sands, and caverns hoar ;
And all the winds wandering along the shore
Undulate with the undulating tide :
There are thick woods where sylvan forms abide ;
And many a fountain, rivulet, and pond,
As clear as elemental diamond,
Or serene morning air ; and far beyond,
The mossy tracks made by the goats and deer
(Which the rough shepherd treads but once a year,)
Pierce into glades, caverns, and bowers, and halls
Built round with ivy, which the waterfalls
Illumining, with sound that never fails,
Accompany the noonday nightingales ;
And all the place is peopled with sweet airs ;
The light clear element which the isle wears
Is heavy with the scent of lemon flowers,
Which floats like mist laden with unseen showers,
And falls upon the eyelids like faint sleep ;
And from the moss violets and jonquils peep,
And dart their arrowy odour through the brain
Till you might faint with that delicious pain.
And every motion, odour, beam, and tone,
With that deep music is in unison :
Which is a soul within the soul—they seem
Like echoes of an antenatal dream.—
It is an isle 'twixt Heaven, Air, Earth, and Sea,
Cradled, and hung in clear tranquillity ;
Bright as that wandering Eden Lucifer,
Washed by the soft blue Oceans of young air.
It is a favoured place. Famine or Blight,
Pestilence, War, and Earthquake, never light
Upon its mountain peaks ; blind vultures, they
Sail onward far upon their fatal way :
The winged storms, chaunting their thunder-psalm
To other lands, leave azure chasms of calm

Over this isle, or weep themselves in dew,
From which its fields and woods ever renew
Their green and golden immortality.
And from the sea there rise, and from the sky
There fall clear exhalations, soft and bright,
Veil after veil, each hiding some delight.
Which Sun or Moon or zephyr draw aside,
Till the isle's beauty, like a naked bride
Glowing at once with love and loveliness,
Blushes and trembles at its own excess :
Yet, like a buried lamp, a Soul no less
Burns in the heart of this delicious isle,
An atom of the Eternal, whose own smile
Unfolds itself, and may be felt not seen
O'er the grey rocks, blue waves, and forests green,
Filling their bare and void interstices.—
But the chief marvel of the wilderness
Is a lone dwelling, built by whom or how
None of the rustic island-people know ;
'Tis not a tower of strength, though with its height
It overtops the woods ; but, for delight,
Some wise and tender Ocean-King, ere crime
Had been invented, in the world's young prime,
Reared it, a wonder of that simple time,
And envy of the isles, a pleasure-house
Made sacred to his sister and his spouse.
It scarce seems now a wreck of human art,
But, as it were, Titanic ; in the heart
Of Earth having assumed its form, then grown
Out of the mountains, from the living stone,

Lifting itself in caverns light and high :
For all the antique and learned imagery
Has been erased, and in the place of it
The ivy and the wild vine interknit
The volumes of their many-twining stems ;
Parasite flowers illume with dewy gems
The lampless halls, and when they fade, the sky
Peeps through their winter-woof of tracery
With moonlight patches, or star atoms keen,
Or fragments of the day's intense serene ;
Working mosaic on their Parian floors.
And, day and night, aloof, from the high towers
And terraces, the Earth and Ocean seem
To sleep in one another's arms, and dream
Of waves, flowers, clouds, woods, rocks, and all that we
Read in their smiles, and call reality.

This isle and house are mine, and I have vowed
Thee to be lady of the solitude.
And I have fitted up some chambers there
Looking towards the golden Eastern air,
And level with the living winds, which flow
Like waves above the living waves below.
I have sent books and music there, and all
Those instruments with which high spirits call
The future from its cradle, and the past
Out of its grave, and make the present last
In thoughts and joys which sleep, but cannot die,
Folded within their own eternity.
Our simple life wants little, and true taste
Hires not the pale drudge Luxury to waste
The scene it would adorn, and therefore still,

Nature, with all her children, haunts
  the hill.
The ringdove, in the embowering
  ivy, yet
Keeps up her love-lament, and the
  owls flit
Round the evening tower, and the
  young stars glance
Between the quick bats in their twi-
  light dance ;
The spotted deer bask in the fresh
  moonlight
Before our gate, and the slow silent
  night
Is measured by the pants of their
  calm sleep.
Be this our home in life, and when
  years heap
Their withered hours, like leaves, on
  our decay,
Let us become the overhanging day,
The living soul of this Elysian isle,
Conscious, inseparable, one. Mean-
  while
We two will rise, and sit, and walk
  together,
Under the roof of blue Ionian
  weather,
And wander in the meadows, or
  ascend
The mossy mountains, where the
  blue heavens bend
With lightest winds, to touch their
  paramour ;
Or linger, where the pebble-paven
  shore,
Under the quick faint kisses of the sea
Trembles and sparkles as with
  ecstasy,—
Possessing and possessed by all that is
Within that calm circumference of
  bliss,
And by each other, till to love and
  live
Be one :—or, at the noontide hour,
  arrive
Where some old cavern hoar seems
  yet to keep
The moonlight of the expired night
  asleep,
Through which the awakened day
  can never peep ;
A veil for our seclusion, close as
  Night's,
Where secure sleep may kill thine
  innocent lights ;

Sleep, the fresh dew of languid love,
  the rain
Whose drops quench kisses till they
  burn again.
And we will talk, until thought's
  melody
Become too sweet for utterance, and
  it die
In words, to live again in looks, which
  dart
With thrilling tone into the voiceless
  heart,
Harmonizing silence without a sound.
Our breath shall intermix, our bosoms
  bound,
And our veins beat together ; and our
  lips,
With other eloquence than words,
  eclipse
The soul that burns between them ;
  and the wells
Which boil under our being's inmost
  cells,
The fountains of our deepest life,
  shall be
Confused in passion's golden purity,
As mountain springs under the morn-
  ing Sun.
We shall become the same, we shall
  be one
Spirit within two frames, Oh ! where-
  fore two ?
One passion in twin-hearts, which
  grows and grew
Till like two meteors of expanding
  flame,
Those spheres instinct with it become
  the same,
Touch, mingle, are transfigured ; ever
  still
Burning, yet ever inconsumable :
In one another's substance finding
  food,
Like flames too pure and light and
  unimbued
To nourish their bright lives with
  baser prey,
Which point to Heaven and cannot
  pass away :
One hope within two wills, one will
  beneath
Two overshadowing minds, one life,
  one death,
One Heaven, one Hell, one immor-
  tality,
And one annihilation. Woe is me !

The winged words on which my soul
    would pierce
Into the height of love's rare Uni-
    verse,
Are chains of lead around its flight of
    fire,—
I pant, I sink, I tremble, I expire !

Weak verses, go, kneel at your
    Sovereign's feet,
And say :—" We are the masters of
    thy slave ;
What wouldest thou with us and ours
    and thine ? "
Then call your sisters from Oblivion's
    cave,
All singing loud : " Love's very pain
    is sweet,
But its reward is in the world divine,
Which, if not here, it builds beyond
    the grave."
So shall ye live when I am there.
    Then haste
Over the hearts of men, until ye meet
Marina, Vanna, Primus, and the rest,
And bid them love each other, and be
    blest :
And leave the troop which errs, and
    which reproves,
And come and be my guest,—for I
    am Love's.

ADONAÏS ;

AN ELEGY ON THE DEATH OF
JOHN KEATS,

AUTHOR OF " ENDYMION," " HYPERION,"
ETC.

Ἀστὴρ πρὶν μὲν ἔλαμπες ἐνὶ ζώοισιν ἑῶος;
Νῦν δὲ θανὼν, λάμπεις ἕσπερος ἐν φθιμένοις.

                      PLATO.

PREFACE

Φάρμακον ἦλθε, Βίων, ποτὶ σὸν στόμα, φάρμακον
  εἶδες·
Πῶς τευ τοῖς χείλεσσι ποτέδραμε, κοὐκ ἐγλύκ-
  άνθη ;
Τίς δὲ βροτὸς τοσσοῦτον ἀνάμερος, ἢ κεράσαι
  τοι,
Ἢ δοῦναι λαλέοντι τὸ φάρμακον ; ἔκφυγεν ᾠδάν.
    MOSCHUS, EPITAPH. BION.

IT is my intention to subjoin to the
London edition of this poem, a criticism upon the claims of its lamented
object to be classed among the writers
of the highest genius who have
adorned our age. My known repug-

nance to the narrow principles of
taste on which several of his earlier
compositions were modelled, proves
at least that I am an impartial judge.
I consider the fragment of " Hyperion," as second to nothing that
was ever produced by a writer of the
same years.

John Keats died at Rome, of a consumption, in his twenty-fourth year,
on the 27th of December, 1820, and
was buried in the romantic and lonely
cemetery of the Protestants in that
city, under the pyramid which is the
tomb of Cestius, and the massy walls
and towers, now mouldering and
desolate, which formed the circuit of
ancient Rome. The cemetery is an
open space among the ruins, covered
in winter with violets and daisies.
It might make one in love with death,
to think that one should be buried in
so sweet a place.

The genius of the lamented person
to whose memory I have dedicated
these unworthy verses, was not less
delicate and fragile than it was
beautiful ; and where canker-worms
abound, what wonder, if its young
flower was blighted in the bud ?
The savage criticism on his " Endymion," which appeared in the
Quarterly Review, produced the most
violent effect on his susceptible mind ;
the agitation thus originated ended
in the rupture of a blood-vessel in the
lungs ; a rapid consumption ensued ;
and the succeeding acknowledgments
from more candid critics, of the true
greatness of his powers, were ineffectual to heal the wound thus wantonly
inflicted.

It may be well said, that these
wretched men know not what they
do. They scatter their insults and
their slanders without heed as to
whether the poisoned shaft lights on
a heart made callous by many blows,
or one, like Keats's, composed of
more penetrable stuff. One of their
associates is, to my knowledge, a
most base and unprincipled calum-
niator. As to " Endymion," was it
a poem, whatever might be its defects, to be treated contemptuously
by those who had celebrated with

various degrees of complacency and panegyric, " Paris," and " Woman," and a " Syrian Tale," and Mrs. Lefanu, and Mr. Barret, and Mr. Howard Payne, and a long list of the illustrious obscure ? Are these the men, who in their venal goodnature, presumed to draw a parallel between the Rev. Mr. Milman and Lord Byron ? What gnat did they strain at here, after having swallowed all those camels ? Against what woman taken in adultery dares the foremost of these literary prostitutes to cast his opprobrious stone ? Miserable man ! you, one of the meanest, have wantonly defaced one of the noblest specimens of the workmanship of God. Nor shall it be your excuse, that, murderer as you are, you have spoken daggers, but used none.

The circumstances of the closing scene of poor Keats's life were not made known to me until the Elegy was ready for the press. I am given to understand that the wound which his sensitive spirit had received from the criticism of " Endymion " was exasperated at the bitter sense of unrequited benefits ; the poor fellow seems to have been hooted from the stage of life, no less by those on whom he had wasted the promise of his genius, than those on whom he had lavished his fortune and his care. He was accompanied to Rome, and attended in his last illness by Mr. Severn, a young artist of the highest promise, who, I have been informed, " almost risked his own life, and sacrificed every prospect, to unwearied attendance upon his dying friend." Had I known these circumstances before the completion of my poem, I should have been tempted to add my feeble tribute of applause to the more solid recompense which the virtuous man finds in the recollection of his own motives. Mr. Severn can dispense with a reward from " such stuff as dreams are made of." His conduct is a golden augury of the success of his future career— may the unextinguished Spirit of his illustrious friend animate the crea-

tions of his pencil, and plead against Oblivion for his name !

ADONAÏS

I

I WEEP for ADONAÏS—he is dead !
Oh, weep for Adonaïs ! though our tears
Thaw not the frost which binds so dear a head !
And thou, sad Hour, selected from all years
To mourn our loss, rouse thy obscure compeers,
And teach them thine own sorrow. Say : " With me
Died Adonaïs ; till the Future dares
Forget the Past, his fate and fame shall be
An echo and a light unto eternity !

II

Where wert thou, mighty Mother, when he lay,
When thy son lay, pierced by the shaft which flies
In darkness ? where was lorn Urania
When Adonaïs died ? With veiled eyes,
'Mid listening Echoes, in her Paradise
She sate, while one, with soft enamoured breath,
Rekindled all the fading melodies,
With which, like flowers that mock the corse beneath,
He had adorned and hid the coming bulk of death.

III

Oh, weep for Adonaïs—he is dead !
Wake, melancholy Mother, wake and weep !
Yet wherefore ? Quench within their burning bed
Thy fiery tears, and let thy loud heart keep,
Like his, a mute and uncomplaining sleep ;
For he is gone, where all things wise and fair
Descend :—Oh, dream not that the amorous Deep
Will yet restore him to the vital air ;

Death feeds on his mute voice, and
   laughs at our despair.

IV

Most musical of mourners, weep
   again !
Lament anew, Urania !—He died,
Who was the Sire of an immortal
   strain,
Blind, old, and lonely, when his
   country's pride
The priest, the slave, and the liber-
   ticide,
Trampled and mocked with many
   a loathed rite
Of lust and blood ; he went, un-
   terrified,
Into the gulf of death ; but his clear
   Sprite
Yet reigns o'er earth ; the third among
   the sons of light.

V

Most musical of mourners, weep
   anew !
Not all to that bright station dared
   to climb :
And happier they their happiness
   who knew,
Whose tapers yet burn through
   that night of time
In which suns perished ; others
   more sublime,
Struck by the envious wrath of
   man or God,
Have sunk, extinct in their reful-
   gent prime ;
And some yet live, treading the
   thorny road,
Which leads, through toil and hate,
   to Fame's serene abode.

VI

But now, thy youngest, dearest
   one, has perished,
The nursling of thy widowhood,
   who grew,
Like a pale flower by some sad
   maiden cherished,
And fed with true love tears instead of dew ;
Most musical of mourners, weep
   anew !
Thy extreme hope, the loveliest
   and the last,

The bloom, whose petals nipt
   before they blew
Died on the promise of the fruit, is
   waste ;
The broken lily lies—the storm is
   overpast.

VII

To that high Capital, where kingly
   Death
Keeps his pale court in beauty and
   decay,
He came ; and bought, with price
   of purest breath,
A grave among the eternal.—Come
   away !
Haste, while the vault of blue
   Italian day
Is yet his fitting charnel-roof !
   while still
He lies, as if in dewy sleep he lay ;
Awake him not ! surely he takes
   his fill
Of deep and liquid rest, forgetful of
   all ill.

VIII

He will awake no more, Oh, never
   more !
Within the twilight chamber
   spreads apace
The shadow of white Death, and
   at the door
Invisible Corruption waits to trace
His extreme way to her dim
   dwelling-place ;
The eternal Hunger sits, but pity
   and awe
Soothe her pale rage, nor dares she
   to deface
So fair a prey, till darkness and the
   law
Of change, shall o'er his sleep the
   mortal curtain draw.

IX

Oh, weep for Adonaïs !—The quick
   Dreams,
The passion-winged Ministers of
   thought,
Who were his flocks, whom near the
   living streams
Of his young spirit he fed, and
   whom he taught
The love which was its music,
   wander not,—

Wander no more, from kindling
  brain to brain,
But droop there, whence they
  sprung ; and mourn their lot
Round the cold heart, where, after
  their sweet pain,
They ne'er will gather strength, nor
  find a home again.

X

And one with trembling hand
  clasps his cold head,
And fans him with her moonlight
  wings, and cries,
" Our love, our hope, our sorrow, is
  not dead ;
See, on the silken fringe of his faint
  eyes,
Like dew upon a sleeping flower,
  there lies
A tear some Dream has loosened
  from his brain."
Lost Angel of a ruined Paradise !
She knew not 'twas her own ; as
  with no stain
She faded, like a cloud which had
  outwept its rain.

XI

One from a lucid urn of starry dew
Washed his light limbs, as if em-
  balming them ;
Another clipt her profuse locks, and
  threw
The wreath upon him, like an ana-
  dem,
Which frozen tears instead of pearls
  begem ;
Another in her wilful grief would
  break
Her bow and winged reeds, as if to
  stem
A greater loss with one which was
  more weak ;
And dull the barbed fire against his
  frozen cheek.

XII

Another Splendour on his mouth
  alit,
That mouth whence it was wont to
  draw the breath
Which gave it strength to pierce
  the guarded wit,
And pass into the panting heart
  beneath

With lightning and with music :
  the damp death
Quenched its caress upon its icy
  lips ;
And, as a dying meteor stains a
  wreath
Of moonlight vapour, which the
  cold night clips,
It flushed through his pale limbs, and
  passed to its eclipse.

XIII

And others came,—Desires and
  Adorations,
Winged Persuasions, and veiled
  Destinies,
Splendours, and Glooms, and glim-
  mering Incarnations
Of hopes and fears, and twilight
  Phantasies ;
And Sorrow, with her family of
  Sighs,
And Pleasure, blind with tears, led
  by the gleam
Of her own dying smile instead of
  eyes,
Came in slow pomp ;—the moving
  pomp might seem
Like pageantry of mist on an autum-
  nal stream.

XIV

All he had loved, and moulded into
  thought
From shape, and hue, and odour,
  and sweet sound,
Lamented Adonaïs. Morning
  sought
Her eastern watch-tower, and her
  hair unbound,
Wet with the tears which should
  adorn the ground,
Dimmed the aërial eyes that kindle
  day ;
Afar the melancholy thunder
  moaned,
Pale Ocean in unquiet slumber lay,
And the wild winds flew around, sobbing in their dismay.

XV

Lost Echo sits amid the voiceless
  mountains,
And feeds her grief with his remembered lay,

And will no more reply to winds or
fountains,
Or amorous birds perched on the
young green spray,
Or herdsman's horn, or bell at
closing day ;
Since she can mimic not his lips,
more dear
Than those for whose disdain they
pined away
Into a shadow of all sounds :—a
drear
Murmur, between their songs, is all
the woodmen hear.

XVI

Grief made the young Spring wild,
and she threw down
Her kindling buds, as if she Autumn were,
Or they dead leaves ; since her
delight is flown,
For whom should she have waked
the sullen year ?
To Phœbus was not Hyacinth so
dear,
Nor to himself Narcissus, as to both
Thou Adonaïs ; wan they stand
and sere
Amid the faint companions of their
youth
With dew all turned to tears ; odour,
to sighing ruth.

XVII

Thy spirit's sister, the lorn nightingale,
Mourns not her mate with such
melodious pain ;
Not so the eagle, who like thee
could scale
Heaven, and could nourish in the
sun's domain
Her mighty youth, with morning
doth complain,
Soaring and screaming round her
empty nest,
As Albion wails for thee : the curse
of Cain
Light on his head who pierced thy
innocent breast,
And scared the angel soul that was its
earthly guest !

XVIII

Ah ! woe is me ! Winter is come
and gone,
But grief returns with the revolving year ;
The airs and streams renew their
joyous tone ;
The ants, the bees, the swallows,
re-appear ;
Fresh leaves and flowers deck the
dead Seasons' bier ;
The amorous birds now pair in
every brake,
And build their mossy homes in
field and brere ;
And the green lizard, and the
golden snake,
Like unimprisoned flames, out of
their trance awake.

XIX

Through wood and stream and
field and hill and Ocean,
A quickening life from the Earth's
heart has burst,
As it has ever done, with change
and motion,
From the great morning of the
world when first
God dawned on Chaos ; in its
stream immersed,
The lamps of Heaven flash with a
softer light ;
All baser things pant with life's
sacred thirst ;
Diffuse themselves ; and spend in
love's delight,
The beauty and the joy of their renewed might.

XX

The leprous corpse touched by this
spirit tender,
Exhales itself in flowers of gentle
breath ;
Like incarnations of the stars,
when splendour
Is changed to fragrance, they illumine death,
And mock the merry worm that
wakes beneath ;
Nought we know dies. Shall that
alone which knows
Be as a sword consumed before the
sheath
By sightless lightning ? th' intense
atom glows
A moment, then is quenched in a
most cold repose.

XXI

Alas ! that all we loved of him
should be,
But for our grief, as if it had not
been,
And grief itself be mortal ! Woe
is me !
Whence are we, and why are we ?
of what scene
The actors or spectators ? Great
and mean
Meet massed in death, who lends
what life must borrow.
As long as skies are blue, and fields
are green,
Evening must usher night, night
urge the morrow,
Month follow month with woe, and
year wake year to sorrow.

XXII

He will awake no more, Oh, never
more !
" Wake thou," cried Misery, " child-
less Mother, rise
Out of thy sleep, and slake, in thy
heart's core,
A wound more fierce than his tears
and sighs."
And all the Dreams that watched
Urania's eyes,
And all the echoes whom their
sister's song
Had held in holy silence, cried,
" Arise ! "
Swift as a Thought by the snake
Memory stung,
From her ambrosial rest the fading
Splendour sprung.

XXIII

She rose like an autumnal Night,
that springs
Out of the East, and follows wild
and drear
The golden Day, which, on eternal
wings,
Even as a ghost abandoning a bier,
Has left the Earth a corpse. Sor-
row and fear
So struck, so roused, so rapt,
Urania,
So saddened round her like an
atmosphere
Of stormy mist ; so swept her on
her way,
Even to the mournful place where
Adonaïs lay.

XXIV

Out of her secret Paradise she sped,
Through camps and cities rough
with stone, and steel,
And human hearts, which to her
aëry tread
Yielding not, wounded the invisible
Palms of her tender feet where'er
they fell ;
And barbed tongues, and thoughts
more sharp than they
Rent the soft Form they never
could repel,
Whose sacred blood, like the young
tears of May,
Paved with eternal flowers that un-
deserving way.

XXV

In the death-chamber for a moment Death,
Shamed by the presence of that
living Might,
Blushed to annihilation, and the
breath
Revisited those lips, and life's pale
light
Flashed through those limbs, so
late her dear delight.
" Leave me not wild and drear and
comfortless,
As silent lightning leaves the starless night !
Leave me not ! " cried Urania : her
distress
Roused Death : Death rose and smiled,
and met her vain caress.

XXVI

" Stay yet awhile ! speak to me
once again ;
Kiss me, so long but as a kiss may
live ;
And in my heartless breast and
burning brain
That word, that kiss shall all
thoughts else survive,
With food of saddest memory kept
alive,
Now thou art dead, as if it were a
part
Of thee, my Adonaïs ! I would give
All that I am to be as thou now art,

But I am chained to Time, and cannot thence depart !

XXVII
" O gentle child, beautiful as thou
wert,
Why didst thou leave the trodden
paths of men
Too soon, and with weak hands
though mighty heart
Dare the unpastured dragon in his
den ?
Defenceless as thou wert, oh !
where was then
Wisdom the mirror'd shield, or
scorn the spear ?
Or hadst thou waited the full cycle,
when
Thy spirit should have filled its
crescent sphere,
The monsters of life's waste had fled
from thee like deer.

XXVIII
" The herded wolves, bold only to
pursue ;
The obscene ravens, clamorous o'er
the dead ;
The vultures, to the conqueror's
banner true,
Who feed where Desolation first
has fed,
And whose wings rain contagion ;
—how they fled,
When, like Apollo, from his golden
bow,
The Pythian of the age one arrow
sped
And smiled !—The spoilers tempt
no second blow,
They fawn on the proud feet that
spurn them lying low.

XXIX
" The sun comes forth, and many
reptiles spawn ;
He sets, and each ephemeral insect
then
Is gathered into death without a
dawn,
And the immortal stars awake
again ;
So it is in the world of living men :
A godlike mind soars forth, in its
delight

Making earth bare and veiling
heaven, and when
It sinks, the swarms that dimmed
or shared its light
Leave to its kindred lamps the spirit's
awful night."

XXX
Thus ceased she : and the moun-
tain shepherds came,
Their garlands sere, their magic
mantles rent ;
The Pilgrim of Eternity, whose
fame
Over his living head like Heaven is
bent,
An early but enduring monument,
Came, veiling all the lightnings of
his song
In sorrow ; from her wilds Ierne
sent
The sweetest lyrist of her saddest
wrong,
And love taught grief to fall like
music from his tongue.

XXXI
'Midst others of less note, came one
frail Form,
A phantom among men, companionless
As the last cloud of an expiring
storm,
Whose thunder is its knell ; he, as I
guess,
Had gazed on Nature's naked loveliness,
Actæon-like, and now he fled
astray
With feeble steps o'er the world's
wilderness,
And his own thoughts, along that
rugged way,
Pursued, like raging hounds, their
father and their prey.

XXXII
A pard-like Spirit beautiful and
swift—
A love in desolation masked ;—a
Power
Girt round with weakness ;—it can
scarce uplift
The weight of the superincumbent
hour ;
It is a dying lamp, a falling shower,

A breaking billow ;—even whilst
we speak
Is it not broken ? On the wither-
ng flower
The killing sun smiles brightly : on
a cheek
The life can burn in blood, even while
the heart may break.

XXXIII

His head was bound with pansies
overblown,
And faded violets, white, and pied,
and blue ;
And a light spear topped with a
cypress cone,
Round whose rude shaft dark ivy-
tresses grew
Yet dripping with the forest's noonday dew,
Vibrated, as the ever-beating heart
Shook the weak hand that grasped
it ; of that crew
He came the last, neglected and
apart ;
A herd-abandoned deer, struck by
the hunter's dart.

XXXIV

All stood aloof, and at his partial
moan
Smiled through their tears ; well
knew that gentle band
Who in another's fate now wept
his own ;
As in the accents of an unknown
land
He sang new sorrow ; sad Urania
scanned
The Stranger's mien, and mur-
mured : " Who art thou ? "
He answered not, but with a sud-
den hand
Made bare his branded and ensan-
guined brow,
Which was like Cain's or Christ's.
Oh ! that it should be so !

XXXV

What softer voice is hushed over
the dead ?
Athwart what brow is that dark
mantle thrown ?
What form leans sadly o'er the
white deathbed,
In mockery of monumental stone,

The heavy heart heaving without a
moan ?
If it be he, who, gentlest of the wise,
Taught, soothed, loved, honoured
the departed one ;
Let me not vex, with inharmonious
sighs,
The silence of that heart's accepted
sacrifice.

XXXVI

Our Adonaïs has drunk poison—
Oh !
What deaf and viperous murderer
could crown
Life's early cup with such a draught
of woe ?
The nameless worm would now it-
self disown :
It felt, yet could escape the magic
tone
Whose prelude held all envy, hate
and wrong,
But what was howling in one breast
alone,
Silent with expectation of the song,
Whose master's hand is cold, whose
silver lyre unstrung.

XXXVII

Live thou, whose infamy is not thy
fame !
Live ! fear no heavier chastisement
from me,
Thou noteless blot on a remembered name !
But be thyself, and know thyself to
be !
And ever at thy season be thou free
To spill the venom when thy fangs
o'erflow :
Remorse and Self-contempt shall
cling to thee ;
Hot Shame shall burn upon thy
secret brow,
And like a beaten hound tremble
thou shalt—as now.

XXXVIII

Nor let us weep that our delight is
fled
Far from these carrion-kites that
scream below ;
He wakes or sleeps with the enduring dead ;

Thou canst not soar where he is
    sitting now.
Dust to the dust ! but the pure
    spirit shall flow
Back to the burning fountain
    whence it came,
A portion of the Eternal, which
    must glow
Through time and change, un-
    quenchably the same,
Whilst thy cold embers choke the
    sordid hearth of shame.

XXXIX

Peace, peace ! he is not dead, he
    doth not sleep—
He hath awakened from the dream
    of life—
'Tis we, who, lost in stormy visions,
    keep
With phantoms an unprofitable
    strife,
And in mad trance strike with our
    spirit's knife
Invulnerable nothings—*We* decay
Like corpses in a charnel ; fear and
    grief
Convulse us and consume us day
    by day,
And cold hopes swarm like worms
    within our living clay.

XL

He has outsoared the shadow of our
    night ;
Envy and calumny, and hate and
    pain,
And that unrest which men miscall
    delight,
Can touch him not and torture not
    again ;
From the contagion of the world's
    slow stain
He is secure, and now can never
    mourn
A heart grown cold, a head grown
    grey in vain ;
Nor, when the spirit's self has
    ceased to burn,
With sparkless ashes load an un-
    lamented urn.

XLI

He lives, he wakes—'tis Death is
    dead, not he ;
Mourn not for Adonaïs.—Thou
    young Dawn,

Turn all thy dew to splendour, for
    from thee
The spirit thou lamentest is not
    gone ;
Ye caverns and ye forests, cease
    to moan !
Cease ye faint flowers and foun-
    tains, and thou Air,
Which like a morning veil thy scarf
    hadst thrown
O'er the abandoned Earth, now
    leave it bare
Even to the joyous stars which smile
    on its despair !

XLII

He is made one with Nature :
    there is heard
His voice in all her music, from the
    moan
Of thunder, to the song of night's
    sweet bird ;
He is a presence to be felt and
    known
In darkness and in light, from herb
    and stone,
Spreading itself where'er that
    Power may move
Which has withdrawn his being to
    its own ;
Which wields the world with never
    wearied love,
Sustains it from beneath, and kindles
    it above.

XLIII

He is a portion of the loveliness
Which once he made more lovely :
    he doth bear
His part, while the one Spirit's
    plastic stress
Sweeps through the dull dense
    world, compelling there
All new successions to the forms
    they wear,
Torturing th' unwilling dross that
    checks its flight
To its own likeness, as each mass
    may bear ;
And bursting in its beauty and its
    might
From trees and beasts and men into
    the Heavens' light.

XLIV

The splendours of the firmament of
    time

May be eclipsed, but are extinguished not ;
Like stars to their appointed height
  they climb,
And death is a low mist which cannot blot
The brightness it may veil. When
  lofty thought
Lifts a young heart above its mortal lair,
And love and life contend in it, for
  what
Shall be its earthly doom, the dead
  live there,
And move like winds of light on dark
  and stormy air.

XLV

The inheritors of unfulfilled renown
Rose from their thrones, built beyond mortal thought,
Far in the unapparent. Chatter-
  ton
Rose pale, his solemn agony had
  not
Yet faded from him ; Sidney, as he
  fought
And as he fell and as he lived and
  loved,
Sublimely mild, a Spirit without
  spot,
Arose ; and Lucan, by his death
  approved ;
Oblivion as they rose shrank like a
  thing reproved.

XLVI

And many more, whose names on
  Earth are dark,
But whose transmitted effluence
  cannot die
So long as fire outlives the parent
  spark,
Rose, robed in dazzling immor-
  tality.
" Thou art become as one of us,"
  they cry ;
" It was for thee yon kingless
  sphere has long
Swung blind in unascended ma-
  jesty,
Silent alone amid a Heaven of song.
Assume thy winged throne, thou
  Vesper of our throng ! "

XLVII

Who mourns for Adonaïs ? Oh, come
  forth,
Fond wretch ! and know thyself
  and him aright.
Clasp with thy panting soul the
  pendulous Earth ;
As from a centre, dart thy spirit's
  light
Beyond all worlds, until its spacious might
Satiate the void circumference ·
  then shrink
Even to a point within our day and
  night ;
And keep thy heart light, lest it
  make thee sink
When hope has kindled hope, and
  lured thee to the brink.

XLVIII

Or go to Rome, which is the sepulchre,
Oh, not of him, but of our joy : 'tis
  nought
That ages, empires, and religions,
  there
Lie buried in the ravage they have
  wrought ;
For such as he can lend,—they
  borrow not
Glory from those who made the
  world their prey ;
And he is gathered to the kings of
  thought
Who waged contention with their
  time's decay,
And of the past are all that cannot
  pass away.

XLIX

Go thou to Rome,—at once the
  Paradise,
The grave, the city, and the wilder-
  ness ;
And where its wrecks like shattered
  mountains rise,
And flowering weeds, and fragrant
  copses dress
The bones of Desolation's naked-
  ness
Pass, till the Spirit of the spot shall
  lead
Thy footsteps to a slope of green
  access,

Where, like an infant's smile, over
the dead
A light of laughing flowers along the
grass is spread.

L

And grey walls moulder round, on
which dull Time
Feeds, like slow fire upon a hoary
brand ;
And one keen pyramid with wedge
sublime,
Pavilioning the dust of him who
planned
This refuge for his memory, doth
stand
Like flame transformed to marble ;
and beneath
A field is spread, on which a newer
band
Have pitched in Heaven's smile
their camp of death,
Welcoming him we lose with scarce
extinguished breath.

LI

Here pause : these graves are all
too young as yet
To have outgrown the sorrow which
consigned
Its charge to each ; and if the seal
is set,
Here, on one fountain of a mourning mind,
Break it not thou ! too surely shalt
thou find
Thine own well full, if thou re-
turnest home,
Of tears and gall. From the
world's bitter wind
Seek shelter in the shadow of the
tomb.
What Adonaïs is, why fear we to become ?

LII

The One remains, the many change
and pass ;
Heaven's light for ever shines,
Earth's shadows fly,
Life, like a dome of many-coloured
glass,
Stains the white radiance of Etern-
ity,
Until Death tramples it to frag-
ments.—Die,

If thou wouldst be with that which
thou dost seek !
Follow where all is fled !—Rome's
azure sky,
Flowers, ruins, statues, music,
words are weak
The glory they transfuse with fitting
truth to speak.

LIII

Why linger, why turn back, why
shrink, my Heart ?
Thy hopes are gone before : from
all things here
They have departed ; thou shouldst
now depart !
A light is passed from the revolving
year,
And man, and woman ; and what
still is dear
Attracts to crush, repels to make
thee wither.
The soft sky smiles,—the low wind
whispers near :
'Tis Adonaïs calls ! Oh, hasten
thither,
No more let Life divide what Death
can join together.

LIV

That light whose smile kindles the
Universe,
That Beauty in which all things
work and move,
That Benediction which the eclips-
ing Curse
Of birth can quench not, that sus-
taining Love
Which through the web of being
blindly wove
By man and beast and earth and
air and sea,
Burns bright or dim, as each are
mirrors of
The fire for which all thirst, now
beams on me,
Consuming the last clouds of cold
mortality.

LV

The breath whose might I have invoked in song
Descends on me ; my spirit's bark
is driven
Far from the shore, far from the
trembling throng

Whose sails were never to the tem-
    pest given ;
The massy earth and sphered skies
    are riven !
I am borne darkly, fearfully afar ;
Whilst burning through the inmost
    veil of Heaven,
The soul of Adonaïs, like a star,
Beacons from the abode where the
    Eternal are.

TO EMILIA VIVIANI

MADONNA, wherefore hast thou sent
    to me
    Sweet basil and mignonette ?
Embleming love and health, which
    never yet
In the same wreath might be.
    Alas, and they are wet !
Is it with thy kisses or thy tears ?
    For never rain or dew
    Such fragrance drew
From plant or flower—the very doubt
    endears
    My sadness ever new,
The sighs I breathe, the tears I shed
    for thee.

FROM THE ARABIC

AN IMITATION

MY faint spirit was sitting in the light
    Of thy looks, my love ;
It panted for thee like the hind at
    noon
    For the brooks, my love.
Thy barb, whose hoofs outspeed the
    tempest's flight,
    Bore thee far from me ;
My heart, for my weak feet were
    weary soon,
    Did companion thee.

Ah ! fleeter far than fleetest storm or
    steed,
    Or the death they bear,
The heart which tender thought
    clothes like a dove
    With the wings of care ;
In the battle, in the darkness, in the
    need,
    Shall mine cling to thee,
Nor claim one smile for all the com-
    fort, love,
    It may bring to thee.

TIME

UNFATHOMABLE Sea ! whose waves
    are years,
    Ocean of Time, whose waters of
    deep woe
Are brackish with the salt of human
    tears !
    Thou shoreless flood, which in thy
    ebb and flow
Claspest the limits of mortality !
And sick of prey, yet howling on fo.
    more,
Vomitest thy wrecks on its innos-
    pitable shore ;
Treacherous in calm, and terrible in
    storm,
    Who shall put forth on thee,
    Unfathomable Sea ?

TO NIGHT

SWIFTLY walk over the western wave,
    Spirit of Night !
Out of the misty eastern cave,
Where all the long and lone daylight,
Thou wovest dreams of joy and fear,
Which make thee terrible and dear,—
    Swift be thy flight !

Wrap thy form in a mantle grey,
    Star-inwrought !
Blind with thine hair the eyes of day,
Kiss her until she be wearied out,
Then wander o'er city, and sea, and
    land,
Touching all with thine opiate wand—
    Come, long-sought !

When I arose and saw the dawn,
    I sighed for thee ;
When light rode high, and the dew
    was gone,
And noon lay heavy on flower and
    tree,
And the weary Day turned to his rest,
Lingering like an unloved guest,
    I sighed for thee.

Thy brother Death came, and cried,
    Wouldst thou me ?
Thy sweet child Sleep, the filmy-eyed,
    Murmured like a noontide bee,
Shall I nestle near thy side ?
Wouldst thou me ?—And I replied,
    No, not thee !

Death will come when thou art dead,
    Soon, too soon—
Sleep will come when thou art fled ;
Of neither would I ask the boon
I ask of thee, beloved Night—
Swift be thine approaching flight,
    Come soon, soon !

A FRAGMENT

As a violet's gentle eye
Gazes on the azure sky,
Until its hue grows like what it be-
    holds ;
As a grey and empty mist
Lies like solid Amethyst,
Over the western mountain it en-
    folds,
When the sunset sleeps
    Upon its snow.

As a strain of sweetest sound
Wraps itself the wind around,
Until the voiceless wind be music too ;
    As aught dark, vain and dull,
    Basking in what is beautiful,
Is full of light and love.

LINES

FAR, far away, O ye
    Halcyons of Memory !
Seek some far calmer nest
Than this abandoned breast ;—
No news of your false spring
To my heart's winter bring ;
Once having gone, in vain
    Ye come again.

Vultures, who build your bowers
High in the Future's towers !
Withered hopes on hopes are spread ;
Dying joys, choked by the dead,
Will serve your beaks for prey
    Many a day.

THE FUGITIVES

I

THE waters are flashing,
The white hail is dashing,
The lightnings are glancing,
The hoar-spray is dancing—
    Away !

The whirlwind is rolling,
The thunder is tolling,
The forest is swinging,
The minster bells ringing—
    Come away !

The Earth is like Ocean,
Wreck-strewn and in motion :
Bird, beast, man, and worm,
Have crept out of the storm—
    Come away !

II

" Our boat has one sail,
And the helmsman is pale ;—
A bold pilot I trow,
Who should follow us now,"—
    Shouted He—

And she cried : " Ply the oar ;
Put off gaily from shore ! "—
As she spoke, bolts of death
Mixed with hail, specked their path
    O'er the sea.

And from isle, tower, and rock,
The blue beacon-cloud broke,
Though dumb in the blast,
The red cannon flashed fast
    From the lee.

III

" And fear'st thou, and fear'st thou
And see'st thou, and hear'st thou ?
And drive we not free
O'er the terrible sea,
    I and thou ? "

One boat-cloak did cover
The loved and the lover—
Their blood beats one measure,
They murmur proud pleasure
    Soft and low ;—

While around the lashed Ocean,
Like mountains in motion,
Is withdrawn and uplifted,
Sunk, shattered, and shifted,
    To and fro.

IV

In the court of the fortress
Beside the pale portress,
Like a bloodhound well beaten
The bridegroom stands, eaten
    By shame ;

On the topmost watch-turret,
As a death-boding spirit,
Stands the grey tyrant father,
To his voice the mad weather
    Seems tame ;

And with curses as wild
As e'er cling to child,
He devotes to the blast
The best, loveliest, and last
    Of his name !

TO ———

MUSIC, when soft voices die,
Vibrates in the memory—
Odours, when sweet violets sicken,
Live within the sense they quicken.

Rose leaves, when the rose is dead,
Are heaped for the beloved's bed ;
And so thy thoughts, when thou art
    gone,
Love itself shall slumber on.

TO MARY WOLLSTONECRAFT GODWIN

MINE eyes were dim with tears un-
    shed ;
    Yes, I was firm—thus wert not
    thou ;—
My baffled looks did fear yet dread
    To meet thy looks—I could not
    know
How anxiously they sought to shine
With soothing pity upon mine.

To sit and curb the soul's mute rage
    Which preys upon itself alone.;
To curse the life which is the cage
    Of fettered grief that dares not
    groan,
Hiding from many a careless eye
The scorned load of agony.

Whilst thou alone, then not regarded,
    The [   ] thou alone should be,
To spend years thus, and be re-
    warded,
    As thou, sweet love, requited me
When none were near—Oh ! I did
    wake
From torture for that moment's sake.

Upon my heart thy accents sweet
    Of peace and pity fell like dew
On flowers half dead ;—thy lips did
    meet
    Mine tremblingly ; thy dark eyes
    threw
Their soft persuasion on my brain,
Charming away its dream of pain.

We are not happy, sweet ! our state
    Is strange and full of doubt and
    fear ;
More need of words that ills abate ;—
    Reserve or censure come not near
Our sacred friendship, lest there be
No solace left for thou and me.

Gentle and good and mild thou art,
    Nor can I live if thou appear
Aught but thyself, or turn thine
    heart
    Away from me, or stoop to wear
The mask of scorn, although it be
To hide the love thou feel'st for me.

SONG

RARELY, rarely, comest thou,
    Spirit of Delight !
Wherefore hast thou left me now
    Many a day and night ?
Many a weary night and day
'Tis since thou art fled away.

How shall ever one like me
    Win thee back again ?
With the joyous and the free
    Thou wilt scoff at pain.
Spirit false ! thou hast forgot
All but those who need thee not.

As a lizard with the shade
    Of a trembling leaf,
Thou with sorrow art dismayed ;
    Even the sighs of grief
Reproach thee, that thou art not
    near,
And reproach thou wilt not hear.

Let me set my mournful ditty
    To a merry measure ;—
Thou wilt never come for pity,
    Thou wilt come for pleasure ;—
Pity then will cut away
Those cruel wings, and thou wilt stay.

I love all that thou lovest,
  Spirit of Delight!
The fresh Earth in new leaves drest,
  And the starry night;
Autumn evening, and the morn
When the golden mists are born.

I love snow, and all the forms
  Of the radiant forest;
I love waves, and winds, and storms,
  Every thing almost
Which is Nature's, and may be
Untainted by man's misery.

I love tranquil solitude,
  And such society
As is quiet, wise, and good;
  Between thee and me
What difference? but thou dost pos-
  sess
The things I seek, not love them less.

I love Love—though he has wings,
  And like light can flee,
But, above all other things,
  Spirit, I love thee—
Thou art love and life! O come,
Make once more my heart thy home.

EVENING

PONTE AL MARE, PISA

The sun is set; the swallows are
  asleep;
  The bats are flitting fast in the grey
    air;
The slow soft toads out of damp cor-
  ners creep;
  And evening's breath, wandering
    here and there
Over the quivering surface of the
  stream,
Wakes not one ripple from its summer
  dream.

There is no dew on the dry grass to-
  night,
  Nor damp within the shadow of the
    trees;
The wind is intermitting, dry, and
  light;
  And in the inconstant motion of
    the breeze
The dust and straws are driven up
  and down,
And whirled about the pavement of
  the town.

Within the surface of the fleeting river
  The wrinkled image of the city lay,
Immovably unquiet, and for ever
  It trembles, but it never fades
    away;
Go to the [   ]
You, being changed, will find it then
  as now.

The chasm in which the sun has sunk,
  is shut
  By darkest barriers of enormous
    cloud,
Like mountain over mountain
  huddled—but
  Growing and moving upwards in a
    crowd,
And over it a space of watery blue,
Which the keen evening star is shin-
  ing through.

LINES

WRITTEN ON HEARING THE NEWS OF THE DEATH OF NAPOLEON

What! alive and so bold, O Earth?
  Art thou not over bold?
What! leapest thou forth as of old
In the light of thy morning mirth,
The last of the flock of the starry fold?
Ha! leapest thou forth as of old?
Are not the limbs still when the ghost
  is fled,
And canst thou move, Napoleon being
  dead?

How! is not thy quick heart cold?
  What spark is alive on thy hearth?
How! is not *his* death-knell knolled?
  And livest *thou* still, Mother Earth?
Thou wert warming thy fingers old
O'er the embers covered and cold
Of that most fiery spirit, when it
  fled—
What, Mother, do you laugh now he is
  dead?

" Who has known me of old," replied
  Earth,
  " Or who has my story told?
It is thou who art over bold."
  And the lightning of scorn laughed
    forth
As she sung, " To my bosom I fold
All my sons when their knell is
  knolled,

And so with living motion all are fed,
And the quick spring like weeds out
  of the dead.

" Still alive and still bold," shouted
    Earth,
  " I grow bolder, and still more bold.
The dead fill me ten thousand fold
  Fuller of speed, and splendour, and
    mirth ;
I was cloudy, and sullen, and cold,
Like a frozen chaos uprolled,
Till by the spirit of the mighty dead
My heart grew warm. I feed on
  whom I fed.

" Ay, alive and still bold," muttered
    Earth,
  " Napoleon's fierce spirit rolled,
In terror, and blood, and gold,
  A torrent of ruin to death from his
    birth.
Leave the millions who follow to
    mould
The metal before it be cold,
And weave into his shame, which like
    the dead
Shrouds me, the hopes that from his
  glory fled."

MUTABILITY

THE flower that smiles to-day
    To-morrow dies ;
All that we wish to stay,
    Tempts and then flies ;
What is this world's delight ?
Lightning that mocks the night,
Brief even as bright.

Virtue, how frail it is !
    Friendship too rare !
Love, how it sells poor bliss
    For proud despair !
But we, though soon they fall,
Survive their joy and all
Which ours we call.

Whilst skies are blue and bright,
    Whilst flowers are gay,
Whilst eyes that change ere night
    Make glad the day ;
Whilst yet the calm hours creep,
Dream thou—and from thy sleep
Then wake to weep.

SONNET

POLITICAL GREATNESS

NOR happiness, nor majesty, nor
    fame,
Nor peace, nor strength, nor skill in
    arms or arts,
Shepherd those herds whom tyranny
    makes tame ;
Verse echoes not one beating of their
    hearts :
History is but the shadow of their
    shame ;
Art veils her glass, or from the page-
    ant starts
As to oblivion their blind millions
    fleet,
Staining that Heaven with obscene
    imagery
Of their own likeness. What are
    numbers, knit
By force or custom ? Man who man
    would be,
Must rule the empire of himself ; in it
Must be supreme, establishing his
    throne
On vanquished will, quelling the
    anarchy
Of hopes and fears, being himself
    alone.

LINES

IF I walk in Autumn's even
    While the dead leaves pass.
If I look on Spring's soft heaven,
Something is not there which was.
Winter's wondrous frost and snow,
Summer's clouds, where are they
    now ?

GINEVRA [1]

WILD, pale, and wonder-stricken,
    even as one
Who staggers forth into the air and
    sun
From the dark chamber of a mortal
    fever,
Bewildered, and incapable, and ever
Fancying strange comments in her
    dizzy brain
Of usual shapes, till the familiar train

[1] This fragment is part of a poem which
Shelley intended to write, founded on a story to
be found in the first volume of a book entitled
L'Osservatore Fiorentino.

Of objects and of persons passed like things
Strange as a dreamer's mad imaginings,
Ginevra from the nuptial altar went ;
The vows to which her lips had sworn assent
Rung in her brain still with a jarring din,
Deafening the lost intelligence within.

And so she moved under the bridal veil,
Which made the paleness of her cheek more pale,
And deepened the faint crimson of her mouth,
And darkened her dark locks, as moonlight doth,—
And of the gold and jewels glittering there
She scarce felt conscious, but the weary glare
Lay like a chaos of unwelcome light,
Vexing the sense with gorgeous undelight.
A moonbeam in the shadow of a cloud
Was less heavenly fair—her face was bowed,
And as she passed, the diamonds in her hair
Were mirrored in the polished marble stair
Which led from the cathedral to the street ;
And even as she went her light fair feet
Erased these images.

The bride-maidens who round her thronging came
Some with a sense of self-rebuke and shame,
Envying the unenviable ; and others
Making the joy which should have been another's
Their own by gentle sympathy ; and some
Sighing to think of an unhappy home ;
Some few admiring what can ever lure
Maidens to leave the heaven serene and pure
Of parents' smiles for life's great cheat ; a thing
Bitter to taste, sweet in imagining.

But they are all dispersed—and lo ! she stands
Looking in idle grief on her white hands,
Alone within the garden now her own ;
And through the sunny air with jangling tone,
The music of the merry marriage-bells,
Killing the azure silence, sinks and swells ;—
Absorbed like one within a dream who dreams
That he is dreaming, until slumber seems
A mockery of itself—when suddenly
Antonio stood before her, pale as she.
With agony, with sorrow, and with pride,
He lifted his wan eyes upon the bride,
And said—" Is this thy faith ? " and then as one
Whose sleeping face is stricken by the sun
With light like a harsh voice, which bids him rise
And look upon his day of life with eyes
Which weep in vain that they can dream no more,
Ginevra saw her lover, and forbore
To shriek or faint, and checked the stifling blood
Rushing upon her heart, and unsubdued
Said—" Friend, if earthly violence or ill,
Suspicion, doubt, or the tyrannic will
Of parents, chance, or custom, time, or change,
Or circumstance, or terror, or revenge,
Or wildered looks, or words, or evil speech,
With all their stings and venom, can impeach
Our love,—we love not :—if the grave, which hides
The victim from the tyrant, and divides
The cheek that whitens from the eyes that dart
Imperious inquisition to the heart
That is another's, could dissever ours,
We love not."—" What ! do not the silent hours

Beckon thee to Gherardi's bridal
 bed ?
Is not that ring "——a pledge, he
 would have said
Of broken vows, but she with patient
 look
The golden circle from her finger took
And said—" Accept this token of my
 faith,
The pledge of vows to be absolved by
 death ;
And I am dead or shall be soon—my
 knell
Will mix its music with that merry
 bell ;
Does it not sound as if they sweetly
 said,
' We toll a corpse out of the marriage
 bed ? '
The flowers upon my bridal chamber
 strewn
Will serve unfaded for my bier—so
 soon
That even the dying violet will not
 die   [tasy
Before Ginevra.' " The strong fan-
Had made her accents weaker and
 wore weak,
And quenched the crimson life upon
 her cheek,
And glazed her eyes, and spread an
 atmosphere
Round her, which chilled the burning
 noon with fear,
Making her but an image of the
 thought,
Which, like a prophet or a shadow,
 brought
News of the terrors of the coming
 time.
Like an accuser branded with the
 crime
He would have cast on a beloved
 friend,
Whose dying eyes reproach not to
 the end
The pale betrayer—he then with vain
 repentance
Would share, he cannot now avert,
 the sentence—
Antonio stood and would have
 spoken, when
The compound voice of women and
 of men
Was heard approaching ; he retired,
 while she

Was led amid the admiring company
Back to the palace,—and her maidens
 soon
Changed her attire for the afternoon,
And left her at her own request to
 keep
An hour of quiet and rest : like one
 asleep
With open eyes and folded hands she
 lay,
Pale in the light of the declining day.

Meanwhile the day sinks fast, the
 sun is set,
And in the lighted hall the guests are
 met ;
The beautiful looked lovelier in the
 light
Of love, and admiration, and delight,
Reflected from a thousand hearts and
 eyes
Kindling a momentary Paradise.
This crowd is safer than the silent
 wood,
Where love's own doubts disturb the
 solitude ;
On frozen hearts the fiery rain of wine
Falls, and the dew of music more
 divine
Tempers the deep emotions of the
 time
To spirits cradled in a sunny clime :—
How many meet, who never yet have
 met,
To part too soon, but never to forget ?
How many saw the beauty, power,
 and wit
Of looks and words which ne'er
 enchanted yet !
But life's familiar veil was now with-
 drawn,
As the world leaps before an earth-
 quake's dawn,
And unprophetic of the coming
 hours,
The matin winds from the expanded
 flowers
Scatter their hoarded incense, and
 awaken
The earth, until the dewy sleep is
 shaken
From every living heart which it
 possesses,
Through seas and winds, cities and
 wildernesses,
As if the future and the past were all

Treasured i' the instant ;—so Gherardi's hall
Laughed in the mirth of its lord's festival,
Till some one asked—" Where is the Bride ? " And then
A bridesmaid went, and ere she came again
A silence fell upon the guests—a pause
Of expectation, as when beauty awes
All hearts with its approach, though unbeheld ;
Then wonder, and then fear that wonder quelled ;—
For whispers passed from mouth to ear which drew
The colour from the hearer's cheeks, and flew
Louder and swifter round the company ;
And then Gherardi entered with an eye
Of ostentatious trouble, and a crowd
Surrounded him, and some were weeping loud.

They found Ginevra dead ! if it be death,
To lie without motion, or pulse, or breath,
With waxen cheeks, and limbs cold, stiff, and white,
And open eyes, whose fixed and glassy light
Mocked at the speculation they had owned.
If it be death, when there is felt around
A smell of clay, a pale and icy glare,
And silence, and a sense that lifts the hair
From the scalp to the ankles, as it were
Corruption from the spirit passing forth,
And giving all it shrouded to the earth,
And leaving as swift lightning in its flight
Ashes, and smoke, and darkness : in our night
Of thought we know thus much of death,—no more
Than the unborn dream of our life before

Their barks are wrecked on its inhospitable shore.
The marriage feast and its solemnity
Was turned to funeral pomp—the company,
With heavy hearts and looks, broke up ; nor they
Who loved the dead went weeping on their way
Alone, but sorrow mixed with sad surprise
Loosened the springs of pity in all eyes,
On which that form, whose fate they weep in vain,
Will never, thought they, kindle smiles again.
The lamps which, half extinguished in their haste,
Gleamed few and faint o'er the abandoned feast,
Showed as it were within the vaulted room
A cloud of sorrow hanging, as if gloom
Had passed out of men's minds into the air.
Some few yet stood around Gherardi there,
Friends and relations of the dead,—and he,
A loveless man, accepted torpidly
The consolation that he wanted not,
Awe in the place of grief within him wrought.
Their whispers made the solemn silence seem
More still—some wept, [   ]
Some melted into tears without a sob,
And some with hearts that might be heard to throb
Leant on the table, and at intervals
Shuddered to hear through the deserted halls
And corridors the thrilling shrieks which came
Upon the breeze of night, that shook the flame
Of every torch and taper as it swept
From out the chamber where the women kept ;—
Their tears fell on the dear companion cold
Of pleasures now departed ; then was knolled
The bell of death, and soon the priests arrived,

And finding death their penitent had shrived,
Returned like ravens from a corpse whereon
A vulture has just feasted to the bone.
And then the mourning women came.—

*   *   *

THE DIRGE

OLD winter was gone
In his weakness back to the mountains hoar,
And the spring came down
From the planet that hovers upon the shore
Where the sea of sunlight encroaches
On the limits of wintry night :
If the land, and the air, and the sea,
Rejoice not when spring approaches,
We did not rejoice in thee,
    Ginevra !

She is still, she is cold
    On the bridal couch,
One step to the white deathbed,
    And one to the bier,
And one to the charnel—and one, Oh where ?
    The dark arrow fled
    In the noon.

Ere the sun through heaven once more has rolled
The rats in her heart
Will have made their nest,
And the worms be alive in her golden hair ;
While the spirit that guides the sun
Sits throned in his flaming chair,
    She shall sleep.

*   *   *

TO-MORROW

WHERE art thou, beloved To-morrow ?
  When young and old, and strong and weak,
Rich and poor, through joy and sorrow,
  Thy sweet smiles we ever seek,—
In thy place—ah ! well-a-day !
We find the thing we fled—To-day.

THE BOAT ON THE SERCHIO

OUR boat is asleep on Serchio's stream,
Its sails are folded like thoughts in a dream,
The helm sways idly, hither and thither ;
Dominic, the boatman, has brought the mast,
And the oars, and the sails ; but 'tis sleeping fast,
Like a beast, unconscious of its tether.

The stars burnt out in the pale blue air,
And the thin white moon lay withering there,
To tower, and cavern, and rift, and tree,
The owl and the bat fled drowsily.
Day had kindled the dewy woods
And the rocks above and the stream below,
And the vapours in their multitudes,
And the Apennines' shroud of summer snow,
And clothed with light of aëry gold
The mists in their eastern caves uprolled.

Day had awakened all things that be,
The lark and the thrush and the swallow free ;
And the milkmaid's song and the mower's scythe,
And the matin bell and the mountain bee :
Fireflies were quenched on the dewy corn,
Glow-worms went out on the river's brim,
Like lamps which a student forgets to trim :
The beetle forgot to wind his horn,
The crickets were still in the meadow and hill :
Like a flock of rooks at a farmer's gun,
Night's dreams and terrors, every one,
Fled from the brains which are their prey,
From the lamp's death to the morning ray.

All rose to do the task He set to
each,
Who shaped us to his ends and not
our own ;
The million rose to learn, and one to
teach
What none yet ever knew or can be
known.

        And many rose
Whose woe was such that fear be-
came desire ;—
Melchior and Lionel were not among
those ;
They from the throng of men had
stepped aside,
And made their home under the
green hill side.
It was that hill, whose intervening
brow
Screens Lucca from the Pisan's
envious eye,
Which the circumfluous plain waving
below,
Like a wide lake of green fertility,
With streams and fields and marshes
bare,
Divides from the far Apennines—
which lie
Islanded in the immeasurable air.

" What think you, as she lies in her
green cove,
Our little sleeping boat is dreaming
of ?
If morning dreams are true, why I
should guess
That she was dreaming of our idleness,
And of the miles of watery way
We should have led her by this time
of day."—

       ——" Never mind," said Lionel,
" Give care to the winds, they can
bear it well
About yon poplar tops ; and see !
The white clouds are driving merrily,
And the stars we miss this morn will
light
More willingly our return to-night.—
List, my dear fellow, the breeze blows
fair ;
How it scatters Dominic's long black
hair !
Singing of us, and our lazy motions,
If I can guess a boat's emotions."—

The chain is loosed, the sails are
spread,
The living breath is fresh behind,
As, with dews and sunrise fed,
Comes the laughing morning wind ;—
The sails are full, the boat makes head
Against the Serchio's torrent fierce,
Then flags with intermitting course,
And hangs upon the wave,
Which fervid from its mountain
source
Shallow, smooth, and strong, doth
come,—
Swift as fire, tempestuously
It sweeps into the affrighted sea ;
In morning's smile its eddies coil,
Its billows sparkle, toss, and boil,
Torturing all its quiet light
Into columns fierce and bright.

       The Serchio, twisting forth
Between the marble barriers which
it clove
At Ripafratta, leads through the
dread chasm
The wave that died the death which
lovers love,
Living in what it sought ; as if this
spasm
Had not yet past, the toppling moun-
tains cling,
But the clear stream in full enthusiasm
Pours itself on the plain, until wan-
dering,
Down one clear path of effluence
crystalline
Sends its clear waves, that they may
fling
At Arno's feet tribute of corn and
wine :
Then, through the pestilential deserts
wild
Of tangled marsh and woods of
stunted fir,
It rushes to the Ocean.

THE AZIOLA

" Do you not hear the Aziola cry ?
Methinks she must be nigh,"
    Said Mary, as we sate
In dusk, ere the stars were lit, or
candles brought ;
And I, who thought
This Aziola was some tedious woman,

Asked, " Who is Aziola ? " How
    elate
felt to know that it was nothing
    human,
No mockery of myself to fear and
    hate !
And Mary saw my soul,
And laughed and said, " Disquiet
    yourself not,
    'Tis nothing but a little downy
        owl."

Sad Aziola ! many an eventide
Thy music I had heard
By wood and stream, meadow and
    mountain side,
And fields and marshes wide,—
    Such as nor voice, nor lute, nor
        wind, nor bird,
    The soul ever stirred ;
Unlike and far sweeter than they all :
Sad Aziola ! from that moment I
Loved thee and thy sad cry.

A LAMENT

O WORLD ! O life ! O time !
On whose last steps I climb,
    Trembling at that where I had stood
        before ;
When will return the glory of your
    prime ?
    No more—Oh, never more !

Out of the day and night
A joy has taken flight : ·
    Fresh spring, and summer, and
        winter hoar,
Move my faint heart with grief, but
    with delight
    No more—Oh, never more !

TO EDWARD WILLIAMS

I

THE serpent is shut out from Para-
    dise.
The wounded deer must seek the
    herd no more
    In which its heart-cure lies :
The widowed dove must cease to
    haunt a bower,
Like that from which its mate with
    feigned sighs
    Fled in the April hour.
I too, must seldom seek again
Near happy friends a mitigated pain.

II

Of hatred I am proud,—with scorn
    content ;
Indifference, that once hurt me, now
    is grown
    Itself indifferent.
But, not to speak of love, pity alone
Can break a spirit already more than
    bent.
    The miserable one
Turns the mind's poison into food,—
Its medicine is tears,—its evil good.

III

Therefore if now I see you seldomer,
Dear friends, dear *friend* ! know that
    I only fly
    Your looks because they stir
Griefs that should sleep, and hopes
    that cannot die :
The very comfort that they minister
    I scarce can bear ; yet I,
So deeply is the arrow gone,
Should quickly perish if it were with-
    drawn.

IV

When I return to my cold home, you
    ask
Why I am not as I have ever been ?
    You spoil me for the task
Of acting a forced part on life's dull
    scene,—
Of wearing on my brow the idle mask
    Of author, great or mean,
In the world's Carnival. I sought
Peace thus, and but in you I found
    it not.

V

Full half an hour, to-day, I tried my
    lot
With various flowers, and every one
    still said,
    " She loves me,—loves me not." [1]
And if this meant a vision long since
    fled—
If it meant fortune, fame, or peace
    of thought—
    If it meant—but I dread
To speak what you may know too
    well :
Still there was truth in the sad oracle,

[1] See *Faust.*

VI

The crane o'er seas and forests seeks
her home ;
No bird so wild, but has its quiet nest,
When it no more would roam ;
The sleepless billows on the ocean's
breast
Break like a bursting heart, and die
in foam,
And thus, at length, find rest :
Doubtless there is a place of peace
Where *my* weak heart and all its
throbs will cease.

VII

I asked her, yesterday, if she believed
That I had resolution.   One who *had*
Would ne'er have thus relieved
His heart with words,—but what
his judgment bade
Would do, and leave the scorner
unreprieved.
These verses are too sad
To send to you, but that I know,
Happy yourself, you feel another's
woe.

REMEMBRANCE

SWIFTER far than summer's flight,
Swifter far than youth's delight,
Swifter far than happy night,
Art thou come and gone :
As the earth when leaves are dead,
As the night when sleep is sped,
As the heart when joy is fled,
I am left lone, alone.

The swallow Summer comes again,
The owlet Night resumes her reign,
But the wild swan Youth is fain
To fly with thee, false as thou.
My heart each day desires the
morrow,
Sleep itself is turned to sorrow,
Vainly would my winter borrow
Sunny leaves from any bough.

Lilies for a bridal bed,
Roses for a matron's head,
Violets for a maiden dead,
Pansies let my flowers be ;
On the living grave I bear,
Scatter them without a tear,
Let no friend, however dear,
Waste one hope, one fear for me

THE INDIAN SERENADE

I ARISE from dreams of thee
In the first sweet sleep of night,
When the winds are breathing low,
And the stars are shining bright.
I arise from dreams of thee,
And a spirit in my feet
Has led me—who knows how ?
To thy chamber window, sweet !

The wandering airs they faint
On the dark, the silent stream—
The champak odours fail
Like sweet thoughts in a dream ;
The nightingale's complaint,
It dies upon her heart,
As I must die on thine,
O beloved as thou art !

O lift me from the grass !
I die, I faint, I fail !
Let thy love in kisses rain
On my lips and eyelids pale.
My cheek is cold and white, alas !
My heart beats loud and fast,
Oh ! press it close to thine again,
Where it will break at last.

TO ———

ONE word is too often profaned
For me to profane it,
One feeling too falsely disdained
For thee to disdain it.
One hope is too like despair
For prudence to smother,
And Pity from thee more dear
Than that from another.

I can give not what men call love,
But wilt thou accept not
The worship the heart lifts above
And the Heavens reject not :
The desire of the moth for the star,
Of the night for the morrow,
The devotion to something afar
From the sphere of our sorrow ?

MUSIC

I PANT for the music which is divine,
My heart in its thirst is a dying
flower ;
Pour forth the sound like enchanted
wine,

Loosen the notes in a silver shower ;
Like a herbless plain for the gentle
    rain,
I gasp, I faint, till they wake again.

Let me drink of the spirit of that
    sweet sound,
    More, O more ! I am thirsting yet,
It loosens the serpent which care has
    bound
    Upon my heart, to stifle it :
The dissolving strain, through every
    vein,
Passes into my heart and brain.

As the scent of a violet withered up,
    Which grew by the brink of a silver
    lake,
When the hot noon has drained its
    dewy cup,
    And mist there was none its thirst
    to slake—
And the violet lay dead while the
    odour flew
On the wings of the wind o'er the
    waters blue—

As one who drinks from a charmed
    cup
    Of foaming, and sparkling, and
    murmuring wine,
Whom, a mighty Enchantress filling
    up,
    Invites to love with her kiss divine.
            *   *   *   *
            *   *   *

TO ———

WHEN passion's trance is overpast,
If tenderness and truth could last
Or live, whilst all wild feelings keep
Some mortal slumber, dark and deep,
I should not weep, I should not weep !

It were enough to feel, to see
Thy soft eyes gazing tenderly,
And dream the rest—and burn and be
The secret food of fires unseen,
Couldst thou but be as thou hast been.

After the slumber of the year
The woodland violets re-appear ;
All things revive in field or grove,
And sky and sea ; but two, which
    move,
And for all others, life and love.

A BRIDAL SONG

THE golden gates of sleep unbar
    Where strength and beauty, met
        together,
Kindle their image like a star
    In a sea of glassy weather !
Night, with all thy stars look down,—
    Darkness, weep thy holiest dew,—
Never smiled the inconstant moon
        On a pair so true.
Let eyes not see their own delight ;—
Haste, swift Hour, and thy flight
        Oft renew.

Fairies, sprites, and angels, keep her !
    Holy powers, permit no wrong !
And return to wake the sleeper,
    Dawn, ere it be long.
O joy ! O fear ! what will be done
In the absence of the sun !
        Come along !

A FRAGMENT

THEY were two cousins, almost like
    two twins,
Except that from the catalogue of
    sins
Nature had razed their love—which
    could not be
But by dissevering their nativity.
And so they grew together, like two
    flowers
Upon one stem, which the same
    beams and showers
Lull or awaken in their purple prime,
Which the same hand will gather—
    the same clime
Shake with decay. This fair day
    smiles to see
All those who love,—and who e'er
    loved like thee,
Fiordispina ? Scarcely Cosimo.
Within whose bosom and whose
    brain now glow
The ardours of a vision which obscure
The very idol of its portraiture ;
He faints, dissolved into a sense of
    love ;
But thou art as a planet sphered
    above,
But thou art Love itself—ruling the
    motion
Of his subjected spirit :—such emo-
    tion

Must end in sin or sorrow, if sweet
   May
Had not brought forth this morn—
   your wedding-day.

GOOD-NIGHT

GOOD-NIGHT ? ah ! no ; the hour is ill
   Which severs those it should unite ;
Let us remain together still,
   Then it will be *good* night.

How can I call the lone night good,
   Though thy sweet wishes wing its
     flight ?
Be it not said, thought, understood,
   That it will be *good* night.

To hearts which near each other move
   From evening close to morning
     light,
The night is good ; because, my love,
   They never *say* good-night.

DIRGE FOR THE YEAR

ORPHAN hours, the year is dead,
   Come and sigh, come and weep !

Merry hours, smile instead,
   For the year is but asleep :
See, it smiles as it is sleeping,
Mocking your untimely weeping.

As an earthquake rocks a corse
   In its coffin in the clay,
So White Winter, that rough nurse,
   Rocks the dead-cold year to-day ;
Solemn hours ! wail aloud
For your mother in her shroud.

As the wild air stirs and sways
   The tree-swung cradle of a child,
So the breath of these rude days
   Rocks the year :—be calm and
     mild,
Trembling hours ; she will arise
With new love within her eyes.

January grey is here,
   Like a sexton by her grave ;
February bears the bier,
   March with grief doth howl and
     rave,
And April weeps—but, O ye hours
Follow with May's fairest flowers.

POEMS WRITTEN IN 1822

THE ZUCCA [1]

SUMMER was dead and Autumn was
   expiring,
  And infant Winter laughed upon
   the land
All cloudlessly and cold ;—when I, de-
   siring
  More in this world than any understand,
Wept o'er the beauty, which, like sea
   retiring,
  Had left the earth bare as the wave-
   worn sand
Of my poor heart, and o'er the grass
   and flowers
Pale for the falsehood of the flattering
   hours.

Summer was dead, but I yet lived to
   weep

[1] Pumpkin.

The instability of all but weeping ;
And on the earth lulled in her winter
   sleep
  I woke, and envied her as she was
   sleeping.
Too happy Earth ! over thy face shall
   creep
  The wakening vernal airs, until
   thou, leaping
From unremembered dreams shalt
   [   ] see
No death divide thy immortality.

I loved—O no, I mean not one of ye,
   Or any earthly one, though ye are
   dear
As human heart to human heart may
   be ;—
  I loved, I know not what—but this
   low sphere,
And all that it contains, contains not
   thee,

Thou, whom, seen nowhere, I feel
    everywhere,
Dim object of my soul's idolatry.

          *   *   *

By Heaven and Earth, from all whose
    shapes thou flowest,
  Neither to be contained, delayed,
    or hidden,
Making divine the loftiest and the
    lowest,
  When for a moment thou art not
    forbidden
To live within the life which thou be-
    stowest,
  And leaving noblest things, vacant
    and chidden,
Cold as a corpse after the spirit's
    flight,
Blank as the sun after the birth of
    night.

In winds, and trees, and streams, and
    all things common,
  In music, and the sweet unconscious
    tone
Of animals, and voices which are
    human,
  Meant to express some feelings of
    their own ;
In the soft motions and rare smile of
    woman,
  In flowers and leaves, and in the
    fresh grass shown,
Or dying in the autumn, I the most
Adore thee present, or lament thee
    lost.

And thus I went lamenting, when I
    saw
  A plant upon the river's margin lie,
Like one who loved beyond his Na-
    ture's law,
  And in despair had cast him down
    to die ;
Its leaves which had outlived the
    frost, the thaw
  Had blighted as a heart which
    hatred's eye
Can blast not, but which pity kills ;
    the dew
Lay on its spotted leaves like tears
    too true.

The Heavens had wept upon it, but
    the Earth

Had crushed it on her unmaternal
    breast.
          *   *   *
I bore it to my chamber, and I plant-
    ed
  It in a vase full of the lightest
    mould ;
The winter beams which out of Hea-
    ven slanted
  Fell through the window panes,
    disrobed of cold,
Upon its leaves and flowers ; the star
    which panted
  In evening for the Day, whose car
    has rolled
Over the horizon's wave, with looks
    of light
Smiled on it from the threshold of the
    night.

The mitigated influences of air
  And light revived the plant, and
    from it grew
Strong leaves and tendrils, and its
    flowers fair,
  Full as a cup with the vine's burn-
    ing dew,
O'erflowed with golden colours ; an
    atmosphere
  Of vital warmth, infolded it anew,
And every impulse sent to every part
The unbeheld pulsations of its heart.

Well might the plant grow beautiful
    and strong,
  Even if the sun and air had smiled
    not on it ;
For one wept o'er it all the winter long·
  Tears pure as Heaven's rain, which
    fell upon it
Hour after hour ; for sounds of softest
    song
  Mixed with the stringed melodies
    that won it
To leave the gentle lips on which it
    slept,
Had loosed the heart of him who sat
    and wept ;

Had loosed his heart, and shook the
    leaves and flowers
  On which he wept, the while the
    savage storm
Waked by the darkest of December's
    hours

Was raving round the chamber
    hushed and warm ;
The birds were shivering in their leaf-
    less bowers,
The fish were frozen in the pools,
    the form
Of every summer plant was dead
    [   ]
Whilst this   *   *   *

THE MAGNETIC LADY TO HER
        PATIENT

" SLEEP, sleep on ! forget thy pain ;
    My hand is on thy brow,
My spirit on thy brain ;
My pity on thy heart, poor friend ;
    And from my fingers flow
The powers of life, and like a sign,
    Seal thee from thine hour of woe ;
And brood on thee, but may not
    blend
        With thine.

" Sleep, sleep on ! I love thee not ;
    But when I think that *he*
Who made and makes my lot
As full of flowers, as thine of weeds,
    Might have been lost like thee ;
And that a hand which was not mine
    Might then have chased his agony
As I another's—my heart bleeds
        For thine.

" Sleep, sleep, and with the slumber of
    The dead and the unborn
Forget thy life and love ;
Forget that thou must wake for ever ;
    Forget the world's dull scorn ;
Forget lost health, and the divine
    Feelings which died in youth's brief
    morn ;
And forget me, for I can never
        Be thine.

" Like a cloud big with a May shower,
    My soul weeps healing rain
On thee, thou withered flower ;
It breathes mute music on thy sleep ;
    Its odour calms thy brain !
Its light within thy gloomy breast
    Spreads like a second youth again.
By mine thy being is to its deep
        Possessed. ·

" The spell is done. How feel you
    now ? "
    " Better—Quite well," replied
The sleeper,—" What would do
You good when suffering and awake ?
    What cure your head and side ? "—
" 'Twould kill me what would cure my
    pain ;
    And as I must on earth abide
Awhile, yet tempt me not to break
    My chain."

LINES

WHEN the lamp is shattered,
The light in the dust lies dead—
    When the cloud is scattered,
The rainbow's glory is shed.
    When the lute is broken,
Sweet tones are remembered not ;
    When the lips have spoken,
Loved accents are soon forgot.

    As music and splendour
Survive not the lamp and the lute,
    The heart's echoes render
No song when the spirit is mute :—
    No song but sad dirges,
Like the wind through a ruined cell,
    Or the mournful surges
That ring the dead seaman's knell.

    When hearts have once mingled,
Love first leaves the well-built nest ;
    The weak one is singled
To endure what it once possessed.
    O, Love ! who bewailest
The frailty of all things here,
    Why choose you the frailest
For your cradle, your home, and your
    bier ?

    Its passions will rock thee,
As the storms rock the ravens on high
    Bright reason will mock thee,
Like the sun from a wintry sky.
    From thy nest every rafter
Will rot, and thine eagle home
    Leave thee naked to laughter,
When leaves fall and cold winds come.

WITH A GUITAR, TO JANE

ARIEL to Miranda :—Take
This slave of music, for the sake

Of him, who is the slave of thee ;
And teach it all the harmony
In which thou canst, and only thou,
Make the delighted spirit glow,
Till joy denies itself again,
And, too intense, is turned to pain.
For by permission and command
Of thine own Prince Ferdinand,
Poor Ariel sends this silent token
Of more than ever can be spoken ;
Your guardian spirit, Ariel, who
From life to life must still pursue
Your happiness, for thus alone
Can Ariel ever find his own ;
From Prospero's enchanted cell,
As the mighty verses tell,
To the throne of Naples he
Lit you o'er the trackless sea,
Flitting, on your prow before,
Like a living meteor.
When you die, the silent Moon,
In her interlunar swoon,
Is not sadder in her cell
Than deserted Ariel ;
When you live again on earth,
Like an unseen Star of birth,
Ariel guides you o'er the sea
Of life from your nativity :
Many changes have been run
Since Ferdinand and you begun
Your course of love, and Ariel still
Has tracked your steps and served
        your will
Now in humbler, happier lot,
This is all remembered not ;
And now, alas ! the poor sprite is
Imprisoned for some fault of his
In a body like a grave—
From you, he only dares to crave,
For his service and his sorrow,
A smile to-day, a song to-morrow.

The artist who this idol wrought,
To echo all harmonious thought,
Felled a tree, while on the steep
The woods were in their winter sleep,
Rocked in that repose divine
On the wind-swept Apennine ;
And dreaming, some of autumn past,
And some of spring approaching fast,
And some of April buds and showers,
And some of songs in July bowers,
And all of love ; and so this tree,—
O that such our death may be !—
Died in sleep, and felt no pain,
To live in happier form again :

From which, beneath Heaven's fair-
        est star,
The artist wrought this loved Guitar,
And taught it justly to reply,
To all who question skilfully,
In language gentle as thine own ,
Whispering in enamoured tone
Sweet oracles of woods and dells,
And summer winds in sylvan cells ;
For it had learnt all harmonies
Of the plains and of the skies,
Of the forests and the mountains,
And the many voiced fountains ;
The clearest echoes of the hills,
The softest notes of falling rills,
The melodies of bird, and bees,
The murmuring of summer seas,
And pattering rain, and breathing
        dew,
And airs of evening ; and it knew
That seldom-heard mysterious sound,
Which, driven on its diurnal round
As it floats through boundless day,
Our world enkindles on its way—
All this it knows, but will not tell
To those who cannot question well
The spirit that inhabits it ;
It talks according to the wit
Of its companions ; and no more
Is heard than has been felt before,
By those who tempt it to betray
These secrets of an elder day.
But, sweetly as its answers will
Flatter hands of perfect skill,
It keeps its highest, holiest tone
For our beloved friend alone.

FRAGMENTS OF AN UNFIN-
ISHED DRAMA

THE following fragments are part of a
Drama, undertaken for the amusement
of the individuals who composed our
intimate society, but left unfinished.
I have preserved a sketch of the story
as far as it had been shadowed in the
poet's mind.

    An Enchantress, living in one of the
islands of the Indian Archipelago, saves
the life of a Pirate, a man of savage but
noble nature. She becomes enamoured
of him ; and he, inconstant to his mortal
love, for a while returns her passion ; but
at length, recalling the memory of her
whom he left, and who laments his loss,
he escapes from the enchanted island
and returns to his lady. His mode of life
makes him again go to sea, and the
Enchantress seizes the opportunity to

bring him, by a spirit-brewed tempest, back to her island.

Scene, before the Cavern of the Indian Enchantress.
The Enchantress comes forth.

ENCHANTRESS.

He came like a dream in the dawn of life,
 He fled like a shadow before its noon ;
He is gone, and my peace is turned to strife,
 And I wander and wane like the weary moon.
  O sweet Echo, wake,
  And for my sake
Make answer the while my heart shall break !

But my heart has a music which Echo's lips,
 Though tender and true, yet can answer not,
And the shadow that moves in the soul's eclipse
 Can return not the kiss by his now forgot ;
  Sweet lips ! he who hath
  On my desolate path
Cast the darkness of absence, worse than death !

The Enchantress makes her spell ; she is answered by a Spirit.
 Spirit. Within the silent centre of the earth   \
My mansion is ; where I have lived insphered
From the beginning, and around my sleep
Have woven all the wondrous imagery
Of this dim spot, which mortals call the world
Infinite depths of unknown elements
Massed into one impenetrable mask ;
Sheets of immeasurable fire, and veins
Of gold, and stone, and adamantine iron.
And as a veil in which I walk through Heaven
I have wrought mountains, seas, waves, and clouds,
And lastly light, whose interfusion dawns
In the dark space of interstellar air.

A good Spirit, who watches over the Pirate's fate, leads, in a mysterious manner, the lady of his love to the Enchanted Isle. She is accompanied by a youth, who loves her, but whose passion she returns only with a sisterly affection. The ensuing scene takes place between them on their arrival at the Isle.

INDIAN YOUTH AND LADY

 Indian. And if my grief should still be dearer to me
Than all the pleasures in the world beside,
Why would you lighten it ?—
 Lady.   I offer only
That which I seek, some human sympathy
In this mysterious island.
 Indian.   Oh ! my friend,
My sister, my beloved ! What do I say ?
My brain is dizzy, and I scarce know whether
I speak to thee or her.
 Lady.   Peace, perturbed heart !
I am to thee only as thou to mine,
The passing wind which heals the brow at noon,
And may strike cold into the breast at night,
Yet cannot linger where it soothes the most,
Or long soothe could it linger.
 Indian.   But you said
You also loved ?
 Lady.   Loved ! Oh, I love.—
Methinks
This world of love is fit for all the world,
And that for gentle hearts another name '
Would speak of gentler thoughts than the world owns.
I have loved.
 Indian. And thou lovest not ?
If so
Young as thou art, thou canst afford to weep.
 Lady. Oh ! would that I could claim exemption
From all the bitterness of that sweet name.
I loved, I love, and when I love no more
Let joys and grief perish, and leave despair

To ring the knell of youth.   He stood
    beside me,
The embodied vision of the brightest
    dream,
Which like a dawn heralds the day of
    life;
The shadow of his presence made my
    world
A paradise.   All familiar things he
    touched,
All common words he spoke, became
    to me
Like forms and sounds of a diviner
    world.
He was as is the sun in his fierce youth,
As terrible and lovely as a tempest;
He came, and went, and left me what
    I am.
Alas! Why must I think how oft
    we two
Have sat together near the river
    springs,
Under the green pavilion which the
    willow
Spreads on the floor of the unbroken
    fountain, *   [there,
Strewn by the nurslings that linger
Over that islet paved with flowers
    and moss,
While the musk-rose leaves, like
    flakes of crimson snow,
Showered on us, and the dove mourned
    in the pine,
Sad prophetess of sorrows not her own.
    Indian. Your breath is like soft
    music, your words are
The echoes of a voice which on my
    heart
Sleeps like a melody of early days.
But as you said—
    Lady.   He was so awful, yet
So beautiful in mystery and terror,
Calming me as the loveliness of hea-
    ven
Soothes the unquiet sea :—and yet
    not so,
For he seemed stormy, and would
    often seem
A quenchless sun masked in porten-
    tous clouds ;
For such his thoughts, and even his
    actions were ;
But he was not of them, nor they of
    him,
But as they hid his splendour from
    the earth.

Some said he was a man of blood and
    peril,
And steeped in bitter infamy to the
    lips.
More need was there I should be inno-
    cent ;
More need that I should be most true
    and kind ;
And much more need that there
    should be found one
To share remorse, and scorn, and soli-
    tude,
And all the ills that wait on those who
    do
The tasks of ruin in the world of life.
He fled, and I have followed him.
    Indian.   Such a one
Is he who was the winter of my peace.
But, fairest stranger, when didst thou
    depart
From the far hills, where rise the
    springs of India,
How didst thou pass the intervening
    sea ?
    Lady. If I be sure I am not dream-
    ing now,
I should not doubt to say it was a
    dream.

A SONG

A WIDOW bird sate mourning for her
        love
    Upon a wintry bough ;
The frozen wind crept on above,
    The freezing stream below.

There was no leaf upon the forest bare,
    No flower upon the ground,
And little motion in the air
    Except the mill-wheel's sound.

TO JANE—THE INVITATION

BEST and brightest, come away,
Fairer far than this fair day,
Which like thee to those in sorrow,
Comes to bid a sweet good-morrow
To the rough year just awake
In its cradle on the brake.
The brightest hour of unborn spring,
Through the winter wandering,
Found it seems the halcyon morn,
To hoar February born ;
Bending from Heaven, in azure mirth,
It kissed the forehead of the earth,

And smiled upon the silent sea,
And bade the frozen streams be free ;
And waked to music all their foun-
    tains,
And breathed upon the frozen moun-
    tains,
And like a prophetess of May,
Strewed flowers upon the barren way,
Making the wintry world appear
Like one on whom thou smilest, dear.

Away, away, from men and towns,
To the wild wood and the downs—
To the silent wilderness
Where the soul need not repress
Its music, lest it should not find
An echo in another's mind,
While the touch of Nature's art
Harmonizes heart to heart.
I leaves this notice on my door
For each accustomed visitor :—
" I am gone into the fields
To take what this sweet hour yields:—
Reflection, you may come to-mor-
    row,
Sit by the fireside of Sorrow.—
You with the unpaid bill, Despair,
You, tiresome verse-reciter, Care,
I will pay you in the grave,
Death will listen to your stave.—
Expectation too, be off !
To-day is for itself enough ;
Hope in pity mock not woe
With smiles, nor follow where I go ;
Long having lived on thy sweet food,
At length I find one moment good
After long pain—with all your love,
This you never told me of."

Radiant Sister of the Day,
Awake ! arise ! and come away !
To the wild woods and the plains,
To the pools where winter rains
Image all their roof of leaves,
Where the pine its garland weaves
Of sapless green, and ivy dun,
Round stems that never kiss the sun,
Where the lawns and pastures be
And the sandhills of the sea,
Where the melting hoar-frost wets
The daisy-star that never sets,
And wind-flowers and violets,
Which yet join not scent to hue,
Crown the pale year weak and new ;
When the night is left behind
In the deep east, dim and blind,

And the blue noon is over us,
And the multitudinous
Billows murmur at our feet,
Where the earth and ocean meet,
And all things seem only one,
In the universal sun.

THE ISLE

THERE was a little lawny islet
By anemone and violet,
    Like mosaic, paven :
And its roof was flowers and leaves
Which the summer's breath enweaves,
Where nor sun nor showers nor breeze
Pierce the pines and tallest trees,
    Each a gem engraven.
Girt by many an azure wave
With which the clouds and moun-
        tains pave
    A lake's blue chasm.

TO JANE—THE RECOLLECTION

Now the last day of many days,
All beautiful and bright as thou,
The loveliest and the last, is dead,
Rise, Memory, and write its praise !
Up, do thy wonted work ! come, trace
The epitaph of glory fled,
For now the Earth has changed its
        face,
A frown is on the Heaven's brow.

I

We wandered to the Pine Forest
    That skirts the Ocean's foam,
The lightest wind was in its nest,
    The tempest in its home.
The whispering waves were half asleep,
    The clouds were gone to play,
And on the bosom of the deep,
    The smile of Heaven lay ;
It seemed as if the hour were one
    Sent from beyond the skies,
Which scattered from above the sun
    A light of Paradise.

II

We paused amid the pines that stood
    The giants of the waste,
Tortured by storms to shapes as rude
    As serpents interlaced.
And soothed by every azure breath,
    That under heaven is blown,
To harmonies and hues beneath,
    As tender as its own ;

Now all the tree tops lay asleep,
　Like green waves on the sea,
As still as in the silent deep
　The ocean woods may be.

III

How calm it was !—the silence there
　By such a chain was bound,
That even the busy woodpecker
　Made stiller by her sound
The inviolable quietness ;
　The breath of peace we drew
With its soft motion made not less
　The calm that round us grew.
There seemed from the remotest seat
　Of the wide mountain waste,
To the soft flower beneath our feet,
　A magic circle traced,
A spirit interfused around
　A thrilling silent life,
To momentary peace it bound
　Our mortal nature's strife ;—
And still I felt the centre of
　The magic circle there,
Was one fair form that filled with love
　The lifeless atmosphere.

IV

We paused beside the pools that lie
　Under the forest bough,
Each seemed as 'twere a little sky
　Gulfed in a world below ;
A firmament of purple light,
　Which in the dark earth lay,
More boundless than the depth of
　night,
And purer than the day—
In which the lovely forests grew,
　As in the upper air,
More perfect both in shape and hue
　Than any spreading there.
There lay the glade and neighbouring
　lawn,
And through the dark-green wood
The white sun twinkling like the
　dawn
　Out of a speckled cloud.
Sweet views which in our world above
　Can never well be seen,
Were imaged by the water's love
　Of that fair forest green.
And all was interfused beneath
　With an Elysian glow,
An atmosphere without a breath,
　A softer day below.

Like one beloved, the scene had lent
　To the dark water's breast,
Its every leaf and lineament
　With more than truth expressed,
Until an envious wind crept by,
　Like an unwelcome thought,
Which from the mind's too faithful eye
　Blots one dear image out.
Though thou art ever fair and kind,
　The forests ever green,
Less oft is peace in Shelley's mind,
　Than calm in waters seen.

A DIRGE

Rough wind, that moanest loud
　Grief too sad for song ;
Wild wind, when sullen cloud
　Knells all the night long ;
Sad storm, whose tears are vain,
Bare woods, whose branches stain,
Deep caves and dreary main,
　Wail, for the world's wrong !

THE TRIUMPH OF LIFE

Swift as a spirit hastening to his task
Of glory and of good, the Sun sprang
　forth
Rejoicing in his splendour, and the
　mask

Of darkness fell from the awakened
　Earth—
The smokeless altars of the mountain
　snows
Flamed above crimson clouds, and at
　the birth

Of light, the Ocean's orison arose,
To which the birds tempered their
　matin lay.
All flowers in field or forest which un-
　close

Their trembling eyelids to the kiss of
　day,
Swinging their censers in the element,
With orient incense lit by the new ray

Burned slow and inconsumably, and
　sent
Their odorous sighs up to the smiling
　air ;
And, in succession due, did continent,

Isle, ocean, and all things that in them
wear

The form and character of mortal
mould,

Rise as the sun their father rose, to
bear

Their portion of the toil, which he of
old

Took as his own and then imposed
on them ;

But I, whom thoughts which must
remain untold

Had kept as wakeful as the stars that
gem

The cone of night, now they were laid
asleep

Stretched my faint limbs beneath the
hoary stem

Which an old chestnut flung athwart
the steep

Of a green Apennine : before me fled

The night ; behind me rose the day ;
the deep

Was at my feet, and Heaven above
my head,

When a strange trance over my fancy
grew

Which was not slumber, for the shade
it spread

Was so transparent that the scene
came through

As clear as, when a veil of light is
drawn

O'er evening hills, they glimmer ; and
I knew

That I had felt the freshness of that
dawn

Bathe in the same cold dew my brow
and hair,

And sate as thus upon that slope of
lawn

Under the selfsame bough, and heard
as there

The birds, the fountains, and the
ocean hold

Sweet talk in music through the enamoured air,

And then a vision on my brain was
rolled.

As in that trance of wondrous thought
I lay,

This was the tenour of my waking
dream :—

Methought I sate beside a public way

Thick strewn with summer dust, and a
great stream

Of people there was hurrying to and
fro,

Numerous as gnats upon the evening
gleam,

All hastening onward, yet none seemed
to know

Whither he went, or whence he came,
or why

He made one of the multitude, and so

Was borne amid the crowd, as through
the sky

One of the million leaves of summer's
bier ;

Old age and youth, manhood and infancy,

Mixed in one mighty torrent did appear :

Some flying from the thing they
feared, and some

Seeking the object of another's fear ;

And others as with steps towards the
tomb,

Pored on the trodden worms that
crawled beneath,

And others mournfully within the
gloom

Of their own shadow walked and
called it death ;

And some fled from it as it were a
ghost,

Half fainting in the affliction of vain
breath :

But more, with motions which each
other crossed,

Pursued or spurned the shadows the
clouds threw

Or birds within the noonday ether
lost,

Upon that path where flowers never
grew,—

And weary with vain toil and faint for
   thirst,
Heard not the fountains, whose melodious dew

Out of their mossy cells for ever burst;
Nor felt the breeze which from the
   forest told
Of grassy paths and wood, lawn-
   interspersed,

With over-arching elms and caverns
   cold,
And violet banks where sweet dreams
   brood, but they
Pursued their serious folly as of old.

And as I gazed, methought that in
   the way
The throng grew wilder, as the woods
   of June
When the south wind shakes the extinguished day,

And a cold glare intenser than the
   noon,
But icy cold, obscured with blinding
   light
The sun, as he the stars. Like the
   young moon

When on the sunlit limits of the night
Her white shell trembles amid crimson air,
And whilst the sleeping tempest
   gathers might,

Doth, as the herald of its coming, bear
The ghost of its dead mother, whose
   dim form
Bends in dark ether from her infant's
   chair,—

So came a chariot on the silent storm
Of its own rushing splendour, and a
   Shape
So sate within, as one whom years
   deform,

Beneath a dusky hood and double
   cape,
Crouching within the shadow of a
   tomb;
And o'er what seemed the head a
   cloud-like crape

Was bent, a dun and faint ethereal
   gloom
Tempering the light: upon the
   chariot beam
A Janus-visaged shadow did assume

The guidance of that wonder-winged
   team;
The shapes which drew it in thick
   lightnings
Were lost:—I heard alone on the air's
   soft stream

The music of their ever-moving wings.
All the four faces of that charioteer
Had their eyes banded; little profit
   brings

Speed in the van and blindness in the
   rear,
Nor then avail the beams that quench
   the sun
Or that with banded eyes could pierce
   the sphere

Of all that is, has been, or will be
   done;
So ill was the car guided—but it
   passed
With solemn speed majestically on.

The crowd gave way, and I arose
   aghast,
Or seemed to rise, so mighty was the
   trance,
And saw like clouds upon the thunder's blast,

The million with fierce song and
   maniac dance
Raging around—such seemed the
   jubilee
As when, to meet some conqueror's
   advance,

Imperial Rome poured forth her living sea
From senate-house, and forum, and
   theatre,
When [   ] upon the free

Had bound a yoke, which soon they
   stooped to bear.
Nor wanted here the just similitude
Of a triumphal pageant, for where'er

The chariot rolled, a captive multitude

Was driven ;—all those who had
    grown old in power
Or misery,—all who had their age
    subdued

By action or by suffering, and whose
    hour
Was drained to its last sand in weal or
    woe,
So that the trunk survived both fruit
    and flower :—

All those whose fame or infamy must
    grow
Till the great winter lay the form and
    name
Of this green earth with them for ever
    low ;—

All but the sacred few who could not
    tame
Their spirits to the conquerors—but
    as soon
As they had touched the world with
    living flame,

Fled back like eagles to their native
    noon,
Or those who put aside the diadem
Of earthly thrones or gems [   ]

Were there, of Athens or Jerusalem
Were neither 'mid the mighty cap-
    tives seen,
Nor 'mid the ribald crowd that fol-
    lowed them,

Nor those who went before fierce and
    obscene.
The wild dance maddens in the van,
    and those
Who lead it—fleet as shadows on the
    green,

Outspeed the chariot, and without
    repose
Mix with each other in tempestuous
    measure
To savage music, wilder as it grows,

They, tortured by their agonizing
    pleasure,
Convulsed and on the rapid whirl-
    winds spun
Of that fierce spirit whose unholy
    leisure

Was soothed by mischief since the
    world begun,—
Throw back their heads and loose
    their streaming hair ;
And in their dance round her who
    dims the sun,

Maidens and youths fling their wild
    arms in air ;
As their feet twinkle they recede, and
    now
Bending within each other's atmo-
    sphere

Kindle invisibly—and as they glow,
Like moths by light attracted and
    repelled,
Oft to their bright destruction come
    and go,

Till like two clouds into one vale im-
    pelled
That shake the mountains when their
    lightnings mingle
And die in rain—the fiery band which
    held

Their natures, snaps—the shock still
    may tingle,
One falls and then another in the path
Senseless—nor is the desolation
    single,

Yet ere I can say *where*—the chariot
    hath
Passed over them, nor other trace I
    find
But as of foam after the ocean's
    wrath

Is spent upon the desert shore ;—be-
    hind,
Old men and women foully disarrayed,
Shake their grey hairs in the insulting
    wind,

And follow in the dance, with limbs
    decayed,
Seeking to reach the light which
    leaves them still
Farther behind and deeper in the
    shade.

But not the less with impotence of
    will
They wheel, though ghastly shadows
    interpose

Round them and round each other,
  and fulfil

Their part, and in the dust from
  whence they rose
Sink, and corruption veils them as
  they lie,
And past in these performs what
  [   ] in those.

Struck to the heart by this sad page-
  antry,
Half to myself I said—"And what
  is this ?
Whose shape is that within the car ?
  And why "—

I would have added—" is all here
  amiss ? "—
But a voice answered—" Life ! "—I
  turned, and knew
(O Heaven, have mercy on such
  wretchedness !)

That what I thought was an old root
  which grew
To strange distortion out of the hill
  side,
Was indeed one of those deluded
  crew,

And that the grass, which methought
  hung so wide
And white, was but his thin discoloured hair,
And that the holes it vainly sought to
  hide,

Were or had been eyes :—" If thou
  canst, forbear
To join the dance, which I had well
  forborne ! "
Said the grim Feature (of my thought
  aware) ;

" I will unfold that which to this deep
  scorn
Led me and my companions, and relate
The progress of the pageant since the
  morn ;

" If thirst of knowledge shall not then
  abate,
Follow it thou even to the night,
  but I

Am weary."—Then like one who with
  the weight
Of his own words is staggered, wearily
He paused ; and, ere he could resume,
  I cried,
" First, who art thou ? "—" Before
  thy memory,

" I feared, loved, hated, suffered, did
  and died,
And if the spark with which Heaven
  lit my spirit
Had been with purer sentiment sup-
  plied,

" Corruption would not now thus
  much inherit
Of what was once Rousseau,—nor
  this disguise
Stained that which ought to have disdained to wear it ;

" If I have been extinguished, yet
  there rise
A thousand beacons from the spark I
  bore "—
" And who are those chained to the
  car ? "—" The wise,

" The great, the unforgotten,—they
  who wore
Mitres and helms and crowns, or
  wreaths of light,
Signs of thought's empire over
  thought—their lore

" Taught them not this, to know
  themselves ; their might
Could not repress the mystery within,
And for the morn of truth they
  feigned, deep night

" Caught them ere evening."—"Who
  is he with chin
Upon his breast, and hands crossed
  on his chain ? "—
" The child of a fierce hour ; he sought
  to win

" The world, and lost all that it did
  contain
Of greatness, in its hope destroyed ;
  and more
Of fame and peace than virtue's self
  can gain

" Without the opportunity which bore
Him on his eagle pinions to the peak
From which a thousand climbers have
　　before

" Fallen, as Napoleon fell."—I felt
　　my check
Alter to see the shadow pass away,
Whose grasp had left the giant world
　　so weak,

That every pigmy kicked it as it lay ;
And much I grieved to think how
　　power and will
In opposition rule our mortal day,

And why God made irreconcilable
Good and the means of good ; and for
　　despair
I half disdained mine eyes' desire to
　　fill

With the spent vision of the times
　　that were
And scarce have ceased to be.—" Dost
　　thou behold,"
Said my guide, " those spoilers
　　spoiled, Voltaire,

" Frederick, and Paul, Catherine, and
　　Leopold,
And hoary anarchs, demagogues, and
　　sage—
——names which the world thinks
　　always old ?

" For in the battle life and they did
　　wage,
She remained' conqueror. I was
　　overcome
By my own heart alone, which neither
　　age,

" Nor tears, nor infamy, nor now the
　　tomb
Could temper to its object."—" Let
　　them pass,"
I cried, " the world and its mysteri-
　　ous doom

" Is not so much more glorious than it
　　was,
That I desire to worship those who
　　drew
New figures on its false and fragile
　　glass

" As the old faded."—" Figures ever
　　new
Rise on the bubble, paint them as
　　you may ;
We have but thrown, as those before
　　us threw,

"Our shadows on it as it passed away.
But mark how chained to the trium-
　　phal chair
The mighty phantoms of an elder day ;

" All that is mortal of great Plato
　　there
Expiates the joy and woe his master
　　knew not :
The star that ruled his doom was far
　　too fair,

" And life, where long that flower of
　　Heaven grew not,
Conquered that heart by love, which
　　gold, or pain,
Or age, or sloth, or slavery could sub-
　　due not.

" And near him walk the [　　　]
　　twain,
The tutor and his pupil, whom Do-
　　minion
Followed as tame as vulture in a
　　chain.

" The world was darkened beneath
　　either pinion
Of him whom from the flock of con-
　　querors
Fame singled out for her thunder-
　　bearing minion ;

" The other long outlived both woes
　　and wars,
Throned in the thoughts of men, and
　　still had kept
The jealous key of truth's eternal
　　doors,

" If Bacon's eagle spirit had not lept
Like lightning out of darkness—he
　　compelled
The Proteus shape of Nature as it
　　slept

" To wake, and lead him to the caves
　　that held

The treasure of the secrets of its
reign.
See the great bards of elder time,
who quelled

" The passions which they sung, as
by their strain
May well be known : their living
melody
Tempers its own contagion to the vein

" Of those who are infected with it—I
Have suffered what I wrote, or viler
pain.
And so my words have seeds of misery ! "——

[There is a chasm here in the MS. which it
is impossible to fill up. It appears from
the context, that other shapes pass, and
that Rousseau still stood beside the
dreamer, as]

———— he pointed to a company,
'Midst whom I quickly recognised the
heirs
Of Cæsar's crime, from him to Con-
stantine ;
The anarch chiefs, whose force and
murderous snares

Had founded many a sceptre-bearing
line,
And spread the plague of gold and
blood abroad :
And Gregory and John, and men divine,

Who rose like shadows between
man and God ;
Till that eclipse, still hanging over
heaven,
Was worshipped by the world o'er
which they strode,

For the true sun it quenched—
" Their power was given
But to destroy," replied the leader :—
" I
Am one of those who have created,
even

If it be but a world of agony."—
" Whence comest thou ? and whither
goest thou ?
How did thy course begin ? " I said,
" and why ?

" Mine eyes are sick of this perpetual
flow
Of people, and my heart sick of one
sad thought—
Speak ! "—" Whence I am, I partly
seem to know,

" And how and by what paths I have
been brought
To this dread pass, methinks even
thou mayst guess ;—
Why this should be, my mind can
compass not ;

" Whither the conqueror hurries me,
still less ;—
But follow thou, and from spectator
turn
Actor or victim in this wretchedness,

" And what thou wouldst be taught I
then may learn
From thee. Now listen :—In the
April prime,
When all the forest tips began to burn

" With kindling green, touched by
the azure clime
Of the young year's dawn, I was laid
asleep
Under a mountain, which from unknown time

" Had yawned into a cavern, high
and deep ;
And from it came a gentle rivulet,
Whose water, like clear air, in its
calm sweep

" Bent the soft grass, and kept for
ever wet
The stems of the sweet flowers, and
filled the grove
With sounds, which whoso hears
must needs forget

" All pleasure and all pain, all hate
and love,
Which they had known before that
hour of rest ;
A sleeping mother then would dream
not of

" Her only child who died upon her
breast

At eventide—a king would mourn no
    more
The crown of which his brows were
    dispossessed

" When the sun lingered o'er his
    ocean floor
To gild his rival's new prosperity.
Thou wouldst forget thus vainly to
    deplore

" Ills, which if ills can find no cure
    from thee,
The thought of which no other sleep
    will quell,
Nor other music blot from memory,

" So sweet and deep is the oblivious
    spell ;
And whether life had been before that
    sleep
The heaven which I imagine, or a hell

" Like this harsh world in which I
    wake to weep,
I know not.   I arose, and for a space
The scene of woods and waters seem
    to keep,

" Though it was now broad day, a
    gentle trace
Of light diviner than the common sun
Sheds on the common earth, and all
    the place

" Was filled with magic sounds woven
    into one
Oblivious melody, confusing sense
Amid the gliding waves and shadows
    dun ;

" And, as I looked, the bright omni-
    presence
Of morning through the orient cavern
    flowed,
And the sun's image radiantly in-
    tense

" Burned on the waters of the well
    that glowed
Like gold, and threaded all the for-
    est's maze
With winding paths of emerald fire ;
    there stood

" Amid the sun,—as he amid the
    blaze
Of his own glory, on the vibrating
Floor of the fountain paved with
    flashing rays,—

" A Shape all light, which with one
    hand did fling
Dew on the earth, as if she were the
    dawn,
And the invisible rain did ever sing

" A silver music on the mossy lawn ;
And still before me on the dusky
    grass,
Iris her many-coloured scarf had
    drawn :

" In her right hand she bore a crystal
    glass,
Mantling with bright Nepenthe ; the
    fierce splendour
Fell from her as she moved under
    the mass

" Out of the deep cavern, with palms
    so tender,
Their tread broke not the mirror of
    its billow ;
She glided along the river, and did
    bend her

" Head under the dark boughs, till,
    like a willow,
Her fair hair swept the bosom of the
    stream
That whispered with delight to be its
    pillow.

" As one enamoured is upborne in
    dream
O'er lily-paven lakes 'mid silver mist,
To wondrous music, so this shape
    might seem

" Partly to tread the waves with feet
    which kissed
The dancing foam ; partly to glide
    along
The air which roughened the moist
    amethyst,

" Or the faint morning beams that fell
    among
The trees, or the soft shadows of the
    trees ;

And her feet, ever to the ceaseless
  song

" Of leaves, and winds, and waves,
    and birds, and bees,
And falling drops moved to a measure
    new,
Yet sweet, as on the summer evening
    breeze,

" Up from the lake a shape of golden
    dew
Between two rocks, athwart the ris-
    ing moon,
Dances i' the wind, where never eagle
    flew ;

" And still her feet, no less than the
    sweet tune
To which they moved, seemed as they
    moved to blot
The thoughts of him who gazed on
    them ; and soon

" All that was, seemed as if it had
    been not ;
And all the gazer's mind was strewn
    beneath
Her feet like embers ; and she, thought
    by thought,

" Trampled its sparks into the dust of
    death,
As day upon the threshold of the east
Treads out the lamps of night, until
    the breath

" Of darkness re-illumine even the
    least
Of heaven's living eyes !—like day she
    came,
Making the night a dream ; and ere
    she ceased

" To move, as one between desire and
    shame
Suspended, I said—' If, as it doth
    seem,
Thou comest from the realm without
    a name,

" ' Into this valley of perpetual dream
Show whence I came, and where I
    am, and why—
Pass not away upon the passing
    stream.'

" ' Arise and quench thy thirst,' was
    her reply,
And as a shut lily, stricken by the
    wand
Of dewy morning's vital alchemy,

" I rose ; and, bending at her sweet
    command,
Touched with faint lips the cup she
    raised,
And suddenly my brain became as
    sand,

" Where the first wave had more than
    half erased
The track of deer on desert Labrador ;
Whilst the wolf, from which they fled
    amazed,

" Leaves his stamp visibly upon the
    shore,
Until the second bursts ;—so on my
    sight
Burst a new vision, never seen before,

" And the fair shape waned in the
    coming light,
As veil by veil the silent splendour
    drops
From Lucifer, amid the chrysolite

" Of sunrise, ere it tinge the moun-
    tain tops ;
And as the presence of that fairest
    planet,
Although unseen, is felt by one who
    hopes

" That his day's path may end, as he
    began it,
In that star's smile, whose light is like
    the scent
Of a jonquil when evening breezes fan
    it,

" Or the soft note in which his dear
    lament
The Brescian shepherd breathes, or
    the caress
That turned his weary slumber to
    content ; [1]

" So knew I in that light's severe
    excess

[1] The favourite song, " Stanco di pascolar le
pecorelle," is a Brescian national air.

The presence of that shape which on
    the stream
Moved, as I moved along the wilder-
    ness,

" More dimly than a day-appearing
    dream,
The ghost of a forgotten form of sleep ;
A light of heaven, whose half-extin-
    guished beam

" Through the sick day in which we
    wake to weep,
Glimmers, for ever sought, for ever
    lost ;
So did that shape its obscure tenour
    keep

" Beside my path, as silent as a ghost;
But the new Vision, and the cold
    bright car,
With solemn speed and stunning
    music, crossed

" The forest, and as if from some
    dread war
Triumphantly returning, the loud
    million
Fiercely extolled the fortune of her
    star.

" A moving arch of victory, the ver-
    milion
And green and azure plumes of Iris
    had
Built high over her wind-winged
    pavilion,

" And underneath ethereal glory clad
The wilderness, and far before her
    flew
The tempest of the splendour, which
    forbade

" Shadow to fall from leaf and stone ;
    the crew
Seemed in that light, like atomies to
    dance
Within a sunbeam ;—some upon the
    new

" Embroidery of flowers, that did en-
    hance
The grassy vesture of the desert,
    played,

Forgetful of the chariot's swift ad
    vance ;

" Others stood gazing, till within the
    shade
Of the great mountain its light left
    them dim ;
Others outspeeded it ; and others
    made

"Circles around it, like the clouds
    that swim
Round the high moon in a bright sea
    of air ;
And more did follow, with exulting
    hymn,

" The chariot and the captives fet-
    tered there :
But all like bubbles on an eddying
    flood
Fell into the same track at last, and
    were

" Borne onward. I among the multi-
    tude
Was swept—me, sweetest flowers
    delayed not long ;
Me, not the shadow nor the solitude ;

" Me, not that falling stream's Le-
    thean song ;
Me, not the phantom of that early
    form,
Which moved upon its motion—but
    among

" The thickest billows of that living
    storm
I plunged, and bared my bosom to
    the clime
Of that cold light, whose airs too soon
    deform.

" Before the chariot had begun to
    climb
The opposing steep of that mysterious
    dell,
Behold a wonder worthy of the rhyme

" Of him who from the lowest depths
    of hell,
Through every paradise and through
    all glory,
Love led serene, and who returned to
    tell

" The words of hate and care ; the
 wondrous story
How all things are transfigured except Love ;
(For deaf as is a sea, which wrath
 makes hoary,

" The world can hear not the sweet
 notes that move
The sphere whose light is melody to
 lovers)
A wonder worthy of his rhyme—the
 grove

" Grew dense with shadows to its inmost covers,
The earth was grey with phantoms,
 and the air
Was peopled with dim forms, as when
 there hovers

" A flock of vampire-bats before the
 glare
Of the tropic sun, bringing, ere evening,
Strange night upon some Indian vale ;
 —thus were

" Phantoms diffused around ; and
 some did fling
Shadows of shadows, yet unlike themselves,
Behind them ; some like eaglets on
 the wing

" Were lost in the white day ; others
 like elves
Danced in a thousand unimagined
 shapes
Upon the sunny streams and grassy
 shelves ;

" And others sate chattering like restless apes
On vulgar hands, [   ]
Some made a cradle of the ermined
 capes

" Of kingly mantles ; some across the
 tire
Of pontiffs rode, like demons ; others
 played
Under the crown which girt with
 empire

" A baby's or an idiot's brow, and
 made
Their nests in it.   The old anatomies
Sate hatching their bare broods under
 the shade

" Of demon wings, and laughed from
 their dead eyes
To re-assume the delegated power,
Arrayed in which those worms did
 monarchise,

" Who made this earth their charnel.
 Others more
Humble, like falcons, sat upon the fist
Of common men, and round their
 heads did soar ;

" Or like small gnats and flies, as
 thick as mist
On evening marshes, thronged about
 the brow
Of lawyers, statesmen, priest, and
 theorist ;—

" And others, like discoloured flakes
 of snow
On fairest bosoms and the sunniest
 hair,
Fell, and were melted by the youthful
 glow

" Which they extinguished ; and, like
 tears, they were
A veil to those from whose faint lids
 they rained
In drops of sorrow.   I became aware

" Of whence those forms proceeded
 which thus stained
The track in which we moved.   After
 brief space,
From every form the beauty slowly
 waned ;

" From every firmest limb and fairest
 face
The strength and freshness fell like
 dust, and left
The action and the shape without the
 grace

" Of life.   The marble brow of youth
 was cleft
With care ; and in those eyes where
 once hope shone,
Desire. like a lioness bereft

" Of her last cub, glared ere it died ;
   each one
Of that great crowd sent forth
   incessantly
These shadows, numerous as the dead
   leaves blown

" In autumn evening from a poplar
   tree,
Each like himself and like each other
   were
At first ; but some distorted seemed
   to be,—

" Obscure clouds, moulded by the
   casual air ;
And of this stuff the car's creative ray
Wrapt all the busy phantoms that
   were there,

" As the sun shapes the clouds. Thus
   on the way
Mask after mask fell from the countenance
And form of all ; and long before the
   day

" Was old, the joy which waked like
   heaven's glance
The sleepers in the oblivious valley
   died ;
And some grew weary of the ghastly
   dance,

" And fell, as I have fallen, by the
   wayside ;—
Those soonest from whose forms most
   shadows pâssed,
And least of strength and beauty did
   abide."

" Then, what is life ? " I cried.—

TO JANE

THE keen stars were twinkling,
And the fair moon was rising among
   them,
     Dear Jane !
The guitar was tinkling,
But the notes were not sweet till you
   sung them
     Again.
As the moon's soft splendour

O'er the faint cold starlight of heaven
     Is thrown,
So your voice most tender
To the strings without soul had then
     given
     Its own.

The stars will awaken,
Though the moon sleep a full hour
     later,
     To-night ;
No leaf will be shaken
Whilst the dews of your melody scat-
     ter
     Delight.
Though the sound overpowers,
Sing again, with your dear voice re-
     vealing
     A tone
Of some world far from ours,
Where music and moonlight and feel-
     ing
     Are one.

LINES WRITTEN IN THE BAY OF LERICI

SHE left me at the silent time
When the moon had ceased to climb
The azure path of heaven's steep,
And, like an albatross asleep,
Balanced on her wings of light,
Hovered in the purple night,
Ere she sought her ocean nest
In the chambers of the west.
She left me ; and I stayed alone,
Thinking over every tone,
Which, though silent to the ear,
The enchanted heart could hear,
Like notes which die when born, but
   still
Haunt the echoes of the hill,
And feeling ever—Oh, too much !—
The soft vibration of her touch,
As if her gentle hand even now
Lightly trembled on my brow.
And thus, although she absent were,
Memory gave me all of her
That even Fancy dares to claim.
Her presence had made weak and
   tame
All passions, and I lived alone
In the time which is our own ;
The past and future were forgot,
As they had been, and would be, not.

But soon, the guardian angel gone,
The dæmon reassumed his throne
In my faint heart.   I dare not speak
My thoughts ; but thus disturbed and
    weak
I sat, and saw the vessels glide
Over the ocean bright and wide,
Like spirit-wingèd chariots sent
O'er some serenest element
For ministrations strange and far,
As if to some Elysian star
They sailed for drink to medicine
Such sweet and bitter pain as mine.
And the wind that winged their flight

From the land came fresh and light ;
And the scent of wingèd flowers,
And the coolness of the hours
Of dew, and sweet warmth left by day,
Were scattered o'er the twinkling bay ;
And the fisher, with his lamp
And spear, about the low rocks damp
Crept, and struck the fish which came
To worship the delusive flame.
Too happy they, whose pleasure
    sought
Extinguishes all sense and thought
Of the regret that pleasure leaves,--
Destroying life alone, not peace !

FRAGMENTS [1]

1

TO ——

HERE, my dear friend, is a new book
    for you ;
I have already dedicated two
To other friends, one female and one
    male,
What you are, is a thing that I must
    veil ;
What can this be to those who praise
    or rail
I never was attached to that great sect
Whose doctrine is that each one
    should select
Out of the world a mistress or a friend,
And all the rest, though fair and wise,
    commend
To cold oblivion—though it is the
    code
Of modern morals, and the beaten
    road
Which those poor slaves with weary
    footsteps tread
Who travel to their home among the
    dead,
By the broad highway of the world—
    and so

With one sad friend, and many a
    jealous foe,
The dreariest and the longest journey
    go.

Free love has this, different from gold
    and clay
That to divide is not to take away.
Like ocean, which the general north
    wind breaks
Into ten thousand waves, and each
    one makes
A mirror of the moon ; like some great
    glass,
Which did distort whatever form
    might pass,
Dashed into fragments by a playful
    child,
Which then reflects its eyes and fore-
    head mild,
Giving for one, which it could ne'er
    express,
A thousand images of loveliness.

If I were one whom the loud world
    held wise,
I should disdain to quote authorities

[1] These fragments do not properly belong to the poems of 1822. They are gleanings from Shelley's manuscript books and papers ; preserved not only because they are beautiful in themselves, but as affording indications of his feelings and virtues.

In the support of this kind of love ;—
Why there is first the God in heaven
    above,
Who wrote a book called Nature, 'tis
    to be
Reviewed I hear in the next *Quar-
    terly* ;
And Socrates, the Jesus Christ of
    Greece ;
And Jesus Christ himself did never
    cease
To urge all living things to love each
    other,
And to forgive their mutual faults,
    and smother
The Devil of disunion in their souls.

   *   *   *

It is a sweet thing, friendship, a dear
    balm,
A happy and auspicious bird of calm,
Which rides o'er life's ever tumultu-
    ous Ocean ;
A God that broods o'er chaos in com-
    motion ;
A flower which fresh as Lapland roses
    are,
Lifts its bold head into the world's
    pure air,
And blooms most radiantly when
    others die,
Health, hope, and youth, and brief
    prosperity
And, with the light and odour of its
    bloom,
Shining within the dungeon and the
    tomb ;
Whose coming is as light and music
    are
'Mid dissonance and gloom—a star
Which moves not 'mid the moving
    heavens alone,
A smile among dark frowns—a gentle
    tone
Among rude voices, a beloved light,
A solitude, a refuge, a delight.

If I had but a friend ! why I have
    three,
Even by my own confession ; there
    may be
Some more, for what I know ; for 'tis
    my mind
To call my friends all who are wise and
    kind,
And these, Heaven knows, at best
    are very few,

But none can ever be more dear than
    you.
Why should they be ? my muse has
    lost her wings,
Or, like a dying swan, who soars and
    sings,
I should describe you in heroic style,
But as it is—are you not void of guile?
A lovely soul, formed to be blessed
    and bless ;
A well of sealed and secret happiness ;
A lute, which those whom love has
    taught to play
Make music on, to cheer the roughest
    day ?

   *   *   *

II

TO WILLIAM SHELLEY

Thy little footsteps on the sands
    Of a remote and lonely shore ;
The twinkling of thine infant hands
    Where now the worm will feed no
        more :
        Thy mingled look of love and glee
        When we returned to gaze on
        thee.

III

And who feels discord now or sorrow ;
    Love is the universe to-day—
These are the slaves of dim to-
    morrow,
    Darkening Life's labyrinthine way.

IV

A gentle story of two lovers young,
    Who met in innocence and died in
        sorrow,
And of one selfish heart, whose ran-
    cour clung
        Like curses on them ; are ye slow to
            borrow
        The lore of truth from such a
            tale ?
        Or in this world's deserted vale,
        Do ye not see a star of gladness
        Pierce the shadows of its sadness,
When ye are cold, that love is a light
    sent
From heaven, which none shall
    quench, to cheer the innocent ?

V

I am drunk with the honey wine
Of the moon-unfolded eglantine,

Which fairies catch in hyacinth
     buds :—
The bats, the dormice, and the moles
Sleep in the walls or under the sward
Of the desolate Castle yard ;
And when 'tis spilt on the summer
     earth,
Or its fumes arise among the dew,
Their jocund dreams are full of mirth,
They gibber their joy in sleep ; for few
Of the fairies bear those bowls so new !

VI

YE gentle visitations of calm
     thought—
   Moods like the memories of happier
     earth,
   Which come arrayed in thoughts of
     little worth,
Like stars in clouds by the weak
     winds enwrought,
   But that the clouds depart and
     stars remain,
   While they remain, and ye, alas,
     depart !

VII

   THE world is dreary,
   And I am weary
Of wandering on without thee, Mary ;
   A joy was crewhile
   In thy voice and thy smile,
And 'tis gone, when I should be gone
     too, Mary.
   1819.

VIII

MY dearest Mary, wherefore hast
     thou gone,
And left me in this dreary world
     alone !
Thy form is here indeed—a lovely
     one—
But thou art fled, gone down the
     dreary road,
That leads to Sorrow's most obscure
     abode ;
Thou sittest on the hearth of pale
     despair,
          Where
For thine own sake I cannot follow
     thee.
   1819.

IX

WHEN a lover clasps his fairest,
Then be our dread sport the rarest.

Their caresses were like the chaff
In the tempest, and be our laugh
His despair—her epitaph !

When a mother clasps her child,
Watch till dusty Death has piled
His cold ashes on the clay ;
She has loved it many a day—
She remains,—it fades away.

x

ONE sung of thee who left the tale
     untold,
   Like the false dawns which perish in
     the bursting :
Like empty cups of wrought and dæ-
     dal gold,
   Which mock the lips with air, when
     they are thirsting.

XI

AND where is truth ?   On tombs ? for
     such to thee
Has been my heart—and thy dead
     memory
Has lain from childhood, many a
     changeful year—
Unchangingly preserved and buried
     there.

XII

IN the cave which wild weeds cover
Wait for thine ethereal lover ;
For the pallid moon is waning,
O'er the spiral cypress hanging
And the moon no cloud is staining.

It was once a Roman's chamber,
Where he kept his darkest revels,
And the wild weeds twine and clam-
     ber ;
It was then a chasm for devils.

XIII

THERE is a warm and gentle atmo-
     sphere   [thus
About the form of one we love, and
As in a tender mist our spirits are
Wrapt in the —— of that which is to
     us
The health of life's own life.

XIV

How sweet it is to sit and read the
     tales
Of mighty poets, and to hear the
     while

Sweet music, which when the attention fails
Fills the dim pause——

XV

WHAT men gain fairly—that they
should possess
And children may inherit idleness,
From him who earns it—This is
understood ;
Private injustice may be general good.
But he who gains by base and armed
wrong,
Or guilty fraud, or base compliances,
May be despoiled ; even as a stolen
dress
Is stript from a convicted thief, and
he
Left in the nakedness of infamy.

XVI

WAKE the serpent not—lest he
Should not know the way to go,—
Let him crawl which yet lies sleeping
Through the deep grass of the mea-
dow !
Not a bee shall hear him creeping,
Not a Mayfly shall awaken,
From its cradling bluebell shaken,
Not the starlight as he's sliding
Through the glass with silent gliding.

XVII

ROME has fallen, ye see it lying
Heaped in undistinguished ruin :
Nature is alone undying.

XVIII

THE fitful alternations of the rain,
When the chill wind, languid as with
pain
Of its own heavy moisture, here and
there
Drives through the grey and beamless
atmosphere.

XIX

I WOULD not be a king—enough
Of woe it is to love !
The path to power is steep and rough,
And tempests reign above.

I would not climb the imperial
throne ;
Tis built on ice which fortune's sun
Thaws in the height of noon.

Then farewell, king, yet were I one,
Care would not come so soon.
Would he and I were far away
Keeping flocks on Himelay !

XX

O THOU immortal deity
Whose throne is in the depth of hu-
man thought,
I do adjure thy power and thee
By all that man may be, by all that
he is not,
By all that he has been and yet
must be !

XXI

HE wanders, like a day-appearing
dream,
Through the dim wildernesses of
the mind ;
Through desert woods and tracts,
which seem
Like ocean, homeless, boundless,
unconfined.

XXII

ON KEATS

WHO DESIRED THAT ON HIS TOMB
SHOULD BE INSCRIBED—

" Here lieth One whose name was
writ on water ! "
But ere the breath that could erase it
blew,
Death, in remorse for that fell slaugh-
ter,
Death, the immortalising winter flew,
Athwart the stream, and time's
monthless torrent grew
A scroll of crystal, blazoning the
name
Of Adonaïs !——

XXIII

THE rude wind is singing
The dirge of the music dead,
The cold worms are clinging
Where kisses were lately fed.

XXIV

WHAT art thou, Presumptuous, who
profanest
The wreath to mighty poets only
due,

Even whilst like a forgotten moon
  thou wanest ?
  Touch not those leaves which for
  the eternal few,
Who wander o'er the paradise of fame,
  In sacred dedication ever grew,—
One of the crowd thou art without a
  name.
Ah, friend, 'tis the false laurel that I
  wear ;
  Bright though it seem, it is not the
  same
As that which bound Milton's immor-
  tal hair ;
  Its dew is poison and the hopes
  that quicken
Under its chilling shade, though seem-
  ing fair,
  Are flowers which die almost before
  they sicken.

XXV

WHEN soft winds and sunny skies
With the green earth harmonize,
And the young and dewy dawn,
Bold as an unhunted fawn,
Up the windless heaven is gone—
Laugh—for ambushed in the day,
Clouds and whirlwinds watch their
  prey.

XXVI

THE babe is at peace within the womb
The corpse is at rest within the tomb,
  We begin in what we end.

XXVII

EPITAPH

THESE are two friends whose lives
  were undivided ;
So let their memory be, now they
  have glided
Under their grave ; let not their bones
  be parted,
For their two hearts in life were single-
  hearted.

XXVIII

OTHO

THOU wert not, Cassius, and thou
  couldst not be,
  "Last of the Romans,"—though
  thy memory claim

From Brutus his own glory, and on
  thee
  Rests the full splendour of his
  sacred fame :
Nor he who dared make the foul
  tyrant quail
  Amid his cowering senate with thy
  name ;
Though thou and he were great, it will
  avail
To thine own fame that Otho's should
  not fail.

'Twill wrong thee not : thou wouldst
  if thou couldst feel,
  Abjure such envious fame.   Great
  Otho died
Like thee : he sanctified his country's
  steel,
  At once the tyrant and tyrannicide,
In his own blood.   A deed it was to
  wring
  Tears from all men—though full of
  gentle pride,
Such pride as from impetuous love
  may spring
That will not be refused its offering.

Dark is the realm of grief : but human things
  Those may not know who cannot
  weep for them.

1817.

XXIX

O MIGHTY mind, in whose deep stream
  this age
  Shakes like a reed in the unheeding
  storm,
Why dost thou curb not thine own
  sacred rage ?

1818.

XXX

SILENCE ! Oh well are Death and
  Sleep and Thou
Three brethren named, the guardians
  gloomy-winged
Of one abyss, where life and truth and
  joy
Are swallowed up.   Yet spare me,
  Spirit, pity me !
Until the sounds I hear become my
  soul,
And it has left these faint and weary
  limbs,

To track along the lapses of the air
This wandering melody until it rests
Among lone mountains in some. . . .
1818.

XXXI

THE fierce beasts of the woods and
wildernesses
Track not the steps of him who drinks
of it ;
For the light breezes, which for ever
fleet
Around its margin, heap the sand
thereon.

1818.

XXXII

MY head is wild with weeping for a
grief
Which is the shadow of a gentle
mind.
I walk into the air, (but no relief
To seek,—or haply, if I sought, to
find ;
It came unsought) ;—to wonder that
a chief
Among men's spirits should be cold
and blind.

1818.

XXXIII

Flourishing vine, whose kindling clus-
ters glow
Beneath the autumnal sun, none
taste of thee ;
For thou dost shroud a ruin, and below
The rotting bones of dead antiquity.

1818..

XXXIV

SCENE FROM TASSO

MADDALO	. . . .	a Courtier
MALPIGLIO	. . . .	a Poet
PIGNA	. . . .	a Minister
ALBANO	. . . .	an Usher

Mad. No access to the Duke ! You
have not said
That the Count Maddalo would speak
with him ?
Pigna. Did you inform his Grace
that Signor Pigna
Waits with state papers for his signa-
ture ?

Mal. The Lady Leonora cannot
know
That I have written a sonnet to her
fame.
In which I . . . Venus and Adonis.
You should not take my gold, and
serve me not.
Alb. In truth I told her ; and she
smiled and said,
" If I am Venus, thou, coy Poesy,
Art the Adonis whom I love, and he
The Erymanthian boar that wounded
him."
Oh trust to me, Signor Malpiglio,
Those nods and smiles were favours
worth the zechin.
Mal. The words are twisted in some
double sense
That I reach not : the smiles fell not
on me.
Pigna. How are the Duke and
Duchess occupied ?
Alb. Buried in some strange talk.
The Duke was leaning—
His finger on his brow, his lips un-
closed,
The Princess sate within the window-
seat,
And so her face was hid ; but on her
knee
Her hands were clasped, veinèd, and
pale as snow,
And quivering. Young Tasso, too,
was there.
Mad. Thou seest on whom from
thine own worshipped heaven
Thou draw'st down smiles—they did
not rain on thee.
Mal. Would they were parching
lightnings, for his sake
On whom they fell !

SONG FOR TASSO

I LOVED—alas ! our life is love ;
But, when we cease to breathe and
move,
I do suppose love ceases too.
I thought (but not as now I do)
Keen thoughts and bright of linkèd
lore,—
Of all that men had thought before,
And all that Nature shows, and more.

And still I love, and still I think,
But strangely, for my heart can drink

The dregs of such despair, and live,
And love.
And, if I think, my thoughts come fast;
I mix the present with the past,
And each seems uglier than the last.

Sometimes I see before me flee
A silver spirit's form, like thee,
O Leonora ! and I sit
. . . still watching it,
Till by the grated casement's ledge
It fades, with such a sigh as sedge
Breathes o'er the breezy streamlet's
    edge.
    1818.

XXXV

SUCH hope as is the sick despair of
    good,
  Such fear as is the certainty of ill,
Such doubt as is pale Expectation's
    food,
  Turned while she tastes to poison,
    when the will
Is powerless, and the spirit . . .
    1820.

XXXVI

MY head is heavy, my limbs are
    weary,
And it is not life that makes me
    move.
    1820.

XXXVII

PROLOGUE TO HELLAS

HERALD OF ETERNITY

IT is the day when all the Sons of God
Wait in the roofless senate-house
    whose floor
Is chaos and the immovable abyss
Frozen by his steadfast word to hya-
    line.
    .   .   .
The shadow of God, and delegate
Of that before whose breath the uni-
    verse
Is as a print of dew.
              Hierarchs and kings,
Who from your thrones pinnacled on
    the past
Sway the reluctant present, ye who
    sit

Pavilioned on the radiance or the
    gloom
Of mortal thought, which, like an ex-
    halation
Steaming from earth, conceals the
    . . of heaven   [here
Which gave it birth, . . . assemble
Before your Father's throne. The
    swift decree
Yet hovers, and the fiery incarnation
Is yet withheld, clothed in which i*
    shall
    .   .   .   .   annul
The fairest of those wandering isles
    that gem
The sapphire space of interstellar air—
That green and azure sphere, that
    earth-enwrapped
Less in the beauty of its tender light
Than in an atmosphere of living spirit
Which interpenetrating all the. . .
. . . it rolls from realm to realm
And age to age, and in its ebb and flow
Impels the generations
To their appointed place,
Whilst the high Arbiter
Beholds the strife, and at the appointed
    time
Sends his decrees veiled in eternal. . .
Within the circuit of this pendent orb
There lies an antique region, on which
    fell
The dews of thought, in the world's
    golden dawn
Earliest and most benign ; and from
    it sprung
Temples and cities and immortal
    forms,
And harmonies of wisdom and of song,
And thoughts, and deeds worthy of
    thoughts so fair.
And, when the sun of its dominion
    failed,
And when the winter of its glory came,
The winds that stripped it bare blew
    on, and swept
That dew into the utmost wildernesses
In wandering clouds of sunny rain
    that thawed
The unmaternal bosom of the North.
Haste, Sons of God, . . . for ye be-
    held,
Reluctant or consenting or aston-
    ished,
The stern decrees go forth which
    heaped on Greece

Ruin and degradation and despair.
A fourth now waits.   Assemble, Sons
    of God,
To speed or to prevent or to suspend
(If, as ye dream, such power be not
    withheld)
The unaccomplished destiny.

> .   .   .

CHORUS.

The curtain of the universe
    Is rent and shattered,
The splendour-wingèd worlds disperse
    Like wild doves scattered.

Space is roofless and bare,
And in the midst a cloudy shrine,
    Dark amid thrones of light,
In the blue glow of hyaline
Golden worlds revolve and shine.
In   .   .   .   flight
From every point of the Infinite,
Like a thousand dawns on a single
    night
The splendours rise and spread.
    And through thunder and darkness
    dread
    Light and music are radiated,
And, in their pavilioned chariots led
By living wings, high overhead
    The giant Powers move,
Gloomy or bright as the thrones they
    fill.

> .   .   .

A chaos of light and motion
Upon that glassy ocean.

The senate of the Gods is met,
Each in his rank and station set ;
    There is silence in the spaces—
Lo ! Satan, Christ, and Mahomet,
    Start from their places !

> .   .   .

CHRIST.

            Almighty Father !
Low-kneeling at the feet of Destiny

> .   .   .

There are two fountains in which
    spirits weep
When mortals err, Discord and
    Slavery named ;
And with their bitter dew two Des-
    tinies
Filled each their irrevocable urns.
    The third,

Fiercest and mightiest, mingled both,
    and added
Chaos and death, and slow oblivion's
    lymph,
And hate and terror, and the poisoned
    rain

> .   .   .

The Aurora of the nations.   By this
    brow
Whose pores wept tears of blood ; by
    these wide wounds ;
By this imperial crown of agony ;
By infamy and solitude and death,
(For this I underwent) ; and by the
    pain
Of pity for those who would . . . for
    me
The unremembered joy of a revenge,
(For this I felt) ; by Plato's sacred
    light,
Of which my spirit was a burning
    morrow ;
By Greece, and all she cannot cease to
    be,
Her quenchless words, sparks of
    immortal truth,
Stars of all night—her harmonies
    and forms,
Echoes and shadows of what Love
    adores
In thee ; I do compel thee, send forth
    Fate,
Thy irrevocable child ! Let her de-
    scend,
A seraph-wingèd victory [arrayed]
In tempest of the omnipotence of God
Which sweeps through all things.
From hollow leagues, from Tyranny
    which arms
Adverse miscreeds and emulous
    anarchies
To stamp, as on a wingèd serpent's
    seed,
Upon the name of Freedom ; from
    the storm
Of faction, which like earthquake
    shakes and sickens
The solid heart of enterprise ; from all
By which the holiest dreams of high-
    est spirits
Are stars beneath the dawn . . .

. . . . She shall arise
Victorious as the world arose from
    chaos !

And, as the heavens and the earth arrayed
Their presence in the beauty and the light
Of thy first smile, O Father ; as they gather
The spirit of thy love, which paves for them
Their path o'er the abyss, till every sphere
Shall be one living spirit; so shall Greece——

SATAN.

Be as all things beneath the empyrean,
Mine ! Art thou eyeless like old Destiny,
Thou mockery-king, crowned with a wreath of thorns,
Whose sceptre is a reed, the broken reed
Which pierces thee, whose throne a chair of scorn ?
For seest thou not beneath this crystal floor
The innumerable worlds of golden light
Which are my empire, and the least of them
. . . which thou wouldst redeem from me ?
Knowst thou not them my portion ?
Or wouldst rekindle the . . . strife
Which our great Father then did arbitrate
When he assigned to his competing sons
Each his apportioned realm ?
                    Thou Destiny,
Thou who art mailed in the omnipotence
Of Him who sends thee forth, whate'er thy task,
Speed, spare not to accomplish ! and be mine
Thy trophies, whether Greece again become
The fountain in the desert whence the earth
Shall drink of freedom, which shall give it strength
To suffer, or a gulf of hollow death
To swallow all delight, all life, all hope.
Go, thou vicegerent of my will, no less
Than of the Father's. But, lest thou shouldst faint,

The wingèd hounds famine and pestilence
Shall wait on thee ; the hundred-forkèd snake
Insatiate superstition still shall . . .
The earth behind thy steps ; and war shall hover
Above, and fraud shall gape below, and change
Shall flit before thee on her dragon wings,
Convulsing and consuming. And I add
Three phials of the tears which demons weep
When virtuous spirits through the gate of death
Pass triumphing over the thorns of life,—
Sceptres and crowns, mitres and swords and snares,
Trampling in scorn, like him and Socrates.
The first is anarchy ; when power and pleasure,
Glory and science and security,
On freedom hang like fruit on the green tree,
Then pour it forth, and men shall gather ashes.
The second, tyranny—

CHRIST.

                    Obdurate spirit !
Thou seest but the past in the to-come.
Pride is thy error and thy punishment.
Boast not thine empire, dream not that thy worlds
Are more than furnace-sparks or rainbow-drops
Before the Power that wields and kindles them.
True greatness asks not space ; true excellence
Lives in the Spirit of all things that live,
Which lends it to the worlds thou callest thine.

.   .   .

MAHOMET.

.   .   .

Haste thou, and fill the waning crescent
With beams as keen as those which pierced the shadow

Of Christian night rolled back upon
the West
When the orient moon of Islam rode
in triumph
From Tmolus to the Acroceraunian
snow.

.   .

          Wake, thou word
Of God, and from the throne of Des-
tiny
Even to the utmost limit of thy way
May triumph

.   .

      Be thou a curse on them whose
creed
Divides and multiplies the most high
God !

1821.

XXXVIII

SONNET TO BYRON

[I AM afraid these verses will not
please you, but]
If I esteemed you less, Envy would
kill
   Pleasure, and leave to Wonder and
   Despair
The ministration of the thoughts that
fill
   The mind which, like a worm whose
   life may share
A portion of the unapproachable,
   Marks your creations rise as fast
   and fair
As perfect worlds at the Creator's will.
But such is my regard that nor your
power
   To soar above the heights where
   others [climb],
Nor fame, that shadow of the unborn
hour
   Cast from the envious future on the
   time,
   Move one regret for his unhonoured
   name
Who dares these words :—the worm
   beneath the sod
May lift itself in homage of the God.

1821.

XXXIX

I FAINT ! I perish with my love ! I
grow

Frail as a cloud whose [splend-
ours] pale
Under the evening's ever-changing
glow :
   I die like mist upon the gale,
And like a wave under the calm I fail.

XL

GREAT Spirit whom the sea of boundless thought
Nurtures within its unimagined caves,
   In which thou sittest sole, as in my
   mind,
Giving a voice to its mysterious
waves.

XLI

      FAINT with love, the Lady of
the South
Lay in the paradise of Lebanon
Under a heaven of cedar boughs ; the
drought
Of love was on her lips ; the light
was gone
Out of her eyes.

XLII

CHARLES THE FIRST

SCENE I.—*The Masque of the Inns of
Court.*

   A Pursuivant. PLACE for the Mar-
   shal of the Masque !
   First Citizen. What thinkest thou
   of this quaint masque, which
   turns,
Like morning from the shadow of the
night,
The night to day, and London to a
place
Of peace and joy ?
   Second Citizen. And hell to heaven !
Eight years are gone,
And they seem hours, since in this
populous street
I trod on grass made green by sum-
mer's rain ;
For the red plague kept state within
that palace
Where now that vanity reigns. In
nine years more
The roots will be refreshed with civil
blood ;

And thank the mercy of insulted
    Heaven
That sin and wrongs wound, as an
    orphan's cry,
The patience of the great Avenger's
    ear.
   A Youth. Yet, father, 'tis a happy
    sight to see,—
Beautiful, innocent, and unforbidden
By God or man. 'Tis like the bright
    procession
Of skyey visions in a solemn dream
From which men wake as from a para-
    dise,
And draw new strength to tread the
    thorns of life.
If God be good, wherefore should this
    be evil ?
And, if this be not evil, dost thou not
    draw
Unseasonable poison from the flowers
Which bloom so rarely in this barren
    world ?
Oh ! kill these bitter thoughts which
    make the present
Dark as the future !—

      .   .   .

When Avarice and Tyranny, vigilant
    Fear
And open-eyed Conspiracy, lie sleep-
    ing
As on hell's threshold ; and all gentle
    thoughts
Waken to worship Him who giveth
    joys,
With his own gift.
   Second Citizen. How young art
    thou in this old age of time !
How green in this grey world ! Canst
    thou discern
The signs of seasons, yet perceive
    no hint
Of change in that stage-scene in which
    thou art
Not a spectator but an actor ? or
Art thou a puppet moved by [engin-
    ery] ?
The day that dawns in fire will die in
    storms,
Even though the noon be calm. *My*
    travel's done,
Before the whirlwind wakes I shall
    have found
My inn of lasting rest ; but thou
    must still

Be journeying on in this inclement
    air.
Wrap thy old cloak about thy back ;
Nor leave the broad and plain and
    beaten road,
Although no flowers smile on the trod-
    den dust,
For the violet paths of pleasure. This
    Charles the First
Rose like the equinoctial sun, . . .
By vapours, through whose threaten-
    ing ominous veil
Darting his altered influence he has
    gained
This height of noon—from which he
    must decline
Amid the darkness of conflicting
    storms,
To dank extinction and to latest night
.   .   .   .   . There goes
The apostate Strafford ; he whose
    titles . . .
.   .   . whispered aphorisms
From Machiavel and Bacon : and, if
    Judas
Had been as brazen and as bold as
    he. . . .
   First Citizen.   That
    Is the Archbishop.
   Second Citizen. Rather say the
    Pope :
London will be soon his Rome. He
    walks
As if he trod upon the heads of men :
He looks elate, drunken with blood
    and gold.
Beside him moves the Babylonian
    woman
Invisibly, and with her as with his
    shadow,
Mitred adulterer ! he is joined in sin,
Which turns Heaven's milk of mercy
    to revenge.
   Third Citizen (lifting up his eyes).
    Good Lord ! rain it down upon
    him !
Amid her ladies walks the Papist
    queen
As if her nice feet scorned our English
    earth.
The Canaanitish Jezebel ! I would
    be
A dog if I might tear her with my
    teeth !
There's old Sir Henry Vane, the Earl
    of Pembroke,

Lord Essex, and Lord Keeper Coventry,
And others who made base their English breed
By vile participation of their honours
With Papists, atheists, tyrants, and apostates.
When lawyers masque, 'tis time for honest men
To strip the vizor from their purposes.
A seasonable time for masquers this !
When Englishmen and Protestants should sit
. . . dust on their dishonoured heads,
To avert the wrath of Him whose scourge is felt
For the great sins which have drawn down from heaven
. . . . . and foreign overthrow.
The remnant of the martyred saints in Rochefort
Have been abandoned by their faithless allies
To that idolatrous and adulterous torturer
Lewis of France,—the Palatinate is lost. . . .

Enter LEIGHTON (*who has been branded in the face*) *and* BASTWICK.

Canst thou be—art thou . . . . ?
Leighton. I *was* Leighton : what I *am* thou seest. And yet turn thine eyes,
And with thy memory look on thy friend's mind,
Which is unchanged, and where is written deep
The sentence of my judge.
    Third Citizen. Are these the marks with which
Laud thinks to improve the image of his Maker
Stamped on the face of man ? Curses upon him,
The impious tyrant !
    Second Citizen. It is said besides
That lewd and Papist drunkards may profane
The Sabbath with their . . . .
And has permitted that most heathenish custom
Of dancing round a pole dressed up with wreaths
On May Day.

A man who thus twice crucifies his God
May well . . . his brother.— In my mind, friend,
The root of all this ill is prelacy.
I would cut up the root.
    Third Citizen. And by what means ?
    Second Citizen. Smiting each Bishop under the fifth rib.
    Third Citizen, You seem to know the vulnerable place
Of these same crocodiles.
    Second Citizen. I learnt it in
Egyptian bondages, sir. Your worm of Nile
Betrays not with its flattering tears like they ;
For, when they cannot kill, they whine and weep.
Nor is it half so greedy of men's bodies
As they of soul and all ; nor does it wallow
In slime as they in simony and lies
And close lusts of the flesh.
    A Marshalsman. Give place, give place !
You torchbearers, advance to the great gate,
And then attend the Marshal of the Masque
Into the royal presence.
    A Law Student. What thinkest thou
Of this quaint show of ours, my aged friend ?
Even now we see the redness of the torches
Inflame the night to the eastward, and the clarions
Gasp (?) to us on the wind's wave. It comes !
And their sounds, floating hither round the pageant,
Rouse up the astonished air.
    First Citizen. I will not think but that our country's wounds
May yet be healed. The king is just and gracious,
Though wicked counsels now pervert his will :
These once cast off——
    Second Citizen. As adders cast their skins
And keep their venom, so kings often change ;

Counsels and counsellors hang on one
  another,
Hiding the loathsome . . . ,
Like the base patchwork of a leper's
  rags.
  A Youth. Oh ! still those disson-
    ant thoughts !—List how the
    music
Grows on the enchanted air ! And
  see, the torches
Restlessly flashing, and the crowd
  divided
Like waves before an admiral's prow !

.   .   .

  A Marshalsman. Give place
To the Marshal of the Masque !
  A Pursuivant. Room for the King !
  A Youth. How glorious ! See
those thronging chariots
Rolling, like painted clouds before
  the wind,
Behind their solemn steeds : how
  some are shaped
Like curved sea-shells dyed by the
  azure depths
Of Indian seas ; some like the new-
  born moon ;
And some like cars in which the Ro-
  mans climbed
(Canopied by Victory's eagle wings
  outspread)
The Capitolian ! See how gloriously
The mettled horses in the torchlight
  stir
Their gallant riders, while *they* check
  their pride,
Like shapes of some diviner element
Than English air, and beings nobler
  than
The envious and admiring multitude.
  Second Citizen. Ay, there they
    are—
Nobles, and sons of nobles, patentees,
Monopolists, and stewards of this poor
  farm
On whose lean sheep sit the prophetic
  crows.
Here is the pomp that strips the
  houseless orphan,
Here is the pride that breaks the deso-
  late heart.
These are the lilies glorious as Solo-
  mon,
Who toil not neither do they spin—un-
  less

It be the webs they catch poor rogues
  withal.
Here is the surfeit which to them who
  earn
The niggard wages of the earth scarce
  leaves
The tithe that will support them till
  they crawl
Back to her cold hard bosom. Here
  is health
Followed by grim disease, glory by
  shame,
Waste by lame famine, wealth by
  squalid want,
And England's sin by England's pun-
  ishment.
And, as the effect pursues the cause
  foregone,
Lo, giving substance to my words, be-
  hold
At once the sign and the thing signi-
  fied—
A troop of cripples, beggars, and lean
  outcasts,
Horsed upon stumbling jades, carted
  with dung,
Dragged for a day from cellars and low
  cabins
And rotten hiding-holes, to point the
  moral
Of this presentment, and bring up the
  rear !
  A Youth. 'Tis but
The anti-masque, and serves as dis-
  cords do
In sweetest music. Who would love
  May flowers
If they succeeded not to winter's
  flaw ?
Or day unchanged by night, or joy it-
  self
Without the touch of sorrow ?
  Second Citizen. I and thou . . .
  A Marshalsman. Place, give place !

SCENE II.—*A Chamber in Whitehall.*

Enter the KING, QUEEN, LAUD, LORD
STRAFFORD, LORD COTTINGTON,
and other Lords ; ARCHY ; *also*
ST. JOHN, *with some Gentlemen of
the Inns of Court.*

  The King. Thanks, gentlemen. I
    heartily accept
This token of your service : your gay
  masque

Was performed gallantly. And it
shows well
When subjects twine such flowers of
observance (?)
With the sharp thorns that deck the
English crown.
A gentle heart enjoys what it confers,
Even as it suffers that which it inflicts,
Though Justice guides the stroke.
Accept my hearty thanks.
   The Queen.   And, gentlemen,
Call your poor Queen your debtor.
Your quaint pageant
Rose on me like the figures of past
years,
Treading their still path back to in-
fancy,
More beautiful and mild as they draw
nearer
The quiet cradle. I could have al-
most wept
To think I was in Paris, where these
shows   [yet
Are well devised—such as I was ere
My young heart shared a portion of
the burthen,
The careful weight, of this great mon-
archy.
There, gentlemen, between the sove-
reign's pleasure
And that which it regards, no clamour
lifts
Its proud interposition.
In Paris ribald censurers dare not
move
Their poisonous tongues against these
sinless sports ;
And *his* smile
Warms those who bask in it, as ours
would do '
If . . . Take my heart's thanks : add
them, gentlemen,
To those good words which, were he
King of France,
My royal lord would turn to golden
deeds.
   St. John. Madam, the love of
Englishmen can make
The lightest favour of their lawful
king
Outweigh a despot's.—We humbly
take our leaves,
Enriched by smiles which France can
never buy.
   [*Exeunt* St. John *and the Gentlemen
of the Inns of Court.*

The King. My lord Archbishop,
Mark you what spirit sits in St.
John's eyes ?
Methinks it is too saucy for this presence.
   Archy. Yes, pray your Grace look :
for, like an unsophisticated . . . sees
everything upside down, you who are
wise will discern the shadow of an
idiot in lawn sleeves and a rochet setting springes to catch woodcocks in
haymaking time. Poor Archy, whose
owl eyes are tempered to the error of
his age, and because he is a fool, and
by special ordinance of God forbidden
ever to see himself as he is, sees now
in that deep eye a blindfold devil sitting on the ball, and weighing words
out between king and subjects. One
scale is full of promises, and the other
full of protestations : and then another devil creeps behind the first out
of the dark windings [of a] pregnant
lawyer's brain, and takes the bandage
from the other's eyes, and throws a
sword into the left hand scale, for all
the world like my Lord Essex's there.
   Strafford. A rod in pickle for the
Fool's back !
   Archy. Ay, and some are now smiling whose tears will make the brine ;
for the Fool sees . . .
   Strafford. Insolent ! You shall
have your coat turned and be whipped
out of the palace for this.
   Archy. When all the fools are
whipped, and all the Protestant
writers, while the knaves are whipping
the fools ever since a thief was set to
catch a thief. If all turncoats were
whipped out of palaces, poor Archy
would be disgraced in good company.
Let the knaves whip the fools, and all
the fools laugh at it. [Let the] wise
and godly slit each other's noses and
ears (having no need of any sense of
discernment in their craft) ; and the
knaves, to marshal them, join in a procession to Bedlam, to entreat the madmen to omit their sublime Platonic
contemplations, and manage the state
of England. Let all the honest men
who lie pinched (?) up at the prisons
or the pillories, in custody of the
pursuivants of the High-Commission
Court, marshal them.

Enter Secretary LYTTELTON, *with papers.*

The King (looking over the papers). These stiff Scots
His Grace of Canterbury must take order
To force under the Church's yoke.—
You, Wentworth,
Shall be myself in Ireland, and shall add
Your wisdom, gentleness, and energy,
To what in me were wanting.—My Lord Weston,
Look that those merchants draw not without loss
Their bullion from the Tower; and, on the payment
Of Ship Money, take fullest compensation
For violation of our royal forests,
Whose limits, from neglect, have been o'ergrown
With cottages and cornfields. The uttermost
Farthing exact from those who claim exemption
From knighthood : that which once was a reward
Shall thus be made a punishment, that subjects
May know how majesty can wear at will
The rugged mood.—My Lord of Coventry,
Lay my command upon the Courts below
That bail be not accepted for the prisoners
Under the warrant of the Star Chamber.
The people shall not find the stubbornness
Of Parliament a cheap or easy method
Of dealing with their rightful sovereign :
And doubt not this, my Lord of Coventry,
We will find time and place for fit rebuke.—
My Lord of Canterbury.
    Archy.   The fool is here.
    Laud. I crave permission of your Majesty
To order that this insolent fellow be
Chastised : he mocks the sacred character,

Scoffs at the state, and——
    The King.   What, my Archy?
He mocks and mimics all he sees and hears,
Yet with a quaint and graceful license. Prithee
For this once do not as Prynne would, were he
Primate of England. With your Grace's leave,
He lives in his own world ; and, like a parrot
Hung in his gilded prison from the window
Of a queen's bower over the public way,
Blasphemes with a bird's mind :—his words, like arrows
Which know no aim beyond the archer's wit
Strike sometimes what eludes philosophy.—
[*To Archy.*] Go, sirrah, and repent of your offence
Ten minutes in the rain : be it your penance
To bring news how the world goes there.—Poor Archy !
                    [*Exit Archy.*
He weaves about himself a world of mirth
Out of the wreck of ours.
    Laud. I take with patience, as my Master did,
All scoffs permitted from above.
    The King.   My lord,
Pray overlook these papers. Archy's words
Had wings, but these have talons.
    The Queen.   And the lion
That wears them must be tamed. My dearest lord,
I see the newborn courage in thine eye
Armed to strike dead the Spirit of the Time,
Which spurs to rage the many-headed beast.
Do thou persist : for faint but in resolve,
And it were better thou hadst still remained
The slave of thine own slaves, who tear like curs
The fugitive, and flee from the pursuer,
And opportunity, that empty wolf,

Flies at his throat who falls.   Subdue
thy actions
Even to the disposition of thy purpose,
And be that tempered as the Ebro's
steel ;
And banish weak-eyed Mercy to the
weak,
Whence she will greet thee with a gift
of peace,
And not betray thee with a traitor's
kiss,
As when she keeps the company of
rebels,
Who think that she is Fear.   This do,
lest we
Should fall as from a glorious pinnacle
In a bright dream, and wake, as from
a dream,
Out of our worshipped state.
   The King.   Belovèd friend,
God is my witness that this weight of
power,
Which He sets me my earthly task to
wield
Under His law, is my delight and pride
Only because thou lovest that and me.
For a king bears the office of a God
To all the under world ; and to his
God
Alone he must deliver up his trust,
Unshorn of its permitted attributes.
[It seems] now as the baser elements
Had mutinied against the golden sun
That kindles them to harmony, and
quells
Their self-destroying rapine.   The
wild million
Strike at the eye that guides them ;
like as humours
Of the distempered body that conspire
Against the spirit of life throned in
the heart,—
And thus become the prey of one an-
other,
And last of death. . . .
   Strafford.   That which would be
ambition in a subject
Is duty in a sovereign ; for on him,
As on a keystone, hangs the arch of
life,
Whose safety is its strength.   Degree
and form,
And all that makes the age of reason-
ing man
More memorable than a beast's, de-
pend

On this—that Right should fence it-
self inviolably
With power ; in which respect the
state of England
From usurpation by the insolent Com-
mons
Cries for reform.
Get treason, and spare treasure.   Fee
with coin
The loudest murmurers ; feed with
jealousies
Opposing factions,—be thyself of
none ;
And borrow gold of many, for those
who lend
Will serve thee till thou payest them ;
and thus
Keep the fierce spirit of the hour at
bay,
Till time, amid its coming generations
Of nights and days unborn, bring
some one chance,

Or war or pestilence or Nature's self,
By some distemperature or terrible
sign,
Be as an arbiter betwixt themselves.
. . . Nor let your Majesty
Doubt here the peril of the unseen
event.
How did your brother kings, coheri-
tors
In your high interest in the subject
earth,
Rise past such troubles to that height
of power
Where now they sit, and awfully se-
rene
Smile on the trembling world ? Such
popular storms
Philip the Second of Spain, this Lewis
of France,
And late the German head of many
bodies,
And every petty lord of Italy,
Quelled or by arts or arms.   Is Eng-
land poorer
Or feebler ? or art thou who wield'st
her power
Tamer than they ? or shall this island
be—
[Girdled] by its inviolable waters—
To the world present and the world to
come
Sole pattern of extinguished mon-
archy ?

Not if thou dost as I would have thee
do.
The King. Your words shall be my
deeds :
You speak the image of my thought.
My friend
(If kings can have a friend, I call thee
so),
Beyond the large commission which
belongs (?)
Under the great seal of the realm, take
this :
And, for some obvious reasons, let
there be
No seal on it, except my kingly word
And honour as I am a gentleman.
Be—as thou art within my heart and
mind—
Another self, here and in Ireland :
Do what thou judgest well, take am-
plest license,
And stick not even at questionable
means.
Hear me, Wentworth. My word is as
a wall
Between thee and this world thine
enemy—
That hates thee, for thou lovest me.
Strafford. I own
No friend but thee, no enemies but
thine :
Thy lightest thought is my eternal law.
How weak, how short, is life to
pay. . .
The King. Peace, peace !
Thou ow'st me nothing yet.—[*To
Laud*]. My lord, what say
Those papers ?
Laud. Your Majesty has ever inter-
posed,
In lenity towards your native soil,
Between the heavy vengeance of the
Church
And Scotland. Mark the consequence
of warming
This brood of northern vipers in your
bosom.
The rabble, instructed no doubt
By Loudon, Lindsay, Hume, and false
Argyll,
(For the waves never menace heaven
until
Scourged by the wind's invisible ty-
ranny)
Have in the very temple of the Lord
Done outrage to His chosen ministers.

They scorn the liturgy of the holy
Church,
Refuse to obey her canons, and deny
The apostolic power with which the
Spirit
Has filled its elect vessels, even from
him
Who held the keys with power to loose
and bind,
To him who now pleads in this royal
presence.
Let ampler powers and new instruc-
tions be
Sent to the High Commissioners in
Scotland.
To death, imprisonment, and confis-
cation,
Add torture, add the ruin of the kin-
dred
Of the offender, add the brand of in-
famy,
Add mutilation : and, if this suffice
not,
Unleash the sword and fire, that, in
their thirst,
They may lick up that scum of schis-
matics.
I laugh at those weak rebels who, de-
siring
What we possess, still prate of Chris-
tian peace :
As if those dreadful arbitrating mes-
sengers
Which play the part of God 'twixt
right and wrong
Should be let loose against the inno-
cent sleep
Of templed cities and the smiling fields
For some poor argument of policy
Which touches our own profit or our
pride
(Where it indeed were Christian char-
ity
To turn the cheek even to the smiter's
hand) ;
And, when our great Redeemer, when
our God,
When He who gave, accepted, and re-
tained,
Himself in propitiation of our sins,
Is scorned in His immediate ministry,
With hazard of the inestimable loss
Of all the truth and discipline which is
Salvation to the extremest generation
Of men innumerable, they talk of
peace !

Such peace as Canaan found, let Scot-
    land now :
For, by that Christ who came to bring
    a sword,
Not peace, upon the earth, and gave
    command
To his disciples at the passover
That each should sell his robe and buy
    a sword,—
Once strip that minister of naked
    wrath,
And it shall never sleep in peace again
Till Scotland bend or break.
    The King. My Lord Archbishop,
Do what thou wilt and what thou
    canst in this.
Thy earthly even as thy heavenly
    King
Gives thee large power in his unquiet
    realm.
But we want money, and my mind
    misgives me
That for so great an enterprise, as yet,
We are unfurnished.
    Strafford. Yet it may not long
Rest on our wills.
    Cottington. The expenses
Of gathering Ship Money, and of dis-
    training
For every petty rate (for we encounter
A desperate opposition inch by inch
In every warehouse and on every
    farm),
Have swallowed up the gross sum of
    the imposts ;
So that, though felt as a most grievous
    scourge
Upon the land, they stand us in small
    stead
As touches the receipt.
    . Strafford. 'Tis a conclusion
Most arithmetical : and thence you
    infer
Perhaps the assembling of a Parlia-
    ment.
Now, if a man should call his dearest
    enemies
To sit in licensed judgment on his life,
His Majesty might wisely take that
    course.
[*Aside to Cottington.*] It is enough to
    expect from these lean imposts
That they perform the office of a
    scourge,
Without more profit. [*Aloud.*] Fines
    and confiscations,

And a forced loan from the refractory
    City,
Will fill our coffers : and the golden
    love
Of loyal gentlemen and noble friends
For the worshipped father of our com-
    mon country,
With contributions from the catholics,
Will make Rebellion pale in our ex-
    cess.
Be these the expedients until time
    and wisdom
Shall frame a settled state of govern-
    ment.
    Laud. And weak expedients they !
    Have we not drained
All, till the . . . which seemed
A mine exhaustless ?
    Strafford. And the love which *is*,
If loyal hearts could turn their blood
    to gold.
    Laud. Both now grow barren : and
    I speak it not
As loving Parliaments, which, as they
    have been,
In the right hand of bold bad mighty
    kings,
The scourges of the bleeding Church,
    I hate.
Methinks they scarcely can deserve
    our fear.
    Strafford. O my dear liege, take
    back the wealth thou gavest :
With that, take all I held, but as in
    trust
For thee, of mine inheritance : leave
    me but
This unprovided body for thy service,
And a mind dedicated to no care
Except thy safety :—but assemble
    not   [like me,
A Parliament. Hundreds will bring,
Their fortunes, as they would their
    blood, before . . .
    The King. No ! thou who judgest
    them art but one. Alas !
We should be too much out of love
    with heaven,
Did this vile world show many such
    as thee,
Thou perfect just and honourable
    man !
Never shall it be said that Charles of
    England
Stripped those he loved for fear of
    those he scorns ;

Nor will he so much misbecome his throne
As to impoverish those who most adorn
And best defend it. That you urge, dear Strafford, ·
Inclines me rather . . .

    The Queen.   To a Parliament ?
Is this thy firmness ? and thou wilt preside
Over a knot of . . . censurers,
To the unswearing of thy best resolves,
And choose the worst, when the worst comes too soon
Plight not the worst before the worst must come.
Oh ! wilt thou smile whilst our ribald foes,
Dressed in their own usurped authority,
Sharpen their tongues on Henrietta's fame ?
It is enough ! Thou lovest me no more ! [*Weeps.*]

    The King. O Henrietta !
                [*They talk apart.*
    Cottington [*to Laud*]. Money we have none :
And all the expedients of my Lord of Strafford
Will scarcely meet the arrears.

    Laud.   Without delay
An army must be sent into the north ;
Followed by a Commission of the Church,
With amplest power to quench in fire and blood,
And tears and terror, and the pity of hell,
The intenser wrath of Heresy. God will give
Victory ; and victory over Scotland give
The lion England tamed into our hands.
That will lend power, and power bring gold.

    Cottington.   Meanwhile
We must begin first where your Grace leaves off.
Gold must give power, or . . .

    Laud   I am not averse
From the assembling of a Parliament
Strong actions and smooth words might teach them soon

The lesson to obey. And are they not
A bubble fashioned by the monarch's mouth,
The birth of one light breath ? If they serve no purpose,
A word dissolves them.

    Strafford.   The engine of Parliaments
Might be deferred until I can bring over
The Irish regiments : they will serve to assure
The issue of the war against the Scots.
And, this game won—which if lost, all is lost—
Gather these chosen leaders of the rebels,
And call them, if you will, a parliament.

    The King. Oh be our feet still tardy shed blood,
Guilty though it may be ! I would still spare
The stubborn country of my birth, and ward
From countenances which I loved in youth
The wrathful Church's lacerating hand.
[*To Laud.*] Have you o'erlooked the other articles ?
             [*Re-enter* ARCHY.

    Laud. Hazlerig, Hampden, Pym, young Harry Vane,
Cromwell, and other rebels of less note,
Intend to sail with the next favouring wind
For the Plantations.

    Archy.   Where they think to found
A commonwealth like Gonzalo's in the play,
Gynæcocœnic and pantisocratic.

    The King. What's that, sirrah ?
    Archy.   New devil's politics.
Hell is the pattern of all commonwealths :
Lucifer was the first republican.
Will you hear Merlin's prophecy, how three posts (?)
" In one brainless skull, when the whitethorn is full,
    Shall sail round the world, and come back again :
    Shall sail round the world in a brainless skull,

And come back again when the moon
    is at full " :—
When, in spite of the Church,
They will hear homilies of whatever
    length
Or form they please.
    Cottington(?). So please your Majesty
        to sign this order
For their detention.
    Archy. If your Majesty were tor-
mented night and day by fever, gout,
rheumatism, and stone, and asthma,
&c., and you found these diseases had
secretly entered into a conspiracy to
abandon you, should you think it necessary to lay an embargo on the port
by which they meant to dispeople
your unquiet kingdom of man ?
    The King. If fear were made for
    kings, the Fool mocks wisely ;
But in this case . . . [*writing*] Here,
    my lord, take the warrant,
And see it duly executed forthwith.—
That imp of malice and mockery shall
    be punished.
[*Exeunt all but the King, the Queen,
                    and Archy.*
    Archy. Ay, I am the physician of
whom Plato prophesied, who was to
be accused by the confectioner before
a jury of children, who found him,
guilty without waiting for the sum-
ming-up, and hanged him without
benefit of clergy. Thus Baby Charles,
and the Twelfth Night Queen of Hearts
and the overgrown schoolboy Cottington, and that little urchin Laud—who
would reduce a verdict of " guilty,
death," by famine, if it were impregnable by compósition—all impannelled
against poor Archy for presenting
them bitter physic the last day of the
holidays.
    The Queen. Is the rain ver, sirrah ?
    The King.   When it rains
And the sun shines, 'twill rain again
    to-morrow :
And therefore never smile till you've
    done crying.
    Archy. But 'tis all over now : like
the April anger of woman, the gentle
sky has wept itself serene.
    The Queen. What news abroad? how
looks the world this morning ?
    Archy. Glóriously as a grave covered
with virgin flowers. There's a rain-

bow in the sky.   Let your Majesty
look at it, for
    " A rainbow in the morning
        Is the shepherd's warning " ;
and the flocks of which you are the
pastor are scattered among the mountain tops, where every drop of water
is a flake of snow, and the breath of
May pierces like a January blast.
    The King. The sheep have mistaken
the wolf for their shepherd, my poor
boy ; and the shepherd, the wolves
for the watchdogs.
    The Queen. But the rainbow was a
good sign, Archy : it says that the
waters of the deluge are gone, and can
return no more.
    Archy. Ay, the salt-water one :
but that of tears and blood must yet
come down, and that of fire follow, if
there be any truth in lies.—The rainbow hung over the city with all its
shops, . . . and churches, from north
to south, like a bridge of congregated
lightning pieced by the masonry of
heaven—like a balance in which the
angel that distributes the coming hour
was weighing that heavy one whose
poise is now felt in the lightest hearts,
before it bows the proudest heads
under the meanest feet.
    The Queen. Who taught you this
trash, sirrah ?
    Archy. A torn leaf out of an old
book trampled in the dirt.—But for the
rainbow. It moved as the sun moved,
and . . . until the top of the Tower. . .
of a cloud through its left hand tip,
and Lambeth Palace look as dark as
a rock before the other.   Methought I
saw a crown figured upon one tip, and
a mitre on the other. So, as I had
heard treasures were found where the
rainbow quenches its points upon the
earth, I set off, and at the Tower ——
But I shall not tell your Majesty what
I found close to the closet-window on
which the rainbow had glimmered.
    The King. Speak ! I will make my
Fool my conscience.
    Archy. Then conscience is a fool.—
I saw there a cat caught in a rat-trap.
I heard the rats squeak behind the
wainscots : it seemed to me that the
very mice were consulting on the
manner of her death.

The Queen. Archy is shrewd and bitter.

Archy. Like the season, so blow the winds.—But at the other end of the rainbow, where the grey rain was tempered along the grass and leaves by a tender interfusion of violet and gold in the meadows beyond Lambeth, what think you that I found instead of a mitre ?

The King. Vane's wits perhaps.

Archy. Something as vain. I saw a gross vapour hovering in a stinking ditch over the carcass of a dead ass, some rotten rags, and broken dishes—the wrecks of what once administered to the stuffing-out and the ornament of a worm of worms. His Grace of Canterbury expects to enter the New Jerusalem some Palm Sunday in triumph on the ghost of this ass.

The Queen. Enough, enough ! Go desire Lady Jane
She place my lute, together with the music
Mari received last week from Italy,
In my boudoir, and . . .
　　　　　　　　[*Exit Archy.*

The King. I'll go in.

The Queen. My beloved lord,
Have you not noted that the Fool of late
Has lost his careless mirth, and that his words
Sound like the echoes of our saddest fears ?
What can it mean ? I should be loth to think
Some factious slave had tutored him.

The King. Oh no !
He is but Occasion's pupil. Partly 'tis
That our minds piece the vacant intervals
Of his wild words with their own fashioning,—
As in the imagery of summer clouds,
Or coals of the winter fire, idlers find
The perfect shadows of their teeming thoughts ;
And, partly, that the terrors of the time
Are sown by wandering Rumour in all spirits, 　　　　　　[best
And in the lightest and the least may

Be seen the current of the coming wind

The Queen. Your brain is overwrought with these deep thoughts.
Come, I will sing to you ; let us go try
These airs from Italy ; and, as we pass
The gallery, we'll decide where that Correggio
Shall hang—the Virgin Mother
With her child, born the King of heaven and earth,
Whose reign is men's salvation. And you shall see
A cradled miniature of yourself asleep,
Stamped on the heart by never-erring love ;
Liker than any Vandyke ever made,
A pattern to the unborn age of thee,
Over whose sweet beauty I have wept for joy
A thousand times,—and now should weep for sorrow,
Did I not think that after we were dead
Our fortunes would spring high in him, and that
The cares we waste upon our heavy crown
Would make it light and glorious as a wreath
Of heaven's beams for his dear innocent brow.

The King. Dear Henrietta !

SCENE III.—*The Star Chamber.* LAUD, JUXON, STRAFFORD, *and others, as Judges.* PRYNNE *as a Prisoner, and then* BASTWICK.

Laud. Bring forth the prisoner Bastwick : let the clerk
Recite his sentence.

Clerk. " That he pay five thousand
Pounds to the king, lose both his ears, be branded
With red-hot iron on the cheek and forehead,
And be imprisoned within Lancaster Castle
During the pleasure of the Court."

Laud. 　　　　　　Prisoner,
If you have aught to say wherefore this sentence
Should not be put into effect, now speak.

Juxon. If you have aught to plead in mitigation,

Speak.

Bastwick. Thus, my lords. If, like the prelates, I
Were an invader of the royal power,
A public scorner of the word of God,
Profane, idolatrous, popish, super-
   stitious,
Impious in heart and in tyrannic act,
Void of wit, honesty, and temperance ;
If Satan were my lord, as theirs,—our
   God
Pattern of all I should avoid to do ;
Were I an enemy of my God and King
And of good men, as ye are ;—I should
   merit
Your fearful state and gilt prosperity,
Which, when ye wake from the last
   sleep, shall turn
To cowls and robes of everlasting fire.
But, as I am, I bid ye grudge me not
The only earthly favour ye can yield,
Or I think worth acceptance at your
   hands,—
Scorn, mutilation, and imprisonment.
   . . . . . Even as my Master
   did,
Until Heaven's kingdom shall des-
   cend on earth,
Or earth be like a shadow in the light
Of Heaven absorbed. Some few
   tumultuous years
Will pass, and leave no wreck of what
   opposes
His will whose will is power.

Laud. Officer, take the prisoner from the bar,
And be his tongue slit for his insolence.

Bastwick. While this hand holds a pen . . .

Laud.   Be his hands . . .

Juxon.   Stop !
Forbear, my lord ! The tongue, which now can speak
No terror, would interpret, being
   dumb,
Heaven's thunder to our harm ; . . .
And hands, which now write only their
   own shame,
With bleeding stumps might sign our
   blood away.

Laud. Much more such " mercy " among men would be,
Did all the ministers of Heaven's re-
   venge

Flinch thus from earthly retribution. I
Could suffer what I would inflict.
[*Exit Bastwick guarded.*] Bring up
The Lord Bishop of Lincoln.—[*To
   Strafford*] Know you not
That, in distraining for ten thousand
   pounds
Upon his books and furniture at Lin-
   coln,
Were found these scandalous and se-
   ditious letters
Sent from one Osbaldistone, who is
   fled ?
I speak it not as touching this poor
   person ;
But of the office which should make
   it holy,
Were it as vile as it was ever spotless.
Mark too, my lord, that this expres-
   sion strikes
His Majesty, if I misinterpret not.

Enter BISHOP WILLIAMS *guarded.*

Strafford. 'Twere politic and just that Williams taste
The bitter fruit of his connexion with
The schismatics. But you, my Lord
   Archbishop,
Who owed your first promotion to his
   favour,
Who grew beneath his smile——

Laud.   Would therefore beg
The office of his judge from this High
   Court,—
That it shall seem, even as it is, that I
In my assumption of this sacred robe,
Have put aside all worldly prefer-
   ence,
All sense of all distinction of all per-
   sons,
All thoughts but of the service of the
   Church.—
Bishop of Lincoln !

Williams. Peace, proud hierarch !
I know my sentence, and I own it just.
Thou wilt repay me less than I deserve,
In stretching to the utmost.

. . . . . .

SCENE IV.—HAMPDEN, PYM, CROM-
WELL, *his Daughter, and young*
SIR HARRY VANE.

Hampden. England, farewell !
   Thou, who hast been my cradle,

Shalt never be my dungeon or my
  grave !
I held what I inherited in thee
As pawn for that inheritance of free-
  dom
Which thou hast sold for thy de-
  spoiler's smile ;
How can I call thee England, or my
  country ?—
Does the wind hold ?
    Vane.   The vanes sit steady
Upon the Abbey towers. The silver
  lightnings
Of the Evening Star, spite of the City's
  smoke,
Tell that the north wind reigns in the
  upper air.
Mark too that fleet of fleecy-wingèd
  cloud
Sailing athwart St. Margaret's.
    Hampden.   Hail, fleet herald
Of tempest ! that rude pilot who shall
  guide
Hearts free as his to realms as pure as
  thee,
Beyond the shot of tyranny,
Beyond the webs of that swoln spi-
  der . . .
Beyond the curses, calumnies, and
  lies (?)
Of atheist priests ! . . . And thou
Fair star, whose beam lies on the wide
    Atlantic,   [calm,
Athwart its zones of tempest and of
Bright as the path to a belovèd home,
Oh, light us to the isles of the evening
  land !
Like floating Edens cradled in the
  glimmer
Of sunset, through the distant mist of
  years.
Touched by departing hope, they
  gleam ! lone regions,
Where power's poor dupes and vic-
    tims yet have never
Propitiated the savage fear of kings
With purest blood of noblest hearts ;
  whose dew
Is yet unstained with tears of those
  who wake
To weep each day the wrongs on which
  it dawns ;
Whose sacred silent air owns yet no
  echo
Of formal blasphemies ; nor impious
  rites

Wrest man's free worship, from the
  God who loves,
To the poor worm who envies us his
  love !
Receive, thou young . . . of Para-
  dise,
These exiles from the old and sinful
  world !

This glorious clime ; this firmament,
  whose lights
Dart mitigated influence through
  their veil
Of pale blue atmosphere, whose tears
  keep green
The pavement of this moist all-feed-
  ing earth ;
This vaporous horizon, whose dim
  round
Is bastioned by the circumfluous sea,
Repelling invasion from the sacred
  towers ;
Presses upon me like a dungeon's
  grate,
A low dark roof, a damp and narrow
  wall.
The boundless universe
Becomes a cell too narrow for the soul
That owns a master ; while the loath-
  liest ward
Of this wide prison, England, is a nest
Of cradling peace built on the moun-
  tain tops,—
To which the eagle spirits of the free,
Which range through heaven and
    earth, and scorn the storm
Of time, and gaze upon the light of
  truth,
Return to brood on thoughts that can-
  not die
And cannot be repelled.
Like eaglets floating in the heaven of
  time,
They soar above their quarry, and
  shall stoop
Through palaces and temples thunder-
  proof.

SCENE V.

Archy. I'll go live under the ivy
that overgrows the terrace, and court
the tears shed on its old roots (?), as
the [wind ?] plays the song of

  " A widow bird sate mourning
    Upon a wintry bough."

[*Sings*] Heigho! the lark and the owl!
One flies the morning, and
one lulls the night :—
Only the nightingale, poor
fond soul,
Sings like the fool through
darkness and light.

· " A widow bird sate mourning for her
love
Upon a wintry bough ;
The frozen wind crept on above,
The freezing stream below.
There was no leaf upon the forest bare,
No flower upon the ground,
And little motion in the air
Except the millwheel's
sound."

1822.

XLIII

LINES

WE meet not as we parted ;
We feel more than all may see ;
My bosom is heavy-hearted,
And thine full of doubt for me.
One moment has bound the free.

That moment is gone for ever ;
Like lightning that flashed and died,
Like a snowflake upon the river,
Like a sunbeam upon the tide,
Which the dark shadows hide.

That moment from time was singled
As the first of a life of pain ;
The cup of its joy was mingled
—Delusion too sweet though vain !
Too sweet to be mine again.

Sweet lips, could my heart have hidden
That its life was crushed by you,
Ye would not have then forbidden
The death which a heart so true
Sought in your briny dew.

Methinks too little cost
For a moment so found, so lost !
1822.

XLIV

Bright wanderer, fair coquette of
heaven
To whom alone it has been given
To change and be adored for ever,
Envy not this dim world, for never
But once within its shadow grew
One fair as ——

TRANSLATIONS

HYMNS OF HOMER

HYMN TO MERCURY.

I

SING, Muse, the son of Maia and of
Jove,
The Herald-child, king of Arcadia
And all its pastoral hills, whom in
sweet love   [May
Having been interwoven, modest
Bore Heaven's dread Supreme—an
antique grove
Shadowed the cavern where the
lovers lay
In the deep night, unseen by gods or
men,
And white-armed Juno slumbered
sweetly then.

II

Now, when the joy of Jove had its
fulfilling,
And Heaven's tenth moon chroni-
cled her relief,
She gave to light a babe all babes ex-
celling,
A schemer subtle beyond all belief ;
A shepherd of thin dreams, a cow-
stealing,
A night-watching, and door-way-
laying thief,
Who 'mongst the gods was soon
about to thieve,
And other glorious actions to achieve

III

The babe was born at the first peep of
  day ;
He began playing on the lyre at
  noon,
And the same evening did he steal
  away
Apollo's herds ;—the fourth day of
  the moon
On which him bore the venerable May,
  From her immortal limbs he leaped
  full soon,
Nor long could in the sacred cradle
  keep,
But out to seek Apollo's herds would
  creep.

IV

Out of the lofty cavern wandering
  He found a tortoise, and cried out
  —" A treasure ! "
(For Mercury first made the tortoise
  sing)
  The beast before the portal at his
  leisure
The flowery herbage was depasturing,
  Moving his feet in a deliberate mea-
  sure
Over the turf. Jove's profitable son
Eyeing him laughed, and laughing
  thus begun :—

V

" A useful godsend are you to me
  now,
  King of the dance, companion of
  the feast,
Lovely in all your nature ! Welcome,
  you
Excellent plaything ! Where, sweet
  mountain beast,
Got you that speckled shell ? Thus
  much I know,
  You must come home with me and
  be my guest ;
You will give joy to me, and I will do
All that is in my power to honour you.

VI

"Better to be at home than out of door ;
  So come with me, and though it has
  been said
That you alive defend from magic
  power,
  I know you will sing sweetly when
  you're dead."

Thus having spoken, the quaint in-
  fant bore,
  Lifting it from the grass on which it
  fed,
And grasping it in his delighted hold,
His treasured prize into the cavern old.

VII

Then scooping with a chisel of grey
  steel,
  He bored the life and soul out of the
  beast—
Not swifter a swift thought of woe or
  weal
  Darts through the tumult of a
  human breast
Which thronging cares annoy—not
  swifter wheel
  The flashes of its torture and unrest
Out of the dizzy eyes—than Maia's
  son
All that he did devise hath featly
  done.

VIII

And through the tortoise's hard
  strong skin
  At proper distances small holes he
  made,
And fastened the cut stems of reeds
  within,
And with a piece of leather over-
  laid
The open space and fixed the cubits in,
Fitting the bridge to both, and
  stretched o'er all
Symphonious chords of sheep-gut
  rhythmical.

IX

When he had wrought the lovely in-
  strument,
  He tried the chords, and made divi-
  sion meet
Preluding with the plectrum, and
  there went
  Up from beneath his hand a tumult
  sweet
Of mighty sounds, and from his lips
  he sent
  A strain of unpremeditated wit
Joyous and wild and wanton—such
  you may
Hear among revellers on a holiday.

X

He sung how Jove and May of the
    bright sandal
Dallied in love not quite legitimate ;
And his own birth, still scoffing at
    the scandal,
    And naming his own name, did cele-
    brate ;
His mother's cave and servant maids
    he planned all
    . In plastic verse, her household stuff
    and state,
Perennial pot, trippet, and brazen
    pan—
But singing he conceived another
    plan.

XI

Seized with a sudden fancy for fresh
    meat,
    He in his sacred crib deposited
The hollow lyre, and from the cavern
    sweet
    Rushed with great leaps up to the
    mountain's head,
Revolving in his mind some subtle
    feat
Of thievish craft, such as a swindler
    might
Devise in the lone season of dun night.

XII

Lo ! the great Sun under the ocean's
    bed has
    Driven steeds and chariot—the
    child meanwhile strode
O'er the Pierian mountains clothed
    in shadows,
    Where the immortal oxen of the
    god
Are pastured in the flowering unmown
    meadows,
    And safely stalled in a remote
    abode—
The archer Argicide, elate and proud,
Drove fifty from the herd, lowing
    aloud.

XIII

He drove them wandering o'er the
    sandy way,
    But, being ever mindful of his craft,
Backward and forward drove he them
    astray,
    So that the tracks, which seemed
    before, were aft :

His sandals then he threw to the
    ocean spray,
    And for each foot he wrought a
    kind of raft
Of tamarisk, and tamarisk-like sprigs,
And bound them in a lump with withy
    twigs.

XIV

And on his feet he tied these sandals
    light,
    The trail of whose wide leaves
    might not betray
His track ; and then, a self-sufficing
    wight,
    Like a man hastening on some dis-
    tant way,
He from Pieria's mountain bent his
    flight ;
But an old man perceived the infant
    pass
Down green Onchestus, heaped like
    beds with grass.

XV

The old man stood dressing his sunny
    vine :
    " Halloo ! old fellow with the
    crooked shoulder !
You grub those stumps ? Before
    they will bear wine
    Methinks even you must grow a
    little older !
Attend, I pray, to this advice of mine,
    As you would 'scape what might
    appal a bolder—
Seeing, see not—and hearing, hear
    not—and—
If you have understanding—under-
    stand."—

XVI

So saying, Hermes roused the oxen
    vast ;
    O'er shadowy mountain and re-
    sounding dell,
And flower-paven plains, great Hermes
    passed ;
    Till the black night divine, which
    favouring fell
Around his steps, grew grey, and
    morning fast
    Wakened the world to work, and
    from her cell,
Sea-strewn, the Pallantean Moon
    sublime

Into her watch-tower just began to
climb.

XVII

Now to Alpheus he had driven all
  The broad foreheaded oxen of the
  Sun ;
They came unwearied to the lofty
  stall
  And to the water troughs which
  ever run
Through the fresh fields—and when
  with rushgrass
  Lotus and all sweet herbage, every
  one
Had pastured been, the great god
  made them move
Towards the stall in a collected drove.

XVIII

A mighty pile of wood the god then
  heaped,
  And having soon conceived the
  mystery
Of fire, from two smooth laurel
  branches stripped
  The bark, and rubbed them in his
  palms,—on high
Suddenly forth the burning vapour
  leaped,
  And the divine child saw delight-
  edly—
Mercury first found out for human
  weal
Tinder-box, matches, fire-irons, flint,
  and steel.

XIX

And fine dry logs and roots innumer-
  ous
  He gathered in a delve upon the
  ground—
And kindled them—and instantane-
  ous
  The strength of the fierce flame
  was breathed around
And whilst the might of glorious Vulcan thus
  Wrapt the great pile with glare
  and roaring sound,
Hermes dragged forth two heifers,
  lowing loud,
Close to the fire—such might was in
  the god.

XX

And on the earth upon their backs
  he threw
  The panting beasts, and rolled them
  o'er and o'er,
And bored their lives out. Without
  more ado
  He cut up fat and flesh, and down
  before
The fire on spits of wood he placed
  the two,
  Toasting their flesh and ribs, and
  all the gore
Pursed in the bowels ; and while this
  was done
He stretched their hides over a craggy
  stone.

XXI

We mortals let an ox grow old, and
  then
  Cut it up after long consideration,—
But joyous-minded Hermes from the
  glen
  Drew the fat spoils to the more
  open station
Of a flat smooth space, and portioned
  them ; and when
  He had by lot assigned to each a
  ration
Of the twelve gods, his mind became
  aware
Of all the joys which in religion are.

XXII

For the sweet savour of the roasted
  meat
  Tempted him, though immortal.
  Natheless
He checked his haughty will and did
  not eat,
  Though what it cost him words can
  scarce express,
And every wish to put such morsels
  sweet
  Down his most sacred throat, he
  did repress ;
But soon within the lofty portalled
  stall
He placed the fat and flesh and bones
  and all.

XXIII

And every trace of the fresh butchery
  And cooking, the god soon made
  disappear,

As if it all had vanished through the
sky ;
  He burned the hoofs and horns and
    head and hair,—
The insatiate fire devoured them hun-
grily ;
  And when he saw that everything
    was clear,
He quenched the coals and trampled
    the black dust,
And in the stream his bloody sandals
    tossed.

XXIV

All night he worked in the serene
    moonshine—
  But when the light of day was
    spread abroad
He sought his natal mountain peaks
    divine.
  On his long wandering, neither man
    nor god
Had met him, since he killed Apollo's
    kine,
  Nor house-dog had barked at him
    on his road ;
Now he obliquely through the key-
    hole passed,
Like a thin mist, or an autumnal
    blast.

XXV

Right through the temple of the
    spacious cave
  He went with soft light feet—as
    if his tread
Fell not on earth ; no sound their fall-
    ing gave ;
  Then to his cradle he crept quick,
    and spread
The swaddling clothes about him ;
    and the knave
  Lay playing with the covering of
    the bed,
With his left hand about his knees—
    the right
Held his beloved tortoise-lyre tight.

XXVI

There he lay innocent as a newborn
    child,
  As gossips say ; but, though he was
    a god,
The goddess, his fair mother, unbe-
    guiled

Knew all that he had done, being
    abroad ;
" Whence come you, and from what
    adventure wild,
  You cunning rogue, and where
    have you abode
All the long night, clothed in your im-
    pudence ?
What have you done since you de-
    parted hence ?

XXVII

" Apollo soon will pass within this
    gate,
  And bind your tender body in a
    chain
Inextricably tight, and fast as fate,
  Unless you can delude the god
    again,
Even when within his arms—ah,
    runagate !
  A pretty torment both for gods and
    men
Your father made when he made
    you ! "—" Dear mother,"
Replied sly Hermes, " wherefore scold
    and bother ?

XXVIII

" As if I were like other babes as old,
  And understood nothing of what is
    what ;
And cared at all to hear my mother
    scold.
  I in my subtle brain a scheme have
    got,
Which, whilst the sacred stars round
    Heaven are rolled,
  Will profit you and me—nor shall
    our lot
Be as you counsel, without gifts or
    food,
To spend our lives in this obscure
    abode.

XXIX

" But we will leave this shadow-
    peopled cave,
  And live among the gods, and pass
    each day
In high communion, sharing what
    they have
  Of profuse wealth and unexhausted
    prey ;
And, from the portion which my
    father gave

To Phœbus, I will snatch my share
    away,
Which if my father will not—nathe-
    less I,
Who am the king of robbers, can but
    try.

XXX

" And, if Latona's son should find me
    out,
    I'll countermine him by a deeper
        plan ;
I'll pierce the Pythian temple-walls,
    though stout,
    And sack the fane of everything I
        can—
Cauldrons and tripods of great worth
    no doubt,
    Each golden cup and polished
        brazen pan,
All the wrought tapestries and gar-
    ments gay."—
So they together talked ;—mean-
    while the Day

XXXI

Ethereal born, arose out of the flood
    Of flowing Ocean, bearing light to
        men.
Apollo passed toward the sacred wood,
    Which from the inmost depths of
        its green glen
Echoes the voice of Neptune,—and
    there stood
    On the same spot in green Onches-
        tus then
That same old animal, the vine-
    dresser,
Who was employed hedging his vine-
    yard there.

XXXII

Latona's glorious Son began :—" I
    pray
    Tell, ancient hedger of Onchestus
        green,
Whether a drove of kine has passed
    this way,
    All heifers with crooked horns ? for
        they have been
Stolen from the herd in high Pieria,
    Where a black bull was fed apart,
        between
Two woody mountains in a neigh-
    bouring glen,
And four fierce dogs watched there,
    unanimous as men.

XXXIII

" And what is strange, the author of
    this theft
    Has stolen the fatted heifers every
        one,
But the four dogs and the black bull
    are left :—
    Stolen they were last night at set of
        sun,
Of their soft beds and their sweet food
    bereft—
    Now tell me, man born ere the
        world begun,
Have you seen anyone pass with the
    cows ? "
To whom the man of overhanging
    brows,—

XXXIV

" My friend, it would require no com-
    mon skill
    Justly to speak of everything I see ;
On various purposes of good or ill
    Many pass by my vineyard,—and
        to me
'Tis difficult to know the invisible
    Thoughts, which in all those many
        minds may be :—
Thus much alone I certainly can say,
I tilled these vines till the decline of
    day,

XXXV

" And then I thought I saw, but dare
    not speak
    With certainty of such a wondrous
        thing,
A child, who could not have been
    born a week,
    Those fair-horned cattle closely
        following,
And in his hand he held a polished
    stick :
    And, as on purpose, he walked
        wavering
From one side to the other of the
    road,
And with his face opposed the steps
    he trod."

XXXVI

Apollo, hearing this, passed quickly
    on—
    No winged omen could have shown
        more clear

That the deceiver was his father's
son.
  So the god wraps a purple atmosphere
Around his shoulders, and like fire is
gone
  To famous Pylos, seeking his kine
there,
And found their track and his, yet
hardly cold,
And cried—" What wonder do mine
eyes behold !

XXXVII

" Here are the footsteps of the horned
herd
  Turned back towards their fields of
asphodel ;
But these ! are not the tracks of beast
or bird,
  Grey wolf, or bear, or lion of the
dell,
Or maned Centaur—sand was never
stirred
  By man or woman thus ! Inexplicable !
Who with unwearied feet could e'er
impress
The sand with such enormous vestiges ?

XXXVIII

" That was most strange—but this is
stranger still ! "
  Thus having said, Phœbus impetu-
ously
Sought high Cyllene's forest-cinctured
hill,
  And the deep cavern where dark
shadows lie,
And where the ambrosial nymph with
happy will
  Bore the Saturnian's love-child,
Mercury—
And a delighted odour from the dew
Of the hill pastures, at his coming,
flew.

XXXIX

And Phœbus stooped under the
craggy roof
  Arched over the dark cavern :—
Maia's child
Perceived that he came angry, far
aloof,
  About the cows of which he had
been beguiled,

And over him the fine and fragrant
woof
  Of his ambrosial swaddling-clothes
he piled—
As among firebrands lies a burning
spark
Covered, beneath the ashes cold and
dark.

XL

There, like an infant who had sucked
his fill,
  And now was newly washed and put
to bed,
Awake, but courting sleep with weary
will
  And gathered in a lump, hands,
feet, and head,
He lay, and his beloved tortoise still
  He grasped and held under his
shoulder-blade ;
Phœbus the lovely mountain goddess
knew,
Not less her subtle, swindling baby,
who

XLI

Lay swathed in his sly wiles. Round
every crook
Of the ample cavern, for his kine
Apollo
Looked sharp ; and when he saw
them not, he took
  The glittering key, and opened
three great hollow
Recesses in the rock—where many a
nook
  Was filled with the sweet food im-
mortals swallow,
And mighty heaps of silver and of
gold
Were piled within—a wonder to be-
hold !

XLII

And white and silver robes, all overwrought
  With cunning workmanship of
tracery sweet—
Except among the gods there can be
nought
  In the wide world to be compared
with it.
Latona's offspring, after having
sought
  His herds in every corner, thus did
greet

Great Hermes :—" Little cradled
rogue, declare,
Of my illustrious heifers, where they
are !

XLIII

" Speak quickly ! or a quarrel be-
tween us
Must rise, and the event will be,
that I
Shall haul you into dismal Tartarus,
In fiery gloom to dwell eternally !
Nor shall your father nor your mother
loose
The bars of that black dungeon—
utterly
You shall be cast out from the light
of day,
To rule the ghosts of men, unblest as
they."

XLIV

To whom thus Hermes slily answered:
—" Son
Of great Latona, what a speech is
this !
Why come you here to ask me what
is done
With the wild oxen which it seems
you miss ?
I have not seen them, nor from any-
one
Have heard a word of the whole
business ;
If you should promise an immense re-
ward,
I could not tell more than you now
have heard.

XLV

" An ox-stealer should be both tall
and strong,
And I am but a little newborn
thing,
Who, yet at least, can think of nothing wrong :—
My business is to suck, and sleep,
and fling
The cradle-clothes about me all day
long,—
Or, half asleep, hear my sweet
mother sing,
And to be washed in water clean and
warm,
And hushed and kissed and kept secure from harm.

XLVI

" Oh, let not e'er this quarrel be
averred !
The astounded gods would laugh
at you, if e'er
You should allege a story so absurd,
As that a newborn infant forth
could fare
Out of his home after a savage herd.
I was born yesterday—my small
feet are
Too tender for the roads so hard and
rough :—
And if you think that this is not
enough,

XLVII

" I swear a great oath, by my father's
head,
That I stole not your cows, and
that I know
Of no one else who might, or could,
or did.—
Whatever things cows are I do not
know,
For I have only heard the name."—
This said,
He winked as fast as could be, and
his brow
Was wrinkled, and a whistle loud
gave he,
Like one who hears some strange ab-
surdity.

XLVIII

Apollo gently smiled and said :—
" Ay, ay,—
You cunning little rascal, you will
bore
Many a rich man's house, and your
array
Of thieves will lay their siege be-
fore his door.
Silent as night, in night ; and many
a day
In the wild glens rough shepherds
will deplore
That you or yours, having an appe-
tite,
Met with their cattle, comrade of the
night !

XLIX

" And this among the gods shall be
your gift,
To be considered as the lord of
those

Who swindle, housebreak, sheep-
steal, and shoplift ;—
But now if you would not your last
sleep doze,
Crawl out ! "—Thus saying, Phœbus
did uplift
The subtle infant in his swaddling-
clothes,
And in his arms, according to his
wont,
A scheme devised the illustrious Argiphont.

L

*　　*　　*　　*
　*　　*　　*　　*

And sneezed and shuddered—Phœbus on the grass
Him threw, and whilst all that he
had designed
He did perform—eager although to
pass,
Apollo darted from his mighty
mind
Towards the subtle babe the following
scoff :
" Do not imagine this will get you off,

LI

" You little swaddled child of Jove
and May ! "
And seized him :—" By this omen I
shall trace
My noble herds, and you shall lead
the way."—
Cyllenian Hermes from the grassy
place,
Like one in earnest haste to get away,
Rose, and with hands lifted towards his face,
Round both his ears up from his
shoulders drew
His swaddling-clothes, and—" What
mean you to do

LII

" With me, you unkind god ? "—
said Mercury :
" Is it about these cows you tease
me so ?
I wish the race of cows were perished !
—I
Stole not your cows—I do not even
know
What things cows are. Alas ! I well
may sigh,

That, since I came into this world
of woe,
I should have ever heard the name of
one—
But I appeal to the Saturnian's
throne."

LIII

Thus Phœbus and the vagrant Mercury
Talked without coming to an ex-
planation,
With adverse purpose. As for Phœbus, he
Sought not revenge, but only information,
And Hermes tried with lies and roguery
To cheat Apollo.—But when no
evasion
Served—for the cunning one his
match had found—
He paced on first over the sandy
ground.

LIV

He of the Silver Bow, the child of
Jove,
Followed behind, till to their hea-
venly sire
Came both his children—beautiful as
Love,
And from his equal balance did re-
quire
A judgment in the cause wherein they
strove.
O'er odorous Olympus and its snows
A murmuring tumult as they came
arose,—

LV

And from the folded depths of the
great Hill,
While Hermes and Apollo reverent
stood
Before Jove's throne, the indestruct-
ible
Immortals rushed in mighty multitude ;
And, whilst their seats in order due
they fill,
The lofty Thunderer in a careless
mood
To Phœbus said :—" Whence drive
you this sweet prey,
This herald-baby, born but yesterday !—

LVI

" A most important subject, trifler,
    this
   To lay before the gods ! "—" Nay,
    father, nay,
When you have understood the busi-
    ness,
   Say not that I alone am fond of
    prey.
I found this little boy in a recess
   Under Cyllene's mountains far
    away—
A manifest and most apparent thief,
A scandalmonger beyond all belief.

LVII

" I never saw his like either in heaven
   Or upon earth for knavery or
    craft :—
Out of the field my cattle yestereven,
   By the low shore on which the loud
    sea laughed,
He right down to the river-ford had
    driven ;
   And mere astonishment would
    make you daft
To see the double kind of footsteps
    strange
He has impressed wherever he did
    range.

LVIII

" The cattle's track on the black dust
    full well
   Is evident, as if they went towards
The place from which they came—
    that asphodel
   Meadow, in which I feed my many
    herds ;
His steps were most incomprehens-
    ible—
   I know not how I can describe in
    words
Those tracks—he could have gone
    along the sands
Neither upon his feet nor on his
    hands ;—

LIX

" He must have had some other
    stranger mode
   Of moving on : those vestiges im-
    mense,
Far as I traced them on the sandy
    road,
   Seemed like the trail of oak-top-
    pings :—but thence

No mark nor track denoting where
    they trod
   The hard ground gave !—but,
    working at his fence,
A mortal hedger saw him as he past
To Pylos, with the cows, in fiery haste.

LX

" I found that in the dark he quietly
   Had sacrificed some cows, and be-
    fore light
Had thrown the ashes all disper-
    sedly
   About the road—then, still as
    gloomy night,
Had crept into his cradle, either eye
   Rubbing, and cogitating some new
    sleight.
No eagle could have seen him as he
    lay
Hid in his cavern from the peering
    day.

LXI

" I taxed him with the fact, when he
    averred
   Most solemnly that he did neither
    see
Nor even had in any manner heard
   Of my lost cows, whatever things
    cows be ;
Nor could he tell, though offered a
    reward,
   Not even who could tell of them
    to me."
So speaking, Phœbus sate ; and
    Hermes then
Addressed the Supreme Lord of gods
    and men :

LXII

" Great Father, you know clearly be-
    forehand
   That all which I shall say to you is
    sooth ;
I am a most veracious person, and
   Totally unacquainted with un-
    truth.
At sunrise Phœbus came, but with no
    band
   Of gods to bear him witness, in
    great wrath
To my abode, seeking his heifers
    there,
And saying that I must show him
    where they are,

LXIII

" Or he would hurl me down the dark
abyss.

I know that every Apollonian limb
Is clothed with speed and might and
manliness,

As a green bank with flowers—but
unlike him

I was born yesterday, and you may
guess

He well knew this when he in-
dulged the whim

Of bullying a poor little newborn
thing

That slept, and never thought of cow-
driving.

LXIV

" Am I like a strong fellow who steals
kine ?

Believe me, dearest Father, such
you are,

This driving of the herds is none of
mine ;

Across my threshold did I wander
ne'er,

So may I thrive ! I reverence the
divine

Sun and the gods, and I love you,
and care

Even for this hard accuser—who
must know

I am as innocent as they or you.

LXV

" I swear by these most gloriously-
wrought portals—

(It is, you will allow, an oath of
might)

Through which the multitude of the
Immortals

Pass and repass for ever, day and
night,

Devising schemes for the affairs of
mortals—

That I am guiltless ; and I will requite,

Although mine enemy be great and
strong,

His cruel threat—do thou defend the
young ! "

LXVI

So speaking, the Cyllenian Argiphont
Winked, as if now his adversary
was fitted :—

And Jupiter, according to his wont,
Laughed heartily to hear the subtle-
witted

Infant give such a plausible account,
And every word a lie. But he remitted

Judgment at present—and his exhor-
tation

Was, to compose the affair by arbitra-
tion.

LXVII

And they by mighty Jupiter were
bidden

To go forth with a single purpose
both,

Neither the other chiding nor yet
chidden :

And Mercury with innocence and
truth

To lead the way, and show where he
had hidden

The mighty heifers.—Hermes, nothing loth,

Obeyed the Ægis-bearer's will—for he
Is able to persuade all easily.

LXVIII

These lovely children of Heaven's
highest Lord

Hastened to Pylos and the pastures
wide

And lofty stalls by the Alphean ford,
Where wealth in the mute night is
multiplied

With silent growth. Whilst Hermes
drove the herd

Out of the stony cavern, Phœbus
spied

The hides of those the little babe had
slain,

Stretched on the precipice above the
plain.

LXIX

" How was it possible," then Phœbus
said,

" That you, a little child, born
yesterday,

A thing on mother's milk and kisses
fed,

Could two prodigious heifers ever
flay ?

E'en I myself may well hereafter
dread

Your prowess, offspring of Cylle-
nian May,
When you grow strong and tall."—
He spoke, and bound
Stiff withy bands the infant's wrists
around.

LXX

He might as well have bound the oxen
wild :
The withy bands, though starkly
interknit,
Fell at the feet of the immortal child,
Loosened by some device of his
quick wit.
Phœbus perceived himself again beguiled,
And stared—while Hermes sought
some hole or pit,
Looking askance and winking fast as
thought,
Where he might hide himself, and not
be caught.

LXXI

Sudden he changed his plan, and with
strange skill
Subdued the strong Latonian, by
the might
Of winning music, to his mightier will;
His left hand held the lyre, and in
his right
The plectrum struck the chords—unconquerable
Up from beneath his hand in circling flight
The gathering music rose—and sweet
as Love
The penetrating notes did live and
move

LXXII

Within the heart of great Apollo—he
Listened with all his soul, and
laughed for pleasure.
Close to his side stood harping fear-
lessly
The unabashed boy ; and to the
measure
Of the sweet lyre, there followed loud
and free
His joyous voice ; for he unlocked
the treasure
Of his deep song, illustrating the birth
Of the bright gods and the dark des-
ert Earth ;

LXXIII

And how to the Immortals every one
A portion was assigned of all that
is ;
But chief Mnemosyne did Maia's son
Clothe in the light of his loud melo-
dies ;—
And, as each god was born or had be-
gun,
He in their order due and fit de-
grees
Sung of his birth and being—and did
move
Apollo to unutterable love.

LXXIV

These words were winged with his
swift delight :
" You heifer-stealing schemer, well
do you
Deserve that fifty oxen should requite
Such minstrelsies as I have heard
even now.
Comrade of feasts, little contriving
wight,
One of your secrets I would gladly
know,
Whether the glorious power you now
show forth
Was folded up within you at your
birth,

LXXV

" Or whether mortal taught or god
inspired
The power of unpremeditated song?
Many divinest sounds have I admired
The Olympian gods and mortal men
among ;
But such a strain of wondrous,strange,
untired,
And soul-awakening music, sweet
and strong,
Yet did I never hear except from thee,
Offspring of May, impostor Mercury !

LXXVI

" What Muse, what skill, what unimagined use,
What exercise of subtlest art, has
given
Thy songs such power ?—for these
who hear may choose
From three, the choicest of the gifts
of Heaven,

Delight, and love, and sleep, sweet
sleep, whose dews
Are sweeter than the balmy tears of
even :—
And I, who speak this praise, am that
Apollo
Whom the Olympian Muses ever fol-
low :

LXXVII

" And their delight is dance, and the
blithe noise
Of song and overflowing poesy ;
And sweet, even as desire, the liquid
voice
Of pipes, that fills the clear air
thrillingly ;
But never did my inmost soul rejoice
In this dear work of youthful
revelry,
As now I wonder at thee, son of Jove;
Thy harpings and thy song are soft as
love.

LXXVIII

" Now since thou hast, although so
very small,
Science of arts so glorious, thus I
swear,—
And let this cornel javelin, keen and
tall,
Witness between us what I prom-
ise here,—
That I will lead thee to the Olympian
Hall,
Honoured and mighty, with thy
mother dear,
And many glorious gifts in joy will
give thee,
And even at the end will ne'er de-
ceive thee."

LXXIX

To whom thus Mercury with prudent
speech :—
" Wisely hast thou inquired of my
skill :
I envy thee no thing I know to teach
Even this day :—for both in word
and will
I would be gentle with thee ; thou
canst reach
All things in thy wise spirit, and
thy sill
Is highest in heaven among the sons
of Jove,

Who loves thee in the fulness of his
love.

LXXX

" The Counsellor Supreme has given
to thee
Divinest gifts, out of the ampli-
tude
Of his profuse exhaustless treasury ;
By thee, 'tis said, the depths are
understood
Of his far voice ; by thee the mystery
Of all oracular fates,—and the
dread mood
Of the diviner is breathed up, even I—
A child—perceive thy might and
majesty—

LXXXI

" Thou canst seek out and compass
all that wit
Can find or teach ;—yet since thou
wilt, come, take
The lyre—be mine the glory giving
it—
Strike the sweet chords, and sing
aloud, and wake
Thy joyous pleasure out of many a fit
Of tranced sound—and with fleet
fingers make
Thy liquid-voiced comrade talk with
thee,—
It can talk measured music eloquently.

LXXXII

" Then bear it boldly to the revel
loud,
Love-wakening dance, or feast of
solemn state,
A joy by night or day—for those endowed
With art and wisdom who interrogate
It teaches, babbling in delightful
mood,
All things which make the spirit
most elate,
Soothing the mind with sweet familiar
play,
Chasing the heavy shadows of dismay.

LXXXIII

" To those who are unskilled in its
sweet tongue,
Though they should question most
impetuously

Its hidden soul, it gossips something
wrong—
  Some senseless and impertinent
    reply.
But thou who art as wise as thou art
    strong,
  Canst compass all that thou desir-
    est. I
Present thee with this music-flowing
  shell,
Knowing thou canst interrogate it
  well,

LXXXIV

" And let us two henceforth together
    feed
  On this green mountain slope and
    pastoral plain,
The herds in litigation—they will
    breed
  Quickly enough to recompense our
    pain,
If to the bulls and cows we take good
    heed ;—
  And thou, though somewhat over
    fond of gain,
Grudge me not half the profit."—
  Having spoke,
The shell he proffered, and Apollo
  took.

LXXXV

And gave him in return the glittering
    lash,
  Installing him as herdsman ;—from
    the look
Of Mercury then laughed a joyous
    flash ;
  And then Apollo with the plectrum
    strook
The chords, and from beneath his
    hands a crash
  Of mighty sounds rushed up, whose
    music shook
The soul with sweetness, and like an
  adept
His sweeter voice a just accordance
  kept.

LXXXVI

The herd went wandering o'er the
    divine mead,
  Whilst these most beautiful Sons of
    Jupiter
Won their swift way up to the snowy
  head

Of white Olympus, with the joyous
    lyre
Soothing their journey ; and their
    father dread
  Gathered them both into familiar
Affection sweet,—and then, and now,
    and ever,
Hermes must love Him of the Golden
  Quiver,

LXXXVII

To whom he gave the lyre that sweetly
    sounded,
  Which skilfully he held and played
    thereon.
He piped the while, and far and wide
    rebounded
  The echo of his pipings ; every one
Of the Olympians sat with joy as-
    tounded,
  While he conceived another piece of
    fun,
One of his old tricks—which the god
    of Day
Perceiving, said :—" I fear thee, Son
    of May ;—

LXXXVIII

" I fear thee and thy sly chameleon
    spirit,
  Lest thou shouldst steal my lyre
    and crooked bow ;
This glory and power thou dost from
    Jove inherit,
  To teach all craft upon the earth
    below ;
Thieves love and worship thee—it is
    thy merit
  To make all mortal business ebb and
    flow
By roguery :—now, Hermes, if you
    dare
By sacred Styx a mighty oath to
    swear,

LXXXIX

" That you will never rob me, you
    will do
  A thing extremely pleasing to my
    heart."
Then Mercury sware by the Stygian
    dew,
  That he would never steal his bow
    or dart,
Or lay his hands on what to him was
    due.

Or ever would employ his powerful
    art
Against his Pythian fane. Then
    Phœbus swore
There was no god or man whom he
    loved more.

XC

" And I will give thee as a good-will
    token
    The beautiful wand of wealth and
    happiness ;
A perfect three-leaved rod of gold un-
    broken,
    Whose magic will thy footsteps ever
    bless ;
And whatsoever by Jove's voice is
    spoken
Of earthly or divine from its recess,
It like a loving soul to thee will speak,
And more than this do thou forbear
    to seek :

XCI

" For, dearest child, the divinations
    high
    Which thou requirest, 'tis unlawful
    ever
That thou, or any other deity,
    Should understand—and vain were
    the endeavour ;
For they are hidden in Jove's mind,
    and I,
    In trust of them, have sworn that I
    would never
Betray the counsels of Jove's inmost
    will
To any god—the oath was terrible.

XCII

⁂ Then, golden-wanded brother, ask
    me not
    To speak the fates by Jupiter de-
    signed ;
But be it mine to tell their various lot
    To the unnumbered tribes of hu-
    man kind.
Let good to these and ill to those be
    wrought
    As I dispense—but he who comes
    consigned
By voice and wings of perfect augury
To my great shrine, shall find avail
    in me.

XCIII

" Him will I not deceive, but will as-
    sist ;
    But he who comes relying on such
    birds
As chatter vainly, who would strain
    and twist
    The purpose of the gods with idle
    words,
And deems their knowledge light, he
    shall have missed
    His road—whilst I among my other
    hoards
His gifts deposit. Yet, O son of May,
I have another wondrous thing to say :

XCIV

" There are three Fates, three virgin
    Sisters, who,
    Rejoicing in their wind-outspeed-
    ing wings,
Their heads with flour snowed over
    white and new,
    Sit in a vale round which Parnas-
    sus flings
Its circling skirts—from these I have
    learned true
    Vaticinations of remotest things.
My father cared not. Whilst they
    search out dooms,
They sit apart and feed on honey-
    combs.

XCV

" They, having eaten the fresh honey,
    grow
    Drunk with divine enthusiasm,
    and utter
With earnest willingness the truth
    they know ;
    But, if deprived of that sweet food,
    they mutter
All plausible delusions ;—these to you
    I give ;—if you inquire, they will
    not stutter ;
Delight your own soul with them :—
    any man
You would instruct may profit if he
    can.

XCVI

" Take these and the fierce oxen,
    Maia's child—
    O'er many a horse and toil-endur-
    ing mule,

O'er jagged-jawed lions, and the wild
  White-tusked boars, o'er all, by
  field or pool,
Of cattle which the mighty Mother
  mild
  Nourishes in her bosom, thou shalt
  rule—
Thou dost alone the veil of death uplift—
Thou givest not—yet this is a great
  gift."

XCVII

Thus King Apollo loved the child of
  May
  In truth, and Jove covered them
  with love and joy.
Hermes with gods and men even
  from that day
  Mingled, and wrought the latter
  much annoy,
And little profit, going far astray
  Through the dun night. Farewell,
  delightful Boy,
Of Jove and Maia sprung,—never by
  me,
Nor thou, nor other songs, shall un-
  remembered be.

TO CASTOR AND POLLUX

YE wild-eyed Muses, sing the Twins
  of Jove,
Whom the fair-ankled Leda mixed in
  love
With mighty Saturn's heaven-ob-
  scuring Child,
On Taygetus, that lofty mountain
  wild,
Brought forth in joy, mild Pollux
  void of blame,
And steel-subduing Castor, heirs of
  fame.
These are the Powers who earth-born
  mortals save
And ships, whose flight is swift along
  the wave.
When wintry tempests o'er the sav-
  age sea
Are raging, and the sailors tremblingly
Call on the Twins of Jove with prayer
  and vow,
Gathered in fear upon the lofty prow,
And sacrifice with snow-white lambs,
  the wind

And the huge billow bursting close
  behind,
Even then beneath the weltering
  waters bear
The staggering ship—they suddenly
  appear,
On yellow wings rushing athwart the
  sky,
And lull the blasts in mute tranquillity,
And strew the waves on the white
  ocean's bed,
Fair omen of the voyage ; from toil
  and dread,
The sailors rest, rejoicing in the sight,
And plough the quiet sea in safe delight.

TO MINERVA

I SING the glorious Power with azure
  eyes,
Athenian Pallas ! tameless, chaste,
  and wise,
Trilogenia, town-preserving maid,
Revered and mighty ; from this awful
  head
Whom Jove brought forth, in warlike
  armour dressed,
Golden, all radiant ! wonder strange
  possessed
The everlasting gods that shape to
  see,
Shaking a javelin keen, impetuously
Rush from the crest of Ægis-bearing
  Jove ;
Fearfully Heaven was shaken, and
  did move
Beneath the might of the Cerulean-
  eyed ;
Earth dreadfully resounded, far and
  wide,
And lifted from its depths, the sea
  swelled high
In purple billows, the tide suddenly
Stood still, and great Hyperion's sun
  long time
Checked his swift steeds, till where
  she stood sublime,
Pallas from her immortal shoulders
  threw
The arms divine ; wise Jove rejoiced
  to view.
Child of the Ægis-bearer, hail to thee,
Nor thine nor others' praise shall un-
  remembered be.

TO THE SUN

OFFSPRING of Jove, Calliope, once more
To the bright Sun, thy hymn of music pour ;
Whom to the child of star-clad Heaven and Earth
Euryphaessa, large-eyed nymph, brought forth ;
Euryphaessa, the famed sister fair
Of great Hyperion, who to him did bear
A race of loveliest children ; the young Morn,
Whose arms are like twin roses newly born,
The fair-haired Moon, and the immortal Sun,
Who, borne by heavenly steeds his race doth run
Unconquerably, illuming the abodes
Of mortal men and the eternal gods.

Fiercely look forth his awe-inspiring eyes,
Beneath his golden helmet, whence arise
And are shot forth afar clear beams of light ;
His countenance with radiant glory bright,
Beneath his graceful locks far shines around,
And the light vest with which his limbs are bound,
Of woof ethereal, delicately twined
Glows in the stream of the uplifting wind.
His rapid steeds soon bear him to the west ;
Where their steep flight his hands divine arrest,
And the fleet car with yoke of gold, which he
Sends from bright heaven beneath the shadowy sea.

TO THE MOON

DAUGHTERS of Jove, whose voice is melody,
Muses, who know and rule all minstrelsy !
Sing the wide-winged Moon. Around the earth,
From her immortal head in Heaven shot forth,

Far light is scattered—boundless glory springs,
Where'er she spreads her many-beaming wings
The lampless air glows round her golden crown.
But when the Moon divine from Heaven is gone
Under the sea, her beams within abide,
Till, bathing her bright limbs in Ocean's tide,
Clothing her form in garments glittering far,
And having yoked to her immortal car
The beam-invested steeds, whose necks on high   [sky
Curve back, she drives to a remoter
A western Crescent, borne impetuously.
Then is made full the circle of her light,
And as she grows, her beams more bright and bright,
Are poured from Heaven, where she is hovering then,
A wonder and a sign to mortal men.
The Son of Saturn with this glorious Power
Mingled in love and sleep—to whom she bore,
Pandeia, a bright maid of beauty rare
Among the gods, whose lives eternal are.
Hail Queen, great Moon, white-armed Divinity,
Fair-haired and favourable, thus with thee,
My song beginning, by its music sweet
Shall make immortal many a glorious feat
Of demigods, with lovely lips, so well
Which minstrels, servants of the muses, tell.

TO THE EARTH, MOTHER OF ALL

O UNIVERSAL mother, who dost keep
From everlasting thy foundations deep,
Eldest of things, Great Earth, I sing of thee ;
All shapes that have their dwelling in the sea,
All things that fly, or on the ground divine

Live, move, and there are nourished—
    these are thine ;
These from thy wealth thou dost sus-
    tain ; from thee
Fair babes are born, and fruits on
    every tree
Hang ripe and large, revered Divin-
    ity !
    The life of mortal men beneath thy
        sway
Is held ; thy power both gives and
    takes away !
Happy are they whom thy mild fa-
    vours nourish,
All things unstinted round them grow
    and flourish.   [field
For them, endures the life-sustaining
Its load of harvest, and their cattle
    yield
Large increase, and their house with
    wealth is filled.
Such honoured dwell in cities fair and
    free,
The homes of lovely women, pros-
    perously ;
Their sons exult in youth's new bud-
    ding gladness,
And their fresh daughters free from
    care or sadness,
With bloom-inwoven dance and
    happy song,
On the soft flowers the meadow-grass
    among,
Leap round them sporting—such de-
    lights by thee
Are given, rich Power, revered
    Divinity.
    Mother of gods, thou wife of starry
        Heaven,
Farewell ! be thou propitious, and be
    given
A happy life for this brief melody,
Nor thou nor other songs shall unre-
    membered be.

THE CYCLOPS

A Satyric Drama

TRANSLATED FROM THE GREEK OF EURIPIDES

Silenus
Chorus of Satyrs
Ulysses
The Cyclops

Silenus. O Bacchus, what a world
    of toil, both now

And ere these limbs were overworn
    with age,
Have I endured for thee ! First,
    when thou fledst
The mountain nymphs who nursed
    thee, driven afar
By the strange madness Juno sent
    upon thee ;
Then in the battle of the sons of
    Earth,
When I stood foot by foot close to
    thy side,
No unpropitious fellow combatant,
And, driving through his shield my
    winged spear,
Slew vast Enceladus. Consider now,
Is it a dream of which I speak to thee?
By Jove it is not, for you have the
    trophies !
And now I suffer more than all before.
For, when I heard that Juno had de-
    vised
A tedious voyage for you, I put to sea
With all my children quaint in search
    of you,
And I myself stood on the beaked
    prow
And fixed the naked mast ; and all my
    boys,
Leaning upon their oars, with splash
    and strain
Made white with foam the green and
    purple sea,—
And so we sought you, king. We
    were sailing
Near Malea, when an eastern wind
    arose,
And drove us to this wild Ætnean
    rock ;
The one-eyed children of the Ocean
    god,
The man-destroying Cyclopses in-
    habit,
On this wild shore, their solitary
    caves ;
And one of these, named Polypheme,
    has caught us
To be his slaves ; and so, for all de-
    light
Of Bacchic sports, sweet dance and
    melody,
We keep this lawless giant's wander-
    ing flocks,
My sons indeed, on far declivities,
Young things themselves, tend on
    the youngling sheep,

But I remain to fill the water casks,
Or sweeping the hard floor, or minis-
tering
Some impious and abominable meal
To the fell Cyclops.   I am wearied of
it !
And now I must scrape up the littered
floor
With this great iron rake, so to receive
My absent master and his evening
sheep
In a cave neat and clean.   Even now
I see
My children tending the flocks hither-
ward.
Ha ! what is this ? are your Sicin-
nian measures
Even now the same as when with
dance and song
You brought young Bacchus to
Athæa's halls ?

*   *   *

CHORUS OF SATYRS.

Strophe.

Where has he of race divine
Wandered in the winding rocks ?
Here the air is calm and fine
For the father of the flocks ;—
Here the grass is soft and sweet,
And the river eddies meet
In the trough beside the cave,
Bright as in their fountain wave.—
Neither here, nor on the dew
Of the lawny uplands feeding,
Oh, you come !—a stone at you
Will I throw to mend your breed-
ing ;—
Get along, you horned thing,
Wild, seditious, rambling !

Epode.[1]

An Iacchic melody
To the golden Aphrodite
Will I lift, as erst did I
Seeking her and her delight
With the Mænads, whose white feet
To the music glance and fleet.
Bacchus, O beloved, where,
Shaking wide thy yellow hair,
Wanderest thou alone, afar ?
To the one-eyed Cyclops, we,

[1] The Antistrophe is omitted.

Who by right thy servants are,
Minister in misery,
In these wretched goat-skins clad,
Far from thy delights and thee.

Silenus. Be silent, sons ; command
the slaves to drive
The gathered flocks into the rock-
roofed cave.
Chorus. Go ! But what needs this
serious haste, O father ?
Silenus. I see a Grecian vessel on
the coast,
And thence the rowers with some
general,
Approaching to this cave. About
their necks
Hang empty vessels, as they wanted
food,
And water-flasks.— O miserable
strangers !
Whence come they, that they know
not what and who
My master is, approaching in ill hour
The inhospitable roof of Polypheme,
And the Cyclopian jaw-bone, man-
destroying ?
Be silent, Satyrs, while I ask and hear,
Whence coming, they arrive the
Ætnean hill.
Ulysses. Friends, can you show me
some clear water spring,
The remedy of our thirst ?   Will any
one
Furnish with food seamen in want of
it ?
Ha ! what is this ?   We seem to be
arrived
At the blithe court of Bacchus.   I ob-
serve
This sportive band of Satyrs near the
caves.
First let me greet the elder.—Hail !
Silenus.   Hail thou,
O Stranger ! Tell thy country and
thy race.
Ulysses. The Ithacan Ulysses and
the king
Of Cephalonia.
Silenus.   Oh ! I know the man,
Wordy and shrewd, the son of Sisy-
phus.
Ulysses. I am the same, but do not
rail upon me.—
Silenus. Whence sailing do you
come to Sicily ?

Ulysses. From Ilion, and from the Trojan toils.

Silenus. How touched you not at your paternal shore ?

Ulysses. The strength of tempests bore me here by force.

Silenus. The self-same accident occurred to me.

Ulysses. Were you then driven here by stress of weather ?

Silenus. Following the pirates who had kidnapped Bacchus.

Ulysses. What land is this, and who inhabit it ?—   [Sicily

Silenus. Ætna, the loftiest peak in

Ulysses. And are there walls, and tower-surrounded towns ?

Silenus. There are not. These lone rocks are bare of men.

Ulysses. And who possess the land? the race of beasts ?

Silenus. Cyclops, who live in caverns, not in houses.

Ulysses. Obeying whom ? Or is the state popular ?

Silenus. Shepherds : no one obeys any in aught.

Ulysses. How live they ? do they sow the corn of Ceres ?

Silenus. On milk and cheese, and on the flesh of sheep. ·

Ulysses. Have they the Bromian drink from the vine's stream ?

Silenus. Ah ! no ; they live in an ungracious land.

Ulysses. And are they just to strangers ?—hospitable ?

Silenus. They think the sweetest thing a stranger brings,

Is his own flesh.

Ulysses. What ! do they eat man's flesh ?

Silenus. No one comes here who is not eaten up.

Ulysses. The Cyclops now—where is he ? Not at home ?

Silenus. Absent on Ætna, hunting with his dogs.

Ulysses. Knowst thou what thou must do to aid us hence ?

Silenus. I know not : we will help you all we can.

Ulysses. Provide us food, of which we are in want.

Silenus. Here is not anything, as I said, but meat.

Ulysses. But meat is a sweet remedy for hunger.

Silenus. Cow's milk there is, and store of curdled cheese.

Ulysses. Bring out : I would see all before I bargain.

Silenus. But how much gold will you engage to give ?

Ulysses. I bring no gold, but Bacchic juice.

Silenus.   O joy !
'Tis long since these dry lips were wet with wine.

Ulysses. Maron, the son of the god, gave it me.

Silenus. Whom I have nursed a baby in my arms.

Ulysses. The son of Bacchus, for your clearer knowledge.

Silenus. Have you it now ? or is it in the ship ?

Ulysses. Old man, this skin contains it, which you see.

Silenus. Why this would hardly be a mouthful for me.

Ulysses. Nay, twice as much as you can draw from thence.

Silenus. You speak of a fair fountain, sweet to me.

Ulysses. Would you first taste of the unmingled wine ?

Silenus. 'Tis just—tasting invites the purchaser.

Ulysses. Here is the cup, together with the skin.

Silenus. Pour : that the draught may fillip my remembrance.

Ulysses. See !

Silenus.   Papaiapæx ! what a sweet smell it has !

Ulysses. You see it then ?—

Silenus.   By Jove, no ! but I smell it.

Ulysses. Taste, that you may not praise it in words only.

Silenus. Babai ! Great Bacchus calls me forth to dance !

Joy ! joy !

Ulysses. Did it flow sweetly down your throat ?

Silenus. So that it tingled to my very nails.

Ulysses. And in addition I will give you gold.

Silenus. Let gold alone ! Only unlock the cask.

Ulysses. Bring out some cheeses now, or a young goat.

Silenus. That will I do, despising any master.
Yes, let me drink one cup, and I will give
All that the Cyclops feed upon their mountains.

* * *

Chorus. Ye have taken Troy, and laid your hands on Helen ?

Ulysses. And utterly destroyed the race of Priam.

Silenus. * * * *
The wanton wretch ! She was bewitched to see
The many-coloured anklets and the chain
Of woven gold which girt the neck of Paris,
And so she left that good man Menelaus.
There should be no more women in the world
But such as are reserved for me alone.—
See, here are sheep, and here are goats, Ulysses ;
Here are unsparing cheeses of pressed milk ;
Take them ; depart with what good speed ye may ;
First leaving my reward, the Bacchic dew
Of joy-inspiring grapes.

Ulysses.   Ah me ! Alas !
What shall we do ? the Cyclops is at hand !
Old man, we perish ! whither can we fly ?

Silenus. Hide yourselves quick within that hollow rock.

Ulysses. 'Twere perilous to fly into the net.

Silenus. The cavern has recesses numberless ;
Hide yourselves quick.

Ulysses.   That will I never do :
The mighty Troy would be indeed disgraced
If I should fly one man. How many times
Have I withstood with shield immovable,
Ten thousand Phrygians !—If I needs must die,

Yet will I die with glory ;—if I live,
The praise which I have gained will yet remain.

Silenus. What, ho ! assistance, comrades, haste, assistance !

The CYCLOPS, SILENUS, ULYSSES ; CHORUS.

Cyclops. What is this tumult ? Bacchus is not here,
Nor tympanies nor brazen castanets.
How are my young lambs in the cavern ? Milking
Their dams, or playing by their sides ? And is
The new cheese pressed into the bulrush baskets ?
Speak ! I'll beat some of you till you rain tears—
Look up, not downwards, when I speak to you.

Silenus. See ! I now gape at Jupiter himself,
I stare upon Orion and the stars.

Cyclops. Well, is the dinner fitly cooked and laid ?

Silenus. All ready, if your throat is ready too.

Cyclops. Are the bowls full of milk besides ?

Silenus: O'erbrimming ;
So you may drink a tunful if you will.

Cyclops. Is it ewe's milk, or cow's milk, or both mixed ?—

Silenus. Both, either ; only pray don't swallow me.

Cyclops. By no means.——

* * *

What is this crowd I see beside the stalls ?
Outlaws or thieves ? for near my cavern home   [two
I see my young lambs coupled two by
With willow bands ; mixed with my cheeses lie
Their implements ; and this old fellow here
Has his bald head broken with stripes.

Silenus.   Ah me !
I have been beaten till I burn with fever.

Cyclops. By whom ? Who laid his fist upon your head ?

Silenus. Those men, because I would not suffer them
To steal your goods.

Cyclops. Did not the rascals know
I am a god, sprung from the race of heaven ?
Silenus. I told them so, but they bore off your things,
And ate the cheese in spite of all I said,
And carried out the lambs,—and said, moreover,
They'd pin you down with a three-cubit collar,
And pull your vitals out through your one eye,
Torture your back with stripes ; then, binding you,
Throw you as ballast into the ship's hold,
And then deliver you, a slave, to move
Enormous rocks, or found a vestibule.
Cyclops. In truth ? Nay, haste, and place in order quickly
The cooking knives, and heap upon the hearth,
And kindle it, a great faggot of wood.—
As soon as they are slaughtered, they shall fill
My belly, broiling warm from the live coals,
Or boiled and seethed within the bubbling cauldron.
I am quite sick of the wild mountain game ;
Of stags and lions I have gorged enough,
And I grow hungry for the flesh of men.
Silenus. Nay, master, something new is very pleasant
After one thing for ever, and of late
Very few strangers have approached our cave.
Ulysses. Hear, Cyclops, a plain tale on the other side.
We, wanting to buy food, came from our ship
Into the neighbourhood of your cave, and here
This old Silenus gave us in exchange
These lambs for wine, the which he took and drank,
And all by mutual compact, without force.
There is no word of truth in what he says,

For slily he was selling all your store.
Silenus. I ? May you perish, wretch—
Ulysses. If I speak false !
Silenus. Cyclops, I swear by Neptune who begot thee,
By mighty Triton and by Nereus old,
Calypso and the glaucous ocean Nymphs,
The sacred waves and all the race of fishes—
Be these the witnesses, my dear sweet master,
My darling little Çyclops, that I never
Gave any of your stores to these false strangers.—
If I speak false may those whom most I love,
My children, perish wretchedly !
Chorus. There stop !
I saw him giving these things to the strangers.
If I speak false, then may my father perish,
But do not thou wrong hospitality.
Cyclops. You lie ! I swear that he is juster far
Than Rhadamanthus—I trust more in him.
But let me ask, whence have ye sailed, O strangers ?
Who are you ? and what city nourished ye ?
Ulysses. Our race is Ithacan.— Having destroyed
The town of Troy, the tempests of the sea
Have driven us on thy land, O Polypheme.
Cyclops. What, have ye shared in the unenvied spoil
Of the false Helen, near Scamander's stream ?
Ulysses. The same, having endured a woeful toil.
Cyclops. O basest expedition ! Sailed ye not
From Greece to Phrygia for one woman's sake ?
Ulysses. 'Twas the gods' work— no mortal was in fault.
But, O great offspring of the Ocean King !
We pray thee and admonish thee with freedom,

That thou dost spare thy friends who visit thee,

And place no impious food within thy jaws.

For in the depths of Greece we have upreared

Temples to thy great father, which are all

His houses. The sacred bay of Tænarus

Remains inviolate, and each dim recess

Scooped high on the Malean promontory,

And aëry Sunium's silver-veined crag,

Which divine Pallas keeps unprofaned ever,

The Gerastian asylums, and whate'er

Within wide Greece our enterprise has kept

From Phrygian contumely; and in which

You have a common care, for you inhabit

The skirts of Grecian land, under the roots

Of Ætna and its crags, spotted with fire.

Turn then to converse under human laws;

Receive us shipwrecked suppliants, and provide

Food, clothes, and fire, and hospitable gifts;

Nor, fixing upon oxen-piercing spits

Our limbs, so fill your belly and your jaws.

Priam's wide land has widowed Greece enough;

And weapon-winged murder heaped together

Enough of dead, and wives are husbandless,

And ancient women and grey fathers wail

Their childless age:—if you should roast the rest,

And 'tis a bitter feast that you prepare,

Where then would any turn?   Yet be persuaded;

Forgo the lust of your jaw-bone; prefer

Pious humanity to wicked will;

Many have bought too dear their evil joys.

Silenus. Let me advise you; do not spare a morsel

Of all his flesh.   If you should eat his tongue

You would become most eloquent, O Cyclops.

Cyclops. Wealth, my good fellow, is the wise man's god;

All other things are a pretence and boast.

What are my father's ocean promontories,

The sacred rocks whereon he dwells, to me?

Stranger, I laugh to scorn Jove's thunderbolt,

I know not that his strength is more than mine

As to the rest I care not.—When he pours

Rain from above, I have a close pavilion

Under this rock, in which I lie supine,

Feasting on a roast calf or some wild beast,

And drinking pans of milk, and gloriously

Emulating the thunder of high heaven.

And when the Thracian wind pours down the snow,

I wrap my body in the skins of beasts,

Kindle a fire, and bid the snow whirl on.

The earth by force, whether it will or no,

Bringing forth grass, fattens my flocks and herds,

Which, to what other god but to myself

And this great belly, first of deities,

Should I be bound to sacrifice?   I well know

The wise man's only Jupiter is this,

To eat and drink during his little day,

And give himself no care.   And as for those

Who complicate with laws the life of man,

I freely give them tears for their reward.

I will not cheat my soul of its delight,

Or hesitate in dining upon you:—

And that I may be quit of all demands,

These are my hospitable gifts;—fierce fire

And yon ancestral cauldron, which o'erbubbling
Shall finely cook your miserable flesh.
Creep in !—

*   *   *

Ulysses. Ay, ay ! I have escaped the Trojan toils,
I have escaped the sea, and now I fall
Under the cruel grasp of one impious man.
O Pallas, mistress, goddess, sprung from Jove,
Now, now, assist me ! Mightier toils than Troy
Are these ;—I totter on the chasms of peril ;—
And thou who inhabitest the thrones
Of the bright stars, look, hospitable Jove,
Upon this outrage of thy deity,
Otherwise be considered as no god.

CHORUS (*alone*).
For your gaping gulf and your gullet wide
The ravine is ready on every side ;
The limbs of the strangers are cooked and done,
There is boiled meat, and roast meat, and meat from the coal,
You may chop it, and tear it, and gnash it for fun,
A hairy goat's skin contains the whole.
Let me but escape, and ferry me o'er
The stream of your wrath to a safer shore.

The Cyclops Ætnean is cruel and bold,
     He murders the strangers
       That sit on his hearth,
     And dreads no avengers
       To rise from the earth.

He roasts the men before they are cold,
He snatches them broiling from the coal.
And from the cauldron pulls them whole,
And minces their flesh and gnaws their bone
With his cursed teeth, till àll be gone.

     Farewell, foul pavilion !
      Farewell, rites of dread !
     The Cyclops vermilion,

     With slaughter uncloying,
       Now feasts on the dead,
     In the flesh of strangers joying !

Ulysses. O Jupiter ! I saw within the cave
Horrible things ; deeds to be feigned in words,
But not believed as being done.
Chorus. What ! sawest thou the impious Polypheme
Feasting upon your loved companions now ?
Ulysses. Selecting two, the plumpest of the crowd,
He grasped them in his hands.—
     Chorus.   Unhappy man !

*   *   *

Ulysses. Soon as we came into this craggy place,
Kindling a fire, he cast on the broad hearth
The knotty limbs of an enormous oak,
Three waggon-loads at least, and then he strewed
Upon the ground, beside the red fire light,
His couch of pine leaves ; and he milked the cows,
And pouring forth the white milk, filled a bowl
Three cubits wide and four in depth, as much
As would contain four amphoræ, and bound it
With ivy wreaths ; then placed upon the fire
A brazen pot to boil, and make red hot
The points of spits, not sharpened with the sickle,
But with a fruit-tree bough, and with the jaws
Of axes for Ætnean slaughterings.[1]
And when this god-abandoned cook of hell
Had made all ready, he seized two of us.
And killed them in a kind of measured manner ;
For he flung one against the brazen rivets
Of the huge cauldron, and seized the other

---

[1] I confess I do not understand this. *Note of the Author*

By the foot's tendon, and knocked
  out his brains
Upon the sharp edge of the craggy
  stone:
Then peeled his flesh with a great
  cooking knife,
And put him down to roast. The
  other's limbs
He chopped into the cauldron to be
  boiled.
And I, with the tears raining from
  my eyes,
Stood near the Cyclops, ministering
  to him;
The rest, in the recesses of the cave,
Clung to the rock like bats, bloodless
  with fear.
When he was filled with my compan-
  ions' flesh,
He threw himself upon the ground,
  and sent
A loathsome exhalation from his maw.
Then a divine thought came to me. I
  filled
The cup of Maron, and I offered him
To taste, and said :—" Child of the
  Ocean-god,
Behold what drink the vines of Greece
  produce,
The exultation and the joy of Bac-
  chus."
He, satiated with his unnatural food,
Received it, and at one draught drank
  it off,
And, taking my hand, praised me :—
  " Thou hast given
A sweet draught after a sweet meal,
  dear guest."
And I, perceiving that it pleased him,
  filled
Another cup, well knowing that the
  wine
Would wound him soon and take a
  sure revenge.
And the charm fascinated him, and I
Plied him cup after cup, until the
  drink
Had warmed his entrails, and he sang
  aloud
In concert with my wailing fellow-
  seamen
A hideous discord—and the cavern
  rung.
I have stolen out, so that if you will
You may achieve my safety and your
  own.

But say, do you desire, or not, to fly
This uncompanionable man, and
  dwell,
As was your wont, among the Grecian
  nymphs,
Within the fanes of your beloved god ?
Your father there within agrees to it,
But he is weak and overcome with
  wine,
And caught as if with birdlime by the
  cup,
He claps his wings and crows in dot-
  ing joy,
You who are young escape with me,
  and find
Bacchus your ancient friend ; un-
  suited he
To this rude Cyclops.
    Chorus.   O my dearest friend,
That I could see that day, and leave
  for ever
The impious Cyclops.
            *   *   *
    Ulysses. Listen then what a punish-
  ment I have
For this fell monster, how secure a
  flight
From your hard servitude.
    Chorus.   Oh ! sweeter far
Than is the music of an Asian lyre
Would be the news of Polypheme
  destroyed.
    Ulysses. Delighted with the Bac-
  chic drink, he goes
To call his brother Cyclops—who in-
  habit
A village upon Ætna not far off.
    Chorus. I understand : catching
  him when alone,
You think by some measure to dis-
  patch him,
Or thrust him from the precipice.
    Ulysses.   Oh no ;
Nothing of that kind ; my device is
  subtle.
    Chorus. How then ? I heard of old
  that thou wert wise.
    Ulysses. I will dissuade him from
  this plan, by saying
It were unwise to give the Cyclopses
This precious drink, which if enjoyed
  alone
Would make life sweeter for a longer
  time.
When vanquished by the Bacchic
  power, he sleeps,

There is a trunk of olive-wood within,
Whose point, having made sharp with
    this good sword,
I will conceal in fire, and when I see
It is alight, will fix it, burning yet,
Within the socket of the Cyclops' eye,
And melt it out with fire—as when a
    man
Turns by its handle a great auger
    round,
Fitting the framework of a ship with
    beams.
So will I in the Cyclops' fiery eye
Turn round the brand, and dry the
    pupil up.
    Chorus. Joy! I am mad with joy
    at your device.
    Ulysses. And then with you, my
    friends, and the old man,
We'll load the hollow depth of our
    black ship,
And row with double strokes from this
    dread shore.
    Chorus. May I, as in libations to a
    god,
Share in the blinding him with the
    red brand?
I would have some communion in his
    death.
    Ulysses. Doubtless; the brand is
    a great brand to hold.
    Chorus. Oh! I would lift a hundred
    waggon-loads,
If like a wasp's nest I could scoop the
    eye out
Of the detested Cyclops.
    Ulysses.   Silence now!
Ye know the close device—and when
    I call,
Look ye obey the masters of the craft.
I will not save myself and leave be-
    hind
My comrades in the cave: I might
    escape,
Having got clear from that obscure
    recess,
But 'twere unjust to leave in jeopardy
The dear companions who sailed here
    with me.

CHORUS.

Come! who is first, that with his hand
Will urge down the burning brand
Through the lids, and quench and
    pierce
The Cyclops' eye so fiery fierce?

SEMI-CHORUS I.—*Song within.*

Listen! listen! he is coming,
A most hideous discord humming,
Drunken, museless, awkward, yelling,
Far along his rocky dwelling;
Let us with some comic spell
Teach the yet unteachable.
By all means he must be blinded,
If my counsel be but minded.

SEMI-CHORUS II.

Happy those made odorous
With the dew which sweet grapes
    weep,
To the village hastening thus,
Seek the vines that soothe to sleep,
Having first embraced thy friend,
There in luxury without end,
With the strings of yellow hair,
Of thy voluptuous leman fair,
Shall sit playing on a bed!—
Speak, what door is opened?

CYCLOPS.

Ha! ha! ha! I'm full of wine,
Heavy with the joy divine,
With the young feast oversated.
Like a merchant's vessel freighted
To the water's edge, my crop
Is laden to the gullet's top.
The fresh meadow grass of spring
Tempts me forth, thus wandering
To my brothers on the mountains,
Who shall share the wine's sweet
    fountains.
Bring the cask, O stranger, bring!

CHORUS.

One with eyes the fairest
Cometh from his dwelling;
Some one loves thee, rarest,
Bright beyond my telling.
In thy grace thou shinest
Like some nymph divinest,
In her caverns dewy;—
All delights pursue thee,
Soon pied flowers, sweet-breathing,
Shall thy head be wreathing.

    Ulysses. Listen, O Cyclops, for I am
    well skilled
In Bacchus, whom I gave thee of to
    drink.
    Cyclops. What sort of god is Bac-
    chus then accounted?

Ulysses. The greatest among men
for joy of life.

Cyclops. I gulped him down with
very great delight.

Ulysses. This is a god who never
injures men.

Cyclops. How does the god like
living in a skin?

Ulysses. He is content wherever he
is put.

Cyclops. Gods should not have their
body in a skin.

Ulysses. If he give joy, what is his
skin to you?

Cyclops. I hate the skin, but love
the wine within.

Ulysses. Stay here; now drink,
and make your spirit glad.

Cyclops. Should I not share this
liquor with my brothers?

Ulysses. Keep it yourself, and be
more honoured so.

Cyclops. I were more useful, giving
to my friends.

Ulysses. But village mirth breeds
contests, broils, and blows.

Cyclops. When I am drunk none
shall lay hands on me.

Ulysses. A drunken man is better
within doors.

Cyclops. He is a fool, who drinking
loves not mirth.

Ulysses. But he is wise who, drunk,
remains at home.

Cyclops. What shall I do, Silenus?
Shall I stay?

Silenus. Stay—for what need have
you of pot companions?

Cyclops. Indeed this place is close-
ly carpeted
With flowers and grass.

Silenus. And in the sun-warm
noon
'Tis sweet to drink. Lie down beside
me now,
Placing your mighty sides upon the
ground.

Cyclops. What do you put the cup
behind me for?

Silenus. That no one here may
touch it.

Cyclops. Thievish one!
You want to drink;—here, place it in
the midst.
And thou, O stranger, tell how art
thou called?

Ulysses. My name is Nobody.
What favour now
Shall I receive to praise you at your
hands?

Cyclops. I'll feast on you the last of
your companions.

Ulysses. You grant your guest a
fair reward, O Cyclops.

Cyclops. Ha! what is this? Stealing the wine, you rogue!

Silenus. It was this stranger kissing me, because
I looked so beautiful.

Cyclops. You shall repent
For kissing the coy wine that loves
you not.

Silenus. By Jupiter! you said that
I am fair.

Cyclops. Pour out, and only give
me the cup full.

Silenus. How is it mixed? Let me
observe.

Cyclops. Curse you!
Give it me so.

Silenus. Not till I see you wear
That coronal, and taste the cup to you.

Cyclops. Thou wily traitor!

Silenus. But the wine is sweet.
Ay, you will roar if you are caught in
drinking.

Cyclops, See now, my lip is clean
and all my beard.

Silenus. Now put your elbow right,
and drink again.
As you see me drink— * * *

Cyclops. How now?

Silenus. Ye gods, what a delicious gulp!

Cyclops. Guest, take it;—you pour
out the wine for me.

Ulysses. The wine is well accustomed to my hand.

Cyclops. Pour out the wine!

Ulysses. I pour; only be silent.

Cyclops. Silence is a hard task to
him who drinks.

Ulysses. Take it and drink it off;
leave not a dreg.
Oh, that the drinker died with his own
draught!

Cyclops. Papai! the vine must be
a sapient plant.

Ulysses. If you drink much after a
mighty feast,
Moistening your thirsty maw, you
will sleep well;

If you leave aught, Bacchus will dry
   you up.
  Cyclops. Ho! ho! I can scarce
  rise. What pure delight!
The heavens and earth appear to
  whirl about
Confusedly. I see the throne of Jove
And the clear congregation of the
  gods.
Now if the Graces tempted me to kiss,
I would not, for the loveliest of them
  all
I would not leave this Ganymede.
Silenus.   Polypheme,
I am the Ganymede of Jupiter.
Cyclops. By Jove! you are; I bore
  you off from Dardanus.

      ULYSSES *and the* CHORUS.

  Ulysses. Come, boys of Bacchus,
  children of high race,
This man within is folded up in sleep,
And soon will vomit flesh from his fell
  maw;
The brand under the shed thrusts out
  its smoke,
No preparation needs, but to burn out
The monster's eye;—but bear your-
  selves like men.
  Chorus. We will have courage like
  the adamant rock.
All things are ready for you here; go
  in,   [noise.
Before our father shall perceive the
  Ulysses. Vulcan, Ætnean king!
  burn out with fire
The shining eye of this thy neighbour-
  ing monster!
And thou, O Sleep, nursling of gloomy
  night,
Descend unmixed on this god-hated
  beast,
And suffer not Ulysses and his com-
  rades,
Returning from their famous Trojan
  toils,
To perish by this man, who cares not
  either
For god or mortal; or I needs must
  think
That Chance is a supreme divinity,
And things divine are subject to her
  power.

        CHORUS.
Soon a crab the throat will seize
 Of him who feeds upon his guest,

Fire will burn his lamp-like eyes
  In revenge of such a feast!
A great oak stump now is lying
  In the ashes yet undying.

Come, Maron, come!
Raging let him fix the doom,
Let him tear the eyelid up,
 Of the Cyclops—that his cup
  May be evil!
Oh, I long to dance and revel
With sweet Bromian, long desired,
In loved ivy-wreaths attired;
  Leaving this abandoned home—
  Will the moment ever come?

  Ulysses. Be silent, ye wild things!
  Nay, hold your peace,
And keep your lips quite close; dare
  not to breathe,
Or spit, or e'en wink, lest ye wake the
  monster,
Until his eye be tortured out with fire.
  Chorus. Nay, we are silent, and we
  chaw the air.
  Ulysses. Come now, and lend a
  hand to the great stake
Within—it is delightfully red hot.
  Chorus. You then command who
  first should seize the stake
To burn the Cyclops' eye, that all may
  share
In the great enterprise.
  Semi-Chorus I.   We are too few;
We cannot at this distance from the
  door
Thrust fire into his eye.
  Semi-Chorus II.   And we just
  now
Have become lame; cannot move
  hand nor foot.
  Chorus. The same thing has oc-
  cured to us;—our ankles
Are sprained with standing here, I
  know not how.
  Ulysses. What, sprained with stand-
  ing still?
  Chorus.   And there is dust
Or ashes in our eyes, I know not
  whence.
  Ulysses. Cowardly dogs, ye will
  not aid me, then?
  Chorus. With pitying my own back
  and my backbone,
And with not wishing all my teeth
  knocked out!

This cowardice comes of itself—but
stay,
I know a famous Orphic incantation
To make the brand stick of its own
accord
Into the skull of this one-eyed son of
Earth.

Ulysses. Of old I knew ye thus by
nature ; now
I know ye better.—I will use the aid
Of my own comrades—yet though
weak of hand
Speak cheerfully, that so ye may
awaken
The courage of my friends with your
blithe words·

Chorus. This I will do with peril of
my life, ·
And blind you with my exhortations,
Cyclops.

Hasten and thrust,
And parch up to dust,
The eye of the beast,
Who feeds on his guest.
Burn and blind
The Ætnean hind !
Scoop and draw,
But beware lest he claw
Your limbs near his maw.

Cyclops. Ah me ! my eyesight is
parched up to cinders.
Chorus. What a sweet pæan ! sing
me that again !
Cyclops. Ah me ! indeed, what woe
has fallen upon me !
But, wretched nothings, think ye not
to flee
Out of this rock ; I, standing at the
outlet,
Will bar the way, and catch you as
you pass.
Chorus. What are you roaring out,
Cyclops ?
Cyclops. I perish !
Chorus. For you are wicked.
Cyclops. And besides miserable.
Chorus. What, did you fall into the
fire when drunk ?
Cyclops. 'Twas Nobody destroyed
me.
Chorus. Why then no one
can be to blame.
Cyclops. I say 'twas Nobody
Who blinded me.

Chorus. Why then, you are not
blind !
Cyclops. I wish you were as blind
as I am.
Chorus. Nay,
It cannot be that no one made you
blind.
Cyclops. You jeer me ; where, I
ask, is Nobody ?
Chorus. No where, O Cyclops * * *
Cyclops. It was that stranger
ruined me :—the wretch
First gave me wine, and then burnt
out my eye,
For wine is strong and hard to
struggle with.
Have they escaped, or are they yet
within ?
Chorus. They stand under the dark-
ness of the rock,
And cling to it.
Cyclops. At my right hand or
left ?
Chorus. Close on your right.
Cyclops. Where ?
Chorus. Near the rock itself.
You have them.
Cyclops. Oh, misfortune on
misfortune !
I've crack'd my skull.
Chorus. Now they escape you
there.
Cyclops. Not there, although you
say so.
Chorus. Not on that side.
Cyclops. Where then ?
Chorus. They creep about you
on your left.
Cyclops. Ah ! I am mocked ! They
jeer me in my ills.
Chorus. Not there ! he is a little
there beyond you.
Cyclops. Detested wretch ! where
are you ?
Ulysses. Far from you
I keep with care this body of Ulysses.
Cyclops. What do you say ? You
proffer a new name.
Ulysses. My father named me so ;
and I have taken
A full revenge for your unnatural
feast ;
I should have done ill to have burned
down Troy,
And not revenged the murder of my
comrades.

Cyclops. Ai ! ai ! the ancient oracle
is accomplished ;
It said that I should have my eye-
sight blinded
By you coming from Troy; yet it fore-
told
That you should pay the penalty for
this
By wandering long over the homeless
sea.
Ulysses. I bid thee weep—con-
sider what I say,
I go towards the shore to drive my
ship
To mine own land, o'er the Sicilian
wave.
Cyclops. Not so, if whelming you
with this huge stone
I can crush you and all your men to-
gether ;
I will descend upon the shore, though
blind,
Groping my way adown the steep
ravine.
Chorus. And we, the shipmates of
Ulysses now,
Will serve our Bacchus all our happy
lives.

EPIGRAMS

SPIRIT OF PLATO

FROM THE GREEK

"EAGLE! why soarest thou above that
tomb ?
To what sublime and star-ypaven
home
Floatest thou ? "
" I am the image of swift Plato's
spirit,
Ascending heaven—Athens does in-
herit
His corpse below."

FROM THE GREEK

A MAN who was about to hang himself,
Finding a purse, then threw away his
rope ;
Th owner coming to reclaim his pelf,
The halter found and used it. So is
Hope
Changed for Despair—one laid upon
the shelf,

We take the other. Under heaven's
high cope
Fortune is God—all you endure and
do
Depends on circumstance as much as
you.

TO STELLA

FROM PLATO

THOU wert the Morning Star among
the living,
Ere thy fair light had fled ;—
Now, having died, thou art as Hes-
perus, giving
New splendour to the dead.

FROM PLATO

KISSING Helena, together
With my kiss, my soul beside it
Came to my lips, and there I kept it,—
For the poor thing had wandered
thither,
To follow where the kiss should guide
it ;—
O, cruel I, to intercept it !

SONNETS FROM THE GREEK OF MOSCHUS

Τὰν ἄλα τὰν γλαυκὰν ὅταν ωνεμος ἀτρέμα
βάλλῃ,—κ. τ. λ.

I

WHEN winds that move not its calm
surface sweep
The azure sea, I love the land no more;
The smiles of the serene and tranquil
deep
Tempt my unquiet mind.—But when
the roar
Of ocean's grey abyss resounds, and
foam
Gathers upon the sea, and vast waves
burst,
I turn from the drear aspect to the
home
Of earth and its deep woods, where,
interspersed,
When winds blow loud, pines make
sweet melody ;
Whose house is some lone bark, whose
toil the sea,

Whose prey, the wandering fish, an
    evil lot
Has chosen.—But I my languid limbs
    will fling
Beneath the plane, where the brook's
    murmuring
Moves the calm spirit but disturbs it
    not.

II

PAN loved his neighbour Echo, but
    that child
Of Earth and Air pined for the Satyr
    leaping ;
The Satyr loved with wasting madness
    wild
The bright nymph Lyda—and so the
    three went weeping.
As Pan loved Echo, Echo loved the
    Satyr ;
The Satyr, Lyda, and thus love con-
    sumed them.
And thus to each—which was a woe-
    ful matter
To bear what they inflicted, justice
    doomed them ;
For, inasmuch as each might hate the
    lover,
Each, loving, so was hated.—Ye that
    love not
Be warned ; in thought turn this ex-
    ample over,
That, when ye love, the like return
    ye prove not.

SONNET FROM THE ITALIAN
OF DANTE

DANTE ALIGHIERI TO GUIDO CAVAL-
CANTI

GUIDO, I would that Lappo, thou, and
    I,
Led by some strong enchantment,
    might ascend
A magic ship, whose charmed sails
    should fly
With winds at will where'er our
    thoughts might wend,
So that no change, nor any evil
    chance,
Should mar our joyous voyage ; but
    it might be,
That even satiety should still en-
    hance

Between our hearts their strict com-
    munity ;
And that the bounteous wizard then
    would place
Vanna and Bice and my gentle love,
Companions of our wandering, and
    would grace
With passionate talk, wherever we
    might rove,
Our time, and each were as content
    and free
As I believe that thou and I should
    be.

SCENES

FROM

"THE MAGICO PRODIGIOSO" OF
CALDERON

CYPRIAN *as a Student ;* CLARIN *and*
MOSCON *as poor Scholars, with*
books

Cyprian. IN the sweet solitude of
    this calm place,
This intricate wild wilderness of trees
And flowers and undergrowth of odor-
    ous plants,
Leave me ; the books you brought
    out of the house
To me are ever best society.
And whilst with glorious festival and
    song
Antioch now celebrates the consecra-
    tion
Of a proud temple to great Jupiter,
And bears his image in loud jubilee
To its new shrine, I would consume
    what still
Lives of the dying day, in studious
    thought,
Far from the throng and turmoil.
    You, my friends,
Go and enjoy the festival ; it will
Be worth the labour, and return for
    me
When the sun seeks its grave among
    the billows,
Which among dim grey clouds on the
    horizon
Dance like white plumes upon a
    hearse ;—and here
I shall expect you.
    Moscon. I cannot bring my
    mind,
Great as my haste to see the festival

Certainly is, to leave you, Sir, without
Just saying some three or four hun-
    dred words.
How is it possible that on a day
Of such festivity, you can bring your
    mind
To come forth to a solitary country
With three or four old books, and turn
    your back
On all this mirth ?

    Clarin.   My master's in the
right ;
There is not anything more tiresome
Than a procession day, with troops of
    men,
And dances, and all that.

    Moscon.   From first to last,
Clarin, you are a temporising flatterer;
You praise not what you feel, but
    what he does ;—
Toad-eater !

    Clarin.   You lie—under a mis-
take—
For this is the most civil sort of lie
That can be given to a man's face. I
    now
Say what I think.

    Cyprian.   Enough, you foolish
    fellows,
Puffed up with your own doting ig-
    norance,   [question.
You always take the two sides of one
Now go, and as I said, return for me
When night falls, veiling in its
    shadows wide
This glorious fabric of the universe.

    Moscon. How happens it, although
    you can maintain
The folly of enjoying festivals,
That yet you go there ?

    Clarin.   Nay, the consequence
Is clear :—who ever did what he ad-
    vises
Others to do ?—

    Moscon.   Would that my feet
    were wings,
So would I fly to Livia.   [*Exit.*

    Clarin.   To speak truth,
Livia is she who has surprised my
    heart ;
But he is more than half way there.—
    'Soho !
Livia, I come ; good sport, Livia,
    soho !   [*Exit.*

    Cyprian. Now since I am alone, let
    me examine

The question which has long disturbed
    my mind
With doubt, since first I read in Plinius
The words of mystic import and deep
    sense
In which he defines God.   My intel-
    lect
Can find no God with whom these
    marks and signs
Fitly agree. It is a hidden truth
Which I must fathom.   [*Reads.*

Enter the DEVIL, *as a fine Gentleman.*

    Dæmon.   Search even as thou
    wilt,
But thou shalt never find what I can
    hide.

    Cyprian. What noise is that among
    the boughs ? Who moves ?
What art thou ?—

    Dæmon.   'Tis a foreign gentle-
    man.
Even from this morning I have lost
    my way
In this wild place, and my poor horse,
    at last
Quite overcome, has stretched him-
    self upon
The enamelled tapestry of this mossy
    mountain,
And feeds and rests at the same time.
    I was
Upon my way to Antioch upon busi-
    ness
Of some importance, but wrapt up in
    cares
(Who is exempt from this inherit-
    ance ?)
I parted from my company, and lost
My way, and lost my servants and
    my comrades.

    Cyprian. 'Tis singular, that, even
    within the sight
Of the high towers of Antioch, you
    could lose
Your way. Of all the avenues and
    green paths
Of this wild wood there is not one but
    leads,
As to its centre, to the walls of Anti-
    och ;
Take which you wil you cannot miss
    your road.

    Dæmon. And such is ignorance !
    Even in the sight

Of knowledge it can draw no profit
    from it.
But, as it still is early, and as I
Have no acquaintances in Antioch,
Being a stranger there, I will even
    wait
The few surviving hours of the day,
Until the night shall conquer it.   I
    see,
Both by your dress and by the books
    in which
You find delight and company, that
    you
Are a great student ;—for my part,
    I feel
Much sympathy with such pursuits.
    Cyprian.   Have you
Studied much ?—
    Dæmon.   No ;—and yet I know
    enough
Not to be wholly ignorant.
    Cyprian.   Pray, sir,
What science may you know ?—
    Dæmon.   Many.
    Cyprian.   Alas !
Much pains must we expend on one
    alone,
And even then attain it not ;—but you
Have the presumption to assert that
    you
Know many without study.
    Dæmon.   And with truth.
For, in the country whence I come,
    sciences
Require no learning,—they are known.
    Cyprian.   Oh, would
I were of that bright country! for in
    this
The more we study, we the more dis-
    cover
Our ignorance.
    Dæmon.   It is so true, that I
Had so much arrogance as to oppose
The chair of the most high Professor-
    ship,
And obtained many votes, and though
    I lost,
The attempt was still more glorious
    than the failure
Could be dishonourable : if you be-
    lieve not,
Let us refer it to dispute respecting
That which you know best, and al-
    though I
Know not the opinion you maintain,
    and though

It be the true one, I will take the con-
    trary.
    Cyprian. The offer gives me plea-
    sure.   I am now
Debating with myself upon a passage
Of Plinius, and my mind is racked
    with doubt
To understand and know who is the
    God
Of whom he speaks.
    Dæmon.   It is a passage, if
I recollect it right, couched in these
    words :
" God is one supreme goodness, one
    pure essence,
One substance, and one sense, all
    sight, all hands."
    Cyprian. 'Tis true.
    Dæmon.   What difficulty find
    you here ?
    Cyprian. I do not recognise among
    the gods
The God defined by Plinius : if he
    must
Be supreme goodness, even Jupiter
Is not supremely good ; because we see
His deeds are evil, and his attributes
Tainted with mortal weakness.   In
    what manner
Can supreme goodness be consistent
    with
The passions of humanity ?
    Dæmon.   The wisdom
Of the old world masked with the
    names of gods
The attributes of Nature and of Man ;
A sort of popular philosophy.
    Cyprian. This reply will not satisfy
    me, for
Such awe is due to the high name of
    God,
That ill should never be imputed.
    Then,
Examining the question with more
    care,
It follows, that the gods should always
    will
That which is best, were they su-
    premely good.
How then does one will one thing,
    one another ?
And you may not say that I allege
Poetical or philosophic learning :—
Consider the ambiguous responses
Of their oracular statues ; from two
    shrines

Two armies shall obtain the assur-
ance of
One victory. Is it not indisputable
That two contending wills can never
lead
To the same end? And, being op-
posite,
If one be good is not the other evil?
Evil in God is inconceivable;
But supreme goodness fails among
the gods
Without their union.

Dæmon. I deny your major.
These responses are means towards
some end
Unfathomed by our intellectual beam.
They are the work of Providence, and
more
The battle's loss may profit those
who lose,
Than victory advantage those who
win.

Cyprian. That I admit, and yet
that God should not
(Falsehood is incompatible with deity)
Assure the victory, it would be enough
To have permitted the defeat; if God
Be all sight,—God, who beheld the
truth,
Would not have given assurance of an
end
Never to be accomplished; thus, al-
though
The Deity may according to his attri-
butes
Be well distinguished into persons, yet
Even in the minutest circumstance,
His essence must be one.

Dæmon. To attain the end,
The affections of the actors in the
scene
Must have been thus influenced by his
voice.

Cyprian. But for a purpose thus
subordinate
He might have employed genii, good
or evil,—
A sort of spirits called so by the
learned,
Who roam about inspiring good or
evil,
And from whose influence and existence we
May well infer our immortality :—
Thus God might easily, without descending

To a gross falsehood in his proper
person,
Have moved the affections by this
mediation
To the just point.

Dæmon. These trifling contra-
dictions
Do not suffice to impugn the unity
Of the high gods; in things of great
importance
They still appear unanimous; con-
sider
That glorious fabric—man, his work-
manship,
Is stamped with one conception.

Cyprian. Who made man
Must have, methinks, the advantage
of the others
If they are equal, might they not
have risen
In opposition to the work, and being
All hands, according to our author
here,
Have still destroyed even as the other
made?
If equal in their power, and only un-
equal
In opportunity, which of the two
Will remain conqueror?

Dæmon. On impossible
And false hypothesis, there can be
built
No argument. Say, what do you
infer
From this?

Cyprian. That there must be a
mighty God
Of supreme goodness and of highest
grace,
All sight all hands, all truth, infall-
ible
Without an equal and without a
rival ;
The cause of all things and the effect
of nothing,
One power, one will, one substance,
and one essence.
And, in whatever persons, one or two,
His attributes may be distinguished,
one
Sovereign power, one solitary essence,
One cause of all cause. [*They rise.*

Dæmon. How can I impugn
So clear a consequence?

Cyprian. Do you regret
My victory?

Dæmon.   Who but regrets a check
In rivalry of wit ? I could reply
And urge new difficulties, but will
    now
Depart, for I hear steps of men ap-
    proaching,
And it is time that I should now pur-
    sue
My journey to the city.
    Cyprian.   Go in peace !
    Dæmon. Remain in peace ! Since
    thus it profits him
To study, I will wrap his senses up
In sweet oblivion of all thought but of
A piece of excellent beauty ; and, as I
Have power given me to wage enmity
Against Justina's soul, I will extract
From one effect two vengeances.
                            [*Exit.*
    Cyprian.   I never
Met a more learned person.   Let me
    now
Revolve this doubt again with careful
    mind.   [*He reads.*

    Enter LELIO *and* FLORO.

    Lelio. Here stop.   Those toppling
    rocks and tangled boughs,
Impenetrable by the noonday beam,
Shall be sole witnesses of what we—
    Floro.   Draw !
If there were words, here is the place
    for deeds.
    Lelio. Thou needest not instruct
    me ; well I know
That in the field the silent tongue of
    steel
Speaks thus.   [*They fight.*
    Cyprian. Ha ! what is this ? Lelio,
    Floro,
Be it enough that Cyprian stands be-
    tween you,
Although unarmed.
    Lelio. Whence comest thou, to
    stand
Between me and my vengeance ?
    Floro.   From what rocks
And desert cells ?

    Enter MOSCON *and* CLARIN.

    Moscon. Run, run, for where we
    left my master,
We hear the clash of swords.
    Clarin.   I never
Run to approach things of this sort,
    but only

To avoid them.   Sir ! Cyprian ! Sir !
    Cyprian. Be silent, fellows ! What !
    two friends who are
In blood and fame the eyes and hope
    of Antioch ;
One of the noble men of the Colatti,
The other son of the Governor, adven-
    ture
And cast away, on some slight cause
    no doubt,
Two lives, the honour of their coun-
    try ?
    Lelio.   Cyprian,
Although my high respect towards
    your person
Holds now my sword suspended, thou
    canst not
Restore it to the slumber of its scab-
    bard.
Thou knowest more of science than
    the duel ;
For when two men of honour take the
    field,
No counsel nor respect can make
    them friends,
But one must die in the pursuit.
    Floro.   I pray
That you depart hence with your
    people, and   [gun
Leave us to finish what we have be-
Without advantage.
    Cyprian. Though you may imagine
That I know little of the laws of duel,
Which vanity and valour instituted,
You are in error.   By my birth I am
Held no less than yourselves to know
    the limits
Of honour and of infamy, nor has
    study
Quenched the free spirit which first
    ordered them ;
And thus to me, as to one well experi-
    enced
In the false quicksands of the sea of
    honour,
You may refer the merits of the case ;
And if I should perceive in your rela-
    tion
That either has the right to satisfac-
    tion
From the other, I give you my word
    of honour
To leave you.
    Lelio. Under this condition then
I will relate the cause, and you will
    cede

And must confess th' impossibility
Of compromise ; for the same lady is
Beloved by Floro and myself.
   Floro.   It seems
Much to me that the light of day
    should look
Upon that idol of my heart—but he—
Leave us to fight, according to thy
    word.
   Cyprian. Permit one question fur-
    ther : is the lady
Impossible to hope or not ?
   Lelio.   She is
So excellent, that if the light of day
Should excite Floro's jealousy, it were
Without just cause, for even the light
    of day
Trembles to gaze on her.
   Cyprian.   Would you for your
Part marry her ?
   Floro.   Such is my confidence.
   Cyprian. And you ?
   Lelio. O, would that I could lift
    my hope
So high ! for, though she is extremely
    poor,
Her virtue is her dowry.
   Cyprian.   And if you both
Would marry her, is it not weak and
    vain,
Culpable and unworthy, thus before-
    hand
To slur her honour ? What would
    the world say
If one should slay the other, and if she
Should afterwards espouse the mur-
    derer ?

    [*The rivals agree to refer their
    quarrel to* CYPRIAN ; *who, in
    consequence, visits* JUSTINA,
    and becomes enamoured of her :
    she disdains him, and he retires
    to a solitary sea-shore.*

SCENE II

CYPRIAN.

O memory ! permit it not
That the tyrant of my thought
Be another soul that still
Holds dominion o'er the will ;
That would refuse, but can no more,
To bend, to tremble, and adore.
Vain idolatry !—I saw,
And gazing became blind with error ;
Weak ambition, which the awe

Of her presence bound to terror !
So beautiful she was—and I
Between my love and jealousy,
Am so convulsed with hope and fear,
Unworthy as it may appear ;—
So bitter is the life I live,
That, hear me, Hell ! I now would
    give,
To thy most detested spirit
My soul, for ever to inherit,
To suffer punishment and pine,
So this woman may be mine.
Hear'st thou, Hell ! dost thou reject
    it ?
My soul is offered !
   Dæmon (unseen).   I accept it.
    [*Tempest with thunder and lightning.*

CYPRIAN.

What is this ! ye heavens, for ever
    pure,
At once intensely radiant and ob-
    scure !
    Athwart the ethereal halls
The lightning's arrow and the thun-
    der balls
    The day affright,
    As from the horizon round,
    Burst with earthquake sound,
In mighty torrents the electric foun-
    tains :—
Clouds quench the sun, and thunder
    smoke
Strangles the air, and fire eclipses
    heaven.
Philosophy, thou canst not even
Compel their causes underneath thy
    yoke,
From yonder clouds even to the waves
    below
The fragments of a single ruin choke
    Imagination's flight ;
For, on flakes of surge, like feathers
    light,
The ashes of the desolation cast
    Upon the gloomy blast,
Tell of the footsteps of the storm ;
And nearer see the melancholy form
Of a great ship, the outcast of the sea,
    Drives miserably !
And it must fly the pity of the port,
Or perish, and its last and sole resort
Is its own raging enemy.
The terror of the thrilling cry
Was a fatal prophecy
Of coming death, who hovers now

Upon that shattered prow,
That they who died not may be dying
  still.
And not alone the insane elements
Are populous with wild portents,
But that sad ship is as a miracle
Of sudden ruin, for it drives so fast
It seems as if it had arrayed its form
With the headlong storm.
It strikes—I almost feel the shock,—
It stumbles on a jagged rock,—
Sparkles of blood on the white foam
  are cast.
      [A tempest—All exclaim within.
We are all lost !
  Dæmon (within). Now from this
    plank will I
Pass to the land, and thus fulfil my
  scheme.
  Cyprian. As in contempt of the
    elemental rage
A man comes forth in safety, while
  the ship's
Great form is in a watery eclipse
Obliterated from the ocean's page,
And round its wreck the huge sea
  monsters sit,
A horrid conclave, and the whistling
  wave
Is heaped over its carcase, like a
  grave.

The DÆMON enters, as escaped from the
    sea.

  Dæmon (aside). It was essential to
    my purposes
To wake a tumult on the sapphire
  ocean,
That in this unknown form I might
  at length ⁊
Wipe out the blot of the discomfiture
Sustained upon the mountain, and
  assail
With a new war the soul of Cyprian,
Forging the instruments of his des-
  truction
Even from his love and from his wis-
  dom.—O
Beloved earth, dear mother, in thy
  · bosom
I seek a refuge from the monster who
Precipitates itself upon me.
  Cyprian.   Friend,
Collect thyself ; and be the memory
Of thy late suffering, and thy greatest
  sorrow

But as a shadow of the past,—for
  nothing
Beneath the circle of the moon but
  flows
And changes, and can never know
  repose.
  Dæmon. And who art thou, before
    whose feet my fate
Has prostrated me ?
  Cyprian.   One who, moved with
    pity,
Would sooth its stings.
  Dæmon. Oh ! that can never be !
No solace can my lasting sorrows find.
  Cyprian. Wherefore ?
  Dæmon.   Because my happi-
    ness is lost.   [be
Yet I lament what has long ceased to
The object of desire or memory,
And my life is not life.
  Cyprian.   Now, since the fury
Of this earthquaking hurricane is still,
And the crystalline heaven has re-
  assumed
Its windless calm so quickly, that it
  seems
As if its heavy wrath had been awak-
  ened
Only to overwhelm that vessel,—
  speak,
Who art thou, and whence comest
  thou ?
  Dæmon.   Far more
My coming hither cost than thou hast
  seen,
Or I can tell.   Among my misadven-
  tures
This shipwreck is the least. Wilt
  thou hear ?
  Cyprian.   Speak.
  Dæmon. Since thou desirest, I will
    then unveil
Myself to thee ;—for in myself I am
A world of happiness and misery ;
This I have lost, and that I must
  lament
For ever.   In my attributes I stood
So high and so heroically great,
In lineage so supreme, and with a
  genius
Which penetrated with a glance the
  world
Beneath my feet, that won by my
  high merit
A king—whom I may call the King of
  kings,

Because all others tremble in their
  pride
Before the terrors of his countenance,
In his high palace roofed with bright-
  est gems
Of living light—call them the stars of
  Heaven—
Named me his counsellor. But the
  high praise
Stung me with pride and envy, and I
  rose
In mighty competition, to ascend
His seat, and place my foot trium-
  phantly
Upon his subject thrones. Chastised,
  I know
The depth to which ambition falls;
  too mad
Was the attempt, and yet more mad
  were now
Repentance of the irrevocable deed:—
Therefore I chose this ruin with the
  glory
Of not to be subdued, before the
  shame
Of reconciling me with him who reigns
By coward cession.—Nor was I alone,
Nor am I now, nor shall I be alone;
And there was hope, and there may
  still be hope,
For many suffrages among his vassals
Hailed me their lord and king, and
  many still
Are mine, and many more perchance
  shall be.
Thus vanquished, though in fact vic-
  torious,
I left his seat of empire, from mine eye
Shooting forth poisonous lightning,
  while my words
With inauspicious thunderings shook
  Heaven,
Proclaiming vengeance, public as my
  wrong,
And imprecating on his prostrate
  slaves
Rapine, and death, and outrage.
  Then I sailed
Over the mighty fabric of the world,
A pirate ambushed in its pathless
  sands,
A lynx crouched watchfully among
  its caves
And craggy shores; and I have wan-
  dered over
The expanse of these wild wildernesses

In this great ship, whose bulk is now
  dissolved
In the light breathings of the invisible
  wind,
And which the sea has made a dust-
  less ruin,
Seeking ever a mountain, through
  whose forests
I seek a man, whom I must now
  compel
To keep his word with me. I came
  arrayed
In tempest, and, although my power
  could well
Bridle the forest winds in their
  career—
For other causes I forbore to soothe
Their fury to Favonian gentleness;
I could and would not: (thus I wake
  in him   [Aside.
A love of magic art.) Let not this
  tempest,
Nor the succeeding calm excite thy
  wonder;
For by my art the sun would turn as
  pale -   [fear;
As his weak sister with unwonted
And in my wisdom are the orbs of
  Heaven
Written as in a record. I have
  pierced
The flaming circles of their wondrous
  spheres,
And know them as thou knowest
  every corner
Of this dim spot. Let it not seem to
  thee
That I boast vainly; wouldst thou
  that I work
A charm over this waste and savage
  wood,
This Babylon of crags and aged trees,
Filling its leafy coverts with a horror
Thrilling and strange? I am the
  friendless guest
Of these wild oaks and pines—and as
  from thee
I have received the hospitality
Of this rude place, I offer thee the
  fruit
Of years of toil in recompense; what-
  e'er
Thy wildest dream presented to thy
  thought
As object of desire, that shall be thine.

*   *   *   *

And thenceforth shall so firm an amity
'Twixt thou and me be, that neither fortune,
The monstrous phantom which pursues success,
That careful miser, that free prodigal,
Who ever alternates with changeful hand
Evil and good, reproach and fame; nor Time,
That lodestar of the ages, to whose beam
The winged years speed o'er the intervals
Of their unequal revolutions ; nor
Heaven itself, whose beautiful bright stars
Rule and adorn the world, can ever make
The least division between thee and me,
Since now I find a refuge in thy favour.

SCENE III. — *The* DÆMON *tempts* JUSTINA, *who is a Christian.*

Dæmon. Abyss of Hell ! I call on thee,
Thou wild misrule of thine own anarchy !
From thy prison-house set free
The spirits of voluptuous death,
That with their mighty breath
They may destroy a world of virgin thoughts ;
Let her chaste mind with fancies thick as motes
Be peopled from thy shadowy deep,
Till her guiltless phantasy
Full to overflowing be !
And, with sweetest harmony,
Let birds, and flowers, and leaves, and all things move
To love, only to love.
Let nothing meet her eyes
But signs of Love's soft victories ;
Let nothing meet her ear
But sounds of Love's sweet sorrow ;
So that from faith no succour may she borrow
But, guided by my spirit blind,
And in a magic snare entwined,
She may now seek Cyprian,
Begin, while I in silence bind

My voice, when thy sweet song thou hast begun.
A Voice within. What is the glory far above
All else in human life ?
All.   Love ! love !
[*While these words are sung, the* DÆMON *goes out at one door, and* JUSTINA *enters at another.*
The First Voice. There is no form in which the fire
Of love its traces has impressed not.
Man lives far more in love's desire
Than by life's breath soon possessed not.
If all that lives must love or die,
All shapes on earth, or sea, or sky,
With one consent to Heaven cry
That the glory far above
All else in life is—
All.   Love ! O love !
Justina. Thou melancholy thought, which art
So fluttering and so sweet, to thee
When did I give the liberty
Thus to afflict my heart ?
What is the cause of this new power
Which doth my fevered being move,
Momently raging more and more ?
What subtle pain is kindled now
Which from my heart doth overflow
Into my senses ?—
All.   Love ! O love !
Justina.   'Tis that enamoured nightingale
Who gives me the reply :
He ever tells the same soft tale
Of passion and of constancy
To his mate, who, rapt and fond,
Listening sits, a bough beyond.

Be silent, nightingale !—No more
Make me think, in hearing thee
Thus tenderly thy love deplore,
If a bird can feel his so,
What a man would feel for me.
And, voluptuous vine, O thou
Who seekest most when least pursuing,—
To the trunk thou interlacest
Art the verdure which embracest,
And the weight which is its ruin,—
No more, with green embraces, vine,
Make me think on what thou lovest,—
For whilst thou thus thy boughs entwine.

I fear lest thou shouldst teach me, sophist,
How arms might be entangled too.

Light-enchanted sunflower, thou
Who gazest ever true and tender
On the sun's revolving splendour,
Follow not his faithless glance
With thy faded countenance,
Nor teach my beating heart to fear,
If leaves can mourn without a tear,
How eyes must weep! O nightin-
   gale,
Cease from thy enamoured tale,—
Leafy vine, unwreath thy bower,
Restless sunflower, cease to move,—
Or tell me all what poisonous power
Ye use against me.
   All.   Love! love! love!
Justina. It cannot be! Whom
   have I ever loved?
Trophies of my oblivion and disdain,
Floro and Lelio did I not reject?
And Cyprian?—
   [*She becomes troubled at the name
         of* CYPRIAN.
         Did I not requite him
With such severity, that he has fled
Where none has ever heard of him
   again?—
Alas! I now begin to fear that this
May be the occasion whence desire
   grows bold,
As if there were no danger. From
   the moment
That I pronounced to my own listen-
   ing heart,
"Cyprian is absent," O miserable me!
I know not what I feel! [*More calmly.*
         It must be pity
To think that such a man, whom all
   the world
Admired, should be forgot by all the
   world,
And I the cause.
   [*She again becomes troubled.*
         And yet if it were pity,
Floro and Lelio might have equal
   share,
For they are both imprisoned for my
   sake.   [*Calmly.*
Alas! what reasonings are these? It is
Enough I pity him, and that, in vain,
Without this ceremonious subtlety.
And woe is me! I know not where to
   find him now,

Even should I seek him through this
   wide world.

        Enter DÆMON.

Dæmon. Follow, and I will lead
   thee where he is.
Justina. And who art thou, who
   hast found entrance hither,
Into my chamber, through the doors
   and locks?
Art thou a monstrous shadow which
   my madness
Has formed in the idle air?
Dæmon.   No. I am one
Called by the thought which tyran-
   nizes thee
From his eternal dwelling; who this
   day
Is pledged to bear thee unto Cyprian.
Justina. So shall thy promise fail.
   This agony
Of passion which afflicts my heart
   and soul,
May sweep imagination in its storm;
The will is firm.
Dæmon.   Already half is done
In the imagination of an act.
The sin incurred, the pleasure then
   remains;
Let not the will stop half-way on the
   road.
Justina. I will not be discouraged,
   nor despair,
Although I thought it, and although
   'tis true
The thought is but a prelude to the
   deed:—
Thought is not in my power, but
   action is,
I will not move my foot to follow
   thee.
   Dæmon. But a far mightier wis-
   dom than mine own
Exerts itself within thee, with such
   power   [*clines*
Compelling thee to that which it in-
That it shall force thy step; how wilt
   thou then
Resist, Justina?
Justina.   By my free will.
Dæmon.   I
Must force thy will.
Justina.   It is invincible;
It were not free if thou hadst power
   upon it.
   [*He draws, but cannot move her.*

Dæmon. Come, where a pleasure waits thee.

Justina.   It were bought Too dear.

Dæmon. 'Twill soothe thy heart to softest peace.

Justina. 'Tis dread captivity.

Dæmon.   'Tis joy, 'tis glory.

Justina. 'Tis shame, 'tis torment, 'tis despair.

Dæmon.   But how Canst thou defend thyself from that or me,

If my power drags thee onward ?

Justina.   My defence Consists in God.

[He vainly endeavours to force her, and at last releases her.

Dæmon. Woman, thou hast subdued me,

Only by not owning thyself subdued.
But since thou thus findest defence in God,
I will assume a feigned form, and thus
Make thee a victim of my baffled rage.
For I will mask a spirit in thy form
Who will betray thy name to infamy,
And doubly shall I triumph in thy loss,
First by dishonouring thee, and then by turning
False pleasure to true ignominy.

[Exit.

Justina.   I Appeal to Heaven against thee ! so that Heaven
May scatter thy delusions, and the blot
Upon my fame, vanish in idle thought,
Even as flame dies in the envious air,
And as the flow'ret wanes at morning frost,
And thou shouldst never——But, alas ! to whom
Do I still speak ?—Did not a man but now   [alone,
Stand here before me ?—No, I am
And yet I saw him. Is he gone so quickly ?
Or can the heated mind engender shapes
From its own fear ? Some terrible and strange
Peril is near. Lisander ! father ! lord !

Livia !—

Enter LISANDER *and* LIVIA.

Lisander. O my daughter ! what ?

Livia.   What ?

Justina.   Saw you A man go forth from my apartment now ?—
I scarce sustain myself !

Lisander.   A man here !

Justina. Have you not seen him ?

Livia.   No, lady.

Justina. I saw him.

Lisander. 'Tis impossible ; the doors
Which led to this apartment were all locked.

Livia (aside). I dare say it was Moscon whom she saw,
For he was locked up in my room.

Lisander.   It must Have been some image of thy phantasy.
Such melancholy as thou feedest is
Skilful in forming such in the vain air
Out of the motes and atoms of the day.

Livia. My master's in the right.

Justina.   Oh, would it were Delusion ! but I fear some greater ill.
I feel as if out of my bleeding bosom
My heart was torn in fragments ; ay,
Some mortal spell is wrought against my frame ;
So potent was the charm, that had not God
Shielded my humble innocence from wrong,
I should have sought my sorrow and my shame
With willing steps.—Livia, quick, bring my cloak,
For I must seek refuge from these extremes
Even in the temple of the highest God
Which secretly the faithful worship.

Livia. Here.

Justina (putting on her cloak). In this, as in a shroud of snow, may I
Quench the consuming fire in which I burn,
Wasting away !

Lisander. And I will go with thee.

Livia. When I once see them safe out of the house,
I shall breathe freely.

Justina.   So do I confide
In thy just favour, Heaven !
    Lisander.   Let us go.
    Justina. Thine is the cause, great
    God I Turn, for my sake
And for thine own, mercifully to me !

SCENES FROM THE "FAUST" OF GOETHE

PROLOGUE IN HEAVEN

The LORD *and the Host of Heaven.*

Enter Three Archangels.

RAPHAEL.

THE sun makes music as of old
    Amid the rival spheres of Heaven,
On its predestined circle rolled
    With thunder speed : the Angels
    even
Draw strength from gazing on its
    glance,
    Though none its meaning fathom
    may ;—
The world's unwithered countenance
    Is bright as at creation's day.

GABRIEL.

And swift and swift, with rapid light-
    ness,
    The adorned Earth spins silently,
Alternating Elysian brightness
    With deep and dreadful night ; the
    sea
Foams in broad billows from the deep
    Up to the rocks ; and rocks and
    ocean,
Onward, with spheres which never
    sleep,
    Are hurried in eternal motion.

MICHAEL.

And tempests in contention roar
    From land to sea, from sea to land ;
And, raging, weave a chain of power
    Which girds the earth as with a
    band,
A flashing desolation there
    Flames before the thunder's way ;
But thy servants, Lord, revere
    The gentle changes of thy day.

CHORUS OF THE THREE.

The Angels draw strength from thy
    glance,
    Though no one comprehend thee
    may :—

Thy world's unwithered countenance
Is bright as on creation's day.[1]

Enter MEPHISTOPHELES.

Mephistcphles. As thou, O Lord,
    once more art kind enough
To interest thyself in our affairs—
And ask, " How goes it with you
    there below ? "
And as indulgently at other times
Thou tookedst not my visits in ill part,
Thou seest me here once more among
    thy household.
Though I should scandalize this com-
    pany,
You will excuse me if I do not talk
In the high style which they think
    fashionable ;
My pathos certainly would make you
    laugh too,
Had you not long since given over
    laughing,
Nothing know I to say of suns and
    worlds ;

[1] RAPHAEL.
The sun sounds, according to ancient custom,
In the song of emulation of his brother-spheres,
And its fore-written circle
Fulfils with a step of thunder.
Its countenance gives the Angels strength,
Though no one can fathom it.
The incredible high works
Are excellent as at the first day.

GABRIEL.
And swift, and inconceivably swift
The adornment of earth winds itself round,
And exchanges Paradise-clearness
With deep dreadful night.
The sea foams in broad waves
From its deep bottom up to the rocks,
And rocks and sea are torn on together
In the eternal swift course of the spheres.

MICHAEL.
And storms roar in emulation
From sea to land, from land to sea,
And make, raging, a chain
Of deepest operation round about.
There flames a flashing destruction
Before the path of the thunderbolt.
But thy servants, Lord, revere
The gentle alternations of thy day.

CHORUS.
Thy countenance gives the Angels strength,
Though none can comprehend thee :
And all thy lofty works
Are excellent as at the first day.

Such is the literal translation of this astonishing Chorus ; it is impossible to represent in another language the melody of the versification ; even the volatile strength and delicacy of the ideas escape in the crucible of translation, and the reader is surprised to find a *caput mortuum.—Author's Note.*

I observe only how men plague themselves ;—

The little god o' the world keeps the
same stamp,

As wonderful as on creation's day :—
A little better would he live, hadst
thou

Not given him a glimpse of Heaven's
light

Which he calls reason, and employs it
only

To live more beastily than any beast.

With reverence to your Lordship be it
spoken,

He's like one of those long-legged
grasshoppers.

Who flits and jumps about, and sings
for ever

The same old song i' the grass. There
let him lie,   [dung.

Burying his nose in every heap of

The Lord. Have you no more to
say ? Do you come here

Always to scold, and cavil, and complain ?

Seems nothing ever right to you on
earth ?

Mephistopheles. No, Lord ; I find
all there, as ever, bad at best.

Even I am sorry for man's days of
sorrow ;

I could myself almost give up the
pleasure

Of plaguing the poor things.

The Lord. Knowest thou Faust ?

Mephistopheles. The Doctor ?

The Lord. Ay ; my servant Faust.

Mephistopheles.   In truth

He serves you in a fashion quite his
own,

And the fool's meat and drink are not
of earth.

His aspirations bear him on so far

That he is half aware of his own folly,

For he demands from Heaven its fairest star,

And from the earth the highest joy it
bears ;

Yet all things far, and all things near,
are vain

To calm the deep emotions of his
breast.

The Lord. Though he now serves
me in a cloud of error,

I will soon lead him forth to the clear
day.

When trees look green, full well the
gardener knows

That fruits and blooms will deck the
coming year.

Mephistopheles. **What will you
bet ?—now I am sure of winning—**

**Only observe you give me full per-
mission**

To lead him softly on my path.

The Lord.   As long

As he shall live upon the earth, so
long

Is nothing unto thee forbidden.—Man
Must err till he has ceased to struggle.

Mephistopheles.   Thanks.

And that is all I ask ; for willingly
**I never make acquaintance with the
dead.**

**The full fresh cheeks of youth are food
for me,**

**And if a corpse knocks, I am not at
home.**

For I am like a cat—I like to play
A little with the mouse before I eat it.

The Lord. Well, well, it is permitted thee. Draw thou

His spirit from its springs ; as thou
find'st power,

Seize him and lead him on thy downward path ;

And stand ashamed when failure
teaches thee

That **a good man, even in his darkest
longings,**

Is well aware of the right way.

Mephistopheles.   Well and good.
I am not in much doubt about my bet
And, if I lose, then 'tis your turn to
crow ;

Enjoy your triumph then with a full
breast.

Ay ; dust shall he devour, and **that
with pleasure,**

Like my old paramour, the famous
Snake.

The Lord. Pray come here when it
suits you ; for I never

Had much dislike for people of your
sort.

And, among all the Spirits who re-
belled,

The knave was ever the least tedious
to me.

The active spirit of man soon sleeps,
and soon

He seeks unbroken quiet ; therefore I
Have given him the Devil for a com-
    panion,
Who may provoke him to some sort of
    work,
And must create for ever.—But ye,
    pure
Children of God, enjoy eternal
    beauty;—
Let that which ever operates and
    lives
Clasp you within the limits of its love ;
And seize with sweet and melancholy
    thoughts
The floating phantoms of its loveli-
    ness.

[*Heaven closes ; the Archangels exeunt.*

  Mephistopheles. From time to time
    I visit the old fellow,
And I take care to keep on good
    terms with him.
Civil enough is this same God Al-
    mighty,
To talk so freely with the Devil him-
    self.

SCENE.—*May Day Night.—The Harz
  Mountain, a desolate Country.*

FAUST, MEPHISTOPHELES.

  Mephistopheles. Would you not
    like a broomstick ?   As for me
I wish I had a good stout ram to ride ;
For we are still far from th' appointed
    place.
  Faust. This knotted staff is help
    enough for me,
Whilst I feel fresh upon my legs.
    What good
Is there in making short a pleasant
    way—
To creep along the labyrinths of the
    vales,
And climb those rocks, where ever-
    babbling springs
Precipitate themselves in waterfalls,
In the sport that seasons such a
    path ?
Already Spring kindles the birchen
    spray,
And the hoar pines already feel her
    breath :
Shall she not work also within our
    limbs ?
  Mephistopheles. Nothing of such an
    influence do I feel.

My body is all wintry, and I wish
The flowers upon our path were frost
    and snow.
But see, how melancholy rises now,
Dimly uplifting her belated beam,
The blank unwelcome round of the
    red moon,
And gives so bad a light, that every
    step
One stumbles 'gainst some crag. With
    your permission
I'll call an Ignis fatuus to our aid :
I see one yonder burning jollily.
Halloo, my friend ! may I request
    that you
Would favour us with your bright
    company ?
Why should you blaze away there to
    no purpose ?
Pray be so good as light us up this
    way.
  Ignis-fatuus. With reverence be it
    spoken, I will try
To overcome the lightness of my
    nature ;
Our course, you know, is generally
    zigzag.
  Mephistopheles. Ha, ha ! your wor-
    ship thinks you have to deal
With men. Go straight on in the
    Devil's name,
Or I shall puff your flickering life out.
  Ignis fatuus.   Well,
I see you are the master of the house ;
I will accommodate myself to you.
Only consider that to-night this moun-
    tain
Is all-enchanted, and if Jack a-lantern
Shows you his way, though you
    should miss your own,
You ought not to be too exact with
    him.

FAUST, MEPHISTOPHELES, *and* IGNIS
  FATUUS *in alternate Chorus.*

The limits of the sphere of dream,
  The bounds of true and false, are
    passed.
Lead us on, thou wandering Gleam,
  Lead us onward far and fast,
  To the wide, the desert waste.
But see, how swift advance and shift
  Trees behind trees, row by row,—
How, clift by clift, rocks bend and
    lift
  Their frowning foreheads as we go.

The giant-snouted crags, ho! ho!
How they snort, and how they
    blow!

Through the mossy sods and stones,
Stream and streamlet hurry down,
A rushing throng! A sound of
    song
Beneath the vault of Heaven is
    blown!
Sweet notes of love, the speaking
    tones
Of this bright day, sent down to say
That Paradise on Earth is known,
Resound around, beneath, above;
All we hope and all we love
Finds a voice in this blithe strain,
Which wakens hill and wood and
    rill,
And vibrates far o'er field and vale,
And which Echo, like the tale
Of old times, repeats again.

To-whoo! to-whoo! near, nearer
    now
The sound of song, the rushing
    throng!
Are the screech, the lapwing, and
    the jay,
All awake as if 'twere day?
See, with long legs and belly wide,
A salamander in the brake!
Every root is like a snake,
And along the loose hill side,
With strange contortions through
    the night,
Curls, to seize or to affright;
And animated, strong, and many,
They dart forth polypus-antennæ,
To blister with their poison spume
The wanderer. Through the dazzl-
    ing gloom
The many-coloured mice that
    thread
The dewy turf beneath our tread,
In troops each other's motions
    cross,
Through the heath and through the
    moss;
And in legions intertangled,
The fireflies flit, and swarm, and
    throng,
Till all the mountain depths are
    spangled.

Tell me, shall we go or stay?
Shall we onward? Come along!

Everything around is swept
Forward, onward, far away!
Trees and masses intercept
The sight, and wisps on every side
Are puffed up and multiplied.

Mephistopheles. Now vigorously
    seize my skirt, and gain
This pinnacle of isolated crag.
One may observe with wonder from
    this point
How Mammon glows among the
    mountains.
Faust.   Ay—
And strangely through the solid depth
    below
A melancholy light, like the red dawn,
Shoots from the lowest gorge of the
    abyss
Of mountains, lighting hitherward;
    there, rise
Pillars of smoke; here, clouds float
    gently by;
Here the light burns soft as the en-
    kindled air,
Or the illumined dust of golden
    flowers;
And now it glides like tender colours
    spreading;
And now bursts forth in fountains
    from the earth;   [light,
And now it winds one torrent of broad
Through the far valley with a hun-
    dred veins;
And now once more within that nar-
    row corner
Masses itself into intensest splendour.
And near us see sparks spring out of
    the ground,
Like golden sand scattered upon the
    darkness;
The pinnacles of that black wall of
    mountains
That hems us in are kindled.
    Mephistopheles.   Rare, in faith!
Does not Sir Mammon gloriously
    illuminate
His palace for this festival—it is
A pleasure which you had not known
    before.
I spy the boisterous guests already.
    Faust.   How
The children of the wind rage in the
    air!
With what fierce strokes they fall
    upon my neck!

Mephistopheles. Cling tightly to
the old ribs of the crag.
Beware ! for if with them thou war-
rest
In their fierce flight towards the
wilderness,
Their breath will sweep thee into dust,
and drag
Thy body to a grave in the abyss.
A cloud thickens the night.
Hark ! how the tempest crashes
through the forest !
The owls fly out in strange affright ;
The columns of the evergreen palaces
Are split and shattered ;
The roots creak, and stretch, and
groan ;
And, ruinously overthrown,
The trunks are crushed and shat-
tered
By the fierce blast's unconquerable
stress.
Over each other crack and crash
they all
In terrible and intertangled fall ;
And through the ruins of the shaken
mountain
    The airs hiss and howl—
It is not the voice of the fountain,
    Nor the wolf in his midnight
        prowl.

    Dost thou not hear ?
    Strange accents are ringing
Aloft, afar, anear ;
    The witches are singing !
The torrent of a raging wizard's
    song
Streams the whole mountain
    along.

CHORUS OF WITCHES.
The stubble is yellow, the corn is
green,
Now to the Brocken the witches go ;
The mighty multitude here may be
seen
Gathering, wizard and witch, below.
Sir Urean is sitting aloft in the air ;
Hey over stock ! and hey over stone !
'Twixt witches and incubi, what shall
be done ?
Tell it who dare ! tell it who dare !
    A Voice. Upon a sow-swine, whose
        farrows were nine,
Old Baubo rideth alone.

CHORUS.
Honour her to whom honour is due,
Old mother Baubo, honour to you !
An able sow with old Baubo upon her,
Is worthy of glory, and worthy of
    honour !
The legion of witches is coming be-
    hind,
Darkening the night and outspeeding
    the wind—

    A Voice. Which way comest thou ?
    A Voice.   Over Ilsenstein ;
The owl was awake in the white
    moonshine ;
I saw her at rest in her downy nest,
And she stared at me with her broad
    bright eyne.
    Voices. And you may now as well
        take your course on to Hell,
Since you ride by so fast on the head-
    long blast.
    A Voice. She dropped poison upon
        me as I past.
Here are the wounds—

CHORUS OF WITCHES.
        Come away ! come along !
The way is wide, the way is long,
But what is that for a Bedlam throng?
Stick with the prong, and scratch
    with the broom.
The child in the cradle lies strangled
    at home,
And the mother is clapping her
    hands.—

SEMI-CHORUS OF WIZARDS I.
                We glide in
Like snails when the women are all
    away ;
And from a house once given over to
    sin
Woman has a thousand steps to stray.

SEMI-CHORUS II.
A thousand steps must a woman take,
Where a man but a single spring will
    make.

    Voices above. Come with us, come
        with us, from Felunsee.
    Voices below. With what joy would
        we fly through the upper sky ;

We are washed, we are 'nointed, stark
   naked are we !
But our toil and our pain are for ever
   in vain.

BOTH CHORUSES.

The wind is still, the stars are fled,
The melancholy moon is dead ;
The magic notes, like spark on spark,
Drizzle, whistling through the dark.
   Come away !
   Voices below. Stay, oh stay !
   Voices above. Out of the crannies
     of the rocks
Who calls ?
   Voices below. O, let me join your
   flocks !
I, three hundred years have striven
To catch your skirt and mount to
   Heaven,—
And still in vain.   Oh, might I be
With company akin to me !

BOTH CHORUSES.

Some on a ram and some on a prong,
On poles and on broomsticks we
   flutter along ;
Forlorn is the wight who can rise not
   to-night.
   A half-witch below. I have been
   tripping this many an hour :
Are the others already so far before ?
No quiet at home, and no peace
   abroad !
And less methinks is found by the
   road.

CHORUS OF WITCHES.

Come onward, away ! aroint thee,
   aroint ! ?
A witch to be strong must anoint—
   anoint—
Then every trough will be boat
   enough ;
With a rag for a sail we can sweep
   through the sky,
Who flies not to-night, when means
   he to fly ?

BOTH CHORUSES.

We cling to the skirt, and we strike
   on the ground ;
Witch legions thicken around and
   around ;
Wizard swarms cover the heath all
   over.   [*They descend.*

Mephistopheles. What thronging,
   dashing, raging. rustling !
What whispering, babbling, hissing,
   bustling !
What glimmering, spurting, stinking,
   burning !
As Heaven and earth were overturn-
   ing.
There is a true witch element about
   us ;
Take hold on me, or we shall be di-
   vided :—
Where are you ?
   Faust (from a distance). Here !
   Mephistopheles.   What !
I must exert my authority in the
   house.
Place for young Voland !   Pray make
   way, good people.
Take hold on me, doctor, and with one
   step
Let us escape from this unpleasant
   crowd :
They are too mad for people of my
   sort.   [light—
Just there shines a peculiar kind of
Something attracts me in those
   bushes.—Come
This way ; we shall slip down there in
   a minute.
   Faust. Spirit of Contradiction !
   Well, lead on—
'Twere a wise feat indeed to wander
   out
Into the Brocken upon May Day night,
And then to isolate oneself in scorn.
Disgusted with the humours of the
   time.
   Mephistopheles. See yonder, round
   a many-coloured flame
A merry club is huddled altogether :
Even with such little people as sit
   there
One would not be alone.
   Faust.   Would that I were
Up yonder in the glow and whirling
   smoke
Where the blind million rush impetu-
   ously
To meet the evil ones ; there might I
   solve
Many a riddle that torments me !
   Mephistopheles.   Yet
Many a riddle there is tied anew
Inextricably.   Let the great world
   rage !

We will stay here safe in the quiet dwellings.

'Tis an old custom. Men have ever built

Their own small world in the great world of all.

I see young witches naked there, and old ones

Wisely attired with greater decency.

Be guided now by me, and you shall buy

A pound of pleasure with a dram of trouble.

I hear them tune their instruments—one must

Get used to this damned scraping. Come, I'll lead you

Among them ; and what there you do and see,

As a fresh compact 'twixt us two shall be.

How say you now ? this space is wide enough—

Look forth, you cannot see the end of it—

A hundred bonfires burn in rows, and they

Who throng around them seem innumerable :

Dancing and drinking, jabbering, making love,

And cooking, are at work. Now tell me, friend,

What is there better in the world than this ?

Faust. In introducing us, do you assume

The character of wizard or of devil ?

Mephistopheles. In truth, I generally go about

In strict incognito ; and yet one likes

To wear one's orders upon gala days.

I have no ribbon at my knee ; but here

At home the cloven foot is honourable.

See you that snail there ?—she comes creeping up,

And with her feeling eyes hath smelt out something :

I could not, if I would, mask myself here.

Come now we'll go about from fire to fire :

I'll be the pimp, and you shall be the lover.

[*To some old Women, who are sitting round a heap of glimmering coals.*

Old gentlewomen, what do you do out here ?

You ought to be with the young rioters

Right in the thickest of the revelry—

But every one is best content at home.

General. Who dare confide in right or a just claim ?

So much as I had done for them !—and now—

With women and the people 'tis the same,

Youth will stand foremost ever,—age may go

To the dark grave unhonoured.

Minister. Nowadays

People assert their rights ; they go too far ;

But, as for me, the good old times I praise.

Then we were all in all ; 'twas something worth

One's while to be in place and wear a star ;

That was indeed the golden age on earth.

Parvenu.[1] We too are active, and we did and do

What we ought not perhaps ; and yet we now

Will seize, whilst all things are whirled round and round,

A spoke of Fortune's wheel, and keep our ground.

Author. Who now can taste a treatise of deep sense

And ponderous volume ? 'Tis impertinence

To write what none will read, therefore will I

To please the young and thoughtless people try.

Mephistopheles. (*Who at once appears to have grown very old.*)—

I find the people ripe for the last day,

Since I last came up to the wizard mountain ;

---

[1] A sort of fundholder.

And as my little cask runs turbid now,
So is the world drained to the dregs.
    Pedlar-witch.   Look here,
Gentlemen ; do not hurry on so fast,
And lose the chance of a good penny-
    worth.
I have a pack full of the choicest
    wares
Of every sort, and yet in all my bundle
Is nothing like what may be found on
    earth ;
Nothing that in a moment will make
    rich
Men and the world with fine malicious
    mischief.——
There is no dagger drunk with blood ;
    no bowl
From which consuming poison may
    be drained
By innocent and healthy lips ; no
    jewel,
The price of an abandoned maiden's
    shame ;
No sword which cuts the bond it can-
    not loose,
Or stabs the wearer's enemy in the
    back ;
No——
    Mephistopheles. Gossip, you know
    little of these times.
What has been, has been ; what is
    done, is past.
They shape themselves into the inno-
    vations
They breed, and innovation drags us
    with it.
The torrent of the crowd sweeps over
    us :
You think to impel, and are yourself
    impelled.
    Faust. Who is that yonder ?
    Mephistopheles.   Mark her well. It
    is
Lilith.
    Faust. Who ?
    Mephistopheles. Lilith, the first
    wife of Adam.
Beware of her fair hair, for she excels
All women in the magic of her locks ;
And when she winds them round a
    young man's neck,
She will not ever set him free again.
    Faust. There sit a girl and an old
    woman—they
Seems to be tired with pleasure and
    with play.

    Mephistopheles. There is no rest to-
    night for anyone :
When one dance ends another is be-
    gun ;
Come, let us do it. We shall have
    rare fun.

[FAUST *dances and sings with a Girl,
and* MEPHISTOPHELES *with an old
Woman.*]

    Procto-Phantasmist. What is this
    cursed multitude about ?
Have we not long since proved to
    demonstration
That ghosts move not on ordinary
    feet !
But these are dancing just like men
    and women.
    The Girl. What does he want, then,
    at our ball ?
    Faust.   Oh ! he
Is far above us all in his conceit :
Whilst we enjoy, he reasons of enjoy-
    ment ;
And any step which in our dance we
    tread,
If it be left out of his reckoning,
Is not to be considered as a step.
There are few things that scandalize
    him not ;
And, when you whirl round in the
    circle now,
As he went round the wheel in his old
    mill,
He says that you go wrong in all re-
    spects,
Especially if you congratulate him
Upon the strength of the resem-
    blance.
    Procto-phantasmist.   Fly !
Vanish ! Unheard of impudence !
    What, still there !
In this enlightened age too, since you
    have been
Proved not to exist !—But this in-
    fernal brood
Will hear no reason and endure no
    rule.
Are we so wise, and is the *pond* still
    haunted ?
How long have I been sweeping out
    this rubbish
Of superstition, and the world will not
Come clean with all my pains !—it is
    a case
Unheard of !

The Girl. Then leave off teasing us so.

Procto-phantasmist. I tell you, spirits, to your faces now,

That I should not regret this despotism

Of spirits, but that mine can wield it not.

To-night I shall make poor work of it,

Yet I will take a round with you, and hope

Before my last step in the living dance

To beat the poet and the devil together.

Mephistopheles. At last he will sit down in some foul puddle—

That is his way of solacing himself,—

Until some leech, diverted with his gravity,

Cures him of spirits and the spirit together.

[*To* FAUST, *who has seceded from the dance.*

Why do you let that fair girl pass from you,

Who sang so sweetly to you in the dance ?

Faust. A red mouse in the middle of her singing

Sprang from her mouth,

Mephistopheles. That was all right, my friend :

Be it enough that the mouse was not grey.

Do not disturb your hour of happiness

With close consideration of such trifles.

Faust. Then saw I—

Mephistopheles. What ?

Faust. Seest thou not a pale

Fair girl, standing alone, far, far away?

She drags herself now forward with slow steps,

And seems as if she moved with shackled feet :

I cannot overcome the thought that she

Is like poor Margaret.

Mephistopheles. Let it be—pass on—

No good can come of it—it is not well

To meet it—it is an enchanted phantom,

A lifeless idol ; with its numbing look,

It freezes up the blood of man ; and they

Who meet its ghastly stare are turned to stone,

Like those who saw Medusa.

Faust. O, too true !

Her eyes are like the eyes of a fresh corpse

Which no beloved hand has closed. Alas !

That is the breast which Margaret yielded to me—

Those are the lovely limbs which I enjoyed !

Mephistopheles. It is all magic, poor deluded fool !

She looks to everyone like his first love.

Faust. O what delight ! what woe ! I cannot turn

My looks from her sweet piteous countenance.

How strangely does a single blood-red line.

Not broader than the sharp edge of a knife,

Adorn her lovely neck !

Mephistopheles. Ay, she can carry

Her head under her arm upon occasion ;

Perseus has cut it off for her. These pleasures

End in delusion,—Gain this rising ground ;

It is as airy here as in a [   ]

And, if I am not mightily deceived,

I see a theatre.—What may this mean ?

Attendant. Quite a new piece, the last of seven, for 'tis

The custom now to represent that number.

'Tis written by a Dilettante, and

The actors who perform are Dilettanti ;

Excuse me, gentlemen ; but I must vanish.

I am a Dilettante curtain-lifter.

INDEX TO FIRST LINES